Writing is the act of saying *I*, of imposing oneself upon other people, of saying *listen to me, see it my way, change your mind.*

–Joan Didion

A writer . . . is someone who has found a process that will bring about new things.

–William Stafford

I think best with a pencil in my hand.

–Anne Morrow Lindbergh

I am never as clear about any matter as when I have finished writing about it.

–James Van Allen

Writing keeps me from believing everything I read.

–Gloria Steinem

Don't tear up the page and start over again when you write a bad line—try to write your way out of it. Make mistakes and plunge on. . . . Writing is a means of discovery, always.

–Garrison Keillor

5th EDITION

The St. Martin's Guide to Writing

RISE B. AXELROD

California State University, San Bernardino

CHARLES R. COOPER

University of California, San Diego

ST. MARTIN'S PRESS

New York

Director of development: Carla Kay Samodulski
Sponsoring editor: Donna Erickson
Marketing managers: Tony Mathias, Karen Melton
Managing editor: Patricia Mansfield Phelan
Senior project editor: Erica Appel
Production supervisor: Joe Ford
Art direction and cover design: Lucy Krikorian
Text design: Brand X Studios/Robin Hoffmann

Library of Congress Catalog Card Number: 95-73176

Manufactured in the United States of America.

1 0 9 8
f e d c

For information, write:
St. Martin's Press, Inc.
175 Fifth Avenue
New York, NY 10010

ISBN: 0-312-13326-X

Acknowledgments

Acknowledgments and copyrights can be found at the back of the book on pages 652–53, which constitute an extension of the copyright page.

ADVISORY BOARD

We owe an enormous debt to all the rhetoricians and composition specialists whose theory, research, and pedagogy have informed *The St. Martin's Guide to Writing*. We would be adding many pages to an already long book if we were to name everyone to whom we are indebted.

The members of the advisory board for the fifth edition, a group of dedicated composition instructors from across the country, have provided us with extensive insights and suggestions for the chapters in Part I and have given us the benefit of their advice on new features, in many cases testing them in their own classrooms. *The St. Martin's Guide to Writing* has been greatly enhanced by their contributions.

RICHARD BOYD
University of California at Riverside

JAMES L. BROWN
Kansas City Kansas Community College

RICHARD BULLOCK
Wright State University

SANDY CAVANAH
Hopkinsville Community College

ROBERT CORRIGAN
Baltimore City Community College

JOAN KUZMA COSTELLO
Inver Hills Community College

JANET KAY DILLON
Kansas State University

NANCY B. ETHERIDGE
Boise State University

JUDITH GARDNER
University of Texas at San Antonio

MICHAEL A. MILLER
Longview Community College

DONNA PADGETT
Georgia Southern University

VICTORIA F. SARKISIAN
Marist College

NANCY W. SHANKLE
Abilene Christian University

LENORA P. SMITH
University of Houston

ROSEMARY WINSLOW
Catholic University of America

A BRIEF CONTENTS

PART 3 WRITING STRATEGIES

PART 4 RESEARCH STRATEGIES

PART 5 WRITING FOR ASSESSMENT

CONTENTS

PART 1 WRITING ACTIVITIES

5 EXPLAINING A CONCEPT 157

PART 2 CRITICAL THINKING STRATEGIES

PART 3 WRITING STRATEGIES

PART 5 WRITING FOR ASSESSMENT

READINGS

PREFACE

The first four editions of *The St. Martin's Guide to Writing* have taught a generation of students how to write. Over the years, students have shared their experiences with it and have testified to its success. About the fourth edition, one student wrote, "It broadened my abilities to think and learn." Another student concluded, "It made me both confident about my work and interested in the work I was doing." After working through Chapter 9, "Speculating about Causes," still another student wrote, "It walked you through the neighborhood of causal argument, stopping at every corner to make sure you weren't left behind." The enthusiastic reception of the *Guide* in its previous four editions testifies to the dedication and seriousness of many instructors who share our conviction that writing can and should be taught. We are deeply grateful to everyone who has helped to make it the most widely used college rhetoric today. With such success and praise, we might be tempted to approach this latest revision cautiously. Instead, encouraged and emboldened, we have strived to increase both the pleasure and the usefulness of our popular tour through the neighborhoods of written discourse.

When we first wrote *The St. Martin's Guide to Writing,* we tried to design a flexible composition textbook for instructors and a helpful guide for students. We took what we had learned from classical rhetoric as well as from contemporary composition theory and research and did our best to make it accessible to students. We wanted to write a book that would help students to learn to write, not one that just talked about writing.

Although *The St. Martin's Guide* has changed over the years, our basic goals remain unchanged. From the beginning, we have tried to continue the classical tradition of teaching writing not only as a method of composing rhetorically effective prose but also as a powerful heuristic for thinking creatively and critically. To the best insights from that tradition, we have with each new edition added what we believed to be some promising developments in composition theory and research. In particular, we have tried to emphasize the idea that writing is both a social act and a way of knowing. We try to teach students that form emerges from context as well as content, that knowledge of writing comes not from analyzing genres alone but also from participating in a community of writers and readers.

Our principal aim is to demystify writing and authorize students as writers. To this end, we seek to teach students how to use the composing process as a means of seeing what they know as well as how they know it. We want students to learn to use writing to think critically and communicate effectively with others. Finally, we hope to inspire students with the desire to question their own certainties and provide them with the strategies for doing so.

AN OVERVIEW OF THE BOOK

As a rhetoric and reader, *The St. Martin's Guide* can serve as a comprehensive introduction to discursive practice. It comprises several parts:

Part I, Writing Activities, presents nine different essay assignments, all reflecting actual writing situations that students may encounter both in and out of college, kinds of discourse that they should learn to read critically and to write intelligently. Among the types of essays included are autobiography, explanation, position paper, proposal, and literary interpretation.

You may choose among these chapters and teach them in any sequence you wish, though they are sequenced here to move students from writing based on personal experience and observation to writing calling for the analysis and synthesis of ideas and information derived from a variety of sources.

Each chapter follows the same organizational plan.

Chapter Organization for Part I

- Three brief **scenarios** identifying the kind of discourse covered in the chapter and suggesting the range of occasions when such writing is done
- A **collaborative activity** that gets students working with the kind of discourse taught in that chapter
- A set of **readings** accompanied by a **critical apparatus** designed to help students to explore connections to their culture and experience and to analyze strategies used in this genre
- A summary of the **purpose and audience** and the **basic features** of this kind of discourse
- A flexible **guide to writing** that escorts students through all the stages of the composing process
- **Editing and proofreading guidelines** to help students to check for several sentence-level problems likely to occur in that kind of writing
- A look at one **writer at work,** focusing on some aspect of the process of writing the student essay featured in that chapter
- A trio of **critical thinking activities** designed to help students to reflect on and consolidate what they learned about writing and reading and to consider the social dimensions of the genre of writing taught in that chapter

Part II, Critical Thinking Strategies, collects in two separate chapters practical heuristics for invention and reading. The catalog of invention strategies includes clustering, looping, dramatizing, and questioning, while the catalog of reading strategies includes annotating, summarizing, exploring the significance of figurative language, and evaluating the logic of an argument.

Part III, Writing Strategies, looks at a wide range of essential writers' strategies: paragraphing and coherence, logic and reasoning, and the familiar modes of presenting information, such as narrating, defining, and classifying. Examples and exercises are almost all taken from contemporary nonfiction, and many exercises deal with reading selections appearing in Part I. Because of the extensive cross-referencing between Parts I and III, instructors will find it easier to teach writing strategies in the context of purpose and audience.

Part IV, Research Strategies, discusses field as well as library and Internet research and includes thorough guidelines for using and documenting sources, with detailed examples of the Modern Language Association (MLA) and American Psychological Association (APA) documentation styles. The part concludes with a sample student research paper.

Part V, Writing for Assessment, covers essay examinations, showing students how to analyze different kinds of exam questions and offering strategies for writing answers. It also addresses portfolios, helping students to assemble a representative sample of their writing.

Proven Features

Several proven features have made *The St. Martin's Guide to Writing* such an effective textbook: the practical guides to writing, the systematic integration of reading and writing, activities to promote group discussion and inquiry, and activities that encourage students to reflect on what they have learned.

Practical Guides to Writing. We do not merely talk about the composing process; rather, we offer practical, flexible guides that escort students through the entire process, from invention through revision and self-evaluation. Thus, this book is more than just a rhetoric that students will refer to occasionally. It is a guidebook that will help them to write. Commonsensical and easy to follow, these writing guides teach students to assess a rhetorical situation, identify the kinds of information they will need, ask probing questions and find answers, and organize their writing to achieve their purpose.

Systematic Integration of Reading and Writing. Because we see a close relationship between the ability to read critically and the ability to write intelligently, *The St. Martin's Guide* combines reading instruction with writing instruction. Each chapter in Part I introduces one kind of discourse, which students are led to consider both as readers and as writers. Readings are followed by questions that make students aware of how they as readers respond and at the same time help them to understand the decisions that writers make. Students are then challenged to apply these insights to their own writing as they imagine their prospective readers, set goals, and write and revise their drafts.

Activities to Promote Group Discussion and Inquiry. At the start of each of the writing chapters is a collaborative activity that invites students to try out some of the thinking and planning they will be doing for the kind of writing covered in that chapter. Then, following each reading comes Connecting to Culture and Experience, designed to provoke thoughtful responses about the social and political dimensions of the reading. In the Guide to Writing is another collaborative activity that gets students to discuss their work in progress with one another and a Critical Reading Guide, which guides students as they read and comment on each other's drafts. Finally, a discussion activity invites students to explore the social dimensions of the genre they have been learning to write. All of these materials include questions and prompts to guide students to work productively together.

Thinking Critically about What You Have Learned. Each chapter in Part I concludes with three metacognitive activities to help students to become aware of what they have learned about the process of writing, about the influence of reading on writing, and about the social and political dimensions of the genres they have learned to write. These activities are based on research showing that reflecting on what they have learned deepens students' understanding and improves their recall.

Changes in the Fifth Edition

We have tried in this new edition to continue our tradition of turning current theory and research into practical classroom activities—with a minimum of jargon. We have also incorporated guidelines for using the new technologies that are increasingly available to students. Chief among these new features are encouragement to write essays on identity and community and on work and career, coverage of the new opportunities for research available on the Internet, updated and improved MLA and APA guidelines, and a new, more colorful design.

New Topic Choices. The Guide to Writing in each chapter in Part I now includes topic suggestions in two broad areas: "identity and community" and "work and career." These two themes are also reflected in a number of the readings in Part I. In addition, *Who Are We? Readings in Identity and Community and Work and Career* provides additional readings for classroom discussion. The two themes are useful for instructors who prefer a thematic approach, and the topic suggestions also broaden the possibilities for all students.

Activities Connecting Themes in the Readings to Students' Culture and Experience. Immediately following each reading, an activity, Connecting to Culture and Experience, relates students' cultural knowledge and personal experience to a central theme of that reading. The activity identifies and usually elaborates on the theme and contextualizes it further to ensure that students see its cultural implications and importance in their own lives. Students are then invited to consider the theme in small group discussion. The goals for the discussion are clearly defined so that students can maintain a shared focus while at the same time exploring freely the various meanings of the theme for their individual lives. Many themes relate to the broad topic areas of "identity and community" and "work and career."

Activities for Analyzing Writing Strategies in Every Reading. In this edition, we have reduced the number of tasks for analyzing writing that follow each reading from four to two. We have also refined and focused them so that students can learn more from each reading about strategies they will need to succeed with their own essays.

Students are directed to a particular strategy in one part of a reading, given directions for carrying out a close analysis of the strategy, and asked to evaluate its effectiveness, given the writer's purpose and readers. Taken together, the eight activities in each chapter, two after each of the four readings, provide students with a comprehensive introduction to the features and strategies of a genre, an introduction they can complete on their own or with the help of other students. In each activity, the strategy of interest is identified in bold type.

A Section on Internet Research. An extensive new section in Chapter 21 describes the World Wide Web and other tools for accessing the Internet, including Telnet, FTP, Archie, and Gopher, and provides suggestions for using newsgroups, discussion groups, and E-mail as part of invention and research. A "search in progress" on the topic of censorship on the Internet demonstrates how to use various search strategies to locate information.

Improved MLA and APA Guidelines. Updated to reflect the latest editions of the *MLA Handbook for Writers of Research Papers* and the *Publication Manual of the American Psychological Association,* the guidelines are now separated for easier reference. Guidelines for citing electronic sources, including Web sites, E-mail correspondence, and postings to newsgroups or discussion groups, are also provided.

Full Color Design. The new design highlights collaborative activities, lists of basic features, guidelines for peer review, and other important activities and information throughout the text.

ADDITIONAL RESOURCES

Numerous resources accompany *The St. Martin's Guide to Writing.*

The *Instructor's Resource Manual,* by Rise B. Axelrod, Charles R. Cooper, and Lenora P. Smith of the University of Houston, includes a catalog of helpful advice for new instructors (by Alison M. Warriner, Sacred Heart University), guidelines on common teaching practices such as assigning journals and setting up group activities, guidelines on responding to and evaluating student writing (by Charles Cooper), guidelines on helping students to prepare for writing assessment tests, suggested course plans, detailed chapter plans, an annotated bibliography in composition and rhetoric, and a selection of background readings. New to this edition are service-learning projects and two new articles on collaborative writing and using computers in the classroom.

Free Falling and other student essays, Third Edition, edited by Paul Sladky (Augusta College), formerly *The Great American Bologna Festival and other student essays,* is a collection of essays written by students across the nation using *The St. Martin's Guide.* The ten chapters in the book correspond to those in Part I of the *Guide.* The book includes forms for the submission of students' essays so that we may consider them for possible publication in future editions.

Who Are We? Readings in Identity and Community and Work and Career, prepared by Rise B. Axelrod and Charles R. Cooper, contains selections that expand on the two new themes in the fifth edition. Full of ideas for classroom discussion and writing, the readings offer students additional perspectives and thought-provoking analysis.

The St. Martin's Guide for Writing in the Disciplines: A Guide for Faculty, by Richard Bullock (Wright State University), is a handy reference for faculty, with ideas for using writing in courses across the curriculum. Among the topics covered are designing assignments that get students writing, using informal writing activities to help students to learn, assigning portfolios, and responding to student writing.

Designed to support classroom instruction, a packet of *transparencies* includes lists of important features for each genre, critical reading guides, collaborative activities, and checklists—all adapted from the text.

Student Writer Software is an easy-to-use process writing program with exercises and an online handbook.

MicroGrade: A Teacher's Gradebook is an easy-to-use new software program for tracking grades and producing progress reports. It can be used on any computer system.

ACKNOWLEDGMENTS

We owe an enormous debt to all the rhetoricians and composition specialists whose theory, research, and pedagogy have informed *The St. Martin's Guide to Writing*. We would be adding many pages to an already long book if we were to name everyone to whom we are indebted; suffice it to say that we have been eclectic in our borrowing.

We must also acknowledge immeasurable lessons learned from all the writers, professional and student alike, whose work we analyzed and whose writing we used in this and earlier editions.

So many instructors and students have contributed ideas and criticism over the years. We want especially to thank the staff, instructors, and students in the Third College Writing Program at the University of California at San Diego, where from 1979 to 1991 we developed and revised the *Guide*. We are still benefiting from the astute insights of M. A. Syverson, Kate Gardner, Kristin Hawkinson, Michael Pemberton, Irv Peckham, Keith Grant-Davie, Evelyn Torres, Gesa Kirsch, James Degan, and other teaching assistants and lecturers from these years. Others who have made special contributions to this edition are Kathryn O'Rourke, California State University, San Bernardino; Steven Axelrod, University of California, Riverside; and Jeremiah Axelrod, University of California, Irvine.

The members of the advisory board for the fifth edition, a group of dedicated composition instructors from across the country, have provided us with extensive insights and suggestions for the chapters in Part I and have given us the benefit of their advice on new features, in many cases testing them in their own classrooms. For all of their many contributions, we would like to thank Richard Boyd, University of California, Riverside; James L. Brown, Kansas City Kansas Community College; Richard Bullock, Wright State University; Sandy Cavanah, Hopkinsville Community College; Robert Corrigan, Baltimore City Community College; Joan Kuzma Costello, Inver Hills Community College; Janet Kay Dillon, Kansas State University; Nancy B. Etheridge, Boise State University; Judith Gardner, University of Texas, San Antonio; Michael A. Miller, Longview Community College; Donna Padgett, formerly of Macon College; Victoria F. Sarkisian, Marist College; Nancy W. Shankle, Abilene Christian University; Lenora P. Smith, University of Houston; and Rosemary Winslow, Catholic University of America.

Many instructors across the nation have helped us to improve the book. For responding to detailed questionnaires about the fourth edition, we thank Mary Helen Adams, Hopkinsville Community College; Laura J. Adamson, Stephen F. Austin State University; Helen Aling, Northwestern College; Cathryn Amdahl, Harrisburg Area Community College; Bill Anderson, Black Hawk College; Connie Anish, Elgin Community College; Mary Bagley; Terry Baker, Pennsylvania State University, York; Rita Barkey, Indiana University, Kokomo; Helen Bauer, Iona College; Charles Beall, San Diego Mesa College; Robert D. Becker, Standing Rock College; Miriam E. Beebe, Weber State University; Todd W. Bersley, California State University, Northridge; Bruce Boeckel, Northwestern College; Suzanne Borowicz, Erie Community College; Herbert Botbyl, Montclair State University; Carol Boyd, Black Hawk College; Richard Boyd, University of California, Riverside; Carol Brown, South Puget Sound Community College; James L. Brown, Kansas City Kansas Community College; Phil Brown, Kirkwood Community College; Christopher C. Burnham, New Mexico State University; Terre Burton, Dixie College; J. Cannon, San Bernardino Valley College; Jo-Anne Cappelutti, Fullerton College; Thomas Carstensen, Delta College; Sandy Cavanah, Hopkinsville Community College; David V. Chevalier, Weber State University; Deborah Collins, Holy Names College; Marie Conte, California State University; Robert Corrigan, Baltimore City Community College; Joan Kuzma Costello, Inver Hills Community College; Rita Coyne, Black Hawk College; Gladys Craig, Russell Sage College; Gaylene Croker, Oxnard College; Sharon Cumberland, Seattle University; Carol Ann Curthoys, University of Portland; Helen Dale, University of Wisconsin, Eau Claire; Michelle W. Dega, Boise State University; Debra L. Frank Dew, University of Oklahoma; Janet Kay Dillon, Kansas State University; Margaret A. Dodson, Boise State University; Carolyn Engdahl, Fitchburg State College; Nancy B. Etheridge, Boise State University; Prescott Evarts, Monmouth University; Barbara L. Farley, Ocean County College; Terri Faut, Erie Community College; Evelyn Frazier, Kentucky State University; Kathy Frederickson, Quinsigamond Community College; Phyllis Gilbert, Mira Costa College; Jacquelin Glenny, Northwestern College; Michael B. Gracey, University of Maryland, Baltimore County; Albert J. Griffith, Our Lady of the Lake University; Barbara Grogan-Barone, George Mason University; Mitzi Harris, Western Wyoming Community College; Gerald Haslam, Sonoma State University; Arthur Henne, Pennsylvania State University, York; Fred Holzknecht, Gavilan College; Dorothy W. Howell, University of North Carolina, Charlotte; Maurice Hunt, Baylor University; William R. Hunter, Edinboro University; Diane Hyer, Truett-McConnell College; Johnny R. Johnston, California State University, Long Beach; Phyllis Karas, North Shore Community College; Lisa Kilczewski, North Idaho College; Connie Kirk, Corning Community College; Linda Kissler, Westmoreland County Community College; Katy Koenen, Seattle University; Cynthia Leavelle, Mississippi College; Edna Maye Loveless, La Sierra University; Michael T. Lueker, Boise State University; David Mair, University of Oklahoma; Joan Marcus, Genesee Community College; David Martin, Shoreline Community College; Joe Mason, University of Alaska, Northwest Campus; Phil Mayfield, Fullerton College; Marcia A. McDonald, Belmont University; Timothy F. McGinn, Oakland University; Michael McIrvin, University of Wyoming; Jackie McNamara, Spokane Community College; Michael A. Miller, Longview Community College; Mary Natali, Coconino Community

College; Tom Newhouse, Buffalo State College; Kathleen Nigro, Saint Louis University; Bebe Nockolai, Maryville University; Kathryn O'Hehir, Brainerd Community College; Anthony O'Keeffe, Bellarmine College; Juilene Osborne-McKnight, Northampton Community College; Anne Panning, University of Hawaii, Manoa; Carole Clark Papper, Ball State University; Carole C. Pfeffer, Bellarmine College; Robbie Pinter, Belmont University; Karen Polanski, Erie Community College; Carol Flanagan Propp, Erie Community College, South Campus; Steven J. Rayshich, Westmoreland County Community College; Donald T. Rhoads Jr., Elizabethtown College; James Robinson, Kapi'olani Community College; Shirley K. Rose, Purdue University; Meena Sachdeva, Kapi'olani Community College; Isa Sage, Monmouth College; Alyce H. Salmon, Monmouth University; Nadine S. St. Louis, University of Wisconsin, Eau Claire; Victoria F. Sarkisian, Marist College; Stephanie Satie, California State University, Northridge; Peter C. Schwartz, Elmira College; Don Schweda, Quincy University; Nancy W. Shankle, Abilene Christian University; Michael T. Sita Jr., Pima County Community College; Virginia M. Skinner-Linnenberg, North Central Michigan College; Nina Skokut, West Coast University; Lenora P. Smith, University of Houston; Patricia M. Smith, Metropolitan Community College; Katie Stahlnecker, Creighton University; Beckey Stamm, Columbus State Community College; Joanne T. Stauffer, Millersville University; Richard Steiger, Murray State University; Sandra Sullivan, Purdue University; Ann H. Sweetman, Quinsigamond Community College; John A. Walsh, University of Guam; Tom Walsh, St. Anselm College; William R. Walters, Rock Valley College; Alison Warriner, Sacred Heart University; Rose Williams, McMurray University; Charlotte Wilmeth-Street, Victor Valley College; Sheila Wood, North Idaho College; Janet Yu, Santa Monica College; and Jean Zipke, University of New Hampshire, Manchester.

For reviewing new readings, we thank Richard Bullock, Wright State University; Elizabeth H. Curtin, Salisbury State University; Michele Harris, Western Wyoming Community College; Maurice Hunt, Baylor University; David Mair, University of Oklahoma; Riki Matthews, Metropolitan State College; Mary Meiser, University of Wisconsin, Eau Claire; Michael A. Miller, Longview Community College; Fred Poe, Murray State College; Steven J. Rayshich, Westmoreland County Community College; Duane Roen, Arizona State University; Shirley K. Rose, Purdue University; Nancy W. Shankle, Abilene Christian University; Virginia M. Skinner-Linnenberg, North Central Michigan College; Lenora P. Smith, University of Houston; and Alison Warriner, Sacred Heart University.

Finally, we would like to thank Laura J. Gurak, University of Minnesota; Michael Meeker, Winona State University; Victoria F. Sarkisian, Marist College; and Stuart A. Selber, Texas Tech University, for useful comments on the new section about the Internet. We are also grateful to the following instructors for their insightful comments and suggestions: Saralinda Blanning, Tamara I. Dozier, Tammy J. Metcalf, and Stacy Harper Wolkwitz of Wright State University and Judith M. Davis, Chad Engbers, and Felicia Pattison of Catholic University of America.

For this new edition of *The St. Martin's Guide*, we also gratefully acknowledge the special contributions of several people. Debora Person, of the University of Wyoming Law Library, provided useful comments on the section on using the library. M. A. Syverson, of the University of Texas, Austin, wrote the section on using the

Internet to conduct research and Victoria F. Sarkisian, of Marist College, added strategies for conducting research on the Internet. Andrew Harnack and Eugene Kleppinger have graciously given us permission to adapt their guidelines for citing Internet sources, for which we thank them. Finally, we are especially grateful to the student authors for allowing us to reprint their work in *Free Falling and other student essays* and in *The St. Martin's Guide.*

Carla Samodulski, our editor, deserves more praise and applause than we can express. She has proved to be a creative, supportive colleague and collaborator. She has written more than a few sentences for this new edition and has participated in all aspects of our work. And she is a superb editor of our writing and a fine writer herself. Thanks, Carla. We would also like to thank Jimmy Fleming for his insights and support, Erica Appel for her meticulous attention to detail and for cheerfully coping with a complex project and a demanding schedule, and Chris Helms, Tony Mathias, Karen Melton, and Janice Wiggins for their creativity and marketing know-how. Susan Cottenden deserves praise for skillfully organizing and editing *Free Falling and other student essays* as does Angela Saragusa for managing several components of the ancillary program. Finally, we would like to thank Sandy Schechter and Kevin Glass for their work in clearing permissions.

The St. Martin's Guide to Writing is enriched also by the work of several people who have written materials to accompany the book. We want to thank Richard Bullock for contributing *The St. Martin's Guide for Writing in the Disciplines: A Guide for Faculty;* Paul Sladky for editing the third edition of our collection of student essays, *Free Falling and other student essays;* Alison Warriner for composing the opening section of the *Instructor's Resource Manual;* and Lenora Smith for helping to update other sections of the manual.

Charles wishes to thank his wife, Mary Anne, for all the decades of support, affection, understanding, and good humor. It's been a great time, sweetheart, and it's not over yet. Rise wishes to thank her husband, Steven, for the loving care with which he so artfully cultivates their garden, and their son, Jeremiah, who blossoms more wondrously with each new year.

The St. Martin's Guide to Writing

CHAPTER 1

Introduction

Why is writing important? What is the connection between writing and thinking? Does reading have something to do with learning to write? How can I learn to write more effectively and efficiently? These are some of the questions you may be asking as you begin this writing course. Read on—for *The St. Martin's Guide to Writing* offers some answers to these and other questions you may have.

WHY WRITING IS IMPORTANT

Writing has wide-ranging implications for the way we think and learn as well as for our chances of success, our personal development, and our relationships with other people.

Writing Influences the Way People Think

First, writing encourages us to be organized, logical, even creative, in our thinking. Moreover, it urges us to ask questions, to look critically at what others have to say as well as what we ourselves think.

The rules, or conventions, of writing impose a certain kind of order on our thinking. To write comprehensible sentences and paragraphs, we need to put words in a certain order: to combine subjects with predicates, coordinate parallel ideas, and subordinate the particular to the general. From different kinds of writing, we learn different ways of developing our thoughts: how to reflect critically on our own behavior in autobiography; how to distinguish fact from opinion in concept explanations; how to make judgments about opposing points of view in position papers. Further, we learn to analyze ideas and to synthesize what we learn from others with what we experience firsthand. The process of writing actually fosters new ways of thinking.

> Writing keeps me from believing everything I read.
> —Gloria Steinem

> Those who are learning to compose and arrange their sentences with accuracy and order are learning, at the same time, to think with accuracy and order.
> —Hugh Blair

Writing Contributes to the Way We Learn

When we take notes in class or as we read, writing helps us to sort information, to highlight what is important, and to remember what we are learning. Taking notes also yields a written record that we can review later. Outlining or summarizing provides an overview of a new subject and fosters close analysis of it. By underlining and making marginal comments as we read, we become involved in conversation—even debate—with other writers. Thus, writing helps us to learn effectively and think critically.

Writing allows us to bring together new and old ideas: As we discover and understand new concepts, writing helps us relate them to other ideas. In this way, writing clarifies and extends our understanding of the world.

> I write to understand as much as to be understood.
>
> —Elie Wiesel

> The mere process of writing is one of the most powerful tools we have for clarifying our own thinking. I am never as clear about any matter as when I have just finished writing about it.
>
> —James Van Allen

Writing Promotes Success in College and on the Job

Because writing encourages us to think critically and to learn, it also makes a significant contribution to academic and professional success. Students whose writing is logically organized, well-supported, and inventive usually do well in courses throughout the curriculum. Job seekers who write persuasive application letters improve their chances of finding positions, and many professionals must be able to write effective letters, speeches, reports, and proposals in order to advance in their fields.

> The aim of school is to produce citizens who are able to communicate with each other, to defend points of view, and to criticize. . . . Writing is not just another subject. There is a symbiotic relationship between writing and thinking.
>
> —Albert Shanker

Writing Fosters Personal Development

Through writing, we learn to reflect deeply on our personal experience and to examine critically our most basic assumptions. Thus, writing enables us to understand ourselves better. Moreover, becoming an author confers authority. It gives us the confidence to assert our own ideas, even when others may question or challenge us.

> Writing is the act of saying *I*, of imposing oneself upon other people, of saying *listen to me, see it my way, change your mind.*
>
> —Joan Didion

> Writing has been for a long time my major tool for self-instruction and self-development.
> —Toni Cade Bambara

Writing Connects Us to the World

As writing contributes to the way we think, it also impels us to communicate our thoughts and feelings, to take part in the conversations around us. The impulse to write can be as urgent as the need to share an experience with a friend, to question an argument in a book, or to respond to a provocative comment in class discussion.

As writers, we speak out for many different reasons: to entertain, to let readers know what we think or how we feel, to influence readers' decisions, actions, or beliefs. We may even confront readers, criticizing their attitudes and behaviors.

> Writing is a struggle against silence.
> —Carlos Fuentes

> My starting point [in writing] is always a feeling of partisanship, a sense of injustice. . . . I write because there is some lie I want to expose, some fact to which I wish to draw attention, and my initial concern is to get a hearing.
> —George Orwell

Exercise 1.1

Write a page or so about how writing has affected your life, and use specific examples. Before you begin, reflect on the role writing has played in your education and personal life. Maybe you can recall a time—writing for yourself or for a school assignment—when writing enabled you to think in a way that surprised you. What kind of writing were you doing and what did you discover? Or think of an occasion when you did extremely well on a writing assignment. How did this success come about and what did you achieve? Or perhaps you once needed to communicate anger, love, hope, jealousy, or disagreement to someone, and writing seemed the best way to do it. What caused this situation, what did you say, and what was the response? These are just some examples of what you might write about.

HOW WRITING IS LEARNED

Writing is important. But can it be learned? This question is crucial because for centuries writing has been veiled in mystery. Many people think good writing is the result of natural talent. They assume "real" writers can dash off a perfect draft in one sitting with minimal effort. They believe that if you do not write brilliantly from the start, you will never learn to write well. Research shows, however, that these assumptions are wrong. Writing can be learned. In fact, while some people may seem to have a gift for writing, virtually anyone can learn to write well enough to handle the writing required in college, at work, and in personal life.

> I believe in miracles in every area of life *except* writing.
> —Isaac Bashevis Singer

Learning to write well takes time and much effort, but it can be done.
—Margaret Mead

As you learn to write, you need to understand three basic ways of thinking about writing:

How written texts work

How the writing process works

How to think critically about your writing

Your development as a writer depends on your knowing all three kinds of learning and understanding their interdependence. Because writing situations differ, writers use different writing processes to produce different kinds of texts. In this way, process and product are inextricably related, but the relationship is complex because the situations that call for writing are so varied. As you write the different assignments in this book, you should reflect on what you are doing and learning. Such reflection reinforces and extends your learning.

How Written Texts Work

How a text works is a function of what it is for—its purpose and audience. Some texts—position papers, for example—try to convince readers to take the writer's point of view seriously. Other kinds of texts serve different purposes: An autobiographical essay conveys the significance of a particular event in the writer's life; a proposal urges readers to take certain actions to solve a problem; an explanation provides readers with information. Texts, then, can be categorized by their purposes and audiences. These categories are called writing *genres.*

Each genre has its own distinctive formal features and content. An autobiographical event essay, for example, is narrative in form and includes descriptive detail and an indication of the event's significance. In contrast, a proposal is argumentative in form, giving reasons why readers should adopt the proposed solution.

Although texts vary within the same genre (no two autobiographies, for example, are the same), texts in a genre nonetheless follow a general pattern. This patterning allows for a certain amount of predictability, without which communication would be difficult, if not impossible. Language—whether spoken or written—is a system of social interaction. Everyone who speaks the same language learns to recognize certain patterns—what particular words mean when used in different contexts, how words should be ordered to make sentences comprehensible, how sentences can be related to one another to make coherent paragraphs and essays, and so forth. These language patterns make communication possible.

To learn to read and write, we have to become familiar with the patterns or conventions of written texts. As readers, we develop expectations that enable us to anticipate where a text is going so that we can make sense of it as we read. Similarly, as writers we learn how to order and present our thoughts in language patterns that readers can recognize and follow. If you are writing a position paper, for example, you need to know that readers expect claims to be supported by relevant reasons and evidence.

Working within a genre does not mean, however, that writing must be mechanical or follow a set formula. Each genre has basic features, but these are broad frameworks within which writers are free to create. Most writers, in fact, find that working within a framework allows them to be more creative, not less. Some even blur the boundaries between genres, creating new forms of expression. Thus, we see that change as well as predictability are built into the language system.

> A writer is a reader moved to emulation.
>
> —Saul Bellow

> You would learn very little in this world if you were not allowed to imitate. And to repeat your imitations until some solid grounding . . . was achieved and the slight but wonderful difference—that made you *you* and no one else—could assert itself.
>
> —Mary Oliver

How We Learn to Write Texts That Work. To learn the conventions of a particular genre, you need to read examples of that genre. At the same time, you should also practice writing in the genre.

> Read, read, read. . . . Just like a carpenter who works as an apprentice and studies the master. Read!
>
> —William Faulkner

Reading is crucial. As you read examples of a genre, you begin to recognize its predictable patterns as well as the possibilities for innovation. This knowledge is stored in your memory and used both when you read and when you write in that genre.

Experienced writers read and learn from positive examples as well as negative ones. Sometimes, they focus on a particular problem—how to write realistic-sounding dialogue, for example. They do not look for answers in a single model. Instead, they sample many texts to see how different writers work with a certain feature of the genre. This sampling is not imitation, but education. Like artists and craftspeople, writers have always learned from other writers.

> I went back to the good nature books that I had read. And I analyzed them. I wrote outlines of whole books—outlines of chapters—so that I could see their structure. And I copied down their transitional sentences or their main sentences or their closing sentences or their lead sentences. I especially paid attention to how these writers made transitions between paragraphs and scenes.
>
> —Annie Dillard

Exercise 1.2

Make two lists: (1) the genres you have *read* recently, such as explanations of how to do something, stories, autobiographies, reports of current events, opinion pieces, reviews of television programs or films; and (2) the genres you have *written* recently, both for college courses and for other purposes. Based on your experience, write a few sentences speculating about how your reading influences your writing.

How the Writing Process Works

Have you ever tried the dangerous method of writing? You begin by writing the first word of the introduction and write straight through to the last word of the conclusion. No planning or trying out ideas before writing; no adding, cutting, or revising as you write; no help from friends or teachers; no second drafts or second thoughts.

The night before a paper is due, desperate students may try the dangerous method. But it is not a very smart way to write. All writers need to develop a process that will help them think critically about a subject. They need to make writing a true process of discovery.

> I don't see writing as a communication of something already discovered, as "truths" already known. Rather, I see writing as a job of experiment. It's like any discovery job; you don't know what's going to happen until you try it.
>
> —William Stafford

Research on how writers write indicates that the writing process is recursive rather than linear. In other words, instead of going from one word to the next, from introduction straight through to conclusion, the experience of writing is more like taking a steep trail with frequent switchbacks; it appears that you are retracing old ground even though you are rising to a new level.

Few writers begin with a complete understanding of a subject. Most use writing as a process of learning, recording ideas and information they have collected, exploring connections and implications, letting the writing lead them to greater understanding. As they develop ideas and plan a draft, writers set goals for their writing: goals for the whole essay (to confront readers or inspire them, for example) and goals for particular passages (to make a sentence emphatic or include details in a paragraph). While writing, they often pause to reread what they have written to see whether they are satisfactorily fulfilling their goals. Rereading may lead writers to further invention and problem solving, to rewording or reorganizing, or even to reconsidering some goals. This continual shifting of attention is what makes the process recursive. Invention does not stop when drafting begins; it continues throughout drafting and revising. Most writers plan and revise their plans, draft and revise their drafts, write and read what they have written, and then write some more. Even when they have a final draft, most writers reread it one more time—proofreading to edit for clarity, grammar, and spelling.

> You are always going back and forth between the outline and the writing, bringing them closer together, or just throwing out the outline and making a new one.
>
> —Annie Dillard

Experienced writers depend on drafting and revising to lead them to new ideas and insights. Many writers claim that they write in order to discover what they think.

> How do I know what I think until I see what I say?
>
> —E. M. Forster

Seasoned writers do not wait for inspiration. They work at their writing, knowing it takes time and perseverance. The hard work comes in thinking things out. Writers all have promising ideas, but until they develop them in writing, they cannot know whether their ideas make sense or lead anywhere.

> Don't think and then write it down. Think on paper.
> —Harvey Kemelman

Once immersed in invention—figuring out what they want to say about the subject, contemplating what readers already think about it, and so forth—most writers find that they continue inventing even when away from their desks. Taking a walk, having a conversation, even dreaming can help the mind see connections or solve problems that had proved frustrating earlier.

> I never quite know when I'm not writing.
> —James Thurber

Like most creative activities, writing is a form of problem-solving. As they work on a draft, most writers continually discover and try to solve writing problems—how to bring a scene to life, how to handle objections, whether to begin with this point or that. The more writers know about their subjects and genres, the better they can anticipate and solve problems. Experienced writers develop a repertoire of strategies for solving problems they are likely to encounter. These are the tools of the trade, and this text provides you with a full toolbox.

> Writing is probably like a scientist thinking about some scientific problem, or an engineer about an engineering problem.
> —Doris Lessing

> You have to work problems out for yourself on paper. Put the stuff down and read it—to see if it works.
> —Joyce Cary

Although writers often work alone, writing does not have to be a solitary activity. Most writers share their ideas as well as their writing, actively seeking constructive critical comments from friends and colleagues. Playwrights, poets, and novelists depend on other writers to read their drafts and offer suggestions for revising. Engineers, business executives, scientists, and government workers plan much of their writing in teams; and when the drafting begins, the writers count on the other team members for advice and support.

> For excellence, the presence of others is always required.
> —Hannah Arendt

> I like working collaboratively from time to time. I like fusing ideas into one vision. I like seeing that vision come to life with other people who know exactly what it took to get there.
> —Amy Tan

Exercise 1.3

Read the following quotes. The first one contains a simile (writing is like _____), and the second a metaphor (writing is _____).

> Writing is like jumping into a freezing lake and slowly coming to the surface.
>
> —A student

> To me, writing is a horseback ride into heaven and hell and back. I am grateful if I can crawl back alive.
>
> —Thomas Sanchez

Write a simile or a metaphor that best expresses your experience with writing. Compare your simile or metaphor with those of your classmates. What do they suggest about your experiences with writing?

How We Develop a Writing Process That Works. As a student learning to write, you need to develop a writing process that is flexible and yet provides structure. It should be a process that neither oversimplifies nor overwhelms, one that helps you learn about a subject and write a successful essay. The Guides to Writing in Part I of this book are designed to meet this need. These guides suggest what you need to think about for each different writing situation. The first few times you write in a new genre, you can rely on these guidelines. They provide a scaffolding to support your work until you become more familiar with each genre.

When engaging in any new and complex activity—driving, playing an instrument, skiing, or writing—we have to learn how to break down the activity into a series of stages or steps. In learning to play tennis, for example, you can isolate lobbing from volleying, or work on your backhand or serve. Similarly, in writing about an autobiographical event, you might first recall what happened, then fill in details of the scene or reflect on the event's significance. At each point you focus on one problem or issue at a time. Dividing the process in this way makes a complex writing task manageable without oversimplifying it.

> You know when you think about writing a book, you think it is overwhelming. But, actually, you break it down into tiny little tasks any moron could do.
>
> —Annie Dillard

Exercise 1.4

Write a page or so describing how you usually proceed with an ambitious writing project. Think of the last time you wrote something fairly difficult, long, or complicated. Do not choose a writing project completed in class or under strict time limits. Describe the process you followed as fully as you can. Begin by describing your purpose for writing and the assumptions you made about your readers' knowledge of the subject or their expectations about your writing.

Use the following questions to help you remember what you did, but do not feel compelled to answer all of them. Say whatever you want about how you went about completing the writing project.

- How much time passed before you started putting your ideas on paper? What were you doing during this time?
- What kind of plan did you begin with? How did your plan change as you worked?
- What discoveries did you make as you were writing your first draft? What major problems did you encounter, and how did you solve them? What changes, if any, did you make after completing your first draft?
- With whom did you discuss your ideas and plans, and who helped you with your writing?

How to Think Critically about Your Writing

Research indicates that when you think about what you are learning, you remember it better. Thinking also helps you to continue learning by bringing to mind what you had forgotten or did not realize you knew.

Learning to write is like learning a foreign language. As young children, we are immersed in spoken language and acquire it naturally, almost effortlessly. In contrast, learning to write requires conscious effort. Beginners need to think about what they are doing—what verb tense to use, whether to concede a point or try to refute it, whether to use slang or more formal words, and so on.

As you practice different kinds, or genres, of writing, you will find that many of your decisions do not require conscious effort. When writing in any one genre, you will rely on familiar strategies that usually produce effective writing for you in that genre. But these strategies will not work in every case simply because every writing situation is unique.

To solve unexpected problems, you have to think about your knowledge of the genre and the writing process. Experienced writers often reread what they have written in order to evaluate the approach they have taken to a writing problem. When writers reflect on what works and what does not, it helps them anticipate and solve problems. Reflection also helps writers feel more competent and in charge of the process.

> Blot out, correct, insert, refine,
> Enlarge, diminish, interline,
> Be mindful, when invention fails,
> To scratch your head, and bite your nails.
> —Jonathan Swift

How We Learn to Think Critically about Our Writing. The exercises in this chapter are designed to help you think, write, and talk with others about your reading and writing experiences. As we have seen, such self-reflection is a key to becoming a better writer. Each chapter in Part I of this book concludes with a section entitled Thinking Critically about What You Have Learned, which gives you an opportunity to look back and reflect on three aspects of what you have written:

1. Your own problem-solving process
2. The influence your reading of other texts in the genre has had on your own text
3. What you have learned about the social dimensions of the genre—how thinking and writing both affect and are affected by society

> I may remember some of the things that were said by the countless millions of words I've read, but finally what I've taken away . . . are habits of understanding, methods of reasoning, points of view, ranges of feeling . . . my mind is not merely mine, but is inhabited by a multitude of borrowed voices.
>
> —William Gass

> To speak [or write] English is to think in that language, to adopt the ideology of the people whose language it is and to be "inhabited" by their discourses.
>
> —Gloria Anzaldúa

Exercise 1.5

Make one list of your strengths as a writer and another of your weaknesses. Then, write a few sentences explaining how you developed your strengths. Describe certain strengths and try to account for their beginnings and recent refinements. Consider the possible influences on each of your writing strengths.

USING THIS BOOK

This book is divided into five major sections.

Part I offers writing assignments for several important genres of nonfiction prose: autobiography, firsthand biography, profile, explanation, position paper, proposal, evaluation, causal analysis, and literary interpretation.

Parts II through V provide strategies for invention and critical reading, writing, and research. Also included are guidelines for writing research papers, using sources, taking essay exams, and assembling a portfolio.

Each chapter in Part I provides readings that demonstrate how written texts of that genre work and a Guide to Writing that leads you through the process of writing your own essays. Each chapter in Part I also includes a separate discussion of purpose and audience and a summary of the basic features of the genre. As we have mentioned, a section on Thinking Critically about What You Have Learned concludes each chapter.

Previewing the Writing Assignments

Pause now to preview each of the writing assignments in this text. On the first page of the Guide to Writing in Chapters 2 through 10 you will find The Writing Assignment. Read this assignment in each chapter to get a quick sense of the genre. Also skim the first invention activity, which you will find immediately after the assignment. It usually provides examples of essay topics or subjects. Then, write several sentences responding to the following questions:

- Which of these kinds of essays have you written before?
- With which of these genres have you had the most experience?
- Of the genres you have never written, which one would you most like to write? Explain briefly why it interests you.

The Readings in each chapter were written by professional writers as well as by students who have used earlier editions of this book. They were selected to reflect a wide range of topics and strategies. If you read these selections with a critical eye, you will see the many different ways writers use a genre.

Each reading selection is accompanied by three groups of questions and some commentary to help you learn how texts in that genre work. Connecting to Culture and Experience invites you to explore with other students an issue or question raised by the text; Analyzing Writing Strategies focuses on key textual features; Considering Topics for Your Own Essay offers ideas you might write about; and the Commentary points out additional features and strategies. Bold type identifies the features focused on in Analyzing Writing Strategies and Commentary so that you can readily identify them.

The Guide to Writing in each assignment chapter provides detailed guidelines for writing an essay in that genre. Included are the following sections: Invention and Research, Planning and Drafting, a Critical Reading Guide, Revising, and Editing and Proofreading. We will now preview these various types of guidelines.

Invention and Research

Each guide begins with invention activities. These are designed to help you find a topic, discover what you already know about it, consider your purpose and audience, research the topic further to see what others have written about it, and develop your ideas.

Most of the assignments in this book provide opportunities to explore your connections to the world. When you are choosing a topic to write about, you might consider suggestions listed under "Identity and Community" and "Work and Career" in the Invention section. These topics enable you to explore your personal connections to the various communities of which you are a part, visit and learn more about places in your community, debate issues important to your community, examine your ideas and attitudes about your present work, and consider issues related to your future career.

Invention is not a stage you can skip. It is the basic, ongoing preoccupation of all writing. As writers, we cannot choose *whether* to invent; we can only decide *how*.

Invention can be especially productive when it is systematic—and when it is written down. Not only does it focus your attention on your purpose and audience, but it then helps you identify and solve problems. Exploratory invention writing can free you for a while from the responsibility of composing coherent and grammatical prose and thus allow you to write more freely about your topic—turning writing into a mode of discovery.

Invention may help you at several stages: while exploring your topic, while drafting, and while revising. The special advantage of the invention activities is that they focus on the features and possibilities of a particular kind of writing in each Part I chapter.

Use Writing to Explore Your Ideas. You can use writing to gather your thoughts and see where they lead. The key to exploratory writing is to refrain from censoring yourself. Simply try writing for five to ten minutes. Explore your ideas freely, letting one idea lead to another. Later, you can reread what you have written and select the most promising ideas to develop.

Focus on One Issue at a Time. Explore your topic systematically by dividing it into its component parts and exploring them one at a time. For example, instead of trying to think of your whole argument, focus on one reason and the support you would give for it, or focus on how you might refute one objection to your argument.

Give Your Ideas Time to Percolate. Begin the invention process far enough ahead of the deadline so that your thinking can develop fully. Spread your invention over several days, allowing your mind time to work on the topic.

Previewing a Guide to Writing

Turn to the Guide to Writing in any of the assignment chapters (Chapters 2 through 10), and skim it from beginning to end to get an idea of what it offers.

Planning and Drafting

Once an initial period of invention is completed, review what you have learned about your topic and start to plan your essay. At this stage, the Guides to Writing help you to set goals and to organize your ideas and information to achieve those goals. When you plan, you put your ideas into a coherent, purposeful order that is appropriate for your readers; when you draft, you choose the words that those readers will understand and find interesting. Invention continues as you draft, for you will make further discoveries about your topic as you work. When you draft, though, you shift your focus from generating new ideas and gathering further information to forging meaningful connections among your ideas and information.

As you begin your first draft, try to keep in mind the following practical points, many of which assist professional writers as they begin drafting.

Choose the Best Time and Place. You can write a draft anytime and anyplace, as you probably already know. People write under the most surprising or arduous conditions. Drafting is likely to go smoothly, however, if you choose a time and place ideally suited for sustained and thoughtful work. Many professional writers suggest that you need a place where you can concentrate for a few hours without repeated interruptions. Writers often find one place where they write best, and they return there whenever they have to write. Try to find such a place for yourself.

Make Revision Easy. If possible, compose on a word processor. If you do not have access to one and must write out or type your text, write on only one side of the page. Leave wide margins. Write on every other line or triple-space your typing. If you arrange your draft on the page in this way, it will be easier for you to change, add, cut, and rearrange material when you revise.

Set Reasonable Goals. Divide your task into manageable portions. The goal of completing a long essay may be so intimidating that it prevents you from starting. Just aim to complete a small part of the essay—one section or paragraph—at a time.

Lower Your Expectations. Be satisfied with less than perfect writing, and do not be overly critical. Remember, you are working on a draft that you will revise. Approach the draft as an experiment or an exercise. Try things out. Follow digressions. Later, you can go back and delete or cross out a sentence or a section, or make other changes.

Do the Easy Parts First. Try not to agonize over the first sentence or paragraph. Just write. If you have trouble with the introduction, write an anecdote or example or assertion first, if that seems easier. If you have a lot of information, start with the part you understand best. If you get stuck at a difficult spot, skip over it and go on to an easier part. Just getting started can be difficult, so doing the simple parts first is often a good approach. If you put off getting started, your work will be rushed and late; your ideas will not grow and change; and thus you will not acquire new insights about your topic. If you start late, your fear of writing will probably increase. If you start early, however, you will find writing easier and more enjoyable. You will also do your best work.

Guess at Words, Spelling, and Facts. If you cannot think of just the right word, or if you have forgotten an important fact, just continue drafting. You can search out the fact or find the elusive word at another time. If you cannot remember how to spell a word, guess and keep going. Later, you can look it up in a dictionary. Inexperienced writers lose large amounts of thinking and drafting time puzzling over a word or trying to recall a specific fact.

Write Quickly. If you set reasonable goals, keep your expectations low, and do the easy parts first, then you should be able to draft quickly. Say what you want to say and move on.

Review your notes, make a plan, and then put your notes aside. You can always refer to them later if you need an exact quote or fact. Now and then, of course, you will want to reread what you have written, but do not reread obsessively. Return to drafting new material as soon as possible. Avoid editing or revising during this stage. You need not have everything exactly right in the first draft. If you want to delete a phrase or sentence, draw a line through it or use your word processor's strikeout function, in case you want to use the phrase or sentence later.

Take Short Breaks—and Reward Yourself! Drafting can be hard work, and you may need to take a break to refresh yourself. But be careful not to wander off for too long or you may lose momentum. Set small goals and reward yourself regularly. That makes it easier to stay at the task of drafting.

Critical Reading Guide

After you have finished drafting your essay, you may want to show it to someone else for comments on how to improve it. Experienced writers often seek advice from others.

To evaluate someone else's draft, you need to read with a critical eye. You must be both positive and skeptical—positive in that you want to identify what is workable and promising in the draft, skeptical in that you need to question the writer's assumptions and decisions.

Here is some general advice on reading any draft critically.

Make a Record of Your Reading. Although talking about a draft may be useful and even fun, you can be most helpful to the writer if you put your ideas on paper. When you write down your comments and suggestions—either on the draft or on another piece of paper—you leave a record that can be used later when the writer revises the material.

Read First for an Overall Impression. On first reading, try not to be distracted by errors of spelling, punctuation, or word choice. Look at the big issues: clear focus, compelling presentation, forcefulness of argument, novelty and quality of ideas. What seems particularly good? What problems do you see? Focus on the overall goal of the draft and how well it was met. Write just a few sentences expressing your initial reaction.

Read Again to Analyze the Draft. For the second reading, focus on individual parts of the draft, bringing to bear what you know about the genre and the subject.

When you read the draft at this level, you must shift your attention from one aspect of the essay to another. Consider how well the opening paragraphs introduce the essay and prepare the reader for what follows. Pay attention to specific writing strategies, like narration or argument. Notice whether the parts seem logically sequenced. Look for detailing, reasoning, or other kinds of support.

As you analyze, you are evaluating as well as describing, but a critical reading involves more than criticism of the draft. A good critical reader helps a writer see how each part of an essay works and how all the parts work together. By describing what you see, you help the writer view the draft more objectively, a perspective that is necessary for thoughtful revising.

Offer Advice, but Do Not Rewrite. As a critical reader, you may be tempted to rewrite the draft—to change a word here, correct an error there, add your ideas everywhere. Resist the impulse. Your role is to read carefully, to point out what you think is or is not working, to make suggestions and ask questions. Leave the revising to the writer.

In turn, the writer has a responsibility to listen to your comments but is under no obligation to do as you suggest. "Then why go to all the trouble?" you might ask. There are at least two reasons. First, when you read someone else's writing critically, you learn more about writing—about the decisions writers make, how a thoughtful reader reads, and the constraints of particular kinds of writing. Second, as a critical reader you embody for the writer the abstraction called "audience." By sharing your reactions with the writer, you complete the circuit of communication.

Revising

Productive invention and smooth drafting rarely result in the essay a writer has imagined. Experienced writers are not surprised or disappointed, however, because they expect revision to be necessary. They know that revising will bring them closer to the essay they really want to write. When writers read their drafts thoughtfully and critically—and perhaps reflect on the advice of others—they are able to see many opportunities for improvement. They may notice misspelled words or garbled sentences. Most important, however, they discover ways to delete, move, rephrase, and add material in order to say what they want to say more clearly.

View the Draft Objectively. To revise, you must first read your draft objectively, to see what it actually says instead of what you intended it to say. If you can, put the draft aside for a day or two. Getting advice from a critical reader will also help you view the draft more objectively.

Reconsider Your Purpose and Audience. Remind yourself of what you are trying to accomplish. Think carefully about what your readers know and believe. How can you interest them in your essay? How, specifically, do you hope to influence them?

Revise in Stages. Do not try to do everything at once. Begin by looking at the whole essay and then move to an analysis of each part. As we suggest in the following sections, focus initially on identifying and solving the major problems; consider possible solutions only after you have a general understanding of how the draft fails to achieve its purpose. Then, focus on clarity and coherence.

Look at Major Problems First. Identify any major problems that are preventing the draft from achieving its purpose. Major problems might include a lack of awareness of your audience, inadequate development of key parts, missing or incomplete sections, the need for further invention or research, or a low level of surprise or interest for readers.

Focus Next on Clarity and Coherence. Consider the beginning of your essay. Think about how well it prepares readers for the parts that follow. Look at each section of the essay in turn. The paragraphs should proceed in a logical order, with appropriate transitions to help readers connect the points you are making. Generalizations should be firmly and explicitly supported by specific details, examples, or evidence. Adjust sentences that do not yet say what you intend.

Editing and Proofreading

Once you have finished revising, your next step is to edit carefully to make sure that every word, phrase, and sentence is clear and correct. Using language and punctuation correctly is an essential part of good writing. Errors will distract readers and lessen your credibility as a writer.

Be sure to save editing until the end—*after* you have planned and worked out a revision. Too much editing too early in the writing process can limit, or even block, invention and drafting.

Keep a List of Your Common Errors. Note the grammatical and spelling errors you discover in your own writing. You will probably start to recognize error patterns to check for as you edit your work.

Begin Proofreading with the Last Sentence. To focus your attention on grammar and spelling, it may help to read backwards, beginning with the last sentence. When you read backwards, it is harder to pay attention to content and thus easier to recognize grammatical and spelling errors.

Exchange Drafts with Another Student. Because it is usually easier to see errors in someone else's writing than in your own, consider trading essays with a classmate and proofreading one another's writing.

Thinking Critically about What You Have Learned

Each chapter in Part I concludes with a set of activities to help you think about what you have learned studying the genre in that chapter. There are three different activities:

- Reflecting on Your Writing asks you to consider how you solved problems writing that particular kind of essay.
- Reviewing What You Learned from Reading helps you to discover what specific influence your reading had on your writing.
- Considering the Social Dimensions of the genre leads you to explore how thinking and writing reflect the cultural context in which they occur.

If you are compiling a portfolio on your coursework to hand in at the end of the term, these activities may help you assess your work.

In his college application, a student relates an experience that made him want to study wildlife biology. He explains that during a family visit to North Carolina the previous summer, his cousin invited him to help her with her graduate-school research project on black bears. He recalls how fearful, yet energized he was when he saw the first bear, a hefty 125-pound animal struggling to free itself from a specially designed trap. He describes how, following his cousin's instructions, he gathered the courage to draw the bear's attention to himself while his cousin used a long jabstick to inject the bear with tranquilizer. Then he details how he helped to tag the bear, measure and weigh it, identify its sex and estimate its age, take its temperature, rub the bear's rump where his cousin had made the injection, and hold the bear's lips open while his cousin counted the teeth and impressed a tattoo on the bear's lips. He concludes the story dramatically by describing the exhilarating moment when, sitting with the bear's head in his lap, his eyes and the bear's met as the bear began to awaken.

In her autobiography, an African-American writer recalls her high school graduation from a segregated all-black school in rural Arkansas in 1940. She writes about how proud she felt until a white superintendent of schools made a condescending speech. Describing his speech and the feelings it inspired in her, she remembers thinking initially that she was the only one in the audience insulted and angered by the speech. When she noticed the proud defiance in her classmates' eyes, the way they stiffened and sat up taller in their seats, and their polite but restrained applause at the end of the speech, she felt sure that they also took offense. But they were too well brought up, too proud, and also too wary to express their outrage openly. Thus the incident, in many ways so grim, actually strengthened her sense of pride.

Asked to recall for a psychology class a significant childhood memory that affected his sense of self-esteem, a student writes about a fishing trip he took when he was nine. He reflects that the trip was doubly significant because it was the first one he ever took alone with his father and the first time he was expected to do something difficult on his own. He remembers wanting to go fishing but being afraid that he would do something wrong, like getting seasick or losing the rod, and disappoint his dad. He focuses the essay on one particular incident—his attempt to land a big fish. He writes that at first he panicked and tried to hand the rod to his father, but his dad insisted that he bring in the fish on his own. During a struggle that seemed to last an hour but probably took only ten minutes, his dad sat beside him, offering advice and encouragement. Afterward, his dad said how proud he was and took his picture with the fish, a five-pound bass.

CHAPTER 2

Remembering Events

Why do people write about remembered events? Perhaps out of nostalgia for the past, but also to understand their past experiences. The "presences of the past," as essayist Carlos Fuentes observed, "are there in the center of your life today." For this reason, probably the most common advice given new writers is to write from experience: Write about what you know best.

When you write about events you remember, you not only write about what you know, but you also come to know yourself better. The Guide to Writing in this chapter will help you to search your memory and to reflect on the meaning of your experience. You will examine the forces within yourself and within society that have helped you become the person you are.

In addition to writing about yourself, you also will read about other people. Reading about significant events in their lives may lead you to think in new ways about your own life, but it can also lead you to better understand other people. Sometimes other people's stories resonate for you, echoing your own remembered feelings and thoughts. At other times, the differences in experience are striking. Probing these differences can be instructive. You may, for example, come to understand how certain conditions—such as whether you are rich or poor, male or female, young or old, black or white—can profoundly affect people's lives and perspectives.

Writing about your life for others to read is not the same as writing for yourself. As a writer, you must remember that autobiography is public, not private. While it invites self-presentation and contributes to self-knowledge, it does not require you to make unwanted self-disclosures. You choose the events and decide how you will portray yourself.

When you write about a remembered event, how you choose to present yourself depends on who you expect to read your essay (your audience) and what you want to communicate to them (your purpose). In the first scenario that opened this chapter, the student applying to college has a well-defined purpose and audience: to make a good impression on the board of admissions. He chose an event that enables him to portray himself as both capable of and excited about scientific work. His story shows that he is observant, remembers details, and writes clearly—qualities valued in a scientist. Although he is writing to impress his readers, he is honest about his feelings, not worrying that his readers might think him naive.

In the second scenario, the writer may have chosen to relate this painful event because it reveals her and her classmates' dignity and moral strength as well as their vulnerability. Perhaps as well she wanted to express openly the outrage she could only express indirectly at the time the event occurred and to give her younger readers some understanding of what their elders had to endure.

The last scenario suggests still another purpose for writing autobiographically: to help you to learn. Educators know that one of the best ways to learn something new is to relate it to something you already know. When the psychology student is asked to apply the concept of self-esteem to an event in his life, his personal experience helps him to grasp the abstract idea he is studying.

These scenarios show that writers purposefully use their personal experiences in different ways for different writing situations. They do not just pour out their memories and feelings. They reflect deeply on the meaning and importance of an experience—what we call its autobiographical significance. Autobiographers compose themselves for readers; they fashion a self in words, much as a novelist constructs a character. As readers, we come to "know" the people we read about by the way they act, look, talk, think, and feel.

As you work through this chapter, you too will learn to write purposefully for your readers. You will learn to tell a story that entertains readers and lets them know something important about how you came to be the person you are now. You also will learn to describe people and places vividly so that readers can see what makes them memorable to you. Finally, you will learn to use writing to help you know yourself and, in the process, you will develop confidence in yourself as a writer.

As you learn to write well about a remembered event, you will also be practicing two of the most basic writing strategies—narration and description. These strategies are needed for almost every kind of writing. Writing is often organized narratively like a story, but even writing that is organized topically may require narration, such as brief stories (or anecdotes) to illustrate the main ideas. Like narration, description is used to illustrate and explain abstract ideas and information. Narration and description are important in explanatory reports and persuasive arguments as well as in remembered events essays.

Writing in Your Other Courses

In some of your other college courses, you may be asked to write essays based on your personal experience. Here are some examples from actual assignments:

- *For a psychology course:* Erik Erikson observed that "young people . . . are sometimes preoccupied with what they appear to be in the eyes of others as compared with what they feel they are." Test this idea against your own experience as an adolescent. Recount a single event when you cared tremendously about what your peers thought about you. In your essay, explain how their judgments influenced your behavior and your sense of self.
- *For a political science course:* Voter apathy is known to be a widespread problem, but not much is known about the origins of voting behavior. Write about the first time you were interested in an election, regardless of whether you were able to vote. Indicate when you first became aware of the election, who told you about

it, how you formed your opinions, and how you felt about the election results. Looking back on the experience, reflect on how that first experience has influenced your voting behavior.

- *For a linguistics course:* Deborah Tannen concludes that because men and women learn to value different conversational styles, they often find conversations with one another frustrating. In particular, Tannen's research reports that women and men have different expectations when they talk about problems. Women expect to spend a lot of time talking about the problem itself, especially about their feelings. Men, in contrast, typically want to cut short the analysis and the talk about feelings; they would rather discuss solutions to the problem. Test Tannen's hypothesis against your own experience. Write about a conversation you had with a member of the opposite sex concerning some problem. Reconstruct as much of the conversation as you can remember, and determine which parts constitute feelings talk and which indicate problem-solving talk.

→ Practice Remembering an Event: A Collaborative Activity

The scenarios that open this chapter suggest some occasions for writing about events in one's life. Think of an event in your life that you would feel comfortable describing to others in your class. The only requirements are that you remember the event well enough to tell the story and that the story lets your classmates learn something about you. Here are some guidelines to follow:

Part 1. Consider several events and choose one you feel comfortable telling in this situation. Then, for two or three minutes, make notes about how you will tell your story.

Now, get together with two or three other students, and take turns telling your stories. Be brief—each story should take only a few minutes.

Part 2. Take ten minutes or so to discuss what happened when you told about a remembered event:

- Tell each other how you chose your particular story. What did you think about when you were choosing an event? How did your purpose and audience—what you wanted your classmates to know and think about you—influence your choice?
- Review what each of you decided to include in your story. Did you plunge right into telling what happened, or did you first provide some background information? Did you decide to leave any of the action out of your story? If so, what did you leave out and why? Did you include a physical description of the scene? Did you describe any of the people, including yourself, or mention any specific dialogue? Did you tell your listeners how you felt at the time the event occurred or did you say how you feel now looking back on it?
- What was the easiest part of telling a story about a remembered event in your life? What was the most difficult?

READINGS

Annie Dillard won the Pulitzer prize for her very first book, *Pilgrim at Tinker Creek.* In that book, she describes herself as "no scientist," merely "a wanderer with a background in theology and a penchant for quirky facts." She has since written many other books, including collections of poetry, essays, and literary theory, as well as her autobiography, *An American Childhood*, from which this selection is taken.

In "Handed My Own Life," we see the early stirrings of Dillard's life-long enthusiasm for learning and fascination with nature. As you read her story, think about why she wrote it. What do you think she wanted to tell readers about herself? What impression do you have of Annie Dillard from reading her story?

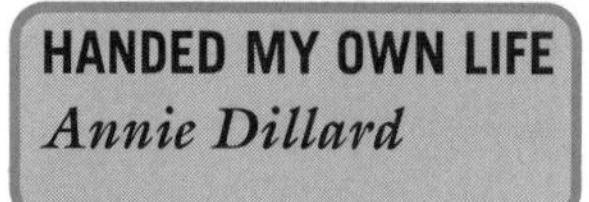

HANDED MY OWN LIFE
Annie Dillard

1 After I read *The Field Book of Ponds and Streams* several times, I longed for a microscope. Everybody needed a microscope. Detectives used microscopes, both for the FBI and at Scotland Yard. Although usually I had to save my tiny allowance for things I wanted, that year for Christmas my parents gave me a microscope kit.

2 In a dark basement corner, on a white enamel table, I set up the microscope kit. I supplied a chair, a lamp, a batch of jars, a candle, and a pile of library books. The microscope kit supplied a blunt black three-speed microscope, a booklet, a scalpel, a dropper, an ingenious device for cutting thin segments of fragile tissue, a pile of clean slides and cover slips, and a dandy array of corked test tubes.

3 One of the test tubes contained "hay infusion." Hay infusion was a wee brown chip of grass blade. You added water to it, and after a week it became a jungle in a drop, full of one-celled animals. This did not work for me. All I saw in the microscope after a week was a wet chip of dried grass, much enlarged.

4 Another test tube contained "diatomaceous earth." This was, I believed, an actual pinch of the white cliffs of Dover. On my palm it was an airy, friable chalk. The booklet said it was composed of the siliceous bodies of diatoms—one-celled creatures that lived in, as it were, small glass jewelry boxes with fitted lids. Diatoms, I read, come in a variety of transparent geometrical shapes. Broken and dead and dug out of geological deposits, they made chalk, and a fine abrasive used in silver polish and toothpaste. What I saw in the microscope must have been the fine abrasive—grit enlarged. It was years before I saw a recognizable, whole diatom. The kit's diatomaceous earth was a bust.

5 All that winter I played with the microscope. I prepared slides from things at hand, as the books suggested. I looked at the transparent membrane inside an onion's skin and saw the cells. I looked at a section of cork and saw the cells, and at scrapings from the inside of my cheek, ditto. I looked at my blood and saw not much; I looked at my urine and saw long iridescent crystals, for the drop had dried.

6 All this was very well, but I wanted to see the wildlife I had read about. I wanted especially to see the famous amoeba, who had eluded me. He was supposed to live in the hay infusion, but I hadn't found him there. He lived outside in warm ponds and streams, too, but I lived in Pittsburgh, and it had been a cold winter.

7 Finally late that spring I saw an amoeba. The week before, I had gathered puddle water from Frick Park; it had been festering in a jar in the basement. This June night

after dinner I figured I had waited long enough. In the basement at my microscope table I spread a scummy drop of Frick Park puddle water on a slide, peeked in, and lo, there was the famous amoeba. He was as blobby and grainy as his picture; I would have known him anywhere.

Before I had watched him at all, I ran upstairs. My parents were still at table, drinking coffee. They, too, could see the famous amoeba. I told them, bursting, that he was all set up, that they should hurry before his water dried. It was the chance of a lifetime. 8

Father had stretched out his long legs and was tilting back in his chair. Mother sat with her knees crossed, in blue slacks, smoking a Chesterfield. The dessert dishes were still on the table. My sisters were nowhere in evidence. It was a warm evening; the big dining-room windows gave onto blooming rhododendrons.

Mother regarded me warmly. She gave me to understand that she was glad I had found what I had been looking for, but that she and Father were happy to sit with their coffee, and would not be coming down. 10

She did not say, but I understood at once, that they had their pursuits (coffee?) and I had mine. She did not say, but I began to understand then, that you do what you do out of your private passion for the thing itself. 11

I had essentially been handed my own life. In subsequent years my parents would praise my drawings and poems, and supply me with books, art supplies, and sports equipment, and listen to my troubles and enthusiasms, and supervise my hours, and discuss and inform, but they would not get involved with my detective work, nor hear about my reading, nor inquire about my homework or term papers or exams, nor visit the salamanders I caught, nor listen to me play the piano, nor attend my field hockey games, nor fuss over my insect collection with me, or my poetry collection or stamp collection or rock collection. My days and nights were my own to plan and fill. 12

When I left the dining room that evening and started down the dark basement stairs, I had a life; I sat to my wonderful amoeba, and there he was, rolling his grains more slowly now, extending an arc of his edge for a foot and drawing himself along by that foot, and absorbing it again and rolling on. I gave him some more pond water. 13

I had hit pay dirt. For all I knew, there were paramecia, too, in that pond water, or daphniae, or stentors, or any of the many other creatures I had read about and never seen: volvox, the spherical algal colony; euglena with its one red eye; the elusive, glassy diatom; hydra, rotifers, water bears, worms. Anything was possible. The sky was the limit. 14

Connecting to Culture and Experience

The story Dillard tells about her experience may be seen as a coming-of-age story. People in cultures around the world tell coming-of-age stories to celebrate a young person's passage into adulthood. In some cultures, adolescents must pass an actual test of endurance and ability before they are admitted into the adult community. This ritual testing is often called a rite of passage. It usually tests the person's spiritual strength as well as physical prowess and know-how. The person must pass the test alone, without the help of friends or relatives. A coming-of-age story typically includes these rites-of-passage elements.

With other students in your class, find these elements in Dillard's essay. With these elements in mind, discuss how seeing Dillard's experience in terms of a coming-of-age story helps you understand why Dillard considers such an apparently trivial event important enough to write an essay about and pivotal enough to title "Handed My Own Life."

Finally, consider what cultural values and attitudes Dillard's coming-of-age story promotes.

Analyzing Writing Strategies

1. At the beginning of this chapter, we make the following assertions about remembered event essays. Consider which of these are true of Dillard's essay.
   - It tells an entertaining story.
   - It is vivid—letting readers see what makes the event as well as the people and places memorable for the writer.
   - It is purposeful, trying to give readers an understanding of why this particular event was significant in the writer's life.
   - It includes self-presentation but not unwanted self-disclosures.
   - It can lead readers to think in new ways about their own experiences or about how other people's lives differ from their own.
2. **Visual description**—naming objects and detailing their colors, shapes, sizes, and textures—is an important writing strategy in remembered event essays. To see how Dillard uses this strategy to describe scenes and people, skim paragraphs 2–5 and 9, underlining the names of objects or people and also bracketing the visual details. Here is an example from the first sentence of paragraph 2: [dark basement] corner. Then, reread these paragraphs, trying to imagine what the effect would be if the visual details you bracketed had been left out.

Considering Topics for Your Own Essay

Recall some occasions when you learned something important or made a significant discovery. List them. Then, choose one occasion that you would be interested in writing about for readers who do not know you. What would you want them to learn about you from reading your essay?

Commentary

"Handed My Own Life" illustrates all of the basic features of remembered event essays: It is a well-told story with autobiographical significance and vivid descriptions of scenes and people. A good story is vivid and lively, but first it must attract our interest and make us want to find out what happened.

One of the ways writers attract readers' interest is by arousing curiosity. From the very first sentence of Dillard's essay, she tells us about herself: "After I read *The Field Book of Ponds and Streams* several times, I longed for a microscope." Not only do we want to know what will happen, but we also want to know more about this girl who wants a microscope. We may not share her particular enthusiasm, but we can identify with her because we have all desired something as much as she "longed for" a microscope. Identification with the writer may get us to start reading, but what makes us continue is curiosity. We wonder whether she will get the microscope and, if she does, what will happen.

In addition to arousing our curiosity, a story also has to have a point: It has to lead somewhere. Good stories do not merely present a series of actions. They provide a **dramatic structure** for the action: a beginning that arouses readers' **curiosity,** a

For more on shaping narrative structure, see pp. 485–88.

For more on scratch outlining, see pp. 450–51.

middle that builds **suspense,** and an ending that completes the action and brings the story to a **climax.** The search for the amoeba gives Dillard's story a simple structure, like that of a mystery.

We can see this simple narrative **organization** in the following paragraph-by-paragraph scratch outline:

1. gives history of her desire to have a microscope and tells when she got one
2. describes workplace and supplies
3. tells of failed efforts to see one-celled animals in hay infusion
4. tells of failed efforts to see diatoms—one-celled creatures—in diatomaceous earth
5. summarizes what she saw or failed to see in microscope during the winter
6. explains that what she wanted to see but failed repeatedly to find was the amoeba (the one-celled animal that lives in the hay infusion and elsewhere)
7. announces that in late spring she saw the amoeba; tells what led up to her seeing the amoeba; describes the amoeba
8. tells that as soon as she found the amoeba, she ran upstairs to show her parents
9. describes father and mother lounging after dinner
10. summarizes what her mother said
11. explains what she understood her mother to mean
12. reflects on the significance of what she had learned from her mother by telling what happened in the years that followed this event
13. returns to the time of the event to tell what she did that night—studied the amoeba and gave him pond water
14. recalls looking forward to seeing many other creatures through the microscope

From this outline, we can see that although the story focuses on the evening when Dillard finally saw the elusive amoeba, the narrative actually spans several months from before Christmas to late spring. Notice, however, that Dillard includes only action and information that enhance the drama or contribute to our understanding of why finding the amoeba was so significant. She leaves out everything she did during the winter except her experiments with the microscope (paragraphs 3–5). Her narrative follows a simple chronology and moves forward through time—beginning some time before the climactic action and, at the conclusion, projecting into the future.

The action leads to Dillard's finding the amoeba, but this discovery is not the end of the story or even the point of the story. The event has **autobiographical significance** because Dillard learns something important about herself and about her relationship with her parents.

Dillard explains that she only "began to understand" the event's significance after talking with her mother (paragraph 11). She does not say how long it took her to understand fully what this event meant in her life. Perhaps writing the story helped Dillard in the process. As novelist Toni Morrison explains: "Some very small incident that takes place today may be the most important event that happens to you this year, but you don't know that when it happens. You don't know it until much later." As you will see, writing gives us the opportunity to think about our experiences and, in hindsight, to figure out what they mean.

The last basic feature of remembered event essays is vivid description of scenes and people. In answering question 2 of Analyzing Writing Strategies, you may have already analyzed two of the three **describing strategies: naming** and **detailing.** You have probably seen that Dillard not only names objects such as the microscope but that she also adds specific details (italicized) to describe them: "*a blunt black three-speed* microscope" (paragraph 2). You should be able to recognize the third describing strategy—**comparing**—in the form of **simile** or **metaphor.** For example, Dillard describes the hay infusion as "a jungle in a drop" (paragraph 3), and diatoms as creatures living in "small glass jewelry boxes" (paragraph 4). A metaphor implies a comparison by calling one object (such as "hay infusion") by the name of another ("a jungle"). Simile, another method of comparing found in remembered event essays, makes the comparison explicit by using the word *as* or *like.* (Dillard, for example, could have written "the hay infusion looks like a jungle in a drop.") In your own writing, you will want to choose from the full palette of describing strategies.

For more on describing strategies, turn to Chapter 15.

Tobias Wolff is probably best known for his short stories and for a novel, *The Barracks Thief*, for which he won the 1985 PEN/Faulkner award. Wolff has written two autobiographical works, *In Pharaoh's Army* (1996) and *A Boy's Life* (1989), which was made into a movie in 1993 and from which "On Being a Real Westerner" comes. Reflecting on his writing process, Wolff has said that it is "part memory, part invention. I can no longer tell where one ends and the other begins. The very act of writing has transformed the original experience into another experience, more 'real' to me than what I started with."

The story Wolff tells here is based on an actual experience that occurred when he was ten years old. He and his mother had just moved west from Florida to Salt Lake City, followed by Roy, his divorced mother's boyfriend. "Roy was handsome," Wolff writes, "in the conventional way that appeals to boys. He had a tattoo. He'd been to war and kept a silence about it that was full of heroic implication." As you read, notice how Wolff's storytelling skills make this event come to life in the reader's imagination.

ON BEING A REAL WESTERNER
Tobias Wolff

1 Just after Easter Roy gave me the Winchester .22 rifle I'd learned to shoot with. It was a light, pump-action, beautifully balanced piece with a walnut stock black from all its oilings. Roy had carried it when he was a boy and it was still as good as new. Better than new. The action was silky from long use, and the wood of a quality no longer to be found.

2 The gift did not come as a surprise. Roy was stingy, and slow to take a hint, but I'd put him under siege. I had my heart set on that rifle. A weapon was the first condition of self-sufficiency, and of being a real Westerner, and of all acceptable employment—trapping, riding herd, soldiering, law enforcement, and outlawry. I needed that rifle, for itself and for the way it completed me when I held it.

3 My mother said I couldn't have it. Absolutely not. Roy took the rifle back but promised me he'd bring her around. He could not imagine anyone refusing him anything and treated the refusals he did encounter as perverse and insincere. Normally mute, he

became at these times a relentless whiner. He would follow my mother from room to room, emitting one ceaseless note of complaint that was pitched perfectly to jelly her nerves and bring her to a state where she would agree to anything to make it stop.

After a few days of this my mother caved in. She said I could have the rifle if, and only if, I promised never to take it out or even touch it except when she and Roy were with me. Okay, I said. Sure. Naturally. But even then she wasn't satisfied. She plain didn't like the fact of me owning a rifle. Roy said he had owned several rifles by the time he was my age, but this did not reassure her. She didn't think I could be trusted with it. Roy said now was the time to find out. 4

For a week or so I kept my promises. But now that the weather had turned warm Roy was usually off somewhere and eventually, in the dead hours after school when I found myself alone in the apartment, I decided that there couldn't be any harm in taking the rifle out to clean it. Only to clean it, nothing more. I was sure it would be enough just to break it down, oil it, rub linseed into the stock, polish the octagonal barrel and then hold it up to the light to confirm the perfection of the bore. But it wasn't enough. From cleaning the rifle I went to marching around the apartment with it, and then to striking brave poses in front of the mirror. Roy had saved one of his army uniforms and I sometimes dressed up in this, together with martial-looking articles of hunting gear: fur trooper's hat, camouflage coat, boots that reached nearly to my knees. 5

The camouflage coat made me feel like a sniper, and before long I began to act like one. I set up a nest on the couch by the front window. I drew the shades to darken the apartment, and took up my position. Nudging the shade aside with the rifle barrel, I followed people in my sights as they walked or drove along the street. At first I made shooting sounds—kyoo! kyoo! Then I started cocking the hammer and letting it snap down. 6

Roy stored his ammunition in a metal box he kept hidden in the closet. As with everything else hidden in the apartment, I knew exactly where to find it. There was a layer of loose .22 rounds on the bottom of the box under shells of bigger caliber, dropped there by the handful the way men drop pennies on their dressers at night. I took some and put them in a hiding place of my own. With these I started loading up the rifle. Hammer cocked, a round in the chamber, finger resting lightly on the trigger, I drew a bead on whoever walked by—women pushing strollers, children, garbage collectors laughing and calling to each other, anyone—and as they passed under my window I sometimes had to bite my lip to keep from laughing in the ecstasy of my power over them, and at their absurd and innocent belief that they were safe. 7

But over time the innocence I laughed at began to irritate me. It was a peculiar kind of irritation. I saw it years later in men I served with, and felt it myself, when unarmed Vietnamese civilians talked back to us while we were herding them around. Power can be enjoyed only when it is recognized and feared. Fearlessness in those without power is maddening to those who have it. 8

One afternoon I pulled the trigger. I had been aiming at two old people, a man and a woman, who walked so slowly that by the time they turned the corner at the bottom of the hill my little store of self-control was exhausted. I had to shoot. I looked up and down the street. It was empty. Nothing moved but a pair of squirrels chasing each other back and forth on the telephone wires. I followed one in my sight. Finally it stopped for a moment and I fired. The squirrel dropped straight into the road. I pulled back into the shadows and waited for something to happen, sure that someone must have heard the shot or seen the squirrel fall. But the sound that was so loud to me probably seemed to our neighbors no more than the bang of a cupboard slammed shut. After a while I 9 sneaked a glance into the street. The squirrel hadn't moved. It looked like a scarf someone had dropped.

When my mother got home from work I told her there was a dead squirrel in the street. Like me, she was an animal lover. She took a cellophane bag off a loaf of bread and we went outside and looked at the squirrel. "Poor little thing," she said. She stuck her hand in the wrapper and picked up the squirrel, then pulled the bag inside out away from her hand. We buried it behind our building under a cross made of popsicle sticks, and I blubbered the whole time. 10

I blubbered again in bed that night. At last I got out of bed and knelt down and did an imitation of somebody praying, and then I did an imitation of somebody receiving divine reassurance and inspiration. I stopped crying. I smiled to myself and forced a feeling of warmth into my chest. Then I climbed back in bed and looked up at the ceiling with a blissful expression until I went to sleep. 11

For several days I stayed away from the apartment at times when I knew I'd be alone there. 12

Though I avoided the apartment, I could not shake the idea that sooner or later I would get the rifle out again. All my images of myself as I wished to be were images of myself armed. Because I did not know who I was, any image of myself, no matter how grotesque, had power over me. This much I understand now. But the man can give no help to the boy, not in this matter nor in those that follow. The boy moves always out of reach. 13

Connecting to Culture and Experience

Wolff shows us that he took great delight in playing the role of a soldier—looking at himself in the mirror dressed in camouflage and "striking brave poses." Another part of the attraction of playing soldier, he admits, is the sense of power he experienced. Still another part may have been that soldiers are generally considered heroes to many people in our culture and often serve as cultural role models, especially for young boys.

With other students in your class, discuss role playing and identity. Begin by telling one another one or two roles you liked to play when you were younger. Then, discuss how you think you got the idea to play these particular roles and what attracted you to them. If you enjoyed dressing up and posing—either for yourself or for others—try to explain why doing so was pleasurable. How did your role playing make you feel—powerful, smart, talented, sophisticated? Finally, discuss whether any of the roles you liked to play are typical role models in our society. What do you think children learn to value about themselves and about others when they play these particular roles?

Analyzing Writing Strategies

1. Writers convey the **significance** of autobiographical events by telling how they felt at the time the event occurred and also by telling how they feel now as they look back on the event. Skim paragraphs 7–13, noting where Wolff expresses his feelings and thoughts about the event. Try to distinguish between (1) what he remembers thinking and feeling at the time and (2) what he thinks and feels as he looks back on the event. What impression do you get of the young Wolff? What does the older Wolff seem to think about his younger self?

2. Good stories show people in action—what we call **specific narrative action.** Analyze paragraphs 5, 7, and 9 by underlining the narrative actions and then bracketing the verb in each narrative action that specifically names the action. For example, here are the narrative actions (underlined) and their action verbs (bracketed) in paragraph 6: [set up] a nest, [drew] the shades, [took up] my position, [nudging] the shade aside, [followed] people, [walked] or [drove], [started cocking] the hammer, [letting] it snap down.

   Now that you have completed your analysis, how do you think specific narrative action and action verbs contribute to autobiographical stories?

Considering Topics for Your Own Essay

In this selection, Wolff describes experiencing what he calls the "ecstasy of my power" to inflict harm on others (paragraph 7). Try to recall several occasions when you were in a position to exercise power over another person or when you were subject to someone else's power. Pick one such instance. Think about how you would present it, explaining what you did and how you felt.

Commentary

This is a gripping story. One factor that makes it so dramatic is the subject: Putting a rifle in a child's hands immediately alerts readers to the possibility that something dreadful could happen. Thus, the potential for suspense is great. But what makes the story so dramatic is Wolff's use of narrating strategies, including narrative cueing devices that move the action through time and help readers keep track of what happened.

For more on specific narrative action, turn to pp. 486–87.

Specific narrative action is the principal technique for dramatically **pacing** a story. One way Wolff uses specific narrative action is to create, in writing, the effect of a slow-motion close-up. Notice how your attention is focused on each distinct action (italicized): "*Hammer cocked, a round in the chamber, finger resting lightly on the trigger,* I drew a bead on whoever walked by . . ." (paragraph 7). To get this effect, Wolff combines specific narrative action with a special kind of phrase that draws our attention to each distinct action. Each phrase explains a different aspect of the central activity presented in the main subject and verb of the sentence, "I drew a bead. . . ." In other words, the main clause gives us an overall picture of the boy aiming the rifle, while the phrases give us close-ups of things we could never see except on film or in our imaginations.

Wolff also uses specific narrative action to intensify the pace. Once the boy gets the rifle, the pace picks up. The narrative rushes headlong from one action to the next until finally the result we fear most happens: The gun goes off and something dies. Wolff creates this headlong rush by bombarding readers with specific narrative actions loaded with action verbs. In analyzing Wolff's story you have already seen for yourself how action verbs work. As they accumulate, they propel the narrative through time, creating excitement and heightening suspense.

If we look closely at Wolff's narration, we can see how two narrative **cueing devices**—verb tense markers and time marker transitions—create the impression of time passing. We call them cueing devices because, like road signs, they enable readers to follow the action. These cues indicate the order in which each action takes place as well as the duration of particular actions. Knowing the order is essential even when a narrative follows a simple chronology. But, as you will see, even a simple narrative like Wolff's interrupts the forward movement at certain points to present earlier or later actions.

For more on verb tense markers, see pp. 483–84.

One important cuing device is the **verb tense marker.** Verb tenses signal when the action occurred—in the past, present, or future. Because remembered event essays tell about past events, most of the verbs are in the past tense. Looking at the verbs in Wolff's essay, we can find several different kinds of past tense signaled by the verb tense markers. In the first sentence of the essay, for example, Wolff shows an action that occurred at one point in the past (underlined) together with an action that was already completed (bracketed): "Just after Easter Roy gave me the Winchester .22 rifle [I'd learned to shoot] with." ("I'd learned" is a shortened form of "I had learned.") A second example shows an earlier action that was still going on (bracketed) when the more recent action occurred (underlined): "One afternoon I pulled the trigger. I [had been aiming] at two old people . . ." (paragraph 9).

Our final example is a little more complicated: "Roy took the rifle back but promised me [he'd bring] her around" (paragraph 3). (Here "he'd" is a short form of "he would," the past tense of "he will.") This example presents three past actions. Whereas the first two actions (underlined) occurred at roughly the same time, the third predicts a future action (bracketed) that occurred after the first two actions were completed.

As an English speaker, you probably do not know the technical names for these tenses, nor do you need to know them. However, you do need to know what the different verb tenses mean and how to use them. In your remembered event essay, you will want to be sure that the verb tenses you use accurately indicate the time relations among various actions in your story.

For more on transitions, see Cueing the Reader on pp. 479–80 and Narrating on p. 483.

In addition to using verb tense to show time, writers also use **time markers,** transitions, to move the narrative action forward in time and to keep readers oriented. Wolff uses many transitional words and phrases to locate an action at a particular point in time or to relate an action at one point in time to an action at another time. He uses three in the first paragraph alone: *just after, when,* and *still.* Time markers may appear at the beginning of a sentence or within a sentence. Notice how many paragraphs in Wolff's story include such a transition in the opening sentence: "Just after" (paragraph 1), "After a few days" (4), "For a week or so" (5), "before long" (6), "One afternoon" (9), "When" (10), "again" (11), and "For several days" (12). This extensive use of time markers is not unusual in remembered event essays. You will want to use them liberally in your own essay to orient readers and propel your narrative through time.

Paul Auster is best known for his novels *The New York Trilogy, In the Country of Last Things,* and *Moon Palace.* He has also written collections of essays (*The Art of Hunger*), poems (*Disappearances*), and at least one screenplay (*Smoke*). He won the French prize for foreign literature in 1988 and was nominated for the Edgar Award for mystery writing in 1986.

The following essay first appeared in the *New Yorker* in 1996 as part of a series of remembered event essays by Auster. As you read the essay, consider how writing may have helped Auster deal with this traumatizing event.

WHY WRITE?
Paul Auster

I was fourteen. For the third year in a row, my parents had sent me to a summer camp in New York State. I spent the bulk of my time playing basketball and baseball, but as it was a co-ed camp there were other activities as well: evening "socials," the first awkward grapplings with girls, panty raids, the usual adolescent shenanigans. I also remember smoking cheap cigars on the sly, "Frenching" beds, and massive water-balloon fights. 1

None of this is important. I simply want to underscore what a vulnerable age fourteen can be. No longer a child, not yet an adult, you bounce back and forth between who you were and who you are about to become. In my own case, I was still young enough to think that I had a legitimate shot at playing in the major leagues, but old enough to be questioning the existence of God. I had read the "Communist Manifesto," and yet I still enjoyed watching Saturday-morning cartoons. Every time I saw my face in the mirror, I seemed to be looking at someone else. 2

There were about sixteen or eighteen boys in my group. Most of us had been together for several years, but a couple of newcomers had also joined us that summer. One was named Ralph. He was a quiet kid without much enthusiasm for dribbling basketballs and hitting the cutoff man, and while no one gave him a particularly hard time, he had trouble blending in. He had flunked a couple of subjects that year, and most of his free periods were spent being tutored by one of the counsellors. It was a little sad, and I felt sorry for him—but not too sorry, not sorry enough to lose any sleep over it. 3

Our counsellors were all New York college students from Brooklyn and Queens. Wisecracking basketball players, future dentists, accountants, and teachers, city kids to their very bones. Like most true New Yorkers, they persisted in calling the ground the "floor," even when all that was under their feet was grass, pebbles, and dirt. The trappings of traditional summer-camp life were as alien to them as the I.R.T. is to an Iowa farmer. Canoes, lanyards, mountain climbing, pitching tents, singing around the campfire were nowhere to be found in the inventory of their concerns. They could drill us on the finer points of setting picks and boxing out for rebounds; otherwise they horsed around and told jokes. 4

Imagine our surprise, then, when one afternoon our counsellor announced that we were going for a hike in the woods. He had been seized by an inspiration and wasn't going to let anyone talk him out of it. Enough basketball, he said. We're surrounded by nature, and it's time we took advantage of it and started acting like real campers—or words to that effect. And so, after the rest period that followed lunch, the whole gang of sixteen or eighteen boys, along with two counsellors, set off into the woods. 5

It was late July, 1961. Everyone was in a fairly buoyant mood, I remember, and half an hour or so into the trek most people agreed that the outing had been a good idea. No one had a compass, of course, or the slightest clue as to where we were going, but we were all enjoying ourselves, and if we happened to get lost, what difference would that make? Sooner or later we'd find our way back. 6

Then it began to rain. At first, it was barely noticeable, a few light drops falling between the leaves and branches, nothing to worry about. We walked on, unwilling to let a little water spoil our fun, but a couple of minutes later it started coming down in earnest. Everyone got soaked, and the counsellors decided that we should turn around and head back. The only problem was that no one knew where the camp was. The woods were thick, dense with clusters of trees and thorn-studded bushes, and we had woven this way and that, abruptly shifting directions in order to move on. To add to the confusion, it was becoming hard to see. The woods had been dark to begin with, but, with 7 the rain falling and the sky turning black, it felt more like night than three or four in the afternoon.

8 Then the thunder started. And after the thunder the lightning started. The storm was directly on top of us, and it turned out to be the summer storm to end all summer storms. I have never seen weather like that before or since. The rain poured down on us so hard that it actually hurt; each time the thunder exploded, you could feel the noise vibrating inside your body. When the lightning came, it danced around us like spears. It was as if weapons had materialized out of thin air—a sudden flash that turned everything a bright, ghostly white. Trees were struck, and their branches began to smolder. Then it would go dark again for a moment, there would be another crash in the sky, and the lightning would return in a different spot.

9 The lightning was what scared us, of course, and in our panic we tried to run away from it. But the storm was too big, and everywhere we went we were met by more lightning. It was a helter-skelter stampede, a headlong rush in circles. Then, suddenly, someone spotted a clearing in the woods. A brief dispute broke out over whether it was safer to go into the open or continue to stand under the trees. The voice arguing for the open won, and we ran in the direction of the clearing.

10 It was a small meadow, most likely a pasture that belonged to a local farm, and to get to it we had to crawl under a barbed-wire fence. One by one, we got down on our bellies and inched our way through. I was in the middle of the line, directly behind Ralph. Just as he went under the barbed wire, there was another flash of lightning. I was two or three feet away, but, because of the rain pounding against my eyelids, I had trouble making out what happened. All I knew was that Ralph had stopped moving. I figured that he had been stunned, so I crawled past him under the fence. Once I was on the other side, I took hold of his arm and dragged him through.

11 I don't know how long we stayed in that field. An hour, I would guess, and the whole time we were there the rain and lightning and thunder continued to crash down upon us. It was a storm ripped from the pages of the Bible, and it went on and on and on, as if it would never end.

12 Two or three boys were hit by something—perhaps by lightning, perhaps by the shock of lightning as it struck the ground near them—and the meadow began to fill with their moans. Other boys wept and prayed. Still others, fear in their voices, tried to give sensible advice. Get rid of everything metal, they said; metal attracts the lightning. We all took off our belts and threw them away from us.

13 I don't remember saying anything. I don't remember crying. Another boy and I kept ourselves busy trying to take care of Ralph. He was still unconscious. We rubbed his hands and arms, we held down his tongue so he wouldn't swallow it, we told him to hang in there. After a while, his skin began to take on a bluish tinge. His body seemed colder to my touch, but in spite of the mounting evidence it never occurred to me that he wasn't going to come around. I was only fourteen years old, after all, and what did I know? I had never seen a dead person before.

14 It was the barbed wire that did it, I suppose. The other boys hit by the lightning went numb, felt pain in their limbs for an hour or so, and then recovered. But Ralph had been under the fence when the lightning struck, and he had been electrocuted on the spot.

15 Later on, when they told me he was dead, I learned that there was an eight-inch burn across his back. I remember trying to absorb this news and telling myself that life would never feel the same to me again. Strangely enough, I didn't think about how I had been right next to him when it happened. I didn't think, one or two sec-

onds later and it would have been me. What I thought about was holding his tongue and looking down at his teeth. His mouth had been set in a slight grimace, and, with his lips partly open, I had spent an hour looking down at the tips of his teeth. Thirty-four years later, I still remember them. And his half-closed, half-open eyes. I remember those, too.

Connecting to Culture and Experience

Like Auster, many people experience adolescence as a time of uncertainty, when their sense of identity seems to vary daily: "Every time I saw my face in the mirror, I seemed to be looking at someone else" (paragraph 2). Auster, for example, sees himself as a budding intellectual (reading Karl Marx's *Communist Manifesto* and thinking about the existence of God), but at the same time he sees himself as a kid who lives in a world of make-believe (watching cartoons and fantasizing about being a professional ballplayer).

With other students, discuss how adolescence unsettled your sense of identity. What changed? What remained the same? What contradictions, if any, do you remember feeling?

Analyzing Writing Strategies

1. To examine the **organization** and understand what the opening paragraphs of Auster's essay contribute to his story, make a paragraph-by-paragraph scratch outline of this essay. (For an example, see the outline of Dillard's essay on p. 25.) What do you think would be lost or gained if Auster's essay opened instead with the first sentence of paragraph 6, beginning "It was late July, 1961"? For comparison, look at the way the next writer, Jean Brandt, opens her remembered event essay. Looking at these various openings will help you decide how much background information, or context, to provide in your own essay before starting the action.
2. Analyze Auster's description of the storm in paragraphs 7, 8, and 11 by marking his use of the describing strategies of naming, detailing, and comparing. Underline the objects he names, bracket each detail of those objects, and use a dotted underline to mark the comparisons—similes and metaphors. Here is an example of naming and detailing from paragraph 7 to get you started: "The woods were [thick], [dense with clusters] of trees and [thorn-studded] bushes. . . ." An example of comparing occurs later in that paragraph: "it felt more like night. . . ."

   When you have completed your analysis, reread the descriptive word images you have marked and consider the feelings and thoughts they suggest to you. What is the **dominant impression** you get from Auster's description of the storm?

Considering Topics for Your Own Essay

After reading Auster's essay, you might want to consider writing about a traumatic event in your own life, such as a death, serious illness, accident, war experience, or other act of violence. Be sure, however, that you feel comfortable writing about something so personal in the public forum of a class. You should also evaluate carefully whether you have sufficient emotional distance from the experience to focus your attention on writing issues.

Instead of choosing a traumatic event, you might pick an event that started out one way but quickly turned into something very different. Or perhaps there is something that you witnessed happening to someone else but that has had a lasting effect on you.

Commentary

Auster's essay illustrates the two main ways writers convey the autobiographical significance of a remembered event: telling and showing. Auster expresses directly his remembered feelings and thoughts at the time of the event as well as his current feelings and thoughts as he looks back on the experience. In addition, Auster shows the event's significance by using descriptive language to create a dominant impression.

Auster intersperses **remembered feelings and thoughts** throughout the essay. He is surprisingly open about some of his feelings. He admits, for example, that although he felt "sorry" for Ralph, he did not feel "too sorry, sorry enough to lose any sleep over" (paragraph 3). Most of his feelings about the storm are expressed indirectly through descriptive images, such as "it felt more like night than three or four in the afternoon" (paragraph 7), but he also states directly that the "lightning was what scared us" (paragraph 9). In addition, he explains what he was thinking at the time: "I had trouble making out what happened. All I knew was that Ralph was not moving. I figured he had been stunned . . ."(paragraph 10).

Auster also tells us what he thinks now as he looks back on the event. His **present perspective** is evident from the beginning of the story, as when he explains: "None of this is important. I simply want to underscore what a vulnerable age fourteen can be . . ."(paragraph 2). In the last three paragraphs, Auster makes some powerful contrasts between what he remembers thinking and feeling at the time and what he thinks and feels "thirty-four years later" (paragraph 15). Perhaps the most startling contrast is this: "Strangely enough, I didn't think about how I had been right next to him when it happened. I didn't think, one or two seconds later and it would have been me"(paragraph 15). Auster enhances the contrast between his remembered and current feelings by repeating the key phrase "I don't remember" (paragraph 13) and then making one small but significant change: "I remember" (paragraph 15).

What Auster says helps us to understand and appreciate his feelings, but he does not drown us in a torrent of emotion. He does not dwell on how shocked he was or how terrible it is for someone so young to die so horribly. His writing expresses feeling but is not overly sentimental. This is an important distinction because sentimentality generally implies insincerity, a performance to impress others rather than the expression of genuine, deeply felt emotion.

For a discussion of dominant impression, turn to pp. 491–92.

Auster combines showing with telling to evoke the event's profound emotional significance. In addition to showing us the rainstorm in a series of vivid visual details, he uses similes and metaphors ("thunder exploded," lightning "like spears" [paragraph 8]) to create a **dominant impression,** thus transforming the literal storm into a symbolic one. It is up to the reader to interpret what the storm symbolizes because symbols suggest various meanings. For example, you might see the storm as symbolizing the struggle between life and death, as nature's mastery over human beings, or even as the wrath of God. The point is that Auster uses showing and telling to make his story meaningful as well as graphic.

Jean Brandt wrote this essay as a first-year college student. It tells about something she did when she was thirteen. Reflecting on how she felt at the time, Brandt writes: "I was afraid, embarrassed, worried, mad." As you read, look for places where these tumultuous and contradictory remembered feelings are expressed.

CALLING HOME
Jean Brandt

As we all piled into the car, I knew it was going to be a fabulous day. My grandmother was visiting for the holidays; and she and I, along with my older brother and sister, Louis and Susan, were setting off for a day of last-minute Christmas shopping. On the way to the mall, we sang Christmas carols, chattered, and laughed. With Christmas only two days away, we were caught up with holiday spirit. I felt light-headed and full of joy. I loved shopping—especially at Christmas. 1

The shopping center was swarming with frantic last-minute shoppers like ourselves. We went first to the General Store, my favorite. It carried mostly knickknacks and other useless items which nobody needs but buys anyway. I was thirteen years old at the time, and things like buttons and calendars and posters would catch my fancy. This day was no different. The object of my desire was a 75-cent Snoopy button. Snoopy was the latest. If you owned anything with the Peanuts on it, you were "in." But since I was supposed to be shopping for gifts for other people and not myself, I couldn't decide what to do. I went in search of my sister for her opinion. I pushed my way through throngs of people to the back of the store where I found Susan. I asked her if she thought I should buy the button. She said it was cute and if I wanted it to go ahead and buy it. 2

When I got back to the Snoopy section, I took one look at the lines at the cashiers and knew I didn't want to wait thirty minutes to buy an item worth less than one dollar. I walked back to the basket where I found the button and was about to drop it when suddenly, instead, I took a quick glance around, assured myself no one could see, and slipped the button into the pocket of my sweatshirt. I hesitated for a moment, but once the item was in my pocket, there was no turning back. I had never before stolen anything; but what was done was done. A few seconds later, my sister appeared and asked, "So, did you decide to buy the button?" 3

"No, I guess not." I hoped my voice didn't quaver. As we headed for the entrance, my heart began to race. I just had to get out of that store. Only a few more yards to go and I'd be safe. As we crossed the threshold, I heaved a sigh of relief. I was home free. I thought about how sly I had been and I felt proud of my accomplishment. 4

An unexpected tap on my shoulder startled me. I whirled around to find a middle-aged man, dressed in street clothes, flashing some type of badge and politely asking me to empty my pockets. Where did this man come from? How did he know? I was so sure that no one had seen me! On the verge of panicking, I told myself that all I had to do was give this man his button back, say I was sorry, and go on my way. After all, it was only a 75-cent item. 5

Next thing I knew, he was talking about calling the police and having me arrested and thrown in jail, as if he had just nabbed a professional thief instead of a terrified kid. I couldn't believe what he was saying. 6

"Jean, what's going on?" 7

The sound of my sister's voice eased the pressure a bit. She always managed to get me out of trouble. She would come through this time too. 8

"Excuse me. Are you a relative of this young girl?" 9

"Yes, I'm her sister. What's the problem?" 10

"Well, I just caught her shoplifting and I'm afraid I'll have to call the police." 11

"What did she take?" 12

"This button." 13

"A button? You are having a thirteen-year-old arrested for stealing a button?" 14

"I'm sorry, but she broke the law." 15

The man led us through the store and into an office, where we waited for the police officers to arrive. Susan had found my grandmother and brother, who, still shocked, didn't say a word. The thought of going to jail terrified me, not because of jail itself, but because of the encounter with my parents afterward. Not more than ten minutes later, two officers arrived and placed me under arrest. They said that I was to be taken to the station alone. Then, they handcuffed me and led me out of the store. I felt alone and scared. I had counted on my sister being with me, but now I had to muster up the courage to face this ordeal all by myself. 16

As the officers led me through the mall, I sensed a hundred pairs of eyes staring at me. My face flushed and I broke out in a sweat. Now everyone knew I was a criminal. In their eyes I was a juvenile delinquent, and thank God the cops were getting me off the streets. The worst part was thinking my grandmother might be having the same thoughts. The humiliation at that moment was overwhelming. I felt like Hester Prynne being put on public display for everyone to ridicule. 17

That short walk through the mall seemed to take hours. But once we reached the squad car, time raced by. I was read my rights and questioned. We were at the police station within minutes. Everything happened so fast I didn't have a chance to feel remorse for my crime. Instead, I viewed what was happening to me as if it were a movie. Being searched, although embarrassing, somehow seemed to be exciting. All the movies and television programs I had seen were actually coming to life. This is what it was really like. But why were criminals always portrayed as frightened and regretful? I was having fun. I thought I had nothing to fear—until I was allowed my one phone call. I was trembling as I dialed home. I didn't know what I was going to say to my parents, especially my mother. 18

"Hi, Dad, this is Jean." 19

"We've been waiting for you to call." 20

"Did Susie tell you what happened?" 21

"Yeah, but we haven't told your mother. I think you should tell her what you did and where you are." 22

"You mean she doesn't even know where I am?" 23

"No, I want you to explain it to her." 24

There was a pause as he called my mother to the phone. For the first time that night, I was close to tears. I wished I had never stolen that stupid pin. I wanted to give the phone to one of the officers because I was too ashamed to tell my mother the truth, but I had no choice. 25

"Jean, where are you?" 26

"I'm, umm, in jail." 27

"Why? What for?" 28

"Shoplifting." 29

"Oh no, Jean. Why? Why did you do it?" 30

"I don't know. No reason. I just did it." 31

"I don't understand. What did you take? Why did you do it? You had plenty of money with you." 32

"I know but I just did it. I can't explain why. Mom, I'm sorry." 33

"I'm afraid sorry isn't enough. I'm horribly disappointed in you." 34

Long after we got off the phone, while I sat in an empty jail cell, waiting for my parents to pick me up, I could still distinctly hear the disappointment and hurt in my mother's voice. I cried. The tears weren't for me but for her and the pain I had put her through. I felt like a terrible human being. I would rather have stayed in jail than confront my mom right then. I dreaded each passing minute that brought our encounter closer. When the officer came to release me, I hesitated, actually not wanting to leave. We went to the front desk, where I had to sign a form to retrieve my belongings. I saw my parents a few yards away and my heart raced. A large knot formed in my stomach. I fought back the tears. 35

Not a word was spoken as we walked to the car. Slowly, I sank into the back seat anticipating the scolding. Expecting harsh tones, I was relieved to hear almost the opposite from my father. 36

"I'm not going to punish you and I'll tell you why. Although I think what you did was wrong, I think what the police did was more wrong. There's no excuse for locking a thirteen-year-old behind bars. That doesn't mean I condone what you did, but I think you've been punished enough already." 37

As I looked from my father's eyes to my mother's, I knew this ordeal was over. Although it would never be forgotten, the incident was not mentioned again. 38

Connecting to Culture and Experience

In paragraph 17, Brandt gives us a vivid portrait of how excruciating the feeling of shame can be: "I sensed a hundred pairs of eyes staring at me. My face flushed and I broke out in a sweat." Shame, as this description indicates, involves a desire for the community's approval or dread of its disapproval.

With other students in your class, discuss the feeling of shame, specifically its social dimensions. Identify one occasion when you felt ashamed. Take turns briefly explaining what happened and why you were ashamed. In whose eyes did you feel the most shame? (Note that Brandt, for example, feels shame at being thought of as a criminal by strangers in the shopping mall, but she feels even more ashamed with her grandmother and perhaps most ashamed with her mother.)

Shame can serve as a deterrent against wrongdoing, but some people believe that guilt is an even stronger deterrent. The words *shame* and *guilt* are often used interchangeably, but they have different connotations: Shame involves anxiety about social acceptance, whereas guilt is a more private, inward-looking emotion, associated with morality. Discuss your understanding of the difference between shame and guilt. Which one is a stronger deterrent against wrongdoing for you—the dread of social disapproval or your conscience? Do you ask yourself, am I going to get caught or am I going to do wrong? In explaining your views, contrast a particular occasion of guilt with the occasion of shame you described earlier.

Analyzing Writing Strategies

1. Reread the essay, paying particular attention to Brandt's use of **dialogue.** What do you learn about her from what she says and how she says it? What do you learn about her relationship with her parents?

2. The story begins and ends in a car, with the two car rides framing the story. **Framing** is a narrative device of echoing something from the beginning in the ending. What effect does this device have on your reaction to the story?
3. The Writer at Work section on pp. 55–60 includes some of Brandt's invention notes and her complete first draft. These materials show how her focus shifted gradually from the theft and subsequent arrest in her first draft to her emotional confrontation with her parents in the final version.

   Read over the notes and draft, and comment on this shift in focus. Why do you think Brandt decided to stress her confrontation with her parents? Why do you think she decided, against the advice of the student who commented on her draft, to cut the scenes in the police car and station? Notice, in particular, that she left out of the final version the vivid image of herself handcuffed to the table (see p. 59, paragraph 5).

Considering Topics for Your Own Essay

Think of a few occasions when you did something uncharacteristic. Perhaps you acted on impulse or took a chance you would not ordinarily take. The events do not have to be reckless, dangerous, or illegal; they could be quite harmless or even pleasant. Pick one occasion you might like to write about. What would you want your readers to recognize about you on the basis of reading your story?

Commentary

What is perhaps most notable about Brandt's essay is that, like Wolff, she displays herself in a rather uncomplimentary light. All autobiographers have to decide just how candid their self-disclosures will be. We can see in her Writer at Work materials some of Brandt's decisions about what to disclose. She indicates in her invention writing that she had always been too "ashamed to tell anyone" about this particular event (p. 57). She seems to have decided to go ahead, in part, because she expects readers will readily recognize the event's significance. She also assumes some readers will identify with her and be sympathetic. But her primary reason for choosing this event seems to be that she hopes writing will help her come to terms with what she did and how she was treated. Without oversimplifying her feelings or fully understanding them, Brandt ultimately admits that what she did was wrong, but she also takes pride in how she acted afterward.

For more on dialogue, see pp. 487–88.

To present the people involved in the event and especially to dramatize her relationship with her parents, Brandt depends on **dialogue.** We can see from her use of dialogue the two ways writers typically present remembered conversations: **quoting** and **summarizing.** Compare the following examples. The first passage quotes a brief exchange between Brandt and her sister as they were leaving the store (paragraphs 3 and 4):

> A few seconds later, my sister appeared and asked, "So, did you decide to buy the button?"
> "No, I guess not." I hoped my voice didn't quaver.

The second example summarizes what the store manager said to Brandt as she left the store (paragraphs 5 and 6):

> An unexpected tap on my shoulder startled me. I whirled around to find a middle-aged man, dressed in street clothes, flashing some type of badge and politely asking me to empty my pockets. . . .
>
> Next thing I knew, he was talking about calling the police and having me arrested. . . .

As these examples indicate, writers usually summarize rather than quote when they need to give only the gist of what was said. Brandt apparently decided that the manager's actual words and way of speaking were not important for her purpose. However, presenting her response to her sister's question was important because it shows how she felt at the time. When you write a remembered event essay, you too will have to decide what to summarize and what to quote in light of your overall purpose.

While we are looking at Brandt's quoted dialogue, you should note a few of the conventions readers expect writers to follow when quoting dialogue. Use quotation marks for quoted dialogue but not for summarized dialogue. If you include one or two exact words in a summarized dialogue and want to call attention to the fact that they were actually spoken, put quotes only around those particular words. Indicate each change of speaker with a new paragraph. Put a concluding period, question mark, or exclamation point that is part of the quotation inside the quotation marks; otherwise place it after the closing quotation marks. Do not conclude a sentence with one punctuation mark inside the quotation marks and a second one outside the marks.

PURPOSE AND AUDIENCE

Writers have various reasons for writing about their experiences. Reminiscing makes it possible to relive moments of pleasure and pain, but it also helps them to gain insight, to learn who they are now by examining who they used to be and the forces that shaped them. Reflecting on the past can lead to significant self-discovery. Nevertheless, writing about personal experience is public, not private. The autobiographer writes to be read and is therefore as much concerned with self-presentation as with self-discovery. Writers present themselves to readers in the way they want to be perceived. The rest they keep hidden, though readers may read between the lines.

We read about others' experiences for much the same reason that we write about our own—to learn how to live our lives. Reading autobiography can validate our sense of ourselves, particularly when we see our own experience reflected in another's life. Reading about others' lives can also challenge our complacency and help us appreciate other points of view. It can enlarge our sympathies by awakening our humanity. When we read about other people's lives, we are invited to empathize with their values and feelings and thus break the shell of our own isolation.

SUMMARY OF BASIC FEATURES

A Well-Told Story

An essay about a remembered event should tell an interesting story. Whatever else the writer may attempt to do, he or she must shape the experience into a story that is entertaining and memorable. This is done primarily by building suspense, which leads us to wonder, for example, whether Tobias Wolff will shoot the rifle or Jean Brandt will get caught for shoplifting. The principal technique for propelling the narrative and heightening suspense is specific narrative action with its action verbs and their tense markers. Suspense increases, for instance, when Wolff shows specific narrative action by giving a detailed close-up of his play with the rifle. In addition, writers use time markers, or temporal transitions, to move the narrative through time and cue readers. Finally, they often use dialogue to convey immediacy and drama, as when Brandt uses dialogue to dramatize her confrontation with her mother on the phone.

A Vivid Presentation of Significant Scenes and People

Instead of giving a generalized impression, skillful writers actually re-create the scene and let us hear what people say. Vivid language and specific details make the event—and the writing—memorable, leaving readers with a dominant impression. By moving in close, a writer can name specific objects in a scene, such as when Brandt catalogs the store's knickknacks, calendars, and buttons. Good writers also provide details about some of the objects, as when Brandt describes the coveted button as a "75-cent Snoopy button." Finally, writers use simile and metaphor to draw comparisons that help readers to understand the point. When Brandt says she felt "like Hester Prynne being put on public display," for example, readers familiar with *The Scarlet Letter* can imagine how embarrassed Brandt must have felt.

To present people who played an important role in a remembered event, autobiographers often provide some descriptive details and a snatch of dialogue. They detail the person's appearance, for example, as Dillard does by describing her mother sitting "with her knees crossed, in blue slacks, smoking a Chesterfield." Dialogue—

quoted and summarized—can be an especially effective way of giving readers a vivid impression of someone. Wolff, for example, describes his mother by combining specific narrative actions with her empathetic words: "She took a cellophane bag off a loaf of bread and we went outside and looked at the squirrel. 'Poor little thing,' she said. She stuck her hand in the wrapper and picked up the squirrel, then pulled the bag inside out away from her hand."

An Indication of the Event's Significance

There are two ways a writer can communicate an event's autobiographical significance: by showing us that the event was important or by telling us directly what it meant. Most writers do both. Showing is necessary because the event must be dramatized if readers are to appreciate its importance and understand the writer's feelings about it. Seeing the important scenes and people from the writer's point of view naturally leads readers to identify with the writer. We can well imagine what that "unexpected tap on [the] shoulder" must have felt like for Brandt and how Dillard felt running upstairs to tell her parents about her great discovery. As we have seen in analyzing Auster's essay, an especially effective way to show significance is by creating a dominant impression with carefully orchestrated descriptive language.

Telling also contributes to a reader's understanding, so most writers explain something about the event's meaning and importance. They may tell us how they felt at the time or how they feel now as they look back on the experience. Often writers do both. Wolff, for example, tells us some of his remembered feelings when he recalls feeling "like a sniper" and delighting in the "ecstasy" of power. He also tells us what he thinks looking back on the experience: "Because I did not know who I was, any image of myself, no matter how grotesque, had power over me. This much I understand now." Telling is the main way that writers interpret the event for readers, but skillful writers are careful not to append these reflections artificially, like a moral tagged on to a fable.

GUIDE TO WRITING

THE WRITING ASSIGNMENT

Write an essay about a significant event in your life. Choose an event that will be engaging for readers and that will, at the same time, tell them something about you. Tell your story dramatically and vividly, giving a clear indication of its autobiographical significance.

INVENTION

The following invention activities will help you to choose an appropriate event, recall specific details, sketch out the story, test your choice, and explore the event's autobiographical significance. Each activity is easy to do and takes only a few minutes. If you can spread out the activities over several days, it will be easier for you to recall details and to reflect deeply on the event's meaning in your life. Keep a written record of your invention work to use when you draft the essay and also when you revise.

Choosing an Event

Finding the best possible event to write about requires some time and reflection.

Listing Remembered Events. *Make a list of significant events from your past.* Begin your list now and add to it over the next few days. Include possibilities suggested by the Considering Topics for Your Own Essay activities following the readings. Considering several possibilities rather than choosing the first event that comes to mind will help you make the very best choice. Following are some more ideas:

Set a timer for ten minutes, and brainstorm your lists with the monitor brightness turned all the way down. Enter as many possibilities as you can think of. Then, turn the brightness up, make sure all the items make sense, and save them as an invention file. Print out a copy to make notes on.

- A "first," such as when you first realized you had a special skill, ambition, or problem; when you first felt needed or rejected; or when you first became aware of your own feelings of altruism or injustice
- A difficult situation, such as when you had to make a tough choice, when someone you admired let you down (or you let someone else down), or when you struggled to learn or understand something hard
- An occasion when things did not turn out as expected, such as when you expected to be praised but were criticized or ignored, or when you were convinced you would fail but succeeded
- An incident charged with strong emotions, such as love, fear, anger, embarrassment, guilt, frustration, hurt, pride, happiness, or joy
- Something that you saw happen to another person but that affected you deeply

Listing Events concerning Identity and Community Whenever you write about events in your life, you are likely to reveal important aspects of your sense of identity and your relationships with others. The suggestions that follow, however, will help you recall events that are particularly revealing of your efforts to know yourself and to discover your place in the communities to which you belong.

- An event that shaped you in a particular way or revealed an aspect of your personality you had not seen before—for example, that you are independent, insecure, ambitious, or jealous
- An incident that made you reexamine one of your basic values or beliefs, such as when you were expected to do something that went against your better judgment, or when your values conflicted with someone else's values
- An occasion when others' actions led you to consider seriously a new idea or point of view
- An incident that made you feel the need to identify yourself with a particular community, such as an ethnic or cultural group, a political action committee, or a group of coworkers trying to improve working conditions
- An event that made you realize that the role you were playing did not conform to social norms and expectations, perhaps with what was expected of you as a student, as a male or female, as a parent or sibling, as a believer in a particular religious faith, or as a member of a particular community
- An incident in which a single encounter with another person changed the way you view yourself or changed your ideas about how you fit into a particular community

Listing Events concerning Work and Career The following suggestions will help you think of events involving your work experiences as well as your career aspirations:

- An event that made you aware of your capacity for or interest in a particular kind of work or career, or an event that convinced you that you were not cut out for a particular kind of work or career
- An incident of harassment or mistreatment at work that led you to reflect on how power can be abused
- An event that revealed to you other people's assumptions, attitudes, or prejudices about you as a worker, your fitness for a particular job, or your career goals
- An incident of conflict or serious misunderstanding with a customer, fellow employee, supervisor, or someone you supervise

Making a Choice. *Look over your list of possibilities and choose one event that you think will make an interesting story.* You should be eager to explore the significance of the event and comfortable about sharing the event with your instructors and classmates. You may find that the choice is easy to make, or you may have several equally promising possibilities from which to choose. Make the best choice you can now. If this event does not work out, you can try a different one later.

Describing the Scene

These activities will help you decide which scenes are important to your story and what you remember about them. Take the time now to explore your memory and imagination. This exploration will yield a treasure trove of images you can use as you draft your story and later when you revise it to create a strong dominant impression.

Listing Scenes. *Make a list of all the places where the event occurred, skipping a few lines after each entry on your list.* Your event may have occurred in only one locale or in many. For now, list all the places you remember without worrying about whether they should be included in your story.

Describing Key Scenes. *In the space after each entry on your list, make some notes describing each scene.* Imagine yourself stepping into an old photograph or movie. As you picture each scene, what do you see (excluding people for the moment)? Are the objects you see large or small, green or brown, square or oblong? Do you hear any whispering or laughter? Do you detect any pungent odors? Does any taste come to mind? Do you see anything soft or hard, smooth or rough?

If you can, save these details on a word processor. Later, as you begin to draft, you can call up the file on a second screen and easily transfer details you want to use in your draft.

Your memory may be only a trickle at first, but once you have begun priming the pump, more memories will come flooding back. Keep paper and pen handy to jot down whatever you remember. At this point, do not worry about whether your memory is accurate or whether any of this material will be useful. Just try to recall as much as you can.

Recalling Key People

These activities will help you to remember the people who played a role in the event—what they looked like, did, and said.

Listing People. *List the people who played more than a casual role in the event.* You may have only one person to list, or you may have several.

Describing Key People. *Write a brief description of the people who played major roles in the event.* For each person, name and detail a few distinctive physical features or items of dress. Use specific narrative action to describe the person's way of talking or gesturing. Briefly explain how the person helped to make the event significant.

Re-creating Conversations. *Reconstruct any important conversations you had during or immediately before or after the event.* Try to recall any especially memorable comments, any unusual choice of words, or any telling remarks that you made or were made to you. Reconstruct one or more conversations, setting up the dialogue as Jean Brandt does on p. 55. (Do not worry about accuracy at this point; just try to capture the spirit of the conversations. Unless the conversations were recorded, the dialogue is bound to be imagined to some extent.)

Sketching the Story

Write for about five minutes, telling what happened. Do not try to tell the story dramatically or even coherently. Just put down whatever you remember. Over the next few days you can add to this rough sketch, but your aim now is simply to start writing the story. (You may find it easier to outline what happened rather than writing complete sentences and paragraphs. Any way you can put the main action on paper is fine.)

Testing Your Choice

Now, you need to decide whether you recall enough detail to write a good story about this particular event. Reread your invention notes to see whether your initial memories seem promising. If you can recall clearly what happened and what the important scenes and people were like, then you have probably made a good choice.

As you go on to explore the event's significance and to consider what readers will learn about you from reading the story, you may have second thoughts. Remember, you must decide what you wish to disclose about yourself and your life. If at any point you feel uncomfortable or lose confidence in your choice, return to your list and choose another event. Starting over can be frustrating but will save time and energy in the long run.

→ Testing Your Choice: A Collaborative Activity

At this point, you will find it useful to get together with two or three other students to try out your stories. Their reactions will help you determine whether you have chosen an event you can present in an interesting way.

Storytellers: Each of you take turns telling your story briefly. Try to make your story dramatic (by piquing your listeners' curiosity and building suspense) and vivid (by using a few specific descriptive details to set the scene and describe key people).

Listeners: Briefly tell each storyteller what you found most intriguing about the story. For example, were you eager to know how it would turn out? Were you curious about any of the people? Were you able to identify with the storyteller? Could you visualize the scene? Could you understand why the event is so memorable and significant for the storyteller?

Reflecting on the Event's Significance

You should now feel fairly confident that you can tell an interesting story about the event you have chosen. The following activities will help you understand the meaning the event holds in your life and develop ways to convey this significance to your readers.

Recalling Your Remembered Feelings and Thoughts. *Write for ten minutes about your feelings and thoughts during and immediately after the event.* The following questions may help stimulate your memory:

- What was my first reaction to the event as it was happening and right after it ended?
- How did I show my feelings? What did I say?
- What did I want the people involved to think of me? Why did I care what they thought of me?
- What did I think of myself at the time?
- How long did these initial feelings last?
- What were the immediate consequences of the event for me personally?

At this point, if you have the time, pause in your invention work and return to it a little later. When you return, reread what you have written in this section and write another sentence or two, commenting on what your remembered feelings and thoughts reveal to you about the event's significance.

Exploring Your Present Perspective. *Write for ten minutes about your current feelings and thoughts as you look back on the event.* These questions may help you to start writing:

- Looking back, how do I feel about this event? If I understand it differently now than I did then, what is the difference?
- What do my actions at the time of the event say about the kind of person I was then? In what ways am I different now? How would I respond to the same event if it occurred today?
- How can looking at the event historically or culturally help to explain what happened and why? For example, was I playing a socially acceptable but personally uncomfortable role? Was I upsetting gender expectations? Was I feeling torn between two cultures or ethnic identities? Was I feeling displaced or out of place?
- Do I now see that a conflict was underlying the event? For example, was I struggling with contradictory desires within myself? Was I feeling pressured by others or by society in general? Was the conflict between my rights and someone else's? Was it about power or responsibility?

Pause again at this point to reflect on what you have written in this section. When you return, write another sentence or two, commenting on the meaning this event now holds for you.

Defining the Significance of the Event. *Write for five minutes, defining your purpose in writing about this particular event for your readers.* Use these questions to focus your thoughts:

Print out your reflections to read over and make notes on before trying to define the event's significance.

- How do I want my readers to feel about what happened? What is the dominant impression or mood I want my story to create?
- What specifically do I want my readers to think of me? What do I expect or fear they might think?
- What do I want readers to learn about themselves or about society in general from reading my story?

PLANNING AND DRAFTING

This section will help you to write a well-developed, detailed draft based on your invention writing.

Seeing What You Have

You have now done a lot of thinking and writing about the basic elements of a remembered event essay: what happened, where it happened, who was involved, what was said, and how you felt. You have also begun to develop your understanding of why the event is so important to you—what we call its autobiographical significance.

In order to write a story that not only interests readers but also makes them think and feel, you will need to select material from your invention writing that contributes to the dominant impression you are trying to make.

It is a good idea at this point to print out a hard copy of what you have written on a word processor for easier reviewing.

Reread what you have written so far to see what you have. As you read through your invention materials, watch for specific narrative actions, vivid descriptive details, choice bits of dialogue. Note any language that resonates with feeling or that seems especially insightful. Highlight any writing you think could be used in your draft.

If you do not find much that is promising, you are not likely to be able to write a good draft. Starting over with another event is certainly a setback, but there is no sense trying to draft a story without good material.

If, however, your invention writing has a little promising material, it would be wise to take the time now to develop some additional material. The following activities may help you generate invention writing you can use:

- To remember more of what actually happened, discuss the event with someone who was there or who remembers hearing about it at the time.
- To imagine an important scene in more vivid detail, look at photographs or visit a place that reminds you of the scene and write about what you observe.
- To recall additional details about a person who played an important role in the event, look at photographs or letters if any are available. You may also be able to talk with the person or with someone who remembers the person. If that is impossible, you might imagine having a conversation with the person today about the event: What would you say? How do you think the person would respond?
- To remember how you felt at the time of the event, try to recall what else was happening in your life during that period. What music, television shows, movies, sports, books, and magazines did you like? What concerns did you have at home, school, work, play?
- To develop your present perspective on the event, try viewing your experience as a historical event. If you were writing a news story or documentary about it, what would you want people to know?
- To decide on the dominant impression you want your story to have on readers, imagine that you are making a film based on this event. What would your film look like? What mood or atmosphere would you try to create? Alternatively, imagine writing a song or poem about the event. Think of an appropriate image or refrain. What kind of song would you write—blues, hip-hop, country, ranchera, hard rock?

Setting Goals

Before starting to draft, set goals for yourself. Some goals should deal with the story as a whole, such as maintaining suspense or creating a dominant impression. Other goals should involve smaller issues—how much to say about the context of the event, which dialogue to summarize and which to quote, which narrative transitions to use. Setting goals will help you make decisions and solve problems as you draft and revise. The following questions will help in your goal-setting process.

Your Purpose and Readers

- What do I want my readers to think of me and my experience? If I want them to identify with me, should I tell them how I felt and what I thought at the time? Should I tell them how my perspective has changed, as Auster does?
- If my readers are likely to have had similar experiences, how can I convey the uniqueness of my experience or its special importance in my life? Should I tell them more about my background or the particular context of the event? Should I give them a glimpse, as Dillard does, of its impact years later?
- If my readers are not likely to have had similar experiences, how can I help them understand what happened and appreciate its importance? Should I reveal the cultural influences acting on me, as Wolff does?
- If my readers may be alarmed by my disclosures or may judge me harshly, what can I do to get them to see my point of view? Should I encourage them to question their own preconceptions, as Wolff does with his observations about the "ecstasy" of power? Should I present my experience without apology or explanation, as Brandt does?

The Beginning

- What can I do in the opening sentences to arouse readers' curiosity? Should I begin with a surprising announcement, as Dillard and Wolff do? Should I establish the setting and situation, as Brandt does?
- How can I get readers to identify with me? Should I tell readers a few things about myself, as Auster does?
- Should I do something unusual, such as begin in the middle of the action or with a funny bit of dialogue?

The Story

See Chapter 14 for information on structuring the narrative.

- What should be the climax of my story, the point readers anticipate with trepidation or eagerness?
- How can I build the suspense leading to the climax? What specific narrative actions should I use to propel the narrative forward? What narrative transitions will enable me to pace the action dramatically? Will dialogue intensify the drama of the story?
- Should I follow strict chronological order? Or would flashback or flashforward make the narrative more interesting?
- How can I use vivid descriptive detail to dramatize the story, as Auster does?

The Ending

- If I conclude with some reflections on the meaning of the experience, how can I avoid tagging on a moral or being too sentimental?
- If I want readers to think well of me, should I conclude with a philosophical statement, as Wolff does? Should I be satirical? Should I be self-critical to avoid seeming smug?
- If I want to underscore the event's continuing significance in my life, can I show that the conflict was never fully resolved, as Brandt does? Could I contrast my remembered and current feelings and thoughts, as Auster does?

- Should I frame the essay by echoing something from the beginning to give readers at least a superficial sense of closure, as Brandt does by setting the last scene, like the first, in the family car?

Outlining

Outlining on a word processor makes it particularly easy to experiment with different ways of sequencing your narrative.

The goals you have set should help you draft your essay, but first you might want to make a quick scratch outline to refocus on the basic storyline. List the order of actions leading to the climax. You could also note on your outline where you will describe the scene, introduce particular people, present dialogue, and insert remembered or current feelings and thoughts. Use this outline to guide your drafting, but do not feel tied to it. As you draft, you may find a better way to sequence the action and integrate these features.

Drafting

If you can shift between windows, you might call up invention material on an alternate screen as you draft on the main screen, shifting back and forth to cut and paste invention material into your draft.

Before you begin writing, you might want to review the general advice on drafting in Chapter 1 (pp. 12–13). Perhaps the most important advice to remember is to write quickly without worrying about details or grammar and spelling. Later, as you revise and edit, you can fill in details and make corrections. Also remember that you have a wealth of written invention material, which you can draw on either as you draft or as you revise.

Start drafting your essay, keeping in mind the goals you have set for yourself, especially the goal of telling the story dramatically. Refer to your outline to help you sequence the action. If you get stuck, either make a note of what you need to fill in later or see if you can use something from your invention writing.

CRITICAL READING GUIDE

Swap copies of your drafts with another student, either by exchanging disks or sending the computer files over a network. Add your comments either next to the essay, if you can divide the screen, or at the end of the document.

Now is the time to try to get a good critical reading. Most writers find it helpful to have someone else read and comment on their drafts, and your instructor may schedule such a reading as part of your coursework. If not, you can ask a classmate, friend, or family member to read your essay. If your campus has a writing center, you might ask a tutor there to comment on your draft. The guidelines in this section are designed to be used by anyone. (If you are unable to have someone else read your draft, turn ahead to the section on Revising, which includes guidelines for reading your own draft with a critical eye.)

If You Are the Writer. To provide helpful comments, your reader needs to know your intended audience and purpose. Briefly write this information at the top of your draft, answering the following questions:

- *Audience.* Who are your readers? How do you expect them to react to your story? Will they be sympathetic, critical, amused, surprised?
- *Purpose.* What do you want your readers to learn about you from reading this story? What do you want them to understand about the event's significance in your life?

continued

continued

If You Are the Reader. Use the following guidelines to help you give critical comments to others on remembered event essays:

1. *Read for a First Impression.* Begin by reading a draft quickly, to enjoy the story and get a sense of its significance. Then, in just a few sentences, describe the dominant impression you got from reading the story. If you have any insights about the meaning or importance of the event that are not reflected in the draft, share your thoughts.
2. *Analyze the Effectiveness of the Storytelling.* Review the story, looking at the way the suspense leads to the climax. Identify what you think is the climax of the story, or indicate if you are not sure where the climax is. Point to any places where the drama loses intensity—perhaps where the suspense slackens, where specific narrative action is sparse or action verbs are needed, where narrative transitions would help readers, or where dialogue could be added to dramatize a scene.

See pp. 40–41 to review the basic features.

3. *Consider How Vividly the Scenes and People Are Described.* Point to any descriptive details, similes, or metaphors that are especially effective and that help create a dominant impression. Also indicate any description that contradicts the story's dominant impression. Note any scenes or people that need more specific description. Identify any dialogue that should have been summarized instead of quoted or dialogue that does not seem relevant.
4. *Assess Whether the Autobiographical Significance Is Clear.* Explain briefly what you have learned about the writer from reading this story. If you think an underlying conflict is dramatized by the story, identify what the conflict is. Point to any passages that impress you with their clarity or eloquence. Also mention any places where the feelings are so overstated that they seem sentimental or so understated that they seem insignificant. Assess whether the dominant impression given by the descriptive language reinforces or contradicts the significance of the story.
5. *Suggest How the Organization Could Be Improved.* Consider the *overall plan,* perhaps by making a scratch outline. Pay special attention to the narrative transitions and verb tense markers so that you can identify any places where the order of the action is unclear. Also indicate any places where you think the description or background information interrupts the action. If you can, suggest other locations for this material.

   Look at the *beginning.* If it does not arouse curiosity, point to language elsewhere in the essay that might serve as a better opening—for example, a bit of dialogue, a striking image, or a remembered feeling.

   Look at the *ending.* Indicate whether the conflict in the story is too neatly resolved at the end, whether the writer has tagged on a moral, or whether the essay abruptly stops without really coming to a conclusion. If there is a problem with the ending, try to suggest something different, such as framing the story with a reference to something from the beginning or projecting into the future.

REVISING

This section will help you identify problems in your draft and revise to solve them.

Identifying Problems

To identify problems in your draft, you need to read it with a critical eye, analyze its basic features, and study any comments you have received from others.

Getting an Overview. Consider the draft as a whole, following these two steps:

Even if your essay is saved to a computer file, reread from a hard copy. Add notes to yourself and quick revisions as you read through the draft.

1. *Reread.* If at all possible, put the draft aside for a day or two. When you do reread it, start by reconsidering your purpose. Then, read the draft straight through, trying to see it as your intended readers will.
2. *Outline.* Make a quick scratch outline, indicating the basic features as they appear in the essay.

Charting a Plan for Revision. You may want to make a double-column chart to keep track of any problems you need to solve. In the left-hand column, list the basic features of writing about remembered events. As you analyze your draft and study any comments from others, note the problems you want to solve in the right-hand column. Here is an example:

Basic Features	*Problems to Solve*
The story	
Scenes and people	
Autobiographical significance	
Organization	

Analyzing the Basic Features of Your Own Draft. Turn to the Critical Reading Guide on the preceding pages. Using this guide, identify problems you now see in your draft. Note the problems on your chart.

Studying Critical Comments. Review all of the comments you have received from other readers. For each comment, refer to the draft to see what might have led the reader to make that particular point. Try to be objective about any criticism. Ideally, these comments will help you to see your draft as others see it (rather than as you hoped it would be) and to identify specific problems.

Solving the Problems

Having identified problems, you now need to figure out solutions and—most important—to carry them out. Basically, there are three ways to find solutions:

1. Review your invention and planning notes for material you can add to your draft.
2. Do additional invention writing to provide material you or your readers thought was needed.
3. Look back at the readings in this chapter to see how other writers have solved similar problems.

The following suggestions, which are organized according to the basic features on the revision chart, will get you started solving some common writing problems.

Before revising, or sharing your draft with another reader, copy your original draft to a second file. Then, should you change your mind about material you delete while revising, it will still be available to you.

The Story

- **Is the climax hard to identify?** Check to be sure your story has a climax. Perhaps it is the point when you get what you were striving for (Dillard), when you do what you were afraid you might do (Wolff), when something startling happens (Auster), or when you are caught (Brandt). If you cannot find a climax in your story or reconstruct your story so that it has one, then you may have a major problem. If this is the case, you should discuss with your instructor the possibility of starting over again with another event.
- **Does the suspense slacken instead of building to the climax?** Try intensifying the pace—by adding specific narrative actions with action verbs, by adding narrative transitions to propel the action through time, or by substituting dramatic quoted dialogue for summarized dialogue.

Scenes and People

- **Do any scenes or people need more specific description?** Try naming objects and adding sensory details to help readers to imagine what the objects look, feel, smell, taste, and sound like. For people, describe a physical feature or mannerism that shows the role the person plays in your story.
- **Does any dialogue seem irrelevant or poorly written?** Eliminate any unnecessary dialogue or summarize quoted dialogue that has no distinctive language or dramatic purpose. Liven up quoted dialogue with faster repartee to make it more dramatic. Instead of introducing each comment with the dialogue cue "he said," describe the speaker's attitude or personality with phrases like "she gasped" or "he muttered under his breath."
- **Do any descriptions weaken the dominant impression?** Omit extraneous details or reconsider the impression you want to make. Add similes and metaphors that strengthen the dominant impression you want your story to have.

Autobiographical Significance

- **Are readers getting a different image of you from the one you wanted to make?** Look closely at the language you have used to express your feelings and thoughts. If you have projected an aspect of yourself you did not intend to, reconsider what the story reveals about you. Ask yourself once again why the event stands out in your memory. What do you want readers to know about you from reading this essay?
- **Are your remembered or current feelings and thoughts about the event coming across clearly and eloquently?** If not, look in your invention writing for

Use your word processor's cut-and-paste or block-and-move functions to shift material around. Make sure that you revise transitions so that material fits smoothly in its new spot.

more expressive language. If your writing seems sentimental to readers, try to express your feelings more directly and simply. Let yourself show ambivalence or uncertainty.

- **Do readers appreciate the event's uniqueness or special importance in your life?** If not, consider giving them more insight into your background or cultural heritage. Also consider whether they need to know what has happened since the event to appreciate why it is so memorable for you.

Organization

- **Is the overall plan ineffective or the story hard to follow?** Look carefully at the way the action unfolds. Fill in any gaps. Eliminate unnecessary digressions. Add or clarify narrative transitions. Fix confusing verb tense markers.
- **Does description or other information disrupt the flow of the narrative?** Try integrating this material by adding smoother transitions. If that doesn't help, consider removing the disruptive parts or placing them elsewhere.
- **Is the beginning weak?** See if there is a better way to start. Review the draft and your notes for an image, a bit of dialogue, or a remembered feeling that might catch readers' attention or spark their curiosity.
- **Does the ending work?** If not, think about a better place to end—a memorable image, perhaps, or a provocative assertion. Consider whether you can frame the essay by referring back to something in the beginning.

EDITING AND PROOFREADING

Now is the time to check for errors in usage, punctuation, and mechanics, and also to consider matters of style. Our research has identified several errors that often occur in narrative writing. Check your draft for three patterns in particular: missing commas after introductory elements, fused sentences, and the misuse of past-perfect verbs.

Use your word processor's spell-check function cautiously. Keep in mind that it will not find all misspellings, particularly misused homonyms (such as *there, their,* and *they're*), typographical errors that are themselves words (such as *fro* and *for*), and many proper nouns and specialized terms. Proofread these carefully yourself. Also proofread for words that should have been deleted when you revised a sentence.

Checking for Missing Commas after Introductory Elements. Introductory elements in a sentence can be words, phrases, or clauses. A comma tells readers that the introductory information is ending and the main part of the sentence is about to begin. If there is no danger of misreading, you can omit the comma after single words or short phrases or clauses, but you will never be wrong to include the comma. The following sentences, taken from drafts done by college students using this book, show several ways to edit introductory sentence elements:

> **Through the nine-day run of the play, the acting just kept getting better and better.**

> **Knowing that the struggle was over, I felt through my jacket to find tea bags and cookies the robber had taken from the kitchen.**

> **As I stepped out of the car, I knew something was wrong.**

Checking for Fused Sentences. Fused sentences occur when two independent clauses are joined with no punctuation or connecting word between them. When you write about a remembered event, you try to re-create a scene. In so doing, you might write a fused sentence like this one:

Sleet glazed the windshield the wipers were frozen stuck.

There are several ways to edit fused sentences:

- Make the clauses separate sentences.

The

Sleet glazed the windshield. ~~the~~ wipers were frozen stuck.

- Join the two clauses with a comma and *and, but, or, nor, for, so,* or *yet.*

, and

Sleet glazed the windshield the wipers were frozen stuck.

- Join the two clauses with a semicolon.

Sleet glazed the windshield; the wipers were frozen stuck.

- Rewrite the sentence, subordinating one clause.

As sleet became

~~Sleet~~ glazed the windshield, the wipers ~~were~~ frozen stuck.

Checking Your Use of the Past Perfect. Verb tenses indicate the time an action takes place. As a writer, you will generally use the present tense for actions occurring at the time you are writing (we *see*), the past tense for actions completed in the past (we *saw*), and the future tense for actions that will occur in the future (we *will see*). When you write about a remembered event, you will often need to use various forms of the past tense: the past perfect to indicate an action that was completed at the time of another past action (she *had finished* her work when we saw her) and the past progressive to indicate a continuing action in the past (she *was finishing* her work). One common problem in writing about a remembered event is the failure to use the past perfect when it is needed. For example:

had

I had three people in the car, something my father told me not to do on several occasions.

In the following sentence, the meaning is not clear without the past perfect:

had run

Coach Kernow told me I ~~ran~~ faster than ever before.

A Common ESL Problem. It is important to remember that the past perfect is formed with had followed by a past participle. Past participles usually end in *-ed, -d, -en, -n,* or *-t: worked, hoped, eaten, taken, bent.*

spoken

Before Tania went to Moscow last year, she had not really ~~speak~~ Russian.

A WRITER AT WORK

FROM INVENTION TO DRAFT TO REVISION

In this section we look at the writing process that Jean Brandt followed in composing her essay, "Calling Home." You will see some of her invention writing and her complete first draft, which you can then compare to the final draft, printed on pp. 35–37.

Invention

Brandt's invention produced about nine handwritten pages, but it took her only two hours, spread out over four days. Here is a selection of her invention writings. She begins by choosing an event and then recalling specific sensory details of the scene and the other people involved. She writes two dialogues, one with her sister Sue and the other with her father. Following is the one with her sister.

Re-creating Conversations

```
SUE: Jean, why did you do it?
ME:  I don't know. I guess I didn't want to wait in that long
     line. Sue, what am I going to tell Mom and Dad?
SUE: Don't worry about that yet, the detective might not real-
     ly call the police.
ME:  I can't believe I was stupid enough to take it.
SUE: I know. I've been there before. Now when he comes back
     try crying and act like you're really upset. Tell him how
     sorry you are and that it was the first time you ever
     stole something but make sure you cry. It got me off the
     hook once.
ME:  I don't think I can force myself to cry. I'm not really
     that upset. I don't think the shock's worn off. I'm more
     worried about Mom.
SUE: Who knows? Maybe she won't have to find out.
ME:  God, I hope not. Hey, where's Louie and Grandma? Grandma
     doesn't know about this, does she?
SUE: No, I sort of told Lou what was going on so he's just
     taking Grandma around shopping.
ME:  Isn't she wondering where we are?
SUE: I told him to tell her we would meet them in an hour.
ME:  How am I ever going to face her? Mom and Dad might possi-
     bly understand or at least get over it, but Grandma? This
     is gonna kill her.
SUE: Don't worry about that right now. Here comes the
     detective. Now try to look like you're sorry. Try to cry.
```

This dialogue helps Brandt to recall an important conversation with her sister. Dialogues are an especially useful form of invention for they enable writers to remember their feelings and thoughts.

Brandt writes this dialogue quickly, trying to capture the language of excited talk, keeping the exchanges brief. She includes a version of this dialogue in her second draft but excludes it from her revision. The dialogue with her father does not appear in any of her drafts. Even though she eventually decides to feature other completely different conversations, these invention dialogues enable her to evaluate how various conversations would work in her essay.

Next, Brandt makes her first attempt to bring the autobiographical significance of the event into focus. She explores her remembered as well as her current feelings and thoughts about the experience:

Being arrested for shoplifting was significant because it changed some of my basic attitudes. Since that night I've never again considered stealing anything. This event would reveal how my attitude toward the law and other people has changed from disrespectful to very respectful.

Brandt begins by stating tentatively that the importance of the event was the lesson it taught her. Reading this statement might lead us to expect a moralistic story of how someone learned something the hard way. As we look at the subsequent invention activities and watch the draft develop, however, we will see how her focus shifts to her relations with other people.

Recalling Remembered Feelings and Thoughts

I was scared, humiliated, and confused. I was terrified when I realized what was happening. I can still see the manager and his badge and remember what I felt when I knew who he was. I just couldn't believe it. I didn't want to run. I felt there wasn't anything I could do--I was afraid, embarrassed, worried, mad that it happened. I didn't show my feelings at all. I tried to look very calm on the outside, but inside I was extremely nervous. The nervousness might have come through in my voice a little. I wanted the people around me to think I was tough and that I could handle the situation. I was really disappointed with myself. Getting arrested made me realize how wrong my actions were. I felt very ashamed. Afterward I had to talk to my father about it. I didn't say much of anything except that I was wrong and I was sorry. The immediate consequence was being taken to jail and then later having to call my parents and tell them what happened. I hated to call my parents. That was the hardest part. I remember how much I dreaded that. My mom was really hurt.

Brandt's exploration of her first reaction is quite successful. Naming specific feelings, she focuses on the difference between what she felt and how she acted. She remembers her humiliation at being arrested as well as the terrible moment when she had to tell her parents. As we will see, this concern with her parents' reaction, more than her own humiliation, becomes the most important theme in her essay.

In exploring her first response to the event, Brandt writes quickly, jotting down memories as they come to mind. Next, she rereads this first exploration and attempts to state briefly what the incident really reveals about her:

I think it reveals that I was not a hard-core criminal. I was trying to live up to Robin Files's (supposedly my best girlfriend) expectations, even though I actually knew that what I was doing was wrong.

Stopping to focus her thoughts like this helps Brandt to see the point of what she has just written in her longer pieces of exploratory writing. Specifically, it helps her to connect diverse invention writings to her main concern: discovering the autobiographical significance of the event. She reflects on what her remembered feelings of the event reveal about the kind of person she was at the time: not a hard-core criminal. She identifies a friend, who will disappear from the writing after one brief mention. Next, she looks at her present perspective on the event.

Exploring Present Perspective

At first I was ashamed to tell anyone that I had been arrested. It was as if I couldn't admit it myself. Now I'm glad it happened, because who knows where I'd be now if I hadn't been caught. I still don't tell many people about it. Never before have I written about it. I think my response was appropriate. If I'd broken down and cried, it wouldn't have helped me any, so it's better that I reacted calmly. My actions and responses show that I was trying to be tough. I thought that that was the way to gain respectability. If I were to get arrested now (of course it wouldn't be for shoplifting), I think I'd react the same way because it doesn't do any good to get emotional. My current feelings are ones of appreciation. I feel lucky because I was set straight early. Now I can look back on it and laugh, but at the same time know how serious it was. I am emotionally distant now because I can view the event objectively rather than subjectively. My feelings are settled now. I don't get upset thinking about it. I don't feel angry at the manager or the police. I think I was more upset about my parents than about what was happening to me. After the first part of it was over I mainly worried about what my parents would think.

By writing about her present perspective, Brandt reassures herself that she feels comfortable enough to write for class about this event. Having achieved a degree of emotional distance, she no longer feels humiliated, embarrassed, or angry. Reassessing her reaction at the time, she is obviously pleased to recall that she did not lose control and show her true feelings. Staying calm, not getting emotional, looking tough—these are the personal qualities Brandt wants others to see in her.

Exploring her present perspective seems to have led to a new, "respectable" self-image she can proudly display to her readers:

My present perspective shows that I'm a reasonable person. I can admit when I'm wrong and accept the punishment that was due me. I find that I can be concerned about others even when I'm in trouble.

Next, Brandt reflects on what she has written in order to express the meaning of the event for her.

Defining the Event's Autobiographical Significance

The event was important because it entirely changed one aspect of my character. I will be disclosing that I was once a thief, and I think many of my readers will be able to identify with my story, even though they won't admit it.

After the first set of invention work, completed in about forty-five minutes on two separate days, Brandt is confident she has chosen an event with personal significance. She knows what she will be disclosing about herself and feels comfortable doing it. In her brief focusing statements she begins by moralizing ("my attitude . . . changed") and blaming others (Robin Files) but concludes by acknowledging what she did. She is now prepared to disclose it to readers ("I was once a thief"). Also, she thinks readers will like her story because she suspects many of them will recall doing something illegal and feeling guilty about it, even if they never got caught.

The First Draft

The day after completing the invention writing, Brandt reviews her invention and writes her first draft. It takes her about an hour.

Her draft is handwritten and contains few erasures or other changes, indicating that she writes steadily, probably letting the writing lead her where it will. She knows this will not be her only draft.

Before you read the first draft, reread the final draft, "Calling Home," in the Readings section of this chapter. Then, as you read the first draft, consider what part it played in the total writing process.

It was two days before Christmas and my older sister and brother, my grandmother, and I were rushing around doing last-minute shopping. After going to a few stores we decided to go to Lakewood Center shopping mall. It was packed with other frantic shoppers like ourselves from one end to the other. The first store we went to (the first and last for me) was the General Store. The General Store is your typical gift shop. They mainly have the cutesy knick-knacks, posters, frames and that sort. The store is decorated to resemble an old-time western general store but the appearance doesn't quite come off. 1

We were all browsing around and I saw a basket of buttons so I went to see what the different ones were. One of the first ones I noticed was a Snoopy button. I'm not sure what it said on it, something funny I'm sure and besides I was in love with anything Snoopy when I was 13. I took it out of the basket and showed it to my sister and she said "Why don't you buy it?" I thought about it but the lines at the cashiers were outrageous and I didn't think it was worth it for a 75 cent item. Instead I figured just take it and I did. I thought I was so sly about it. I casually slipped it into my pocket and assumed I was home free since no one pounced on me. Everyone was ready to leave this shop so we made our way through the crowds to the entrance. 2

My grandmother and sister were ahead of my brother and I. They were almost to the entrance of May Co. and we were about 5 to 10 yards behind when I felt this tap on my shoulder. I turned around already terror struck, and this man was flashing some kind of badge in my face. It happened so fast I didn't know what was going on. Louie finally noticed I wasn't with him and came back for me. Jack explained I was being arrested for shoplifting and if my parents were here then Louie should go find them. Louie ran to get Susie and told her about it but kept it from Grandma. By the time Sue got back to the General Store I was in the back office and Jack was calling the police. I was a little scared but not really. It was sort of exciting. My sister was telling me to try and cry but I couldn't. About 20 minutes later two cops came and handcuffed me, led me through the mall outside to the police car. I was kind of embarrassed when they took me through the mall in front of all those people. 3

When they got me in the car they began questioning me, while driving me to the police station. Questions just to fill out the report--age, sex, address, color of eyes, etc. 4

Then when they were finished they began talking about Jack and what a nuisance he was. I gathered that Jack had every single person who shoplifted, no matter what their age, arrested. The police were getting really fed up with it because it was a nuisance for them to have to come way out to the mall for something as petty as that. To hear the police talk about my "crime" that way felt good because it was like what I did wasn't really so bad. It made me feel a bit relieved. When we walked into the station I remember the desk sergeant joking with the arresting officers about "well we got another one of Jack's hardened criminals." Again, I felt my crime lacked any seriousness at all. Next they handcuffed me to a table and questioned me further and then I had to phone my mom. That was the worst. I never was so humiliated in my life. Hearing the disappointment in her voice was worse punishment than the cops could ever give me. 5

This first draft establishes the main sequence of actions. About a third of it is devoted to the store manager, an emphasis that disappears by the final draft. What is to have prominence in the final draft—Brandt's feelings about telling her parents and her conversations with them—appears here only in a few lines at the very end. But mentioning the interaction suggests its eventual importance, and we are reminded of its prominence in Brandt's invention writing.

Brandt writes a second draft for another student to read critically. In this draft, she includes dialogues with her sister and with the policemen. She also provides more information about her actions as she considered buying the Snoopy button and then decided to steal it instead. She includes visual details of the manager's office. This draft is not much different in emphasis from the first draft, however, still ending with a long section about the policemen and the station. The parents are mentioned briefly only at the very end.

The reader tells Brandt how much he likes her story and admires her frankness. However, he does not encourage her to develop the dramatic possibilities in calling her parents and meeting them afterward. In fact, he encourages her to keep the dialogue with the policemen about the manager and to include what the manager said to the police.

Brandt's revision shows that she does not take her reader's advice. She reduces the role of the police officers, eliminating any dialogue with them. She greatly expands the role of her parents: The last third of the essay is now focused on her remembered feelings about calling them and seeing them afterward. In terms of dramatic importance, the phone call home now equals the arrest. When we recall Brandt's earliest invention writings, we can see that she was headed toward this conclusion all along; but she needed invention, three drafts, a critical reading, and about a week to get there.

THINKING CRITICALLY ABOUT WHAT YOU HAVE LEARNED

Now that you have worked extensively in autobiography—reading it, talking about it, writing it—take some time to reflect on what you have learned: What problems did you have while you were writing, and how did you solve them? How did reading about events in other people's lives help you write about a remembered event in your own life? Finally, you might stop to think critically about autobiography as a genre of writing: How does it influence the way we think about ourselves?

Reflecting on Your Writing

Write a brief explanation (a page or so) for your instructor about how you discovered and solved a problem as you wrote your essay. Before you begin, gather all of your writing—invention, planning notes, outlines, drafts, comments from other readers, revision plans, and final revision. Review these materials as you complete this writing task.

1. Identify one major problem you needed to solve as you wrote about a remembered event. Do not be concerned with grammar and punctuation; concentrate on problems unique to writing a story about your experience. For example: Did you puzzle over how to present a particular scene or person? Was it difficult to structure the narrative so that it builds to a climax? Did you find it hard (or uncomfortable) to convey the event's autobiographical significance?

2. Determine how you came to recognize the problem. When did you first discover it? What called it to your attention? Did you notice it yourself, or did another reader point it out? Can you now see hints of it in your invention writing, your planning notes, or an earlier draft? If so, where specifically?
3. Reflect next on how you went about solving the problem. Did you work on a particular passage, cut or add details, or reorganize the essay? Did you reread one of the essays in the chapter to see how another writer handled similar material? Did you look back at the invention guidelines? Did you discuss the problem with another student, a tutor, or your instructor? If so, how did talking about it help, and how useful was the advice you got?
4. Finally, write your explanation of the problem and your solution. Be as specific as possible in reconstructing your efforts. Quote from your invention notes or early drafts, from readers' comments, from your revision plan, and from your final revision to show the various changes your writing underwent as you worked to solve the problem. Taking the time now to think about how you recognized and solved a real writing problem will help you to become more aware of what works and does not work, making you a more confident writer.

Reviewing What You Learned from Reading

Your own essay about a remembered event has no doubt been influenced by the essays you have read in this chapter. These readings may have helped you decide which of your own experiences would seem significant to your readers, or they may have given you ideas about how to evoke a vivid sense of place or how to convey your feelings about the event. Write a page or so explaining to your instructor how the readings in this chapter influenced your essay. Before you start, take some time to reflect on what you have learned from these selections.

1. Reread the final revision of your essay; then review the selections you read before completing your own essay, looking for specific influences. If you were impressed, for example, with the way one of the readings set a scene or used dialogue, dramatized the action or conveyed autobiographical significance, look to see where you might have been striving for similar effects in your own essay. Look also for ideas you got from your reading: writing strategies you were inspired to try, specific details you were led to include, effects you sought to achieve.
2. Now write an explanation of these influences. Did a single reading selection influence you, or were you influenced by several selections? Quote from the selections and your final revision to show how your story was influenced by the other essays. If, in reviewing the selections, you have found another way to improve your own essay, indicate briefly what you would change and which of the selections inspired the change.

Considering the Social Dimensions of Autobiography

"The unexamined life is not worth living," declared the Greek philosopher Socrates more than two thousand years ago, and few people would disagree today. One way to examine your life is by writing about events that have special significance for you. Contemplating this significance can lead you to recognize personal strengths and weaknesses and to clarify your beliefs and values.

At the same time, reading others' autobiographical writing can help forge connections among people. Another person's life often reflects our own experience, enabling us to identify and empathize. Just as often, however, another person's life does not resemble ours, and we learn that people can have radically different experiences, even within the same society. Think of the dramatic contrast between Paul Auster's experience and Annie Dillard's, or between Dillard's and Tobias Wolff's. Reading their autobiographical essays makes us realize how factors such as gender, age, health, race, class, religion, and sexual orientation influence all our lives.

Wolff's experience, for example, gives us insight into how the American myth of the cowboy has defined manliness partly in terms of guns and power. Reading about such events in other people's lives may not completely bridge the differences that separate us, but it can help us to better understand one another and the circumstances affecting our lives. Striving as readers and as writers to forge connections with other people is important, but so is recognizing the differences—welcome as well as unwelcome—that exist in our diverse society.

These ideas about autobiographical writing lead to some basic questions about how we understand ourselves and our relationships with others.

Autobiography and Self-Discovery. If autobiography leads to self-discovery, what do we mean by the "self"? Should we think of the self as our "true" essence or as the different roles we play in different situations? Put another way, does what you are define what you do, or does what you do define who you are?

If we accept the idea of an essential self, autobiographical writing helps us in the search to discover who we truly are. Given this idea of the self, we might see Tobias Wolff, for example, as searching to understand whether he is the kind of person who shoots squirrels or the kind of person who cries over dead animals. If, on the other hand, we accept the idea that the various roles we play are what create the self, then autobiographical writing allows us to reveal the many sides of our personalities. This view of the self assumes that we present different self-images to different people in different situations. Given this idea, we might see Wolff as presenting his sympathetic side to his mother but keeping his aggressive, "manly" side hidden from her.

Also recall Wolff's comment in the headnote prior to the reading: that autobiography for him is "part memory, part invention," that "the very act of writing has transformed the original experience into another experience more 'real' to me than what I started with." Here, he brings up another essential question about autobiography and self-discovery. How "true" is autobiography? Surely when we relate past experience through the distorting lens of memory, there are bound to be discrepancies between what we write and what "actually" happened. Moreover, in the interest of telling a good story—or presenting a particular image of themselves—autobiographers inevitably edit or embellish the event in some way, whether consciously or not.

Ways of Interpreting Our Experience. Finally, how do we interpret autobiography? Do we view it psychologically, in terms of personal feelings, relationships, conflicts, and desires, or more publicly, in terms of the social, political, and cultural conditions of our lives? You can understand these different perspectives by applying them to the selections in this chapter. Wolff's essay, for example, could be seen in psychological terms as a family drama, the story of an adolescent boy trying to assert his manhood. Or it could be seen in political terms as a critique of power and war. Brandt's essay could be interpreted psychologically, either in terms of her childish desire to have what she wants when she wants it or in terms of her conflict with her mother. It also could be interpreted politically, perhaps in terms of class, race, or gender: Imagine how the arrest might have gone differently, for example, if Brandt were anything other than a young middle-class woman.

For Discussion. Here are some questions that might spark thinking and discussion about the ways we represent our experiences in autobiographical essays. Note your thoughts as you read the questions or discuss them in class. Then, write a page or so for your instructor exploring your own ideas and conclusions.

1. Many people believe that reading autobiographical essays opens our minds to new experiences and a fuller understanding of people who are different from us. Recall one essay, either from this chapter or by one of

your classmates, that portrays an experience quite different from your own.

How do you respond to this difference: Does it arouse your curiosity? Your compassion? Are you put off by the strangeness? Do you have contradictory feelings? What value, if any, do you see in reading about the lives of people who are different from you? As a writer, how do you feel about presenting your own life to readers who may be different from you?

2. What thoughts do you now have about autobiography and self-discovery? Do you think your own autobiographical writing reveals your single, essential, true self? Or does it show different aspects of your personality? When you were writing your essay about a remembered event, did you try to discover who you truly are? Were you aware of contradictions between how you acted at certain moments and how you like to think of yourself? Did you see yourself as playing different roles for different people?

   Think about how you describe yourself in your invention notes and drafts. We can see from A Writer at Work that Brandt, for example, thought of herself in several different ways. Confronted by her mother's disapproval, Brandt writes in the final draft that she is a "terrible human being." But in her invention notes, she describes herself as basically a "reasonable" person who simply did something stupid.

   Also think about how true or how fictional your story is. In what ways did you embellish memories, as Wolff says he did?

3. Consider how you have generally interpreted other people's essays about remembered events. Have you understood the essays primarily in personal, psychological terms? Or in social, possibly political terms? Or in some of both? When you read Annie Dillard's essay, for example, did you wonder why she was so intent on finding the amoeba? Did you see her behavior as obsessive or her need for approval as indicating low self-esteem? Or did you think of her essay more in social terms: perhaps seeing Dillard's childhood as privileged, or thinking about her parents' style of child-raising, or whether they would have encouraged her scientific curiosity more if she had been a boy.

   When you were writing about your own life, how did you think about your experience? Did you see yourself as being motivated by certain personal needs or fears? Or did you see yourself as being influenced more by external forces? What do you think we gain or lose by looking at experience in these different ways?

Invited by a sports magazine to write an article about the person who most influenced him, a professional football player writes about his high school football coach. He admits that his coach had such a powerful influence that he still finds himself doing things to win his approval and admiration, even though he never was able to please him in high school. He describes his coach's short, sturdy build, ever-present aviator's sunglasses, and exasperated gestures during practice. He relates several anecdotes to show how the coach pressured and criticized him: mimicking his clumsiest moves during a practice, challenging him to an arm-wrestling match and laughing at him when he lost, and once making him do so many push-ups and run so many laps that he collapsed in exhaustion.

A novelist writes in her autobiography about an aunt who was notorious for lying. She tells anecdotes about some of her aunt's most fantastic lies and the hilarious trouble they caused. The woman's behavior annoyed and embarrassed most of the family, but the writer acknowledges that she secretly sympathized with her. As she describes her aunt, the writer points out the resemblances between them: Not only does she look like her aunt, sharing her red hair and broad shoulders, but she too has a vivid imagination and likes to embellish reality.

For his political science class, a college junior writes a term paper about his internship as a campaign worker for an unsuccessful candidate for the state legislature. In one part of the paper he focuses on the candidate, whom he came to know and to admire. He describes the woman's energy and ambition, her broad understanding of issues and attention to detail. The student writes about the anger and bitterness he felt when she lost. He reconstructs a conversation they had wherein the candidate seemed genuinely philosophical about her defeat, a detachment that amazed him.

CHAPTER 3

Remembering People

Since people are so important in our lives, they are worth writing about. As these scenarios suggest, in this chapter you will be reading and writing firsthand biography, not the more formal researched biography of a widely known person. Firsthand biography describes someone who played a significant role in the writer's life. Like writing about remembered events, it is autobiographical. The aim is twofold: to portray the person vividly so that readers can imagine what he or she was like, and to show how the person was significant in your life.

Although your writing will reveal aspects of yourself and your relationship with the person, the focus should be on the person you are describing—physical appearance, mannerisms, way of speaking, typical behavior toward you and others. You should also relate specific anecdotes that illustrate character traits and give insight into the nature of your relationship. You may, like the football player, decide to write about someone who was once in a position of authority over you. Or you may, like the novelist, choose to describe a lovable but eccentric aunt. The person you select may have been a passing acquaintance, like the unsuccessful candidate, or someone you knew for a long time, like the aunt. The possibilities are endless.

Writing firsthand biography encourages you to consider the different roles others play in your life and the complexity of personal relationships. Many of us tend to oversimplify, to remember only the very best or the very worst. We may demonize those who have mistreated or frustrated us and idealize those who have helped or inspired us. Writing thoughtfully about another person may help you to avoid thinking of others as caricatures and stereotypes. When you search your memory for descriptive details and illustrative anecdotes, you are likely to portray your subjects as complex individuals with both vulnerabilities and strengths. Through this process, you may discover qualities you had overlooked, nuances you had not appreciated. Writing can even help you to sort through and to better understand your own feelings, perhaps making you realize that they are less certain than you had previously thought.

Writing in Your Other Courses

Writing about other people and their significance in your life is not a typical academic writing assignment, but you may encounter it in a few college courses. Here are some assignments requiring this kind of writing:

- *For an education class:* Write about a teacher who was unusually effective, focusing on qualities that contributed to this effectiveness. Relate at least three specific occasions that show this teacher's effectiveness. What, exactly, did the teacher do, and how did she or he help you to learn?

- *For a history class focusing on American ethnic groups:* Describe an older family member who has helped you to understand your ethnic roots. Relate two or three anecdotes that you think best represent what he or she taught you.
- *For a philosophy class:* What constitutes living a life according to Aristotle's Golden Mean? Write about a person you know who comes close to accomplishing this goal. Include specific examples to show how this person lives.
- *For a nursing class:* Describe a nurse who cared for you during a hospital stay. (If you have never been hospitalized, describe a nurse who assisted a doctor when you made an office visit.) Describe the room or office as you remember it. In your writing, focus on the nurse's appearance, movements, tone of voice, and way of dealing with you. Try to include specific events: what happened and who said what to whom.

→ Practice Remembering a Person: A Collaborative Activity

The scenarios that open this chapter suggest some occasions for writing about people important in your life. Imagine that you have been asked to write about someone who had a significant effect on your childhood. The person can be either another child or someone older, someone you still know or someone who long ago passed out of your life. The only requirements are that the relationship seems important to you now and that you remember the person well.

Part 1. Consider the possibilities, and choose a person. Then, for a few minutes, make notes about what you want to tell other students about this person.

Now, get together with two or three other students; each of you should take just a few minutes to describe your person.

Part 2. As a group, take ten minutes or so to discuss what happened when you told about a remembered person:

- How did each of you choose a person? Did you agonize over several possibilities, or settle easily on the obvious choice? Try to account for the main influences on your choice.
- Review what each of you decided to say about your person. Did you think it important to describe the person's appearance or way of moving, gesturing, or talking? Did you focus in a general way on the history of your relationship? Did you tell any specific anecdotes involving the two of you? Did you tell your listeners what to think about this person, or did you let them decide for themselves?
- What were the easiest and most difficult aspects of telling your classmates about an important person in your life?

READINGS

Maya Angelou, a poet as well as an autobiographer, has also worked as an actress, singer, editor, professor, and administrator of the Southern Christian Leadership Conference. In 1993 she was honored by President Clinton when he asked her to write a poem for his inauguration. Her poem celebrated the ethnic diversity of the United States. She has said of her writing: "I speak to the black experience, but I am always talking about the human condition."

Angelou grew up during the 1930s in the small Arkansas town of Stamps, where she lived with her brother Bailey; her grandmother, the "Momma" mentioned in this selection; and her Uncle Willie. Momma and Willie operated a small grocery store. In this selection, from *I Know Why the Caged Bird Sings* (1970), Angelou writes about her memories of her uncle, from her perspective as an adult of forty. As you read, notice how she describes him and selects specific anecdotes to reveal their relationship.

UNCLE WILLIE
Maya Angelou

When Bailey was six and I a year younger, we used to rattle off the times tables with the speed I was later to see Chinese children in San Francisco employ on their abacuses. Our summer-gray pot-bellied stove bloomed rosy red during winter, and became a severe disciplinarian threat if we were so foolish as to indulge in making mistakes. 1

Uncle Willie used to sit, like a giant black Z (he had been crippled as a child), and hear us testify to the Lafayette County Training Schools' abilities. His face pulled down on the left side, as if a pulley had been attached to his lower teeth, and his left hand was only a mite bigger than Bailey's, but on the second mistake or on the third hesitation his big overgrown right hand would catch one of us behind the collar, and in the same moment would thrust the culprit toward the dull red heater, which throbbed like a devil's toothache. We were never burned, although once I might have been when I was so terrified I tried to jump onto the stove to remove the possibility of its remaining a threat. Like most children, I thought if I could face the worst danger voluntarily, and *triumph,* I would forever have power over it. But in my case of sacrificial effort I was thwarted. Uncle Willie held tight to my dress and I only got close enough to smell the clean dry scent of hot iron. We learned the times tables without understanding their grand principle, simply because we had the capacity and no alternative. 2

The tragedy of lameness seems so unfair to children that they are embarrassed in its presence. And they, most recently off nature's mold, sense that they have only narrowly missed being another of her jokes. In relief at the narrow escape, they vent their emotions in impatience and criticism of the unlucky cripple. 3

Momma related times without end, and without any show of emotion, how Uncle Willie had been dropped when he was three years old by a woman who was minding him. She seemed to hold no rancor against the baby-sitter, nor for her just God who allowed the accident. She felt it necessary to explain over and over again to those who knew the story by heart that he wasn't "born that way." 4

In our society, where two-legged, two-armed strong Black men were able at best to eke out only the necessities of life, Uncle Willie, with his starched shirts, shined shoes and shelves full of food, was the whipping boy and butt of jokes of the underemployed and underpaid. Fate not only disabled him but laid a double-tiered barrier 5 in his path. He was also proud and sensitive. Therefore he couldn't pretend that he wasn't crippled, nor could he deceive himself that people were not repelled by his defect.

Only once in all the years of trying not to watch him, I saw him pretend to himself and others that he wasn't lame. 6

Coming home from school one day, I saw a dark car in our front yard. I rushed in to find a strange man and woman (Uncle Willie said later they were school teachers from Little Rock) drinking Dr. Pepper in the cool of the Store. I sensed a wrongness around me, like an alarm clock that had gone off without being set. 7

I knew it couldn't be the strangers. Not frequently, but often enough, travelers pulled off the main road to buy tobacco or soft drinks in the only Negro store in Stamps. When I looked at Uncle Willie, I knew what was pulling my mind's coattails. He was standing erect behind the counter, not leaning forward or resting on the small shelf that had been built for him. Erect. His eyes seemed to hold me with a mixture of threats and appeal. 8

I dutifully greeted the strangers and roamed my eyes around for his walking stick. It was nowhere to be seen. He said, "Uh . . . this this . . . this . . . uh, my niece. She's . . . uh . . . just come from school." Then to the couple—"You know . . . how, uh, children are . . . th-th-these days . . . they play all d-d-day at school and c-c-can't wait to get home and pl-play some more." 9

The people smiled, very friendly. 10

He added, "Go on out and pl-play, Sister." 11

The lady laughed in a soft Arkansas voice and said, "Well, you know, Mr. Johnson, they say, you're only a child once. Have you children of your own?" 12

Uncle Willie looked at me with an impatience I hadn't seen in his face even when he took thirty minutes to loop the laces over his high-topped shoes. "I . . . I thought I told you to go . . . go outside and play." 13

Before I left I saw him lean back on the shelves of Garret Snuff, Prince Albert and Spark Plug chewing tobacco. 14

"No, ma'am . . . no ch-children and no wife." He tried a laugh. "I have an old m-m-mother and my brother's t-two children to l-look after." 15

I didn't mind his using us to make himself look good. In fact, I would have pretended to be his daughter if he wanted me to. Not only did I not feel any loyalty to my own father, I figured that if I had been Uncle Willie's child I would have received much better treatment. 16

The couple left after a few minutes, and from the back of the house I watched the red car scare chickens, raise dust and disappear toward Magnolia. 17

Uncle Willie was making his own way down the long shadowed aisle between the shelves and the counter—hand over hand, like a man climbing out of a dream. I stayed quiet and watched him lurch from one side, bumping to the other, until he reached the coal-oil tank. He put his hand behind that dark recess and took his cane in the strong fist and shifted his weight on the wooden support. He thought he had pulled it off. 18

I'll never know why it was important to him that the couple (he said later that he'd never seen them before) would take a picture of a whole Mr. Johnson back to Little Rock. 19

He must have tired of being crippled, as prisoners tire of penitentiary bars and the guilty tire of blame. The high-topped shoes and the cane, his uncontrollable muscles and thick tongue, and the looks he suffered of either contempt or pity had simply worn him out, and for one afternoon, one part of an afternoon, he wanted no part of them. 20

I understood and felt closer to him at that moment than ever before or since. 21

Connecting to Culture and Experience

Racial tension plays a part in several episodes of Maya Angelou's autobiography. In this story, however, all of the characters are African-American. The motive for Uncle Willie's unexpected behavior seems to be shame for his deformity, especially before strangers of a higher social class. (The travelers are both big-city school teachers, while Uncle Willie is a lowly storekeeper in a tiny town.) The shame leads to pretense, which few readers will find strange or inappropriate. In this situation, it is not surprising that Uncle Willie pretends to be someone he is not.

Discuss with other students the temptation to appear to be someone else. Think about why people are motivated to pretend. Shame and feelings of inferiority are two reasons. What other reasons come to mind?

Try to think of a specific time when you pretended to be someone else. It could be a serious or humorous incident. (You may not be able to think of such a time, or you may not recall a situation you feel comfortable sharing with others.) Tell what happened and who else was there. Speculate about what motivated you.

With your classmates, reflect on what your experiences reveal about pretense and its social and personal motivations.

Analyzing Writing Strategies

1. At the beginning of this chapter, we make the following generalizations about firsthand biography. Which of these assertions are true of Angelou's essay?
   - It focuses on a person with whom the writer had a significant, rather than casual, relationship.
   - It portrays the person vividly so that readers can imagine what he or she was like.
   - It relies on description and anecdote to reveal important aspects of the person and the relationship.
   - It confronts the writer's inevitable ambivalent feelings toward the person, rather than oversimplifying or sentimentalizing the relationship.
   - It makes clear the significance of the relationship and reveals something important about the writer.
   - It leads readers to reflect on people who have been important to their own lives.
2. In paragraphs 9–15, **dialogue** plays an important part in Angelou's narrative. Reread these paragraphs and consider what the dialogue reveals about Uncle Willie and his visitors. Notice what is said and the way it is said. In what ways does dialogue contribute to Angelou's presentation of her uncle?

For more on dialogue, see pp. 487–88.

Considering Topics for Your Own Essay

Consider writing a portrait of an adult who has significantly influenced your life. Think about someone who is outside your immediate family—a grandparent, aunt or uncle, teacher, or coach. Begin by listing two or three possibilities. Choose one, and then consider the following questions: How would you engage your readers' interest and disclose the person's significance in your life? What details would you include? What anecdotes might you relate?

Commentary

We know that Uncle Willie was a very significant person in Angelou's life, yet she never tells us that directly. Instead, she shows us his **significance** through specific anecdotes, remembered feelings, and reflection. She might have begun the essay by stating her main point, announcing just how Uncle Willie was important to her. Instead, she uses a much more engaging and effective strategy: She tells a story about how Uncle Willie forced her and her brother to memorize the multiplication tables. Learning about Uncle Willie's actions and her reactions at the time, we begin right away to understand why their relationship is significant to Angelou.

Their relationship was not easy, but relationships with parents, guardians, or mentors rarely are. We have mixed feelings about people we love, and autobiographers often explore these feelings frankly. Angelou shows us that Uncle Willie was proud, sensitive, and relatively prosperous. He and Momma provided a home for her, and he cared about her education. Yet Angelou is not at all sentimental about him. She admits that he sometimes scared her and that she did not always feel close to him. Had she been his child, she believed, he would have treated her better. Clearly he was not a perfect guardian, and she tells us so.

For more on naming and detailing, see pp. 492–95.

To learn more about firsthand biography, look carefully at Angelou's **description** of Uncle Willie. Notice how she describes his posture, face, hands; his shined high-top shoes, starched shirts, and cane. She describes objects in the scene with the same precision: the stove is "summer-gray" and in winter "rosy red." Uncle Willie leans back on shelves of "Garret Snuff, Prince Albert [smoking tobacco] and Spark Plug chewing tobacco." Coming home from school, Angelou finds not a couple from out of town drinking sodas, but schoolteachers from Little Rock drinking Dr. Pepper.

For more on simile and metaphor, see pp. 495, 496.

Throughout her essay Angelou relies on inventive **word images** to describe people, scenes, and feelings. Uncle Willie sits "like a giant black Z" and makes his way down the aisle "like a man climbing out of a dream." When Angelou enters the store, she senses something wrong, "like an alarm clock that had gone off without being set." These images, sometimes called **similes,** reveal Angelou's feelings more fully and concretely. Similes and metaphors are not mere decoration; they enable the reader to see with the writer's sensibility.

For more on scratch outlining, see pp. 431–32.

Devising an organizational plan is important when you write an essay about a remembered person. **Organization** poses special challenges in this genre. How do you impose a workable plan on your scattered memories and diverse invention notes? How do you begin? At what point do you describe the person? How do you sequence your anecdotes and narrate each one smoothly? How do you reveal the significance of the relationship? Should it be done only in one place or woven throughout the essay? This scratch outline of Angelou's essay shows one way of organizing:

Anecdote 1

description of times-table practice with Uncle Willie

the consequence of making a times-table mistake

explanation of Uncle Willie's lameness

Anecdote 2

finding the visitors in the store with Uncle Willie

noticing Uncle Willie's pretense

the visitors leave

observing Uncle Willie retrieving his cane

comment on the significance of the pretense anecdote for understanding their relationship

This successful, simple plan explains in large part why readers have no difficulty following Angelou's portrait of Uncle Willie. There are two anecdotes: the briefer one about math practice and the longer one about Uncle Willie's pretending that he was not crippled. Both anecdotes are smoothly narrated: Readers move through each one without feeling confused. After the first anecdote, the explanation of Uncle Willie's lameness prepares readers both for the pretense anecdote and the comment that concludes the essay. Vivid descriptions of Uncle Willie are woven throughout the essay; we hear him talk and see him move. All of the basic features of firsthand biography are here, and they are organized in a satisfying way. There are many ways to organize, however, as you will discover when you read the other essays in this chapter.

Gerald Haslam, a professor of English at Sonoma State University in California, is known for his advocacy of western literature. He has published several short-story collections, including *Okies: Selected Stories* (1973) and *Hawk Flights: Visions of the West* (1983). This essay, from *California Childhood* (1988), is about his great-grandmother. Notice how he relies on specific anecdotes and dialogues to present a subject from his childhood.

GRANDMA
Gerald Haslam

1 *"Expectoran su sangre!"* exclaimed Great-grandma when I showed her the small horned toad I had removed from my breast pocket. I turned toward my mother, who translated: "They spit blood."

2 *"De los ojos,"* Grandma added. "From their eyes," mother explained, herself uncomfortable in the presence of the small beast.

3 I grinned, "Awwwwww."

4 But my Great-grandmother did not smile. *"Son muy toxicos,"*[1] she nodded with finality. Mother moved back an involuntary step, her hands suddenly busy at her breast. "Put that thing down," she ordered.

5 "His name's John," I said.

6 "Put John down and not in your pocket, either," my mother nearly shouted. "Those things are very poisonous. Didn't you understand what Grandma said?"

7 I shook my head.

8 "Well . . ." mother looked from one of us to the other—spanning four generations of California, standing three feet apart—and said, "of course you didn't. Please take him back where you got him, and be careful. We'll all feel better when you do." The tone of her voice told me that the discussion had ended, so I released the little reptile where I'd captured him.

9 I later learned that my great-grandmother—whom we simply called "Grandma"—had been moving from house to house within the family, trying to find a place she'd

[1] They're very poisonous.

accept. She hated the city, and most of the aunts and uncles lived in Los Angeles. Our house in Oildale was much closer to the open country where she'd dwelled all her life. She had wanted to come to our place right away because she had raised my mother from a baby when my own grandmother died. But the old lady seemed unimpressed with Daddy, whom she called *"ese gringo."*

10 In truth, we had more room, and my dad made more money in the oil patch than almost anyone else in the family. Since my mother was the closest to Grandma, our place was the logical one for her, but Ese Gringo didn't see it that way, I guess, at least not at first. Finally, after much debate, he relented.

11 In any case, one windy afternoon, my Uncle Manuel and Aunt Toni drove up and deposited four-and-a-half feet of bewigged, bejeweled Spanish spitfire: a square, pale face topped by a tightly-curled black wig that hid a bald head—her hair having been lost to typhoid nearly sixty years before—her small white hands veined with rivers of blue. She walked with a prancing bounce that made her appear half her age, and she barked orders in Spanish from the moment she emerged from Manuel and Toni's car. Later, just before they left, I heard Uncle Manuel tell my dad, "Good luck, Charlie. That old lady's dynamite." Daddy only grunted.

12 She had been with us only two days when I tried to impress her with my horned toad. In fact, nothing I did seemed to impress her, and she referred to me as *el malcriado,*[2] causing my mother to shake her head. Mom explained to me that Grandma was just old and lonely for Grandpa and uncomfortable in town. Mom told me that Grandma had lived over half a century in the country, away from the noise, away from clutter, away from people. She refused to accompany my mother on shopping trips, or anywhere else. She even refused to climb into a car, and I wondered how Uncle Manuel had managed to load her up in order to bring her to us.

13 She disliked sidewalks and roads, dancing across them when she had to, then appearing to wipe her feet on earth or grass. Things too civilized simply did not please her. A brother of hers had been killed in the great San Francisco earthquake and that had been the end of her tolerance of cities. Until my Great-grandfather died, they lived on a small rancho near Arroyo Cantua, north of Coalinga. Grandpa, who had come north from Sonora as a youth to work as a *vaquero,*[3] had bred horses and cattle, and cowboyed for other ranchers, scraping together enough of a living to raise eleven children.

14 He had been, until the time of his death, a lean, dark-skinned man with wide shoulders, a large nose, and a sweeping handlebar mustache that was white when I knew him. His Indian blood darkened all his progeny so that not even I was as fair-skinned as my Great-grandmother, Ese Gringo for a father or not.

15 As it turned out, I didn't really understand very much about Grandma at all. She was old, of course, yet in many ways my parents treated her as though she were younger than me, walking her to the bathroom at night and bringing her presents from the store. In other ways—drinking wine at dinner, for example—she was granted adult privileges. Even Daddy didn't drink wine except on special occasions. After Grandma moved in, though, he began to occasionally join her for a glass, sometimes even sitting with her on the porch for a premeal sip.

16 She held court on our front porch, often gazing toward the desert hills east of us or across the street at kids playing on the lot. Occasionally, she would rise, cross the yard and sidewalk and street, skip over them, sometimes stumbling on the curb, and

[2] the brat
[3] cowboy

wipe her feet on the lot's sandy soil, then she would slowly circle the boundary between the open middle and the brushy sides, searching for something, it appeared. I never figured out what.

17 One afternoon I returned from school and saw Grandma perched on the porch as usual, so I started to walk around the house to avoid her sharp, mostly incomprehensible, tongue. She had already spotted me. *"Venga aqui!"*[4] she ordered, and I understood.

18 I approached the porch and noticed that Grandma was vigorously chewing something. She held a small white bag in one hand. Saying *"Qué deseas tomar?"*[5] she withdrew a large orange gumdrop from the bag and began slowly chewing it in her toothless mouth, smacking loudly as she did so. I stood below her for a moment trying to remember the word for candy. Then it came to me: *"Dulce,"* I said.

19 Still chewing, Grandma replied, *"Mande?"*

20 Knowing she wanted a complete sentence, I again struggled, then came up with *"Deseo dulce."*

21 She measured me for a moment, before answering in nearly perfect English, "Oh, so you wan' some candy. Go to the store an' buy some."

22 I don't know if it was the shock of hearing her speak English for the first time, or the way she had denied me a piece of candy, but I suddenly felt tears warm my cheeks and I sprinted into the house and found Mom, who stood at the kitchen sink. "Grandma just talked English," I burst between light sobs.

23 "What's wrong?" she asked as she reached out to stroke my head.

24 "Grandma can talk English," I repeated.

25 "Of course she can," Mom answered. "What's wrong?"

26 I wasn't sure what was wrong, but after considering, I told Mom that Grandma had teased me. No sooner had I said that than the old woman appeared at the door and hiked her skirt. Attached to one of her petticoats by safety pins were several small tobacco sacks, the white cloth kind that closed with yellow drawstrings. She carefully unhooked one and opened it, withdrawing a dollar, then handed the money to me. *"Para su dulce,"*[6] she said. Then, to my mother, she asked, "Why does he bawl like a motherless calf?"

27 "It's nothing," Mother replied.

28 "Do not weep, little one," the old lady comforted me, "Jesus and the Virgin love you." She smiled and patted my head. To my mother she said as though just realizing it, "Your baby?"

29 Somehow that day changed everything. I wasn't afraid of my Great-grandmother any longer and, once I began spending time with her on the porch, I realized that my father had also begun directing increased attention to the old woman. Almost every evening Ese Gringo was sharing wine with Grandma. They talked out there, but I never did hear a real two-way conversation between them. Usually Grandma rattled on and Daddy nodded. She'd chuckle and pat his hand and he might grin, even grunt a word or two, before she'd begin talking again. Once I saw my mother standing by the front window watching them together, a smile playing across her face.

30 No more did I sneak around the house to avoid Grandma after school. Instead, she waited for me and discussed my efforts in class gravely, telling mother that I was a bright boy, *"muy inteligente,"* and that I should be sent to the nuns who would train me.

[4] Come here!
[5] What do you want to take?
[6] For your candy

I would make a fine priest. When Ese Gringo heard that, he smiled and said, "He'd make a fair-to-middlin' Holy Roller preacher, too." Even Mom had to chuckle, and my great-grandmother shook her finger at Ese Gringo. "Oh you debil, Sharlie!" she cackled.

31 Frequently, I would accompany Grandma to the lot where she would explain that no fodder could grow there. Poor pasture or not, the lot was at least unpaved, and Grandma greeted even the tiniest new cactus or flowering weed with joy. "Look how beautiful," she would croon. "In all this ugliness, it lives." Oildale was my home and it didn't look especially ugly to me, so I could only grin and wonder.

32 Because she liked the lot and things that grew there, I showed her the horned toad when I captured it a second time. I was determined to keep it, although I did not discuss my plans with anyone. I also wanted to hear more about the bloody eyes, so I thrust the small animal nearly into her face one afternoon. She did not flinch. *"Ola señor sangre de ojos,"*[7] she said with a mischievous grin. *"Qué tal?"*[8] It took me a moment to catch on.

33 "You were kidding before," I accused.

34 "Of course," she acknowledged, still grinning.

35 "But why?"

36 "Because the little beast belongs with his own kind in his own place, not in your pocket. Give him his freedom, my son."

37 I had other plans for the horned toad, but I was clever enough not to cross Grandma. "Yes, Ma'am," I replied. That night I placed the reptile in a flower bed cornered by a brick wall Ese Gringo had built the previous summer. It was a spot rich with insects for the toad to eat, and the little wall, only a foot high, must have seemed massive to so squat an animal.

38 Nonetheless, the next morning when I searched for the horned toad it was gone. I had no time to explore the yard for it, so I trudged off to school, my belly troubled. How could it have escaped? Classes meant little to me that day. I thought only of my lost pet—I had changed his name to Juan, the same as my Great-grandfather—and where I might find him.

39 I shortened my conversation with Grandma that afternoon so I could search for Juan. "What do you seek?" the old woman asked me as I poked through flower beds beneath the porch. "Praying mantises," I improvised, and she merely nodded, surveying me. But I had eyes only for my lost pet, and I continued pushing through branches and brushing aside leaves. No luck.

40 Finally, I gave in and turned toward the lot. I found my horned toad nearly across the street, crushed. It had been heading for the miniature desert and had almost made it when an automobile's tire had run over it. One notion immediately swept me: if I had left it on its lot, it would still be alive. I stood rooted there in the street, tears slicking my cheeks, and a car honked its horn as it passed, the driver shouting at me.

41 Grandma joined me, and stroked my back. "The poor little beast," was all she said, then she bent slowly and scooped up what remained of the horned toad and led me out of the street. "We must return him to his own place," she explained, and we trooped, my eyes still clouded, toward the back of the vacant lot. Carefully, I dug a hole with a piece of wood. Grandma placed Juan in it and covered him. We said an Our Father and a Hail Mary, then Grandma walked me back to the house. "Your little Juan is safe with

[7] Hello mister bloody eyes
[8] What's up?

God, my son," she comforted. We kept the horned toad's death a secret, and we visited his small grave frequently.

42 Grandma fell just before school ended and summer vacation began. As was her habit, she had walked alone to the vacant lot but this time, on her way back, she tripped over the curb and broke her hip. That following week, when Daddy brought her home from the hospital, she seemed to have shrunken. She sat hunched in a wheelchair on the porch, gazing with faded eyes toward the hills or at the lot, speaking rarely. She still sipped wine every evening with Daddy and even I could tell how concerned he was about her. It got to where he'd look in on her before leaving for work every morning and again at night before turning in. And if Daddy was home, Grandma always wanted him to push her chair when she needed moving, calling, "Sharlie!" until he arrived.

43 I was tugged from sleep on the night she died by voices drumming through the walls into darkness. I couldn't understand them, but was immediately frightened by the uncommon sounds of words in the night. I struggled from bed and walked into the living room just as Daddy closed the front door and a car pulled away.

44 Mom was sobbing softly on the couch and Daddy walked to her, stroked her head, then noticed me. "Come here, son," he gently ordered.

45 I walked to him and, uncharacteristically, he put an arm around me. "What's wrong?" I asked, near tears myself. Mom looked up, but before she could speak, Daddy said, "Grandma died." Then he sighed heavily and stood there with his arms around his weeping wife and son.

46 The next day my Uncle Manuel and Uncle Arnulfo, plus Aunt Chintia, arrived and over food they discussed with my mother where Grandma should be interred. They argued that it would be too expensive to transport her body home and, besides, they could more easily visit her grave if she was buried in Bakersfield. "They have such nice, manicured grounds at Greenlawn," Aunt Chintia pointed out. Just when it seemed they had agreed, I could remain silent no longer, "But Grandma has to go home," I burst. "She has to! It's the only thing she really wanted. We can't leave her in the city."

47 Uncle Arnulfo, who was on the edge, snapped to Mother that I belonged with the other children, not interrupting adult conversation. Mom quietly agreed, but I refused. My father walked into the room then. "What's wrong?" he asked.

48 "They're going to bury Grandma in Bakersfield, Daddy. Don't let 'em, please."

49 "Well, son . . ."

50 "When my horny toad got killed and she helped me to bury it, she said we had to return him to his place."

51 "Your horny toad?" Mother asked.

52 "He got squished and me and Grandma buried him in the lot. She said we had to take him back to his place. Honest she did."

53 No one spoke for a moment, then my father, Ese Gringo, who stood against the sink, responded: "That's right . . ." he paused, then added, "We'll bury her." I saw a weary smile cross my mother's face. "If she wanted to go back to the ranch then that's where we have to take her," Daddy said.

54 I hugged him and he, right in front of everyone, hugged back.

55 No one argued. It seemed, suddenly, as though they had all wanted to do exactly what I had begged for. Grown-ups baffled me. Late that week the entire family, hundreds it seemed, gathered at the little Catholic church in Coalinga for mass, then drove out to Arroyo Cantua and buried Grandma next to Grandpa. She rests there today.

Connecting to Culture and Experience

Haslam's family seems to have assumed that Grandma should live with one of them (she "had been moving from house to house within the family, trying to find a place she'd accept"). Accommodating older family members poses a challenge for many families, especially since nursing home and health care costs are rising. In addition to costs, a family's decisions about its older members are influenced by its ethnic, cultural, or religious traditions.

With other students in your class, discuss how each of your families has accommodated older members. Identify the older members of your family and explain their current living situations and sources of support. Do they live with other family members? Do they rely solely on federal Social Security and Medicare payments? Does your family contribute financially in any way? Do the elderly members work full or part time? Do they have investments they can rely on? (You may need to interview elderly family members to get answers to these questions.)

Then, as a group, consider these questions: If elderly relatives have lived with your immediate family, what roles did they take? How did their presence influence your family? What did you learn from this experience? If elderly relatives have lived elsewhere, how safe and contented were they? What degree of responsibility did your immediate family take for them? Finally, in a more general way, what are your thoughts about the care and housing of the elderly in our society?

Analyzing Writing Strategies

For more on narrative action, see pp. 486–87.

1. Analyze how Haslam uses **specific narrative action** to present Grandma. (Narrative action shows a person moving and gesturing.) Underline each use of narrative action in paragraphs 4, 16, 18, 26, and 43–45. Then, put brackets around the action verb that specifically identifies the action. For example, here are the narrative actions and their action verbs in paragraph 4: [nodded] with finality, [moved back] an involuntary step, and her hands suddenly busy at her breast. (The last example, a special kind of phrase following a main clause, does not have a verb. In the Commentary section that follows, we discuss this type of phrase further.) After you have completed this exercise, look at the narrative actions as a group and consider the following questions: Which narrative actions best helped you to visualize the person's movements or gestures? Pick two or three of the actions and explain briefly why they seem so vivid to you.
2. As in Maya Angelou's portrait of Uncle Willie, **anecdotes** play a central role in Haslam's portrait of Grandma. (An anecdote is a brief story about a one-time event, occurring within the time span of a day.) In the margin of Haslam's essay, mark where each anecdote occurs. To get you started, the first anecdote is in paragraphs 1–8. Anecdotes carried over to the second day should be considered as two separate anecdotes.

   Review all of the anecdotes and choose *one* to analyze closely. First, summarize what happens in the anecdote, being sure to identify the people involved. Then, explain what the anecdote reveals about Grandma and her relationship with the young Haslam. Finally, comment on what the anecdote contributes to the essay as a whole.

Considering Topics for Your Own Essay

Recall two or three adults who influenced your early childhood and then, for whatever reason, passed out of your life. You might consider, for example, neighbors, parents of friends, teachers, camp counselors, or relatives. Choose one person and think about the following questions: What anecdotes would reveal the important characteristics of this person? List these anecdotes and jot down what each one would reveal. Which anecdote should you develop more fully because it promises to reveal an important aspect of your relationship with the person?

Commentary

For more on narrating anecdotes, see Chapter 14.

Haslam's essay, like Angelou's, illustrates the importance of **anecdotes** in writing about people. Anecdotes usually include dialogue along with descriptive detail and narrative action. With anecdotes, writers can *show* the remembered person rather than simply telling readers about him or her and their relationship. Anecdotes create vivid impressions. They can give readers a glimpse into the person's character, shed light on the writer's feelings about the person, or show how the relationship changed over time.

Haslam shows through a series of anecdotes how he came to know and love his great-grandmother. Haslam does not explain much in these anecdotes: He shows us what his great-grandmother was like through her actions and speech.

Dialogue usually plays an important part in anecdotes, presenting people through their own words. However, since writers recalling something in the past are unlikely to remember everything that was said, they often must invent or reconstruct dialogue. Effective dialogue captures the mood as well as the content of a conversation. In the genre of firsthand biography, the dialogue should give readers an impression of the person's character and how he or she relates to others, particularly to the writer. Written dialogue, unlike actual conversation, also tends to be brief. Seldom does one person hold forth at great length unless the writer wants to emphasize that the person is long-winded. Dialogue should not merely be filler; it should help to portray the person or reveal his or her significance.

Haslam's essay allows us to analyze closely a special kind of sentence—the cumulative sentence—that is used by nearly all contemporary professional writers, especially writers of autobiography. In a **cumulative sentence,** phrases follow a main clause but do not modify a specific word in the clause. Here are examples from paragraphs 38–40:

. . . so I trudged off to school, *my belly troubled.*

I stood rooted there in the street, *tears slicking my cheeks,* . . .

. . . and a car honked its horn as it passed, *the driver shouting at me.*

Autobiographers also often conclude a sentence with a word or phrase that modifies a specific word in a main clause. Here are two examples from paragraphs 39 and 40:

. . . and she merely nodded, *surveying me.*

I found my horned toad nearly across the street, *crushed.*

In the first sentence *surveying me* modifies *she,* and in the second *crushed* modifies *horned toad.*

Sentences like these provide **sentence variety, narrative action,** and **dramatic emphasis**. They provide variety by allowing a writer to avoid a string of predictable brief subject-plus-verb sentences *(I stood rooted there in the street. Tears slicked my cheeks. A car honked its horn as it passed. The driver shouted at me).* In such sentences, two or more actions can be linked together, a device that provides greater immediacy *(car honked/driver shouting, she nodded/surveying me).* Finally, these sentences provide dramatic emphasis by holding off and singling out key elements *(crushed).*

Amy Wu wrote this essay in 1993 when she was seventeen years old, just before becoming a student at New York University, where she majors in political science and journalism. She is campus correspondent for the *New York Daily News* and a columnist for *Asian Week* of San Francisco. This essay was published in *Chinese American Forum,* a national newsletter.

As you read, notice the way Wu relies on contrasts between her mother and other kinds of mothers to help readers understand her special relationship with her mother.

A DIFFERENT KIND OF MOTHER

Amy Wu

1 My best friend once asked me what it was like being brought up by a Chinese mother. Surprisingly, I could find no answer. I found myself describing my mother's beauty—the way my mother's hair was so silky and black, how her eyes were not small and squinty, but shaped like perfect almonds. How her lips and cheeks were bright red even if she put on no makeup.

2 But unlike my friends, who see my mother as a Chinese mother, I see my mother as simply "my" mother. The language between any mother and daughter is universal. Beyond the layers of arguments and rhetoric, and beyond the incidents of humiliation and misunderstandings, there is a love that unites every mother and daughter.

3 I am not blind, however, to the disciplinary differences between a culture from the west and a culture from the east. Unlike American mothers, who encourage their young children to speak whatever is on their mind, my mother told me to hold my tongue. Once, when I was 5 or 6, I interrupted my mother during a dinner with her friends and told her that I disliked the meal. My mother's eyes transformed from serene pools of blackness into stormy balls of fire. "Quiet!" she hissed, "do you not know that silent waters run deep?" She ordered me to turn my chair to the wall and think about what I had done. I remember throwing a red-faced tantrum before my mother's friends, pounding my fists into the rug, and throwing my utensils at the steaming dishes. Not only did I receive a harsh scolding, but a painful spanking. By the end of that evening, I had learned the first of many lessons. I learned to choose my words carefully before I opened my undisciplined mouth.

4 Whenever my friends and I strike up conversations about our mothers in the cafeteria or at slumber parties, I find myself telling them this story. Nevertheless, they respond to my story with straight and pale faces. "How?" one of my friends asked, "can a mother be so cruel?" "You mean she beat you in front of other people?" another

asked. My best friend told me that her mother disciplined her children wisely instead of abusing them. She sat them on her lap, patiently explaining what they had done wrong. She didn't believe in beating children into submission.

5 What my American friends cannot understand, however, is how my mother's lessons have become so embedded within me, while my friends have easily forgotten their mother's words. My mother's eyes are so powerful, her fists so strong, that somehow I cannot erase her words of advice. To this day, I choose my words carefully before I speak, unlike so many of my friends whose words spill out aimlessly when they open their mouths. My mother says that American girls are taught to squabble like chickens, but a Chinese girl is taught how to speak intelligently.

6 Only lately have I also discovered that Chinese mothers show their love in different ways. Ever since I was a little girl, my mother has spent hours cooking intricate dishes. I remember Friday evenings she would lay out the precious china her mother had given her as a wedding present—how she laid down the utensils and glasses so meticulously, how she made sure there was not a crease in the tablecloth.

7 She would spend the entire day steaming fish, baking ribs, cutting beef into thin strips, and rolling dough to make dumplings. In the evening, her work of labor and art would be unveiled. My father and I and a few Chinese neighbors and friends would be invited to feast on my mother's work of art.

8 I remember how silent my mother was as she watched her loved ones devour her labor of love. She would sit back, with a small smile on her face. She would nibble at the food in her dish while urging others to eat more, to take seconds, and thirds and fourths. "Eat, eat!" she would order me. I dared not tell her I was too full.

9 She would fill my bowl with mounds of rice and my dish with endless vegetables, fish, and fried delicacies. A Chinese mother's love flows from the time and energy she puts into forming a banquet. A Chinese mother's love comes through her order to eat more.

10 My American friends laugh so hard that tears come out of their eyes, when I tell them how my Chinese mother displays her love. "So she wants you to get fat!" one screamed. They said that their mothers showed love by hugging them tightly, buying them clothes, and kissing them on the cheeks.

11 Deep inside, I know that my mother does show her love, except she does it when she thinks I am asleep. Every so often, she will tiptoe into my dark room, sit on the edge of my bed, and stroke my hair. When I am awake, however, she is like a professor constantly hounding her prize student and expecting only the best. All throughout my childhood, she drilled me on lessons of cleanliness and respect.

12 A few years ago at my Grandpa Du's 67th birthday party, I ran up to my grandfather and planted a wet, juicy kiss on his right cheek. To this day, I can easily remember the horrified looks on my relatives' faces. My grandfather turned pale for a second and then smiled meekly. He nodded his head and quickly sat down.

13 Later that evening, my mother cornered me against the wall. "Do you not know that respect to elderly is to bow!" she screamed. Her face turned bright purple. My excuses of "I didn't know . . ." were lost in her powerful words.

14 From that day on, I bowed to anyone Chinese and older than I. I have learned that respect for the elderly earns a young person a different kind of respect. These days, my grandfather points to me and tells my little cousins to follow my example. "She has been taught well," he tells them.

15 It saddens me that my Chinese mother is so often misunderstood. After she threw my friends out during my twelfth birthday party, because they refused to take off their shoes, they saw her as a callous, cruel animal. One of my friends went home and told

her father that I had an abusive mother. Her father even volunteered to call the child welfare department. They never dared to step foot in my house again.

16 My mother has given me so many fine values and morals because of her way of teaching me. I choose words carefully before I speak. I am careful to speak and act toward the elderly a certain way. Without my mother's strong words and teachings, I believe that I would be a rather undisciplined person who didn't value life greatly. I would most likely have been spoiled and callous and ignorant. I have also learned that there is more than one definition of love between a mother and a daughter.

Connecting to Culture and Experience

Wu conveys a strong awareness of ethnic differences between herself and her high school friends. In particular, she makes it clear that she believes her mother's way of disciplining her is superior to the way her friends are being raised. She is not simply irritated with them for criticizing her mother; she stops just short of expressing contempt because they do not understand her mother and Wu's relationship with her. In fact, she does express contempt for the neighbors who considered calling the child welfare department after her mother sent home the birthday partygoers who refused to take off their shoes in her home: She announces proudly that not one of these friends was ever allowed to return to her home. Quite clearly, Wu expresses a strong sense of pride in her ethnic identity, even a sense of superiority.

With other students in your class, discuss your reactions to Wu's beliefs. To begin, you may want to take turns talking about your ethnic identity. (People living in the United States belong to a wide variety of ethnic groups—Irish, Polish, African, Italian, German, Caribbean, Swedish, Serbian, Mexican, Ukrainian, and various mixtures of these and other groups.) Think about whether you have a strong or weak sense of ethnic identity. Then, consider these questions: Does your upbringing seem notably different from that of people from other ethnic groups? Do you believe that your parents instilled in you values that are different from those instilled by parents in other ethnic groups? What seems unique about your ethnic group? What makes you most proud of your ethnic identity?

To conclude your discussion, talk with your classmates about the social implications of ethnic identity. Are we a stronger society if we emphasize or blur ethnic differences? What do we gain by cultivating and prizing ethnic differences? What do we lose? We do not expect you to answer these questions in a brief discussion. Thinking about these issues, however, and learning what others think will help you understand why the issues are important in the United States and throughout the world.

Analyzing Writing Strategies

For more on comparing, see pp. 520–25.

1. In order to show readers what her mother was like, Wu compares her perceptions of her mother to her friends' perceptions. Analyze paragraphs 4–10 to see just how she creates this **comparison.** Reread these paragraphs, noting specific language that reveals Wu's and her friends' contrasting attitudes toward her mother. Write a few sentences about what you learn, and include specific examples from the story. From this analysis, how would you say Wu's extended comparison helps readers to better understand her relationship with her mother?

2. Wu makes it clear that she is concerned with the **significance** of her intense and sometimes stormy relationship with her mother. She reveals this significance through anecdotes and recurring activities and through explicit statements—by both showing and telling. Reread the three brief anecdotes in paragraphs 3–4, 12–13, and 15. Also reread the three recurring activities in paragraphs 4, 7–9, and 10. (Recurring activities, unlike anecdotes, are events that repeat themselves over time.) As you read the anecdotes and recurring activities, notice that immediately before or after each one Wu tells readers what is significant about it—what she "learned" from it about her mother and their relationship.

   In the margin, bracket these anecdotes and recurring activities along with the statements that explain their significance. Then, make a double-column list of these pairs. On the left, identify briefly what happened during each anecdote or recurring activity. On the right, note what Wu claims she learned from each incident.

Considering Topics for Your Own Essay

Consider writing about a parent, guardian, or some other older person, like a counselor or minister, who has influenced you deeply, for good or ill. Choose one person and think for a few moments about what you would want readers to know about this person and your relationship. What details of appearance, style, or movement might you select? Which anecdotes would be memorable for readers and most revealing of your relationship with the person?

Commentary

In presenting her mother and exploring their relationship, Wu makes good use of both **anecdotes** and **recurring activities.** Anecdotes are brief stories of one-time events completed in no more than a day, while recurring activities are repeated over a period of time. The anecdote where Wu tells her mother she does not like the food (paragraphs 3–4) and the recurring activity of Wu's mother preparing special banquets for family and friends (paragraphs 7–9) provide a useful contrast of these important autobiographical strategies. The anecdote happens in only a few minutes, we assume; the five- or six-year old Wu announces that she does not like the food, throws a tantrum after being put in a chair to face the wall, and suffers the consequences of a scolding and spanking. There is dialogue and narrative action. Within the few sentences of this very brief anecdote there is drama and even suspense: We wonder what will happen next. By contrast, the recurring activity takes place on many weekends of Wu's childhood. It is always the same. The banquet is an important family ritual—the same china and utensils set out in the same way, the same dishes prepared in the same way. The mother always behaves predictably, as does Wu. There is not a hint that anything unusual ever happened at one of these banquets. No particular dish is lovingly described. Consequently, we imagine few visual details, and there is no action or suspense.

Both of these narrative strategies are important in autobiography. While the most admired recent autobiographies include both anecdotes and recurring activities, anecdotes seem to be privileged, perhaps because they present relationships concretely and vividly. Readers can easily imagine the scenes and people. People moving, gesturing, and talking reveal themselves in interesting ways. Readers are more likely to remember an anecdote than a more general recurring activity or an explicit statement about the significance of a relationship. All the writers in this chapter rely on anecdotes to present their subjects, and you will too.

Wu makes use of another notable strategy: She reveals important aspects of her relationship with her mother through **conversations with others.** These occur in paragraphs 4 and 10, where Wu reports what her friends say about her mother on the basis of stories Wu has told them. This strategy allows Wu to sharpen the contrast between her Chinese mother and mothers of other ethnic groups. In "Grandma," Haslam also makes use of this strategy. He reconstructs conversations with his mother (paragraphs 22–28) and other family members (paragraphs 46–53) so that readers can learn more about his grandmother and his relationship with her.

Jan Gray was a first-year college student when she wrote the next selection, which portrays her father, a man toward whom she has ambivalent but mostly angry feelings. As you read, notice how Gray uses description to convey these feelings.

FATHER
Jan Gray

My father's hands are grotesque. He suffers from psoriasis, a chronic skin disease that covers his massive, thick hands with scaly, reddish patches that periodically flake off, sending tiny pieces of dead skin sailing to the ground. In addition, his fingers are permanently stained a dull yellow from years of chain smoking. The thought of those swollen, discolored, scaly hands touching me, whether it be out of love or anger, sends chills up my spine. 1

By nature, he is a disorderly, unkempt person. The numerous cigarette burns, food stains, and ashes on his clothes show how little he cares about his appearance. He has a dreadful habit of running his hands through his greasy hair and scratching his scalp, causing dandruff to drift downward onto his bulky shoulders. He is grossly overweight, and his pullover shirts never quite cover his protruding paunch. When he eats, he shovels the food into his mouth as if he hasn't eaten for days, bread crumbs and food scraps settling in his untrimmed beard. 2

Last year, he abruptly left town. Naturally, his apartment was a shambles, and I offered to clean it so that my mother wouldn't have to pay the cleaning fee. I arrived early in the morning anticipating a couple hours of vacuuming and dusting and scrubbing. The minute I opened the door, however, I realized my task was monumental: Old yellowed newspapers and magazines were strewn throughout the living room; moldy and rotten food covered the kitchen counter; cigarette butts and ashes were everywhere. The pungent aroma of stale beer seemed to fill the entire apartment. 3

As I made my way through the debris toward the bedroom, I tried to deny that the man who lived here was my father. The bedroom was even worse than the front rooms, with cigarette burns in the carpet and empty bottles, dirty dishes, and smelly laundry scattered everywhere. Looking around his bedroom, I recalled an incident that had occurred only a few months before in my bedroom. 4

I was calling home to tell my mother I would be eating dinner at a girlfriend's house. To my surprise, my father answered the phone. I was taken aback to hear his voice because my parents had been divorced for some time and he was seldom at our house. In fact, I didn't even see him very often. 5

"Hello?" he answered in his deep, scratchy voice. 6

"Oh, umm, hi Dad. Is Mom home?" 7

"What can I do for you?" he asked, sounding a bit too cheerful. 8

"Well, I just wanted to ask Mom if I could stay for dinner here." 9

"I don't think that's a very good idea, dear." I could sense an abrupt change in the tone of his voice. "Your room is a mess, and if you're not home in ten minutes to straighten it up, I'll really give you something to clean." Click. 10

Pedalling home as fast as I could, I had a distinct image of my enraged father. I could see his face redden, his body begin to tremble slightly, and his hands gesture nervously in the air. Though he was not prone to physical violence and always appeared calm on the outside, I knew he was really seething inside. The incessant motion of those hands was all too vivid to me as I neared home. 11

My heart was racing as I turned the knob to the front door and headed for my bedroom. When I opened my bedroom door, I stopped in horror. The dresser drawers were pulled out, and clothes were scattered across the floor. Everything on top of the dresser—a perfume tray, a couple of baskets of hair clips and earrings, and an assortment of pictures—had been strewn about. The dresser itself was tilted on its side, supported by the bed frame. As I stepped in and closed the door behind me, tears welled up in my eyes. I hated my father so much at that moment. Who the hell did he think he was to waltz into my life every few months like this? 12

I was slowly piecing my room together when he knocked on the door. I choked back the tears, wanting to show as little emotion as possible, and quietly murmured, "Come in." He stood in the doorway, one hand leaning against the door jamb, a cigarette dangling from the other, flicking ashes on the carpet, very smug in his handling of the situation. 13

"I want you to know I did this for your own good. I think it's time you started taking a little responsibility around this house. Now, to show you there are no hard feelings, I'll help you set the dresser back up." 14

"No thank you," I said quietly, on the verge of tears again. "I'd rather do it myself. Please, just leave me alone!" 15

He gave me one last look that seemed to say, "I offered. I'm the good guy. If you refuse, that's your problem." Then he turned and walked away. I was stunned at how he could be so violent one moment and so nonchalant the next. 16

As I sat in his bedroom reflecting on what he had done to my room, I felt the utmost disgust for this man. There seemed to be no hope he would break his filthy habits. I could come in and clean his room, but only he could clean up the mess he had made of his life. But I felt pity for him, too. After all, he is my father—am I not supposed to feel some responsibility for him and to love and honor him? 17

Connecting to Culture and Experience

Jan Gray admits that her disgust for her father is mixed with pity. Ambivalence—mixed feelings—is fundamental to our relationships with others. We normally do not feel only hate and fear toward other people. On the other hand, we usually do not feel only unqualified love and devotion. Such feelings are generally considered to be sentimental or pollyannaish. (Pollyanna, a character in a 1913 American novel of the same name, optimistically found good in everything and everybody.)

With students in your class, discuss ambivalence in human relationships. Identify someone for whom you have notably ambivalent feelings—a family member, friend, employer, or anyone else—someone you feel comfortable talking about with your classmates. Your feelings may be mainly negative, mainly positive, or evenly balanced. Take turns describing your relationship with the person you have chosen and speculating about how your ambivalent feelings emerged. Explain also how you have been able to sustain the relationship, if you have.

As a group, what can you conclude about ambivalence in relationships? On the basis of your individual experiences, does it seem that ambivalence is inevitable? Do you think that accepting ambivalence would make families more stable and people in general more tolerant? If so, try to explain how.

Analyzing Writing Strategies

For more on creating a dominant impression, see pp. 491–92.

1. Autobiographers strive to create a **dominant impression** of their subjects: Every detail of appearance, conversation, and gesture contributes to this impression. Gray has this same goal in mind when she opens her essay with two paragraphs of physical description, **naming** and **detailing** certain features of her father's appearance as well as his characteristic habits. The first paragraph, for example, focuses on his hands, naming the features she wants to focus on: psoriasis/skin disease, patches, dead skin, and fingers. She also details what she names; for example, the hands are "grotesque," the skin disease "chronic," the hands "massive." In paragraph 2, Gray focuses on other features of her father's person and appearance.

   In paragraphs 1 and 2, underline all of the features Gray names, and put each detail of the named features in brackets. (Grammatically, the names are nouns, the details adjectives.) Then, look over the detailing and think about the dominant impression it gives of Gray's father.
2. We see Gray's father through precise naming and vivid detailing, but we also learn about him from what he says. Reread the reconstructed **dialogue** in paragraphs 6–10 and 13–16. Pay attention to what the father says and how each conversation develops. Notice also how Gray comments on what her father says and shows his actions as he talks to her. Then, consider these questions: What does each conversation reveal about the father and Gray's relationship with him? Do the conversations confirm what you learn about the father and the relationship elsewhere in the essay, or do they offer new information? If they offer something new, identify exactly what they reveal.
3. The Writer at Work section later in this chapter presents the first draft of this essay. Compare the two versions by making a scratch outline of the draft and the revision. How did Gray change the organization? Why do you think she made these changes, and what effect do they have?

Considering Topics for Your Own Essay

Imagine writing about someone with whom you had a serious conflict. How would you present this person? Which anecdotes might be most revealing? What conversations might you reconstruct that would dramatize the conflict? What dominant impression of this person would you attempt to create?

Commentary

Like the other biographers in this chapter, Gray centers her essay around anecdotes that take place at different times and places. Their sequence defines the **organization** of her essay. Instead of putting them in a simple chronological order, Gray embeds one anecdote within the other, using flashback to heighten the contrast between the two scenes. The last sentence of paragraph 4 provides a smooth transition to the flashback, and the opening phrase of paragraph 17 returns us to the time of the first anecdote.

Not only is the organization of this essay complex; so is Gray's expression of the **significance** of the relationship with her father. She is obviously repulsed by her father's skin condition and habits and by his threatening phone conversation and "smug" destruction of her room. The father comes across as psychologically unstable and possibly dangerous, even though Gray specifically states that "he was not prone to physical violence." Even though everything Gray tells and shows about her father is critical of him, she concludes the essay by expressing sympathy toward him. Some readers could interpret her final sentence—a rhetorical question—as ironic, assuming that she could not possibly love and honor the man she has described. But Gray's own reflections on writing the essay acknowledge her ambivalence, feelings she has not—and may never—fully resolve. One reason we write about significant relationships is to examine such feelings. While the writing process may not resolve our ambivalence, it can help us to understand why we feel as we do.

PURPOSE AND AUDIENCE

A writer of an essay about a remembered person has several purposes in mind. Perhaps the most prominent is to gain a better understanding of the remembered person and of the writer's own relationship with the person. To achieve this purpose, the writer needs to see the complexity of the relationship so as to avoid either demonizing or idealizing the person.

Another purpose is to entertain readers with a vivid portrait of an unusual or engaging person. To achieve this goal, writers present a remembered person through description, dialogue, action, imagery, comparison, and anecdote. All of these strategies are carefully coordinated to create a dominant impression that will enable readers to readily imagine the person and understand why he or she is significant for the writer. By using many concrete, revealing details, writers try to make their portraits come alive. Finally, writers may hope that readers will come to reflect on people who have been important in their own lives.

SUMMARY OF BASIC FEATURES

A Vivid Portrait

For more on naming, detailing, and comparing, see pp. 492–96.

At the center of an essay about a remembered person is a vivid portrait. Writers rely on dialogue and the full range of descriptive strategies—naming, detailing, comparing—to present a person to their readers.

In presenting Uncle Willie, Maya Angelou names many features of his appearance, singling out his posture, hands, face, and clothing. Through concrete visual details and comparisons, she helps us to imagine his face "pulled down on the left side, as if a pulley had been attached to his lower teeth." She also helps us to see his specific movements as he makes his way down an aisle "hand over hand, like a man climbing out of a dream."

For more on dialogue, see pp. 487–88.

Besides presenting their subjects visually, autobiographers let us hear their subjects speak so that we can infer what they are like. All the readings in this chapter include some dialogue. Angelou uses it to present a stuttering Uncle Willie, and Gray gives it prominence in the confrontation with her unpredictable, threatening father.

Detailed Anecdotes, Scenes, and Recurring Activities

In portraying significant relationships, writers almost always need to narrate anecdotes and to describe the scenes in which they take place. Writers often depict recurring activities as well.

For more about narrative, see Chapter 14.

Anecdotes reveal a subject's character and dramatize the writer's relationship with him or her. More than half of Angelou's portrait of Uncle Willie is composed of anecdotes. In the first anecdote, Uncle Willie stops her just short of burning herself during her recitation of the multiplication tables. The second incident demonstrates the power of using an extended anecdote in this type of essay. It dramatizes Uncle Willie's feelings about his lameness and his motives for deceiving the Little Rock couple. The anecdote includes suspense, specific narrative action, dialogue, and statements about its significance. Angelou also describes parts of the scene in each anecdote. For example, the stove warming the arithmetic lesson is a "dull red heater, which throbbed like a devil's toothache."

In addition to narrating anecdotes depicting one-time incidents, autobiographers may also present recurring activities. Wu alternates anecdotes and recurring activities quite successfully in her essay. For example, to show how her mother taught her to think before she spoke, she relies on an anecdote about criticizing her mother's food at a dinner with her mother's friends. To show how her friends do not understand her mother's methods of discipline and teaching, Wu tells about a recurring activity in which she relates the dinner-party anecdote and her friends contrast Wu's mother unfavorably to their own mothers.

An Indication of the Person's Significance

Portrait writers choose as their subjects people they consider significant—those they have loved or feared, those who have influenced them, those they have tried to impress—and they try to make clear exactly what that significance is. Whether or not they state this significance explicitly, they convey it through anecdotes, descriptions of recurring activities, vivid details—or all of these. For example, Haslam never tells us directly that he loved and revered Grandma, though he does say at one point, "I wasn't afraid of my great-grandmother any longer." Instead he shows us—through anecdotes, Grandma's recurring interactions with him and other family members, and her comments—that she had earned his trust and that he had come to love her.

The subjects writers choose are significant to them, but their feelings always involve ambivalence. Angelou's relationship with Uncle Willie is highly ambivalent, for example, as is Gray's with her father. Neither writer tries to force a neat resolution by reducing deep and contradictory feelings to simple love or hate. They acknowledge the ambivalence and accept it. In many portraits, in fact, the significance seems to lie in this inevitable complexity of close relationships. Similarly, good writers avoid sentimentalizing their relationships, neither damning nor idealizing their subjects. Gray comes close to damning her father but stops just short of it by admitting her feelings of pity and responsibility. Angelou sympathizes with Uncle Willie's shame about his lameness and stuttering, but she does not present him as a long-suffering saint.

GUIDE TO WRITING

THE WRITING ASSIGNMENT

Write an essay about a person who has been important in your life. Strive to present a vivid portrait, one that will let your readers see the person's character and the significance of the relationship to you.

INVENTION

The following activities will help you to choose a person, to describe this person, to explore your relationship, and to define the significance of the relationship. Each activity takes no more than a few minutes. Together, they enable you to search your memory and to think deeply about the person you choose to write about. Done one by one over several days' time, they provide a record of your thinking and put you in a strong position for drafting your essay.

Choosing a Person to Write About

You may already have a person in mind. Even if you do, however, it is a good idea to consider other people in order to choose the best possible subject. The following activities will help you to make the choice.

Listing People You Remember. *Make a list of people you could write about.* Include relatives, teachers, coaches, employers, friends, neighbors, and others on your list. Make your list as complete as you can, including people you knew for a long time and those you knew briefly, people you knew long ago and those you knew recently, people you liked and those you disliked. The following categories may give you some ideas:

Set a timer for ten minutes, and brainstorm your list with the monitor brightness turned all the way down. Enter as many possibilities as you can think of. Then, turn the brightness up, make sure all the names make sense, and save them as an invention file. Print out a copy to make notes on.

- Anyone who had authority over you or, conversely, anyone for whom you felt responsible
- Anyone who helped you in difficult times or made life difficult for you
- Anyone whose advice or actions influenced you
- Anyone who taught you something important about yourself
- Anyone who inspired strong emotions in you—admiration, envy, disapproval, fascination
- Anyone whose behavior or values led you to question your own
- Anyone who really surprised or disappointed you
- Anyone who supported you in something you wanted to achieve

Listing People to Explore Identity and Community Think about people who helped you to explore your own identity and sense of community. List only people you remember vividly, people you knew very well over a period of time. Do not overlook the importance of people outside your immediate family.

- Someone who helped you to develop a previously unknown side of yourself or to play a role you had not played before
- Someone who led you to redefine your sense of identity, perhaps by making you aware of your way of talking, appearance, ethnic background, social class, or religious beliefs
- Someone who caused you to reflect on whether you or anyone else can really change
- Someone who led you to question assumptions or stereotypes you had about other people
- Someone who made you feel you were part of a larger community or that you had something worthwhile to contribute or, conversely, someone who made you feel alienated, like an outsider

Listing People to Explore Work and Career The following categories should help you to recall people who have influenced your thoughts about work and career. List only those people about whom you can recall specific details and stories.

- Someone who competed with you at work or someone with whom you learned to work collaboratively
- Someone who served as a positive or negative role model, perhaps leading you to change your attitudes toward work, your willingness to be supervised, or your ability to lead others
- Someone who helped you to reevaluate your attitudes about a career—for example, about the pursuit of money or happiness, about focusing all of your energy in one direction in order to increase your chances of success, or about the value of helping people or protecting the environment
- Someone who helped you to evaluate your choice of a college major or your attitude toward school in light of your career goals

Making a Choice. Look over your list of possible subjects and choose an interesting person to write about. The person should be someone you can describe vividly, whose significance in your life you are eager to explore, and about whom you can interest your readers. You may find that your choice is easy to make, or you may have several subjects that seem equally attractive. Make the best decision you can for now. If the subject does not work out, you can try a different one later.

Describing the Person

If you can, save these lists on a word processor. Later, as you begin to draft, you can call up the file on a second screen and easily transfer details you want to use in your draft.

The following activities will help you to recall specific information you can use to describe the person. If you complete each activity thoughtfully, you will have a wealth of remembered detail to draw on in drafting your essay. Even after you start drafting, you can return to these lists to capture fleeting memories that can be incorporated as you need them.

Appearance. *List and describe aspects of the person's appearance.* Put one aspect of the person's appearance on each line. Then, describe each feature in words or brief phrases, such as "cheeks—round, bright red spots in middle." You might start at the top, with the person's hair and face, and work down to the feet. Or you might start with the person's general appearance or build and then focus on specific details.

Next, think about the person's way of dressing, including jewelry, hats, or other accessories. List these items, including the purpose or occasion if necessary. Then, describe the items in words or brief phrases.

Actions. *Make a list of the ways the person moved and acted.* Again, make your list as extensive as possible, considering the following points and putting one item on each line.

- Any specific gestures or habits you remember
- Ways you recall him or her "in action": walking, running, driving a car, sitting at the kitchen table
- What you observed when the person expressed a mood or emotion—expressions or actions that showed you what the person was feeling

Now go back and describe each item more fully in words or brief phrases if necessary.

Conversation. *Make a list of the times you observed the person in conversation.* What can you remember about the way he or she speaks? Include in your list:

- Any memorable phrases, including slang or regional expressions
- Tone of voice and the manner of speech
- The first thing you remember the person ever saying to you
- The most memorable thing you recall the person saying

Reconstruct one or more brief conversations between the person and yourself or someone else. Set up each conversation as a dialogue, with each person's words starting a new line.

Anecdotes. *Choose an anecdote and describe it in detail, using the following steps.*

- Recall some important events or incidents associated with your subject. Do you associate him or her with a particular location, certain objects or activities, a period of time in your life, or another person? List these items, one per line.
- What specific incidents stand out in your mind? Briefly list as many anecdotes as you can remember, one per line.
- Choose one particularly telling anecdote from your list and write about it for ten minutes, describing what happened in a way that will interest your readers. Give as much detail as you can remember, including dialogue if it is important to the anecdote.

Testing Your Choice

You should now be ready to decide tentatively whether your choice is a good one. Reread your invention work to see whether your initial memories seem promising. If you were able to recall anecdotes and many details, then you have probably made a good choice. Your invention writing and thinking will also allow you to assess whether the person was truly significant in your life.

If at any point you lose confidence in your choice, however, return to your list and consider another subject.

Testing Your Choice: A Collaborative Activity

At this point you will find it useful to get together in a group with two or three other students and present your subjects to one another. In turn, each of you should identify the role the person has played in your life, give a few key details of appearance and manner, and relate one anecdote that reveals something about the person and your relationship. As listeners, briefly tell each presenter what seems most surprising or interesting about the person and the relationship. This collaborative activity will help you to determine whether you have chosen a subject you can present in an interesting way.

Defining the Person's Significance

Now you should consider what significance the person has had in your life. The following activities can help you to discover this significance and to find a way to share it with your readers.

Recalling Your Remembered Feelings and Thoughts. *Write for ten minutes about your earliest memories of the person.* Use the following questions to stimulate your memory:

If You Have Always Known This Person:

- What are my earliest memories of him or her?
- What was our relationship like initially?
- What did we do together? How did we talk to each other?
- In the early part of our relationship, how did we influence each other?

If You Met This Person at a Specific Time in Your Life:

- What do I remember about our first meeting—place, time, occasion, particular incidents, other people, words exchanged?
- Had I heard of this person before our first meeting? If so, what did I expect him or her to be like?
- What was my initial impression?
- How did I act when we met? What impression, if any, was I trying to make?
- Did I talk about the person to anyone after we met? What did I say?

Now stop to focus your thoughts. In a couple of sentences, indicate the person's importance to you early in your relationship.

Exploring Your Present Perspective. *Take ten minutes or so to write about how you feel now in thinking about your relationship with this person.* Try to express your insights about his or her importance in your life. Use these questions as a guide:

- Would I have wanted the person to act differently toward me? How?
- How do I feel about the way I acted toward the person? Would I have behaved any differently had I known then what I know now? How?
- Looking back at our relationship, do I understand it any differently now than I did at the time?
- If my feelings toward the person were ambivalent, how would I describe them? What are my current feelings?

Now focus your thoughts about your present perspective. In two or three sentences, describe your present perspective on the person.

If you have used a word processor to explore the person's significance, you might want to print out a copy of your reflections to read over and make notes on before reflecting on what you have discovered.

Reflecting on the Significance of the Relationship. *Write a few sentences about the significance of your relationship with the person.* Because you are both presenting the person and revealing your relationship, you need to pause here at the end of your invention work to reflect on what you have discovered. You need not arrive yet at a coherent statement about the relationship. For now, experiment with different ways of stating it. Try to answer these questions: What was special or unusual about our relationship? What did I learn from it? What made the relationship significant to me?

PLANNING AND DRAFTING

This section will help you to see what you have accomplished up to this point and to determine what you need to explore more fully. You will also receive some guidance for the next stages of the writing process.

Seeing What You Have

It is a good idea at this point to print out a hard copy of what you have written on a word processor for easier reviewing.

You have now produced a lot of writing for this assignment: descriptions of the person's appearance and behavior, recollections of anecdotes and dialogue, reflections on his or her significance to you. Before going on to plan and draft your essay, reread what you have already written. Look for patterns: evidence of growth or deterioration, harmony or tension, consistency or contradiction in the person or in the relationship. See if you make any new discoveries or gain fresh insights. Jot your ideas in the margins, and underline or star any promising material. Then, ask yourself the following questions:

- Do I remember enough specific details about the person? Will I be able to describe him or her vividly?
- Do I understand how the person was significant to me? Have I been able to state that significance clearly?
- Do my anecdotes and dialogues capture the person's character and portray our relationship effectively?

- Relationships tend to be complex. Will I be able to avoid sentimentality, oversimplifications, or stereotyping?

If your invention writing seems too general or superficial, or if it has not led you to a clear understanding of the significance the person holds in your life, then you may well have difficulty writing a coherent, developed draft. It may be that the person you have chosen is not a good subject after all. The person may not really be important enough to you. Or you may not yet have enough emotional distance to write about the person. As frustrating as it is to start over, it is far better to do so now than later.

If your invention writing looks thin but promising, you may be able to fill it out by doing one or more of the following:

- Think more about your relationship with the person, probing your feelings more deeply.
- Add more descriptive details to your list.
- Recall other important anecdotes.
- Reconstruct additional conversations.

Setting Goals

Before actually beginning to draft, set goals for yourself. These can include overall goals—keeping readers' interest, satisfying any curiosity about the person's significance, creating a vivid portrait of the person. Other goals should involve smaller issues—selecting rich visual details, creating realistic dialogue, finding fresh images, connecting paragraphs to one another. All these goals, large and small, guide the decisions you will make as you draft and revise. Here are some questions that should help you:

Your Purpose and Readers

- Are my readers likely to know someone like this person? If so, how can I help them to imagine this particular person?
- Will my readers be surprised by this person or by our relationship? Might they disapprove of either? If so, how can I break through their preconceptions to get them to see the person as I do?
- How can I help readers to see the significance this person has for me?

The Beginning

- How can I capture my readers' attention with the first sentence? Should I begin as Gray does, with an image of the person? With an anecdote, as Angelou and Haslam do? Should I first present myself, or should I focus immediately on my subject, as Wu does?
- On what note should I open? What tone should I adopt—casual, distant, confiding, mournful, angry, sarcastic?
- Should I provide some background or context, as Wu and Gray do, or jump right into the action, as Angelou and Haslam do? Should I let readers *see* the person right away? Or should I *tell* them about him or her first?

Presenting the Person

- Which descriptive details best present the person?
- What direct statements should I make to characterize the person? What values, attitudes, conduct, or character traits should I emphasize?
- To help my readers to understand my relationship with this person, what can I show them in our conversations and our experiences together?
- What insights or feelings do I need to discuss explicitly so my readers will see the person's significance in my life?

The Ending

- What do I want the ending to accomplish? Should it sum things up? Fix a particular image in readers' minds? Provide a sense of completion? Open up new possibilities?
- How shall I end? With reflection? With a statement of the person's significance, as Wu does? With speculation about my subject's feelings, as Angelou does? With the person's words? With an anecdote, as Haslam does?
- Shall I frame the essay by having the ending echo the beginning, as Haslam does?

Outlining

Outlining on a word processor makes it easy to try different ways of sequencing your material.

After you have set goals for your draft, you might want to make a scratch outline of your essay, indicating a tentative sequence for the material you will cover. Note briefly how you plan to begin; list in order possible anecdotes, descriptions, conversations, or reflections; and note how you might end. As you draft, you may well diverge from your outline if you discover a better way to organize your essay.

Drafting

Call up your invention material on an alternate screen as you draft. Shift back and forth to cut and paste invention material into your draft.

Start drafting your essay, keeping in mind the goals you set while you were planning. As you write, try to describe your subject in a way that makes his or her importance in your life clear for your readers. If you get stuck while drafting, explore the problem by using some of the writing activities in the Invention section of this chapter. You may want to review the general drafting advice on pp. 13–14.

CRITICAL READING GUIDE

Swap copies of your drafts with another student, either by exchanging disks or by sending the computer files over a network. Add your comments either next to the essay, if you can divide the screen, or at the end of the document.

Now is the time to get a good critical reading of your draft. Your instructor may arrange such a reading as part of your coursework. If not, you can ask a classmate, friend, or family member to read your essay. You could also seek comments from your campus writing center. The guidelines in this section can be used by *anyone* reviewing an essay about a remembered person. (If you are unable to have someone else read your draft, turn ahead to the section on Revising, where you will find guidelines for reading your own draft critically.)

If You Are the Writer. In order to provide focused, helpful comments, your reader must know your intended audience and purpose. Briefly write out this information at the top of your draft, answering the following questions:

- *Audience.* Who are your readers? How do you assume they will react to your writing?
- *Purpose.* What impression do you want readers to have of your subject? What do you want them to see about his or her significance in your life?

If You Are the Reader. The following guidelines can be useful for approaching a draft with a well-focused, questioning eye.

1. *Read for a First Impression.* Begin by reading the draft straight through to get a general impression. Read for enjoyment, ignoring spelling, punctuation, and usage errors for now. Try to imagine the person and to understand his or her significance for the writer.

   When you have finished this first quick reading, write a few sentences about your overall impression. Summarize the person's significance as you understand it. If you have any insights about the person or the relationship that are not reflected in the draft, write down these thoughts.
2. *Consider How Vividly the Person Is Described.* Strong descriptive writing is specific and detailed. Note any places where you would like greater specificity or more detail. Point out any particularly effective descriptions as well as any that seem to contradict the overall impression the rest of the essay gives about the person.

   Does the writer tell us too much about the person's character and conduct through general statements rather than showing us through anecdotes, dialogues, and descriptions? Point out vague or unnecessary statements as well as those that need illustration. Also indicate any statements that seem to be contradicted by anecdotes or dialogues. Note any particularly revealing passages that help you to understand the person's character or significance.
3. *Consider the Effectiveness of the Anecdotes.* Review the anecdotes, noting any that are particularly effective and any that seem unnecessary or confusing. Is each anecdote dramatic and well paced, or is more specific narrative action needed to show people moving, gesturing, and talking? Could anything else be well illustrated by anecdote?

continued

continued

Review the dialogues, pointing out any that are particularly effective as well as any that sound artificial or stilted, that move too slowly, or that seem undramatic.

4. *Assess Whether the Autobiographical Significance Is Clear.* What did you learn about the writer from reading this essay? Does the essay sentimentalize the person or the relationship? State the person's significance and suggest ways of indicating this significance more precisely. Perhaps it is overstated, understated, or unclear. Assess whether all details and anecdotes contribute to showing the significance.
5. *Analyze the Effectiveness of the Organization.* Now that you have thought about the essay, do you consider the *beginning* effective? Did it capture your interest and set up the right expectations? Point out any other passages that might make a better beginning, and explain why.

   Look at the *ending*. Is it satisfying? Does it repeat what you already know? Does it oversimplify or reduce the meaning of the relationship to a platitude? Could the essay end at an earlier point? Does the ending frame the essay by referring back to the beginning? If not, can you suggest a way that it might? Try to suggest a different ending.

   Consider the *overall plan,* perhaps by making a scratch outline. Decide whether the essay might be strengthened by shifting parts around, perhaps changing the order of anecdotes or moving the descriptions of the person. Point out spots where your momentum slowed as you read.
6. *Give the Writer Your Final Thoughts.* These questions may help you to summarize your final thoughts: What effect did the essay have on you personally? How did you react to the subject and the relationship? Did the subject remind you of people you know well? If so, briefly explain the connection. What general ideas about people and life in America does the essay suggest to you? What aspect of the essay is most memorable? What part needs further work?

REVISING

The following guidelines will help you to identify and to solve problems as you revise your draft.

Identifying Problems

To identify problems in your draft, you need to read it objectively, analyze its basic features, and study any comments you have received from others.

Even if your essay is saved to a computer file, reread from a hard copy. Add notes to yourself and quick revisions as you read through the draft.

Getting an Overview. Consider your draft as a whole, trying to see it with a critical eye. It may help to follow these two simple steps:

1. *Reread.* If at all possible, put the draft aside for a day or two. When you do reread it, start by reconsidering your purpose. Then, read the draft straight through, trying to see it as your intended readers will.

2. *Outline.* Make a scratch outline to get an overview of the essay's development. This outline can be sketchy—words and phrases instead of complete sentences—but it should identify the basic features as they appear in the essay.

Charting a Plan for Revision. You may want to make a double-column chart like the following one to help you to keep track of any problems you need to solve. In the left-hand column, list the basic features of writing about remembered people. As you analyze your draft and study any comments you have received from others, note the problems you want to solve in the right-hand column.

Basic Features	*Problems to Solve*
Presentation of the subject	
Anecdotes and scenes	
Autobiographical significance	
Organization	

Analyzing the Basic Features of Your Own Draft. Turn to the Critical Reading Guide on the preceding pages. Use this guide to help you to identify problems in your draft. Note anything you need to solve on your chart.

Studying Critical Comments. Review any comments you have received. For each comment, refer to the draft to determine what led readers to make that particular point. Try not to react defensively. Ideally, these comments will help you to see your draft for what it is (rather than what you hoped it would be) and to identify specific problems.

Solving the Problems

Having identified problems in your draft, you now need to figure out solutions and—most important—to carry them out. Basically, you have three options:

1. Review your invention and planning notes for material you can add to the draft.
2. Do additional invention writing to answer specific questions you or other readers have.
3. Look back at the readings in this chapter to see how other writers have solved similar problems.

Before revising, copy your original draft to a second file. Then, should you change your mind about material you delete while revising, it will still be available to you.

Here are some suggestions on how you might respond to several of the problems common to writing about remembered people. The suggestions are organized according to the basic features on your revision chart.

Presentation of the Subject

- **Do you need more visual detail?** Try naming things more specifically and adding sensory details to bring your subject to life. Choose concrete, specific words rather than abstract, general ones. When you make comparisons, perhaps with similes and metaphors, you can tell readers a good deal about your subject. Review your invention notes for details to add.

- **Do any details seem irrelevant to the dominant impression you wish to give about your subject and your relationship?** If so, eliminate these details.
- **Do you need additional dialogue?** Review your notes on your subject's speech patterns for memorable phrases or expressions. Try reconstructing a conversation between the two of you that might "say something" important about your subject. Review the dialogues in the readings to help you to get ideas.
- **Do any of the dialogues weaken the dominant impression you want to give?** If so, eliminate or revise them.

Anecdotes and Scenes

- **Do any of the anecdotes seem dull?** Try adding more specific narrative details to show movements and gestures.
- **Do any of the anecdotes weaken the point you are trying to make?** If so, eliminate them, or reconsider your point.
- **Could the essay use more anecdotes?** Look over your notes for other incidents worth telling about. Try to think of incidents that will help to characterize your subject as well as the relationship between the two of you.
- **Do you need to elaborate on a scene?** Try naming specific objects and providing more sensory details to help readers see, hear, smell, and otherwise experience the scene.

Autobiographical Significance

- **Do you need to clarify the significance this person has had in your life?** Try to think of dialogue or anecdotes that might show readers more about your relationship. If any anecdotes or descriptive details seem irrelevant or contradictory, cut them or reconsider the significance you are trying to show. Review any notes you made concerning your feelings about your subject.
- **Is your portrait either too sentimental or too dismissive?** Readers will question a portrait that is either all positive or all negative. It is important to acknowledge any ambivalent feelings you have about the relationship. Consider introducing some complexity into your portrayal.

Organization

Use your word processor's cut-and-paste or block-and-move functions to shift material around. Make sure that you revise transitions so that material fits smoothly into its new spot.

- **Is the beginning weak?** See whether there is a better way to begin. Look for engaging dialogue, an intriguing anecdote, or a colorful description. Try to find something that will capture readers' attention.
- **Does the essay have any slow spots?** Perhaps you have described something too thoroughly or become sidetracked telling an anecdote. You may be able to speed things along by eliminating some detail.
- **Is the ending flat?** Review your draft to see if there is a better place to end your essay. You might try ending with a question, to leave readers with something to ponder. Or see whether there is something at the outset that you could refer to again at the end, thus framing the essay.

EDITING AND PROOFREADING

Use your word processor's spell-check function cautiously. Keep in mind that it will not find all misspellings, particularly misused homonyms (such as *there, their,* and *they're*), typographical errors that are themselves words (such as *fro* for *for*), and many proper nouns and specialized terms. Proofread these carefully yourself. Also proofread for words that should have been deleted when you edited a sentence.

Now is the time to check your draft for errors in style, usage, punctuation, and mechanics. Our research has identified several errors that frequently occur in first-hand biography. Check your draft for these common errors: sentence fragments, missing hyphens in compound adjectives that precede nouns, and subject/pronoun repetition. The following guidelines will help you.

Checking for Sentence Fragments. A sentence fragment is a group of words that is punctuated as a sentence but that lacks some necessary sentence element, usually either a subject or a verb. Writing about a remembered person seems to encourage sentence fragments such as the following:

> I felt sorry for Lucy. Not because of her weight problem but because of her own discomfort with herself.

The first five words are a sentence, containing a subject *(I)* and a verb *(felt)*. The next fourteen words constitute a fragment; although they are punctuated like a sentence, beginning with a capital letter and ending with a period, they include neither a subject nor a verb. This kind of fragment seems to occur when writers try to present many specific details so that readers can imagine the person. The following examples have been edited to attach the fragment to the sentence preceding it.

- **I felt sorry for Lucy/ ^not ~~Not~~ because of her weight problem but because of her own discomfort with herself.**
- **Frank turned over the tarot cards one at a time/ ^each ~~Each~~ time telling me something about my future.**
- **There she stood at the door to our summer cabin/ ^the ~~The~~ spare, dimly lit space where we were to become closest friends and then bitter enemies.**

Checking for Hyphens. When you use compound adjectives (two adjectives together) that are not in a dictionary, you have to decide whether or not to use a hyphen. In general, you should hyphenate most compound adjectives that precede a noun but not those that follow a noun.

> Coach Brega was a feared but well-respected man. He was feared but well respected.

You may have used some compound adjectives as you were adding vivid details to your essay. Check your draft carefully to see that you have hyphenated compound adjectives correctly. Here are some more examples taken from student essays about remembered people:

- **The intruder turned out to be a fifteen year old runaway.**

- **One of my musician friends had a four channel mixing board.**

- **I bought a high powered Honda CRX.**

A Common ESL Problem. Unlike some languages, English does not allow a subject to be repeated by a pronoun *(he, she, it, you, we, they)*.

- **Great-Aunt Sonia ~~she~~ taught me to pick mushrooms.**

- **The person I miss the most from my country ~~he~~ is Luis Paulo.**

- **In Rio, the rivalry between Flamengo and Fluminense ~~it~~ is as strong as the one here between the Yankees and the Red Sox.**

A WRITER AT WORK

REVISING A DRAFT AFTER A CRITICAL READING

In this section we look at the way Jan Gray's essay about her father evolved from draft to revision. Included here are her first draft and a written critique of it by one of her classmates. Read the draft and critique, and then reread her final version, "Father," printed earlier in this chapter.

The First Draft

Gray drafted her essay after spending a couple of hours on the invention and planning activities. She had no difficulty choosing a subject, since she had such strong feelings about and vivid memories of her father. She wrote the draft quickly in one sitting, not worrying about punctuation or usage. Though she wrote in pencil, her draft appears here typed.

My father is a large intelligent, overpowering man. He's well-respected in the food-processing trade for his clever but shrewd business tactics but I find his manipulative qualities a reflection of the maturity that he lacks. For as long as I can remember he's always had to be in control, decision-maker of the family and what he said was law. There was no compromising with this man and for that reason I've always feared him. 1

When I was little and he used to still live with us, everytime he came home from work I avoided him as best I could. If he came in the kitchen I went in the livingroom and 2 if he came into the livingroom I went upstairs to my bedroom just to avoid any confrontation.

3 Family trips were the worst. There was nowhere to go, I was locked up with him in a camper or motel for 1 week, 2 weeks or however long the vacation lasted. I remember one trip in particular. It was the summer after my 12th Birthday and the whole family (5 kids, 2 adults and one dog) were going to go "out west" for a month. We travelled through Wyoming, North and South Dakota, Colorado and other neighboring states were on the agenda. My father is the type who thinks he enjoys these family outings because as a loyal husband and father that's what he should do. Going to the state parks and the wilderness was more like a business trip than a vacation. He had made the agenda so no matter what we were to stick to it. That meant at every road sign like Yellowstone Nat'l Park we had to stop, one or more of the kids would get out stand by the sign and he'd take a picture just so he could say we've been there. Get in and get out as quick as possible was his motto to cover as much ground in as little time as he could. I hated having to take those pictures because it seemed so senseless--who cares about the dumb signs anyway? But dad is a very impatient man and any sign of non conformity was sure to put him in a rage. Not a physical violence, no, my father never did get violent but you always knew when he was boiling up inside. I could sense it in the tone of his voice and the reddish glaze that would cover his eyes. He would always stay very calm yet he was ready to explode. He never physically hurt anyone of us kids--sure we've all been spanked before but only when we were younger. Although he constrained himself from inflicting harm on people he didn't hold back from damaging objects.

4 I remember one time I was calling my mother from a girlfriend's house to ask if I could stay over for dinner when my father unexpectedly answered the phone. "Hello?" he said, in his usually gruffy manner.

5 "Oh, hi dad. Is Mom around?"

6 "What can I do for you?"

7 "Well, I just wanted to ask her if I could eat dinner over here at Shana's."

8 "I don't think that's a very good idea. Your room is a shambles and if your not home in 10 minutes I'm really going to make a mess for you to clean up." Click.

9 I was in shock. I hadn't expected him to be there because at this time my parents were divorced but I knew he was serious so I jumped on my bike and pedalled home as fast as I could. I know I was there within ten minutes but apparently he didn't think so. I walked in the front door and headed straight for my room. When I opened my bedroom door I couldn't believe what I saw. My dresser drawers were all pulled out and clothes strewn about the room, the

dresser was lying on its side and everything on top of the dresser had been cast aside in a fit of anger. I closed my door and tears began to well up in my eyes. I hated him so much at the moment. All those years of fear suddenly turned to anger and resentment. Who the hell was this man to do this when he didn't even live in the house anymore? I was slowly piecing my room back together when he knocked on the door. I choked back the tears because I didn't want him to know that his little outrage had gotten to me and quietly said, "Come in."

10 He opened the door and stood in the doorway one arm leaning on the door jamb and a cigarette with ashes falling on the carpet dangling from his other hand.

11 "I want you to know I did this for your own good" He said. "I think its time you started taking a little responsibility around this house. Now let me help you put the dresser back up."

12 "No thanks. I'd rather do it myself."

13 "Aw, come on. Let's not have any hard feelings now."

14 "Please, I said. I'd rather do it myself so would you please leave me alone." By this time I was shaking and on the verge of breaking out in tears. He gave me one last look that seemed to say, "I offered, I did the right thing, I'm the good guy and she refused me so now it's her problem" and he walked out.

15 I was so upset that he could be so violent one moment and then turn around and patronize me by offering to help clean up what he had done. That one incident revealed his whole character to me.

16 My father is a spiteful, manipulative, condescending, malicious man and from that day on I knew I would never understand him or want to.

Gray opens her draft with a series of direct statements describing her father's character and stating her feelings about him. The second paragraph illustrates what she tells us in the first. Paragraph 3 also serves as illustration, showing her father's domination over the family and concluding with a physical description and a suggestion of his potential for violence.

In paragraphs 4–15, Gray relates an anecdote. Though long, it is fast-paced and dramatic. She uses dialogue to show us her father's character and description to let us visualize the damage he did to her room. Then, she ends as she began—with a series of statements explicitly disclosing her feelings.

Critical Comments

A classmate named Tom Schwartz read Gray's draft. He read it through once and quickly wrote down his general impression. Following the Critical Reading Guide, Schwartz then reread the draft to analyze its features closely. It took him a little more than half an hour to complete a full written critique, which appears here. Each point corresponds to a step in the Critical Reading Guide earlier in this chapter.

Read for a First Impression.

Your dad sure seems crazy. I can see he's impossible to live with. Because he's your dad he's naturally significant. You say you hate him and you call him a lot of names. But you also say he thought of himself as a loyal father. Was there anytime he was ok?

Consider How Vividly the Person Is Described.

I can't picture him. What did he look like? I like the description of your messed up room. I'd like even more detail, like what clothes were thrown around and where. Did he break anything when he tipped the dresser? Was the whole room a wreck or just the dresser? Oh yeah, the detail of his cigarette ashes falling on the carpet is great. He's the one who's making the mess, not you.

You make a lot of statements. Most need illustration. I don't get it about there being no compromising with him. What do you expect him to do? My dad is pretty strict too. But he doesn't wreck my room.

Consider the Effectiveness of the Anecdotes.

I don't get the vacation. Was it a birthday trip? Didn't you go to Yellowstone? Or did you just take pictures of signs? Sounds weird. The room anecdote is the best. It's really dramatic. The dialogue works as a frame I think. He had some nerve offering to help pick up the dresser. How smug and self-satisfied. Patronizing is right. Great anecdote.

Assess Whether the Autobiographical Significance Is Clear.

I just said you might have more feelings than you're admitting. You certainly have every reason to hate him. You say he never really hit you. But he certainly was violent, like you said.

I'm not sure why you wrote about your dad. Maybe you just feel strongly about him and need to figure him out. Maybe because he's colorful--unusual, unpredictable, not like other fathers, even divorced ones. I think he was a great choice for an essay. You disclose a lot of unpleasant stuff about your family. You certainly seem honest.

Analyze the Effectiveness of the Organization.

The beginning doesn't lead me to expect the room anecdote. The stuff about his business seems out of place. You're writing about your relationship with him not about his business. I don't have any suggestions.

```
     The ending may be going too far now that I think of
it. Also, even though you say you don't want to understand
him, here you are writing about him. Maybe there's more to
it than you're admitting. You could end with the paragraph
before. The anecdote sure does reveal his character.
```

Give the Writer Your Final Thoughts.

```
I guess it makes me feel lucky my dad and I get along.
I don't know what I'd do if he was like your dad. I still
wonder if your dad was all that bad. He must have some
good sides.
```

This critique helped Gray a great deal in revising her draft. Reread her revision now to see what she changed; it is obvious that many of her changes were suggested by Schwartz.

In writing about what she learned from writing this essay, Gray remarked: "Tom's criticism helped me a lot. He warned me against making too many statements without illustrating them. He said I needed more showing and less telling. He also questioned the vacation anecdote. I guess it didn't have much of a point. And the incident with my room seemed to work so well I decided to add the part about my dad's apartment."

Gray realized that the heart of her essay was in the anecdote about her room. She also saw, from Schwartz's comments, that the opening paragraphs were not working. Responding to his request for more physical description of her father, Gray returned to the invention activity in which she listed important details about her father's appearance. From this exploration, she came up with the detailed description that now opens the essay. As she was describing her father, she remembered the incident of cleaning his apartment and decided to use the description of his filthy apartment to frame the description of her own ransacked room.

Perhaps Schwartz's greatest contribution, however, was to help Gray to reexamine her father's real significance in her life. Specifically, Schwartz made her realize that her feelings were more complicated than she let on in her first draft. In writing about what she learned, Gray concluded, "The feelings I wanted to express didn't come across. I had a hard time writing the paper because I held back on a lot of things. I'm pretty ambivalent in my feelings toward my father right now." Gray discovered she could disclose her feelings by showing her father, his room, and the confrontation over her room. Gray's portrait of her father turned out to be more sympathetic than her comments about him, expressing some ambivalence—pity as well as fury.

THINKING CRITICALLY ABOUT WHAT YOU HAVE LEARNED

Now that you have spent considerable time reading and discussing essays about remembered people, and writing such an essay yourself, you should reflect on what you have learned. What problems did you have as a writer, and how did you solve them? How did reading other essays influence your own essay? Think critically about the genre of firsthand biography. What ideas do you have about the social and cultural dimensions of this kind of writing?

Reflecting on Your Writing

Write a one-page explanation, telling your instructor about a problem you encountered in writing your essay and how you solved it. Before you begin, gather all of your writing—invention, planning notes, drafts, critical comments, revising notes and plans, and final revision. Review these materials as you complete this writing task.

1. Identify *one* writing problem you needed to solve as you wrote about a remembered person. Do not be concerned with grammar and punctuation; concentrate on problems unique to developing an essay in this genre. For example: Did you puzzle over how to create a vivid portrait or present revealing anecdotes and scenes? Was it difficult for you to probe the significance of the relationship?
2. How did you recognize the problem? When did you first discover it? What called it to your attention? If someone else pointed out the problem to you, can you now see hints of it in your invention writings? If so, where specifically? When you first recognized the problem, how did you respond?
3. Think about how you solved the problem. Did you change the wording of a passage, cut or add details, or move paragraphs around? Did you reread one of the essays in this chapter to see how another writer handled a similar problem, or did you look back at the invention suggestions? If you talked about your writing problem with another student, a tutor, or your instructor, did talking about it help? How useful was the advice you received?
4. Now, write a brief explanation of the problem and your solution. Be as specific as possible in reconstructing your efforts. Quote from your invention or draft, others' critical comments, your revision plan, or your revised essay to show the various changes in your writing as you solved the problem. This is time well spent. If you can identify a particular problem, explain how you solved it, and understand what you learned from the experience, you will be able to solve future writing problems more easily.

Reviewing What You Learned from Reading

Your own essay about a remembered person has been influenced to some extent by the essays in this chapter as well as by classmates' essays that you have read. These other essays may have helped you to choose your subject, suggested ideas for using anecdote and dialogue, shown you how to reveal ambivalence, or assisted you in some other way. Write a page or so explaining to your instructor how the readings in this chapter influenced your final draft. Before you write, take some time to think about what you have learned from these selections.

1. Reread the final revision of your essay; then look back at the selections you read before completing it. Do you see any specific influences? For example, if you were impressed with the way one of the readings avoided sentimentality, acknowledged ambivalent feelings, detailed a scene, or compared two people, look to see where you might have been striving for similar effects in your own writing. Also look for ideas you got from your reading: writing strategies you were

inspired to try, specific details you were led to include, effects you sought to achieve.

2. Now write an explanation of these influences. Did one selection have a particularly strong influence on your essay, or were several selections influential in different ways? Quote from the other essays and from your final revision to show how your portrait was influenced by the other selections. Finally, point out anything you would now do to improve your own essay, based on reviewing the reading selections again.

Considering the Social Dimensions of Autobiography

Since writing about remembered people and writing about remembered events (Chapter 2) are both kinds of autobiography, they offer the promise of self-knowledge. Reflecting on how a particular person influenced you in the past, either positively or negatively, can help you to understand some of your current attitudes, feelings, and values. Similarly, as you look back on a significant relationship, you may discover how you usually respond in certain types of relationships and what you need and expect from other people. Moreover, writing about significant people requires that you look at yourself as a participant in dynamic, reciprocal relationships. Thus, such writing encourages you to acknowledge that you are not solely responsible for all of your achievements or all of your failings. It shows you how others have helped as well as hindered you, taught as well as thwarted you.

Empathy and Distance. Because they focus on interpersonal relationships, essays about remembered people can help you to cross the boundary between yourself and others and to understand other points of view. Maya Angelou, for example, writes about an incident that helped her to understand Uncle Willie's deepest feelings. When she senses his vulnerability, she begins to see him not simply in terms of how he treats her but in terms of his own needs and frustrations. Her empathy allows her to feel closer to him, but it does not erase her other feelings of anger and resentment. In fact, she realizes that her feelings toward her uncle are more complicated than she had recognized. Because writing thoughtfully about others reveals them to be complex human beings rather than simple stereotypes, writers often discover that their true feelings are, at least to some extent, ambivalent.

Yet, while firsthand biography can help you to develop empathy, it is nonetheless true that, as with any autobiography, you are still writing about yourself. You focus, of course, on what the person was like, but you also reveal the person's significance in your life. Moreover, however detailed and forthright the portrait, it will always be partial and biased. You can only present what *you* experienced and remember; you can never fully understand another person or completely escape your own point of view.

Ways of Understanding Other People. As we read and write essays about remembered people, we are influenced by other factors, such as whether we tend to understand people psychologically—as acting out personal fears and desires—or socially—as embodying learned values and attitudes. For example, we could interpret Maya Angelou's portrait of Uncle Willie psychologically, seeing in it a child's resentment of a father-surrogate or an adult's inability to show affection. But we could also explain it in terms of a larger social context. Uncle Willie's behavior toward Angelou and her brother might be connected to his position as an oppressed African-American man in the segregated South of the 1930s and 1940s. Or we could easily attribute his behavior to the fact that he has a marked physical disability in a society intolerant of physical differences. Depending on how you interpret behavior, you could see Uncle Willie's bullying either as a neurotic assertion of power or as an effort to stand tall.

Views of the Self. Finally, if we assume that reading and writing about remembered people can contribute to self-discovery, we must consider how the "self" is defined and how it may be affected by significant relationships.

Many people think that the self is formed early in life and remains basically unchanged by later circumstances. If you accept this view, then you are likely to see people as fundamentally unaffected by personal relationships. For example, you might see Jan Gray as emotionally independent of her father, secure in her own sense of herself: She seems neither to need his praise nor to care about his criticism. On the other hand, you may think of the self as more fluid and variable, believing that the various roles we play constitute different aspects of the self and that the self changes when we interact with other people. If you read Gray's essay from this perspective, you might see her relationship with her father as changing over time and Gray herself as different at various stages in the relationship. You might conclude that after her father wrecked her room, she was not the same person, that she was changed by the experience. You might also speculate that seeing her father's pathetic apartment was a turning point, enabling her to distance herself from him emotionally.

For Discussion. Following are some questions about the way we understand relationships and represent them in essays about remembered people. Jot down your thoughts as you read through these questions or discuss them in class. Then, write a page or so for your instructor exploring your own ideas and conclusions.

1. We have said that writing about an important person from your past can help you to understand some of your current attitudes, feelings, and values. Test this assertion against your writing experience in this chapter. What, if anything, did you learn about the kind of person you are today?

   Then, reflect on what your answer suggests about the nature of the self: Do you think of yourself as essentially the same as you were in the past, or do you think you have changed as a result of past relationships and experiences?

2. Think about the role empathy plays in writing about remembered people. We have suggested that Maya Angelou's essay hinges on her developing empathy for her uncle. Do you agree with this analysis? Why or why not?

   Is empathy central to any other essay in this chapter? If so, explain its role. Was empathy a part of your own essay? What can you conclude about the value of empathy in writing about remembered people?

3. We have also suggested that empathizing with the remembered person does not erase other feelings but allows the writer to accept ambivalent feelings toward the person. Recall a few examples of ambivalence in your own essay or in the other essays you read. How does the ambivalence in these essays help to create portraits that are not stereotyped?

4. How have you tended to interpret the essays in this chapter? Do you think of them primarily in psychological terms? Political and social terms? A little of both? In what terms do you interpret the relationship you wrote about? What do you think we gain or lose when we use these different perspectives to try to understand relationships between people?

5. Based on your reading of Jan Gray's essay, do you think she changes as her relationship with her father evolves, or do you see her as basically the same throughout? What in the essay makes you think as you do? Reread her first draft in the Writer at Work section and think about what it reveals about her childhood. Think about your own essay in the same terms. Does it reveal a single, unified self or one that is composed of different sides and changes over time?

   What can you conclude about the impact of relationships on the self? Do relationships provide an opportunity for us to act out who we already are? Or do they change us by giving us different roles to play?

A college student, a reporter for her campus newspaper, decides to profile a local radio station popular with students. In several visits, she observes the station's inner workings and interviews the manager, technicians, and disk jockeys. The disk jockeys are known by name to many students at the college. As several days pass during her visits to the station, she listens to the station itself more than she usually does and talks to two of her close friends about what she is observing. Reviewing her many pages of observation and interview notes, she decides to focus her profile on how the most popular disk jockey prepares for her four-hour show. As the student describes the disk jockey's well-practiced but increasingly frenzied activities as show time approaches, she fills in many details of the station's operation and management. Her story ends as the disk jockey plays the first recorded song of the show. Her profile shows how this popular disk jockey, known for her humor and her lively stories about musicians she knows personally, is nevertheless engaged in routine day-to-day work.

A student in an art history class writes a profile of a local artist recently commissioned to paint outdoor murals for the city. The student visits the artist's studio and talks with him about the process of painting murals. The artist invites the student to spend the following day as part of a team of local art students and neighborhood volunteers working on the mural under his direction. This firsthand experience helps the student to describe the process of mural painting almost from an insider's point of view. She organizes her profile around the main stages of this collaborative mural project, from conception to completion. As she describes each stage, she weaves in details about the artist, his helpers, and the site of their work, seeking to convey an impression of their talent and civic spirit.

A newspaper reporter gets approval from his city editor to profile a farmers' market that has recently opened near the city center. He calls the market manager and asks him to identify the market's most popular and most successful farmer. After making arrangements, the reporter goes to the farm the afternoon before market day and observes and actually participates in picking, packing, and loading the market produce. Early the next morning, he meets the farmer and his family at a café near the market where many of the farmers have breakfast before the market opens. During the morning, he spends part of the time in or near the farmer's stall and the rest of the time roaming the market talking to other farmers and to patrons. In his profile, which is published in the newspaper's Sunday magazine, the reporter describes the scene, the produce, and the people. He organizes the profile around his own Saturday morning activities. He orchestrates the details to convey his respect for the farmers and to give readers an impression of a lively and enjoyable activity for a Saturday morning.

CHAPTER 4

Writing Profiles

Magazines and newspapers are filled with profiles. Unlike conventional news stories, which report current events, profiles tell about people, places, and activities. Some profiles take us behind the scenes of familiar places, giving us a glimpse of their inner workings. Others introduce us to the exotic—peculiar hobbies, unusual professions, bizarre personalities. Still others probe the social, political, and moral significance of our institutions.

Because profiles share many features with autobiography, such as narrative, anecdote, description, and dialogue, you may use some of the strategies learned in writing about a remembered event (Chapter 2) or a person (Chapter 3). Yet profiles differ significantly from autobiography. Whereas an autobiographer reflects on remembered personal experience, a profile writer synthesizes and presents newly acquired observations. In writing a profile, you practice the field research methods of observing, interviewing, and notetaking commonly used by investigative reporters, social scientists, and naturalists. You also learn to analyze and synthesize the information you have collected.

Whatever their subjects or whatever information may be available to them, profile writers strive first and foremost to present a person, a place, or an activity vividly to their readers. They succeed only by presenting many concrete details that will enable readers to imagine the scene and the people. Most important, writers orchestrate the details carefully to convey an attitude toward their subjects and to offer an interpretation of them.

The scope of your profile may be large or small, depending on your assignment and your subject. You could attend a single event such as a parade or a convention and write up your observations of the place, people, and activities. Or you might conduct an interview with a person who has an unusual hobby or occupation and write up a profile based on your interview notes. If you have the time to do more extensive research, you might write a full-blown profile based on several observations and interviews with various people.

Writing in Your Other Courses

Profiles are familiar reading and writing assignments in various college courses. Here are some typical college profile assignments:

- *For a business course:* Report on the organizational structure of a particular place of business, first visiting the business and interviewing employees at various levels.
- *For an education course:* Observe a class where students are learning cooperatively, taking careful notes about what the teacher and students say and do. Based on what you know about cooperative learning principles, evaluate the teacher's effectiveness in applying them. Write a report on your conclusions, supported with specific details from your observations.
- *For an anthropology course:* In "Deep Play: Notes on the Balinese Cockfight," Clifford Geertz argues that to acquire deep insights into a culture, an anthropologist should study everyday experiences as if they were printed texts. Geertz's own "close reading" of the Balinese cockfight, for example, provides insights into Balinese status hierarchy and self-regard. Closely observe some instance of play or leisure in our culture, and write an essay presenting your own "close reading" of this cultural text.

→ Practice Choosing a Profile Subject: A Collaborative Activity

The scenarios that open this chapter suggest some occasions for writing profiles. Imagine that you have been assigned to write a profile of a person, a place, or an activity on your campus or in your community. Think of subjects that you would like to know more about.

Part 1. List several subjects. Consider local personalities (flamboyant store owner, distinguished teacher, newspaper columnist, talk show host), places on campus (student health center, research center, machine shop, police department, student newspaper office, day-care center, exercise or sports facility, women's resource center, campus tour office, office of telecommunications services), and businesses or activities in the community (comic-book store, auto wrecking company, motorcycle dealer, commercial fishing boat, local brewery or winery, eating disorder and treatment center, abortion alternatives or services, specialized building contractor, dance studio, private tutoring service, dog kennel).

Get together with two or three other students, and read your lists to one another. The other group members will tell you which item on your list they personally found most interesting and discuss with you briefly any questions they have about it.

Part 2. After you have all read your lists and received responses, discuss these questions:

- Were you surprised by which items on your list the other members of the group found most interesting?
- Were you surprised by any of their questions about this subject?
- How might these questions influence your approach to the subject?

READINGS

"Soup" is an unsigned profile that initially appeared in the "Talk of the Town" section of the *New Yorker* magazine (January 1989). The *New Yorker* regularly features brief, anonymous profiles like this one, whose subject is the fast-talking owner/chef of a takeout restaurant specializing in soup. In 1995, Albert Yeganeh, the subject of this profile, also inspired an episode of the television series *Seinfeld*. As you read, notice the prominence given to dialogue.

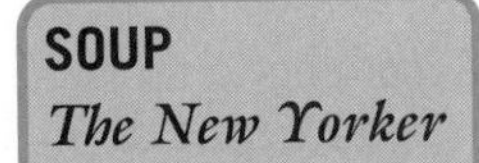

1 When Albert Yeganeh says "Soup is my lifeblood," he means it. And when he says "I am extremely hard to please," he means that, too. Working like a demon alchemist in a tiny storefront kitchen at 259-A West Fifty-fifth Street, Mr. Yeganeh creates anywhere from eight to seventeen soups every weekday. His concoctions are so popular that a wait of half an hour at the lunchtime peak is not uncommon, although there are strict rules for conduct in line. But more on that later.

2 "I am psychologically kind of a health freak," Mr. Yeganeh said the other day, in a lisping staccato of Armenian origin. "And I know that soup is the greatest meal in the world. It's very good for your digestive system. And I use only the best, the freshest ingredients. I am a perfectionist. When I make a clam soup, I use three different kinds of clams. Every other place uses canned clams. I'm called crazy. I am not crazy. People don't realize why I get so upset. It's because if the soup is not perfect and I'm still selling it, it's a torture. It's *my* soup, and that's why I'm so upset. First you clean and then you cook. I don't believe that ninety-nine per cent of the restaurants in New York know how to clean a tomato. I tell my crew to wash the parsley *eight* times. If they wash it five or six times, I scare them. I tell them they'll go to jail if there is sand in the parsley. One time, I found a mushroom on the floor, and I fired the guy who left it there." He spread his arms, and added, "This place is the only one like it in . . . in . . . the whole earth! One day, I hope to learn something from the other places, but so far I haven't. For example, the other day I went to a very fancy restaurant and had borscht. I had to send it back. It was *junk*. I could see all the chemicals in it. I never use chemicals. Last weekend, I had lobster bisque in Brooklyn, a very well-known place. It was *junk*. When I make a lobster bisque, I use a whole lobster. You know, I never advertise. I don't have to. All the big-shot chefs and the kings of the hotels come here to see what *I'm* doing."

3 As you approach Mr. Yeganeh's Soup Kitchen International from a distance, the first thing you notice about it is the awning, which proclaims "Homemade Hot, Cold, Diet Soups." The second thing you notice is an aroma so delicious that it makes you want to take a bite out of the air. The third thing you notice, in front of the kitchen, is an electric signboard that flashes, say, "Today's Soups . . . Chicken Vegetable . . . Mexican Beef Chili . . . Cream of Watercress . . . Italian Sausage . . . Clam Bisque . . . Beef Barley . . . Due to Cold Weather . . . For Most Efficient and Fastest Service the Line Must . . . Be Kept Moving . . . Please . . . Have Your Money . . . Ready . . . Pick the Soup of Your Choice . . . Move to Your Extreme . . . Left After Ordering."

4 "I am not prejudiced against color or religion," Mr. Yeganeh told us, and he jabbed an index finger at the flashing sign. "Whoever follows that I treat very well. My regular customers don't say anything. They are very intelligent and well educated. They know I'm just trying to move the line. The New York cop is very smart—he sees everything

but says nothing. But the young girl who wants to stop and tell you how nice you look and hold everyone up—*yah!*" He made a guillotining motion with his hand. "I tell you, I hate to work with the public. They treat me like a slave. My philosophy is: The customer is always wrong and I'm always right. I raised my prices to try to get rid of some of these people, but it didn't work."

The other day, Mr. Yeganeh was dressed in chefs' whites with orange smears across his chest, which may have been some of the carrot soup cooking in a huge pot on a little stove in one corner. A three-foot-long handheld mixer from France sat on the sink, looking like an overgrown gardening tool. Mr. Yeganeh spoke to two young helpers in a twisted Armenian-Spanish barrage, then said to us, "I have no overhead, no trained waitresses, and I have the cashier here." He pointed to himself theatrically. Beside the doorway, a glass case with fresh green celery, red and yellow peppers, and purple eggplant was topped by five big gray soup urns. According to a piece of cardboard taped to the door, you can buy Mr. Yeganeh's soups in three sizes, costing from four to fifteen dollars. The order of any well-behaved customer is accompanied by little waxpaper packets of bread, fresh vegetables (such as scallions and radishes), fresh fruit (such as cherries or an orange), a chocolate mint, and a plastic spoon. No coffee, tea, or other drinks are served. 5

"I get my recipes from books and theories and my own taste," Mr. Yeganeh said. "At home, I have several hundreds of books. When I do research, I find that I don't know anything. Like cabbage is a cancer fighter, and some fish is good for your heart but some is bad. Every day, I should have one sweet, one spicy, one cream, one vegetable soup—and they *must* change, they should always taste a little different." He added that he wasn't sure how extensive his repertoire was, but that it probably includes at least eighty soups, among them African peanut butter, Greek moussaka, hamburger, Reuben, B.L.T., asparagus and caviar, Japanese shrimp miso, chicken chili, Irish corned beef and cabbage, Swiss chocolate, French calf's brain, Korean beef ball, Italian shrimp and eggplant Parmesan, buffalo, ham and egg, short rib, Russian beef Stroganoff, turkey cacciatore, and Indian mulligatawny. "The chicken and the seafood are an addiction, and when I have French garlic soup I let people have only one small container each," he said. "The doctors and nurses love that one." 6

A lunch line of thirty people stretched down the block from Mr. Yeganeh's doorway. Behind a construction worker was a man in expensive leather, who was in front of a woman in a fur hat. Few people spoke. Most had their money out and their orders ready. 7

At the front of the line, a woman in a brown coat couldn't decide which soup to get and started to complain about the prices. 8

"You talk too much, dear," Mr. Yeganeh said, and motioned to her to move to the left. "Next!" 9

"Just don't talk. Do what he says," a man huddled in a blue parka warned. 10

"He's downright rude," said a blond woman in a blue coat. "Even abusive. But you can't deny it, his soup is the best." 11

Connecting to Culture and Experience

A popular book recently urged American business executives to "search for excellence," claiming that profit will follow. Albert Yeganeh is a prime example of this philosophy.

Discuss with two or three other students your experiences with excellence as workers on the job and in school. How have your work values been shaped by the situations in which you have worked? On the job, for example, what kinds of attitudes encourage—or discourage—high-quality work? In school, what has inspired you to do your best work or prevented or discouraged you from doing it? Focus on specific examples of school and work experiences.

Analyzing Writing Strategies

1. At the beginning of this chapter, we make generalizations about **profile essays.** Consider which of these are true of the *New Yorker* essay and if so, in what ways.
   - Profile essays are based on a writer's newly acquired observations.
   - They take readers behind the scenes of familiar places or introduce them to unusual places and people.
   - They provide information while at the same time arousing readers' curiosity.
   - They present scenes and people vividly and concretely through description, action, and dialogue.
   - They reveal an attitude toward their subjects and offer—implicitly or explicitly—an interpretation of them.
   - They create a dominant impression of their subjects.
2. In addition to profiling a person, this essay shows us his place of business. Reread paragraphs 1, 3, and 5, underlining **details** that present the soup kitchen itself, inside and outside. For example, in paragraph 3 you would underline *awning* and also what is written on the awning: *"Homemade Hot, Cold, Diet Soups."* You need not worry about whether you are underlining too many or too few details. Try to catch every detail that expands your image of the place.

   Review the details you have underlined, and think about the **dominant impression** they create of the kitchen. Then, try to summarize the impression you get in two or three sentences.

For more on detailing, see pp. 494–95.

Considering Topics for Your Own Essay

List several unusual people or places on campus or in your community that you could profile. Which of these would be most interesting to you? Why? What seems special about your choice?

Commentary

"Soup" illustrates one solution to the problems writers face in **organizing** a profile. A writer may decide to impose order by grouping bits of information and sequencing them in some helpful way. This kind of organization is called *topical,* as distinct from chronological or narrative. (The next reading illustrates chronological organization.)

"Soup" is a good example of **topical organization.** The following scratch outline reveals the various topics and their sequence:

Introduction to Yeganeh and his soup kitchen (paragraph 1)

Yeganeh asserts his perfectionism (2)

An outside view of the soup kitchen (3)

Yeganeh expresses his attitude toward customers (4)

A view of Yeganeh at work inside the soup kitchen (5)

Rules of the house (5)

Yeganeh describes his soup-making repertoire (6)

A lineup of customers outside and inside and their interactions with Yeganeh (7–11)

This plan alternates interview segments with observations of the soup kitchen. There are three interview topics: perfectionism (paragraph 2), attitudes toward customers (4), and soup-making repertoire (6). Observational topics present the soup kitchen from three different vantage points: outside, approaching from a distance (3); inside the kitchen (5); and within the line of customers waiting to be served (7–11). Instead of organizing chronologically by telling a story of one visit to the soup kitchen, the writer reports topic by topic what was learned on several visits. The writer probably first grouped related topics and then came up with a sensible plan of alternating them, perhaps assuming that readers would remain more engaged if the relatively large blocks of quoted material alternated with descriptions of the soup kitchen. When you plan your profile essay, you will want to decide right away whether to organize your first draft topically or chronologically.

Profiles reflect a writer's personal preferences for what is worth learning and writing about. Even so, writers, like the writer of "Soup," sometimes try to remain invisible, adopting a "they" rather than an "I" **point of view.** There is no *I* in "Soup," only *us,* mentioned twice. This use of *us* in paragraphs 4 and 5 probably comes from the convention of the editorial *we* that some magazines and newspapers adopt, though the writer could have taken another writer along or perhaps just a friend, as is common among restaurant reviewers. As you read the remaining essays, notice whether the writer seems visible or invisible. Depending on your subject and your purpose, you can adopt either point of view in your own profile essay.

David Noonan, the freelance journalist who wrote the following selection, started with a surefire subject, guaranteed to intrigue readers: a team of brain surgeons as they perform a complicated operation. His profile provides a direct look at something very few of us are likely ever to see—the human brain. He had to handle this subject with some delicacy, however, to avoid making readers uncomfortable with overly explicit description or excessive technical terminology. Think about your own responses as you read this piece, which was published in *Esquire* in 1983. Are you uneasy with any of the graphic detail or overwhelmed by the terminology?

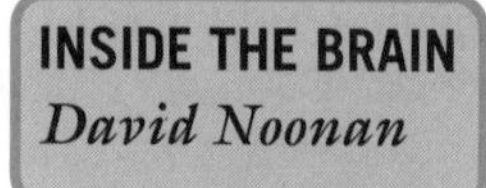

INSIDE THE BRAIN
David Noonan

1 The patient lies naked and unconscious in the center of the cool, tiled room. His head is shaved, his eyes and nose taped shut. His mouth bulges with the respirator that is breathing for him. Clear plastic tubes carry anesthetic into him and urine out of him. Belly up under the bright lights he looks large and helpless, exposed. He is not dreaming; he is too far under for that. The depth of his obliviousness is accentuated by the urgent activity going on all around him. Nurses and technicians move in and out

of the room preparing the instruments of surgery. At his head, two doctors are discussing the approach they will use in the operation. As they talk they trace possible incisions across his scalp with their fingers.

2 It is a Monday morning. Directed by Dr. Stein, Abe Steinberger is going after a large tumor compressing the brainstem, a case that he describes as "a textbook beauty." It is a rare operation, a suboccipital craniectomy, supracerebellar infratentorial approach. That is, into the back of the head and over the cerebellum, under the tentorium to the brainstem and the tumor. Stein has done the operation more than fifty times, more than any other surgeon in the United States.

3 Many neurosurgeons consider brainstem tumors of this type inoperable because of their location and treat them instead with radiation. "It's where you live," says Steinberger. Breathing, heartbeat, and consciousness itself are some of the functions connected with this primary part of the brain. Literally and figuratively, it is the core of the organ, and operating on it is always very risky. . . .

4 The human skull was not designed for easy opening. It takes drills and saws and simple force to breach it. It is a formidable container, and its thickness testifies to the value of its contents. Opening the skull is one of the first things apprentice brain surgeons get to do on their own. It is sometimes called cabinet work, and on this case Steinberger is being assisted in the opening by Bob Solomon.

5 The patient has been clamped into a sitting position. Before the first incision is made he is rolled under the raised instrument table and he disappears beneath sterile green drapes and towels. The only part of him left exposed is the back of his head, which is orange from the sterilizing agent painted on it. Using a special marker, Steinberger draws the pattern of the opening on the patient's head in blue. Then the first cut is made into the scalp, and a thin line of bright-red blood appears.

6 The operation takes place within what is called the sterile field, a small germfree zone created and vigilantly patrolled by the scrub nurses. The sterile field extends out and around from the surgical opening and up over the instrument table. Once robed and gloved, the doctors are considered sterile from the neck to the waist and from the hands up the arms to just below the shoulders. The time the doctors must spend scrubbing their hands has been cut from ten minutes to five, but this obsessive routine is still the most striking of the doctor's preparations. Leaning over the trough-like stainless-steel sink with their masks in place and their arms lathered to the elbow, the surgeons carefully attend to each finger with the brush and work their way up each arm. It is the final pause, the last thing they do before they enter the operating room and go to work. Many at NI are markedly quiet while they scrub; they spend the familiar minutes running through the operation one more time. When they finish and their hands are too clean for anything but surgery they turn off the water with knee controls and back through the OR door, their dripping hands held high before them. They dry off with sterile towels, step into long-sleeved robes, and then plunge their hands down into their thin surgical gloves, which are held for them by the scrub nurse. The gloves snap as the nurse releases them around the doctors' wrists. Unnaturally smooth and defined, the gloved hands of the neurosurgeons are now ready; they can touch the living human brain.

7 "Drill the hell out of it," Steinberger says to Solomon. The scalp has been retracted and the skull exposed. Solomon presses the large stainless-steel power drill against the bone and hits the trigger. The bit turns slowly, biting into the white skull. Shavings drop from the hole onto the drape and then to the floor. The drill stops automatically when it is through the bone. The hole is about a half inch in diameter. Solomon drills

four holes in a diamond pattern. The skull at the back of the head is ridged and bumpy. There is a faint odor of burning bone.

8 The drilling is graphic and jarring. The drill and the head do not go together; they collide and shock the eye. The tool is too big; its scale and shape are inappropriate to the delicate idea of neurosurgery. It should be hanging on the wall of a garage. After the power drill, a hand drill is used to refine the holes in the skull. It is a sterilized stainless-steel version of a handyman's tool. It is called a perforator, and as Solomon calmly turns it, more shavings hit the floor. Then, using powerful plierlike tools called Leksell rongeurs, the doctors proceed to bite away at the skull, snapping and crunching bone to turn the four small holes into a single opening about three inches in diameter. This is a *craniectomy;* the hole in the skull will always be there, protected by the many layers of scalp muscle at the back of the head. In a *craniotomy* a flap of bone is preserved to cover the opening in the skull.

9 After the scalp and the skull, the next layer protecting the brain is the dura. A thin, tough, leathery membrane that encases the brain, the dura (derived from the Latin for *hard*) is dark pink, almost red. It is rich with blood vessels and nerves (when you have a headache, it's the dura that aches), and now it can be seen stretching across the expanse of the opening, pulsing lightly. The outline of the cerebellum bulging against the dura is clear. With a crease in the middle, the dura-sheathed cerebellum looks oddly like a tiny pair of buttocks. The resemblance prompts a moment's joking. "Her firm young cerebellum," somebody says. . . .

10 The dura is carefully opened and sewn back out of the way. An hour and fifteen minutes after the drilling began, the brain is exposed.

11 The brain exposed. It happens every day on the tenth floor, three, four, and five times a day, day after day, week in and week out, month after month. The brain exposed. Light falls on its gleaming surface for the first time. It beats lightly, steadily. It is pink and gray, the brain, and the cerebellar cortex is covered with tiny blood vessels, in a web. In some openings you can see the curve of the brain, its roundness. It does not look strong, it looks very soft, soft enough to push your finger through. When you see it for the first time you almost expect sparks, tiny sparks arcing across the surface, blinking lights, the crackle of an idea. You stare down at it and it gives nothing back, reveals nothing, gives no hint of how it works. As soon as they see it the doctors begin the search for landmarks. They start talking to each other, describing what they both can see, narrating the anatomy.

12 In the operating room the eyes bear much of the burden of communication. With their surgical masks and caps in place, the doctors and nurses resort to exaggerated stares and squints and flying eyebrows to emphasize what they are saying. After more than two decades in the operating room, Dr. Stein has developed this talent for nonverbal punctuation to a fine art. His clear blue eyes narrow now in concentration as he listens to Abe explain what he wants to do next. They discuss how to go about retracting the cerebellum. "Okay, Abe," Stein says quietly. "Nice and easy now."

13 The cerebellum (the word means *little brain*) is one of the most complicated parts of the brain. It is involved in the processing of sensory information of all kinds as well as balance and motor control, but in this case it is simply in the way. With the dura gone the cerebellum bulges out of the back of the head; it can be seen from across the room, protruding into space, striated and strange-looking.

14 When the cerebellum is retracted, the microscope is rolled into place and the operation really begins. It is a two-man scope, with a cable running to a TV monitor and a

videotape machine. Sitting side by side, looking through the scope into the head, Steinberger and Stein go looking for the tumor.

15 It is a long and tedious process, working your way into the center of the human brain. The joke about the slip of the scalpel that wiped out fifteen years of piano lessons is no joke. Every seen and unseen piece of tissue does something, has some function, though it may well be a mystery to the surgeon. In order to spend hour after hour at the microscope, manipulating their instruments in an area no bigger than the inside of a juice can, neurosurgeons must develop an awesome capacity for sustained concentration.

16 After two hours of talking their way through the glowing red geography of the inner brain, Stein and Steinberger come upon the tumor. "Holy Toledo, look at that," exclaims Steinberger. The tumor stands out from the tissue around it, purple and mean-looking. It is the end of order in a very small, orderly place. It does not belong. They pause a moment, and Abe gives a quick tour of the opening. "That's tumor, that's the brainstem, and that's the third ventricle," he says. "And that over there, that's memory."

17 A doctor from the pathology department shows up for a piece of the tumor. It will be analyzed quickly while the operation is under way so the surgeons will know what they are dealing with. The type of tumor plays an important part in decisions about how much to take out, what risks to take in the attempt to get it all. A more detailed tissue analysis will be made later.

18 It turns out to be a brainstem glioma, an invasive intrinsic tumor actually growing up out of the brainstem. It is malignant. They get a lot of it but it will grow back. With radiation the patient could live fifteen years or even longer, and he will be told so. Abe Steinberger, in fact, will tell him. More than six hours after the first incision, the operation ends.

19 When the operation is over it is pointed out to Steinberger that he is the same age as the patient. "Really?" he says. "It's funny, I always think of the patients as being older than me."

20 How they think of the patients is at the center of the residents' approach to neurosurgery. It is a sensitive subject, and they have all given it a lot of thought. They know well the classic preconceived notion of the surgeon as a cold and arrogant technician. "You think like a surgeon" is a medical-school insult. Beyond that, the residents actually know a lot of surgeons, and though they say most of them don't fit the stereotype, they also say that there are some who really do bring it to life.

21 In many ways the mechanics of surgery itself create a distance between the surgeon and the patient. A man with a tumor is a case, a collection of symptoms. He is transformed into a series of X rays, CAT scans, and angiograms. He becomes his tumor, is even referred to by his affliction. "We've got a beautiful meningioma coming in tomorrow," a doctor will say. Once in the operating room the patient disappears beneath the drapes and is reduced to a small red hole. Though it is truly the ultimate intimacy, neurosurgery can be starkly impersonal.

22 "The goal of surgery is to get as busy as you can doing good cases and making people *better* by operating on them," says Phil Cogen. "That automatically cuts down the time you spend with patients." Though this frustrates Cogen, who has dreams and nightmares about his patients "all the time," he also knows there is a high emotional price to pay for getting too close. "One of the things you learn to do as a surgeon in any field is disassociate yourself from the person you're operating on. I never looked under

the drapes at the patient until my third year in neurosurgery, when it was too late to back out."

23 While Cogen prides himself on not having a "surgical personality," Abe Steinberger believes that his skills are best put to use in the operating room and doesn't worry too much about the problems of patient relations. "I sympathize with the patients," he says. "I feel very bad when they're sick and I feel great when they're better. But what I want to do is operate. I want to get in there and do it."

Connecting to Culture and Experience

At the end of "Inside the Brain," Noonan raises the issue of how surgeons cope with their own feelings as well as with those of their patients, an issue that has broader implications. "One of the things you learn to do as a surgeon in any field," Cogen says, "is disassociate yourself from the person you're operating on" (paragraph 22). Disassociating may be useful and sometimes even necessary, as this profile demonstrates. It is widely recognized, however, that it also has costs, both psychological and social. Psychologically, it denies feelings. It may become habitual, turning people into automatons. Socially, it leads practitioners to think of others as objects rather than people: "'We've got a beautiful meningioma coming in tomorrow,' a doctor will say." Disassociating yourself from others' emotions and your own may reflect a fear of feeling rather than serve as a practical strategy for dealing with feelings. There is no reason to believe, however, that people who can disassociate in certain situations, like the surgeons in this profile, are incapable of normal feelings in other situations.

Think of a time when you felt the need to put aside your feelings in order to get on with the task before you. For example, has there ever been a time in school, during a sporting activity, or at work when you had to cut off your feelings in order to get something important done? Were you conscious at the time of what you were doing? What were the advantages and disadvantages of disassociating yourself from your feelings?

Analyzing Writing Strategies

For a discussion of narration, see Chapter 14.

1. "Inside the Brain" is a good example of **chronological organization,** a profile plan that follows the stages of an activity unfolding in time. The operation actually lasts six hours, but Noonan does not tell us everything that happens. Instead, he selects certain events to create a chronology, or **narration.** To see how Noonan translates clock time into narrative time—with its special qualities of suspense and drama—and how he alternates narration with information, make a scratch outline of the essay. For convenience, identify the subject of each paragraph with a brief phrase identifying either the information presented or the stage in the unfolding operation. For example, paragraph 1 narrates (tells part of the story of the operation), paragraphs 2 through 4 primarily provide information, and the narrative picks up again in paragraph 5. The narrative ends with paragraph 19.

   Review your scratch outline, and consider each of the following questions: How many paragraphs are primarily narrative, with most of their sentences describing the scene in the operating room and detailing the operation, and how many primarily give information about the brain or brain surgery in general? Where do the informational paragraphs fall in the sequence of paragraphs? Among the narrative paragraphs, where does the suspense rise for you as a reader? Where do you think the climax—the most dramatic moment in the story—occurs? Finally, how successful do you think Noonan has been in striking a balance between engaging readers with a dramatic story and informing them about a complex subject?

2. Noonan quotes both Dr. Stein and Dr. Steinberger, letting us hear what they say during the operation (paragraphs 3, 7, 12, and 16). What do these **quotations** add to the essay? How might the essay have been different had Noonan paraphrased rather than quoted?

Considering Topics for Your Own Essay

If you were asked to profile a highly skilled specialist at work, what specialty would you choose? Who would you need to talk to, and how would you gain access? What kind of information would you need to gather? How might you go about getting it?

Commentary

Some profiles, like Noonan's, require that the writer **research** the subject in order to understand it well. Although most of Noonan's information obviously comes from observing and interviewing, he must also have done some reading to familiarize himself with surgical terminology and procedures. Noonan does not cite the sources for his information because he is not writing a formal research report but rather is telling a story about a specific brain surgery.

Just as important as the actual information a writer provides is the way he or she arranges and presents it. **Information** must be organized in a way appropriate to the audience as well as to the content itself. It must be readily accessible to readers. Readers are willing to learn from a profile, but they do not want to feel that they are reading an encyclopedia entry. Noonan inserts bits of information into the narrative, as in paragraph 8 when he tells us that a hand drill is used after the power drill and how a craniotomy differs from a craniectomy. Sometimes the information takes only a second to read and is subordinated in a clause or a brief sentence. At other times, it seems to suspend the narrative altogether, as when Noonan explains the idea of a sterile field and describes the scrubbing-up process in paragraph 6.

For a discussion of sentence definition strategies, see pp. 506–508.

Defining concisely and explaining clearly are essential to successful profiles. If you profile a technical or little-known specialty, you will need to define terms, tools, and procedures likely to be unfamiliar to your readers. However, the definitions and explanations must not divert readers' attention for too long from the details of a scene or the drama of an activity.

If you examine Noonan's **sentences** closely, you can learn much that will help you in your own profile writing. For example, he occasionally opens sentences with modifying phrases called participial phrases:

Using a special marker, Steinberger draws the pattern of the opening on the patient's head in blue. (paragraph 5)

Sitting side by side, looking through the scope into the head, Steinberger and Stein go looking for the tumor. (14)

Once robed and gloved, the doctors are considered sterile from the neck to the waist and from the hands up the arms to just below the shoulders. (6)

Directed by Dr. Stein, Abe Steinberger is going after a large tumor compressing the brainstem. . . . (2)

As sentence openers, participial phrases are efficient and readable. They reduce the number of separate sentences needed, provide pleasing variety in sentence patterns, and are easy for readers to follow.

Catherine S. Manegold is a staff writer for the *New York Times.* She was formerly Southeast Asia bureau chief for the *Philadelphia Inquirer* and general foreign desk editor at *Newsweek.* Her reporting has been nominated for the Pulitzer prize four times, and she won the Overseas Press Award for her coverage of the 1991 Gulf War. This profile appeared in a 1993 *Times* series, "The Children of the Shadows," focusing on the struggle of poor urban children and teenagers.

SCHOOL SERVES NO PURPOSE

Catherine S. Manegold

Crystal Rossi wears two streaks of bright magenta in her hair. They hang, stains of Kool-Aid, down her loose, long strands of blonde like a seventh grader's twist of punk: Don't come too close. Don't mess with me. Don't tell me what to do. I'm not like you. 1

At her Brooklyn public school, a kaleidoscope of teen-age rage, Crystal's teachers see a young girl with an attitude. They focus on her slouch, her Kool-Aid streaks, her grunge clothes and sullen anger and see all the signs of trouble. But those vivid slashes say the most, communicating a basic paradox of adolescence, the double-edged message: "bug off" and "LOOK AT ME." 2

This is the time, this tender age of 12, when every major decision on the treacherous road to adulthood looms. It is also the time, in the sixth and seventh grades, when some students start a long, slow fall away from school. 3

On the surface, Crystal hardly seems the sort of child who would stumble. 4

Her family is stable. Her stepfather works. Her mother takes care of the home. Her father lives just blocks away. Her school is typical, chaotic, underfinanced and overcrowded, but it is clean and relatively safe. 5

But in a competition between the street and schoolyard, the street seems to be winning. 6

"The classes are boring!" Crystal exploded one afternoon. "And the teachers are mean!" Her eyes downcast, she complained that too much class time was spent on discipline. "They are always yelling," she said. "I wish they would all just shut up." 7

Her face to the world is one of toughness. But in fact she is a child trying to navigate a difficult and often lonely road. In a whisper one day, her head cast down and fingers playing across a desk top, she admitted that she was often nervous. 8

"Sometimes I can't even sleep," she said. "I stay up all night, and then I'm too tired to get up in the morning." 9

She rarely allows herself to express such vulnerability. Instead, she tends toward bravado; in a rare moment of exuberance she tells her mother that she is a "leader" 10 who sets the pace in school. Her mother does not buy it. "No," her mother says as she shakes her head. "You are a follower."

11 Such deflations are consistent. What is absent is a quiet, steady voice of encouragement, a single figure to lead Crystal through the minefields of a childhood in Bensonhurst. Pressures abound, applied by teachers, parents and even friends, but Crystal seems without a touchstone to guide her and give her a sense of her potential.

12 At home, three other daughters occupy her mother's time and worry. Crystal's sister, Colette, 15, is failing the ninth grade. Her halfsisters, Candice, 5, and Jovan, 2, demand attention and dominate family life, especially when their dad comes home and lifts them in a warm embrace. Crystal, lonely and lackluster, hides in plain sight.

13 Crystal says she wants to be a lawyer. But she has never actually met a lawyer and is now flunking most of her classes. That career appeals because, she says, "you get to talk back to people" and "you make a lot of money."

14 Her teachers worry that she might not even make it to her high school graduation. They already see the signs. In class she ducks competition and is losing focus. Outside of school hers is a childhood of temptations and dangers: drugs, alcohol, gangs and older kids who linger on street corners wanting everything from sex to the coat off a 12-year-old's back.

15 There was a fleeting moment when Crystal's academic future seemed full of promise. Her 34-year-old mother, Colleen Ficalora, said Crystal was once slated for a kindergarten for gifted students, "but she would have had to take a bus." Now, in the seventh grade at the Joseph B. Cavallaro Junior High School in Bensonhurst, Crystal is often restless, angry and tuned out.

16 Mrs. Ficalora wants Crystal to break a family pattern. Not one of her own 14 brothers and sisters graduated from high school. Neither did she. Nor did Crystal's father or stepfather. If Crystal gets her diploma she will stand apart.

17 At school, some teachers are trying to help. But sitting in one class, a "resource room" tailored to give troubled students individual attention, Crystal slumped on her desk. "We just sit there," she said later. "They are supposed to help you with stuff you don't understand. But I understand everything so I just sit there."

18 "Kids who study are all nerds," she said dismissively. "Who'd want to be like that? Everybody makes fun of them."

19 But the kids make fun of one another for failing, too.

20 "Stooopid," Crystal taunted a friend in the resource room one morning.

21 "No, you're stupid, stupid," the girl retorted.

22 "No. You. You're stupid," Crystal shot back, her head resting on her desk top.

23 Most days, Crystal says, she is usually happy only at lunch, when she and her friends bend over pizza and sandwiches "just talking." The time brings them together, jostling and punching and trading stories of their day. Sometimes they vanish into a bathroom and plant thick lipstick kisses—perfect O's—on one another's foreheads. Their mark of solidarity against a world too often hostile.

24 Of the 950 or so students at Cavallaro Junior High School on any given day, says Rose P. Molinelli, the principal, 300 or more are at risk of everything from dropping out to doping up to slashing their wrists and watching their lives literally drain right out of them. One of the school's seventh-grade classes last year had five suicide attempts. This year has been quieter, but the threats remain.

25 "You can walk out this door any afternoon and get hurt," Mrs. Molinelli said as she stooped on a busy stairwell to scoop up a bit of litter. Other pressures are subtler.

"The kids all know who is abused and who is having trouble at home and who is in a gang," Mrs. Molinelli said. "They know who gets high. They know who gets killed. It gets to them. I think all kids today are at risk. And parents are overwhelmed. A lot of kids get lost." 26

Crystal glides through the environment as though untouched. When a fight breaks out in the hall, she slips around the corner. But privately, she whispers about the gangs, the kids who have been robbed or hurt or are threatened by bullies, and of friends with "troubles" at home. 27

"I know a kid who just got shot," she said starkly. "He got shot and he is dead." 28

Classes run at or near their maximum of 30 children each, and teachers have to struggle just to keep order, much less provide individual attention. Budget cuts have whittled resources, and although Mrs. Molinelli says her teachers have come up with creative ways to compensate for the shortages, she knows the children could use more. 29

"We're on the edge," she said. "We're already on the edge and now they are talking about more funding cuts. Right now, we've only got one guidance counselor for 700 students. That's not enough." 30

Crystal's schedule includes one-on-one tutoring in a "rap class" where Cathy Searao, a school drug counselor, spends time talking with troubled students partly as a mentor and partly as a friend. Shrugging, embarrassed and monosyllabic, Crystal says she likes the program because there "the teacher really talks to you." One afternoon Ms. Searao taught Crystal and a friend how to develop film. It was the one moment in her school day when Crystal smiled. She shyly admits that she also enjoys science and a dance program she goes to after school. 31

Mrs. Molinelli would like to see more individualized programs in the school. But in the meantime, she fights cutbacks. 32

Crystal's mother wants more from the public school as well. "I feel like I try my hardest," she said, "but I still need someone there education-wise who can back me up." 33

In science, as a substitute teacher tried to teach the difference between fact and opinion, Crystal spent her time, lipstick in one hand, a mirror in the other, tracing streaks of red along her lips. 34

The toll of her inattention is already becoming all too clear. In the first semester, Crystal passed every major class but science. But as the school year progressed, she started drifting. In September Crystal made her way to class on time on every day but one. In January she was late 12 days out of 20. 35

Her mother says it is a constant battle just to get Crystal up and out. As she and her husband begin the day, the tone is set. 36

"I start trying to wake her up at 7 A.M.," Mrs. Ficalora said. "By 7:30, I am really screaming." 37

Crystal's February report card included a 65 in social studies. She failed English, math, science, foreign language and physical education. "We have already sent the family an 'at risk' letter," said Diane Costaglioli, the assistant principal in charge of the seventh grade. "She's on a decline." 38

At home, her mother tells her to do her homework but rarely checks, and her stepfather, Louie Ficalora, an electrician at ABC, rarely asks about it. But together they provide a raft of high-tech toys that keep Crystal occupied but unmotivated. 39

The basement room she shares with Colette has all the comforts—and distractions—of a fully equipped apartment. "Sometimes my mom punishes me by making me go to my room," Crystal said. "But that's O.K. We've got a television, a VCR, 40

Nintendo, a radio, books, magazines, our own phone line, and a bunch of other stuff down there."

41 Upstairs, there are distractions, too. The television comes on just after Crystal gets home at 3. It stays on well into the night.

42 Mrs. Ficalora complains that the family is not brought in to the school's daily rhythms. "We don't even have to see the homework," she said. "So we don't know what they're dealing with."

43 Somehow, though, there has been a breakdown in communication. Last fall, Crystal's school gave each student a homework planner that encouraged parents to be involved in each day's assignment. Crystal says she lost hers, and her mother concedes that although she at times helps with homework, she usually is involved only at report-card time.

44 For Crystal, though, homework can seem almost quaint in a life that whirls through a landscape full of real and perceived dangers. Outside school, her world stretches from glass-strewn lots where friends drink and smash bottles against brick walls to street corners where gang members pick fights. Her friends are an ethnic stew of Italian-Americans, Puerto Ricans, blacks, and immigrants—a multiracial bond that in coming years may well be tested.

45 So far, though, they face their fears together. Temptations and highs lurk everywhere. Though Crystal says she has not yet tried marijuana, LSD or crack, she talks about such drugs the way children used to talk of trolls and ice-cream cones. Like most of her friends, she has already sampled alcohol and cigarettes. Other temptations await. "Everybody drinks," she said with a knowing shrug. "They drink and do acid in the park."

46 Crystal knows the varied routes to dropping out. But they do not scare her. "They hang out," she said of the students who leave school. "They do weed. They drink. They do acid. Everybody knows what they are doing."

47 Sex looms, too. So far, boys don't seem to be her problem. Her mother prohibits her from dating. But Crystal points out coolly, "When I'm out there you don't know where I am." Crystal's mother assumes that her 12-year-old can take care of herself. "I let her know that she has an independence," she said.

48 Yet just surviving is a constant struggle. Teachers, the police and parents say they are often stunned by the casualness of the violence both inside and outside school. Hallways are full of a steady stream of students who sniffle that a friend has hit or kicked them. Students are called from class for fighting. Friends poke, trip and slap.

49 On the streets, fights start over nothing. Many boys link up with gangs. Crystal lists their names, neighborhood by neighborhood, including two for girls, Bitches on a Mission and the Five Million Hoodlums, to which some of her friends belong. "They can protect you," Crystal said somewhat admiringly. "They can keep you safe."

50 But it is toward her sister, Colette, that Crystal most often turns for protection. "She watches out for me," she said. "If somebody bothers me, she sends people after them."

51 Colette may be failing, but she has another quality that Crystal values far more than grades. She is the one older person who always listens—and never punishes.

52 Still, anxiety pervades. "I'm always nervous," she said quietly one day at school, her head cast down, her hands clasped tightly between her legs. "I get nervous over nothing. And then I'll get a really big headache."

53 One moment of ease comes in the minutes between school and life after school. When the last bell rings, Crystal and her friends linger outside the building to remind one another that they care. Linking arms and passing gum and cigarettes around, they laugh and poke and share their secrets, their fears, their triumphs. Then they reach forward, one to the next, to kiss, almost somberly, and wish one another well.

Connecting to Culture and Experience

In paragraph 11, Manegold reflects on Crystal's plight: "What is absent is a quiet, steady voice of encouragement, a single figure to lead Crystal through the minefields of a childhood in Bensonhurst. . . . Crystal seems without a touchstone to guide her and give her a sense of her potential."

With two or three other students, discuss your late elementary and junior high school years. Was there someone in your life who provided the kind of guidance Manegold believes Crystal is missing? If someone did serve as a guide for you, what did this person contribute to your "sense of potential"? What social conditions make it possible for a person to help a youngster in this way—resources of time, money, knowledge, materials, technology, and so forth? What is there about Crystal's social world that prevents her from having this sort of help?

Analyzing Writing Strategies

For more on these descriptive and narrative strategies, see Chapters 14 and 15.

1. Manegold relies on **diverse strategies** to present Crystal to readers. These are the principal strategies:
   - Detailing her visually (paragraphs 1, 2, 34)
   - Devising similes and metaphors (1, 8, 11)
   - Reporting what Crystal says (7, 9, 13, 17, 18, 28, 40, 45–47, 49, 50, 52)
   - Narrating her interactions with others (10, 20–22, 31, 34, 47, 53)

   Closely examine each strategy separately in order to determine what it discloses about Crystal. Then, consider how each strategy contributes to the **dominant impression** you have of Crystal.
2. Manegold might have organized her profile around a single, typical day in Crystal's life, following her from early morning when she awakes to the end of the day when the television is finally turned off. Noonan ("Inside the Brain") uses this narrative pattern of organization by following one operation from beginning to end, even though he collected his information during several visits, interviews, and trips to the library to read about brain surgery. Instead, like the author of "Soup," Manegold chooses to employ a **topical organization** that reveals various aspects of Crystal's life at home and at school. Imagine how the information in the profile could have been put together as a typical day in Crystal's life. Given Manegold's purpose, why do you think she chose a topical over a narrative organization?

Considering Topics for Your Own Essay

Consider profiling a child or an early adolescent who has overcome physical, emotional, or socioeconomic problems or achieved something notable by your community's standards. You might also consider profiling a talented child or early adolescent engaged in a sport; a musical, drama, or dance group; a creative writing or journalism project; a budding entrepreneurial enterprise; or volunteer work of some kind. You would need to observe the person in a variety of social interactions in order to account for the contributions others make to the person's achievement. You may want to profile a person you know slightly, perhaps a child in a family you are acquainted with. Because this essay is not about a remembered person, you should probably not choose a member of your immediate family: Profiles rely on fresh observations of someone who is something of a mystery to the writer.

Commentary

A profile is a special kind of research project. Profiles always involve **visits:** meeting with a person or going to a place. Profile writers take notes from **observations** and **interviews** and may pick up reading materials at a place they are profiling. They may even need to conduct library research to gather information about the history and specialized aspects of a place or an activity. Although Manegold seems not to have done any library research, she clearly visited the school several times to follow Crystal around and to talk with her in different school settings. She interviewed several administrators and teachers. She also visited Crystal's home and spoke with her mother. We can easily imagine her arranging visits to the school and home, scheduling enough time on each visit to observe Crystal in different situations during and after school, taking notes as she watched and listened. After each visit, she must have reviewed her notes, adding details and impressions of what she had seen. These notes would have led her to think about what she wanted to discover on her next visit.

Manegold's research seems closer to that of the anonymous *New Yorker* author of "Soup" than to David Noonan's research for "Inside the Brain." Relying entirely on observations and interviews, the *New Yorker* writer includes extended quotations from Mr. Yeganeh and likely used a tape recorder, in addition to a notebook and pencil. By contrast, Noonan, though he includes much observational and interview material, relies to a noticeable extent on library research, where he picked up technical information about brain surgery. Manegold's research project is different from the other two in one important way: Whereas the other profiles focus on a single small location, hers ranges widely across a number of different scenes at the school and in the neighborhood and encompasses Crystal's interactions with a variety of individuals and groups.

Like the author of "Soup," Manegold offers few direct **judgments** or **conclusions.** Instead, she presents Crystal's life from several perspectives. Letting people speak for themselves permits us to make our own inferences about them, although Manegold subtly guides our judgments by her language and by the information she decided to use from her many pages of notes. Still, she leaves much for us to fill in. This filling in occurs in all our reading, as we combine what the text offers with our own memories and knowledge of the world. Not all profile writers leave us to make so many judgments and inferences. Brian Cable, in the next essay, does more to guide our judgments.

Brian Cable wrote the following selection when he was a first-year college student. Cable's profile of a mortuary combines both seriousness and humor. He lets readers know his feelings as he presents information about the mortuary and the people working there. Notice in particular the way Cable uses his visit to the mortuary as an occasion to reflect on death.

THE LAST STOP
Brian Cable

Let us endeavor so to live that when we come to die even the undertaker will be sorry.

—Mark Twain

1 Death is a subject largely ignored by the living. We don't discuss it much, not as children (when Grandpa dies, he is said to be "going away"), not as adults, not even as senior citizens. Throughout our lives, death remains intensely

private. The death of a loved one can be very painful, partly because of the sense of loss, but also because someone else's mortality reminds us all too vividly of our own.

2 Thus did I notice more than a few people avert their eyes as they walked past the dusty-pink building that houses the Goodbody Mortuaries. It looked a bit like a church—tall, with gothic arches and stained glass—and somewhat like an apartment complex—low, with many windows stamped out of red brick.

3 It wasn't at all what I had expected. I thought it would be more like Forest Lawn, serene with lush green lawns and meticulously groomed gardens, a place set apart from the hustle of day-to-day life. Here instead was an odd pink structure set in the middle of a business district. On top of the Goodbody Mortuaries sign was a large electric clock. What the hell, I thought, mortuaries are concerned with time too.

4 I was apprehensive as I climbed the stone steps to the entrance. I feared rejection or, worse, an invitation to come and stay. The door was massive, yet it swung open easily on well-oiled hinges. "Come in," said the sign. "We're always open." Inside was a cool and quiet reception room. Curtains were drawn against the outside glare, cutting the light down to a soft glow.

5 I found the funeral director in the main lobby, adjacent to the reception room. Like most people, I had preconceptions about what an undertaker looked like. Mr. Deaver fulfilled my expectations entirely. Tall and thin, he even had beady eyes and a bony face. A low, slanted forehead gave way to a beaked nose. His skin, scrubbed of all color, contrasted sharply with his jet black hair. He was wearing a starched white shirt, gray pants, and black shoes. Indeed, he looked like death on two legs.

6 He proved an amiable sort, however, and was easy to talk to. As funeral director, Mr. Deaver ("call me Howard") was responsible for a wide range of services. Goodbody Mortuaries, upon notification of someone's death, will remove the remains from the hospital or home. They then prepare the body for viewing, whereupon features distorted by illness or accident are restored to their natural condition. The body is embalmed and then placed in a casket selected by the family of the deceased. Services are held in one of three chapels at the mortuary, and afterward the casket is placed in a "visitation room," where family and friends can pay their last respects. Goodbody also makes arrangements for the purchase of a burial site and transports the body there for burial.

7 All this information Howard related in a well-practiced, professional manner. It was obvious he was used to explaining the specifics of his profession. We sat alone in the lobby. His desk was bone clean, no pencils or paper, nothing—just a telephone. He did all his paperwork at home; as it turned out, he and his wife lived right upstairs. The phone rang. As he listened, he bit his lips and squeezed his Adam's apple somewhat nervously.

8 "I think we'll be able to get him in by Friday. No, no, the family wants him cremated."

9 His tone was that of a broker conferring on the Dow Jones. Directly behind him was a sign announcing "Visa and Master Charge Welcome Here." It was tacked to the wall, right next to a crucifix.

10 "Some people have the idea that we are bereavement specialists, that we can handle the emotional problems which follow a death: Only a trained therapist can do that. We provide services for the dead, not counseling for the living."

11 Physical comfort was the one thing they did provide for the living. The lobby was modestly but comfortably furnished. There were several couches, in colors ranging from earth brown to pastel blue, and a coffee table in front of each one. On one table lay

some magazines and a vase of flowers. Another supported an aquarium. Paintings of pastoral scenes hung on every wall. The lobby looked more or less like that of an old hotel. Nothing seemed to match, but it had a homey, lived-in look.

"The last time the Goodbodies decorated was in '59, I believe. It still makes people feel welcome." 12

And so "Goodbody" was not a name made up to attract customers but the owner's family name. The Goodbody family started the business way back in 1915. Today, they do over five hundred services a year. 13

"We're in *Ripley's Believe It or Not,* along with another funeral home whose owners' names are Baggit and Sackit," Howard told me, without cracking a smile. 14

I followed him through an arched doorway into a chapel that smelled musty and old. The only illumination came from sunlight filtered through a stained glass ceiling. Ahead of us lay a casket. I could see that it contained a man dressed in a black suit. Wooden benches ran on either side of an aisle that led to the body. I got no closer. From the red roses across the dead man's chest, it was apparent that services had already been held. 15

"It was a large service," remarked Howard. "Look at that casket—a beautiful work of craftsmanship." 16

I guess it was. Death may be the great leveler, but one's coffin quickly reestablishes one's status. 17

We passed into a bright, fluorescent-lit "display room." Inside were thirty coffins, lids open, patiently awaiting inspection. Like new cars on the showroom floor, they gleamed with high-gloss finishes. 18

"We have models for every price range." 19

Indeed, there was a wide variety. They came in all colors and various materials. Some were little more than cloth-covered cardboard boxes, others were made of wood, and a few were made of steel, copper, or bronze. Prices started at $400 and averaged about $1,800. Howard motioned toward the center of the room: "The top of the line." 20

This was a solid bronze casket, its seams electronically welded to resist corrosion. Moisture-proof and air-tight, it could be hermetically sealed off from all outside elements. Its handles were plated with 14-karat gold. The price: a cool $5,000. 21

A proper funeral remains a measure of respect for the deceased. But it is expensive. In the United States the amount spent annually on funerals is about $2 billion. Among ceremonial expenditures, funerals are second only to weddings. As a result, practices are changing. Howard has been in this business for forty years. He remembers a time when everyone was buried. Nowadays, with burials costing $2,000 a shot, people often opt instead for cremation—as Howard put it, "a cheap, quick, and easy means of disposal." In some areas of the country, the cremation rate is now over 60 percent. Observing this trend, one might wonder whether burials are becoming obsolete. Do burials serve an important role in society? 22

For Tim, Goodbody's licensed mortician, the answer is very definitely yes. Burials will remain in common practice, according to the slender embalmer with the disarming smile, because they allow family and friends to view the deceased. Painful as it may be, such an experience brings home the finality of death. "Something deep within us demands a confrontation with death," Tim explained. "A last look assures us that the person we loved is, indeed, gone forever." 23

Apparently, we also need to be assured that the body will be laid to rest in comfort and peace. The average casket, with its inner-spring mattress and pleated satin lining, is surprisingly roomy and luxurious. Perhaps such an air of comfort makes it 24 easier for the family to give up their loved one. In addition, the burial site fixes the deceased in the survivors' memory, like a new address. Cremation provides none of these comforts.

Tim started out as a clerk in a funeral home but then studied to become a mortician. "It was a profession I could live with," he told me with a sly grin. Mortuary science might be described as a cross between pre-med and cosmetology, with courses in anatomy and embalming as well as in restorative art. 25

Tim let me see the preparation, or embalming, room, a white-walled chamber about the size of an operating room. Against the wall was a large sink with elbow taps and a draining board. In the center of the room stood a table with equipment for preparing the arterial embalming fluid, which consists primarily of formaldehyde, a preservative, and phenol, a disinfectant. This mixture sanitizes and also gives better color to the skin. Facial features can then be "set" to achieve a restful expression. Missing eyes, ears, and even noses can be replaced. 26

I asked Tim if his job ever depressed him. He bridled at the question: "No, it doesn't depress me at all. I do what I can for people and take satisfaction in enabling relatives to see their loved ones as they were in life." He said that he felt people were becoming more aware of the public service his profession provides. Grade-school classes now visit funeral homes as often as they do police stations and museums. The mortician is no longer regarded as a minister of death. 27

Before leaving, I wanted to see a body up close. I thought I could be indifferent after all I had seen and heard, but I wasn't sure. Cautiously, I reached out and touched the skin. It felt cold and firm, not unlike clay. As I walked out, I felt glad to have satisfied my curiosity about dead bodies, but all too happy to let someone else handle them. 28

Connecting to Culture and Experience

"Death," Cable announces in the opening sentence, "is a subject largely ignored by the living. We don't discuss it much, not as children (when Grandpa dies, he is said to be 'going away'), not as adults, not even as senior citizens." Yet when a family member dies, every family is forced to confront death not only spiritually or philosophically but also practically. Tim, the mortician, would argue that the spiritual and the practical are inseparable, though he is a specialist in the practical aspects of death, removing the body, showing caskets, embalming the body, arranging for burial, and so on.

Discuss with other students the various ways your families and friends arrange the practical aspects of death, including the funeral service itself. Think of the most recent funeral you attended. The following questions may help you to recall some of the details: Was there a formal service? If so, did it take place in a house of worship, a funeral home, a private home, a cemetery, or some other place? Was the body cremated or buried? Who was present? Did people dress formally or informally? Who spoke? What kind of music was played? Did some or all of those attending the funeral gather somewhere else before or afterward?

Finally, speculate about the relation between the practical aspects of the service and your beliefs about death. In what ways did the funeral meet or fail to meet your expectations? What did the service accomplish for you personally? In what ways did the service reflect or fulfill your beliefs or fail to do so?

Analyzing Writing Strategies

1. How does the opening quotation from Mark Twain shape your expectations as a reader? Compare Cable's opening (the quotation and paragraphs 1 and 2) to the openings of the three previous profiles. What can you conclude about the **opening strategies** of these profile writers? Given each writer's subject, materials, and purpose, which opening do you find most effective, and why?
2. During his visit to the mortuary, Cable focuses on three rooms, the lobby (paragraphs 7 and 11), the chapel where funeral services are conducted (15), and the casket display room (18–21). Reread Cable's **descriptions** of these three rooms, and underline details that together convey an impression of each room. Then, explain the impression you get of each room, pointing to specific details to support your explanation. Finally, speculate about the meanings of each room. What does Cable gain by contrasting them so sharply? Together, how do they convey a **dominant impression** of the mortuary and help you understand Cable's attitude toward the place?

For more on describing and creating a dominant impression, see pp. 491–92.

3. We present Cable's interview notes and the preliminary report he prepared from them on pp. 147–52. Read them now. Then, ask yourself how Cable integrated **quotations** from the interviews and descriptive details from his observations into his essay. What do the quotations he chose reveal about his impression of Howard and Tim? What do the descriptive details he uses tell you about the effect the mortuary had on him? How do the quotations and descriptive details shape your reaction to the essay?

Considering Topics for Your Own Essay

Think of a place or an activity about which you have strong preconceptions, and imagine writing a profile about it. What would you choose to tell about? How might you use your preconceptions to capture readers' attention?

Commentary

Cable puts himself inside the scene that he profiles. We accompany him on his tour of the mortuary, listen in on the interviews with Deaver and Tim, and are made privy to his reflections—the feelings and thoughts he has about what he is seeing and hearing. In each of the other profiles in this chapter, the writer remains outside the scene, a more or less disembodied eye through which we see the people and places.

Whereas the first-person **point of view,** with its telltale *I,* is rare or nonexistent in the other profiles, it is an essential part of Cable's rhetorical strategy. Similarly, he shares his preconceptions to establish common ground with his readers, contrasting these preconceptions with the discoveries he makes during his visits to the mortuary.

Though his subject matter is serious, Cable takes a lighthearted approach, injecting humor occasionally, but not at the expense of Deaver or Tim or their work. He reports Deaver's deadpan joke about famous names of mortuaries. He points out that Deaver's desk is "bone clean." He compares the coffins to "new cars on the showroom floor . . . with high-gloss finishes" and tells us that Deaver refers to the most expensive model as "the top of the line." Tim, the mortician, says, "It was a profession I could live with." Clearly, Deaver and Tim are not deadly serious about their work, and Cable seems to have adopted their attitude for his profile. By contrast, the tone of Catherine Manegold's profile of Crystal Rossi is persistently serious, no doubt because of Crystal's difficulties and gloomy prospects. In your own essay, your **attitude** and **tone** will be determined by the nature of your subject, the discoveries you make about it, your preconceptions of it, and your readers' expectations about an engaging, informative presentation of a subject like yours.

PURPOSE AND AUDIENCE

A profile writer's primary purpose is to inform readers. Readers expect profiles to present information in an engaging way, however. Whether profiling people (a soup kitchen owner, a junior high school student), places (a mortuary), or activities (brain surgery), the writer must meet these expectations. Although a reader might learn as much about brain surgery from an encyclopedia entry as from Noonan's profile, reading the profile is sure to be more enjoyable.

Readers of profiles expect to be surprised by unusual subjects. If the subject is familiar, they expect it to be presented from an unusual perspective. When writing a profile, you will have an immediate advantage if your subject is a place, an activity, or a person that is likely to surprise and intrigue your readers. For example, the writer of "Soup" has the double advantage of both a colorful person and an unusual place. Even if your subject is very familiar, however, you can still engage your readers by presenting it in a way they had never before considered.

A profile writer has one further concern: to be sensitive to readers' knowledge of a subject. Since readers must imagine the subject profiled and understand the new information offered about it, the writer must carefully assess what readers are likely to have seen and to know. For a profile of a brain operation, the decisions of a writer whose readers have little medical expertise will be different from those of a writer whose readers are primarily doctors and nurses. Given Noonan's attention to detail, he is clearly writing for a general audience that has never before seen a high-tech operating room.

Profile writers must also consider whether readers are familiar with the terminology they want to use. Because profiles involve information, they inevitably require definitions and illustrations. For example, Noonan carefully defines many terms: *craniectomy, craniotomy, dura, cerebellum*. However, he does not bother to define other technical terms like *angiogram* and *meningioma*. Since profile writers are not writing technical manuals or textbooks, they can choose to define only terms that readers need to know to follow what is going on. Some concepts or activities will require extended illustrations, as when Noonan describes in detail what is involved in "opening the brain" or scrubbing up before entering the operating room.

SUMMARY OF BASIC FEATURES

An Intriguing, Well-Focused Subject

The **subject** of a profile is typically a specific **person, place,** or **activity.** In this chapter, the *New Yorker* writer shows us Albert Yeganeh, soup cook extraordinaire; Manegold shows us Crystal Rossi, a twelve-year-old struggling at school; Brian Cable describes a particular place, the Goodbody Mortuary; and David Noonan presents an activity, brain surgery. Although they focus on a person, a place, or an activity, all of these profiles contain all three elements: certain people performing a certain activity at a particular place.

Skilled profile writers make even the most mundane subjects interesting by presenting them in a new light. They may simply take a close look at a subject usually taken for granted, as Cable does when he examines a mortuary. Or they may surprise readers with a subject they had never thought of, as the *New Yorker* writer does in portraying a fanatical soup cook. Whatever they examine, they bring attention to the uniqueness of the subject, showing what is remarkable about it.

A Vivid Presentation

Profiles particularize their subjects—one junior high school student's life, a surgical operation, an opinionated soup chef, the Goodbody Mortuary—rather than generalize about them. Because profile writers are interested more in presenting individual cases than in making generalizations, they present their subjects vividly and in detail.

Successful profile writers master the writing strategies of **description,** often using **sensory imagery** and **figurative language.** The profiles in this chapter, for example, evoke the senses of **sight** (a "dusty-pink building" that "looked a bit like a church—tall, with gothic arches and stained glass—and somewhat like an apartment complex—low, with many windows stamped out of red brick"), **touch** ("a thin, tough, leathery membrane"), **smell** ("a faint odor of burning bone"), and **hearing** ("snapping and crunching bone"). **Similes** ("handheld mixer . . . looking like an overgrown gardening tool") and **metaphors** ("kaleidoscope of teen-age rage") also abound.

Profile writers often describe people in graphic detail ("The patient lies naked and unconscious in the center of the cool, tiled room. His head is shaved, his eyes and nose taped shut. His mouth bulges with the respirator that is breathing for him"). They reveal personal habits and characteristic poses ("As he listened, he bit his lips and squeezed his Adam's apple somewhat nervously"). They also use **dialogue** to reveal character: "He spread his arms and added, 'This place is the only one like it in . . . in . . . the whole earth! One day, I hope to learn something from the other places, but so far I haven't.'"

A Dominant Impression

Readers expect profile writers to convey a particular impression or interpretation of the subject. They want to know the writer's insights into the subject after having spent time observing the scene and talking to people. Indeed, this interpretation is what separates profiles from mere exercises in description and narration.

continued

continued

To convey a **dominant impression,** writers carefully select details of scene and people and put these details together in a particular way. They also express an **attitude** toward the subject, an attitude that can be implied through details or stated explicitly. For example, a writer may express admiration, concern, detachment, fascination, skepticism, amusement—perhaps even two or three different feelings that complement or contradict one another. The *New Yorker* writer expresses admiration for Mr. Yeganeh. Manegold expresses concern for Crystal Rossi.

Writers also offer **interpretations** of their subjects. An interpretation may be implied or stated directly. It can be announced at the beginning, woven into the ongoing observations, or presented as a conclusion. Noonan, for instance, points out a somewhat startling discrepancy between the impersonality of neurosurgery and the extraordinary intimacy of such an operation. The *New Yorker* writer implies a contrast between Yeganeh's attitude toward his customers and the way customers are supposed to be treated. Cable shares his personal realization that Americans seem to capitalize on death almost as a way of coping with it. Manegold invites us to make inferences about what will happen to Crystal and who is responsible for her plight. In combination with carefully orchestrated details and a clearly expressed attitude, these interpretations give readers a dominant impression of the subject being profiled. The effort to create a dominant impression guides all the writer's decisions about how to select materials and how to organize and present them.

An Engaging and Informative Plan

Successful profile writers know that if they are to keep their readers' attention, they must engage as well as inform. For this reason, they tell their stories dramatically and describe people and places vividly. They also **control the flow of unfamiliar information** carefully. Whether the overall plan is topical or chronological, writers give much thought to where unfamiliar information is introduced and how it is introduced.

Profiles present a great deal of factual detail about their subject. Noonan tells us about the brain's parts (dura, cerebellum, brainstem), about surgical procedures (preparation of the patient, the difference between craniectomy and craniotomy), and about the attitudes of surgeons toward brain surgery. But this information is woven into the essay in bits and pieces—conveyed in dialogue, interspersed throughout the narrative, given in description—rather than presented in one large chunk.

Parceling out information in this way makes it easier to comprehend: Readers can master one part of the information before going on to the next. Perhaps even more important, such control injects a degree of surprise and thus makes readers curious to know what will come next. Controlling the information flow may, in fact, help to keep readers reading, especially when the essay is organized around topics or aspects of the information.

Narration may be even more important, for it is used by many profile writers to organize their essays. Some profiles even read like stories, with **suspense** building to a dramatic **climax.** Noonan's essay has two climaxes, the first when the brain is exposed and the second when the tumor is discovered. The climax of Cable's narrative occurs at the end when he touches a corpse. Both writers organize their narratives to develop and sustain suspense and drama.

GUIDE TO WRITING

THE WRITING ASSIGNMENT

Write an essay about an intriguing person, place, or activity in your community. Your instructor may offer you a choice of options: a brief profile of an event, a place, or an activity observed once or twice; a brief profile of an individual based on one or two interviews; or a longer, more fully developed profile of a person, a place, or an activity based on several observational visits and interviews. Observe your subject closely, and then present what you have learned in a way that both informs and engages readers.

INVENTION AND RESEARCH

Preparing to write a profile involves several activities: choosing a subject, exploring your preconceptions of it, planning your project, posing some preliminary questions, and finding a theme or focus for your profile. Each step takes no more than a few minutes, yet together these activities enable you to anticipate problems likely to arise in a complex project like a profile, arrange and schedule your interviews wisely, and take notes and gather materials in a productive way. There is much to learn about observing, interviewing, and writing about what you have learned, and these activities will support your learning.

Choosing a Subject

When you choose a subject, you consider various possibilities, select a promising one, and check that particular subject's accessibility.

Listing Possibilities. *Make a list of several subjects to consider for your essay.* You may already have a subject in mind for your profile. But take a few minutes to consider some other possible subjects. The more possibilities you consider, the more confident you can be about your choice.

Set a timer for ten minutes, and brainstorm lists on a computer with the monitor brightness turned all the way down. Enter as many possibilities as you can think of. Then turn the brightness up, read to make sure that all the items make sense, and save them as an invention file. If you would like, print out a copy to make notes on.

Before you list possible subjects, consider realistically the time you have available and the amount of observing and interviewing you will be able to accomplish. Whether you have a week to plan and write up one observational visit or interview or a month to develop a full profile will determine what kinds of subjects will be appropriate for you. Consult with your instructor if you need help defining the scope of your writing project.

Here we present some ideas you might use as starting points for your list of subjects. Try to extend your list to ten or twelve possibilities. Consider every subject you can think of, even unlikely ones. Consider unfamiliar subjects—people, places, or activities you find fascinating or bizarre or perhaps even forbidding. Take risks. People like to read about the unusual.

People

- Anyone with an unusual or intriguing job or hobby—a private detective, beekeeper, classic-car owner, dog trainer
- A prominent local personality—parent of the year, labor organizer, politician, consumer advocate, television or radio personality, community activist
- A campus personality—ombudsman, coach, distinguished teacher
- Someone recently recognized for service or achievement
- Someone whose predicament symbolizes that of other people

Places

- A weight reduction clinic, tanning salon, body-building gym, health spa, nail salon
- Small-claims court, juvenile court, consumer fraud office
- A used-car lot, old movie house, used-book store, antique shop, historic site, auction hall, flower show, farmers' market
- A hospital emergency room, hospice, birthing center, psychiatric unit
- A local diner; the oldest, biggest, or quickest restaurant in town; a coffeehouse
- The campus radio station, computer center, agricultural research facility, student center, faculty club, museum, newspaper office, health center
- A book, newspaper, or magazine publisher; florist shop, nursery, or greenhouse; pawnshop; boatyard; automobile restorer or wrecking yard
- A recycling center; fire station; airport control tower; theater, opera, or symphony office; refugee center; orphanage; convent or monastery

Activities

- A citizens' volunteer program—voter registration, public television auction, meals-on-wheels project, tutoring program
- An unconventional sports event—marathon, Frisbee tournament, chess match
- Folk dancing, rollerblading, rock climbing, poetry reading

Listing Subjects Related to Identity and Community Writing a profile about a person or a place in your community can help you to learn more about yourself in relation to others in your community and about institutions and activities fundamental to community life. By "community" we mean both geographic communities, such as towns and neighborhoods, and institutional and temporary communities, such as a church congregation, college students majoring in a certain subject, a volunteer organization, or a sports team. The following suggestions will enable you to list several possible subjects.

People

- Someone who successfully fits into several communities at the same time
- Someone who has made or is currently making an important contribution to a community
- A prominent member of one of the communities you belong to who can help you define and understand that community

- Someone in a community who is generally not liked or respected but tolerated, such as a homeless person, gruff store owner, or unorthodox church member, or someone who has been or is in danger of being shunned or exiled from a community

Places

- A facility that provides a needed service in its community, such as a legal advice bureau, child care center, medical clinic, mission or shelter that offers free meals
- A place where people of different ages, genders, ethnic groups, or some other attribute have formed a kind of ongoing community, such as a chess table in the park, political or social action headquarters, computer class, local coffeehouse, barber or beauty shop. Or a place where people come together because they are of the same age, gender, or ethnic group, such as a seniors-only housing complex, a boathouse for a men's crew team, a campus women's center, an African-American or Asian-American student center
- An Internet site, such as a chat room, game parlor, or bulletin board where people form a virtual community

Activities

- A team practicing—one you can observe as an outsider, not as a participant
- A community improvement project, such as graffiti cleaning, tree planting, house repairing, church painting, highway litter pickup
- Researchers working together on a project

Listing Possibilities Related to Work and Career Choosing a work- or career-related subject from one of these possibilities can help you to learn more about your attitudes toward work and your career goals by examining the way others do their work and pursue their careers.

People

- A college senior or graduate student in a major you are considering
- Someone working in the career you are thinking of pursuing
- Someone who trains people to do the kind of work you would like to do

Places

- A place on campus where students work—library, computer center, cafeteria, bookstore, office, tutoring or learning center
- A place where you could learn more about the kind of career you would like to pursue—law office, medical center or veterinary hospital, research institute, television station, newspaper, school, software manufacturer, engineering firm
- A place where people do a kind of work you would like to know more about—clothing factory, coal mine, dairy farm, racetrack, restaurant, bakery, commercial fishing boat, gardening nursery, nursing home, delicatessen
- A place where people are trained for a certain kind of work or career—police academy, cosmetology program, video repair course, truck drivers' school

Activities

- The actual activities performed by someone doing a kind of work represented on television, like that of a police detective, judge, attorney, newspaper reporter, taxi driver, novelist, or emergency room doctor
- Activities to prepare for a particular kind of work, for example, a boxer preparing for a fight, an attorney preparing for a trial, a teacher or professor preparing a course, an actor rehearsing a role, a musician practicing for a concert

Making a Choice. *Choose a subject to write about.* Look over your list, and select a subject that you find personally fascinating, something you want to know more about. It should also be a subject that you think you can make interesting to readers.

If you choose a subject with which you are familiar, it is a good idea to study it in an unfamiliar setting. Say that you are a rock climber and decide to profile rock climbing. Do not rely on your own knowledge and authority. Seek out other rock-climbing enthusiasts and even some critics of the sport to get a more objective view. Go to a rock-climbing event or training class where you can simply observe, not participate. Unless you can adopt an outsider's perspective on a familiar activity, your writing will very likely be uninspired and unsurprising. Most writers report the greatest satisfaction and the best results when they profile unfamiliar activities.

Stop now to focus your thoughts. In a sentence or two, identify the subject you have chosen and explain why you think it is a good choice for you and for your readers.

Checking on Accessibility. *Take steps to ensure that your subject will be accessible to you.* Having chosen a subject, make sure you will be able to observe it. Find out who might be able to give you information, and make some preliminary phone calls. Explain that you need information for a school research project. You will be surprised how helpful people can be when they have the time. If you are unable to contact knowledgeable people or get access to the place you need to observe, you may not be able to write on this subject. Therefore, try to make initial contact early.

Start a file on your disk that includes names, addresses, and phone numbers of people and places you need to contact.

Testing Your Choice: A Collaborative Activity

You might find it useful to get together in a group with two or three other students and describe your chosen topics to one another. Assess group members' interest in the person, place, or activity you wish to write about, and invite their advice about whether it sounds promising. Does it seem likely to lead to a profile they would care to read? Taking this step will help you decide whether you have chosen a good subject to write about, one that will allow you to proceed confidently to develop your profile.

Exploring Your Preconceptions

Explore your initial thoughts and feelings about your subject in writing before you begin observing or interviewing. Take about ten minutes to write about your thoughts, using the following questions as a guide:

- What do I already know about this subject?
  How would I define or describe it?
  What are its chief qualities or parts?
  Do I associate anyone or anything with it?
  What is its purpose or function?
  How does it compare with other, similar subjects?

- What is my attitude toward this subject?
  Why do I consider this subject intriguing? What about it interests me?
  Do I like it? Respect it? Understand it?

- What do I expect to discover as I observe the subject?
  What would surprise me about it?
  Might I find anything amusing in it?

- How do my preconceptions of the subject compare with other people's?
  What might be unique about my preconceptions?
  What attitudes about this subject do I share with other people?

Planning Your Project

Set up a tentative schedule for your observational and interview visits. Whatever the scope of your project—single observation, interview with follow-up, or repeated observations and interviews—you will want to get the most out of your time with your subject. Chapter 20 offers guidance in observing and interviewing and will give you an idea of how much time you will need to plan, carry out, and write up an observation or interview.

Take time now to consult Chapter 20. Figure out first the amount of time you have to complete your essay; then, decide what visits you will need to make, whom you will need to interview, and what library work you might want to do. Estimate the time necessary for each. You might use a chart like the following one:

Date	*Time Needed*	*Purpose*	*Preparation*
10/23	1 hour	Observe	Bring map and directions, pad
10/25	1½ hours	Library research	Bring reference list, notebook, change for copy machine
10/26	45 minutes	Interview	Read brochure and prepare questions
10/30	2 hours	Observe and interview	Prepare questions, confirm appointment, bring pad

Keeping a schedule in a separate file or on a disk allows for easy modification. As your plans change, you can print out a revised schedule.

You will probably have to modify your plan once you actually begin work, but it is a good idea to keep some sort of schedule in writing.

If you are developing a full profile, your first goal is to get your bearings. Some writers begin by observing; others start with an interview. Many read up on the subject before doing anything else, to get a sense of its main elements. You may also want to read about other subjects similar to the one you have chosen. Save your notes.

Posing Some Preliminary Questions

Write questions to prepare for your first visit. Before beginning your observations and interviews, try writing some questions for which you would like to find answers. These questions will orient you and allow you to focus your visits. As you work, you will find answers to many of these questions. Add to this list as new questions occur to you, and delete any that come to seem irrelevant.

Each subject invites its own special questions, and every writer has particular concerns. For example, one student chose to profile a clinical center of the Women's Health Initiative, a nationwide fifteen-year study of women's health. She learned of the study in her local newspaper and called the local center to get further information. The center administrator faxed her a fact sheet on the study and the local center's special part in it. The student knew that she would need to report on the study and also to profile the local center and key people who work there. She also hoped to interview women who come to the center to participate in the research. Consequently, she devised these questions to launch her research and prepare for her first visit to the center to interview the director:

If you list your questions on a computer, leave at least ten lines between individual questions. When you print out a copy, you will have room to write in answers as you interview and observe.

- Why has so little research been done until now on women's health?
- How did the study come about, and what is the National Institute of Health?
- Why does the study focus only on women between the ages of fifty and eighty?
- Will women from all income levels be involved?
- Why will it take fifteen years to complete the study?
- When was the local center established, and what role does it play in the national study?
- Does the center simply coordinate the study, or does it also provide health and medical advice to women participating in the study?
- Who works at the center, and what are their qualifications to work there?
- Will I be able to interview women who come to the center to participate in the research?

Finding a Tentative Interpretation

Write nonstop for five to ten minutes in order to find a tentative interpretation of your subject. After you have completed your visits, you should be ready to arrive at a tentative interpretation of your subject. Other students have found these questions to be helpful:

If you use a word processor to explore your interpretation, print out a hard copy to review before trying to state your tentative interpretation.

- What visual or other sensory impression is most memorable?
- What does this single impression tell me about the place?
- What is the mood of the place? How do people seem to feel there?
- What is most memorable about the people I observed and talked to?
- What is most striking about the activity I observed? What is most likely to surprise or interest my readers?
- What was the most important thing I learned? Why is it important?

- If I could find out the answer to one more question, what would the question be? Why is this question so crucial?
- What about this subject says something larger about our lives and times?
- What generalization or judgment do these personal reactions lead me to?

Take a few moments to reflect on what you have discovered. Then, in a sentence or two, state what now seems to you to be a promising interpretation of your subject. What do you want readers to see as they read your profile? What do you want them to remember later about your subject?

PLANNING AND DRAFTING

As preparation for drafting, review your invention or research notes to see what you have, set goals for yourself, and organize your profile.

Seeing What You Have

Read over your invention materials to see what you have. You may now have a great deal of material—notes from visits, interviews, or reading; some idea of your preconceptions; a list of questions, perhaps with some answers. You should also have a tentative interpretation. Your aim is to digest all the information you have gathered; to pick out the promising facts, details, anecdotes, and quotations; and to see how it all might come together to present your subject to readers and offer an interpretation of it.

Print out a hard copy of what you have written on a word processor for easier reviewing.

As you sort through your material, look at it in some of the following ways. They may help you find a focus and clarify your interpretation.

- Contrast your preconceptions of the subject with your findings about it.
- Compare what different people say about the subject.
- Look for discrepancies between people's words and their behavior.
- Compare your reactions with those of the people directly involved.
- Consider the place's appearance in light of the activity that occurs there.
- Examine your subject as an anthropologist or archaeologist might, looking for evidence that would explain its role in the society at large.

Setting Goals

The following questions will help to establish goals for your first draft. Consider each one briefly now, and return to them as necessary as you draft.

Your Readers

- Are my readers likely to be at all familiar with my subject? If not, what details do I need to provide to help them visualize it?
- If my readers are familiar with my subject, how can I present it to them in a new and engaging way? What information do I have that is likely to be new or entertaining to them?

- Is there anything I can say about this subject that will lead readers to think about their own lives and values?

The Beginning

The opening is especially important in a profile. Because readers are unlikely to have any particular reason to read a profile, the writer must arouse their curiosity and interest. The best beginnings are surprising and specific; the worst are abstract. Here are some strategies you might consider:

- Should I open with a striking image or vivid scene, as Noonan and Manegold do?
- Should I begin with a statement of the central theme?
- Should I start with an intriguing epigraph, as Cable does?
- Do I have an amazing fact that would catch readers' attention?
- Is there an anecdote that captures the essence of the subject?
- Should I open with a question, perhaps one answered in the essay?
- Do I have any dialogue that would serve as a good beginning, as in the *New Yorker* piece?

The General Organization

Profile writers use two basic methods of organizing their material: They arrange it either chronologically in a narrative or topically by grouping related materials.

If I Organize My Material Chronologically, as Noonan Does:

- How can I make the narrative readable and dramatic?
- What information should I integrate into the narrative?
- What information will I need to suspend the narrative to include? How can I minimize the disruption and resume the dramatic pace?
- What information should I quote, and what should I summarize?
- How can I set the scene vividly?

If I Organize My Material Topically, as Manegold Does:

- What topics in my material best present the subject and inform readers yet hold their interest?
- How can I sequence the topics to bring out comparisons, similarities, or contrasts in my material?
- What transitions will help readers make connections between topics?
- Where and how should I describe the subject so that it will be vivid?

The Ending

- Should I try to frame the essay by repeating an image or phrase from the beginning or by completing an action begun earlier in the profile?
- Would it be effective to end by restating the interpretation?
- Should I end with a telling image, anecdote, or bit of dialogue?

Outlining

For more on clustering and outlining, see pp. 430–34.

If you plan to arrange your material chronologically, plot the key events on a timeline. Star the event you consider the high point or climax.

If you plan to arrange your material topically, by grouping related information, you might use clustering or outlining strategies to get a graphic view of the interconnections. Both these strategies will help you to divide and group your information. After classifying your material, you might list the items in the order in which you plan to present them.

The following outlines illustrate the difference between chronological and topical organization. The first is a *chronological outline* of Noonan's profile on brain surgery:

The operating room and patient
The doctors
The operation (a preview)
The doctor's preparations for the operation
Drilling through the skull
Opening the dura
Retracting the cerebellum
Searching for the tumor
Discovering the tumor
Analyzing the tumor
The doctors' perspectives on brain surgery

If Noonan had wanted to emphasize the tremendous amount of knowledge and sophisticated technology that is involved in brain surgery, he might have chosen a *topical pattern* like this one:

The challenge of brain surgery as a specialty
Who is attracted to it
Special training required
A typical lecture to medical students by an experienced surgeon
The technology of brain surgery (perhaps through a tour of an operating room)
Recent scientific breakthroughs in understanding brain disease
Doctors' relations with their patients (the disassociation problem)
Rewards of a career in brain surgery

Outlining on a word processor makes it particularly easy to experiment with different ways of patterning and ordering your material.

All of the material for this hypothetical topical essay, like the material in the actual chronological essay, would come from observations, interviews, and background reading.

The organization you choose will reflect the possibilities in your material, your purpose, and your readers. At this point, your decision must be tentative. As you begin drafting, you will almost certainly discover new ways of organizing your material. Once you have a first draft, you and others may see ways to reorganize the material to achieve your purpose better with your particular readers.

Drafting

If you can shift between windows, call up your invention material on an alternate window as you draft on the main window. Shift back and forth to cut and paste invention material into your draft.

Start drafting your essay. By now, of course, you are not starting from scratch. If you have followed this guide, you will already have done a great deal of invention and planning. Some of this material may even fit right into your draft with little alteration.

Be careful not to get stuck trying to write the perfect beginning. Start writing anywhere. The time to perfect your beginning is at the revision stage.

Once you are actually writing, try not to be interrupted. Should you find that you need to make additional visits for further observations and interviews, do so after you have completed a first draft. You might look at the general advice on drafting in Chapter 1.

CRITICAL READING GUIDE

Now is the time to get a good critical reading of your draft. Your instructor may arrange such a reading as part of your coursework; if not, you can ask a classmate, friend, or family member to read it over. If your campus has a writing center, you might ask a tutor there to read and comment on your draft. The guidelines that follow can be used by *anyone* reviewing a profile. (If you are unable to have someone else read over your draft, turn ahead to the Revising section, which provides guidelines for reading your own draft critically.)

Swap copies of your drafts with another student, either by exchanging disks or by sending the computer files over a network. Add your comments either next to the essay, if you can divide the window, or at the end of the document.

If You Are the Writer. To provide focused, helpful comments, readers must know your intended audience and purpose. Take time now to reconsider these two elements, jotting down the following information at the top of your draft.

- *Audience.* Who are your readers? What do you assume they already know about your subject? How have you planned to engage and hold their interest?
- *Purpose.* What impression of your subject do you want to give readers?

If You Are the Reader. Reading a draft critically means reading it more than once, first to get a general impression and then to analyze its basic features.

1. *Read for a First Impression.* Read quickly through the draft first to get an overall impression. As you read, try to notice passages that contribute to your first impression. After you have finished reading the draft, note down your immediate reaction. What do you consider most interesting in the essay? What is the dominant impression you get of the subject? What questions do you have about it?

See pp. 130–32 to review the basic features.

2. *Consider Whether the Subject Is Intriguing and Well Focused.* Does the profile contain enough details to identify the subject as a specific person, place, or event? Comment on the effectiveness of descriptive details used to show the subject's uniqueness. Point out any places where vague or general statements fail to hold your interest in the subject.
3. *Decide Whether the Interpretation Seems Clear.* Profiles must offer readers an interpretation of the subject that may be explicit (stated in the essay) or implicit (suggested by the details). If the interpretation is explicit, point out where you find it. If it seems to be implicit, point to details that suggest it to you. State what you believe to be the writer's attitude toward the subject, and note what evidence supports your conclusion.
4. *Consider How Vividly the Subject Is Presented to Readers.* Profiles must present their subjects in specific details rather than general statements. Look at the description of objects, scenes, and people. Point out vivid and specific descriptions as well as places where readers would need further details in order to imagine what the writer is talking about. Also point out any seemingly unnecessary or exaggerated descriptions.

   Consider the use of specific narrative action—people moving, gesturing, talking. Suggest ways to strengthen any sections of specific action, and point out any other places where action might be appropriate.
5. *Assess How Well the Flow of Information Is Controlled.* Profile readers are willing to be informed, but they expect the information load to be manageable. Point out any places where you felt bogged down or overwhelmed with information or where information was not clearly presented or was inadequate. If necessary, look for ways to reduce or add information or to break up long blocks of information with description of scenes or people or narration of events.

   Skim the essay for definitions, and indicate whether any seem unnecessary or unclear. Also point out any other terms that need defining.
6. *Evaluate the Effectiveness of the Organization.* If the profile is organized chronologically, point out any places where the narrative seems to drag as well as where it seems most dramatic and intense. Identify the climax or high point of the narrative.

   If the profile is organized topically, look to see whether the writer has presented too little or too much material for a topic and whether topics might be sequenced differently or connected more clearly.

   Reread the *beginning,* and decide whether it is effective. Did it capture your attention? Is there a quotation, a fact, or an anecdote elsewhere in the draft that might make a better opening?

   Look again at the *ending.* Does it leave you hanging, seem too abrupt, or oversimplify the material? Suggest another ending, possibly by moving a passage or a quotation from elsewhere in the essay.
7. *Give the Writer Your Final Thoughts.* What is the strongest part of this draft? What about the draft is most memorable? What in the draft is weak, most in need of further work?

REVISING

The following guidelines will help you to identify problems in your own draft and to revise and edit to solve them.

Identifying Problems

To identify problems in your draft, you need to read it objectively, analyze its basic features, and study any comments you have received from others.

Getting an Overview. Consider the draft as a whole, trying to see it objectively. It may help to do so in two steps:

Even if the draft of your essay is saved to a computer file, reread from a hard copy. Add notes to yourself and quick revisions as you read through the draft.

1. *Reread.* If at all possible, put the draft aside for a day or two before rereading it. When you do, start by considering your purpose. Then, read the draft straight through, looking mainly for its basic message.
2. *Outline.* Make a scratch outline of the draft that identifies the stages in which you present your subject.

Charting a Plan for Revision. Preparing a two-column list is a good way to start plotting out the course of your revision. The left-hand column lists the basic features of profiles; the right-hand column lists any problems that you or other readers identified with that feature.

Before revising, copy your original draft to a second file. Should you change your mind about material you delete while revising, it will still be available to you.

Basic Features	*Problems to Solve*
Choice of subject	
Interpretation	
Presentation of subject	
Information flow	
Organization	

Analyzing Basic Features. Turn now to the analysis questions just presented in the Critical Reading Guide. Analyze your draft following those questions, adding any specific problems you notice to your chart of problems to solve.

Studying Critical Comments. Review any comments you have received from other readers, and add any points that need attention to the chart. Try not to react too defensively to these comments; by letting you see how others respond to your draft, they provide valuable information about both its strengths and its weaknesses.

Solving the Problems

Having identified problems in your draft, you now need to figure out solutions and to carry them out. Basically, you have three options:

1. Review your observation or interview notes for other information and ideas.

2. Do additional observations or interviews to answer questions you or other readers raised.
3. Look back at the readings in this chapter to see how other writers have solved similar problems.

Here are some suggestions to get you started solving some of the problems common to profiles.

The Subject

- **Does the subject seem lackluster, not intriguing, or unremarkable?** Add specific descriptive details to help readers to see why it is noteworthy.
- **Do any of your statements about your subject seem too general?** Revise them to focus on specific characteristics.

Interpretation

- **Did readers have difficulty recognizing the meanings you found in your subject, your interpretation of it?** Try stating the interpretation more explicitly or eliminating dialogue, description, and anecdotal or factual detail that does not contribute to the interpretation you want to offer or that seems to work against it. Ensure that the dominant impression of the details and your attitude toward the subject are congruent with that interpretation.

Presentation of the Subject

- **Does the subject seem less vivid than it should be?** Add specific words and details so that readers can better imagine it. Look for places where you can include more sensory details—sights, sounds, smells, textures.

Information Flow

- **Did readers feel bogged down by information at any point?** Move, condense, or eliminate some of it. Eliminate any unnecessary definitions.
- **Was there some point that readers could not understand?** Add more information or definitions. Make sure these fit smoothly into your essay and do not interrupt readers' attention to your main points.

Organization

For more on specific narrative action, see pp. 486–87.

- **If your essay is organized chronologically, does it seem to drag or ramble?** Find the climax, or high point, and try to heighten the suspense leading up to it. Add drama through specific narrative action, showing details of movements and gestures.
- **If you organized topically, did readers find the profile disorganized?** Try rearranging topics to see if another order makes more sense. Look at the outlines you have made to get ideas.

Use your word processor's cut-and-paste or block-and-move functions to shift material around. Make sure you revise transitions so that material fits smoothly in its new spot.

- **Does the opening fail to engage readers' attention?** Consider alternatives. Think of questions you could open with, or look for an engaging image or dialogue later in the essay to move to the beginning. Go back to your observation or interview notes for other ideas.
- **Does the ending seem weak?** Consider ending at an earlier point or moving something more striking to the end. Strive to provide a satisfying closure.
- **At any point in your essay, did readers feel that transitions between stages in the narrative or between topics were confusing or too abrupt?** Add appropriate words or phrases or revise sentences to make transitions clearer or smoother.

EDITING AND PROOFREADING

In working on your draft so far, you have probably not paid too much attention to matters of grammar and mechanics. Now, however, you should take time to check over your draft for errors in usage, punctuation, and mechanics. Our research has identified several errors that occur often in profiles. Two in particular are explained here.

Checking the Punctuation of Quotations. Because most profiles are based in part on interviews, you will almost certainly have quoted one or more people. When you quote someone's exact words, enclose those words in quotation marks. There are clear conventions for punctuating quotations; check your draft for your use of the following specific punctuation marks.

All quotations should have quotation marks at the beginning and the end.

Use your word processor's spell-check function cautiously. Keep in mind that it will not find all misspellings, particularly misused homonyms (such as *there* for *their* or *they're*), typos that are themselves words (such as *fro* for *for*), and many proper nouns and specialized terms. Proofread these carefully yourself. Also proofread for words or phrases that should have been deleted when you edited a sentence.

◇ **"What exactly is civil litigation? I asked.**

Commas and periods go *inside* quotation marks.

◇ **"I'm here to see Anna Post", I replied nervously.**

◇ **Tony explained, "Fraternity boys just wouldn't feel comfortable at the Chez Moi Café".**

Question marks and exclamation points go *inside* closing quotation marks if they are part of the quotation, *outside* if they are not.

◇ **After a pause, the patient asked, "Where do I sign"?**

◇ **Willie insisted, "You can *too* learn to play Super Mario"!**

◇ **When was the last time someone you just ticketed said to you, "Thank you, Officer, for doing a great job?"**

Use commas with signal phrases (*he said, she asked,* etc.) that accompany direct quotations.

◇ **"This sound system costs only four thousand dollars," Jorge said.**

◇ **I asked, "So where were these clothes from originally?"**

A Common ESL Problem: Adjective Order. In trying to present the subject of your profile vividly and in detail, you have almost certainly included many descriptive adjectives. When you include more than one adjective in front of a noun, you may have difficulty sequencing them. For example, do you write "a large old ceramic pot" or "an old large ceramic pot"? The following list shows the order in which adjectives are ordinarily arranged in front of a noun.

1. *Amount:* a/an, the, a few, six
2. *Evaluation:* good, beautiful, ugly, serious
3. *Size:* large, small, tremendous
4. *Shape, length:* round, long, short
5. *Age:* young, new, old
6. *Color:* red, black, green
7. *Origin:* Asian, Brazilian, German
8. *Material:* wood, cotton, gold
9. *Noun used as an adjective:* computer (as in *computer program*), cake (as in *cake pan*)
10. *The noun modified*

A WRITER AT WORK

THE INTERVIEW NOTES AND WRITE-UP

Most profile writers take notes when interviewing people. Later, they may summarize their notes in a short write-up. In this section, you will see some of the interview notes and a write-up that Brian Cable prepared for his mortuary profile, one of the readings in this chapter.

Cable toured the mortuary and conducted two interviews, one with the funeral director and one with the mortician. Before each interview, he wrote out a few questions at the top of a sheet of paper and then divided it into two columns; he used the left-hand column for descriptive details and personal impressions and the right-hand column for the information he got directly from the person he was interviewing. We present Cable's notes and write-up for his interview with the funeral director, Howard Deaver.

Cable used the questions as a guide for the interview and then took brief notes during it. He did not concern himself too much with notetaking because he planned to spend a half-hour directly afterward to complete his notes. He kept his attention fixed on Deaver, trying to keep the interview comfortable and conversational and noting down just enough to jog his memory and to catch anything especially quotable. A typescript of Cable's interview notes follows.

The Interview

QUESTIONS

1. How do families of deceased view the mortuary business?
2. How is the concept of death approached?
3. How did you get into this business?

DESCRIPTIVE DETAILS & PERSONAL IMPRESSIONS	INFORMATION
weird-looking tall long fingers big ears low, sloping forehead Like stereotype--skin colorless	"Call me Howard" How things work: Notification, pick up body at home or hospital, prepare for viewing, restore distorted features--accident or illness, embalm, casket--family selects, chapel services (3 in bldg.), visitation room--pay respects, family & friends.
	Can't answer questions about death--"Not bereavement specialists. Don't handle emotional problems. Only a trained therapist can do that." "We provide services for dead, not counseling for the living." (great quote) Concept of death has changed in last 40 yrs (how long he's been in the business) Funeral cost $500-$600, now $2,000
plays with lips blinks plays with Adam's apple desk empty--phone, no paper or pen	Phone call (interruption) "I think we'll be able to get him in on Friday. No, no, the family wants him cremated." Ask about Neptune Society--cremation Cremation "Cheap, quick, easy means of disposal."
angry disdainful of the Neptune Soc.	Recent phenomenon. Neptune Society--erroneous claim to be only one. "We've offered them since the beginning. It's only now it's come into vogue." Trend now back toward burial. Cremation still popular in sophisticated areas 60% in Marin Co. and Florida

DESCRIPTIVE DETAILS & PERSONAL IMPRESSIONS	INFORMATION
	Ask about paperwork--does it upstairs, lives there with wife, Nancy
musty, old stained glass sunlight filtered	Tour around (happy to show me around) Chapel--large service just done, Italian.
man in black suit roses wooden benches	"Not a religious institution--a business." casket--"beautiful craftsmanship" --admires, expensive
contrast brightness fluorescent lights Plexiglass stands	Display room--caskets, about 30 of them Loves to talk about caskets "models in every price range" glossy (like cars in a showroom) cardboard box, steel, copper, bronze $400 up to $1,800. Top of line: bronze, electronically welded, no corrosion--$5,000

Cable's notes include many descriptive details of Deaver as well as of various rooms in the mortuary. Though most entries are short and sketchy, much of the language finds its way into the essay. In describing Deaver, for example, Cable notes that he fits the stereotype of the cadaverous undertaker, a fact that Cable will make much of in his essay.

He puts quotation marks around Deaver's actual words, some of them complete sentences, others only fragments. We will see how he fills these quotes in when he writes up the interview. In only a few instances does he take down more than he can use. Even though profile writers want good quotes, they should not use quotes to present information that can be more effectively expressed in their own words. In profiles, writers use direct quotation both to provide information and to capture the mood or character of the person speaking.

As you can see, Deaver was not able to answer Cable's questions about the families of the deceased and their attitudes toward death or mortuaries. The gap between the questions and Deaver's responses led Cable to recognize one of his own misperceptions about mortuaries—that they serve the living by helping them adjust to the death of their loved ones. This misperception becomes an important theme of his essay.

After filling in his notes following the interview, Cable took some time to reflect on what he had learned. Here are some of his thoughts:

I was surprised how much Deaver looked like the undertakers in scary movies. Even though he couldn't answer any of my questions, he was friendly enough. It's obviously a business for him (he loves to talk about caskets and to point out all their features, like a car dealer kicking a tire). Best quote:

"We offer services to the dead, not counseling
to the living." I have to arrange an interview with the
mortician.

Writing up an account of the interview a short time afterward helped Cable to fill in more details and to reflect further on what he had learned. His write-up shows him already beginning to organize the information he had gained from his interview with Deaver.

A Write-up on the Interview

I. His physical appearance.

Tall, skinny, with beady blue eyes embedded in his bony face. I was shocked to see him. He looked like the undertakers in scary movies. His skin was white and colorless, from lack of sunshine. He has a long nose and a low, sloping forehead. He was wearing a clean white shirt. A most unusual man--have you ever seen those Ames Home Loan commercials? But he was friendly, and happy to talk to me. "Would I answer some questions? Sure."

II. What people want from a mortuary.

A. Well first of all, he couldn't answer my question as to how families cope with the loss of a loved one. "You'd have to talk to a psychologist about that," he said. He did tell me how the concept of death has changed over the last ten or so years.

B. He has been in the business for forty years (forty years?!). One look at him and you'd be convinced he'd been there at least that long. He told me that in the old times, everyone was buried. Embalmed, put in a casket, and paid final homage before being shipped underground forever and ever. Nowadays, many people choose to be cremated instead. Hence comes the success of the Neptune Society and those like it. They specialize in cremation. You can have your ashes dumped anywhere. "Not that we don't offer cremation services. We've offered them since the beginning," he added with a look of disdain. It's just that they've become so popular recently because they offer a "quick, easy, and efficient means of disposal." Cheap too--I think it is a reflection of a "no nonsense" society. The Neptune Society has become so successful because it claims to be the only one to offer cremations as an alternative to expensive burial. "We've offered it all along. It's just only now come into vogue."

Sophisticated areas (I felt "progressive" would be more accurate) like Marin County have a cremation rate of over 60 percent. The phone rang. "Excuse me," he said. As he talked on the phone, I noticed how he played with his lips, pursing and squeezing them. He was blinking all the time too.

Yet he wasn't a schizo or anything like that. I meant to ask him how he got into this business, but I forgot. I did find out his name and title. Mr. Deaver, general manager of Goodbody Mortuaries (no kidding, that's the real name). He lived on the premises upstairs with his wife. I doubt if he ever left the place.

III. It's a business!

Some people have the idea that mortuaries offer counseling and peace of mind--a place where everyone is sympathetic and ready to offer advice. "In some mortuaries, this is true. But by and large, this is a business. We offer services to the dead, not counseling to the living." I too had expected to feel an awestruck respect for the dead upon entering the building. I had also expected green lawns, ponds with ducks, fountains, flowers, peacefulness--you know, a "Forest Lawn" type deal. But it was only a tall, Catholic-looking building. "Mortuaries do not sell plots for burial," he was saying. "Cemeteries do that, after we embalm the body and select a casket. We're not a religious institution." He seemed hung up on caskets--though maybe he was just trying to impress upon me the differences between caskets. "Oh, they're very important. A good casket is a sign of respect. Sometimes if the family doesn't have enough money, we rent them a nice one. People pay for what they get just like any other business." I wonder when you have to return the casket you rent.

I wanted to take a look around. He was happy to give me a tour. We visited several chapels and visiting rooms--places where the deceased "lie in state" to be "visited" by family and friends. I saw an old lady in a "fairly decent casket," as Mr. Deaver called it. Again I was impressed by the simple businesslike nature of it all. Oh yes, the rooms were elaborately decorated, with lots of shrines and stained glass, but these things were for the customers' benefit. "Sometimes we have up to eight or nine corpses here at one time, sometimes none. We have to have enough rooms to accommodate." Simple enough, yet I never realized how much (trouble?) people were after they died. So much money, time, and effort go into their funerals.

As I prepared to leave, he gave me his card. He'd be happy to see me again, or maybe I could talk to someone else. I said I would arrange to call for an appointment with the mortician. I shook his hand. His fingers were long, and his skin was warm.

Writing up the interview helped Cable to probe his subject more deeply. It also helped him to express a humorous attitude toward his subject. Cable's interview notes and write-up are quite informal; later, he integrates these more formally into his full profile of the mortuary.

THINKING CRITICALLY ABOUT WHAT YOU HAVE LEARNED

Now that you have spent several days discussing profiles and writing one of your own, it is a good idea to spend some time reflecting on what you have learned about this genre. First, you should think about your own writing process, discovering what you learned about solving a problem you encountered in writing your profile. Next, review what you learned as a reader of profiles that helped you to write your own. Finally, explore the social dimensions of profiles: In what ways do they influence our thinking about ourselves and the society we live in?

Reflecting on Your Writing

Write a page or so telling your instructor about a problem you encountered in writing your profile and how you solved it. Before you begin, gather all of your writing—invention, planning notes, drafts, any critical comments from classmates and your instructor, revising notes and plans, and final revision. Review these materials as you complete this writing task.

1. Identify *one* writing problem you needed to solve as you worked on your profile. Do not be concerned with grammar or punctuation; concentrate instead on problems unique to developing a profile. For example, did you puzzle over how to organize your diverse observations into a coherent essay? Was it difficult to convey a dominant impression or offer an interpretation? Did you have any concerns about presenting the place and people vividly, controlling the flow of information, or any other aspect of the essay?
2. How did you recognize the writing problem? When did you first discover it? What called it to your attention? If you did not become aware of the problem until someone else pointed it out to you, can you now see hints of it in your invention writings? If so, where specifically? When you first recognized the problem, how did you respond?
3. Reflect on how you went about solving the problem. Did you work on the wording of a passage, cut or add details about the place or people, or move paragraphs or sentences around? Did you reread one of the essays in this chapter to see how another writer handled the problem, or did you look back at the invention suggestions? If you talked about the problem with another student, a tutor, or your instructor, did talking about it help? How useful was the advice you got?
4. Now write your explanation of the problem and your solution. Reconstruct your efforts as specifically as possible. Quote from your invention, your draft, others' critical comments, your revision plan, or your revised essay to show the various changes your writing underwent as you tried to solve the problem. When you have finished, consider how explaining what you have learned about solving this writing problem can help you to solve future writing problems.

Reviewing What You Learned from Reading

Write a page or so explaining to your instructor how the readings in this chapter influenced your revised essay. Before you write, take time to reflect on what you have learned from the reading selections in this chapter, and consider some ways your reading has influenced your writing.

1. Reread the final revision of your essay; then, look back at the profiles you read before completing your own. Do you see any specific influences? For example, if you were impressed with the way one of the readings presented a place through concrete details, made an ordinary activity seem interesting, focused all of the materials around a compelling and unexpected interpretation, or reconstructed dialogue from interview notes, look to see where you might

have been striving for similar effects in your own writing. Also, look for ideas you got from your reading, writing strategies you were inspired to try, specific details you were led to include, effects you sought to achieve.

2. Now write an explanation of these influences. Did one reading in particular influence you, or were you influenced by several readings in different ways? Quote from the readings and from your final revision to show how your essay was influenced by your reading of other profiles in this chapter. Finally, now that you have reviewed the other readings again, point out any ways in which you might improve your profile.

Considering the Social Dimensions of Profiles

Profiles offer some of the same pleasures as autobiographies, novels, and films—good stories, memorable characters, exotic places or familiar places viewed freshly, vivid images of people at work and play. They divert and entertain. They may even shock or fascinate. In addition, by intent and design, they offer information that we nearly always feel we can rely on. This special combination of diversion and information makes profiles unique among all the kinds of reading and writing available to us.

Like travel writing and natural history, profiles nearly always take us to a particular place, usually a place we have never been. For example, Cable provides many visual details of Goodbody Mortuary, with its gothic arches and stained glass, its hotel-like lobby with couches and coffee tables, aquarium, and pastoral paintings. The author of "Soup" describes Soup Kitchen International's appearance from the street so well that we could easily find it even if we did not know its number on West Fifty-fifth Street.

But the larger appeal of profiles is that they present real people most readers will never have a chance to meet. Often, profiles present people the writer admires—and assumes readers will admire—for their achievements, endurance, dedication, skill, or unselfishness. For example, we may find it easy to admire Mr. Yeganeh for his commanding knowledge of the world's soups and his devotion to quality, just as we may be in awe of Noonan's brain surgeons for their great skill and extraordinary concentration. Profiles also present less admirable people; these may occasionally be shown as cruel, greedy, or selfish, but more often they are people, such as Crystal, with whom we can sympathize because of their innocence or bad luck. The strongest profiles present us with neither saints nor monsters nor helpless victims but rather with people of mixed motives, human failings, and some resources even in dire situations. Noonan invites us to admire the brain surgeons but also to question their apparent lack of feeling for their patients, and Manegold's profile suggests that Crystal herself bears some responsibility for her disaffection from school.

Entertain Readers or Show the Whole Picture? Profiles broaden our view of the world by entertaining and informing us with portraits of unusual people in particular places. It is hard to imagine doing without them. We must also recognize, however, that profiles sometimes offer a more limited view of their subjects than they seem to. For example, the impulse to entertain readers may lead a profile writer to focus exclusively on the dramatic, bizarre, colorful, or humorous aspects of a place or an activity, ignoring equally important everyday, humdrum, ironic, or paradoxical aspects. Imagine a profile of a travel agent focusing on the free trips he or she enjoys as part of the job but ignoring the everyday demands of dealing with clients, the energy-draining precision required by computer-based airline reservation systems, and the numbing routine of addressing envelopes and mailing tickets to clients. Such a profile would provide a limited and distorted picture of a travel agent's work. While hardly distorted, Noonan's profile of a brain operation does skip over the more tedious parts of the procedure (the two-hour navigation through the brain before the tumor is found, for example) as a way of keeping readers involved in the drama of the moment.

In addition, by focusing on the dramatic or glamorous aspects of a subject, profile writers tend to ignore economic or social consequences and to slight "supporting players." Profiling the highly praised chef in a trendy new restaurant, a writer might not ask whether the chef participates in the city's leftover-food-collection program for the homeless or find out who the kitchen workers and wait staff are, how the chef treats them, or how much they are paid. Profiling the campus bookstore, a writer might become so entranced by the details of ordering books for hundreds of courses, shelving them so that they can be found easily, and selling them efficiently to hordes of students during the first week of a semester that the writer could forget to ask about textbook costs, pricing policies, profit margins, and payback on used textbooks. (Note that Noonan quotes only the surgeons; the nurses and other technicians involved in the brain operation remain anonymous. Neither do the costs of so elaborate a procedure—and who pays for it and profits from it—concern him.)

Be Aware of the Writer's Viewpoint. Though profiles may seem impartial and objective, they inevitably reflect the views of their writers. The choice of subject, the details observed, the questions asked, the ultimate focus and presentation—all are influenced by the writer's interests and values, gender and ethnicity, and assumptions about social and political issues. We would expect a vegetarian to write a very different profile of a cattle ranch than a beef-lover would. Consequently, profiles should be read critically, particularly because the writer's values are likely to be unstated. For example, we might question elements of Manegold's portrait of Crystal and her family: Might a writer from a background more like Crystal's present the girl and her world differently from the way this well-educated, well-traveled outsider does?

For Discussion. Following are some questions that can help you think critically about the benefits and pleasures as well as the potential distortions of profiles. As you read and, perhaps, discuss these questions in class, note down your thoughts and reactions. Then, write a page or so for your instructor presenting your own ideas about profiles and the way they shape our image of the world.

1. We have asserted that profiles broaden readers' views of life by providing knowledge about diverse people and places. Test that assertion against the profiles you have read while working on this assignment. Consider profiles published here as well as those written by your classmates, and choose one that broadened your view of life and one that did not. How would you explain your response to both of these profiles? Then, think back to the subjects you considered for your profile. Did you intentionally choose a subject that would "broaden readers' view of life"? Explain what motivated your choice.
2. Many Americans seem preoccupied with entertainment and sports stars and with bizarre and sensational events, a fact that influences how profiles are written. Consider whether any of the profiles you have read have glamorized or sensationalized their subjects and ignored less colorful but centrally important everyday activities. Is this a problem with your own profile?
3. Some critics of television blame this preoccupation with the bizarre and the sensational for the decline in serious public debate over social and economic issues: Often, vital concerns are reduced to brief pronouncements during newscasts and talk-show shouting matches. Single out a profile you read that seems to have overlooked potential social or economic consequences of an activity, business, or institution. What has been overlooked? Why do you think the writer omitted these aspects?
4. Have any of the profiles you have read depicted a person of great achievement as solely responsible for his or her accomplishments?

Who has been ignored? What has been left out? What does this reluctance to go behind the scenes and to see who is "doing the dirty work" suggest about a profile writer's interests and values? Why do you think Americans tend to see achievement as an individual effort and to overlook others who contributed?

5. Consider the attitudes, values, and views of the writers of this chapter's profiles. Are these attitudes obvious or hidden? How can you tell? How did your own assumptions, values, gender, and ethnicity influence your choice of a subject to profile, your approach to learning about it, and your attitudes toward it? Are your attitudes obvious or hidden? If obvious, how did you make them so, and did you feel as though you were taking a risk? If hidden, why did you think it best to keep your personal views out of sight?

For a book on "religious fundamentalism," a noted religious scholar writes a chapter in which he compares religious groups around the world to come up with a definition explaining the nature of fundamentalism everywhere. In his introduction, he mentions that the use of the term *fundamentalism* began in 1920 during a dispute among conservative Protestant groups. To explain fundamentalism, he describes the ways fundamentalist religious groups are alike and organizes his chapter around similarities. Among these similarities are a sense of threat and an organized reaction to the threat, reliance on authoritative texts, resistance to ambiguity and ambivalence, an inclination to behave aggressively toward unbelievers, an allegiance to a grand past, and a belief in a bright future. He illustrates each of these features of fundamentalism with many examples from the beliefs and histories of fundamentalist groups around the world. He concludes by pointing out that religious fundamentalism has become a major force at the end of the twentieth century.

A writer for a popular computer magazine presents a new concept known as "hive computing." For context, she reminds readers that in the past few years, separate personal computers (PCs) have replaced shared mainframe computers in businesses and research institutes. She alerts readers that this trend may soon reverse, in part because many PCs sit unused much of the time. Since twenty or thirty PCs offer the computing power of a mainframe, some researchers have dreamed of coordinating and making full use of the PCs. She reports that computer scientists at two universities are developing the hardware and software to realize this dream. She explains that hive computing breaks up a complex task and assigns small parts of it to separate PCs. A PC "owner" may reclaim his or her computer at any time while its hive assignment migrates to an unused PC. She contrasts current networks with hive computing and describes the advantages of the latter.

In a textbook for introductory linguistics, a college professor discusses "syntactic development," tracing children's gradual control of sentences, from the earliest two-word sentences through all basic sentence patterns. After reviewing the research on syntactic development, he divides the information into stages of development and describes what children do within each stage, including brief transcripts of monologues and conversations to illustrate each stage of development. He also discusses the work of key researchers and cites their major publications. Because he is writing for beginning students in this field, he carefully defines all special linguistic terms.

CHAPTER 5

Explaining a Concept

Explanatory writing serves to inform readers. In general, it does not feature its writers' experiences or feelings, as autobiography does (see Chapters 2 and 3). Instead, successful explanatory writing presents information, confidently and efficiently, with the purpose of educating the reader about a topic. This type of writing, required almost every day in virtually every profession, may be based on first-hand observation (Chapter 4), but it always moves beyond describing specific objects and events to explain general principles and patterns of behavior. Since it deals almost exclusively with established information, explanatory writing tends not to present an argument but to present information as if everyone assumes it were true. It does not aspire to be more than it is: a way for readers to find out about a particular subject. Much of what we find in newspapers, encyclopedias, instruction manuals, reference books, and research reports is explanatory writing.

This chapter focuses on one important kind of explanatory writing, explanations of concepts. The chapter readings explain the concepts "love," "contingent workers," "path dependence," and "schizophrenia." These concepts name processes and phenomena under study. Scientists in various fields have studied the body's chemistry during both new romances and long-term relationships to create a "neurochemistry of love." Economists studying trends in the workforce use the concept "contingent workers" to describe the kind of workers, from chief executive officers to office assistants, who go from company to company to work on specific projects for limited amounts of time. Other economists have explained why promising technological developments frequently lose out to inferior ones by creating a concept known as "path dependence." Psychiatrists classify patients with certain symptoms as having the mental illness called "schizophrenia."

Every field of study has its concepts: physics has "entropy," "mass," and "fission"; literature has "irony," "romanticism," and "bildungsroman"; music has "harmony"; art has "perspective"; mathematics has "probability"; and so on. You can see from this brief list that concepts are central to the understanding of virtually every subject. Moreover, when you enter a new field, you are expected to learn a new set of concepts. That is why introductory courses and their textbooks teach a whole new vocabulary of technical terms and specialized jargon. When you read the opening chapter of this textbook, for example, you were introduced to many concepts important to the study of writing, such as "genre," "writing process," "invention," "revision," and "thinking critically."

Learning to explain a concept is especially important to you as a college student. It will help you to read textbooks (which themselves exist to explain concepts); it will prepare you to write a common type of exam and paper assignment; and it will acquaint you with the basic strategies common to all types of explanatory writing—definition, classification, comparison and contrast, cause and effect, and process narration.

Writing in Your Other Courses

In your college courses, you will frequently be asked to explain or apply concepts. These are some typical assignments:

- *For a chemistry course:* In your own words, explain the "law of definite proportions" and show its importance to the field of chemistry.
- *For a government course:* Choose one emerging democracy in eastern Europe, research it, and report on its progress in establishing a democratic government. Consider carefully its present arrangements for "political parties," "majority rule," "minority rights," and "popular consent."
- *For an English course:* Many works of literature depict "scapegoat" figures. Select two written works and two films, and discuss how the authors and directors present the social conflicts that lead to the creation of scapegoats.

→ Practice Explaining a Concept: A Collaborative Activity

The scenarios that open this chapter suggest occasions for writing about concepts. Think of some concepts you are currently studying or have recently studied or concepts connected to a sport or hobby you know a lot about. Here are some possibilities: "hip hop," "squeeze play," "ambition," "creativity," "friendship," "success," "hypertext," "interval training," "job satisfaction," "photosynthesis," "maturity," "community," "civil rights," "manifest destiny."

Part 1. Choose one concept to explain to two or three other students. When you have chosen your concept, think about what others in the group are likely to know about it and how you can inform them about it in two or three minutes. Consider how you will define the concept and what other strategies you might use—description, comparison, and so on—to explain it in an interesting, memorable way.

Get together with two or three other students and explain your concepts to one another. You might begin by indicating where you learned the concept and in what area of study or work or leisure it is usually used.

Part 2. When all group members have explained their concepts, discuss what you learned from the experience of explaining a concept. Begin by asking one another a question or two that would elicit further information you need to understand each concept more fully. Then, consider these questions:

- How did you decide what to include in your explanations and what to leave out?
- How successfully did you estimate listeners' prior knowledge of your concepts?
- If you were to repeat your explanation to a similar group of listeners, what would you add, subtract, or change?

READINGS

Anastasia Toufexis, an associate editor at *Time* since 1978, has written major reports, including some best-selling cover stories, for nearly every section of the magazine: medicine, health and fitness, law, environment, education, science, and national and world news. Toufexis received her bachelor's degree in premedicine from Smith College in 1967 and spent several years reporting for medical and pharmaceutical magazines. She has won a number of awards for her work at *Time* and has lectured on newsmagazine journalism and science writing at Columbia University, the University of North Carolina, and the School of Visual Arts in New York. As you read, notice how Toufexis brings together a variety of sources of information to present a neurochemical perspective on love.

LOVE: THE RIGHT CHEMISTRY
Anastasia Toufexis

Love is a romantic designation for a most ordinary biological—or, shall we say, chemical?—process. A lot of nonsense is talked and written about it.

—Greta Garbo to Melvyn Douglas in *Ninotchka*

O.K., let's cut out all this nonsense about romantic love. Let's bring some scientific precision to the party. Let's put love under a microscope. 1

When rigorous people with Ph.D.s after their names do that, what they see is not some silly, senseless thing. No, their probe reveals that love rests firmly on the foundations of evolution, biology and chemistry. What seems on the surface to be irrational, intoxicated behavior is in fact part of nature's master strategy—a vital force that has helped humans survive, thrive and multiply through thousands of years. Says Michael Mills, a psychology professor at Loyola Marymount University in Los Angeles: "Love is our ancestors whispering in our ears." 2

It was on the plains of Africa about 4 million years ago, in the early days of the human species, that the notion of romantic love probably first began to blossom—or at least that the first cascades of neurochemicals began flowing from the brain to the bloodstream to produce goofy grins and sweaty palms as men and women gazed deeply into each other's eyes. When mankind graduated from scuttling around on all fours to walking on two legs, this change made the whole person visible to fellow human beings for the first time. Sexual organs were in full display, as were other characteristics, from the color of eyes to the span of shoulders. As never before, each individual had a unique allure. 3

When the sparks flew, new ways of making love enabled sex to become a romantic encounter, not just a reproductive act. Although mounting mates from the rear was, and still is, the method favored among most animals, humans began to enjoy face-to-face couplings; both looks and personal attraction became a much greater part of the equation. 4

Romance served the evolutionary purpose of pulling males and females into long-term partnership, which was essential to child rearing. On open grasslands, one parent would have a hard—and dangerous—time handling a child while foraging for food. "If a woman was carrying the equivalent of a 20-lb. bowling ball in one arm and a pile of sticks in the other, it was ecologically critical to pair up with a mate to rear the young," explains anthropologist Helen Fisher, author of *Anatomy of Love.* 5

While Western culture holds fast to the idea that true love flames forever (the movie *Bram Stoker's Dracula* has the Count carrying the torch beyond the grave), nature apparently meant passions to sputter out in something like four years. Primitive pairs 6 stayed together just "long enough to rear one child through infancy," says Fisher. Then each would find a new partner and start all over again.

What Fisher calls the "four-year itch" shows up unmistakably in today's divorce statistics. In most of the 62 cultures she has studied, divorce rates peak around the fourth year of marriage. Additional youngsters help keep pairs together longer. If, say, a couple have another child three years after the first, as often occurs, then their union can be expected to last about four more years. That makes them ripe for the more familiar phenomenon portrayed in the Marilyn Monroe classic *The Seven-Year Itch.* 7

If, in nature's design, romantic love is not eternal, neither is it exclusive. Less than 5% of mammals form rigorously faithful pairs. From the earliest days, contends Fisher, the human pattern has been "monogamy with clandestine adultery." Occasional flings upped the chances that new combinations of genes would be passed on to the next generation. Men who sought new partners had more children. Contrary to common assumptions, women were just as likely to stray. "As long as prehistoric females were secretive about their extramarital affairs," argues Fisher, "they could garner extra resources, life insurance, better genes and more varied DNA for their biological futures. . . ." 8

Lovers often claim that they feel as if they are being swept away. They're not mistaken; they are literally flooded by chemicals, research suggests. A meeting of eyes, a touch of hands or a whiff of scent sets off a flood that starts in the brain and races along the nerves and through the blood. The results are familiar: flushed skin, sweaty palms, heavy breathing. If love looks suspiciously like stress, the reason is simple: the chemical pathways are identical. 9

Above all, there is the sheer euphoria of falling in love—a not-so-surprising reaction, considering that many of the substances swamping the newly smitten are chemical cousins of amphetamines. They include dopamine, norepinephrine and especially phenylethylamine (PEA). Cole Porter knew what he was talking about when he wrote, "I get a kick out of you." "Love is a natural high," observes Anthony Walsh, author of *The Science of Love: Understanding Love and Its Effects on Mind and Body.* "PEA gives you that silly smile that you flash at strangers. When we meet someone who is attractive to us, the whistle blows at the PEA factory." 10

But phenylethylamine highs don't last forever, a fact that lends support to arguments that passionate romantic love is short-lived. As with any amphetamine, the body builds up a tolerance to PEA; thus it takes more and more of the substance to produce love's special kick. After two to three years, the body simply can't crank up the needed amount of PEA. And chewing on chocolate doesn't help, despite popular belief. The candy is high in PEA, but it fails to boost the body's supply. 11

Fizzling chemicals spell the end of delirious passion; for many people that marks the end of the liaison as well. It is particularly true for those whom Dr. Michael Liebowitz of the New York State Psychiatric Institute terms "attraction junkies." They crave the intoxication of falling in love so much that they move frantically from affair to affair just as soon as the first rush of infatuation fades. 12

Still, many romances clearly endure beyond the first years. What accounts for that? Another set of chemicals, of course. The continued presence of a partner gradually steps up production in the brain of endorphins. Unlike the fizzy amphetamines, these are soothing substances. Natural pain-killers, they give lovers a sense of security, peace and calm. "That is one reason why it feels so horrible when we're abandoned or a lover dies," notes Fisher. "We don't have our daily hit of narcotics." 13

Researchers see a contrast between the heated infatuation induced by PEA, along with other amphetamine-like chemicals, and the more intimate attachment fostered 14 and prolonged by endorphins. "Early love is when you love the way the other person makes you feel," explains psychiatrist Mark Goulston of the University of California, Los Angeles. "Mature love is when you love the person as he or she is." It is the difference between passionate and compassionate love, observes Walsh, a psychobiologist at Boise State University in Idaho. "It's Bon Jovi vs. Beethoven."

Oxytocin is another chemical that has recently been implicated in love. Produced by the brain, it sensitizes nerves and stimulates muscle contraction. In women it helps uterine contractions during childbirth as well as production of breast milk, and seems to inspire mothers to nuzzle their infants. Scientists speculate that oxytocin might encourage similar cuddling between adult women and men. The versatile chemical may also enhance orgasms. In one study of men, oxytocin increased to three to five times its normal level during climax, and it may soar even higher in women.

Chemicals may help explain (at least to scientists) the feelings of passion and compassion, but why do people tend to fall in love with one partner rather than a myriad of others? Once again, it's partly a function of evolution and biology. "Men are looking for maximal fertility in a mate," says Loyola Marymount's Mills. "That is in large part why females in the prime childbearing ages of 17 to 28 are so desirable." Men can size up youth and vitality in a glance, and studies indeed show that men fall in love quite rapidly. Women tumble more slowly, to a large degree because their requirements are more complex; they need more time to check the guy out. "Age is not vital," notes Mills, "but the ability to provide security, father children, share resources and hold a high status in society are all key factors."

Still, that does not explain why the way Mary walks and laughs makes Bill dizzy with desire while Marcia's gait and giggle leave him cold. "Nature has wired us for one special person," suggests Walsh, romantically. He rejects the idea that a woman or a man can be in love with two people at the same time. Each person carries in his or her mind a [illegible] subliminal guide to the ideal partner, a "love map," to borrow a term coined [illegible] Money of Johns Hopkins University.

Dr[illegible]ences of childhood, the map is a record of whatever v[illegible]hing and disgusting. Small feet, curly hair. [illegible]hers told a joke. A fireman's unif[illegible]thered while growing up is imp[illegible]s never meet each and every rec[illegible]t up the wires and signal, "It's lo[illegible]overs may have different com- b[illegible]

[illegible] Probably not. To most people— [illegible] the sum of its natural parts. It's [illegible]on, poetry and phenylethylamine. [illegible]at love will never fully yield up its

Connecting to [illegible]

[illegible]phetamines fuel romance; endorphins and oxyto[illegible] Toufexis makes clear, however, these chemical reactions d[illegible]e are initially attracted to each other. Toufexis explains that an initial a[illegible]urs because each of us carries a "unique subliminal guide" or "love map" that lead[illegible]s unerringly to a partner. Moreover, she explains that men look for maximal fertility, whereas women look for security, resources, status, and a willingness to father children.

Discuss these explanations for sexual attraction. Consider where your love map comes from and how much it may be influenced by your family or ethnicity or images in the media or advertising. Consider whether it is possible for an individual's love map to change over time—from adolescence to adulthood, for example.

Analyzing Writing Strategies

1. At the beginning of this chapter, we present generalizations about essays explaining concepts. Consider which of these are true of Toufexis's essay.
   - It seeks to inform readers about a specific subject.
   - It presents information confidently and efficiently.
   - It relies almost exclusively on established information.
   - It does not feature its writer's experiences or feelings.
   - It tends not to argue for its points.
2. To keep readers on track, writers of explanations offer prominent cues. One such cue is the **transition sentence** that opens a new paragraph, referring to information in the preceding paragraph. To see how Toufexis relates information paragraph by paragraph, examine each opening sentence in paragraphs 7–15, underlining any parts that refer to the preceding paragraph. Your underlining will show that these transitions work in a variety of ways. Choose three transitions that function in different ways, and try to explain the differences.

Considering Topics for Your Own Essay

Like Toufexis, you could write an essay about love or romance, but with a different focus: on its history (how and when did it develop as an idea in the West?), its cultural characteristics (how is love regarded presently among different American ethnic groups or world cultures?), its excesses or extremes, its expression between parent and child, or the phases of falling in and out of love. Also consider writing about other concepts involving personal relationships, such as "jealousy," "codependency," "idealization," "stereotyping," or "homophobia."

Commentary

Observing an important requirement of essays explaining concepts, Toufexis provides several different kinds of cues to keep readers on track. In addition to paragraph-opening transitions, Toufexis carefully **forecasts** the topics and direction of her essay in her second paragraph: "Their probe reveals that love rests firmly on the foundations of evolution, biology and chemistry." This forecast helps readers anticipate the types of scientific information Toufexis has selected for her special focus on love.

Besides offering frequent transitions and a forecast, Toufexis also **frames** her explanation. Writers create a frame when they relate the end of an essay to its beginning, providing readers with a satisfying sense of closure. At both the beginning and the end of her essay, Toufexis refers to science, scientists, and Ph.D.'s. She also contrasts romantic feelings themselves with the scientific approach to understanding the neurochemistry of those feelings. Note, however, that she does not simply paraphrase what she said earlier. Instead, she "echoes" the beginning in a subtle way by returning to references, ideas, and key words or phrases the reader will remember.

For more on cueing readers, see Chapter 13.

You can feature all of these cues—transitions, forecasting, framing—in your essay explaining a concept. Whereas forecasting and framing are optional, transitions are essential; without them, your readers will either stumble along resentfully or throw up their hands in confusion and irritation.

Concept explanations are based on authoritative, expert **sources,** on established material gleaned from reputable **publications** or **interviews.** Toufexis uses both these kinds of sources. She apparently arranged phone interviews with six different professors specializing in diverse academic disciplines: psychology, anthropology, psychiatry, and sexology. (She does not identify the discipline of one professor—Walsh, in paragraph 10—but from the title of his book, we might guess that he is a biochemist.) We assume that she read at least parts of the two books she names in paragraphs 5 and 10, and perhaps she also read still other sources, which may have led her to some of the professors she interviewed.

What is obvious about Toufexis's use of sources is that she does not indicate precisely where she obtained all the information she includes. For example, she does not cite the source of the anthropological information in paragraphs 3–5, although a reader might guess that she summarized it from *Anatomy of Love,* cited at the end of paragraph 5. We cannot be certain whether the quote at the end of paragraph 5 comes from the book or from an interview with its author. These liberties in citing sources are acceptable in newspapers and magazines, including the leading ones educated readers count on to keep them up to date on developments in various fields. Experienced readers know that reporters, who write about surprisingly diverse topics as part of their jobs, rely entirely on sources for their articles and essays. They understand that Toufexis is not an expert on the neurochemistry of love; they accept her role as synthesizer and summarizer of authoritative sources.

Part III covers these and other writing strategies in detail.

Toufexis also uses some of the writing strategies that make concept explanations possible: **narrating, classifying,** and **analyzing effects.** Toufexis relies on narrative in paragraphs 3 and 4 to sketch out the evolution of romantic love. She uses past-tense verbs common to narrative *(began, gazed, graduated)* along with clauses and phrases indicating time *(when, in the early days, the first time, as never before)*. She uses classification to organize the information about chemicals in paragraphs 9–15, first setting up the classification in paragraph 9—which is also an example of internal forecasting—and then presenting information about three kinds of chemicals: phenylethylamines (paragraph 13), endorphins (paragraph 14), and oxytocin (paragraph 15). Toufexis analyzes effects in paragraphs 5–8, where she suggests the benefits of romantic love for human evolution.

Janice Castro, a graduate of the University of California at Berkeley, is an associate editor at *Time,* where she writes about politics and business. Some of her major reports have addressed the high cost of medical care, drugs in the workplace, quality in American manufacturing, the state of the U.S. workforce, and Japanese investment in the United States. In the following selection, originally published in *Time* in 1993, Castro discusses changes in the way American companies do business, changes that rely on part-time and freelance workers. Castro uses the concept "contingent workers" to name both the phenomenon and the people it affects.

CONTINGENT WORKERS

Janice Castro

The corporation that is now the largest private employer in America does not have any smokestacks or conveyor belts or trucks. There is no clanging of metal on metal, no rivets or plastic or steel. In one sense, it does not make anything. But then again, it is in the business of making almost everything. 1

Manpower Inc., with 560,000 workers, is the world's largest temporary employment agency. Every morning, its people scatter into the offices and factories of America, seeking a day's work for a day's pay. As General Motors (367,000 workers), IBM (330,500) and other industrial giants struggle to survive by shrinking their payrolls, Manpower, based in Milwaukee, Wisconsin, is booming along with other purveyors of temporary workers, providing the hands and the brainpower that other companies are no longer willing to call their own. 2

Even as its economy continues to recover, the U.S. is increasingly becoming a nation of part-timers and free-lancers, of temps and independent contractors. This "disposable" work force is the most important trend in business today, and it is fundamentally changing the relationship between Americans and their jobs. For companies large and small, the phenomenon provides a way to remain globally competitive while avoiding the vagaries of market cycles and the growing burdens imposed by employment rules, antidiscrimination laws, health-care costs, and pension plans. But for workers, it can mean an end to the security and sense of significance that came from being a loyal employee. One by one, the tangible and intangible bonds that once defined work in America are giving way. 3

Every day, 1.5 million temps are dispatched from agencies like Kelly Services and Manpower—nearly three times as many as 10 years ago. But they are only the most visible part of America's enormous new temporary work force. An additional 34 million people start their day as other types of "contingent" workers. Some are part-timers with some benefits. Others work by the hour, the day or the duration of a project, receiving only a paycheck without benefits of any kind. The rules of their employment vary widely and so do the attempts to label them. They are called short-timers, per-diem workers, leased employees, extra workers, supplementals, contractors—or in IBM's ironic computer-generated parlance, "the peripherals." They are what you might expect: secretaries, security guards, salesclerks, assembly-line workers, analysts and CAD/CAM designers. But these days they are also what you'd never expect: doctors, high school principals, lawyers, bank officers, X-ray technicians, biochemists, engineers, managers—even chief executives. 4

Already, one in every three U.S. workers has joined these shadow brigades carrying out America's business. Their ranks are growing so quickly that they are expected to outnumber permanent full-time workers by the end of this decade. Companies keep chipping away at costs, stripping away benefits or substituting contingent employees for full-time workers. This year alone, U.S. employers are expected to use such tactics to cut the nation's $2.6 billion payroll costs as much as $800 million. And there is no evidence to suggest that such corporate behavior will change with improvement in the economy. 5

No institution is immune to the contingent solution. Imagine the surprise of a Los Angeles woman, seriously injured in an auto accident, when she recently asked a radiology technician at the hospital about a procedure. "Don't ask me," he snapped. "I'm just a temp." In Appleton, Wisconsin, the Aid Association for Lutherans is using temps to keep track of $3.6 million in relief funds for victims of Hurricane Andrew. The State of Maine uses temps as bailiffs and financial investigators. IBM, once the citadel of 6

American job security, has traded 10% of its staff for "peripherals" so far. Says IBM administrative manager Lillian Davis, in words that would have been unimaginable from a Fortune 500 executive 20 years ago: "Now that we have stepped over that line, we have decided to use these people wherever we can."

The number of people employed full time by Fortune 500 companies has shrunk from 19% of the work force two decades ago to less than 10% today. Almost overnight, companies are shedding a system of mutual obligations and expectations built up since the Great Depression, a tradition of labor that said performance was rewarded, loyalty was valued and workers were a vital part of the enterprises they served. In this chilly new world of global competition, they are often viewed merely as expenses. Long-term commitments of all kinds are anathema to the modern corporation. For the growing ranks of contingent workers, that means no more pensions, health insurance or paid vacations. No more promises or promotions or costly training programs. No more lawsuits for wrongful termination or other such hassles for the boss. Says Secretary of Labor Robert Reich: "These workers are outside the traditional system of worker-management relationships. As the contingent work force grows—as many people find themselves working part time for many different employers—the social contract is beginning to fray." 7

As the underpinnings of mutual commitment crumble, time-honored notions of fairness are cast aside for millions of workers. Working temp or part time often means being treated as a second-class citizen by both employers and permanent staff. Says Michelle Lane, a former temp in Los Angeles: "You're just a fixture, a borrowed thing that doesn't belong there." Being a short-timer also can mean doing hazardous work without essential training, or putting up with sexual and racial harassment. Placement officers report client requests for "blond bombshells" or people without accents. Says an agency counselor: "One client called and asked us not to send any black people, and we didn't. We do whatever the clients want, whether it's right or not." 8

Workers have little choice but to cope with such treatment since most new job openings are the labor equivalent of uncommitted relationships. More than 90% of the 365,000 jobs created by U.S. companies last month were part-time positions taken by people who want to work full time. "The fill-ins are always desperate for full-time jobs," says one corporate personnel officer. "They always ask." Richard Belous, chief economist for the National Planning Association in Washington, has studied the proliferation of tenuous jobs. "If there was a national fear index," he says, "it would be directly related to the growth of contingent work." 9

Once contingent workers appear in a company, they multiply rapidly, taking the places of permanent staff. Says Manpower chairman Mitchell Fromstein: "The U.S. is going from just-in-time manufacturing to just-in-time employment. The employer tells us, 'I want them delivered exactly when I want them, as many as I need, and when I don't need them, I don't want them here.'" Fromstein has built his business by meeting these demands. "Can I get people to work under these circumstances? Yeah. We're the ATMs of the job market." 10

In order to succeed in this new type of work, says Carvel Taylor, a Chicago industrial consultant, "you need to have an entrepreneurial spirit, definable skills and an ability to articulate and market them, but that is exactly what the bulk of the population holed up inside bureaucratic organizations doesn't have, and why they are scared to death." Already the temping phenomenon is producing two vastly different classes of untethered workers: the mercenary work force at the top of the skills ladder, who thrive; and the rest, many of whom, unable to attract fat contract fees, must struggle to survive. 11

The flexible life of a consultant or contract worker does indeed work well for a relatively small class of people like doctors, engineers, accountants and financial planners, who can expect to do well by providing highly compensated services to a variety of employers. David Hill, 65, a former chief information systems officer for General Motors, has joined with 17 other onetime auto-industry executives (median salary before leaving their jobs: $300,000) to form a top-of-the-line international consulting group. "In the future," says Hill, "loyalty and devotion are going to be not to a Hughes or Boeing or even an industry, but to a particular profession or skill. It takes a high level of education to succeed in such a free-flowing environment. We are going to be moving from job to job in the same way that migrant workers used to move from crop to crop."

Many professionals like the freedom of such a life. John Andrews, 42, a Los Angeles antitrust attorney, remembers working seven weeks without a day off as a young lawyer. He prefers temping at law firms. Says he: "There's no security anymore. Partnerships fold up overnight. Besides, I never had a rat-race mentality, and being a lawyer is the ultimate rat-race job. I like to travel. My car is paid for. I don't own a house. I'm not into mowing grass."

But most American workers do better with the comfort and security of a stable job. Sheldon Joseph was a Chicago advertising executive until he was laid off in 1989. Now he temps for $10 an hour in a community job-training program. Says the 56-year-old Joseph: "I was used to working in the corporate environment and giving my total loyalty to the company. I feel like Rip Van Winkle. You wake up and the world is all changed. The message from industry is, 'We don't want your loyalty. We want your work.' What happened to the dream?"

Employers defend their new labor practices as plain and simple survival tactics. American companies are evolving from huge, mass-production manufacturers that once dominated markets to a new species of hub-and-network enterprises built for flexibility in a brutally competitive world. The buzz phrase at many companies is "accordion management"—the ability to expand or contract one's work force virtually at will to suit business conditions.

Boardroom discussions now focus on what are called "core competencies"—those operations at the heart of a business—and on how to shed the rest of the functions to subcontractors or nonstaff workers. Managers divide their employees into a permanent cadre of "core workers," which keeps on shrinking, and the contingent workers, who can be brought in at a moment's notice. Most large employers are not even certain at any given time how many of these helpers are working for them—nor do they usually care. Says a manager: "We don't count them. They're not here long enough to matter." Some analysts wonder whether America's celebrated rise in productivity per worker (2.8% last year) is all it seems to be, since so many of those invisible hands are not being counted. So profound is the change that the word *core* has evolved a new meaning, as in "she's core," meaning that she is important and distinctive because she is not part of the contingent work force.

Indeed, managers these days can hire virtually any kind of temp they want. Need an extra lawyer or paralegal for a week or so? Try Lawsmiths in San Francisco or Project Professionals in Santa Monica, California. Need a loan officer? Bank Temps in Denver can help. Engineers? Sysdyne outside Minneapolis, Minnesota. CAD/CAM operators? You don't even need to buy the equipment: in Oakland, California, Western Temporary Services has its own CAD/CAM business, serving such clients as the U.S. Navy, the Air Force, Chevron, Exxon and United Technologies. Doctors and nurses? A firm called

Interim in Fort Lauderdale, Florida, can provide them anywhere in the country. Need to rent a tough boss to clean up a bad situation? Call IMCOR, a Connecticut-based firm that boasts a roster of senior executives expert at turnarounds. Says IMCOR chairman John Thompson: "Services like ours are going to continue to flourish when businesses change so rapidly that it's in no one's interest to make commitments. Moving on to the next place where you're needed is going to be the way it is. We will all be free-lancers."

18 For now, most citizens will have to scramble to adapt to the new age of the disposable worker. Says Robert Schaen, a former comptroller of Chicago-based Ameritech who now runs his own children's publishing business: "The days of the mammoth corporations are coming to an end. People are going to have to create their own lives, their own careers and their own successes. Some people may go kicking and screaming into the new world, but there is only one message there: You're now in business for yourself."

Connecting to Culture and Experience

Janice Castro reports on a surprising change in the employment conditions of American workers. As recently as ten to fifteen years ago, most workers held full-time jobs with health care coverage, paid vacations, and pension plans. Many had virtual job security, continuing in the same job for thirty or forty years until retirement. Now, one-third of American workers are contingent, and Castro predicts that they will outnumber permanent, full-time workers by the year 2000.

Discuss what this change might mean for you personally. First, describe a job that you or others you know have held contingently. Then, speculate about how the increase in contingent work may affect your career plans and life opportunities. Do you hope to avoid contingent work? If so, how might you do so? Could contingent work provide opportunities at certain points in your career? How might you plan for a successful career at which you worked only contingently?

Analyzing Writing Strategies

For more on definition, see Chapter 16.

1. Writers of essays explaining concepts must nearly always create their own **definitions** for the central concept and other key terms. In paragraph 4, Castro tentatively defines "contingent workers." How does she go about constructing this definition? What does it include? How satisfactory do you find this initial definition of the concept?
2. It is likely that you found Castro's essay understandable on first reading and needed only occasionally to reread a sentence or brief section in order to clarify meaning. Reread the essay, making a list of any features that contribute to its **readability.**

Considering Topics for Your Own Essay

Consider writing about the "contingent worker" concept, but with a focus different from Castro's. For example, you could focus on the debate between labor and business over contingent work (sorting out the issues and reporting what you learn but not taking a side yourself), the history of contingent or part-time work in America, or changes brought about in the lives of people who have had to give up full-time jobs and take up contingent work. Or you could write about some other concept central to current discussions of work, such as "career path," "glass ceiling," "burnout," "networking," "mentoring," "management styles," or "collective bargaining."

Commentary

Castro makes good use of a variety of **sources.** As a business reporter, she has access to published materials and computer data sources that provide the many facts and statistics she includes about corporations and employment trends. Since she has written about contingent workers and related topics before, she has developed a store of information. In addition, she apparently interviewed fourteen people for this new report, and some of her facts and statistics may have come from these interviews. Following her magazine's convention for citing sources, she names her interviewees but does not identify other sources of information, perhaps because she knows that her readers will accept the information as well established. Many news media assume that readers and listeners will accept statistics they cite about American business, just as people accept their baseball scores and weather reports.

When you write your essay for this chapter, you too will rely on a variety of authoritative sources to explain a concept to readers who know less about it than you do. You will need to cite your sources more precisely and more fully than Castro does, however, because complete citation of sources is expected in all academic writing by students and professors. Veronica Murayama's essay in this chapter and Chapter 22 provide guidance in using and acknowledging sources.

Writers face special challenges in **planning and organizing** essays that explain concepts. First, they gather a lot of information about a concept. Then, they must find a way to explain the concept that will interest and inform their readers. Finally, writers must organize the information so that readers can understand it without too much uncertainty or frustration.

Consider Castro's plan. Here is a scratch outline of her essay:

For more on scratch outlining, see "Outlining" in Chapter 11.

Manpower Inc. employs more workers than GM. (paragraphs 1–2)

Increase in part-time and freelance employment represents a fundamental change. (3)

The concept of contingent workers is defined. (4)

The number of contingents is growing and not likely to decline when the economy improves. (5)

All kinds of institutions and businesses are relying on contingents. (6)

Mutual obligations between employer and employee are being shed. (7)

Contingents are second-class citizens. (8–9)

Demand for contingents is increasing. (10)

Some contingents find success. (11–13)

But most Americans still prefer a secure job. (14)

Employers have a number of arguments for relying on contingents. (15)

Employers distinguish sharply between core and contingent employees. (16)

Some contingents are highly specialized. (17)

Workers will have to adapt to this change. (18)

At the beginning, Castro contextualizes and defines the concept (paragraphs 1–4). She then reports on the nature of contingent work (5–10) and its mixed impact on employees (11–14). Finally, she presents employers' views (15–17) and concludes with a new way for contingent workers to see themselves—as being in business for themselves (18). Most readers will find this plan easy to follow.

Finally, special kinds of sentence structures enable writers to present information effectively. For example, Castro relies on **appositives** and **parenthetical explanations** that efficiently combine into one sentence information that might otherwise require two:

> IBM, *once the citadel of American job security,* has traded 10% of its staff for "peripherals" so far. (paragraph 6)
>
> Says Michelle Lane, *a former temp in Los Angeles:* "You're just a fixture, a borrowed thing that doesn't belong there." (8)
>
> As General Motors *(367,000 workers),* IBM *(330,500),* and other industrial giants struggle to survive . . . (2)

By combining information into series or lists, writers of explanatory essays can gain further efficiency:

> . . . avoiding the vagaries of market cycles and the growing burden imposed by *employment rules, antidiscrimination laws, health-care costs, and pension plans.* (paragraph 3)
>
> They are called *short-timers, per-diem workers, leased employees, extra workers, supplementals, contractors*—or in IBM's ironic computer-generated parlance, "the peripherals." (4)
>
> They are what you might expect: *secretaries, security guards, salesclerks, assembly-line workers, analysts and CAD/CAM designers.* (4)

Items in a series or list must be grammatically parallel. Lists can be introduced by a colon, as in the last example just given.

Peter Passell holds a Ph.D. in economics from Yale University. Since 1977, he has worked for the *New York Times,* first as a member of the editorial board for several years and now as a reporter and columnist. He has written articles and reviews for the *New York Times Magazine* and *Book Review, The New York Review of Books, The New Republic, The Nation,* and *Le Monde.* His most recent book is *Where to Put Your Money* (1996), a practical guide for the small investor.

Published in the *New York Times Magazine* in 1996, "Path Dependence" explains a new economics concept that enables us to understand why the best inventions sometimes lose out to inferior competitors. As you read, notice how Passell relies on several quite different illustrations of the concept in order to help readers to understand it and see its usefulness.

PATH DEPENDENCE: WHY THE BEST DOESN'T ALWAYS WIN

Peter Passell

Apple Computer, the company that brought you the idiot-friendly Macintosh, is staring at bankruptcy. Meanwhile, the great army of technocrats at Microsoft, which only last year managed to reproduce the look and feel of a 1980's Mac, lumbers on, invincible. 1

A bad break for Apple? A rare exception to the Darwinian rules in which the best products win the hearts and dollars of consumers? No. Economists are finally beginning to acknowledge what others have long suspected: the best doesn't always win. Just as biologists are challenging the idea that natural selection drives evolution along "efficient" and predictable paths, economists are discovering the disorder that lurks in the shadows of their simple, elegant models of capitalist progress. . . . 2

Recent wisdom on this subject dates back to 1985. That's the year Paul David, an economic historian at Stanford University, published an article about QWERTY in *The American Economic Review.* Q-W-E-R-T-Y, of course, are the first six letters on the upper left of the typewriter keyboard—the universal standard since the 1890's. But why these? Why not one of half a dozen other keyboard layouts that are said to permit faster typing? 3

David's answer is that QWERTY was the solution to a fleeting technological problem, an arrangement that would minimize the jamming of keys in primitive typewriters. While this explanation has since been challenged, what matters is that one keyboard, chosen for reasons long irrelevant, remains the standard. For all their ingenuity, competing designs have made about as much headway against QWERTY as Esperanto[1] has made against English. That's because a standardized layout allows typists to learn just one keyboard in order to use all. Once thousands of people had learned to type using QWERTY's merely adequate layout, the technology was effectively locked in. Keyboard design is thus the classic example of "path dependence," the idea that small, random events at critical moments can determine choices in technology that are extremely difficult and expensive to change. 4

In the typical path-dependence scenario, producers or consumers see one technology as slightly superior. This edge quickly snowballs into clear economic advantage: production costs fall with greater experience in manufacturing, and consumer acceptance grows with greater familiarity. And along the way, the weight of numbers makes the leading product more valuable than one based on competing technologies. With more MS-DOS computers around, it pays to write software to the Microsoft standard, which in turn makes it more useful to own an MS-DOS computer. 5

The most familiar example of path dependence is the triumph of Matsushita's VHS standard for videocassette recorders over Sony's Betamax. Betamax was first and, by most accounts, better. But Sony made two strategic marketing errors. To get the product out the door faster, it initially sold Betamax machines that played one-hour tapes—too short for an entire movie. And to sell more Sony machines, the company chose not to license Betamax to competitors. 6

VHS, introduced a year later, in 1976, played two-hour tapes. And since Matsushita freely licensed the technology, half a dozen other brand-name VHS players hit the stores in a matter of months. Sony soon countered with a two-hour machine, but it was too late. 7

While VHS versus Betamax makes great fodder for business school seminars, the outcome hardly made the earth move. The stakes have been much higher in technolo- 8

[1]A simplified international language invented in the late nineteenth century.

gies that are now so entrenched it's hard to imagine the world without them. Take the automobile engine. At the turn of the century, gasoline was locked in a three-way race with steam and electric power. The Stanley Steamer was a technological marvel, setting a world speed record of 122 miles an hour in 1909. But the manufacturer priced the car as a luxury, never trying to achieve the economies of mass production and of "learning by doing" that might have made it the people's car.

Moreover, steam's economic problems were compounded by an outbreak of hoof-and-mouth disease in 1914 that briefly closed public horse troughs and denied steam cars a convenient source of water for their perpetually thirsty boilers. With better technology or simply many more steam cars on the road, this liability would have evaporated. But car buyers had little incentive to make a leap of faith when plausible alternatives were available. One of those alternatives was the electric car, whose weakness was a driving range limited by the storage capacity of its batteries. That problem seemed well on its way to solution around 1915. But innovators in the battery industry were distracted by the more immediate need to perfect a high-amperage battery to crank the new electric starters in cars with gasoline engines. 9

Apparently all the gasoline engine needed to triumph was a brief period in which its technological and price edge led to rapidly expanding sales. This cut production costs, which expanded sales even more—and made it more convenient to fuel and service gasoline vehicles. 10

Today, of course, dependence on gasoline engines is a fact of life. While electric or steam vehicles would reduce air pollution and dependence on imported oil, it would take an investment of tens or even hundreds of billions of dollars to leap the technological chasm. Indeed, California, which has mandated the use of electric cars, is just now facing the reality that the existing technology is wretchedly inadequate to the task. 11

Robin Cowan of the University of Western Ontario offers a second cautionary tale of path dependence. The world is stuck with another functional, but environmentally problematic, technology: the "light water" nuclear reactor, whose momentary superiority over reactors that use inert gases led to the virtual abandonment of alternatives. 12

In the mid-1950's there was no particular reason to believe that light-water reactors were the cheapest to build and operate. But the Navy invested heavily in light water, which was seen as the most compact and reliable design for submarines and aircraft carriers. When Washington pressed for a quick scale-up to commercial nuclear power after the Soviet Union exploded a nuclear weapon, American manufacturers took the route of least technological resistance. 13

Later, Washington used subsidies for design and manufacturing to persuade the Europeans to switch to a light-water standard. And once light-water reactors were produced in quantity, the manufacturers learned-by-doing, cutting costs well below those of competing designs. 14

Perhaps light-water reactors would have prevailed in any event. But there is little doubt that a competing gas-graphite system was safer because it offered greater protection against catastrophic loss of coolant. With global warming now looming, the "lock-in" to atmospherically benign—but widely feared—light-water nuclear technology must count as an opportunity lost. 15

If path dependence is such a big deal, why are college freshmen unlikely to encounter the idea in Econ. 101? Brian Arthur, a pioneer in the field at Stanford in the early 1980's who now does research at the Santa Fe Institute, blames tradition-bound economists. Put it another way: the "technology" of modern economics is itself path dependent, because economists have so much invested elsewhere. 16

Connecting to Culture and Experience

Path dependence explains choices in technology, but Passell's more general point that the best does not always win applies broadly to cultural events. From your own experience and knowledge, think of one illustration of this insight about competition. Perhaps the most creative song never made the charts, the best team failed to win the championship, the most effective legislation won too little support, a challenging and well-organized course did not attract students, the best-qualified student was not awarded a prize or an award, or the most impressive movie was not nominated for an Academy Award.

Discuss with other students your favorite example of the best not winning. In turn, describe your examples briefly. Then, speculate together about why each example might have lost out to an inferior. What generalizations can you make to explain why your separate examples failed? For example, you might generalize that people are often intimidated by excellence or that the first person to gain a foothold is likely to win the competition. Your generalizations need not apply to every example that you discussed.

Analyzing Writing Strategies

See the scratch outline of Castro's essay on p. 168 for an example.

1. To understand how Passell organized the information available to him, make a scratch outline of his explanation. Looking over your outline, and referring to the essay as you need to, notice how the essay begins (paragraphs 1 and 2) and decide how the beginning relates to what follows. Then, consider the role of paragraphs 3–5. Finally, reflect on the sequence of the remaining paragraphs. What patterns do you find? What advantages or disadvantages do you see in Passell's **organization**?
2. Writers who are explaining concepts rely on **examples** to increase readers' understanding. Passell offers four examples to explain path dependence. The first is in paragraphs 1 and 2, the second in paragraphs 6 and 7, the third in paragraphs 8–11, and the fourth in paragraphs 12–15. First, analyze each example to discover its topic. Assuming that Passell decided to provide four examples of path dependence because he believed that each offered new information about the concept, decide what each example adds to your understanding. Finally, identify the example that was most informative and most memorable for you as one reader.

Considering Topics for Your Own Essay

If you have a special interest in business, economics, or technology, consider writing an essay explaining a concept from that field. You need not choose a recently established concept, as Passell does, though readers may find leading-edge topics particularly enticing. Examples might include "glass ceiling" in business, "gross domestic product" in economics, or "genetic engineering" in technology.

Commentary

Like other authors in this chapter, Passell provides readers with a concise **definition** of the concept he is explaining. At the end of paragraph 4, he defines "path dependence" as "the idea that small, random events at critical moments can determine choices in technology that are extremely difficult and expensive to change." Toufexis's concept is the chemical basis of love, which she defines most precisely in this way: "Researchers see a contrast between the heated infatuation induced by PEA, along with other amphetamine-like chemicals, and the more intimate attachment fostered and prolonged by the endorphins" (paragraph 14). Castro's definition of "contingent workers" is slightly more expansive: "Some are part-timers with some benefits. Others work by the hour, the day or the duration of the project, receiving only a paycheck without benefits of any kind. The rules of their employment vary widely and so do the attempts to label them. They are called short-timers, per-diem workers, leased employees, extra workers, supplementals, contractors—or in IBM's computer-generated parlance, 'the peripherals'" (paragraph 4). Concise and accessible, these are like dictionary definitions, and similar definitions for *contingent workers* and *path dependence* may in fact appear soon in dictionaries.

While readers expect a concise definition of the concept at some point in the explanation, they expect much more—they need much more—if they are to understand it: They need **examples.** Examples are integral to Passell's explanation. The essay opens with an example: the likelihood that Apple Computer will be done in by Microsoft Corporation and its clunkier Windows 95 operating system for IBM-compatible personal computers. Indeed, the definition of "path dependence" follows this example so that the definition will seem less abstract and therefore more meaningful. Three other examples follow, all of them developed in some detail so that their relevance and importance will be readily apparent to readers.

Finally, Passell's essay is **focused.** There may be many other explanations for why products fail, but Passell focuses on just one of them, path dependence. We can infer that he focused on this concept because he believed that it should be more widely known. He mentions its recent emergence but stops short of tracing the history of the concept and giving us a biography of Paul David, its originator. He indicates that many economists seem not to know about the concept or perhaps resist its implications for their own field, but he does not speculate at length about the causes of this resistance or quote economists who question the usefulness of the concept. Instead he focuses on introducing it to nonspecialist readers who are curious about how things work in the world at large. As you read and learn about the concept that you will explain in your essay, one of your most important decisions will be to find an appropriate focus for a relatively brief introduction to the concept.

Veronica Murayama wrote this essay as a first-year college student. In it, she defines a psychiatric concept, the debilitating mental illness called schizophrenia. Since this illness has been exhaustively studied and so much has been written about it, Murayama had to find a manageable focus for her essay. As you read, consider how she made this choice. Notice, too, how she seeks to engage your interest in the concept.

SCHIZOPHRENIA: WHAT IT LOOKS LIKE, HOW IT FEELS

Veronica Murayama

1 Some mental illnesses, like depression, are more common than schizophrenia, but few are more severe. A schizophrenic has delusions and hallucinations, behaves in bizarre ways, talks incoherently, expresses little feeling or else feelings inappropriate to the situation, and is incapable of normal social interactions. Because these symptoms are so severe, about half the hospitalized mentally ill in America are schizophrenics.

Only 1 percent of Americans (between 2 and 3 million) are schizophrenic, and yet they occupy about one-fourth of the available beds in our hospitals ("Schizophrenic," 1987, p. 1533). Up to 40 percent of the homeless may be schizophrenic (King, 1989, p. 97).

2 Schizophrenia has been recognized for centuries, and as early as the seventeenth century its main symptoms, course of development, and outcome were described. The term *schizophrenia,* first used in 1908, refers to the disconnection or splitting of the mind that seems basic to all the various forms of the disease. It strikes both men and women, usually during adolescence or early adulthood, and is found all over the world. Treatment may include chemotherapy, electroconvulsive therapy, psychotherapy, and counseling. Hospitalization is ordinarily required, but usually not for more than a few months. It seems that about a third of patients recover completely and the rest can eventually have "a reasonable life adjustment," but some effect of the illness nearly always remains, most commonly lack of feeling and reduced drive or ambition ("Schizophrenic," 1987, pp. 1533, 1537–1539). Schizophrenia hits adolescents especially hard, and the effect on their families can be disastrous.

3 Though much is known about schizophrenia and treatment is reasonably effective, specialists still argue about its causes. For example, various researchers blame an unsatisfactory family life in which one or both parents suffer from some form of mental illness (Lidz, 1973), some combination of genetic inheritance and family life ("Schizophrenic," 1987, p. 1534; "Schizophrenia," 1987, p. 192), or "an early developmental neuropathological process" that results in reduced size of certain brain areas (Suddath, Cristison, Torrey, Casanova, & Weinberger, 1990, p. 793). What is known and agreed on, however, is what schizophrenia looks like to an observer and what it feels like to a sufferer, and these are what I want to focus on in this essay. I have always believed that when people have knowledge about any type of human suffering, they are more likely to be sympathetic with the sufferer. Schizophrenic symptoms are not attractive, but they are easy to understand. The medical manuals classify them approximately as follows: bizarre delusions, prominent hallucinations, confusion about identity, unconnected speech, inappropriate affect, disturbances in psychomotor behavior, impaired interpersonal functioning, and reduced drive.

4 Schizophrenics themselves experience the disease to a large extent as delusional thinking. For example, one woman said, "If I see a phone, I can talk on it without picking it up, immediately, anywhere in the world. But I don't abuse it. I'm authorized by AT&T. In the Yukon. And RCA" (Shane, 1987). It is common for schizophrenics to have delusions that they are being persecuted—that people are spying on them, spreading false stories about them, or planning to harm them. Events, objects, or people may be given special threatening significance, as when a patient believes a television commentator is making fun of him. Other delusions are very likely: "the belief or experience that one's thoughts, as they occur, are broadcast from one's head to the external world so that others can hear them; that thoughts that are not one's own are inserted into one's mind; that thoughts have been removed from one's head; or that one's feelings, impulses, thoughts, or actions are not one's own, but are imposed by some external force" ("Schizophrenia," 1987, p. 188). Sometimes delusions are grandiose, as when a patient thinks that he is the Messiah and will save the world or that she is the center of a conspiracy. A woman patient wrote, "I want a revolution, a great uprising to spread over the entire world and overthrow the whole social order. . . . Not for the love of adventure! No, no! Call it unsatisfied urge to action, if you like, indomitable ambition" (cited in Lidz, 1973, p. 134).

Related to delusions are hallucinations, which are very common in schizophrenics. Usually they hear voices coming from inside or outside the head, making insulting remarks, commenting on behavior, or giving commands that can sometimes be dangerous to others. Sometimes they hear sounds like humming, whistling, or machinery. 5

These false ideas and imaginary sensations leave schizophrenics confused about their identities. Feeling ruled by forces outside themselves, they lack normal feelings of individuality and uniqueness. One patient wrote, "I look at my arms and they aren't mine. They move without my direction. Somebody else moves them. . . . I have no control. I don't live in me. The outside and I are all the same" (cited in Mendel, 1974, p. 111). 6

Besides revealing their delusions and hallucinations, schizophrenics' speech is often rambling and unconnected. It may shift rapidly from one topic to another that is seemingly completely unrelated or only loosely related, and the speaker does not show any awareness of the lack of connection. One patient, a man, said, "I have always believed in the good of mankind but I know I am not a woman because I have an Adam's apple" ("Schizophrenic," 1987). Sometimes the topics are so unrelated that the patient's speech becomes incoherent and incomprehensible. Even when it is connected, schizophrenic speech can sometimes contain very little information because it is vague, abstract, or repetitive. 7

Schizophrenics also present themselves in recognizable ways, referred to as "inappropriate affect." Their voices are often monotonous and their faces expressionless. They may express little if any emotion, and their emotional responses do not seem varied. On the other hand, their responses may seem completely inappropriate to the situation, or there may be unpredictable outbursts of anger. 8

Another visible feature of schizophrenia is disturbed psychomotor behavior. The most severely ill may move around very little or sit rigidly and resist being moved. Here is what one patient felt: "When I was acting so stiff and wasn't talking I had the feeling that if I moved the whole world might collapse. . . . I don't know why, but I seemed like I was the center of everything and everything depended on my not moving" (cited in Mendel, 1974, p. 108). Patients may take up strange postures or engage in rocking or pacing. At the other extreme, they may move excitedly and apparently purposelessly. Unfortunately, violent behavior is possible as well. One manual points out that "grotesque violence, with self-mutilation (often of sexual organs) or murderous attacks, may occur. Matricide [killing one's mother], the rarest form of murder, is most often perpetrated by schizophrenics, as is filicide [killing one's brother or sister]. . . . The risk of suicide is increased in all stages of schizophrenic illness" ("Schizophrenic," 1987, p. 1535). One woman patient wrote, "Death is the greatest happiness in life, if not the only one. Without hope of the end, life would be unendurable" (cited in Mendel, 1974, p. 137). 9

Even if violence does not occur, it is not surprising that the speech and behavioral symptoms I have described are almost invariably accompanied by—and contribute to—impaired interpersonal functioning. Once schizophrenics become obsessed with delusions, hallucinations, and illogical ideas, they are often too distracted and centered on themselves to interact with other people. Such patients are notable for their emotional detachment even from family members or friends they were previously close to. They also withdraw from all other social interactions, dropping out of school or leaving jobs. They simply cannot face the outside world. Some schizophrenics behave quite differently, however, at least during some phases of the illness. They "cling to other people, intrude upon strangers, and fail to recognize that excessive closeness makes people uncomfortable and likely to pull away" ("Schizophrenia," 1987, p. 189). 10

Along with social impairment comes loss of drive or ambition. Schizophrenics typically have difficulty in initiating actions, making decisions, or following through with plans, and their work and other responsibilities often suffer severely as a result. 11

It is important to know that doctors, counselors, and psychoanalysts do not easily label someone schizophrenic. They do not do so unless many of the symptoms I have described are present and unmistakable. Since depression has some of the same symptoms as schizophrenia and the treatment of the two is quite different, doctors have to be especially careful not to confuse them. We have come a long way from the time when schizophrenics were considered dangerous lunatics and were locked away without treatment, sometimes for life. Doctors now recognize the illness and can counsel both patients and families and prescribe drugs that have proven effective. The problem today is that so many of the homeless are believed to be schizophrenic, and it seems unlikely that many of them ever receive treatment. 12

References

King, K. (1989, November). Lost brother. *Life,* 94–98.

Lidz, T. (1973). *The origin and treatment of schizophrenic disorders.* New York: Basic.

Mendel, W. M. (1974). A phenomenological theory of schizophrenia. In A. Burton, J. Lopez-Ibor, & W. M. Mendel (Eds.), *Schizophrenia as a life style* (pp. 106–155). New York: Springer.

Schizophrenia. (1987). *Diagnostic and statistical manual of mental disorders* (3rd ed., pp. 187–198). Washington, DC: American Psychiatric Association.

Schizophrenic disorders. (1987). *The Merck manual of diagnosis and therapy* (15th ed.) (pp. 1532–1539). Rahway, NJ: Merck and Company.

Shane, S. (1987, July 28). Relatives bear demoralizing task of patient care. *Baltimore Sun,* p. 14.

Suddath, R. L., Cristison, G. W., Torrey, E. F., Casanova, M. F., & Weinberger, D. R. (1990). Anatomical abnormalities in the brains of monozygotic twins discordant for schizophrenia. *New England Journal of Medicine, 322,* 791–793.

Connecting to Culture and Experience

Veronica Murayama's essay demonstrates that schizophrenia is a diagnosable medical problem. It is only one of many mental illnesses, perhaps the most widespread being depression, which afflicts 15 percent of Americans. People with mental illness need help because their suffering is acute and the costs to their families and to society are great, yet mental health funds are often the first to be cut in times of budget constraints.

Discuss the mental health resources available on your campus or in your community. Begin by identifying campus or community organizations that provide services for the mentally ill. Share what information you may have about the services these organizations offer. Consider whether these resources are adequate for your campus or community.

Analyzing Writing Strategies

1. Analyze Murayama's use of **sources.** In paragraphs 1 and 3, Murayama summarizes or paraphrases information from sources. She cites them but does not quote from them. In paragraph 2, she summarizes and quotes from the same source. In paragraphs 3, 4, 6, 7, 8, 9, and 10, she quotes from different sources. Contrast her use

of summaries and paraphrases in paragraphs 1, 2, and 3 with her use of quotes in the other paragraphs. When does she seem to use one or the other? When and to what effect does she use quoted material to explain schizophrenia to her readers?

2. How does Murayama **frame** her essay? (*Framing* means referring at the end to something mentioned at the beginning.) Compare Murayama's use of framing with Toufexis's. What advantages do you see in framing an explanatory essay?
3. The Writer at Work section later in this chapter shows how Murayama surveyed sources, found a focus for her essay, and made use of sources in her essay. As you read "Finding Sources" on pages 194–95, highlight or underline the main steps in Murayama's progress toward finding sources and a focus for her explanation. Then answer these questions: Who provided guidance, and how did Murayama discover a focus? How much time do you estimate this process required? What reservations or questions do you have about her search?

Considering Topics for Your Own Essay

Consider writing an essay that would help you learn about another type of mental illness, such as hypochondriasis, mood disorders, bipolarism, phobic behaviors, or autism. The two manuals Murayama cites catalog many such illnesses. You would also want to look for current research and popular articles on your topic.

Commentary

Assuming that her audience knows little about schizophrenia, Murayama tries to **engage readers** by giving them reasons to learn about the illness. Her first sentence acknowledges that readers may be more familiar with more common types of mental illness such as depression. She then implies why it is important to learn about schizophrenia: because it is one of the most "severe" mental diseases. To illustrate what she means by "severe," Murayama briefly lists some of the common symptoms of schizophrenia and indicates that large numbers of people need to be hospitalized for the illness.

By mentioning in the last sentence of paragraph 1 that up to 40 percent of homeless people may suffer from schizophrenia, she implies yet another, more immediate reason for readers to learn about the illness: They may actually witness many of the symptoms when they encounter homeless people on the street. This reason tells us that Murayama wants not only to inform readers about schizophrenia but also to influence how they regard the homeless. She indicates this secondary, but no less important, purpose for explaining schizophrenia in paragraph 3, where she refers to her belief that "knowledge about . . . human suffering" can make people "more likely to be sympathetic with the sufferer."

In paragraph 3, Murayama forecasts the plan of her essay. A **forecast** identifies the main topics or ideas in an essay, usually in the sequence in which they will be discussed. By listing schizophrenic symptoms, Murayama lays out her topics in the order in which she presents them and also identifies the key terms she will rely on throughout the essay. Readers seeking information benefit from such an obvious cue because it prepares them for what is coming.

Throughout her essay, Murayama relies on several basic strategies for explaining concepts: classification, division, cause, and comparison and contrast. She borrows a system of classification and division from the medical manuals she read (see paragraph 3). The **classification,** based on symptoms of schizophrenia, yields eight categories or symptoms. She wisely relies on this division to organize her essay. It enables her to bring together relevant material from several sources. When you plan your essay, you will also have to borrow or discover a way to classify and divide all of your information.

The strategy of **cause** plays a brief but important role in paragraph 3, where Murayama lists the still-debated causes of schizophrenia. Reporting the various causes that specialists continue to argue about sets up her announcement that she will focus her essay on one aspect of the concept that all writers do seem to agree about—its symptoms. Throughout the essay, Murayama relies on the strategy of **comparison or contrast** to explain schizophrenia to her readers. Knowing that readers are more likely to know about depression than schizophrenia, she contrasts the two at the beginning and end of her essay. In paragraphs 8, 9, and 10, she contrasts the surprisingly dissimilar behaviors among patients exhibiting three of the symptoms of schizophrenia.

Part III covers these and other writing strategies in detail.

It is also worth noting some of the ways in which Murayama incorporates quoted material into her own sentences. In some cases, she uses a **dialogue cue,** such as *he said* or *she wrote:*

One *patient, a man, said,* "I have always believed in the good of mankind. . . ." (paragraph 7)

One *woman patient wrote,* "Death is the greatest happiness in life. . . ." (9)

In other cases, she uses a **colon** to introduce dialogue:

Here is what one patient felt: "When I was acting so stiff and wasn't talking . . ." (9)

For more on quoting sources, see pp. 595–603.

She also uses a **noun clause** with *that:*

One manual points out *that* "grotesque violence . . . may occur." (9)

PURPOSE AND AUDIENCE

Though it often seeks to engage readers' interests, explanatory writing gives prominence to the facts about its subject. It aims at readers' intellect rather than their imagination, determined to instruct rather than entertain or argue.

To set out to teach readers about a concept is no small undertaking. To succeed, you must know the concept so well that you can explain it simply, without jargon or other confusing language. You must be authoritative without showing off or talking down. You must also estimate what your readers already know about the concept in order to decide which information will be truly new to them. You want to define unfamiliar words and pace the information carefully so that your readers are neither bored nor overwhelmed.

This assignment requires a willingness to cast yourself in the role of expert, which may not come naturally to you at this stage in your development as a writer. Students are most often asked to explain things in writing to readers who know more than they do—their instructors. When you plan and draft this essay, however, you will be aiming at readers who know less—maybe much less—than you do about the concept you will explain. Like Toufexis and Castro, you could write for a general audience of adults who regularly read a newspaper and subscribe to a few magazines. Even though some of them may be highly educated, you can readily and confidently assume the role of expert after a couple of hours of research into your concept. Your purpose may be to deepen your readers' understanding of a concept they may already be familiar with. You could also write for upper elementary or secondary school students, introducing them to an unfamiliar concept, or to your classmates, demonstrating to them that a concept in an academic discipline they find forbidding can actually be made both understandable and interesting. Even if you are told to consider your instructor your sole reader, you can assume that your instructor is eager to be informed about nearly any concept you choose.

You have spent many years in school reading explanations of concepts: Your textbooks in every subject have been full of concept explanations. Now, instead of receiving these explanations, you will be delivering one. To succeed, you will have to accept your role of expert. Your readers expect you to be authoritative and well informed; they expect that you have limited the focus of your explanation but that you have not excluded anything essential to their understanding.

SUMMARY OF BASIC FEATURES

A Focused Concept

The primary purpose for explaining a concept is to inform readers, but writers of explanatory essays cannot possibly hope to say everything there is to say about a concept, nor would they want to. Instead, they must make choices about what to include, what to emphasize, and what to omit. Most writers focus on one aspect of the concept. Veronica Murayama, for example, focuses on the symptoms of schizophrenia, and Passell focuses on historical examples of path dependence.

An Appeal to Readers' Interests

Most people read explanations of concepts for work or study. Consequently, they do not expect the writing to entertain them, but simply to inform them. Yet readers appreciate explanations that both make clear the concept's importance and keep them awake with lively writing and vivid detail. The essays in this chapter show some of the ways in which writers try to appeal to readers—for example, by using humor and unaffected, everyday language; by giving readers reasons for learning about the concept; by showing how the concept might apply personally to them.

A Logical Plan

Since concept explanations present information that is new to readers and can therefore be hard to understand, writers need to develop a plan that presents new material bit by bit in a logical order. The most effective explanations are carefully organized and give readers all the obvious cues they need, such as forecasting statements, topic sentences, transitions, and summaries. In addition, the writer may try to frame the essay for readers by relating the ending to the beginning. We have seen these features repeatedly in the readings in this chapter. For example, Toufexis frames her essay with references to Ph.D.'s, she forecasts the three sciences from which she has gleaned her information about the neurochemistry of love, and nearly all of her paragraphs begin with a transition sentence.

For more on cueing readers, see Chapter 13.

Good writers never forget that their readers need clear signals. Because writers already know the information and are aware of how the essay is organized, it can be difficult for them to see the essay the way someone reading it for the first time would. That is precisely how it should be seen, however, to be sure that the essay includes all the cues the reader will need.

Clear Definitions

See Chapter 16 for further discussion of definitions.

Essays explaining concepts depend on clear definitions. To relate information clearly, a writer must be sensitive to readers' knowledge; any terms that are likely to be unfamiliar or misunderstood must be explicitly defined, as Toufexis defines *attraction junkies* (paragraph 12) and *endorphins* (paragraph 13). In a sense, all the readings in this chapter are extended definitions of concepts, and all the authors offer relatively concise, clear definitions of their concepts at some point in their essays.

Appropriate Writing Strategies

Many writing strategies are useful for presenting information. The strategies a writer uses are determined by the way he or she focuses the essay and the kind of information available. The following strategies are particularly useful in explaining concepts.

For more about classification, see Chapter 17.

Classification. One way of presenting information is to sort it into groups and discuss the groups one by one. For example, Murayama uses the classification of schizophrenic symptoms as a way of organizing her description of the disease.

For further illustration of these narrative strategies, see Chapter 14.

Process Narration. Process narration typically explains how something is done. Many concepts involve processes that unfold over time, such as the geologic scale, or over both time and space, such as bird migration. Process narration involves some of the basic storytelling strategies covered in Chapters 2 and 3: narrative time signals, actors and action, and transitions showing temporal relationships. For example, Toufexis briefly narrates the development of romantic attraction (paragraphs 3–4), and Passell tells how light-water reactors gained dominance (paragraphs 13–15).

For more about comparison and contrast, see Chapter 18.

Comparison and Contrast. The comparison-and-contrast strategy is especially useful for explaining concepts because it helps readers to understand something new by showing how it is similar to or different from things they already know. Every essayist in this chapter makes use of comparison and contrast. For example, Murayama contrasts schizophrenics who withdraw from others with those who cling and intrude. Castro contrasts Manpower Inc. and General Motors, as well as core and contingent workers.

Cause and Effect. Another useful strategy for explaining a concept is to report its causes or effects. Toufexis explains the evolutionary benefits of romantic love, and Castro describes the effects of contingent employment on workers and the workplace.

Note that writers of explanatory essays ordinarily either report established causes or effects or report others' speculated causes or effects as if they were established facts. They usually do not themselves speculate about possible causes or effects.

Careful Use of Sources

To explain concepts, writers nearly always draw on information from many different sources. Although they often draw on their own experience and observation, they almost always do additional research into what others have to say about their subject. Referring to expert sources always lends authority to an explanation.

For more on reading sources critically, see pp. 591–94. For advice on integrating sources, see pp. 452–55.

How writers treat sources depends on the writing situation. Certain formal situations, such as college assignments or scholarly papers, have rules for citing and documenting sources. Students and scholars are expected to cite their sources formally because readers judge their writing in part by what they have read and how they have used their reading. For more informal writing—magazine articles, for example—readers do not expect page references or publishing information, but they do expect sources to be identified; this identification often appears within the text of the article.

GUIDE TO WRITING

THE WRITING ASSIGNMENT

Write an essay that explains a concept. Choose a concept that interests you and that you want to study further. Consider carefully what your readers already know about it and how your essay might add to what they know.

INVENTION AND RESEARCH

The following guidelines will help you to find a concept, to understand it fully, to select a focus appropriate for your readers, to test your choice, and to devise strategies for presenting what you have discovered in a way that will be truly informative for your particular readers. Each activity is easy to do and takes only a few minutes. If you can spread out the activities over several days, you will have adequate time to understand the concept and decide how to present it. Keep a written record of your invention work to use when you draft the essay and also when you revise.

Finding a Concept

Even if you already have a concept in mind, completing the following activities will help you to be certain of your choice.

Consider the concepts in Considering Topics for Your Own Essay on pp. 162, 167, 172, and 177.

Listing Concepts. *List several concepts.* The longer your list, the more likely you are to find just the right concept to write about. And should your first choice not work out, you will have a ready list of alternatives. Include concepts you already know something about as well as some you know only slightly and would like to research further.

Your courses provide many concepts you will want to consider. These are typical concepts from a number of academic and other subjects. Your class notes or textbooks will suggest many others.

Set a timer for ten minutes, and brainstorm your lists with the monitor brightness turned all the way down. Enter as many possibilities as you can think of. Then turn the brightness up, read to make sure that all the concepts make sense, and save them as an invention file. Print out a copy to make notes on.

- *Literature:* hero, antihero, picaresque, the absurd, canon, representation, figurative language, modernism
- *Philosophy:* existentialism, nihilism, logical positivism, determinism
- *Business management:* autonomous work group, quality circle, cybernetic control system, management by objectives, zero-based budgeting
- *Psychology:* Hawthorne effect, assimilation/accommodation, social cognition, moratorium, intelligence, divergent/convergent thinking, operant conditioning, short-term memory, tip-of-the-tongue phenomenon
- *Government:* majority rule, minority rights, federalism, popular consent, exclusionary rule, political party, political machine, interest group, political action committee

- *Biology:* photosynthesis, morphogenesis, ecosystem, electron transport, plasmolysis, phagocytosis, homozygosity, diffusion
- *Art:* cubism, Dadaism, surrealism, expressionism
- *Math:* Mobius transformation, boundedness, null space, eigenvalue, factoring, Rolle's theorem, continuity, derivative, indefinite integral
- *Physical sciences:* matter, mass, weight, energy, gravity, atomic theory, law of definite proportions, osmotic pressure, first law of thermodynamics, entropy
- *Public health:* alcoholism, seasonal affective disorder, contraception, lead poisoning, prenatal care
- *Environmental studies:* acid rain, recycling, ozone depletion, toxic waste, endangered species
- *Sports:* squeeze play, hit and run (baseball); power play (hockey); nickel defense, wishbone offense (football); serve and volley offense (tennis); setup (volleyball); pick and roll, inside game (basketball)
- *Personal finance:* mortgage, budget, insurance, deduction, revolving credit
- *Law:* tort, contract, garnishment, double indemnity, liability, reasonable doubt
- *Sociology:* norm, deviance, role conflict, ethnocentrism, class, social stratification, conflict theory, functionalist theory

Listing Concepts concerning Identity and Community Many concepts are important in understanding identity and community. As you consider the following concepts, try to think of others in this category: self-esteem, character, personality, autonomy, individuation, narcissism, multiculturalism, ethnicity, race, racism, social contract, communitarianism, community policing, social Darwinism, identity politics, special-interest groups, diaspora, colonialism, public space, the other, agency, difference, yuppie, generation X.

Listing Concepts concerning Work and Career Concepts like the following enable you to gain a deeper understanding of your work experiences and career aspirations: free enterprise, minimum wage, affirmative action, stock option, sweatshop, glass ceiling, downsizing, collective bargaining, service sector, market, entrepreneur, bourgeoisie, underclass, working class, middle class, division of labor, monopoly, automation, robotics, contingent worker, management style, deregulation, multinational corporation.

Choosing a Concept. *Look over your list, and select one concept to explore.* Pick a concept that interests you, one you feel eager to learn more about. Consider also whether it might interest others. You may know very little about the concept now, but the guidelines that follow will help you to research it and to understand it fully.

Researching the Concept

Discovering What You Already Know. *Take a few minutes to write out whatever you know about the concept.* Also say why you have chosen the concept and why you find it interesting and worth knowing about. Write quickly, without planning or organizing. Write phrases or lists as well as sentences. You might also want to make drawings or charts. Ask questions that you hope to answer.

Try keeping computer files for your research notes. Keep one file as a bibliography. Organize your other research files in whatever way makes sense to you—for example, by subtopic or as quote, summary, and paraphrase files. You may be able to download some sources directly onto a disk.

Gathering Information. *Learn more about your concept by taking notes or making copies of relevant material and keeping careful records.* Check any materials you already have at hand that explain your concept. If you are considering a concept from one of your academic courses, you will find explanatory material in your textbook or lecture notes.

To acquire a comprehensive, up-to-date understanding of your concept and to write authoritatively about it, you may also need to know how experts other than your textbook writer and instructor define and illustrate the concept. To find this information, you might locate relevant articles or books in the library, search for resources or make inquiries on the Internet, or consult experts on campus or in the community. Chapter 21 recommends a search strategy and specific sources for researching your concept.

As you get a better understanding of the concept and decide which aspect of it you will focus your essay on, you may need to do additional research to get answers to specific questions.

If you can, make photocopies or print out information you download from CD-ROMs or the Internet. If you must rely on notes, be sure to copy the language exactly so that later you can quote sources accurately.

For MLA and APA guidelines, see pp. 603–20.

Since you do not know what information you will ultimately use, keep a careful record of the author, title, publication date, and page numbers for all the source material you gather. Check with your instructor about whether you should follow the Modern Language Association (MLA) or American Psychological Association (APA) style of acknowledging sources. In this chapter, the Murayama essay follows the APA style.

Focusing the Concept

Once you have done some research on your concept, you must choose a way to focus your essay. Because more is known about most concepts than you can include in an essay and concepts can be approached from so many perspectives (for example, history, definition, significance), you must limit your explanation. Doing so will help you avoid the common problem of trying to explain too much.

Because the focus must reflect both your special interest in the concept and your readers' likely knowledge and interest, you will want to explore both. See "Finding Sources" in the Writer at Work section of this chapter for an illustration of focusing a concept following some preliminary research.

Exploring Your Own Interests. *Make a list of different aspects of the concept that could become a focus for your essay, and evaluate what you know about each aspect.* To consider which aspect of the concept most interests you, review what you know about the concept. As you review this information, make a list of different aspects of the concept, skipping a few lines after each item in the list. (Murayama's list on p. 194 is an example.)

Under each item in your list, indicate whether you know enough to begin writing about that aspect of the concept, what additional questions you would need to answer, and what is important or interesting to you about that particular aspect.

Analyzing Your Readers. *Take about five minutes to analyze your readers in writing.* To decide what aspect of the concept to focus on, you also need to think about who your prospective readers are likely to be and to speculate about their knowledge of and interest in the concept. Even if you are writing only for your instructor, you should give some thought to what he or she knows and thinks about the concept.

The following questions are designed to help you with your analysis:

- Who are my readers, and what are they likely to know about this concept?
- What, if anything, might they know about the field of study to which this concept applies?
- What could I point out that would be useful for them to know about this concept, perhaps something that could relate to their life or work?
- What connections could I make between this concept and others that my readers are likely to be familiar with?

Choosing a Focus. *With your interests and those of your readers in mind, choose an aspect of your concept on which to focus, and write a sentence justifying its appropriateness.*

Testing Your Choice

Pause now to test whether you have chosen a workable concept and focused it appropriately. As painful as it may be to consider, starting fresh with a new concept would be better than continuing with an unworkable one. The following questions can help you test your choice:

- Do I understand my concept well enough to explain it?
- Have I discovered a focus for writing about this concept?
- Have I found enough information for an essay with such a focus?
- Do I see possibilities for engaging my readers' interest in this aspect of my subject?

If you cannot answer yes to all four questions, consider refocusing your subject or selecting another concept to write about.

Testing Your Choice: A Collaborative Activity

Get together with two or three other students to find out what your readers are likely to know about your subject and what might interest them about it.

Presenters: Each of you take turns explaining your concept briefly, describing your intended readers and identifying the aspect of the concept you will focus on.

Listeners: Briefly tell the presenter whether the focus sounds appropriate and interesting for the intended readers. Share what you think readers are likely to know about the concept and what might be especially interesting and informative for them to learn about it.

Considering Explanatory Strategies

Try out potentially useful writing strategies. Before you move on to plan and draft your essay, consider some possible ways of presenting the concept. Try to answer each of the following questions with a sentence or two. Questions that you can answer readily may identify strategies that can help you to explain your concept.

- What term is used to name the concept, and what does it mean? (definition)
- How is this concept like or unlike related concepts? (comparison and contrast)
- How can an explanation of this concept be divided into parts? (classification)
- How does this concept happen, or how does one go about doing it? (process narration)
- What are its known causes or effects? (cause and effect)

PLANNING AND DRAFTING

The following guidelines will help you get the most out of your invention notes, determine specific goals for your essay, and write a first draft.

Seeing What You Have

Reread everything you have written so far. This is a critically important time for reflection and evaluation. Before beginning the actual draft, you must decide whether your subject is worthwhile and whether you have sufficient information for a successful essay.

Print out a hard copy of what you have written on a word processor for easier reviewing.

It may help, as you read, to annotate your invention writings. Look for details that will help you to explain the concept so that your readers can grasp it. Underline or circle key words, phrases, or sentences; make marginal notes. Your goal is to identify the important elements in what you have written so far.

Be realistic. If at this point your notes do not look promising, you may want to refocus your concept or select a different concept to write about. If your notes seem thin but promising, do further research to find more information before continuing.

Setting Goals

Successful writers are always looking beyond the next sentence to larger goals. Indeed, the next sentence is easier to write if you keep larger goals in mind. The following questions can help you set these goals. Consider each one now, and then return to them as necessary while you write.

Your Readers

- How can I build on my readers' knowledge?
- What new information can I present to them?
- How can I organize my essay so that my readers can follow it easily?
- What tone would be most appropriate? Would an informal tone like Toufexis's or a formal one like Murayama's be more appropriate?

The Beginning

- How shall I begin? Should I open with a provocative quotation, as Toufexis does? With a general statement about the concept, as Murayama does? With a surprising or ironic fact, as Castro does? With a question?
- How can I best forecast the plan my explanation will follow? Should I offer a detailed forecast? Or is a brief description sufficient?

Writing Strategies

- What terms do I need to define? Can I rely on brief sentence definitions, or will I need to write extended definitions?
- Are there ways to categorize the information?
- What examples can I use to make the explanation more concrete?
- Would any comparisons or contrasts help readers understand the information?
- Do I need to explain any processes or known causes or effects?

The Ending

- Should I frame the essay by relating the ending to the beginning?
- Should I end the essay with an emphatic or memorable quote, as Castro does?

Outlining

See pp. 431–34 for more on outlining.

Outlining on a word processor makes it particularly easy to experiment with different ways of ordering information and using transitions.

Give some thought now to organization. Many writers find it helpful to outline their material before actually beginning to write. Consider tentative any outlining you do before you begin drafting, however. Never be a slave to an outline. As you draft, you will usually see ways to improve on your original plan. Be ready to revise your outline, to shift parts around, to drop or add parts. Consider the following questions as you plan:

- Which writing strategies should I use to present the information?
- What order might best serve my purpose?
- What kinds of transitions can I use between the various strategies or parts of the essay?

Drafting

Call up invention material on an alternate window as you draft. Shift back and forth to cut and paste invention material into your draft.

Begin drafting your essay, keeping your focus in mind. Remember also the needs and expectations of your readers; organize, define, and explain with them in mind. Work to increase their understanding of your concept. You may want to review the drafting advice on pp. 13–14.

CRITICAL READING GUIDE

Swap copies of your drafts with another student, either by exchanging disks or by sending the computer files over a network. Add your comments either next to the essay, if you can divide the screen, or at the end of the document.

Now is the time to get a good critical reading. All writers find it helpful to have someone else read and comment on their drafts, and your instructor may schedule such a reading as part of your coursework. If not, you can ask a classmate, friend, or family member to read it over. If your campus has a writing center, you might ask a tutor to read and comment on your draft. The guidelines that follow are designed to be used by *anyone* reviewing an explanatory essay. (If you are unable to have someone else read your draft, turn ahead to the Revising section, which gives guidelines for reading your own draft with a critical eye.)

If You Are the Writer. To provide focused, helpful comments, your critical reader must know your intended audience and purpose. Briefly write out this information at the top of your draft.

- *Audience:* Who are your readers? How much do you assume they know about the concept?
- *Purpose:* What information have you focused on, and what is the main thing you want readers to learn?

If You Are the Reader. Reading a draft critically means reading it more than once, first to get a general impression and thereafter to analyze its basic features.

1. *Read for a First Impression.* Read first to get a sense of the concept. Then, briefly give your impressions. Is the concept well focused and clearly explained? Did you find the essay informative and easy to follow? What in the draft do you think would especially interest the intended readers?
2. *Assess Whether the Concept Is Clearly Explained and Focused.* Restate, in one sentence, what you understand the concept to mean. Indicate any confusion or uncertainty you have about its meaning. Given the concept, does the focus seem appropriate, too broad, or too narrow for the intended readers? Can you think of a more interesting aspect of the concept on which to focus the explanation?

See pp. 180–81 to review the basic features.

3. *Consider Whether the Content Is Appropriate for the Intended Readers.* Does it tell them all that they are likely to want to know about this concept? Can you suggest additional information that should be included? What questions that readers are likely to have about the concept are not answered? Point out any information that seems superfluous or too predictable.
4. *Evaluate the Organization.* Look at the way the essay is organized, outlining it briefly. Is the information logically divided? If not, suggest a better way to divide it. Also consider the order—can you suggest a better way of sequencing the information?

    Look at the *beginning*. Will it pull intended readers into the essay and make them want to continue? Does it adequately forecast the direction of the essay? If possible, suggest a better way to begin.

Find the obvious *transitions* in the draft. Are they helpful? If not, try to improve one or two of them. Look for additional places where transitions would be helpful.

Look at the *ending*. Is it effective? Does it frame the essay by referring to something at the beginning? Should it? If you can, suggest a better way to end.

5. *Assess the Clarity of Definitions.* Are any definitions likely to be unclear to readers? Point out any other terms that may need to be defined for the intended readers.
6. *Analyze How Appropriately Writing Strategies Are Used.* Besides definition, what writing strategies has the writer used, and how effective are they? Examine each recognizable use of examples, process narration, comparison and contrast, cause and effect, or classification, and identify any that seem unclear, incomplete, or otherwise ineffective. If you can, suggest ways to improve these, and point out any other places where a writing strategy would enable readers to comprehend the concept more fully.
7. *Evaluate the Use of Sources.* If the writer has used sources, review the list of sources cited. Given the purpose, readers, and focus of the essay, does the list seem balanced, and are the selections appropriate? Try to suggest concerns or questions that readers knowledgeable about the concept might raise. Then, consider the use of sources within the text of the essay. Are there places where summary or paraphrase would be preferable to quoted material or vice versa? Note any places where the writer has inserted quoted material into the text awkwardly, and recommend ways to smooth them out.
8. *Give the Writer Your Final Thoughts.* Which part needs the most work? What do you think the intended readers will find most informative or memorable? What did you like best about the essay?

REVISING

This section will help you identify problems in your draft and to revise and edit to solve them.

Identifying Problems

To identify problems in your draft, you need to get an overview of it, analyze its basic features, and study any comments you have received from other readers.

Even if your essay is saved to a computer file, reread from a hard copy. Add notes to yourself and quick revisions as you read through the draft.

Getting an Overview. First, consider the draft as a whole, trying to see it objectively. It may help to do so in two steps:

1. *Reread.* If possible, put the draft aside for a day or two. When you do reread it, start by reconsidering your audience and purpose. Then, read the draft straight through, trying to see it as your intended readers will.

2. *Outline.* Make a scratch outline to get an overview of the essay's development. This outline can be sketchy—words and phrases instead of complete sentences—but it should identify the main ideas as they appear.

Charting a Plan for Revision. You may want to make a two-column chart to identify the problems you need to solve. In the left-hand column, list the basic features and strategies of concept explanation, skipping several lines between each. As you analyze your draft and study any comments from others, note the problems you want to solve in the right-hand column.

Basic Features	*Problems to Solve*
Concept focus	
Appeal to readers	
Organization	
Definitions	
Writing strategies	
Sources	

Analyzing Basic Features. Using the questions presented in the Critical Reading Guide, reread the draft to identify problems and note them on your chart of problems to solve.

Studying Critical Comments. Review all of the comments you have received from other readers, and add to your chart any other points that need attention. Try to be objective about any criticism. By letting you see how others respond to your draft, the comments provide valuable information about how you might improve it.

Solving the Problems

Before revising, copy your original draft to a second file. Should you change your mind about material you delete while revising, it will still be available to you.

Having identified problems, you now need to figure out solutions and to carry them out. Basically, there are three ways to find solutions:

1. Review your invention and planning notes and sources for additional information and ideas.
2. Do further invention or research to answer questions your readers raised.
3. Look back at the readings in this chapter to see how other writers have solved similar problems.

Here are suggestions to help you solve some of the problems common to explanatory essays. For now, focus on solving the issues identified on your chart. Avoid tinkering with grammar and punctuation; that work can come later when you edit.

Focus

- **Is the focus too broad?** Consider limiting it further so that you can explain one part of the concept in more depth. If readers were uninterested in the aspect you focused on, consider focusing on some other aspect of the concept.

- **Is the focus too narrow?** You may have isolated too minor an aspect. Go back to your invention and look for larger or more significant aspects.

Appeal to Readers

- **Do you think readers will have unanswered questions?** Review your invention writing and sources for further information to satisfy your readers' needs or answer their concerns and questions.
- **Does any of the content seem superfluous?** Eliminate it.
- **Does the content seem predictable?** Search for novel or surprising information to add.

Organization

Use your word processor's cut-and-paste or block-and-move functions to shift material around. Make sure you revise transitions so that material fits smoothly in its new spot.

- **Is the explanation difficult to follow?** Look for a way to reorder the parts so that the essay is easier to follow. Try constructing an alternative outline. Add transitions or summaries to help keep readers on track.
- **Is the beginning weak?** Try making your focus obvious immediately, forecasting the plan of your essay, or opening with an unusual piece of information that would catch readers' interest.
- **Is the ending inconclusive?** Consider moving important information there. Try summarizing highlights of the essay or framing it by referring to something in the beginning. Or you might speculate about the future of the concept or assert its usefulness.

Definitions

- **Does your concept need a clearer or fuller definition?** Add a concise definition early in your essay, or consider adding a brief summary that defines the concept in the middle or at the end. Remove any information that may blur readers' understanding of the concept.
- **Are other key terms inadequately defined?** Supply clear definitions, searching your sources or checking a dictionary if necessary.

Writing Strategies

Use your computer to help you to analyze problems with your essay. For example, if a reader feels that you need more examples to explain your concept, highlight the examples in your paper by putting them in bold type. Then look for places where you need to add more.

- **Does the content seem thin or the definition of the concept blurred?** Consider whether any other writing strategies would improve the presentation.
  - Try comparing or contrasting the concept with a related one that is more familiar to readers.
  - Consider ways to classify the information that would make it easier to understand or provide an interesting perspective on the topic.
  - Add some information about its known causes or effects.
  - See whether adding examples enlivens or clarifies your explanation.
  - Tell more about how the concept works or what people do with it.

Use of Sources

See pp. 595–603 for advice on integrating quotations into your text.

- **Are sources inadequate?** Return to the library or the Internet to find additional ones. Consider dropping weak or less reliable sources. Make sure that your sources cover the aspect on which you focus in a comprehensive, balanced way.
- **Do you rely too much on quoting, summarizing, or paraphrasing?** Change some of your quotations to summaries or paraphrases, or vice versa.
- **Does quoted material need to be more smoothly integrated into your own text?** Revise to make it so.
- **Are there discrepancies in your in-text citations or list of sources?** Compare each in-text citation to examples of your chosen citation style in Chapter 22. Be sure that all of the citations and sources listed follow the style you are using exactly. Check to see that your list of sources has an entry for each in-text citation.

EDITING AND PROOFREADING

Use your word processor's spell-check function cautiously. Keep in mind that it will not find all misspellings, particularly misused homonyms (such as *there* for *their* or *they're*), typos that are themselves words (such as *fro* for *for*), and many proper nouns and specialized terms. Proofread these carefully. Also proofread for words that should have been deleted when you edited a sentence.

In working on your draft so far, you may have corrected some obvious errors, but grammar and style have not been a priority. Now is the time to check carefully for errors in usage, punctuation, and mechanics, as well as to consider matters of style. You may find that studying your draft in separate passes—first for paragraphs, then for sentences, and finally for words—will help you to recognize any problems.

Our research on students' writing has identified several errors that are especially common in writing that explains concepts; the following brief guidelines can help you check and edit your draft for these errors.

Checking the Punctuation of Adjective Clauses. Adjective clauses include both a subject and a verb. They give information about a noun or a pronoun. They often begin with *who, which,* or *that.* Here is an example from Veronica Murayama:

It is common for schizophrenics to have delusions *that they are being persecuted.*

Because adjective clauses add information about the nouns they follow—defining, illustrating, or explaining—they can be useful in writing that explains a concept. Adjective clauses may or may not need to be set off with a comma or commas. To decide, first you have to determine whether or not the clause is essential to the meaning of the sentence. Clauses that are essential to the meaning of a sentence should *not* be set off with a comma; clauses that are not essential to the meaning must be set off with a comma. Here are two examples from Murayama:

Essential It is common for schizophrenics to have delusions *that they are being persecuted.*

The adjective clause defines and limits the word *delusions.* If the clause were removed, the basic meaning of the sentence would change, saying that schizophrenics commonly have delusions of all sorts.

Nonessential Related to delusions are hallucinations, *which are very common in schizophrenics.*

The adjective clause gives information that is not essential to the sentence. Taking away the adjective clause *(which are very common in schizophrenics)* in no way changes the basic meaning of the sentence.

To decide whether an adjective clause is essential or nonessential, mentally delete the clause. If taking out the clause changes the basic meaning of the sentence or makes it unclear, the clause is probably essential and should not be set off with commas. If the meaning of the sentence does not change enormously, the clause is probably nonessential and should be set off with commas.

- **Postpartum neurosis, which can last for two weeks or longer, can adversely affect a mother's ability to care for her infant.**
- **The early stage starts with memory loss, which usually causes the patient to forget recent life events.**
- **Seasonal affective disorders are mood disturbances that occur with a change of season.**
- **The coaches who do the recruiting should be disciplined.**

Adjective clauses following proper nouns always require commas.

- **Nanotechnologists defer to K. Eric Drexler, who speculates imaginatively about the uses of nonmachines.**

Checking for Commas around Interrupting Phrases. When writers are explaining a concept, they need to supply a great deal of information. They add much of this information in phrases that interrupt the flow of a sentence. Words that interrupt are usually set off with commas. Be especially careful with interrupting phrases that fall in the middle of a sentence—such phrases must be set off with two commas, one at the beginning and one at the end:

- **People on the West Coast, especially in Los Angeles, have always been receptive to new ideas.**
- **Alzheimer's disease, named after the German neuropathologist Alois Alzheimer, is a chronic degenerative illness.**
- **These examples, though simple, present equations in terms of tangible objects.**

A WRITER AT WORK

USING SOURCES

This section describes how student writer Veronica Murayama searched for sources and integrated them into one part of her essay on schizophrenia.

Finding Sources

Following directions in the Invention and Research section of this chapter, Murayama went to the library to see what she could find on schizophrenia. She wanted a quick orientation to the concept so that she could decide on a focus for her essay and for further research. This initial search led her right away to two books and four current articles:

Schizophrenia as a Life Style

The Origin and Treatment of Schizophrenic Disorders

"Drug Gains FDA Approval," *Science News*

"Drugs among Young Schizophrenics," *Science News*

"Seeking Source of Schizophrenia," *USA Today*

"Relatives Bear Demoralizing Task of Patient Care," *Baltimore Sun*

She read the articles, skimmed the books, and then talked to a reference librarian. When Murayama explained the assignment—emphasizing her need for an overview—and showed the materials she had already collected, the librarian recommended that she check two basic references on mental illness. The first book is relied on by medical doctors, the second by psychiatrists and other mental health counselors:

The Merck Manual of Diagnosis and Therapy

Diagnostic and Statistical Manual of Mental Disorders

After closely reading the materials on schizophrenia in these two sources, she decided that, given the information in all her sources, she had enough material on these topics:

The history of the description and treatment of schizophrenia

Its effects on families of schizophrenics

The current debate about its causes

The current preferred treatment of it

Current research on it

Its symptoms

She was intrigued by both the debate about causes and the symptoms, but when she discussed these alternatives with a small group in her writing class, she recognized that, like herself before she began her research, the others knew so little about schizophrenia that they would be most engaged and informed by a description of the illness itself—what it looks like to a therapist diagnosing it and what it feels like to a patient experiencing it.

When Murayama met with her instructor, he pointed out that she should seek out recent reports in a respected medical journal such as the *New England Journal of Medicine.* In that journal, she found a research report demonstrating that certain areas of schizophrenics' brains appear to be smaller than the same areas in brains of persons not suffering from the illness. This interesting research finding appears as one clause in paragraph 3 of her essay.

When she returned to the library, she reread the sources that provided information about the symptoms of schizophrenia. The basic information she needed was in the two reference manuals. Her quotes from patients came mainly from one of the books, *Schizophrenia as a Life Style.* She did not use or cite the *Science News* and *USA Today* articles.

Murayama's search for sources was far from comprehensive, but it was adequate for a brief essay. She wisely stopped searching when she felt that she had the information she needed. It turned out that she used only a small part of her information on symptoms.

Integrating Sources

Two paragraphs from Murayama's essay illustrate a sound strategy for integrating sources into your essay, relying on them fully—as you nearly always must do in explanatory writing—and yet making them your own. Here are paragraphs 10 and 11 from Murayama's essay (the sentences are numbered for ease of reference):

(1) Even if violence does not occur, it is not surprising that the speech and behavioral symptoms I have described are almost always accompanied by--and contribute to--impaired interpersonal functioning. (2) Once schizophrenics become obsessed with delusions, hallucinations, and illogical ideas, they are often too distracted and centered on themselves to interact with other people. (3) Such patients are notable for their emotional detachment even from family members or friends they were previously close to. (4) They also withdraw from all other social interactions, dropping out of school or leaving jobs. (5) They simply cannot face the outside world. (6) Some schizophrenics behave quite differently, however, at least during some phases of the illness. (7) They "cling to other people, intrude upon strangers, and fail to recognize that excessive closeness makes other people uncomfortable and likely to pull away" ("Schizophrenia," 1987, p. 189).

(8) Along with social impairment comes loss of drive or ambition. (9) Schizophrenics typically have difficulty in initiating actions, making decisions, or following through with plans, and their work and other responsibilities often suffer severely as a result.

All of the information in these paragraphs comes from the following two sections of the *Diagnostic and Statistical Manual of Mental Disorders.*

> *Volition.* The characteristic disturbances in volition are most readily observed in the residual phase. There is nearly always some disturbance in self-initiated, goal-directed activity, which may grossly impair work or other role functioning. This may take the form of inadequate interest, drive, or ability to follow a course of action to its logical conclusion. Marked ambivalence regarding alternative courses of action can lead to near-cessation of goal-directed activity.
>
> *Impaired interpersonal functioning and relationship to the external world.* Difficulty in interpersonal relationships is almost invariably present. Often this takes the form of social withdrawal and emotional detachment. When the person is severely preoccupied with egocentric and illogical ideas and fantasies and distorts or excludes the external world, the condition has been referred to as "autism." Some with the disorder, during a phase of the illness, cling to other people, intrude upon strangers, and fail to recognize that excessive closeness makes other people uncomfortable and likely to pull away.

Comparing the source and Murayama's paragraphs 10 and 11, we can see that her first sentence introduces the name of the symptom, which she borrows in part from the symptom name in the source. Sentence 2 paraphrases the source. Sentences 3–5 are her own elaborations of the material in the source, basically giving concrete examples of the more abstract discussion in the original source. Sentence 6 again paraphrases the source. Then, she quotes the source. In sentences 8 and 9, she summarizes the information in the source paragraph headed "Volition."

THINKING CRITICALLY ABOUT WHAT YOU HAVE LEARNED

At this point, you have considerable experience with essays explaining concepts—reading them, talking about them, even writing one of your own. Now is a good time to reflect on the act of reading and writing concept essays and to think critically about how explanations of concepts influence the way we think about ourselves and our culture.

Reflecting on Your Writing

Write a page or so telling your instructor about a problem you encountered in explaining a concept and how you solved it. Before you begin, gather all of your writing—invention, planning notes, drafts, any critical comments from classmates and your instructor, revising notes and plans, and final revision. Review these materials closely as you complete this writing task.

1. Identify *one* writing problem you had to solve as you worked to explain the concept in your essay. Do not be concerned with grammar and punctuation; concentrate instead on problems unique to developing a concept explanation. For example, did you puzzle over how to focus your explanation? Did you worry about how to appeal to your readers' interests or how to identify and define the terms your

readers would need explained? Did you have trouble integrating sources smoothly?

2. How did you recognize the writing problem? When did you first discover it? What called it to your attention? If you did not become aware of the problem until someone else pointed it out to you, can you now see hints of it in your invention writings? If so, where specifically? How did you respond when you first recognized the problem?
3. How did you go about solving the problem? Did you work on the wording of a particular passage, cut or add information, move paragraphs or sentences around, add transitions or forecasting statements, use any different writing strategies? Did you reread one of the essays in this chapter to see how another writer handled the problem or look back at the invention suggestions? If you talked about the writing problem with another student, a tutor, or your instructor, did talking about it help? How useful was the advice you got?
4. Now write your explanation of the problem and your solution. Be as specific as possible in reconstructing your efforts, quoting from your invention, your draft, others' critical comments, your revision plan, or your revised essay to show the various changes your writing underwent as you tried to solve the problem. Thinking in detail about how you identified a particular problem, how you went about solving it, and what you have learned from this experience can help you to solve future writing problems.

Reviewing What You Learned from Reading

To some extent, your own essay has been influenced by other concept explanations you have read in this chapter and by your classmates' essays. For example, your reading may have helped you to choose a topic or to realize that you needed to do research. A reading may have suggested how to structure your essay or how to use a strategy like giving examples or comparison. Write a page or so explaining to your instructor how the readings in this chapter influenced your revised essay. Before you begin, take time to reflect on what you have learned about concept explanations from the readings in this chapter and acknowledge some influences they have had on your own writing.

1. Reread the final revision of your essay; then look back at the selections you read before completing your essay. Name any specific influences. For example, if you were impressed by the way one of the readings described the origins or originators of the concept, organized the information, or connected to readers' knowledge through analogy or comparison, look in your revised essay to see where you were striving for similar effects with your own writing. Also, look for ideas you got from your reading, writing strategies you were inspired to try, specific details you were led to include, and effects you sought to achieve.
2. Now write an explanation of these influences. Did one reading have an especially strong influence, or were several readings influential in different ways? Quote from the selections and from your final revision to show how your essay explaining a concept was influenced by your reading of other concept explanations in this chapter. Finally, briefly explain any further improvements you would make in your essay, based on your review of the chapter's readings.

Considering the Social Dimensions of Concept Explanations

"Knowledge is power," the saying goes, and concepts are the building blocks of knowledge, essential to its creation and acquisition. We use concepts to name and organize ideas and information in areas as diverse as snowboarding and psychiatry. Academic disciplines and most of the professions are heavily concept based, enabling newcomers to be introduced efficiently, if abstractly, to the basic knowledge they need to begin to work in a field.

Knowledge and Authority. As you have learned from your reading, research, and writing for this chapter, writers explaining concepts present knowledge as established and uncontested. They presume to be unbiased, objective, and disinterested, and they assume that readers will not doubt or challenge the truth or the value of the knowledge they present. This stance encourages readers to feel confident about the validity of the explanation.

Explanatory writing should not always be accepted at face value, however. Textbooks and reference materials, in particular, often present a limited view of knowledge in an academic discipline. Because introductory textbooks must be highly selective, they necessarily leave out certain sources of information and kinds of knowledge. Thus, textbooks should be read critically, questioningly, with the reader's full participation as an active thinker.

The Power of Authority. At the same time, however, we recognize that concept explanations involve power relations: The writer establishes what is to count as knowledge about a subject and how that knowledge is to be used. Readers, at least when they begin to study a subject, are powerless to judge the accuracy and completeness of the information or to discern the writer's motives or ideology. The writer's decisions about what to include and exclude remain hidden, so readers of an introductory psychology textbook, for example, will simply not know that it neglects recent research suggesting that cognitive development involves major changes in brain physiology. The reader is not invited to question the writer's choices but rather is placed in the passive position of recipient.

You probably recognize this feeling from reading textbooks in subjects you have never studied before. Students reading textbooks generally accept the role of passive recipient because they are eager to learn new information or at least want to show an instructor what they have learned. They work to memorize and understand terms and their definitions if they expect to be tested on what they have learned or on how they can apply concepts to demonstrate their understanding. Students in introductory courses may be unprepared or unwilling to question their textbooks or think critically about the concepts being presented, yet research shows that we learn and remember best when we think critically and questioningly about a text.

For Discussion. Here we present some questions that can help you to think critically about the role of concept explanations. We focus on those found in textbooks because your most direct experience with concept explanations at this point is probably in your academic work. As you read through and, perhaps, discuss these questions in class, note down your thoughts and reactions. Then, write a page or so for your instructor, presenting your own thoughts about the function of concept explanations in your life and in our society.

1. We have said that concept explanations make their knowledge seem to be true. How do they typically do this? Give a few examples from the readings in this chapter and from this or another textbook to illustrate. What can you say about your own attempt to sound authoritative in explaining your concept?
2. We have also said that concept explanations present established knowledge. How do you think knowledge gets established in an academic field such as biology, psychology, or history?
3. Do you think concept explanations should present *only* established knowledge? What if a few experts in a field question some of the concepts in one of your textbooks? Should their questions be included? Given your reasons for reading the textbook and the goals of the textbook writer, what do you think would be gained or lost if such questions were included?

4. In your experience, is it true that teachers, especially in introductory courses, expect students to memorize concepts presented in textbooks without raising questions about the material? As we have mentioned, research on learning suggests that we learn best when we think critically and questioningly about a text. Identify one assumption or assertion you have found in this chapter, either in the reading selections or in the text discussion, that you could question. What do you think such questioning can contribute to your learning?
5. How does your thinking about the preceding questions help you to interpret the aphorism "Knowledge is power"?

A student writes an editorial for the campus newspaper condemning the practice of hazing students who are pledging to join a fraternity. He acknowledges that most hazing is harmless but argues that hazing can get out of hand and even be lethal. He refers specifically to two incidents reported in the national news in which students died as a result of hazing. In one case, the student died of alcohol poisoning after drinking too much liquor; in the other, the student had a heart attack after running the track many times. To show that the potential for similar tragedy exists on his own campus, the writer recounts several anecdotes told to him by students about their experiences pledging for campus fraternities. He concludes with a plea to the fraternities on campus to curtail their hazing practices before someone gets seriously hurt or killed.

For a business magazine, a corporate executive writes an essay arguing that not only is protecting the environment good citizenship, but it is also good business. To support her position, she gives examples of two companies that became successful by developing innovative methods of reducing hazardous wastes: Marine Shale Processors, which turns toxic materials into street paving, and Detox Industries, which uses microorganisms to break down biologically polychlorinated biphenyls (PCBs). She also reminds readers of the decisive action taken in the late 1980s by established corporations to help to solve the problem of ozone depletion, such as Du Pont's decision to discontinue production of chlorofluorocarbons (CFCs) and McDonald's elimination of styrofoam cartons. Finally, she points out that *Fortune* magazine agrees with her position, noting that their annual ranking of "America's Most Admired Corporations" includes "Community and Environmental Responsibility" alongside "Financial Soundness" among the eight deciding factors.

Parents write a letter to the school board protesting a new program, called "Peacekeepers," in their child's middle school. The writers acknowledge that the aim of the program—to avoid conflict among students—is worthwhile. But they argue that the program's methods unduly restrict students' freedoms. Moreover, they claim that the program teaches children to become passive robots who uncritically follow orders rather than thinking adults ready to fight for what is right. To support their argument, they list some of the rules that have been instituted: children must wear the same uniforms to school; when they walk down the hall, students must keep their hands clasped behind their backs; they are not permitted to raise their voices in anger or to use obscenities; and they cannot play aggressive games like dodgeball or contact sports like basketball and football.

CHAPTER 6

Arguing a Position

Arguing a position is intellectually challenging. It requires you to think critically about your own assumptions, to separate fact from opinion, and to respect the right of others to disagree with you as you may disagree with them. You may associate arguing with quarreling—voices raised in anger, doors slammed, people hurting one another but not changing anyone's mind. This kind of arguing may let us vent strong feelings or express ourselves, but it seldom leads us to consider seriously other points of view, let alone to look critically at our own thinking or learn anything new.

There is a more deliberative way of arguing we call *reasoned argument* because it depends on giving reasons rather than raising your voice. It demands that positions be supported rather than merely asserted. Reasoned argument requires more thought than quarreling but no less passion or commitment to an idea, as you will see when you read the essays in this chapter arguing about controversial issues.

Controversial issues are, by definition, issues about which people feel strongly and sometimes disagree vehemently. The opening scenarios suggest the kinds of controversial issues about which people write position papers. The issue may involve a practice that has been accepted for some time, like fraternity hazing, or it may concern a newly proposed or recently instituted policy, like the "Peacekeeper" program. People may agree about goals but disagree about the best way to achieve them, as in the perennial debate over how to guarantee adequate health care for all citizens. Often the issue involves conflicting values or priorities, as in the argument over the "Peacekeeper" program, which pits the need for safe, conflict-free schools against the need to teach children to be independent and assertive.

As you can see from these examples, controversial issues have no obvious "right" answer, no truth that everyone accepts, no single authority on which everyone relies. Simply gathering information—finding the facts or learning from experts—will not settle disputes like these, although the more that is known about an issue, the more informed the positions will be. Writers cannot offer absolute proof in debates about controversial issues because they are matters of opinion and judgment. To some extent, people decide such matters by considering factual evidence, but they also base their position on less objective factors such as values and principles, assumptions and preconceptions about how the world works and how it should work.

Although it is not possible to prove that a position on a controversial issue is right or wrong, it is possible through argument to convince others to accept or reject a position. To be convincing, a position paper must argue for its position and also counter opposing arguments. When arguing for a position, as we have suggested, writers must do more than provide support. They must earn their readers' trust and build their arguments on common values and beliefs. Counterarguing may involve not only refuting flawed arguments but also learning from reasonable opposing arguments and modifying your position to accommodate them. Even when opponents cannot reach consensus, vigorous debate that sets forth arguments and counterarguments on all sides of an issue can advance everyone's thinking.

Learning to make reasoned arguments on controversial issues and to think critically—not only about others' views but also about our own—is not a luxury; it is a necessity if our increasingly diverse society is to survive and flourish. As citizens in a democracy, we have a special duty to inform ourselves about pressing issues and to participate constructively in the public debate. Honing our thinking and arguing skills also has practical advantages in the workplace, where we often need to decide on policy and make difficult choices.

Writing in Your Other Courses

In your college courses, you will frequently be asked to make reasoned arguments supported by information from the discipline. Consider the following typical assignments from actual courses and textbooks.

- *For a prelaw course:* Research one of the nonacademic cases that Goldstein mentions (such as the Bush administration's "gag order" prohibiting doctors from counseling patients on abortion in federally funded clinics), and write a well-documented essay arguing about the legitimacy of free-speech restrictions in this particular case.
- *For a health sciences course:* Gieringer describes his position as favoring "decriminalization" but "not necessarily full legalization." What position would you advocate on legalizing drugs? Present your own best argument, using the course readings as your primary sources of evidence. You may also do additional research. But do not simply summarize other people's arguments; construct a well-reasoned, well-supported, well-organized argument of your own.
- *For a management course:* Daniel Goleman contends that "groupthink" is an "especially dangerous pathology for businesses," and Eugene Fodor has offered strong evidence that business leaders stifle free thought even when they think they are encouraging frank discussion. Write an essay giving your own informed opinion on this issue. Support your position with evidence from the readings as well as from your research profiling a business.
- *For an economics course:* David M. Gordon claims in "Class and the Economics of Crime" that "ghetto crime is committed by people responding quite reasonably to the structure of economic opportunities available to them." Write an essay agreeing or disagreeing with this statement.
- *For a sociology course:* "Organized crime is inevitable as long as drug use is illegal." Drawing on course readings, agree or disagree with this position.

Practice Constructing an Argument for a Position: A Collaborative Activity

To construct an argument, you must assert a position and offer support for it. This activity gives you a chance to practice constructing an argument with other students.

Part 1. Get together with two to three other students and choose an issue. You do not have to be an expert on the issue, but you should be familiar with some of the arguments people typically make about it. If you do not have an issue in mind, the following list might help you think of possibilities:

- Should the practice of giving grades in college courses be abolished?
- Should college athletes be paid a portion of the money the school gains from sports events?
- Should community service be a requirement for graduation from high school or college?

In your group, spend two to three minutes quickly exchanging your personal views on the issue and then agree together to argue for the same position on the issue, whether you personally agree with the position or not. Choose someone in the group to take notes. Write down the issue and position like this:

Issue: Should grades be abolished?

Position: Grades should be abolished.

Take another ten to fifteen minutes to construct an argument for your position, giving several reasons and noting the kinds of support you would need. Also try to anticipate one or two of the arguments people with other views on the issue could make, including objections to your argument and reasons for their positions. Write down what you discover under the following headings: Reasons, Support Needed, and Likely Objections to Your Position. Following is an example of this work for the position that grades should be abolished.

Reasons:

1. Tests are not always the best way to judge students' knowledge because some students become anxious and do poorly on tests even though they understand the material.
2. Tests often evaluate only what is easily measurable, such as whether you remember facts, rather than whether you can use facts to explain something or solve a problem.
3. etc.

Support Needed:

We would try to find research studies on testing anxiety. We could include anecdotes from our own experience with testing anxiety. We might ask a few teachers why they rely on tests and how they feel about alternatives to testing, like group projects.

continued

continued

Likely Objections to Your Position:

1. Tests are efficient—for teachers and for students, especially in comparison with research papers.
2. Tests are evaluated strictly on what you have learned about the subject, not on how well you write or how well your group collaborated.
3. etc.

Part 2. Discuss for about five minutes what you did as a group to construct an argument:

Reasons: Was it difficult to come up with several reasons for your position? If not, to what do you attribute your success? If so, how was it difficult?

Support: What did you learn about supporting an argument? How many different kinds of support (such as research studies and personal experience) did you consider? Which reasons seemed easiest to support? Which hardest?

Objections: What did you learn about anticipating objections to your argument? What was the weightiest objection you thought of? How might you respond to it? How did it influence your thinking about your own reasons and the support you need for them?

READINGS

Richard Estrada writes a syndicated column for the *Dallas Morning News.* He wrote this essay in late October 1995 during the baseball World Series in which the Atlanta Braves played the Cleveland Indians. The series, which was televised, drew attention to the practice of dressing team mascots like Native Americans on the warpath and encouraging fans to rally their team with gestures like the "tomahawk chop" and pep yells like the "Indian chant." The controversy over these practices ignited a long-standing debate over sports teams using names associated with Native Americans. Various high schools and at least one university, Stanford, have changed the names of their sports teams in recent years because of this ongoing controversy.

The title, as you may know, refers to a children's chant: "Sticks and stones will break my bones, but words will never hurt me." As you read, consider why Estrada and his newspaper editor thought this title was appropriate.

STICKS AND STONES AND SPORTS TEAM NAMES

Richard Estrada

1 When I was a kid living in Baltimore in the late 1950s, there was only one professional sports team worth following. Anyone who ever saw the movie *Diner* knows which one it was. Back when we liked Ike, the Colts were the gods of the gridiron and Memorial Stadium was their Mount Olympus.

2 Ah, yes: The Colts. The Lions. Da Bears. Back when defensive tackle Big Daddy Lipscomb was letting running backs know exactly what time it was, a young fan could

easily forget that in a game where men were men, the teams they played on were not invariably named after animals. Among others, the Packers, the Steelers and the distant 49ers were cases in point. But in the roll call of pro teams, one name in particular always discomfited me: the Washington Redskins. Still, however willing I may have been to go along with the name as a kid, as an adult I have concluded that using an ethnic group essentially as a sports mascot is wrong.

3 The Redskins, along with baseball teams like the Atlanta Braves, the Cleveland Indians and the Kansas City Chiefs, should find other names that avoid highlighting ethnicity.

4 By no means were such names originally meant to disparage Native Americans. The noble symbols of the Redskins or college football's Florida Seminoles or the Illinois Illini are meant to be strong and proud. Yet, ultimately, the practice of using a people as mascots is dehumanizing. It sets them apart from the rest of society. It promotes the politics of racial aggrievement at a moment when our storehouse is running over with it.

5 The World Series between the Cleveland Indians and the Atlanta Braves reignited the debate. In the chill night air of October, tomahawk chops and war chants suddenly became far more familiar to millions of fans, along with the ridiculous and offensive cartoon logo of Cleveland's "Chief Wahoo."

6 The defenders of team names that use variations on the Indian theme argue that tradition should not be sacrificed at the altar of political correctness. In truth, the nation's No. 1 P.C. [politically correct] school, Stanford University, helped matters some when it changed its team nickname from "the Indians" to "the Cardinals." To be sure, Stanford did the right thing, but the school's status as P.C. without peer tainted the decision for those who still need to do the right thing.

7 Another argument is that ethnic group leaders are too inclined to cry wolf in alleging racial insensitivity. Often, this is the case. But no one should overlook genuine cases of political insensitivity in an attempt to avoid accusations of hypersensitivity and political correctness.

8 The real world is different from the world of sports entertainment. I recently heard a father who happened to be a Native American complain on the radio that his child was being pressured into participating in celebrations of Braves baseball. At his kid's school, certain days are set aside on which all children are told to dress in Indian garb and celebrate with tomahawk chops and the like.

9 That father should be forgiven for not wanting his family to serve as somebody's mascot. The desire to avoid ridicule is legitimate and understandable. Nobody likes to be trivialized or deprived of their dignity. This has nothing to do with political correctness and the provocations of militant leaders.

10 Against this backdrop, the decision by newspapers in Minneapolis, Seattle and Portland to ban references to Native American nicknames is more reasonable than some might think.

11 What makes naming teams after ethnic groups, particularly minorities, reprehensible is that politically impotent groups continue to be targeted, while politically powerful ones who bite back are left alone. How long does anyone think the name "Washington Blackskins" would last? Or how about "the New York Jews"?

12 With no fewer than 10 Latino ballplayers on the Cleveland Indians' roster, the team could change its name to "the Banditos." The trouble is, they would be missing the point: Latinos would correctly object to that stereotype, just as they rightly protested against Frito-Lay's use of the "Frito Bandito" character years ago.

It seems to me that what Native Americans are saying is that what would be intolerable for Jews, blacks, Latinos and others is no less offensive to them. Theirs is a request not only for dignified treatment, but for fair treatment as well. For America to ignore the complaints of a numerically small segment of the population because it is small is neither dignified nor fair. 13

Connecting to Culture and Experience

As children, we may say, "Sticks and stones will break my bones, but words will never hurt me." Most children, however, recognize the power of words, especially words that make us feel different or inferior.

Discuss with other students your experience of name-calling. List the names given to groups with which you identify yourself, based on ancestry, ethnicity, race, religion, gender, neighborhood, geographic region, or any other factor. Which of these names, if any, do you consider insulting? Why? What does the name connote? Would you consider someone who uses names like these insensitive, as Estrada suggests, or do you think that someone who takes offense at the use of names like these is being hypersensitive? Or if you think the issue is a matter not of sensitivity but of something else, what terms would you use to describe the issue? Consider, for example, the relationship between who is doing the naming and who is being named. Who has the power in this relationship?

Analyzing Writing Strategies

1. At the beginning of this chapter, we make generalizations about **position papers.** Consider which of these are true of Estrada's essay.
   - Controversial issues have no obvious "right" answer, no truth that everyone accepts, no single authority on which everyone relies.
   - Writers cannot offer absolute proof in debates about controversial issues because they are matters of opinion and judgment; positions depend to some extent on factual evidence but depend as well on less objective factors like values and principles, assumptions and preconceptions about how the world works and how it should work.
   - A convincing argument supports its position and also seeks to earn readers' trust by building an argument on common values and beliefs.
   - A convincing argument counterargues opposing arguments but also modifies its position to accommodate reasonable opposing arguments.

For more on using anecdotes in argument, see pp. 533–34.

2. Reread paragraphs 8 and 9, where Estrada presents an **anecdote** about a father he heard complaining on a radio talk show. Explain, in your own words, Estrada's reasoning in this part of his argument. Describe the logical connection he wants his readers to see between the child's experience and his position, which is stated at the end of paragraph 7. Then, speculate about why Estrada assumes that the anecdote might carry some weight with his *Dallas Morning News* readers. Also consider what objections a critical reader might make to Estrada's reasoning here.

Considering Topics for Your Own Essay

List some issues that you could write about involving cultural diversity. For example, should a law be passed to make English the "official language" in this country, requiring that ballots and driver's tests be in English only? Should elementary schools continue bilingual education to help non-English-speaking students to learn subjects like math, science, and history while they are learning to read and write fluently in English? Should there be some form of affirmative action in college admissions for people who are qualified but belong to underrepresented groups?

Commentary

Estrada's essay allows us to introduce all the basic features of position papers: a well-defined issue, a clear position, a reasoned argument, and an appropriate tone. Moreover, looking closely at his essay, we can see that Estrada deploys these features strategically to achieve his purpose with his particular readers, developing what we call an argumentative strategy.

Writers taking a position on a controversial issue develop an **argumentative strategy** based on what they assume readers already think and feel about the issue and what they want readers to think and feel about it. Estrada apparently assumes the readers of his column in the politically conservative *Dallas Morning News* would tend to disregard the issue of sports teams' names as unimportant unless he can bring home to them its significance as a personal rather than a political issue. Therefore, Estrada adopts a strategy of accommodation that seeks not to alienate his readers or make them defensive but to make them empathize with what he calls a "real world" issue (paragraph 8).

Look first at how Estrada establishes the **tone** of this essay. Unlike some position papers that start off on an angry or self-righteous note decrying what the writer thinks is wrong and declaring what he or she thinks is right, Estrada strives for a calmer, more reflective, even nostalgic tone. He opens the essay by remembering his youthful enthusiasm for his hometown football team. Knowing that Dallas is a fanatical sports town and that many Texans encourage children to play ball and root for their favorite teams, Estrada's reminiscence helps to build a bond of common values with his readers. He holds off **defining the issue** until the middle of the second paragraph, as if he were reluctant to bring up a point on which he disagrees with his readers. Even then he frames his position on the issue in personal and moral terms as something that "discomfited" him when he was a child and has led him as an adult to reach a conclusion about right and wrong. In this context, he asserts strongly and clearly what he thinks others (the sports teams) should do. This assertion of his **position** is the thesis of the essay. Estrada restates his position several times throughout the essay and reasserts it again at the end. He argues for his position by providing three well-supported **reasons.**

For more on counterarguing, see pp. 537–42.

In addition to arguing for his position, Estrada also **counterargues** the reasons he expects readers would give for their position. His counterargument **accommodates** his readers' point of view by acknowledging—and implying that he shares—their critical attitude toward "political correctness," but it also **refutes** their argument.

Estrada's attempt at accommodation is evident in word choices like "the politics of racial aggrievement," "the altar of political correctness," and "That father should be forgiven" (paragraphs 4, 6, and 9, respectively). From this language, we can infer that Estrada wants his readers to see that he shares many of their values and assumptions. Nevertheless, Estrada does assert his position unequivocally without hedging or apology, and he rebuts his readers' opposing arguments: "No one should overlook genuine cases of political insensitivity in an attempt to avoid accusations of hypersensitivity and political correctness" (paragraph 6).

The following outline shows how Estrada organizes all the features of his position paper:

Presents the issue and asserts his position (paragraphs 1–3)

Acknowledges good intentions and readers' concerns but reasserts importance of the issue (4, 5)

Counterargues against charges of political correctness and hypersensitivity (6, 7)

Gives first reason with supporting anecdote: real kids are getting hurt (8, 9)

Gives second reason with supporting examples: other newspapers agree (10)

Gives third reason with supporting examples: these kinds of names would be offensive to anyone (11, 12)

Concludes by appealing to readers (13)

Writing about a controversial issue, you too will have to devise an argumentative strategy tailored for your particular readers. To see how to construct an argumentative strategy, let us compare part of Estrada's reasoning and support with the same argument made by another writer, Ward Churchill, for a different audience and purpose. As you will see in the excerpt, Estrada and Churchill are both making the same argument but using it differently to achieve different purposes with their different audiences. Briefly, the argument is that naming sports teams after certain ethnic groups and not others is unfair. It is also cowardly, as Churchill makes explicit and Estrada implies, to pick on a group that lacks political clout.

Churchill, a professor of American Indian studies and an active member of the American Indian Anti-Defamation League, is writing in *Z Magazine,* a politically liberal, even radical, journal. Whereas Estrada assumes that his readers will disagree with him but could be persuaded by the right arguments, Churchill is writing to readers who already agree, perhaps with the intention of entertaining them and stiffening their resolve. Notice that neither of these writers tries to convince readers whose opposition is entrenched. When writers address such readers, it is usually in the context of a political debate or talk show like *Crossfire,* where the primary aim is to rally supporters and incense opponents.

Given their different **purpose** and **audience,** we can understand the different argumentative strategies Estrada and Churchill use. Estrada, in paragraphs 11–13, gingerly cites just a few hypothetical team names, limiting the groups he insults and avoiding the very worst slurs. In contrast, Churchill makes a point of including everyone and using the most insulting names possible. Churchill takes Estrada's argument to the extreme, reducing to absurdity the idea of naming teams after ethnic groups.

You might think he risks alienating his readers, but the risk is small because he explains at the end precisely what he is trying to argue.

Compare this excerpt from Churchill's essay with paragraphs 11–13 in Estrada's essay.

If what they [defenders of Indian team names] say is true, then isn't it time we spread such "inoffensiveness" and "good cheer" around among *all* groups so that *everybody* can participate *equally* in fostering the round of national laughs they call for? . . . Simple consistency demands that anyone who thinks the Tomahawk Chop is a swell pastime must be just as hearty in their endorsement of the following ideas. . . . 1

First, as a counterpart to the Redskins, we need an NFL team called "Niggers" to honor Afro-Americans. Half-time festivities for fans might include a simulated stewing of the opposing coach in a large pot while players and cheerleaders dance around it, garbed in leopard skins and wearing fake bones in their noses. This concept obviously goes along with the kind of gaiety attending the Chop, but also with the actions of the Kansas City Chiefs, whose team members—prominently including black team members—lately appeared on a poster looking "fierce" and "savage" by way of wearing Indian regalia. Just a bit of harmless "morale boosting," says the Chiefs' front office. You bet. . . . 2

And why stop there? There are plenty of other groups to include. "Hispanics"? They can be "represented" by the Galveston "Greasers" and San Diego "Spics." . . . Asian Americans? How about the "Slopes," "Dinks," [and] "Gooks". . . ? Let's see. Who's been left out? Teams like the Kansas City "Kikes," Hanover "Honkies". . . Have a religious belief? . . . The Fighting Irish of Notre Dame can be rechristened the "Drunken Irish." . . . Issues of gender and sexual preference can be addressed through creation of teams like the . . . Detroit "Dykes" and the Fresno "Fags." How about the Gainesville "Gimps" and the Richmond "Retards," so the physically and mentally impaired won't be excluded from our fun and games? 3

Now, don't go getting "overly sensitive" out there. None of this is demeaning or insulting, at least when it's being done to Indians. . . . Let's get just a bit real here. The notion of "fun" embodied in rituals like the Tomahawk Chop must be understood for what it is. There's not a single non-Indian example used above which can be considered socially acceptable in even the most marginal sense. The reasons are obvious enough. So why is it different where American Indians are concerned? One can only conclude that, in contrast to the other groups at issue, Indians are (falsely) perceived as being too few, and therefore too weak, to defend themselves effectively against racist and otherwise offensive behavior. 4

Barbara Ehrenreich has written several books, including a critique of the 1980s, *The Worst Years of Our Lives: Irreverent Notes from a Decade of Greed* (1990), and a study of the middle class, *Fear of Falling* (1989). Her essays are published regularly in *American Scholar, Atlantic, New Republic,* and *Time,* where this selection originally appeared in December 1995. In it, Ehrenreich responds to recent attacks on the immorality of television talk shows by Senator Joseph Lieberman and William Bennett. Bennett served under President Reagan as secretary of education and chair of the National Endowment for the Humanities and under President Bush as director of the Office of National Drug Control Policy, but he is probably best known for his advocacy of "family values" and his literary anthology, *The Book of Virtues: A Treasury of Great Moral Stories* (1993).

If you are familiar with television talk shows, consider as you read Ehrenreich's essay whether her portrayal of the shows seems accurate. If you have never watched talk shows, consider whether Ehrenreich gives you enough specific detail to imagine what they are like.

IN DEFENSE OF TALK SHOWS

Barbara Ehrenreich

Up until now, the targets of Bill *(The Book of Virtues)* Bennett's crusades have at least been plausible sources of evil. But the latest victim of his wrath—TV talk shows of the *Sally Jessy Raphael* variety—are in a whole different category from drugs and gangsta rap. As anyone who actually watches them knows, the talk shows are one of the most excruciatingly moralistic forums the culture has to offer. Disturbing and sometimes disgusting, yes, but their very business is to preach the middle-class virtues of responsibility, reason and self-control. 1

Take the case of Susan, recently featured on *Montel Williams* as an example of a woman being stalked by her ex-boyfriend. Turns out Susan is also stalking the boyfriend and—here's the sexual frisson—has slept with him only days ago. In fact Susan is neck deep in trouble without any help from the boyfriend: she's serving a yearlong stretch of home incarceration for assaulting another woman, and home is the tiny trailer she shares with her nine-year-old daughter. 2

But no one is applauding this life spun out of control. Montel scolds Susan roundly for neglecting her daughter and failing to confront her role in the mutual stalking. A therapist lectures her about this unhealthy "obsessive kind of love." The studio audience jeers at her every evasion. By the end Susan has lost her cocky charm and dissolved into tears of shame. 3

The plot is always the same. People with problems—"her husband says she looks like a cow," "pressured to lose her virginity or else," "mate wants more sex than I do"—are introduced to rational methods of problem solving. People with moral failings—"boy crazy," "dresses like a tramp," "a hundred sex partners"—are introduced to external standards of morality. The preaching—delivered alternately by the studio audience, the host and the ever present guest therapist—is relentless. "This is wrong to do this," Sally Jessy tells a cheating husband. "Feel bad?" Geraldo asks the girl who stole her best friend's boyfriend. "Any sense of remorse?" The expectation is that the sinner, so hectored, will see her way to reform. And indeed, a Sally Jessy update found "boy crazy," who'd been a guest only weeks ago, now dressed in schoolgirlish plaid and claiming her "attitude [had] changed"—thanks to the rough-and-ready therapy dispensed on the show. 4

All right, the subjects are often lurid and even bizarre. But there's no part of the entertainment spectacle, from *Hard Copy* to *Jade,* that doesn't trade in the lurid and bizarre. At least in the talk shows, the moral is always loud and clear: Respect yourself, listen to others, stop beating on your wife. In fact it's hard to see how *The Bill Bennett Show,* if there were to be such a thing, could deliver a more pointed sermon. Or would he prefer to see the feckless Susan, for example, tarred and feathered by the studio audience instead of being merely booed and shamed? 5

There *is* something morally repulsive about the talks, but it's not anything Bennett or his co-crusader Senator Joseph Lieberman has seen fit to mention. Watch for a few 6 hours, and you get the claustrophobic sense of lives that have never seen the light of some external judgment, of people who have never before been listened to, and certainly never been taken seriously if they were. "What kind of people would let themselves be humiliated like this?" is often asked, sniffily, by the shows' detractors. And the answer, for the most part, is people who are so needy—of social support, of education, of material resources and self-esteem—that they mistake being the center of attention for being actually loved and respected.

What the talks are about, in large part, is poverty and the distortions it visits on the human spirit. You'll never find investment bankers bickering on *Rolonda,* or the host of *Gabrielle* recommending therapy to sobbing professors. With few exceptions the guests are drawn from trailer parks and tenements, from bleak streets and narrow, crowded rooms. Listen long enough, and you hear references to unpaid bills, to welfare, to 12-hour workdays and double shifts. And this is the real shame of the talks: that they take lives bent out of shape by poverty and hold them up as entertaining exhibits. An announcement appearing between segments of *Montel* says it all: the show is looking for "pregnant women who sell their bodies to make ends meet." 7

This is class exploitation, pure and simple. What next—"homeless people so hungry they eat their own scabs"? Or would the next step be to pay people outright to submit to public humiliation? For $50 would you confess to adultery in your wife's presence? For $500 would you reveal your 13-year-old's girlish secrets on *Ricki Lake*? If you were poor enough, you might. 8

It is easy enough for those who can afford spacious homes and private therapy to sneer at their financial inferiors and label their pathetic moments of stardom vulgar. But if I had a talk show, it would feature a whole different cast of characters and category of crimes than you'll ever find on the talks: "CEOs who rake in millions while their employees get downsized" would be an obvious theme, along with "Senators who voted for welfare and Medicaid cuts"—and . . . "who dithered about talk shows while trailer-park residents slipped into madness and despair." 9

Connecting to Culture and Experience

Many people consider the United States to be a classless society or at least one that is predominantly middle-class. Ehrenreich, however, assumes that there are different social and economic classes in this country (ranging from "CEOs who rake in millions" to "homeless people"). People on the lowest rungs of the ladder, according to Ehrenreich, are represented on television talk shows.

Discuss with other students this idea that television reveals part, if not all, of America's class structure. Focus your discussion on two or three specific television programs or series (other than talk shows) in which you think people are portrayed in terms of class. The program need not still be on the air; it may be a program you remember seeing in the past. Some possibilities with which you may be familiar are *Lifestyles of the Rich and Famous, Married . . . with Children, All in the Family,* and *Dallas.* Certain kinds of programs, such as police or lawyer shows, may be more likely than others to represent class.

When you have chosen television programs or series that portray class, discuss what class or classes they portray. Consider also how the shows depict people in terms of class. Are they being held up for ridicule or represented fairly, condescended to or respected? What stereotypes about class, if any, do you think the programs promote?

Analyzing Writing Strategies

For more on using cases in argument, see pp. 535–36.

1. In paragraphs 2 and 3, Ehrenreich presents what she calls "the case of Susan." A **case** is an extended, detailed example used as evidence supporting an argument. To be convincing, a case must be specific enough for readers to accept it as something that actually happened, but it also must be typical enough for readers to accept it as a representative, generalizable example. Reread these paragraphs to see how Ehrenreich tries to make the case of Susan both specific and typical.

   Then look closely at paragraph 4, where Ehrenreich offers several other brief **examples.** What role do these examples play in relation to the case of Susan? What do you think would be lost or gained if Ehrenreich had used the case without the follow-up examples or used the examples alone without the case?
2. In the second part of her argument (paragraphs 6–9), Ehrenreich contends that television talk shows are immoral in a way that neither Bennett nor his "co-crusader" Senator Joseph Lieberman has "seen fit to mention." For some readers, word choices like "co-crusader" and "seen fit to mention" convey a particular **tone.** What tone, if any, do these words convey to you?

   Reread paragraphs 6–9, underlining any word choices that seem to you to convey a particular tone. Then describe the tone (or tones, if you think this section has more than one). Given your understanding of Ehrenreich's argumentative strategy—how she is trying to achieve her purpose with her particular readers—evaluate the appropriateness of the tone she adopts in this part of the essay. (To explore tone further, you may wish to read James Wolcott's evaluation in Chapter 8 of the television talk show *Night Stand,* which uses satire to respond to both Ehrenreich and Bennett's positions.)

Considering Topics for Your Own Essay

Consider other controversial issues that involve the media—television, radio, film, music video, recording, computer games, or the Internet. For example, should individuals be able to sell videotapes they have copied from commercial broadcasts? Should prime-time television programs be permitted to show nudity? Should store owners be prohibited from selling "Parental Advisory"–stickered recordings to people under eighteen? Should there be censorship on the Internet? Select one issue on which you have a position, and consider how you would construct a reasoned argument for your position.

Commentary

Ehrenreich's essay allows us to look closely at the central role **defining the issue** plays in position papers. To define the issue, a writer must first establish for readers that there really is a controversy worthy of their attention. Because she is writing for a magazine that includes a news story about Bennett and Lieberman's campaign against the immorality of television talk shows, Ehrenreich can safely assume that her readers already know about the issue. Consequently, she takes the shortcut of simply mentioning their names and the name of the talk show singled out for criticism, *Sally Jessy Raphael.*

In addition to establishing the issue's existence and seriousness, writers also define the issue in a way that supports their position and sets up their argument.

We saw that Estrada, for example, defines the issue in personal and moral terms rather than in the either-or, conservative or liberal terms typical of political debate. He tries to redefine the terms of the issue because he knows his largely conservative audience would not be open to his argument if he declared that he was taking a liberal position on the issue.

Like Estrada, Ehrenreich tries to change the terms of the debate. But whereas Estrada puts the issue into new terms, Ehrenreich keeps the old term, *morality*, but redefines it by reminding readers of a second kind of morality that they seem to have forgotten. Ehrenreich begins, in the first part of her essay, by accepting Bennett's definition of morality as the "virtues of responsibility, reason and self-control" (paragraph 1). But applying this definition leads Ehrenreich to a conclusion diametrically opposed to the one Bennett draws. Instead of agreeing with Bennett that television talk shows promote immorality, she refutes his position, arguing instead that talk shows are "excruciatingly moralistic" and, in fact, "preach the middle-class virtues" (paragraph 1).

With paragraph 6, Ehrenreich shifts the meaning of morality from individual responsibility for oneself to public responsibility for others less fortunate. In paragraphs 1–5, she presents morality as a standard that each person must live up to or suffer the consequences. The consequences, according to Ehrenreich, take the form of public humiliation, with television talk shows serving as a modern-day pillory. Ehrenreich apparently accepts the idea of individual responsibility but objects to the role of scold played by the viewing public. She chastises viewers who are entertained by shaming desperate, misguided people. Moreover, she accuses Bennett and Lieberman of "sniffily" looking down their noses on people's suffering (paragraph 6) when they should be instilling a sense of moral responsibility in members of the public and inspiring them to improve the lives of people "bent out of shape by poverty" (paragraph 7). Ehrenreich argues that talk shows are "morally repulsive" in the sense that they perpetuate attitudes of moral superiority and justify continued neglect.

By analyzing Ehrenreich's sentences, you can also learn many different ways to use **dashes.** Dashes are versatile punctuation marks. They can set off material for emphasis, clarification, illustration, or comment:

> But the latest victim of his wrath—TV talk shows of the *Sally Jessy Raphael* variety—are in a whole different category. . . . (paragraph 1)
>
> Turns out Susan is also stalking the boyfriend and—here's the sexual frisson—has slept with him only days ago. (2)
>
> People with problems—"husband says she looks like a cow," "pressured to lose her virginity or else," "mate wants more sex than I do"—are introduced to rational methods of problem solving. (4)
>
> And indeed, a Sally Jessy update found "boy crazy," who'd been a guest only a few weeks ago, now dressed in schoolgirlish plaid and claiming her "attitude [had] changed"—thanks to the rough-and-ready therapy dispensed on the show. (4)

Dashes tend to work especially well in informal writing, like Ehrenreich's. Notice the informality of some of her word choices—beginning sentences with "Turns out" and "And," as well as using contractions and colloquial language like "the talks."

Guy Molyneux is a public opinion pollster and president of the Next America Foundation, an educational organization founded by sociologist Michael Harrington. He often writes for such newspapers as the *New York Times* and the *Los Angeles Times.* This essay originally appeared in the latter in May 1993.

Molyneux's essay includes many references that his original readers would have recognized but might not be familiar to you. We have footnoted many of them, but at least in some instances you may feel that Molyneux provides enough information for you to understand the point he is making. Molyneux probably assumed that many in his audience would be regular newspaper readers and therefore would catch most of his references.

As you read, think about whether what Molyneux says about political debates applies to arguments with which you are familiar—televised debates among candidates for political office, arguments on talk radio, editorials in newspapers—as well as friendly discussions among friends or family.

THE DECLINING ART OF POLITICAL DEBATE

Guy Molyneux

1 "You just don't get it." . . .

2 One of the earliest appearances of the phrase was during the Anita P. Hill–Clarence Thomas hearings: The 14 white men on the Senate Judiciary Committee "just didn't get it." Many said Dan Quayle's ill-fated attack on Murphy Brown's single parenthood showed that the then–vice president didn't get it. Quayle's reply: "Hollywood just doesn't get it." Zoë Baird and her Administration sponsors didn't "get" the ramifications of her nanny problem. Senate Minority Leader Bob Dole (R-Kan.) even says President Bill Clinton "doesn't get it" when he proposes new government spending. Increasingly, it is used to describe virtually anybody with whom one disagrees.[1]

3 However rhetorically effective, "getting it" is actually emblematic of much that is wrong with today's political dialogue and debate. Arguments often seem designed to stigmatize those who disagree, to shame or embarrass the opposition rather than refute its arguments. The purpose is to end or prevent debate, not open it up. Most fundamentally, it represents an abandonment of what should lie at the heart of political discourse: persuasion of those who now disagree, or don't yet agree. No one seems interested in trying to help anyone else "get it."

4 There is nothing wrong, or new, in believing one's own position is fairer, more realistic or just smarter than the opposition's. But "getting it" suggests something more: possession of a special wisdom denied to others. This sacred knowledge comes in both liberal and conservative versions. Liberals claim a monopoly on racial and sexual "sensitivity"; conservatives on respect for "traditional values."

5 This could have its roots in America's sectarian Protestant culture. It's another version of the search for personal salvation—instead of being "saved," you "get it." Indeed, one of the early uses of the phrase was in the EST self-actualization movement.

[1] Anita Hill accused Supreme Court justice nominee Clarence Thomas of sexual harassment during the Senate hearings on whether or not he should be appointed to the Court. Vice President Dan Quayle criticized a sitcom character, Murphy Brown, for having a child out of wedlock. Zoë Baird's nomination for attorney general had to be withdrawn when it was discovered that she had hired an illegal alien to care for her children.

Participants were not allowed to leave a seminar until they "got it"—the New Age equivalent of being saved.

6 But politics is better likened to missionary work than to the search for a personal state of grace. The priority isn't—or shouldn't be—one's own correctness (sanctity), but winning others over to your viewpoint. That's how political minorities grow to become majorities, creating the possibility of change and progress.

7 The new style of political discourse isn't likely to accomplish that. Instead, it obliterates the essential distinction between a point of view and objective "knowledge." Differing opinions thus become "ignorance." Persuasion is meaningless—the task, instead, is "education." The breathtaking arrogance of such an approach pushes away, rather than attracts, benighted souls who don't agree. Moreover, it encourages intellectual laziness on the part of the "enlightened." If a position's correctness cannot be doubted, it also need not be explained or defended. Basic argumentation skills atrophy. . . .

8 Persuasion depends, mostly, on finding common values. To persuade someone of a view not already held, you must link it to some other argument or value shared by both parties. But today's political debate largely forsakes appeals to common values and understanding. Worse, it often implies that there cannot be any such common ground. Certain people's race, gender, age, etc. make it impossible for them truly to "get it." Though currently popular with political liberals, this is an illiberal notion. Tell men that they can't truly understand sexual harassment, and many will happily return to ignoring the issue. Tell whites they can't comprehend the black experience, and many will decide blacks' problems aren't their concern. Those who want to promote equality, brotherhood and sisterhood must insist on the possibility of understanding one another—even if imperfectly—despite differing life experiences.

9 Sen. Bob Packwood (R-Ore.), ironically, helped show why this is so.[2] Confronted with overwhelming evidence of his inappropriate sexual behavior, he cleverly conceded that he "just didn't get it." The political insult became a defense: You shouldn't punish me, because I didn't get it. But what didn't he "get"? That married men shouldn't pursue other women? That a man shouldn't fondle a woman who has shown no interest? And if Packwood didn't understand the actions were wrong, why did they invariably happen in closed offices or empty corridors?

10 The defense is absurd, but it is abetted by a political culture that gives up the notion of shared values. By saying those we disagree with "don't get it," we actually give them an out while attempting to demonize them—because we give up the notion of shared moral and ethical standards. Without that, there is no accountability. It may well be true that at some profound level, men cannot truly understand the experience of sexual harassment. But the part they can understand—what constitutes harassment and why it is wrong—is far greater, and far more important.

11 Historically, the greatest political rhetoric has emphasized not what we cannot know of one another, but what we can. That is how differences of culture, class and race are bridged. Abraham Lincoln's famous declaration, "As I would not be a slave, so I would not be a master," was in this tradition. Lincoln kept a predominantly white citizenry in the North united through a war devoted, in part, to ending slavery for blacks—an astonishing persuasive feat. He did it with the help of rhetoric such as this: "This is a world of compensations; and he who would be no slave must consent to have no slave. Those who deny freedom to others deserve it not for themselves, and, under a just God, cannot long retain it."

[2] Senator Packwood was forced to retire from the Senate following charges of sexual harassment.

A century later, John F. Kennedy made similar appeals in throwing his support behind the second great chapter in the struggle for racial equality. In arguing for civil rights, he asserted that "every American ought to have the right to be treated as he would wish to be treated, as one would wish his children to be treated." Invoking broadly held concepts of fairness, Kennedy noted that "no one has been barred on account of his race from fighting or dying for America—there are no 'white' or 'colored' signs on the foxholes or graveyards of battle."

Today, much political debate takes the form of either "preaching to the choir" or berating those unfortunate enough not to share the speaker's wisdom. But Kennedy was not speaking to white liberals and blacks, nor [was he speaking] to white racists. He was addressing whites who did not necessarily support civil rights, but might be moved to that view—the people who most needed to hear what he had to say.

The appalling decline of political eloquence over the past generation has been widely noted—especially during the Bush presidency. In part, this reflects a wider coarsening of public speech. But it also has roots in this abandonment of the ideal of persuasion. Persuasion both demands and inspires fine political rhetoric. As our belief in the possibility of changing the minds of our fellow citizens decays, so too does the level of our political debate.

Today's conservative and liberal movements, both prone to self-righteousness, feed these debilitating trends. The largely nonideological center of the electorate, neither spoken to nor [spoken] for, grows increasingly alienated. And the mass media, with its preference for conflict and punchy sound bites, rewards some of the worst forms of debate. The result: a self-reinforcing cycle built on a cynical electorate and negative politics.

Connecting to Culture and Experience

In paragraph 8, Molyneux says that "today's political debate largely forsakes appeals to common values and understanding." He argues that people assume that "race, gender, age, etc. make it impossible" to find common ground.

Discuss with other students an experience when you argued with someone who was different from you in race, gender, age, or some other way. Was it possible to find common values the two of you could share, or was it impossible? What could you have done, if anything, to increase the likelihood of finding common ground?

Analyzing Writing Strategies

1. Molyneux's essay is complex, in part because he is making an argument about arguing. To get an overview of his argument and determine whether he argues in the way he says we should, make a scratch outline like the one in the Commentary section following Estrada's essay.

   After you have outlined the argument, decide whether Molyneux practices what he preaches. Does his **argumentative strategy** establish common values, or does it polarize readers on different sides of the issue? Point to a specific place in the essay to illustrate your judgment.

Scratch outlining is explained and illustrated on pp. 448–51.

2. Look closely at paragraphs 11–13, where Molyneux quotes Presidents Lincoln and Kennedy. How do the **quotations** bolster the argument he is making about the importance of reinforcing the idea that we have or should have common values? Consider both whom he chose to quote as well as the particular language he quotes.

Considering Topics for Your Own Essay

Think of a political issue on which you could write an essay. Consider a local campus issue such as whether a particular instructor should get tenure or be fired, whether funds should be used for computer labs or parking spaces, or whether student athletes should be required to maintain a certain grade point average to participate in sports. Also consider local community issues such as whether a new shelter for abused women and children should be opened, whether parents should be held responsible legally and financially for crimes committed by their children under age eighteen, or whether in-line skating or skateboarding should be permitted downtown or on campus. When you have chosen a topic, think about how you would go about getting information to support your argument.

Commentary

Position papers may use a range of different **writing strategies** to explain the issue as well as to present reasons. To show that the issue really exists and is, in fact, pervasive, Molyneux gives several quick **examples** illustrating recent instances when the phrase "You just don't get it" has been used (paragraph 2). Molyneux uses the Senator Packwood **anecdote** (paragraphs 9 and 10) to show how "You just don't get it"—originally a criticism of people who do not try to understand other people's points of view—was ironically turned into a defense or justification of not even trying to get it.

For more on using anecdotes, see pp. 533–34.

To prove that political debate has declined, Molyneux uses **comparison and contrast,** arguing that the eloquence of Lincoln and Kennedy is sadly missed today. He makes other strategic comparisons and contrasts, such as the comparison between politics and missionary work (paragraph 6) and the contrast between a point of view and objective knowledge (paragraph 7). Molyneux also speculates about the historical and cultural **causes and effects** of the current decline in political debate (paragraph 5). Finally, Molyneux uses **classification** when he refers to the categories of liberal and conservative as well as when he writes at the beginning of paragraph 13: "Today, much political debate takes the form of either 'preaching to the choir' or berating those unfortunate enough not to share the speaker's wisdom." You may not need to use as many different writing strategies as Molyneux, but you should know how to use them to explain and support your argument.

For more on using comparison and contrast, see Chapter 18.

For more on causes and effects, see Chapter 9.

For more on using classification, see Chapter 17.

In addition, Molyneux employs several **cohesive devices** to make his writing flow smoothly from one sentence to another and to help readers follow the thread of his argument. In the second paragraph, for instance, Molyneux relies on **word repetition** to show how often the put-down "You just don't get it" occurs. Paragraph 3 chains **synonyms** to connect important ideas from sentence to sentence: "political dialogue and debate" (sentence 1), "arguments" (2), "political discourse" and "persuasion" (4). Pronouns are also used to link a sentence to the preceding one, as in these sentences from paragraph 4: "But 'getting it' suggests something more: possession of a *special wisdom* denied to others. *This sacred knowledge* . . . ." The pronoun reference chain continues in the next paragraph in the first two sentences: "*This* could have its roots . . . ," "*It's* another version of . . . ." Note that some of these pronoun references work better than others. "This sacred knowledge" in paragraph 4, for example, follows the pronoun *this* with a synonym for the phrase *special wisdom* in the preceding

For more on cohesive devices, see pp. 475–78.

sentence. In the fifth paragraph, however, the pronoun *This* is not preceded by a synonym. Without such a signal, readers may not know to which word or concept in the fourth paragraph the pronoun is supposed to refer. *This* probably refers generally to the process described in paragraph 4 of assuming that one's knowledge is "sacred" or "special," but there is no way to be certain. After you write your own essay, reread it carefully to make sure that you have given readers cueing devices and that they are clear and unambiguous.

Jessica Statsky wrote the following essay about children's competitive sports for her first-year college composition course. Although this essay was written several years ago in 1990, the issue still remains: In 1995, baseball-related injuries alone accounted for 162,100 visits to hospital emergency rooms by children aged five to fourteen. One-third of the injuries were classified as serious and four children died. Before reading, recall your own experiences as an elementary school child playing competitive sports, either in or out of school. If you were not actively involved yourself, did you know anyone who was? Looking back, do you think that winning was unduly emphasized? What value was placed on having a good time? On learning to get along with others? On developing athletic skills and confidence?

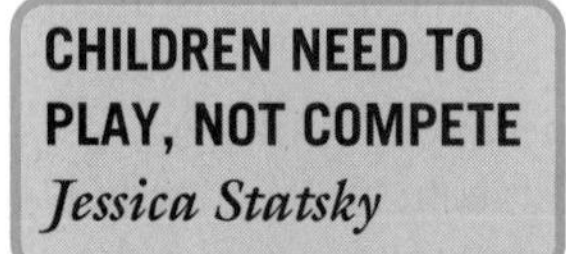

CHILDREN NEED TO PLAY, NOT COMPETE

Jessica Statsky

Over the past three decades, organized sports for children have increased dramatically in the United States. And though many adults regard Little League Baseball and Peewee Football as a basic part of childhood, the games are not always joyous ones. When overzealous parents and coaches impose adult standards on children's sports, the result can be activities that are neither satisfying nor beneficial to children. 1

I'm concerned about all organized sports activities for children between the ages of six and twelve. The damage I see results from noncontact as well as contact sports, from sports organized locally as well as those organized nationally. Highly organized competitive sports such as Peewee Football and Little League Baseball are too often played to adult standards, which are developmentally inappropriate for children and can be both physically and psychologically harmful. Furthermore, because they eliminate many children from organized sports before they are ready to compete, they are actually counterproductive for developing either future players or fans. Finally, because they emphasize competition and winning, they unfortunately provide occasions for some parents and coaches to place their own fantasies and needs ahead of children's welfare. 2

One readily understandable danger of overly competitive sports is that they entice children into physical actions that are bad for growing bodies. For example, a twelve-year-old trying to throw a curve ball may put abnormal strain on developing arm and shoulder muscles, sometimes resulting in lifelong injuries (Koppett 294). Contact sports like football can be even more hazardous. Thomas Tutko, a psychology professor at San Jose State University and co-author of the book *Winning Is Everything and Other American Myths,* writes: 3

> I am strongly opposed to young kids playing tackle football. It is not the right stage of development for them to be taught to crash into other kids. Kids under the age of fourteen are not by nature physical. Their main concern is

> self-preservation. They don't want to meet head on and slam into each other. But tackle football absolutely requires that they try to hit each other as hard as they can. And it is too traumatic for young kids. (qtd. in Tosches A1)

As Tutko indicates, even when children are not injured, fear of being hurt detracts from their enjoyment of the sport. One mother of an eight-year-old Peewee Football player explained, "The kids get so scared. They get hit once and they don't want anything to do with football anymore. They'll sit on the bench and pretend their leg hurts . . ." (qtd. in Tosches A1). Some children are driven to even more desperate measures. For example, in one Peewee Football game, a reporter watched the following scene as a player took himself out of the game: 4

> "Coach, my tummy hurts. I can't play," he said. The coach told the player to get back onto the field. "There's nothing wrong with your stomach," he said. When the coach turned his head the seven-year-old stuck a finger down his throat and made himself vomit. When the coach turned back, the boy pointed to the ground and told him, "Yes there is, coach. See?" (Tosches A33)

Besides physical hazards and anxieties, competitive sports pose psychological dangers for children. Martin Rablovsky, a former sports editor for the *New York Times,* said that in all his years of watching young children play organized sports, he noticed very few of them smiling. "I've seen children enjoying a spontaneous pre-practice scrimmage become somber and serious when the coach's whistle blows," Rablovsky said. "The spirit of play suddenly disappears, and sport becomes joblike" (qtd. in Coakley 94). The primary goal of a professional athlete—winning—is not appropriate for children. Their goals should be having fun, learning, and being with friends. Although winning does add to the fun, too many adults lose sight of what matters and make winning the most important goal. Several studies have shown that when children are asked whether they would rather be warming the bench on a winning team or playing regularly on a losing team, about 90 percent choose the latter (Smith, Smith, and Smoll 11). 5

Winning and losing may be an inevitable part of adult life, but they should not be part of childhood. Too much competition too early in life can affect a child's development. Children are easily influenced, and when they sense that their competence and worth are based on their ability to live up to their parents' and coaches' high expectations—and on their ability to win—they can become discouraged and depressed. According to Dr. Glyn C. Roberts, a professor of kinesiology at the Institute of Child Behavior and Development at the University of Illinois, 80 to 90 percent of children who play competitive sports at a young age drop out by sixteen (Kutner C8). 6

This statistic illustrates another reason I oppose competitive sports for children: because they are so highly selective, very few children get to participate. Far too soon, a few children are singled out for their athletic promise, while many others, who may be on the verge of developing the necessary strength and ability, are screened out and discouraged from trying out again. Like adults, children fear failure, and so even those with good physical skills may stay away because they lack self-confidence. Consequently, teams lose many promising players who with some encouragement and experience might have become stars. The problem is that many parent-sponsored, out-of-school programs give more importance to having a winning team than to developing children's physical skills and self-esteem. 7

Indeed, it is no secret that too often scorekeeping, league standings, and the drive to win bring out the worst in adults who are more absorbed in living out their own 8 fantasies than in enhancing the quality of the experience for children (Smith, Smith, and Smoll 9). Recent newspaper articles on children's sports contain plenty of horror stories. *Los Angeles Times* reporter Rich Tosches, for example, tells the story of a brawl among seventy-five parents following a Peewee Football game (A33). As a result of the brawl, which began when a parent from one team confronted a player from the other team, the teams are now thinking of hiring security guards for future games. Another example is provided by an *L.A. Times* editorial about a Little League manager who intimidated the opposing team by setting fire to one of their team's jerseys on the pitching mound before the game began. As the editorial writer commented, the manager showed his young team that "intimidation could substitute for playing well" (B6).

Although not all parents or coaches behave so inappropriately, the seriousness of the problem is illustrated by the fact that Adelphi University in Garden City, New York, offers a sports psychology workshop for Little League coaches, designed to balance their "animal instincts" with "educational theory" in hopes of reducing the "screaming and hollering," in the words of Harold Weisman, manager of sixteen Little Leagues in New York City (Schmitt B2). In a three-and-one-half-hour Sunday morning workshop, coaches learn how to make practices more fun, treat injuries, deal with irate parents, and be "more sensitive to their young players' fears, emotional frailties, and need for recognition." Little League is to be credited with recognizing the need for such workshops. 9

Some parents would no doubt argue that children can't start too soon preparing to live in a competitive free-market economy. After all, secondary schools and colleges require students to compete for grades, and college admission is extremely competitive. And it is perfectly obvious how important competitive skills are in finding a job. Yet the ability to cooperate is also important for success in life. Before children are psychologically ready for competition, maybe we should emphasize cooperation and individual performance in team sports rather than winning. 10

Many people are ready for such an emphasis. In 1988, one New York Little League official who had attended the Adelphi workshop tried to ban scoring from six-to-eight-year-olds' games—but parents wouldn't support him (Schmitt B2). An innovative children's sports program in New York City, City Sports for Kids, emphasizes fitness, self-esteem, and sportsmanship. In this program's basketball games, every member on a team plays at least two of six eight-minute periods. The basket is seven feet from the floor, rather than ten feet, and a player can score a point just by hitting the rim (Bloch C12). I believe this kind of local program should replace overly competitive programs like Peewee Football and Little League Baseball. 11

Authorities have clearly documented the excesses and dangers of many competitive sports programs for children. It would seem that few children benefit from these programs and that those who do would benefit even more from programs emphasizing fitness, cooperation, sportsmanship, and individual performance. Thirteen- and fourteen-year-olds may be eager for competition, but few younger children are. These younger children deserve sports programs designed specifically for *their* needs and abilities. 12

Works Cited

Bloch, Gordon B. "Thrill of Victory Is Secondary to Fun." *New York Times* 2 Apr. 1990, late ed.: C12.

"The Bad News Pyromaniacs?" Editorial. *Los Angeles Times* 16 June 1990: B6.

Coakley, Jay J. *Sport in Society: Issues and Controversies.* St. Louis: Mosby, 1982.

Koppett, Leonard. *Sports Illusion, Sports Reality.* Boston: Houghton, 1981.

Kutner, Lawrence. "Athletics, through a Child's Eyes." *New York Times* 23 Mar. 1989, late ed.: C8.

Schmitt, Eric. "Psychologists Take Seat on Little League Bench." *New York Times* 14 Mar. 1988, late ed.: B2.
Smith, Nathan, Ronald Smith, and Frank Smoll. *Kidsports: A Survival Guide for Parents.* Reading, MA: Addison-Wesley, 1983.
Tosches, Rich. "Peewee Football: Is It Time to Blow the Whistle?" *Los Angeles Times* 3 Dec. 1988: A1+.

Connecting to Culture and Experience

Statsky makes the point that competition is highly valued in our culture, whereas cooperation tends to be downplayed. Discuss some of the ways in which our society encourages competition, especially among children and through sports or other forms of play. Consider also how cooperation is encouraged. Think about whether, in your own experience, the educational system has encouraged one more than the other.

Then, expand your discussion to include the influence of cultural forces such as advertising, television, and movies. Which of the two, competition or cooperation, seems to be valued more highly in these areas? If you believe that there is a cultural preference for competition or cooperation, reflect on who in the society might benefit most from such a preference. Consider such factors as gender, age, ethnicity, class, and religion. Who loses most?

Analyzing Writing Strategies

For more on forecasting, summaries, and transitions, see Chapter 13.

1. Analyze the **cueing devices** Statsky uses to help readers stay on track as they read her essay. Underline statements forecasting what is to come, summaries of what has just been said, and transitions. Choose one example of each kind of cueing device, and briefly explain what each example does to cue readers. Finally, evaluate how effectively Statsky uses cueing to help you follow her argument.
2. Unlike the other essays in this chapter that were written for magazines and newspapers, Statsky wrote her essay for a college English class. Therefore, she follows the Modern Language Association style of **citing sources** in the essay and appending a "Works Cited" list to the essay.

   Skim Statsky's essay, marking each time she refers to a source. Note where she quotes whole sentences or individual words and phrases. Also try to determine where she summarizes the source instead of quoting it verbatim. Then pick one source you think adds something important to her argument, and briefly explain what it adds.
3. Read the Writer at Work discussion on pp. 240–42 to see how Statsky describes her prospective readers and develops her counterargument with these readers in mind. Then, review the essay to see how she incorporates counterargument into it. Has she left anything out or added anything new? Finally, how well do you think she has anticipated and responded to opposing arguments and objections to her argument?

Considering Topics for Your Own Essay

Make a list of issues related to childhood and adolescence. For example, should elementary and secondary schools be on a year-round schedule? Should children have the right to "divorce" their parents? Should adolescents who commit serious crimes be tried as adults? Then, choose an issue that you think you could write about. What position would you take?

Commentary

Writers of position papers must be especially careful not to **define the issue** too broadly or to overstate their position. Statsky limits the issue by identifying several parameters such as age, geography, school affiliation, and type of sport. For example, she focuses on children between the ages of six and twelve (paragraph 2) and on "parent-sponsored out-of-school" sports (paragraph 7). But she allows for sports organized nationally as well as locally and for all kinds of sports, noncontact as well as contact. Finally, to ensure that her readers know the kind of organized, competitive team sports she is talking about, she gives two familiar examples: Peewee Football and Little League Baseball.

Statsky also **qualifies her position** by avoiding absolute or unconditional language. In the opening paragraph, for example, she uses the words *not always* to soften her assertion: "These games are *not always* joyous ones." Similarly, in the next sentence, instead of saying "the result is," she allows for other possibilities by saying "the result *can be*." Such minor adjustments in word choice can have a major effect on readers because they make the writer's position seem reasonable without making her seem indecisive. Indeed, Statsky presents her argument confidently and assertively.

PURPOSE AND AUDIENCE

You may have a variety of purposes for writing a paper that takes a position on a controversial issue. First and foremost, you will write to take a position. But you will do more than simply state what you think; you will also present an argument explaining and justifying your point of view. Although your position paper will nearly always be written for others to read, writing can also lead you to clarify your own thinking. Anticipating others' views—accepting the points you consider valid and refuting those with which you disagree—will help you to develop your understanding of the issue and confidence in your own point of view.

In addition to stating a position, most position papers are intended to influence other people's thinking on important issues. Assuming that logical argument will prevail over prejudice, writers try to change readers' minds by presenting compelling reasons supported by solid evidence and by pointing out flaws in others' reasoning. They seek common ground in shared interests, values, and principles. They may show that they are reasonable by moderating their own views and urging others to compromise as well.

When agreement seems beyond reach, however, it is highly unlikely that a single essay will be able to change readers' minds, no matter how well written it is. Addressing an audience that is completely opposed to their position, most writers are satisfied if they can simply win their readers' respect for their different point of view. Often, however, all that can be done is to sharpen the differences. Position papers written in these circumstances tend to be more contentious than compromising.

Purpose and audience are thus closely linked when you write a position paper. In defining your purpose and developing an effective argumentative strategy, you also need to analyze your readers. You need to determine where they stand on the issue—whether they oppose your position, are undecided, or basically agree with you. You also need to discern how they think about the issue—for example, whether they see it as a moral issue, an issue of civil liberties, or an issue that affects them personally.

SUMMARY OF BASIC FEATURES

A Well-Defined Issue

Position papers concern controversial issues, matters of policy and principle about which people disagree. These issues must be arguable and not subject to absolute proof. They may involve conflicting values and priorities or disagreements about current practices and procedures.

Although position papers strive primarily to influence readers' views, they also seek to inform readers about issues. In fact, the writer's initial task is usually to define the issue for readers. How writers define the issue depends on what they assume readers already know and what they want readers to think about the issue. Because she is writing in a weekly newsmagazine that contains an article on the issue, Ehrenreich can safely assume that her readers know about it. All she needs to do is mention the people involved in the controversy. Molyneux, by contrast, has to give several examples to establish that his issue—the decline of political debate—actually exists and is worthy of readers' attention. While his examples are chosen primarily to help readers to understand what is at stake, they also support his position.

Writers know that issues can be defined in many ways and that readers' attitudes vary. Therefore, they try to define the issue in a way that promotes their argumentative strategy. Defining an issue essentially means framing it in a particular context. For instance, Estrada defines the issue of naming sports teams after Native Americans in terms of how it affects individuals, especially children, rather than in terms of liberal or conservative politics. Sometimes defining the issue also involves marking its boundaries. Statsky, for example, focuses her issue on organized sports for children between the ages of six and twelve.

A Clear Position

In addition to defining the issue, the essay should also clearly indicate the writer's position on the issue. Writers may qualify their positions to show that they understand the issue's complexity or to accommodate strong objections, but they should avoid vagueness and indecision. Estrada, for example, acknowledges his readers' legitimate concerns about hypersensitivity while emphatically asserting the need to fight "genuine cases of political insensitivity."

For more on thesis statements, see pp. 465–66.

Very often writers declare their position in a thesis statement early in the essay. This strategy has the advantage of letting readers know right away where the writer stands. Statsky states her thesis explicitly in the opening paragraph and forecasts her reasons at the end of the second paragraph. Sometimes, however, writers gain an advantage by postponing the thesis, as in Ehrenreich's case. She begins by refuting

continued

continued

Bennett's position that television talk shows foster immorality and saves her own position about the real immorality of talk shows until the second half of the essay.

A Convincing, Well-Reasoned Argument

To convince readers, writers must develop an argumentative strategy that will enable them to achieve their purpose with their particular readers. The argumentative strategy determines how they will argue for their position and how they will counter opposing arguments.

For more on kinds of support, see pp. 529–37.

Arguing Directly for the Position. Writers argue for their positions by offering reasons and supporting them with examples, facts, statements from authorities, statistics, or personal anecdotes. We have seen all of these kinds of support in this chapter—examples in Ehrenreich, anecdote in Estrada, authorities in Molyneux, and facts and statistics in Statsky.

Even when their arguments are complicated and subtle, writers try to make their reasoning simple and direct. They do not merely hint at their reasons, hoping that readers will figure them out. Instead, they make their reasons explicit and explain their thinking in some detail. They usually also offer several reasons because they know that some will carry more weight with readers than others. For instance, Estrada presents three specific reasons for his position.

For more on counterarguing, see pp. 537–42.

Countering Opposing Arguments. As they argue for their positions, experienced writers also argue against the objections and alternative arguments that readers holding differing positions on the issue are likely to offer. Sometimes counterarguing involves acknowledging readers' objections by simply mentioning them without evaluating or refuting them. More often, writers either accommodate arguments by qualifying their own position, like Estrada, or refute arguments, like Ehrenreich.

Counterarguing can enhance credibility and strengthen the argument. When readers holding an opposing position recognize that a writer takes their reasoning seriously, they are more likely to listen to what the writer has to say. Counterargument can also reassure readers that they share certain important values and attitudes with a writer, building a bridge of common concerns among people who have been separated by difference and antagonism.

An Appropriate Tone

Position papers often concern highly controversial issues about which writers—and readers—feel very strongly. The challenge for writers, therefore, is to find a tone that adequately expresses their feelings without shutting down communication. Ideally, writers gain readers' confidence and respect both by the way they reason and by the language they use. Estrada's calm, thoughtful tone is an important part of his argumentative strategy. Similarly, Ehrenreich's informality is part of her effort to show that unlike Bennett, she is not a snob. Statsky's more formal tone is typical of academic argument.

GUIDE TO WRITING

THE WRITING ASSIGNMENT

Write a position paper on a controversial issue. Present the issue to readers, take a position, and develop a convincing, well-reasoned argument.

INVENTION AND RESEARCH

At this point, you need to choose and explore an issue, consider your purpose and your audience, formulate your thesis, test your choice, develop your reasoning, and anticipate readers' concerns. You will find these activities easy to do and most helpful when spread over several days. Be sure to keep a written record of your invention and research to use when you draft and later revise your essay.

Choosing an Issue

Set a timer for ten minutes, and brainstorm your list with the monitor brightness turned all the way down. Then turn the brightness up, read to make sure that all the items make sense, and save them as an invention file. Print out a copy to make notes on.

You will be spending a good deal of time and effort thinking about the issue, so it is important for you to consider carefully before making a choice. The following activities can help you choose a promising issue and may suggest ways to begin thinking about it.

Listing Issues. *Make a list of issues you might consider writing about.* Begin your list now, and add to it over the next few days. Include issues on which you already have a position and ones you do not know much about but would like to explore further. Put the issues in the form of questions, like the following examples:

- Should local school boards be allowed to ban books (like *The Adventures of Huckleberry Finn* and *Of Mice and Men*) from school libraries?
- Should teenagers be required to get their parents' permission to obtain birth control information and contraceptives?
- Should fathers and mothers have an equal chance of gaining custody of their children after a divorce?
- Should schools teach spiritual and moral values?
- Should undercover police officers be permitted to pose as high school students in order to identify sellers and users of drugs?
- Should training in music performance or art (drawing, painting, sculpting) be required of all high school students?
- Should college admission be based solely on academic achievement in high school?
- Should colleges provide child care facilities for children of students taking classes?
- Should students attending public colleges be required to pay higher tuition fees if they do not graduate in four years?

Listing Issues concerning Identity and Community As the following suggestions indicate, many controversial issues will enable you to explore your understanding of identity and community. List issues that interest you.

- Should girls and boys be treated differently by their families or schools?
- Should our schools continue to emphasize the history, philosophy, literature, and art of western European civilization, or should they give equal time to other cultural traditions (such as Native American, African, Asian, and Latin) that contribute to American civilization?
- Should high schools or colleges require students to perform community service as a condition for graduation?
- Should children of immigrants who do not speak English be taught in their native language while they are learning English?
- Should all materials related to voting, driving, and income tax be written only in English or in other languages read by members of the community?
- Should the racial or ethnic makeup of a police force parallel the makeup of the community it serves?

Listing Issues concerning Work and Career Many current controversial issues have to do with the topic of work and career. Identify issues such as the following that you would consider writing about.

- Should businesses remain loyal to their communities, or should they move to wherever labor costs, taxes, or other conditions are more favorable?
- Should companies be free to replace workers who go on strike for better wages or working conditions, or should they be required to negotiate with workers?
- When they choose careers, should people look primarily for jobs that are well paid or for jobs that are personally fulfilling, morally correct, or socially responsible?
- Should the state or federal government provide job training, temporary employment, or financial aid to people who are unemployed and willing to work?
- Should the primary purpose of college education be job training?
- Should drug testing be mandatory for people in high-risk jobs such as bus drivers, heavy-equipment operators, and airplane pilots?

Choosing an Intriguing Issue. *Select an issue from your list that seems especially interesting, one that you would like to know more about.* It should be an arguable issue with no obvious right answer or absolute proof.

Your choice may be influenced by whether you have time for research or whether your instructor requires it. For example, you would have to research affirmative-action programs before you could argue for or against the continuation of affirmative action in college admissions or in the workplace. Issues like affirmative action that have been debated for years and written about repeatedly make excellent topics for extended research projects. Other issues, such as whether warning labels should be put on potentially offensive recordings, may be approached more confidently from personal experience and limited research. Still other topics, such as separate college organizations for African-American, Asian, and Latino students or special academic assistance for athletes, may be more suitable if your time is limited or your instructor wants you to argue a position without doing research. If you choose to write about an issue currently affecting your community or college, you could explore opposing arguments with classmates and friends.

Exploring the Issue

To explore the issue, you need to define the issue, determine whether to do research, and decide tentatively on your position.

Refer to Chapter 20 for advice on interviewing an expert or surveying opinion and to Chapter 21 for guidelines on doing library research and researching on the Internet.

Defining the Issue. *To begin thinking about the issue, write for about five minutes explaining how you currently understand it.* If you feel strongly about the issue, briefly explain why, but do not present your argument at this time. Focus on defining what you think the issue is by considering questions like these:

- Who has taken a position on this issue, and what positions have they taken?
- How does the issue affect different people? What is at stake for them?
- What kind of issue is it for them and for you—personal, political, economic, moral?
- What is the issue's history? What made it an issue, and what are its consequences?
- How broad is the issue? What other issues are related to it? In what category might it fit?

Keep one file as a bibliography, listing all sources you consult. Organize other files by subtopic or as quote, summary, and paraphrase files. Copy quotations exactly and indicate the source for each. You may be able to download some sources directly onto a disk.

Doing Research. *If you do not know very much about the issue or the various views on it, do some research before continuing.* You can gather information by talking to others or by reading what others have written.

If you do not have time for research and lack confidence in your knowledge of the issue, you should switch your focus to another issue about which you are better informed. Return to your list of possible issues and start over.

Deciding on a Tentative Position. *State the position you are now inclined to take on the issue.* Do not worry over this statement because your position is liable to change as you develop your ideas and learn more about the issue. Your aim now is merely to record your thinking as of this moment.

Considering Your Purpose and Your Audience

Now that you have begun to explore the issue and think at least tentatively about your position, you will benefit from imagining the rhetorical context for your essay—to whom you are writing (your prospective readers) and what you want them to think about the issue (your purpose).

Analyzing Potential Readers. *Write for five minutes describing the readers to whom you are addressing your argument.* Begin by briefly identifying your likely readers, and then use the following questions to help you describe them.

- What position or positions do I expect my readers to take on this issue? How entrenched are these positions likely to be?

- What do I expect my readers to know about the issue? In what contexts are they likely to have encountered it? In what ways might the issue affect them personally?
- How far apart on the issue are my readers and I likely to be? What fundamental differences in worldview or experience might keep us from agreeing? Which of my readers' values or moral principles might influence their view of the issue?
- Why would I choose to address these particular readers about this issue? Why does it matter to me what they think about it?

Reflecting on Your Purpose. *Write for five minutes exploring your purpose and considering an argumentative strategy you could use with these particular readers.* Now that you have some ideas about your likely readers, you are ready to begin formulating an argumentative strategy designed to achieve your purpose with them. As you write, consider these possibilities:

- Explain your purpose in addressing these particular readers. Consider whether you can realistically expect to change their minds or whether you should be satisfied simply to get them to take your argument seriously.
- If you are writing to people sympathetic to your point of view, what do you hope to achieve—encourage them to take some kind of action, give them reasons to commit to your position, arm them with ammunition to make their own arguments, win their respect and admiration?
- If you are writing to people hostile to your point of view, what could you hope to accomplish—get them to concede that other points of view must be taken seriously, make them feel foolish or defend their reasons, show them how knowledgeable and committed you are to your position, show them how well you can argue?
- If you are writing to people who are inclined to take an opposing position but are not staunchly committed to it, what should you try to do—make them think critically about the reasons and the kinds of support they have for their position, give them reasons to change their minds, show them how your position serves their interests better, appeal to their principles and sense of responsibility, disabuse them of their preconceptions and prejudices against your position?
- Explore some ways you might build a bridge of shared values and concerns with these readers by asking yourself, on what, if anything, can you and your readers agree? Do you use similar terms to define the issue, think the issue is important for related reasons, share any assumptions or values in regard to the issue, have any experiences in common that might relate to your positions on the issue?

Testing Your Choice

Decide whether you should proceed with this particular issue. Review your invention notes to see whether you understand the issue well enough to continue working with it and whether you can feel confident that you will be able to construct an argumentative strategy that will appeal to your particular readers. To make that decision, ask yourself the following questions:

- Does this topic really interest me? Have I begun to understand the issue and my own position well enough to begin constructing a reasoned argument?
- Do I have a good enough sense of how my readers view this issue to begin formulating an argumentative strategy that is appropriate for them?

- Do I now know enough about the issue, or can I learn what I need to know in the time I have remaining?

If you cannot answer these questions affirmatively at this point in the process, it might be wise to consider a different issue. Giving up on a topic after you have worked on it is bound to be frustrating, but if you have little interest in the issue and do not have any idea how you could address your readers, starting over may be the wisest course of action. The following collaborative activity may help you decide whether to go on with this issue or begin looking for an alternative.

Testing Your Choice: A Collaborative Activity

At this point in your invention work, you will find it helpful to get together with two or three other students to try out a bit of your argument. Their reactions will help you determine whether you will be able to construct a convincing, well-reasoned argument for your position.

Arguers: Take turns briefly providing the context—the issue, purpose and readers, and your position—followed by one reason for your position. Choose a reason you think will carry weight with your readers, and explain why you think so.

Listeners: Briefly tell each arguer how you think the intended readers are likely to respond to the reason. Also try to help the arguer by suggesting one way in which the reason could be made stronger—for example, by providing a clearer explanation of how the reason supports the position, by showing that the reason is based on common values or beliefs, or by providing a fact, an example, a personal anecdote, or a statement from an authority to support the reason. If you think the reason is weak, explain how readers could argue against it.

Developing Your Argument

To construct a convincing argument, you need to list reasons for your position, choose the strongest ones, and develop them fully.

Listing Reasons. *Write down every plausible reason you could give to convince readers that your position on this issue should be taken seriously.* It might help to state your reasons as part of a thesis statement with *because* or *that* clauses. For example, "My position is X because . . ." or "A reason I believe X is that . . . ."

Choosing the Strongest Reasons. *Review your list with your readers in mind, and put a check by the reasons that would carry the most weight with them and are most important to you.* If none of your reasons seems very strong, you might need to reconsider your position, do some more research, or pick another topic.

Developing Your Best Reasons. *Write for five minutes on each of your strongest reasons, explaining it to your readers and providing support for it.* You may discover that you need some specific information. Do not stop to track it down now; just make a note about what you need and continue writing. If you decide not to include some of these reasons, you may not need the information after all. Later, before drafting or when revising, you will be able to follow up and find any information you still need.

Developing Your Counterargument

Now that you have developed your reasons, you need to anticipate likely opposing arguments and decide which ones you will accommodate and which you will try to refute.

Listing Opposing Arguments. *Make as complete a list as you can of the arguments you expect others to make in response to your argument.* Include in your list possible objections to your argument as well as the reasons typically given for other points of view.

If you cannot recall actual arguments others have made, try talking to someone who disagrees with you. Or try to invent objections by considering where your argument might be vulnerable to criticism. For example, think of an assumption you are making (such as assumptions about what people believe or how they should act) that others might not accept. Imagine how others might define the issue differently from you (for instance, as a question of what is right rather than what feels good). How might people in different situations—different neighborhoods, occupations, age groups, living arrangements—react to your argument? Recognize that others might question an authority you rely on, information you accept as fact, or generalizations you make about specific examples.

Accommodating Legitimate Arguments. *Decide which objections or arguments for different positions make sense to you, and write for ten minutes developing a response.* Remember that you are not merely trying to win an argument; you are trying to advance your own and others' thinking on the issue. Therefore, it is important not to ignore serious criticism, especially if it has some validity. If the criticism does not seriously undermine your position, you may be able simply to acknowledge the point and explain why you think it does not negatively affect your argument.

If the criticism is more serious, try not to let it shake your confidence. Instead, consider how you can accommodate it, perhaps by qualifying your position or changing the way you argue for it. If the criticism is so damaging that you cannot accommodate it into your argument, however, you may need to rethink your position radically or consider writing on a different issue. If you arrive at such an impasse, discuss the problem with your instructor; do not abandon your issue unless it is absolutely necessary.

Refuting Illegitimate Arguments. *Decide which objections or arguments for different positions you need to refute, and write for ten minutes planning your response.* Do not choose to refute an obviously ridiculous argument that no one really takes seriously. Also, do not refute only the weakest, most vulnerable argument while ignoring the strongest one. Finally, be careful not to misrepresent the opposition's reasoning or motives.

See pp. 542–43 and 458–61 for more on logical fallacies.

Do try to get at the heart of your disagreement. You may want to argue that the values, principles, or beliefs on which the opposing argument is based are not widely shared or just plain wrong. Or perhaps you can point out that the reasoning is flawed (for instance, showing that a generalization applies only to certain people or in certain situations). Or maybe you can show that the argument lacks convincing support (for instance, that the opposition's statistics can be interpreted differently or that their expert is contradicted by your expert).

Deciding on an Argumentative Strategy

Now it is time to decide on an argumentative strategy for your essay and to formulate a thesis statement to guide you as you draft the essay.

Considering Your Argumentative Strategy. *Write for five minutes, contemplating your overall strategy for achieving your purpose with your readers.* Now that you have explored possible arguments supporting your position and considered how to handle opposing arguments, you need to reflect on your overall strategy—how the various arguments and counterarguments you have imagined could work together given your purpose and your readers. Try to envision the whole picture rather than its individual parts. Ask yourself: What do I want my readers to remember after reading my essay? What do I want them to think and feel?

Formulating a Thesis Statement. *Write a few sentences formulating a thesis statement that forecasts your argumentative strategy.* Qualify your position if necessary to fit the overall argumentative strategy you have decided to follow. Include in your thesis statement a forecast of your major arguments and counterarguments. Tell your readers simply and directly what you want them to think about the issue and why. Although you will probably refine this thesis statement as you revise your essay, articulating it clearly now will help you to plan and write your first draft.

PLANNING AND DRAFTING

Take some time now to review your invention notes and see what you have, to set goals for your essay, to prepare an outline, and to draft your position paper.

Seeing What You Have

Print out a hard copy of what you have written for easier reviewing.

If you completed all of the invention work, you have accumulated several pages of notes. Review these carefully to see what you might use in your draft. Mark passages that seem especially promising, show conviction, have vivid writing, contain pointed examples, and demonstrate strong reasoning.

If your invention notes are skimpy, you may not have given enough thought to the issue or know enough at this time to write a convincing argument about it. You have several alternatives: You can do more invention and research. You can go on to set goals and plan your essay, hoping that you will develop your thinking as you do so. You can use the drafting process to help you to expand on ideas you already have and hope that your classmates will help you to think of new ideas when they read your draft. Or, after consulting your instructor, you can give up on this topic and try a new issue.

For more on general invention activities, see Chapter 11.

Setting Goals

Experienced writers set overall goals for themselves before drafting their essays. They decide what they will try to achieve and how they will go about it. To help you set realistic goals, consider the following questions now. You may also find it helpful to return to some of these questions as you outline and draft your essay.

Your Purpose and Your Audience

- What can I realistically hope to accomplish by addressing these particular readers? Are they so deeply committed to their own positions that they will be unable to credit my arguments? Should I try, as Ehrenreich and Estrada do, to change readers' perception of the issue?
- Can I appeal to readers on the basis of certain values we share, like Molyneux and Statsky? Can I make readers see, as Estrada does, that a practice they support has bad consequences?
- Can I draw on any common experiences that relate to this issue? Could I share my own experience or tell about other people's experiences, as Estrada does? Should I assume, as Statsky does, that readers will be able to think of examples from their own experience and observations that confirm my argument?
- Should my purpose be to urge my readers to do something about the issue? Do I want them to change their views, like Ehrenreich, as well as their behavior, like Estrada and Molyneux? Am I trying to inspire my readers to mobilize others to make some kind of change, as Statsky appears to be doing?

The Beginning

- How can I involve readers from the start? Can I begin by connecting the issue to my own personal experience, as Estrada does? Perhaps I should consider starting with several specific examples to help readers to grasp what is at issue, as Molyneux does. I might also consider beginning with a rhetorical question or startling statistics to draw readers into the argument.
- How much do I need to explain about the issue at the outset? Should I try to prove to my readers that the issue affects many people, as Statsky does?
- Do I need to define the terms I use to characterize the issue? Should I begin by distinguishing my view of the issue from someone else's, as Ehrenreich does? Should I make clear at the outset, as Statsky does, exactly what my concerns are and how I see the issue?

Your Argument

- If I have more than one reason, how should I sequence the reasons? From strongest to weakest? From most to least predictable? From simplest to most complex? Can I set them out logically, as a chain of linked reasons?
- Which objections to my argument and which arguments for other points of view should I mention, if any? Shall I acknowledge certain arguments as legitimate, as Estrada does? Shall I try to use authorities and statistics to support my counterargument, as Statsky does? What would I gain from conceding something? What would I lose?

The Ending

- How can I conclude my argument effectively? Should I repeat my thesis, as Statsky does? Should I try to amuse my readers by poking fun at my opponents, as Ehrenreich does? Or should I try to unite readers with different allegiances by reminding them of their ideals? Could I conclude by looking to the future or urging readers to take action?

Outlining

Outlining on a word processor makes it easy to experiment with different ways of sequencing your reasons, support, and counterargument.

Some position papers include everything—an extended definition of the issue, an elaborate argument with multiple reasons and support, and several opposing arguments, some of which are accommodated while others are refuted. Your essay may not be so complicated, but you will still have to decide how to arrange the different parts. Once you have considered strategies for beginning and ending your essay and determined a sequence for your argument and counterargument, consider the organization carefully, and prepare a tentative outline.

Here is how Statsky organized her position paper on children's competitive sports:

For another outline of a position paper, see pp. 448–51.

Identifies issue, states thesis, and forecasts reasons

Explains and supports first reason—competing at too early an age is developmentally inappropriate and may be harmful physically

Explains and supports second reason—competing at too early an age may also be harmful psychologically

Refutes opposing argument—that children need to learn to live in a competitive world—by arguing that childhood is just the training period, not the real thing

Explains and supports third reason—because competitive sports are so selective, very few children participate and reap the potential benefits

Explains and supports fourth reason—parents and coaches sometimes use children's sports to act out their own fantasies in ways harmful to the children

Refutes opposing argument—that children need to learn to live in a competitive world—by arguing that cooperation is as important to society as competition and ought to be emphasized

Concludes by reasserting the position and framing the essay

However you choose to arrange your essay, making an outline before drafting will help you to get started. An outline presents a route, neither the only one nor necessarily the best, but one that will get you going in the right direction.

Drafting

With an outline and goals as your guide, begin drafting your essay. As you draft, keep your audience in mind by writing to a particular (real or imaginary) reader; think of your writing as a transcript of what you would say to this person. Also keep in mind your purpose in addressing this particular reader—your argumentative strategy. Remember to establish common ground by acknowledging the intelligence, experience, values, and concerns of your reader.

Call up invention material on an alternate window as you draft on the main window, shifting back and forth to cut and paste invention material into your draft.

Use your outline to guide your drafting, but do not worry if you diverge from your original plan. Writing sometimes has a logic of its own that carries the writer along. As you pick up momentum, you may leave the outline behind. If you get stuck, refer to your outline again. You might want to review the general advice on drafting on pp. 13–14.

CRITICAL READING GUIDE

Swap copies of your drafts with another student, either by exchanging disks or by sending the computer files over a network. Add your comments either next to the essay, if you can divide the window, or at the end of the document.

Now is the time to get a good critical reading of your draft. Your instructor may arrange such a reading as part of your coursework; if not, you can ask a classmate, friend, or family member to read it over. If your school has a writing center, you might ask a tutor there to read and comment on your draft. The guidelines in this section are designed to be used by *anyone* reviewing a position paper. (If you are unable to have someone else review your draft, turn ahead to the Revising section for help reading your own draft with a critical eye.)

If You Are the Writer. To provide focused, helpful comments, your critical reader must know your intended purpose and audience. Briefly write out this information at the top of your draft.

- *Audience.* To whom are you directing your argument? What position do you assume they now take or are inclined to take on this issue?
- *Purpose.* What effect do you realistically expect your argument to have on these particular readers?

If You Are the Reader. Use the following guidelines to help you give constructive, critical comments on position papers.

See pp. 223–24 to review the basic features.

1. *Read for a First Impression.* First read the purpose and audience statement at the top of the draft, and then read the essay quickly to get a sense of the writer's position on the issue and an understanding of the basic argument. Even if you disagree with the writer's position, your primary responsibility is to help the writer to improve the argument for the intended readers. If you disagree, however, you should say so right away so that you will be able to put aside your own views as you go on to analyze and evaluate the argument. Briefly explain what you personally think is most and least convincing in the argument and also what you expect the intended readers to find most and least convincing.
2. *Analyze the Way the Issue Is Presented.* Restate, in one sentence, the issue as you understand it from reading the draft. Then look at the terms the writer uses to define the issue. If you think that most readers would cast the issue in different terms, explain them. If you think that more information is needed to help readers to appreciate the importance of the issue, ask questions to help the writer to fill in whatever is missing. If you think that the issue, as defined, is not really arguable—for example, if it is a question of fact or a matter of faith—let the writer know.
3. *Assess Whether the Position Is Stated Clearly and Unequivocally.* Restate, in one sentence, the writer's position as you understand it from reading the draft. Then underline the sentence or sentences in the draft where the thesis is stated explicitly. If you cannot find an explicit statement of the thesis, let the writer know. Point to any words in the thesis statement that seem unclear or ambiguous.

continued

continued

Given the writer's purpose and audience, consider whether the thesis statement is too strident or too timid and whether it needs to be better qualified, more sharply focused, or asserted more confidently.

4. *Evaluate the Argument for the Writer's Position.* Find the reasons and number them in the margin: "Reason 1," "Reason 2," and so on. Then consider each reason in turn, looking at how it is explained and supported. Point out any reasons that need to be explained more clearly or supported more convincingly. Consider whether any important reasons have been left out or any weak ones have been overemphasized. Think of how the reasons work together, and indicate if you see any contradictions in the argument or leaps in logic that need to be explained more fully. Note any support that seems weak as well as any places where more support is needed.

   Look for faulty reasoning. Note any sweeping generalizations (broad statements asserted without support). Indicate if the writer has oversimplified the issue or is using either-or reasoning (unfairly limiting the argument to only two alternatives).

See pp. 542–43 and 458–61 for more on logical fallacies and faulty reasoning.

5. *Evaluate the Counterargument.* Look for places where other positions on the issue are mentioned, specifically places where objections and opposing arguments are acknowledged. Let the writer know if any of the opposing arguments or objections have been misrepresented—perhaps by being overstated or taken out of context. Note any areas of potential agreement that the writer could emphasize (common values or principles, for example) and any concessions that the writer should consider making (qualifying the position to accommodate individual choice, for example). Suggest how the refutation could be strengthened (indicating where further support could be found or helping the writer to understand the thinking behind an objection or opposing argument, for example).

   Again, look for faulty reasoning. Point out any personal attacks on opponents rather than on their reasoning. Let the writer know if the draft addresses only the weakest objections or opposing arguments and ignores stronger ones.

6. *Comment on How Well the Tone Supports the Essay's Argumentative Strategy.* Describe, in your own words, the tone of the argument (for example, ridiculing, aggressive, condescending, accommodating, apologetic). Look back at the writer's description of the purpose and audience at the top of the draft and your own evaluation of the argument and counterargument. Then tell the writer how well the tone supports the essay's argumentative strategy. Point out any place where the tone undercuts the strategy or where you could suggest word changes that might make the tone more effective.

7. *Suggest How the Organization Could Be Improved.* Consider the overall plan, perhaps by making a scratch outline. Note whether the beginning adequately establishes the issue and forecasts the argument. Review the sequence of arguments and counterarguments, making sure that they are logical and easy to follow. Point out any places where cueing devices—transitions, summaries, and topic sentences—could be clarified or added. If the ending seems especially weak, suggest how the writer might end on a stronger note.

REVISING

This section will help you to identify problems in your draft and to revise to solve them.

Identifying Problems

To discover problems in your draft, you need to read it with a critical eye, analyze its basic features, and study any comments you have received from others.

Getting an Overview. Consider the draft, trying to see it as a whole. It may help to do so in two steps:

Even if your essay is saved to a computer file, reread from a hard copy. Add notes to yourself and revisions as you read through the draft.

1. *Reread.* If at all possible, put the draft aside for a day or two before rereading it. When you return to it, start by reconsidering your purpose. Then read the draft straight through, trying to see it as your intended readers will.
2. *Outline.* Quickly outline the draft to see where the issue is defined, the position is stated, each reason is explained and supported, and any opposing arguments are refuted.

Charting a Plan for Revision. You may want to use a two-column chart to keep track of the work you need to do as you revise. In the left-hand column, list the basic features of position papers. As you analyze your draft and study any comments from other readers, use the right-hand column for noting any problems to solve.

Basic Features	*Problems to Solve*
Definition of the issue	
Thesis statement	
Argument for position	
Counterargument	
Tone	
Organization	

Analyzing Basic Features. Using the questions presented in the Critical Reading Guide, reread your draft to identify specific problems you need to solve and note them on your revision chart.

Studying Critical Comments. Review all of the comments you have gotten from other readers, and add to the chart any that you intend to act on. Try not to react defensively to these comments; by letting you see how other readers respond to your draft, the comments provide valuable information about how you might improve it.

Solving the Problems

Having identified problems in your draft, you now need to come up with solutions and—most important of all—ways to implement them. You have three possible means of finding solutions:

1. Review your invention and planning notes for information and ideas to add to the draft.
2. Do further invention and research to answer questions your readers raised.
3. Look back at the readings in this chapter to see how other writers have solved similar problems.

The following suggestions will help you to start thinking of ways to solve some writing problems typical of position papers.

Definition of the Issue

Before revising, copy your original draft to a second file. Should you change your mind about material you delete while revising, it will still be available to you.

- **Does the reader need more information about the issue?** Consider adding examples, quoting authorities, or simply explaining the issue further.
- **Does the issue strike readers as unimportant?** State explicitly why you think it is important and why you think your readers should think so too. Try to provide an anecdote, a fact, or a quote from an authority that would demonstrate its importance.

Thesis Statement

- **Do you think readers might not find or recognize your thesis?** You may need to rewrite your thesis statement to make it clearer. If your thesis is implied but not directly expressed, consider stating it explicitly so as to avoid misunderstanding.
- **Do you need to qualify your thesis to account for exceptions or strong objections to your argument?** Modify your thesis by limiting its scope.

Argument for Your Position

- **Do you think readers might have difficulty identifying your reasons?** Announce them more explicitly.
- **Do any of your reasons seem vague or weak?** Either delete weak reasons or explain and support them more fully. Consider telling an anecdote or making a comparison or contrast to show how your reasons relate to one another.
- **Does your support seem weak or scanty?** Review your invention notes or do some more research to gather additional facts, statistics, or quotations from authorities.
- **Do you use any unfounded generalizations?** Be more specific and support your statements.
- **Have you oversimplified the argument—for example, by using either-or reasoning?** Add some qualifying language that shows that you are aware of the issue's true complexity.

Counterargument

- **Can you make any concessions to opposing views?** Try to find common ground with readers by acknowledging the legitimacy of their concerns. Show readers where you share their values, interests, and assumptions.

- **Does your attempt to refute an objection seem unconvincing?** Try to strengthen it. Avoid attacking your opponents. Instead, provide solid support—respected authorities, facts and statistics from reputable sources—to convince readers that you can argue credibly.
- **Have you ignored strong opposing arguments?** Take account of them. If you cannot refute them, you might have to acknowledge their legitimacy.

See Chapter 13 for advice about cueing readers so that they can follow your argument easily.

Use your computer to help you to analyze problems with your essay. For example, if a reader feels that your reasons and refutations are not arranged logically, highlight each one by putting it in bold type. Then, reconsider the sequence in which you present your argument and counterargument.

Tone

- **Does the tone seem inappropriate?** Consider altering your language. Think more about your purpose, audience, and argumentative strategy. You may need to express your strong feelings about the issue more directly or indicate why you feel as you do. If you expect readers to dismiss your concerns, you might try a more combative or confrontational style, forcefully refuting their arguments. If you are trying to build a bridge of shared concerns, consider personalizing your writing by using *I* or a personal anecdote.

Organization

- **Does the beginning seem weak or dull?** Consider opening with a striking anecdote or a surprising quotation.
- **Do you think readers might have trouble following your argument?** Consider adding a brief forecast of your main points at the beginning of your essay.
- **Do the reasons and refutations need to be more logically arranged?** Reorder them. Consider announcing each reason and refutation more explicitly.
- **Does the ending seem weak or vague?** Search your invention notes for a strong quotation, or add language that will reach out to readers.

Use your word processor's cut-and-paste or block-and-move functions to shift material around. Make sure you revise transitions so that material fits smoothly in its new spot.

EDITING AND PROOFREADING

Use your spell-check function cautiously. Remember that it will not find all misspellings, particularly misused homonyms (such as *there* for *their* or *they're*), typos that are words (such as *fro* for *for*), and many proper nouns. Proofread these carefully yourself. Also read for words that should have been deleted during editing.

In working on your draft so far, you may have corrected some obvious errors, but grammar and style have not been a priority. Now is the time to edit carefully to correct any errors in mechanics, usage, and punctuation, as well as to consider matters of style. Research has identified several errors that are especially common in essays that argue a position; the following guidelines can help you check and edit your draft for these errors.

Checking for Commas before Coordinating Conjunctions That Link Independent Clauses. An independent clause is a group of words that can stand alone as a complete sentence. Writers often join two or more such clauses with coordinating conjunctions (*and, but, for, or, nor, so,* or *yet*) in order to link related ideas in one sentence. Look at one example from Jessica Statsky's essay:

> Winning and losing may be an inevitable part of adult life, but they should not be part of childhood.

In this sentence, Statsky links two ideas: (1) that winning and losing may be part of adult life and (2) that they should not be part of childhood. In essays that argue a position, writers often join ideas in this way as they set forth the reasons and support for their position.

When you are joining independent clauses, use a comma before the coordinating conjunction so that readers can easily see where one idea stops and the next one starts:

- **The new immigration laws will bring in more skilled people, but their presence will take jobs away from other Americans.**

- **Sexually transmitted diseases are widespread, and many students are sexually active.**

Do not use a comma when the coordinating conjunction joins phrases that are *not* independent clauses:

- **Newspaper reporters have visited pharmacies/ and observed pharmacists selling steroids illegally.**

- **We need people with special talents/ and diverse skills to make the United States a stronger nation.**

Checking the Punctuation of Conjunctive Adverbs. When writers take a position, the reasoning they need to employ seems to invite the use of conjunctive adverbs (*consequently, furthermore, however, moreover, therefore, thus*) to connect sentences and clauses. Conjunctive adverbs that open a sentence should be followed by a comma.

- **Consequently, many local governments have banned smoking.**

- **Therefore, talented nurses will leave the profession because of poor working conditions and low salaries.**

If a conjunctive adverb joins two independent clauses, it must be preceded by a semicolon and followed by a comma.

- **The recent vote on increasing student fees produced a disappointing turnout/; moreover, the presence of campaign literature on ballot tables violated voting procedures.**

- **Children watching television recognize violence but not its intention; thus, they become desensitized to violence.**

Conjunctive adverbs that fall in the middle of an independent clause are set off with commas.

◇ **Due to trade restrictions, however, sales of Japanese cars did not surpass sales of domestic cars.**

A Common ESL Problem. Because the distinctions in meaning among some common conjunctive adverbs are subtle, nonnative speakers often have difficulty using them accurately. For example, the difference between *however* and *nevertheless* is small; each is used to introduce statements that contrast with what precedes it. But *nevertheless* emphasizes the contrast, whereas *however* softens it. Check usage of such terms in an English dictionary rather than a bilingual one. *The American Heritage Dictionary of the English Language* has special usage notes to help to distinguish frequently confused words.

A WRITER AT WORK

DEVELOPING YOUR COUNTERARGUMENT

In this section, we look at how Jessica Statsky tried to anticipate opposing arguments and decide how to counterargue in her essay on the issue of whether sports for children should be competitive.

To understand Statsky's thinking about possible counterarguments, we need first to see who her intended readers are and what she thought she could realistically accomplish with these readers. Here is an excerpt from the part of her invention writing in which she analyzed her potential readers:

```
I think I will write mainly to parents who are considering
letting their children get involved in competitive sports and
to those whose children are already on teams and who don't
know about the possible dangers. Parents who are really into
competition and winning probably couldn't be swayed by my
arguments anyway. I don't know how to reach coaches (but
aren't they parents?) or league organizers. I'll tell parents
some horror stories and also present solid evidence from
psychologists that competitive sports can really harm children
under the age of twelve. I think you'll be impressed with
this scientific evidence.
    I share with parents one important value: the best
interests of children. Competition really works against
children's best interests. Maybe parents' magazines (don't
know of any specific ones) publish essays like mine.
```

To develop her counterargument, Statsky listed arguments she expected her readers would make and decided which of these arguments she could accept and which she needed to refute.

Listing Opposing Arguments

Assuming that most people who favor organized sports for children would defend the emphasis on competition, Statsky listed the following opposing arguments and likely objections to her argument against competitive sports for children:

```
--Competition teaches children how to succeed in later life
--Children who are allowed to feel the thrill of winning
  experience a boost of self-esteem
--Allows children to prove to themselves and others their
  capabilities
--Gives children an incentive to excel
--Children need not be strained and damaged physically
  in competitive sports if research is done to determine their
  limits at different ages and care is taken to observe their
  limits
```

This list appears to pose serious challenges to Statsky's argument, but she benefits considerably by facing up to her readers' objections before she drafts her essay. By preparing this list, she gains insight into how she must develop her own argument in light of these predictable objections, and she can begin thinking about which objections she might accommodate and which she must refute. She gains authority because she can demonstrate in her essay a good understanding of opposing positions. Consequently, her readers—those who agree, are undecided, or oppose—will find her argument more plausible.

Accommodating Legitimate Arguments

Looking over her list of opposing arguments, Statsky decided that she could accommodate readers by conceding that competitive sports can sometimes be fun for children—at least for those who win. Here are her invention notes:

```
     It is true that children do sometimes enjoy getting
prizes and being recognized as winners in competitions adults
set up for them. I remember feeling very excited when our
sixth-grade relay team won a race at our school's sports day.
And I felt really good when I would occasionally win the
candy bar for being the last one standing in classroom
spelling contests. But when I think about these events,
it's the activity itself I remember as the main fun, not
the winning. I think I can concede that winning is exciting
to 6-to-12-year-olds, while arguing that it's not as
important as adults think. I hope this will win me
some friends among readers who are undecided about my
position.
```

In Statsky's revised essay, this accommodation appears in paragraph 5 as the sentence beginning "Although winning does add to the fun. . . ."

Refuting Illegitimate Arguments

Statsky recognized that she must attempt to refute the other objections in her list. She chose one and tried out the following refutation:

```
     It irritates me that adults are so eager to make first
and second graders go into training for getting and keeping
```

```
jobs as adults. I don't see why the pressures on adults
need to be put on children. Anyway, both my parents tell me
that in their jobs, cooperation and teamwork are the keys
to success. You can't get ahead unless you're effective in
working with others. Maybe we should be training children and
even high school and college students in the skills necessary
for cooperation, rather than competition. Sports and physical
activity are important for children, but elementary schools
should emphasize achievement rather than competition--race
against the clock rather than against each other. Rewards
could be given for gains in speed or strength instead of for
defeating somebody in a competition.
```

The major benefit of this brief invention activity was to alert Statsky to the importance of learning more about the effects of competition on children, as well as about the possibilities for more cooperative physical activities and programs. You can see from her revised essay that refuting the benefits of competition is a theme that runs through her entire essay.

While this invention activity did not produce sentences she could use in her draft, it advanced her thinking about her readers and her purpose and brought an early, productive focus to her library research on competition in children's sports.

THINKING CRITICALLY ABOUT WHAT YOU HAVE LEARNED

Now that you have read and discussed several essays that argue a position and written one of your own, it is a good time to think critically about what you have learned. What problems did you encounter as you were writing, and how did you solve them? How did the position papers you read influence your own writing? How do position papers in general reflect cultural attitudes about public debate and controversy?

Reflecting on Your Writing

Write a page or so telling your instructor about a problem you encountered in writing an essay that argues a position, how you discovered it, and how you went about solving it. Before you begin, gather all of your invention and planning notes, drafts and critical comments, revision plan, and final revision. Review these materials as you complete this writing task.

1. Identify *one* writing problem you encountered as you worked on the essay. Do not be concerned with general writing problems; focus on a problem that specifically involves planning and writing a position paper. For example, did you puzzle over how to convince your readers that the issue is important? Did you have trouble asserting your position forcefully while acknowledging other points of view? Was it difficult to refute any objection that readers might raise?
2. At what stage in the process did you first recognize the problem? Was it when you were thinking about your readers' attitudes, trying to decide how to sequence your ideas, reviewing critical comments on a draft, or at some other point? What called the problem to your attention? If you did not become aware of it until rather late in the process, can you now see hints of it in your invention writings or early drafting? If so, where specifically?
3. Reflect on how you tried to solve the problem. Did you reword, reorganize, or simply cut the

part that was problematic? Did you reread your invention writing? Did you need to do more invention or research? Did you seek advice from a classmate or your instructor?

4. Finally, write your explanation of the problem and your solution. Be specific by quoting from your invention writing, drafts, others' critical comments, your own revision plan, and your final revision. Show how your writing and thinking changed as you tried to solve the problem. If you are still uncertain about your solution, say so. The point is not to prove that you have solved the problem perfectly but rather to show what you have learned about problem solving in the process of arguing a position.

Reviewing What You Learned from Reading

The position papers you have read have almost certainly influenced the one you wrote. For example, selections in this chapter may have helped you to decide that you needed to do some library research before you could argue responsibly for your position, that you could use a personal anecdote as part of your support, or that you should try to anticipate readers' objections and questions. Write a page or so explaining to your instructor how your writing has been influenced by how others argue. Before you write, take time to reflect on the possible influences your reading has had on your thinking and writing:

1. Review the readings in this chapter and the final draft of your own essay. Did any of the position papers in the chapter (or by your classmates) influence your choice of topic or argumentative strategy? For example, consider whether any reading influenced how you decided to use authorities, refute objections, or establish common ground. In deciding what tone to adopt—whether to be contentious or to accommodate different points of view—did you think of how others you respect debate this kind of issue? Consider also debates you have seen recently in newspapers and magazines or heard on television or radio. How have these examples of arguing influenced your writing?
2. Now write an explanation of these influences. You may focus on a single influence or discuss how you used different examples of argument to develop your own style of arguing a position. Compare what you did in your essay with what you have seen others do, giving specific examples. Finally, point out anything you would now do to improve your own essay, based on your review of the chapter's readings.

Considering the Social Dimensions of Position Papers

Arguing positions on important social and political issues is essential in a democracy. Doing so gives each of us a voice. Instead of remaining silent and on the margins, we can enter the ongoing debate. We can influence others, perhaps convincing them to change their minds or at least to take a different point of view seriously. Airing our differences also allows us to live together in relative peace. Instead of brawling with each other at school board meetings, in legislative halls, on street corners, or in the classroom, we argue. We may raise our voices in anger and frustration, and our differences may seem insurmountable, but at least no one is physically hurt and, with luck, we can find common ground.

When we take account of opposing viewpoints in presenting an argument, our opposition also influences the way we think, encouraging us to consider issues rationally—to find reasons for our own opinions and to understand the reasons behind opposing opinions. Finding reasons for our views forces us to examine our assumptions—the fundamental ideas we have about how things are or should be—as well as the assumptions of others (which may be the same as our own or very different). Thinking rationally also requires that we find support that grounds our opinions in something other than belief—in facts that can be verified, in the authority of experts, in experiences with which others can identify. Finally, thinking rationally requires that we look seriously at objections to our argument. When we know that we must defend our position, we are presumably more apt to take positions that are defensible. Ideally, then, writing position papers fosters the kind of reasonable debate that enables a diverse society like ours to hold together.

Yet even though rational argument about controversial social issues is a highly valued activity in our society, scholars and others have recently raised questions about its presumed objectivity, its power to exclude people, and its suppression of dissent.

The Illusion of Objectivity. As a society, we value reasoned argument, in part, because we think it allows us to transcend personal bias and narrow self-interest—in other words, it enables us to be objective. Recently, however, philosophers have argued that objectivity itself is only an illusion, that it is impossible to escape one's history and culture to achieve some mythical, purely "objective" stance. Race, nationality, class, gender, religion, region, schooling, access to the media—all these factors influence who we are and what we believe. Everything we learn and know, as well as *how* we learn and know, derives from individual experience and perception. Consequently, according to this viewpoint, the fact that we are able to give objective-*sounding* reasons for our opinions does not guarantee that they are unbiased or even reasonable: What appears to be rational thought may be merely rationalization, a way of justifying fundamentally intuitive personal convictions. In other words, supporting a position with a "well-reasoned" argument may simply be a game we play to trick others—and ourselves—into believing that we are open-minded and our opinions are rational.

Exclusion from Power. A second critique of the kind of argumentation we have presented in this chapter is that by valuing it so highly, our society privileges one mode of thinking and presenting ideas over all others. Since students who hope to succeed in college and gain access to most of the professions that confer status, money, and power in our society must be skilled at rational argument, those whose educational options, cultural traditions, or perhaps even natural ability keep them from mastering logical argumentation are clearly at a disadvantage. Even when they possess other important creative or technical abilities, they may well be excluded from the corridors of power because they cannot participate in rational debate.

Suppressing Dissent. Finally, some critics argue that our society privileges reasoned argument over other modes of discourse in dealing with social issues in order to control dissent. Instead of expressing what may be legitimate outrage and inciting public concern through passionate language, dissenters are urged to be dispassionate and reasonable. They may even be encouraged to reach common ground with those whose views they find repugnant for the sake of peaceful compromise. While it may help to prevent violent confrontation, this emphasis on reasoned argument may also prevent an honest and open exchange of differences. In the end, this way of arguing may serve to maintain the status quo by silencing the more radical voices within the community.

For Discussion. Here are some questions to help you to consider the social dimensions of arguing a position. As you read and, perhaps, discuss these questions in class, write down your thoughts and reactions. Then write a page or so for your instructor, presenting your ideas about the role that writing that takes a position plays in our society.

1. We have said that reasoned argument is the dominant form of debate in our society. Nevertheless, television and radio talk shows like *The Rush Limbaugh Program* and *Crossfire* seem to have replaced calm, reasoned debate with a more contentious, "in your face" style of argumentation. Why do you think this kind of argument is so popular nowadays? How do you respond to Guy Molyneux's point that political debate today "takes the form of either 'preaching to the choir' or berating those unfortunate enough not to share the speaker's wisdom" (paragraph 13)?

2. One critique of reasoned argument is that it pretends to be more objective than it actually is, that the reasons position takers give are really justifications for their personal opinions. How would you respond to this criticism? Do you think that reasoned argument should try to be objective? When you were writing your own position paper, were you trying to be objective? Which of your reasons would you now identify as objective-sounding, chosen because you thought your readers would find it convincing, not because you really believed it?
3. We have said that mastering logical argumentation is necessary for success in school, business, and the professions. Why do you think reasoned argument is so dominant? How would you respond to people who maintain that being required to master this kind of thinking and writing is exclusionary and therefore unfair? What has helped you learn to think and write logically?
4. As a writer and reader of position papers, do you think having to take opposing points of view into account encourages people to moderate their views? In writing your own essay, how did you handle opposing views? Did having to consider them help you to clarify or sharpen differences between your position and opposing positions? Did considering opposing views lead you to modify your own?
5. Unlike actual debate, in position papers the writer represents the opposing views; the people who hold these views cannot speak for themselves. When you were planning your own essay and trying to anticipate other points of view, how did you represent what others think? Did you use their words or your own? What difference might it make whose words are used? When you were deciding how to present other views, did you choose the more or less extreme versions? Consider your reasons for making this choice and what difference it might make.
6. Do you think the emphasis on reasoned argument in our society discourages dissent? Might more passionate approaches to social issues be more effective? For example, suppose that Jessica Statsky's argument against competitive children's sports had instead taken the form of a satiric, highly unflattering portrait of the kinds of parents and coaches who push children to compete too early. Do you think that such alternative ways of expressing opinions on social issues are sometimes appropriate? If not, why not? If so, how would you justify them?

Writing for a national newsmagazine, a professor proposes that since a college education now costs so much, students should be given the option of earning a college degree by passing an examination. He gives three reasons why readers should take his proposal seriously: It would save resources, contribute to social mobility, and free unconventional students to pursue self-education. Anticipating two likely objections to his proposal from his college-educated readers, he argues that some students may prefer to do without the social interaction college can provide and that an inexpensive screening exam could be devised to identify applicants who would be unlikely to succeed on the final degree exam. To allay reader doubts that one exam could really assess all that a student could learn in four years of college, he describes a month-long exam that would test oral and written knowledge and competence in a major field. He proposes charging $3,000 for the degree exam—to pay professors to prepare the exam and evaluate it.

For a political science class, a college senior writes a proposal to solve a problem she sees with the length of the president's term of office. With five other students, she will read her proposal aloud to the class as part of a panel on the United States presidency. Citing examples from recent history, she argues that presidents spend the first year of each term getting organized and the fourth year either running for reelection or weakened by their status as lame ducks. Consequently, they are fully productive for only half of their four-year terms.

She proposes limiting presidents to one six-year term, claiming that this change would solve the problem by giving presidents four or five years to put their programs into effect. She acknowledges that a single term could make presidents less responsive to the public will but insists that the system of legislative checks and balances would make that problem unlikely.

Several students in the predentistry program at a large state university realize that they are uncertain about the requirements, procedures, and strategies for applying to dental school. One of them writes a proposal to the head of the program suggesting that predentistry students need a handbook. To dramatize that a problem exists and that students consider it serious, he points out that dental school admission rates for students in the program are declining and includes an informal survey of current enrollees. He mentions other programs that provide such a guide. Realizing that few faculty members would take time for such a project, he proposes that students write the handbook and handle the printing and distribution; two faculty members would serve as advisers. He asks that the publication costs be borne by the predentistry program, however, pointing out that students would donate their time.

CHAPTER 7

Proposing a Solution

Proposals are vital to a democracy. They inform citizens about problems affecting their well-being and also suggest actions that could be taken to remedy these problems. People write proposals every day in business, government, education, and the professions. Proposals are a basic ingredient of the world's work.

As a special form of argument, proposals have much in common with position papers, described in Chapter 6. Both analyze a subject about which there is disagreement and take a definite stand on it. Both make an argument, giving reasons and support and acknowledging readers' likely objections or questions. Proposals, however, go further: They urge readers to take specific action. They argue for a proposed solution to a problem, succeeding or failing by the strength of that argument.

Problem solving is basic to most disciplines and professions. For example, scientists use the scientific method, a systematic form of problem solving; political scientists and sociologists, using social science methods, propose solutions to troubling political and social problems; engineers regularly employ problem-solving techniques in building bridges, automobiles, and computers; attorneys find legal precedents to solve their clients' problems; teachers continually make decisions about how to help students with learning problems; counselors devote themselves to helping clients solve personal problems; business owners and managers daily solve problems large and small.

Problem solving depends on a questioning attitude—wondering about alternative approaches to bringing about change, puzzling over how a goal might be achieved, questioning why a process unfolds in a particular way, posing challenges to the status quo. In addition, it demands imagination and creativity. To solve a problem, you need to see it anew, to look at it from new angles and in new contexts.

Because a proposal tries to convince readers that its way of defining and solving the problem makes sense, proposal writers must be sensitive to readers' needs and expectations. Readers need to know details of the solution and to be convinced that it will solve the problem and can be implemented. If readers initially favor a different solution, knowing why the writer rejects it will help them to decide whether to support the writer's proposed solution.

As you plan and draft a proposal, you will have to determine whether your readers are aware of the problem and whether they recognize its seriousness, and you will have to consider their views of any other solutions. Knowing what your readers know—their assumptions and biases, the kinds of arguments likely to appeal to them—is a central part of proposal writing.

Writing in Your Other Courses

As the opening writing scenarios illustrate, college students find occasions to propose solutions to problems. Here are some typical assignments calling for problem-solving skills:

- *For an economics class:* The *maquiladora* industry along the U.S.-Mexican border provides foreign exchange for Mexico and low-paying jobs for half a million Mexicans, as well as profits for American manufacturers. Yet this innovative binational arrangement has created serious problems on the Mexican side of the border: inadequate housing, health care, and public services; on-the-job injuries; and environmental damage. Study one of these problems, research it, and propose a solution. Address your proposal to the mayor of Nogales, Tijuana, or Juarez.
- *For a business class:* A corporation wishes to install a workstation network but is unwilling to give up its mainframe computers. Propose a solution to this problem. Research the possibilities of mainframe-workstation integration, explain the problem carefully, and argue convincingly for your solution. Address your proposal to the CEO of the corporation.
- *For a biology class:* Apply the principle of circadian rhythm to the problem of jet lag. Explain circadian rhythm, define jet lag in light of it, and propose several actions readers might take to reduce the effects of jet lag. Present your proposal in the form of an article for the travel section of a newspaper, to be read by the general public.

→ Practice Proposing a Solution to a Problem: A Collaborative Activity

To get a sense of the complexities and possibilities involved in proposing solutions, think through a specific problem, and try to come up with a feasible proposal.

Part 1. Form a group with two or three other students, and select one person to take notes during your discussion.

- First, identify two or three problems within your college or community, and select one that you all recognize and agree needs to be solved.
- Next, consider possible solutions to this problem, and identify one solution that you can all support. You need not all be equally enthusiastic for this solution.
- Finally, determine which individual or group has the authority to take action on your proposed solution and how you would go about convincing this audience that the problem is serious and must be solved and that your proposed solution is feasible and should be supported. Make notes also about questions this audience might have about your proposal and what objections the audience might raise.

Part 2. As a group, discuss your efforts at proposing a solution to a problem. What surprised or pleased you most about this activity? What difficulties did you encounter in coming up with arguments that the problem must be solved and that your proposed solution would solve it? How did the objections you thought of influence your confidence in your proposed solution?

READINGS

Max Frankel writes a weekly column on communications for the *New York Times Magazine*. His long career at the *Times* began in 1952. Since then, he has been a reporter in eastern Europe, the Soviet Union, the Caribbean, and Washington, D.C., where he was diplomatic correspondent, White House correspondent, and head of the *Times* Washington bureau. Returning to New York, he served as editor of the *Times* editorial page (1977–1986) and, prior to his retirement, executive editor (1986–1994). In 1973 he won a Pulitzer prize for his reporting of President Nixon's visit to China the previous year. In the 1996 *New York Times Magazine* column reprinted here, Frankel compares the promise of E-mail to that of the telephone and the postal system. He proposes a way to ensure that E-mail realizes this promise by making it available to all Americans.

UNIVERSAL E-MAIL: WORTHY OF A "NEW FRONTIER" COMMITMENT

Max Frankel

1 It doesn't quite have the ring of John F. Kennedy's vow, 35 years ago this month, to land a man on the moon "before this decade is out." But you'd think a President or candidate for President would by now have hurled a similar challenge, with the promise of raising the nation's literacy, its computer skills and its technical prowess: E-mail for All by 2010!

2 As millions of Americans already know, E-mail is electronic mail that can be sent by anyone with a computer and telephone to everyone similarly equipped, anywhere on earth, almost instantaneously, at virtually no cost. It is by far the most popular feature of the Internet, that amorphous network of computer networks. E-mail's digital messages can be coolly deliberate, like a letter, or warmly spontaneous, like a phone call. They can be sent at any hour and read at the receiver's convenience. They can be addressed to a single person or simultaneously to thousands—thousands chosen by the sender for some shared interest or thousands who asked for a certain type of mail.

3 Although E-mail will eventually carry moving pictures and oral messages, it is now mostly written—typed, to be precise, on keyboards. Its messages are sliced up and wrapped inside small electronic packets, all of which pick their way along the best available Internet routes to an electronic postal station, where they reassemble and wait in storage for an addressee—like frankel@times.com—to check in to read them. E-mail travels as fast as a fax but arrives in much more versatile form. It can be long or short, studied, searched or skimmed, instantly answered or copied, relayed, edited or destroyed.

4 E-mail lets you court a lover, proclaim a credo, organize a rally or circulate a recipe. City Hall can use it to schedule trash collections; politicians can use it to take a poll. E-mail can order groceries or offer clothing discounts to selected customers. It is certain to become a vital new instrument of commerce and the creator of vibrant electronic communities.

5 But like conventional telephone and postal service, E-mail will never fulfill its social and commercial promise until it is universal. The more people it can reach, the greater its value to all. The already visible danger is that E-mail will become the preserve of the affluent and educated classes, bypassing large segments of the population—much as paper mail and telephones once bypassed rural America. Now, as then, the market alone seems unable at first to serve its own best interest.

It took a decree of Congress to require the Postal Service "to bind the Nation together through the personal, educational, literary and business correspondence of the people . . . in all areas and . . . all communities." As a result, paper mail became a powerful stimulus to road building, railroading and aviation. Similarly, governments imposed universal service on telephone companies, requiring them to overcharge urban customers so as to subsidize the extension of phone lines to farflung rural areas.

That mail and phone services can now be profitably privatized and deregulated is not an argument against government intervention and leadership. On the contrary, it is proof of the value of government incubation.

A recent Rand study, with research supported by the Markle Foundation, concluded that in the foreseeable future the free market is likely to deliver E-mail to only half of America. Without a government-led drive toward universality, some E-mail systems may prove to be incompatible with others. And without induced subsidies, perhaps from Internet access fees, the computer industry may never produce the inexpensive technologies that would enable television sets, telephones and computer games to bring E-mail into the home. Interim subsidies and technologies would also be needed if less-affluent citizens are to get their E-mail outside the home, in apartment lobbies, libraries and schools.

There appear to be no technical barriers to achieving universal E-mail once that goal has been proclaimed. Indeed, experiments in a few specially wired communities show that E-mail arouses people's interest in other computer services. In Blacksburg, Va., it has stimulated many to learn more complicated computer skills, to use the Internet for more sophisticated transactions and to create two dozen Net-related businesses.

House Speaker Newt Gingrich was not nearly as "nutty" as he thought when he mused out loud about subsidizing laptops for poor ghetto kids. But he was only scoring debating points and soon abandoned his own insight about how computers threaten to further divide American society.

If political leaders would reflect on the subject, they would recognize a vast constituency of the computerless and computer-challenged. They would recall the rich history of conservatives as well as liberals using government to advance and enlarge the nation's communications and transportation industries. They would summon Microsoft's Bill Gates and I.B.M.'s Lou Gerstner and the other titans of technology who so often deplore our inadequate schooling and seek their commitment to universal E-mail. The computer companies and their charities need to be challenged to underwrite cheaper terminals, to recycle older terminals and to invent pay terminals, like pay phones, for public spaces. They should be asked to consider charging modest fees for profitable private uses of the Internet—a government offspring—to subsidize the Net's penetration of every community.

President Kennedy, of course, could invoke the specter of *Sputnik* and cold war divisions to urge a race against the Russians to the moon. But he set a loftier goal than missile superiority. "Now it is time to take longer strides," he said, "time for a great new American enterprise." We face the more abstract specter of technological partition, a society of computer elites and illiterates drifting apart and losing touch. And we, too, could use a great new enterprise. E-mail for all won't guarantee how well we speak to one another, but it can keep us talking and growing richer together.

Connecting to Culture and Experience

As a result of intervention by the federal government, all Americans now have access to telephones and postal mail, and nearly all use them to stay in touch with others and to do business. Frankel believes that E-mail promises to become an equally powerful socially unifying force while at the same time producing greater prosperity for all. At present, however, few Americans use E-mail and other features of the Internet like the World Wide Web, and Frankel argues that unless the federal government intervenes once again, most Americans will never gain access to E-mail.

With two or three other students, discuss your own experiences with the Internet. Do you have access to E-mail, the World Wide Web, or other features of the Internet like newsgroups and chat groups? How recently did you gain access, and who helped you or taught you? Specifically, what use do you, your friends, or your family make of E-mail? Do you share Frankel's vision for it?

Congress has shown interest in censoring certain materials on the Internet, but it has not taken up the issue of access. What do you think are the merits and potential problems of federal laws to ensure access to E-mail? Do you share Frankel's doubts that private corporations can make widespread access a reality soon?

Analyzing Writing Strategies

1. At the beginning of this chapter, we discuss several attributes of proposals to solve problems. Consider which of these are true of Frankel's proposal.
   - It informs people about a problem affecting their well-being and offers a solution.
   - It argues for the significance or importance of the problem.
   - It both outlines a solution and argues that this solution will solve the problem and can be implemented.
   - It anticipates readers' objections to or questions about the proposed solution.
   - It also anticipates that some readers will prefer solutions other than the one the writer outlines.
2. To convince readers to take his proposal seriously, Frankel relies on several kinds of **support.** He refers to a research study (paragraph 8), gives an example (paragraph 9), and makes a comparison (paragraph 12). Locate each instance of support, and bracket it in the margin. Consider whether each would be clear, accessible, and convincing to *Times* readers. Evaluate how well the details support Frankel's reasoning at the point where they appear in his argument. Which instance of support seems most successful? Explain briefly. What questions might you raise about the other two instances?

Considering Topics for Your Own Essay

Consider proposing a solution to some problem of technology or work. For example, like Frankel, you could propose a way to popularize or distribute some new technology, whether computer-based or automotive or educational or recreational. If you are working part or full time now, you are doubtless aware of some problem at work that needs rethinking and solving. You could write a proposal to your boss, trying to convince him or her to see the problem your way and to consider implementing your proposed solution.

Commentary

The **organization** of Frankel's proposal for universal E-mail reveals the basic two-part plan of all proposals:

Problem

A president needs to challenge the nation to provide E-mail for all. (paragraph 1)

A description of E-mail (2)

How E-mail works (3)

The uses of E-mail (4)

E-mail must become universal. (5)

Solution

Government ensured that postal mail and telephones would be available to all. (6)

Government incubation leads to privatization. (7)

Government subsidies will be required to provide the less affluent with access to E-mail. (8)

There are no technical barriers to universal E-mail. (9)

National politicians must take the lead. (10, 11)

E-mail for all may strengthen community and the economy. (12)

In this scratch outline, Frankel presents the problem first and then the solution. He devotes about a third of the space to the problem and two-thirds to his proposed solution. The problem is that E-mail may not become available to all Americans. The solution is that the federal government must take the lead in providing access to E-mail. Frankel correctly assumes that many of his readers do not use E-mail or even know what it is. Consequently, he describes it carefully at the beginning. He then states the problem concisely in paragraph 5 and announces his proposed solution in paragraph 6. The argument for his solution follows to the end. This plan is simple, obvious, and effective. It allows Frankel to present his argument coherently and readably, and it meets readers' expectations for an argument that proposes a solution to a problem. Readers can move easily from one paragraph to the next. There are no gaps or surprises.

This simple but workable plan makes possible a sophisticated **argumentative strategy,** however. Writing for an influential national newspaper—the *New York Times* is distributed in every major American city—Frankel aims at both educated citizens and political leaders. He appeals to the self-interest of all readers and invites political leaders, "conservatives as well as liberals," to take up the "great new enterprise" of making E-mail available to all by 2010. He reminds political leaders of President Kennedy's great success in posing challenges and setting ambitious goals, and in doing so he suggests that universal E-mail may be as important a national goal as space exploration. We know that this part of his strategy is important because Frankel frames the essay with it. (*Framing* connects the end of an essay to its beginning, putting a frame around it, as a frame encloses a picture.)

Before announcing his solution or even defining the problem, Frankel makes sure that all his readers know what E-mail is, what it does, and how it works. He bases his strategy on the assumption that even readers who do not use E-mail can see its potential if he describes it for them. Even more important than this description, however, is Frankel's insightful analogy in paragraphs 5–7, where he compares E-mail to the telephone and postal mail. He knows that his readers probably cannot imagine life without telephones and daily mail delivery, and he hopes to convince them that E-mail offers even greater potential for keeping people in touch. Because Frankel relies on this analogy to introduce the problem (paragraph 5), announce his proposed solution (paragraph 6), and launch his argument for it (paragraph 7), the analogy seems central to his argumentative strategy.

Frankel argues to support his proposed solution in paragraphs 7–12. His goal is to convince readers that the proposal is worth taking seriously—that it is feasible and better than alternative solutions. One way to think about his strategy is to imagine him anticipating readers' questions and attempting to answer them:

- Shouldn't E-mail be privatized and deregulated, like current mail and phone service? (paragraph 7)
- Won't the free market eventually deliver E-mail to all Americans? (paragraph 8)
- Aren't there formidable technical barriers? (paragraph 9)
- What happened to Speaker Gingrich's well-publicized laptops-for-poor-kids proposal? (paragraph 10)
- What role would corporations play? (paragraph 11)
- Aren't you exaggerating by comparing E-mail to the cold war? (paragraph 12)

Frankel's strategy will succeed only if many readers find his answers convincing. Like Kennedy, Frankel has a grand vision. He believes that much is at stake, and he hopes that his readers will embrace his vision and share his urgency. Most important, he hopes that a prominent political leader will take up his proposal. He must convince readers that the free market cannot solve the problem, even in the long run. Then, to confront a more formidable obstacle, he must convince them that the federal government must do it. To do so, he adopts a wide range of strategies—refuting objections, referring to published research, giving examples, bridging political differences, suggesting a major role for corporations. Throughout, he maintains a positive, even cheerful tone. He does not shout. He is not irritable. He does not exclude.

For more on arguing, see Chapter 19.

When you write your own proposal essay, you, too, will want to adopt an argumentative strategy that will enable you to achieve your purpose with your particular readers. This chapter offers the resources you will need.

Mickey Kaus, a graduate of Harvard University and Harvard Law School, has been writing about public policy for eighteen years. He has worked at *Newsweek* and is now a senior editor for *The New Republic,* a national weekly magazine of news and opinion. His recent book, *The End of Equality,* argues for greater civility (considerateness, politeness) in public life. In the following proposal, Kaus considers the problem of verbal harassment of women by men in public places. He begins by rejecting another solution proposed by a feminist law professor, then sets up the problem as a conflict between an individual's right to free speech (a man's right to make vulgar comments about a passing woman's appearance) and the need for civility in the "public sphere," when people are moving around their communities, shopping, working, or at leisure. The question seems to be whether the First Amendment to the Constitution permits restraints on speech in certain situations. (Passed in 1791 as part of the Bill of Rights, the amendment says, "Congress shall make no law . . .

abridging the freedom of speech.") Some writers on this issue take the position that speech should rarely, if ever, be restricted, while others take the position that speech may be restricted under certain circumstances.

As you read, notice the way Kaus considers and rejects other proposed solutions to public verbal harassment before he proposes his own solution.

The latest issue of the prestigious *Harvard Law Review* features a sixty-page article by Northwestern law professor Cynthia Grant Bowman on the "street harassment" of women. Bowman argues that "wolf-whistles, sucking noises and catcalls" directed at women in public places—as well as comments that "range from 'Hello, baby' to vulgar suggestions and outright threats"—are part of a "spectrum of means by which men objectify women and assert coercive power over them." She wants to make these things illegal, or at least subject the harassers to civil lawsuits. 1

Bowman would seem to offer conservative curmudgeons their fattest target since a liberal judge in New York ruled that beggars had a constitutional right to panhandle in the subways. Her article amply displays many of the annoying aspects of "feminist jurisprudence." There is, first, the tendency to exaggerate the harm done by male misbehavior. "[A]ny incident of harassment, no matter how 'harmless,'" is held to reinforce fear of rape "by demonstrating that any man may choose to invade a woman's personal space, physically or psychologically. . . ." Bowman also implies that men cannot understand what it feels like for a woman to be sexually taunted. In keeping with this assumption, she cites *The Washington Post*'s Courtland Milloy as "one woman" who has eloquently recounted the evils of harassment. Last time I checked, Milloy was a man. And Bowman ignores the possibility that a "reasonable woman" might ever *want* men to hit on her. 2

Take it away, Rush Limbaugh. Or, rather, take it away, TNR.[1] A couple of weeks ago this magazine ran a Notebook item dismissing Bowman's article with the observation that "in a free country, being maddened is a hazard of existence." 3

Sometimes, though, it's too easy to be a curmudgeon. Compare Bowman's arguments with those in that New York subway panhandling case. In the latter, conservatives insisted on preserving order in public spaces, at the expense of a borderline First Amendment claim. Is the case against "street harassment" all that different? One would expect those who most loudly lament the loss of civility and public order to be the most sympathetic to Bowman's complaint. Certainly *Public Interest*-type[2] conservatives such as James Q. Wilson, who argues for "the priority of the good over personal rights," should understand that beggars aren't the only people whose assertion of "rights" can threaten the common sphere of living. Mr. Wilson, meet Ms. Bowman. 4

After reading Bowman's article, I conducted an unscientific survey of female acquaintances, asking if they were in fact bothered by "street harassment." None were as distressed as Bowman is. But almost all said they were regularly harassed, at least on the "hey, baby" level. And while some claimed to enjoy the milder forms of hassling (e.g., the whistles), most said they often changed their routes in order to avoid public spaces where they thought they would be taunted. 5

[1] TNR stands for *The New Republic,* the magazine in which this essay originally appeared.
[2] *Public Interest* is a conservative political journal.

For all her foolishness, Bowman has pointed up a severe violation of civility, one that seems to diminish public life for a large portion of the American population. The problem is what to do about it. The pursuit of civility in public spaces is a peculiarly difficult enterprise for Americans accustomed to framing legal issues in terms of conflicting rights. Quite simply, it is impossible to describe the civil ordering of the public sphere in terms of "rights," or at least in terms of the absolute speechlike rights we're used to. I'm walking down the street talking to a friend. A stranger walks up and begins to harangue me. I turn my back. He keeps haranguing. I have a "right" to be there. He has a "right" to be there too. We both have "rights." But something has to give. 6

Worse, the question of whether we want to restrain the haranguer inevitably hinges on the content of his expression. It makes a difference if he says, "Hello, baby," or "[F——ing] bitch." It even makes a difference if he's funny or trite. The required judgment is almost aesthetic. 7

It won't do to simply note, with liberal communitarians[3] such as William Galston, that "there is a gap between rights and rightness that cannot be closed without a richer moral vocabulary . . . that invokes principles of decency [and] duty." That's true. But how do we get ourselves a public sphere that reflects this decency, when we no longer have a culture that takes care of the problem automatically? 8

At least three approaches seem to be available. First, re-education. Amitai Etzioni, in his forthcoming book, *The Spirit of Community,* despairs of any attempt to put a "notch" in the First Amendment to allow the prohibition of offensive speech. Instead, he suggests, why not require offenders "to attend classes that will teach them civility?" This may make some sense in a university setting (which is the context of Etzioni's discussion). As a remedy for "street harassment," it seems pathetically inadequate. Even if we could send harassers to the moral equivalent of traffic school, it would probably provoke more ridicule than re-education. There's something creepy about the idea of state-sponsored re-education classes, anyway. 9

Second, as Bowman suggests, we might give "targets" of street harassment the right to sue for civil damages, perhaps for "intentional infliction of emotional distress." Yet this seems a recipe for disastrous litigiousness. Do we really want every woman who feels "dissed" to be able to require a judge to determine the "reasonableness" of the dissing? 10

The third, and least unsatisfactory, approach is to delegate the required semi-aesthetic judgments to the police by making "street harassment" a misdemeanor, just as other sorts of public disturbances are misdemeanors. Litigiousness would be avoided by having a third party (a cop) decide on the spot whether civility had been violated. Pennsylvania already has a law penalizing anyone who intentionally "engages in a course of conduct or repeatedly commits acts which alarm or seriously annoy" another person "and which serve no legitimate purpose." The trouble, as Bowman notes, is that this sort of ordinance typically applies only to those who repeatedly harass a single person, not to those who harass a series of passers-by. But this defect can be easily remedied. If it's not a violation of the First Amendment to arrest a man who calls one pedestrian a "bitch" fifteen times, why is it a violation to arrest him if he says it once to fifteen different pedestrians? 11

Few police departments would actually arrest any but the most egregious violators, of course—though female police officers might have interestingly different priorities in 12

[3] Communitarianism is a movement that emphasizes community responsibility over individual freedom.

this regard. But the law would at least give cops a basis for telling offenders to "move along." Most importantly, the law might also stimulate the cultural change that everybody, including Bowman, agrees is the only real solution to the problem. Until then, her argument will be hard to dismiss.

Connecting to Culture and Experience

Consider the times when, in public, a stranger has said something to you that felt like an intrusion or harassment. Perhaps someone asked you for money, threatened you, intimidated you, or just wanted to talk. Make a list of these occasions.

Discuss these incidents with two or three other students. Begin by describing one or two of the incidents from your lists. Together, consider which incidents seem to be clear examples of acceptable speech and which ones violate civility. From your discussion, can you tell whether your group leans toward protecting speech rights or toward guaranteeing a minimal level of public civility, or do you find yourselves divided on this important current issue?

Analyzing Writing Strategies

See pp. 252 and 266 in this chapter for an example of a scratch outline.

1. Make a scratch outline of Kaus's essay. Using your scratch outline as a guide, analyze Kaus's **argumentative strategy** in presenting the problem to be solved. (See the Commentary following the Frankel reading for an analysis of a proposal writer's argumentative strategy.) What do you think he is trying to accomplish with his readers in paragraphs 1–8? How does he use Bowman, Limbaugh (a politically conservative talk-show host), Wilson, and Galston to prepare readers for his solution? Given his purpose and readers, what are the advantages or disadvantages of his argumentative strategy?

See Chapter 13 for a discussion of cues.

2. When Kaus presents three alternative solutions in paragraphs 9–11, he provides obvious cues—a **forecast** and **transitions**—to keep readers on track. Underline these cues, and describe briefly how they guide the reader.

Considering Topics for Your Own Essay

List some social problems in your community that concern you. Many communities are experiencing problems like lack of participation in local politics, limited access to English classes for recent immigrants or to training programs for the unemployed, crime in schools, unsupervised latchkey kids, tension or conflict between ethnic groups, deteriorating streets or school buildings or park facilities and landscaping, or reduced library hours and resources. Choose one social problem you might write about. How would you define and present the problem? What solution would you propose, and what alternative solutions might you evaluate?

Commentary

See pp. 537–42 for more on anticipating readers' concerns.

Kaus's essay illustrates the importance in some proposals of **anticipating and evaluating alternative solutions,** a special strategy of counterargument. Kaus anticipates two alternative solutions to the problem of street hassles: Etzioni's proposal to reeducate people who are uncivil (paragraph 9) and one of Bowman's proposals, to allow victims to sue (paragraph 10). Kaus might have merely acknowledged these alternatives, mentioning them only to let readers know he was aware of them; or he could have accommodated them, integrating parts of all of them into his own proposed solution. Instead, he refutes them, calling Etzioni's solution "pathetically inadequate" and Bowman's "a recipe for disastrous litigiousness."

Like Frankel, Kaus carried out some **research** to learn more about the problem to be solved, in his case talking casually to a few female friends. He uses what he learns to challenge what he considers to be Bowman's exaggerations but also to acknowledge that even the milder street hassles cause women to avoid certain public spaces.

Kaus's essay also illustrates an interesting dilemma faced by many writers who propose solutions to problems: Recognizing that the real solution is out of reach, they propose instead an **interim or partial solution.** For example, in his last paragraph, Kaus acknowledges that the only lasting solution to street hassles is "cultural change," and yet he unapologetically argues for the only change that he thinks is possible at the moment, a law making street hassling a misdemeanor, like running a stop sign. When you plan your essay proposing a solution, you, too, may face the dilemma of proposing an interim solution that can be put into effect immediately or arguing for a more far-reaching solution that would be much harder to implement.

You may have noticed Kaus's aggressive, sharp **tone** in judging various writers. He at first seems especially unkind to Bowman, but he turns out to be as harsh toward Etzioni. He accuses Bowman of being annoying, of exaggerating, of being foolish. He growls that Etzioni's proposal to reeducate offensive speakers is pathetically inadequate, likely to provoke ridicule, and creepy. You may find this tone offensive, or you may deem it simply direct and frank. You might feel that it would so irritate some readers that they would close their minds to Kaus's proposal, or you might believe that tough talk can cut through formal reserve and let readers know where the writer stands. It is worth noting that Kaus explicitly credits Bowman for raising an important issue and concludes his proposal by acknowledging that "her argument will be hard to dismiss." This fairness in assessing Bowman's contribution pulls his argument back from the brink of dismissiveness and nastiness. Political discourse can be much harsher nowadays, as you probably know.

Whatever you may think of Kaus's tone, you should know that it is one of a wide range of tones adopted today by respected writers on public policy. Frankel uses a quite different tone in his proposal to make E-mail universal. Except for his backhanded compliment to House of Representatives Speaker Newt Gingrich—he reminds readers that Gingrich referred to his own idea about computers for the poor as "nutty"—Frankel's tone is sunny and inviting, compared to Kaus's; yet there can be no doubt about each writer's commitment to solving social problems. The tone you adopt in your own proposal will depend on how you want to present yourself in writing to your readers and also on the nature of the problem and its history. Sometimes it seems appropriate to express exasperation. Whenever a proposal writer grates on readers' feelings, however, there is the danger that some will become alienated and refuse to participate in solving the problem.

Adam Paul Weisman wrote this article in 1987 for *The New Republic,* a national news and opinion magazine. It proposes a solution to the problem of teenage pregnancy. As you read, ask yourself how Weisman's admission that his solution is not original—that it has already been tried—affects your reaction to it.

BIRTH CONTROL IN THE SCHOOLS

Adam Paul Weisman

1 Should contraceptives be distributed to teenagers in public schools? A research panel of the National Academy of Sciences spent two years studying adolescent pregnancy in America, and decided they should. Its 1986 report, *Risking the Future,* prompted a new wave of angry debate about how to reduce the high rate of teenage pregnancy in the United States.

2 No one disputes the severity of the problem. Teen pregnancy ruins young lives and perpetuates a tragic cycle of poverty. According to the Alan Guttmacher Institute, the rate of pregnancy among American women aged 15 to 19 was almost ten percent in 1981. That far outstrips the next closest industrialized nation, England, where the rate is less than 5 percent. Guttmacher estimates that more than 80 percent of teenage pregnancies in the United States are unintended and unwanted. Every year about four in 100 women aged 15 to 19 have an abortion. But those looking for ways to reduce these statistics have divided into two distinct camps: one favoring contraception, the other, sexual abstinence.

3 The contraception advocates point out that a majority of teenagers have already rejected abstinence. In 1986, 57 percent of 17-year-olds [said] they have had sex. This camp believes that schools, as a central location in young people's lives, are a good place to make contraceptives available. Three recent studies (by the National Academy of Sciences, the Guttmacher Institute, and the Children's Defense Fund) have taken this view, while also calling for programs geared toward postponing adolescent sexual involvement and including parents in school sex education classes.

4 The abstinence advocates believe the answer lies in inculcating values based on a clear understanding that sex is simply wrong for teenagers. They say that moral lessons are best taught by parents in the home, but that schools should continue the job by teaching a chaste morality. Secretary of Education William Bennett[1] has been the most outspoken proponent of this view. Exposing students to "mechanical" means of pregnancy prevention, he says, encourages "children who do not have sexual intimacy on their minds to . . . be mindful of it."

5 Bennett concedes that "birth control clinics in schools may prevent some births." And indeed, whatever the drawbacks, the contraception advocates have one strong advantage in this debate: their approach works. The only rigorous study of a pregnancy prevention program for urban teenagers was conducted in Baltimore from 1982 to 1983 by researchers from Johns Hopkins Medical School. The Hopkins-run birth-control clinic, located across the street from one school and nearby another, reduced the pregnancy rate in the schools it served by 30 percent while pregnancy rates in control schools soared 58 percent.

6 "Why did this program work?" asks Dr. Laurie Zabin, the program's director, in her report on the experiment. "Access to high-quality, free services was probably crucial to its success. Professional counseling, education, and open communications were, no doubt, also important. All these factors appear to have created an atmosphere that allowed teenagers to translate their attitude into constructive preventive behavior." And what of those students who were virgins? According to Zabin, that group of girls (not very large) delayed initiation of sexual activity an average of seven months longer than those in the control groups, strong evidence that awareness of contraception is not directly linked to promiscuity.

[1] William Bennett was secretary of education during the Reagan administration.

But the existing school-based clinics that distribute or arrange for birth control are not just rooms plastered with Planned Parenthood posters where contraceptives are handed out. They are full-service health clinics that came into existence to provide young people with comprehensive health care. Public health officials, including many who have doubts about distributing contraceptives in schools, agree that in many places, particularly the inner city, health care for adolescents is inadequate. The school-based clinic, like the school lunch program, seeks to make all students healthy enough to get the most out of education. 7

This is not to say that school-based clinics don't do a lot in the way of contraception. According to Douglas Kirby, director of research for the Center for Population Options, a group that advocates and monitors school-based clinics, 15 percent to 20 percent of visits to clinics are for family planning. The majority are for general health care. Twenty-eight percent of the clinics actually dispense contraceptives or other prescription drugs. About half of the clinics write prescriptions that are filled off-campus; the rest diagnose and counsel teens before making referrals to outside health agencies. 8

The clinics also seem to help reduce unintended pregnancies. In St. Paul 33 percent of girls made use of the clinic's contraceptive services, and birth rates dropped by 50 percent. Thanks to the clinic's counseling, four out of five of the girls who did have children stayed in school, and only 1.4 percent of them had another pregnancy before graduation. Nationally, about 17 percent of teenage mothers become pregnant again within a year. 9

Bennett argues that distributing birth control is "not what school is for," and that doing so represents "an abdication of moral authority." Many educators have similar concerns. They fear that communities and government are trying to dump another social problem—like drug counseling and AIDS education—on the schools when they could better be handled in the home. Diane Ravitch, an adjunct professor of history and education at Teachers College in New York, says, "Schools are increasingly being pushed to be social service centers, and they don't do that well." 10

Yet clearly schools do more than teach students the three R's. Schools are where many teenagers learn to drive, weld, and cook. And numerous surveys reveal that over 80 percent of parents think it is a proper place for their children to learn about sex. Dr. Stephen Joseph, health commissioner for New York City, explains that if it weren't for the involvement of schools, the United States never could have achieved 100 percent immunization rates, a worthy goal that "wasn't perceived as the role of the school either at that time." 11

If the pressing health crisis were non-sexual in nature—tuberculosis, for example—it's hard to believe that educators such as Bennett wouldn't be the first to volunteer schools as a locus for a solution. And of course, if the problem of teen pregnancy is one that the schools shouldn't be expected to deal with, that would exclude any program of anti-sex indoctrination as well as the distribution of contraceptives. Putting such indoctrination into the curriculum is, arguably, more intrusive on the schools' basic function than the existence of a birth control or general health clinic. Bennett's speeches rule out the very real possibility that schools could prosecute a moral agenda and *also* support a clinic. 12

Despite the success of Zabin's off-campus model, there is a good reason school-based clinics receive such wide support in the health services community: teenagers are notoriously lazy. As Cheryl Hayes, director of the NAS study, explains, "If teenagers have to wait in the rain for a bus to take them to a clinic, there is a good chance they will never make it to the clinic." If the goal is providing health care and family plan- 13 ning services to teenagers, it is unlikely that anything will work as well as locating those services where most teenagers are: at school.

Of course the real question that excites people isn't whether teenagers should get birth control at school, but whether they should get it at all. There is no hard evidence linking exposure to contraception with promiscuity, and it is unlikely any teenager who watches prime-time television is less than "mindful" (as Bennett puts it) of sexual intimacy. Although Bennett has dismissed the recommendations of *Risking the Future* as "stupid," the opponents of making contraception available to teenagers have yet to offer an effective alternative. As for the "parental authority" that birth control availability is said to undermine, a 1986 Planned Parenthood survey of 1,000 teenagers revealed that 31 percent of parents discuss neither sex nor birth control with their children. The failure of parental authority is manifest in the almost 900,000 unintended teenage pregnancies in 1983. *Risking the Future* only makes that failure painfully clear. 1

Connecting to Culture and Experience

Weisman points out that school-based clinics exist primarily to provide full-service health care. Some clinics also provide information about birth control and dispense contraceptives or prescriptions for drugs. In addition, some schools offer sex education classes. Dispensing contraceptives and, to a lesser extent, giving out information about birth control and offering sex education classes continue to be controversial policies.

With two or three other students, discuss whether school-based health clinics should be permitted to distribute birth-control information and contraceptives. Begin by telling each other briefly whether your high school offered sex education classes and provided a health clinic. Summarize the major topics of the sex education curriculum and the services offered by the clinic at your school. Were your schools much alike, or were they different?

Then exchange views about whether you think it is appropriate for school-based clinics to give out birth-control information or contraceptives, whether or not your school had such a clinic. Do you think it is appropriate for schools to provide these services? If your school had a clinic, was it controversial? What are the advantages or dangers of schools' ensuring that all students have access to information about birth control and contraception? What are the advantages or dangers of distributing contraceptives?

Analyzing Writing Strategies

For more on anticipating readers' concerns, see pp. 537–42.

1. How does Weisman set the stage for his argument in the title and the first two paragraphs? What advantages or disadvantages do you see in his opening? Compare Weisman's title and two opening paragraphs to the title and the four opening paragraphs in Frankel's proposal and to the title and the three opening paragraphs in Kaus's essay. What can you conclude about strategies for **titling and opening** essays that propose solutions to problems?
2. Consider how Weisman presents the advantages of his solution to increase its appeal to supporters of the abstinence solution. Keep in mind that his primary audiences are educational policymakers and parents of high school students.

Focus on paragraphs 7–13. Underline details, statements, and ideas that reveal Weisman's understanding of the abstinence solution and his attempt to **find common values** or common ground with its advocates. For example, at the beginning of paragraph 7, he reminds readers that school-based health clinics were founded to give students access to adequate health care. What other common values and concerns does Weisman call on? Where is he most successful in identifying common values? Where is he least successful?

Considering Topics for Your Own Essay

Teenagers are part of the problem in this proposal, but they can also be part of the solution to social problems. For example, high school students can refurbish playgrounds and parks or teach illiterate adults to read. Think of a problem that teenagers might be able to help to solve. If you were to propose a solution to this problem, how would you explain the problem? How would you go about convincing teenagers that they should participate?

Commentary

Weisman's essay illustrates a strategy that is often important in proposals: **acknowledging an alternative solution,** evaluating that alternative, and then refuting it.

After establishing the problem, Weisman introduces the two solutions that have been proposed: encouraging teenagers to abstain from sexual activity and providing them with birth-control information. To demonstrate his fairness, Weisman presents the abstinence solution objectively, even sympathetically. He accepts the legitimacy of this proposed solution and objects only on the grounds that it does not work.

The fact that Weisman's proposed solution does appear to be more effective is the cornerstone of his argument. He uses Secretary Bennett's own words to argue that the contraception solution works in at least some cases, then cites the Johns Hopkins study as the centerpiece of his argument. Furthermore, by noting that birth-control counseling "delayed initiation of sexual activity" for some of the teenagers, he makes a forceful appeal to those in favor of abstinence.

Not only does Weisman support his solution with reasons and evidence, but he also **anticipates and refutes a major objection** to it. This objection, that schools should not be used to solve social and moral problems, he refutes in two ways. First, he reasons that the problem of teenage pregnancy is a health crisis and that there is ample precedent for dealing with such problems through the schools. This argument appeals to humanitarian concerns but is unlikely to convince people who consider teenage pregnancy a moral issue. To those readers, he offers a second argument: If birth-control information is excluded from the schools, then "any program of anti-sex indoctrination" must also be excluded. In other words, the argument against school-based birth-control clinics could also be made against teaching sexual abstinence. Both are forms of sex education.

Weisman's **argumentative strategy** is to show that he understands and respects the values of those who advocate an alternative solution and that he shares their desire to remedy the problem. He appeals to them on practical grounds, arguing that his solution will get the job done.

Patrick O'Malley wrote the following proposal while he was a first-year college student. He proposes that college professors give students frequent brief examinations in addition to the usual midterm and final exams. After discussing with his instructor his unusual rhetorical situation—a student advising professors—he decided to revise the essay into the form of an open letter to professors on his campus, a letter that might appear in the campus newspaper.

O'Malley's essay may strike you as unusually authoritative. This air of authority is due in large part to what O'Malley learned about the possibilities and problems of frequent exams as he interviewed two professors (his writing instructor and the writing program director) and talked with several students. As you read, notice particularly how he anticipates professors' likely objections to his proposals and their preferred solutions to the problem he identifies.

MORE TESTING, MORE LEARNING

Patrick O'Malley

It's late at night. The final's tomorrow. You got a *C* on the midterm, so this one will make or break you. Will it be like the midterm? Did you study enough? Did you study the right things? It's too late to drop the course. So what happens if you fail? No time to worry about that now—you've got a ton of notes to go over. 1

Although this last-minute anxiety about midterm and final exams is only too familiar to most college students, many professors may not realize how such major, infrequent, high-stakes exams work against the best interests of students both psychologically and intellectually. They cause unnecessary amounts of stress, placing too much importance on one or two days in the students' entire term, judging ability on a single or dual performance. They don't encourage frequent study, and they fail to inspire students' best performance. If professors gave additional brief exams at frequent intervals, students would be spurred to study more regularly, learn more, worry less, and perform better on midterms, finals, and other papers and projects. 2

Ideally, a professor would give an in-class test or quiz after each unit, chapter, or focus of study, depending on the type of class and course material. A physics class might require a test on concepts after every chapter covered, while a history class could necessitate quizzes covering certain time periods or major events. These exams should be given weekly, or at least twice monthly. Whenever possible, they should consist of two or three essay questions rather than many multiple-choice or short-answer questions. To preserve class time for lecture and discussion, exams should take no more than 15 or 20 minutes. 3

The main reason why professors should give frequent exams is that when they do, and when they provide feedback to students on how well they are doing, students learn more in the course and perform better on major exams, projects, and papers. It makes sense that in a challenging course containing a great deal of material, students will learn more of it and put it to better use if they have to apply or "practice" it frequently on exams, which also helps them find out how much they are learning and what they need to go over again. A recent Harvard study notes students' "strong preference for frequent evaluation in a course." Harvard students feel they learn least in courses that have "only a midterm and a final exam, with no other personal evaluation." They believe they learn most in courses with "many opportunities to see how they are doing" (Light, 1990, p. 32). In a review of a number of studies of student learning, Frederiksen (1984) reports that students who take weekly quizzes achieve higher scores on final 4 exams than students who take only a midterm exam and that testing increases retention of material tested.

5 Another, closely related argument in favor of multiple exams is that they encourage students to improve their study habits. Greater frequency in test taking means greater frequency in studying for tests. Students prone to cramming will be required—or at least strongly motivated—to open their textbooks and notebooks more often, making them less likely to resort to long, kamikaze nights of studying for major exams. Since there is so much to be learned in the typical course, it makes sense that frequent, careful study and review are highly beneficial. But students need motivation to study regularly, and nothing works like an exam. If students had frequent exams in all their courses, they would have to schedule study time each week and gradually would develop a habit of frequent study. It might be argued that students are adults who have to learn how to manage their own lives, but learning history or physics is more complicated than learning to drive a car or balance a checkbook. Students need coaching and practice in learning. The right way to learn new material needs to become a habit, and I believe that frequent exams are key to developing good habits of study and learning. The Harvard study concludes that "tying regular evaluation to good course organization enables students to plan their work more than a few days in advance. If quizzes and homework are scheduled on specific days, students plan their work to capitalize on them" (Light, 1990, p. 33).

6 By encouraging regular study habits, frequent exams would also decrease anxiety by reducing the procrastination that produces anxiety. Students would benefit psychologically if they were not subjected to the emotional ups and downs caused by major exams, when after being virtually worry-free for weeks they are suddenly ready to check into the psychiatric ward. Researchers at the University of Vermont found a strong relationship between procrastination, anxiety, and achievement. Students who regularly put off studying for exams had continuing high anxiety and lower grades than students who procrastinated less. The researchers found that even "low" procrastinators did not study regularly and recommended that professors give frequent assignments and exams to reduce procrastination and increase achievement (Rothblum, Solomon, & Murakami, 1986, pp. 393, 394).

7 Research supports my proposed solution to the problems I have described. Common sense as well as my experience and that of many of my friends support it. Why, then, do so few professors give frequent brief exams? Some believe that such exams take up too much of the limited class time available to cover the material in the course. Most courses meet 150 minutes a week—three times a week for 50 minutes each time. A 20-minute weekly exam might take 30 minutes to administer, and that is one-fifth of each week's class time. From the student's perspective, however, this time is well spent. Better learning and greater confidence about the course seem a good trade-off for another 30 minutes of lecture. Moreover, time lost to lecturing or discussion could easily be made up in students' learning on their own through careful regular study for the weekly exams. If weekly exams still seem too time-consuming to some professors, their frequency could be reduced to every other week or their length to 5 or 10 minutes. In courses where multiple-choice exams are appropriate, several questions take only a few minutes to answer.

8 Another objection professors have to frequent exams is that they take too much time to read and grade. In a 20-minute essay exam a well-prepared student can easily write two pages. A relatively small class of 30 students might then produce 60

pages, no small amount of material to read each week. A large class of 100 or more students would produce an insurmountable pile of material. There are a number of responses to this objection. Again, professors could give exams every other week or make them very short. Instead of reading them closely they could skim them quickly to see whether students understand an idea or can apply it to an unfamiliar problem; and instead of numerical or letter grades they could give a plus, check, or minus. Exams could be collected and responded to only every third or fourth week. Professors who have readers or teaching assistants could rely on them to grade or check exams. And the Scantron machine is always available for instant grading of multiple-choice exams. Finally, frequent exams could be given *in place of* a midterm exam or out-of-class essay assignment.

9 Since frequent exams seem to some professors to create too many problems, however, it is reasonable to consider alternative ways to achieve the same goals. One alternative solution is to implement a program that would improve study skills. While such a program might teach students how to study for exams, it cannot prevent procrastination or reduce "large test anxiety" by a substantial amount. One research team studying anxiety and test performance found that study skills training was "not effective in reducing anxiety or improving performance" (Dendato & Diener, 1986, p. 134). This team, which also reviewed other research that reached the same conclusion, did find that a combination of "cognitive/relaxation therapy" and study skills training was effective. This possible solution seems complicated, however, not to mention time-consuming and expensive. It seems much easier and more effective to change the cause of the bad habit rather than treat the habit itself. That is, it would make more sense to solve the problem at its root: the method of learning and evaluation.

10 Still another solution might be to provide frequent study questions for students to answer. These would no doubt be helpful in focusing students' time studying, but students would probably not actually write out the answers unless they were required to. To get students to complete the questions in a timely way, professors would have to collect and check the answers. In that case, however, they might as well devote the time to grading an exam. Even if it asks the same questions, a scheduled exam is preferable to a set of study questions because it takes far less time to write in class, compared to the time students would devote to responding to questions at home. In-class exams also ensure that each student produces his or her own work.

11 Another possible solution would be to help students prepare for midterm and final exams by providing sets of questions from which the exam questions will be selected or announcing possible exam topics at the beginning of the course. This solution would have the advantage of reducing students' anxiety about learning every fact in the textbook, and it would clarify the course goals, but it would not motivate students to study carefully each new unit, concept, or text chapter in the course. I see this as a way of complementing frequent exams, not as substituting for them.

12 From the evidence and from my talks with professors and students, I see frequent, brief in-class exams as the only way to improve students' study habits and learning, reduce their anxiety and procrastination, and increase their satisfaction with college. These exams are not a panacea, but only more parking spaces and a winning football team would do as much to improve college life. Professors can't do much about parking or football, but they can give more frequent exams. Campus administrators should get behind this effort, and professors should get together to consider giving exams more frequently. It would make a difference.

For information on using and acknowledging sources, see Chapter 22.

References

Dendato, K. M., & Diener, D. (1986). Effectiveness of cognitive/relaxation therapy and study-skills training in reducing self-reported anxiety and improving the academic performance of test-anxious students. *Journal of Counseling Psychology, 33,* 131–135.

Frederiksen, N. (1984). The real test bias: Influences of testing on teaching and learning. *American Psychologist, 39,* 193–202.

Light, R. J. (1990). *Explorations with students and faculty about teaching, learning, and student life.* Cambridge, MA: Harvard University Graduate School of Education and Kennedy School of Government.

Rothblum, E. D., Solomon, L., & Murakami, J. (1986). Affective, cognitive, and behavioral differences between high and low procrastinators. *Journal of Counseling Psychology, 33,* 387–394.

Connecting to Culture and Experience

O'Malley advocates frequent brief exams as a solution to the problems of midterm and final exam anxiety, poor study habits, and disappointing exam performance.

With two or three other students, discuss O'Malley's proposal in light of your own experience in your courses. Which of your high school or college courses have included frequent exams? Did they offer the benefits O'Malley claims? Did you learn more because of them? Did courses without frequent exams produce the problems he identifies?

Analyzing Writing Strategies

1. Reread paragraph 3 carefully to discover how O'Malley **defines and qualifies the solution.** Underline key words and phrases that indicate what kind of exams he advocates. For his purpose and readers, does he adequately qualify the solution? Does anything seem unnecessary? Should anything be added? Does each key term hold up usefully throughout the essay?
2. O'Malley argues directly for his proposed solution in paragraphs 4–6. Reread these paragraphs to understand his reasoning—the **reasons and support** he provides for his proposed solution. Begin by underlining the first sentence in each paragraph, where O'Malley identifies each of his three major reasons. What do you think he gains by making these statements so prominent? What clues does he give you in each statement about its relation to the others?

   Then analyze the support he provides for each reason. Notice first that he provides several sentences of support for each reason. What kinds of support does he offer, and what are the sources of this support? For O'Malley's readers—college professors—what is likely to be most and least convincing about this support?

   For more on supporting reasons in argument, see Chapter 19.
3. Turn to the Writer at Work discussion on pp. 284–86. Compare the last paragraph in the section of O'Malley's draft with paragraph 4 in his revision, and list specific changes he made from draft to revision. Knowing his purpose and readers, what advantages do you see in his changes?

Considering Topics for Your Own Essay

Much of what happens in high school and college is predictable and conventional. Examples of conventional practices that have changed very little over the years are exams, group instruction, graduation ceremonies, required courses, and lower admission requirements for athletes. Think of additional examples of established practices in high school or college; then select one that you believe needs to be improved or refined in some way. What changes would you propose? What individual or group might be convinced to take action on your proposal for improvement? What questions or objections should you anticipate? How could you discover whether others have previously proposed improvements in the practice you are concerned with? Whom might you interview to learn more about the practice and the likelihood of changing it?

Commentary

O'Malley's essay demonstrates the importance of **taking readers seriously.** Not only did he interview both those who would carry out his proposal (professors) and those who would benefit from it (students), but he featured in his essay what he had learned in these interviews. Paragraphs 7–11 directly acknowledge professors' objections, their questions, and the alternative solutions they would probably prefer. If at all possible, it is good to interview possible readers and thus to find out their likely objections, questions, and preferred solutions.

O'Malley's **organization** is also worth noting:

Opening: a scenario to introduce the problem (paragraph 1)
Presentation of the problem and introduction of the solution (2)
Details of the solution (3)
Reason 1: improved learning and performance (4)
Reason 2: improved study habits (5)
Reason 3: decreased procrastination and anxiety (6)
Accommodation of objection 1: limited class time (7)
Accommodation of objection 2: too much work (8)
Refutation of alternative solution 1: study skills training (9)
Refutation of alternative solution 2: study questions (10)
Accommodation of alternative solution 3: sample exam questions (11)
Closing: reiteration of the proposed solution and advice on implementing it (12)

See Chapter 13 for a discussion of cues.

The essay follows an appropriate order for O'Malley's purpose and readers. It is especially easy to follow because of explicit cues given to readers: forecasts (previews of what comes next), paragraph breaks, transitions, and summaries. Most important, the plan is logical and convincing. It is not the only possible plan—the alternative solutions might have been acknowledged before O'Malley argues for his solution, for example—but it is a very effective plan. This orderly plan was developed over several days of invention, drafting, and revising.

PURPOSE AND AUDIENCE

Most proposals are calls to action. Because of this clear purpose, a writer must anticipate readers' needs and concerns more when writing a proposal than in any other kind of writing. The writer attempts not only to convince readers but also to inspire them, to persuade them to support or implement the proposed solution. What your particular readers know about the problem and what they are capable of doing to solve it determine how you address them.

Readers of proposals are often unaware of the problem. In this case, your task is clear: to present them with facts that will convince them of its existence. These facts may include statistics, testimony from witnesses or experts, and examples, including the personal experiences of people involved with the problem. You can also speculate about the cause of the problem and describe its ill effects.

Sometimes readers recognize the existence of a problem but fail to take it seriously. When readers are indifferent, you may need to connect the problem closely to their own concerns. For instance, you might show how much they have in common with the people directly affected by it or how it affects them indirectly. However you appeal to readers, you must do more than alert them to the problem; you must also make them care about it. You want to touch readers emotionally as well as intellectually.

At other times, readers concerned about the problem may assume that someone else is taking care of it and that they need not become personally involved. In this situation, you might want to demonstrate that the people they thought were taking care of the problem have failed. Another assumption readers might make is that a solution they supported in the past has already solved the problem. You might point out that the original solution has proved unworkable or that new solutions have become available through changed circumstances or improved technology. Your aim is to rekindle these readers' interest in the problem.

Perhaps the most satisfying proposals are addressed to parties who can take immediate action to remedy the problem. Your chances of writing such a proposal are good if you choose a problem faced by a group to which you belong. Not only do you have a firsthand understanding of the problem but you also have a good idea what solution other members of the group will support. (You might informally survey some of them before you submit your proposal in order to test your definition of the problem and your proposed solution.) When you address readers who are in a position to take action, you obviously want to assure them that it is wise to do so. You must demonstrate that the solution is feasible—that it can be implemented and that it will work.

SUMMARY OF BASIC FEATURES

A Well-Defined Problem

A proposal is written to offer a solution to a problem. Before presenting the solution, the writer must be sure that readers know what the problem is. Patrick O'Malley, for example, spends his first three paragraphs defining the problem. It is wise to state the problem explicitly, as all the writers in this chapter do. For example, Max Frankel demonstrates that few Americans have access to E-mail, and Adam Paul Weisman identifies the problem directly as teenage pregnancy.

Stating the problem is not enough, however; the writer also must establish the problem as serious enough to need solving. Sometimes a writer can assume that readers will recognize the problem. For example, Weisman can assume that readers are aware of the high rate of teenage pregnancy and acknowledge its seriousness, even if they disagree about a solution. At other times, readers may not be aware of the problem and will need to be convinced that it deserves their attention. O'Malley, for example, explicitly says that many professors do not realize the harmful effects of infrequent exams.

In addition to stating the problem and establishing its seriousness, a proposal writer may have to analyze the problem, exploring its causes, consequences, history, and past efforts at dealing with it.

A Proposed Solution

For more on thesis statements, see pp. 526–29.

Once the problem is established, the writer must present and argue for a particular solution. Announcing the solution is the thesis of the proposal. O'Malley states his thesis thus: "If professors gave additional brief exams at frequent intervals, students would be spurred to study more regularly, learn more, worry less, and perform better."

A Convincing Argument

The main purpose of a proposal is to convince readers that the writer's solution is the best way of solving the problem. Proposal writers argue for their solutions by trying to demonstrate all of the following:

- The proposed solution will solve the problem.
- It is a feasible way of solving the problem and can be easily implemented.
- It stands up against anticipated objections or reservations.
- It is better than alternative solutions.

Arguing That the Proposed Solution Will Solve the Problem. A writer must give reasons and support to show that the proposed solution will solve the problem. To this end, Weisman cites the Johns Hopkins study as evidence that the program he proposes will work, and Frankel, proposing intervention by the federal government to ensure access for all to E-mail, offers the analogy that such intervention was required to ensure that telephones and postal mail became available to all Americans.

Arguing That the Proposed Solution Is Feasible. In arguing that the proposal is feasible, the writer must demonstrate how it can be implemented. The easier it seems to implement, the more likely it is to win readers' support. Therefore, writers generally set out the steps required to put the proposal into practice, an especially important strategy when the solution might seem difficult, time-consuming, or expensive to enact. All the writers in this chapter except Kaus offer specific suggestions for implementing their proposals. For example, O'Malley offers professors several specific ways to give their students frequent, brief exams.

For illustrations of other ways to anticipate readers' reservations and objections, see pp. 537–42.

Anticipating Reservations and Objections. A writer who is arguing for a proposal must anticipate objections or reservations that readers may have about the proposed solution. Weisman anticipates the objection that schools should not be used as "social service centers." He attempts to refute it by arguing that schools have provided health-related services in the past and that if birth-control information is banned from the schools, teaching sexual abstinence should also be banned.

Considering and Rejecting Alternative Solutions. Finally, the writer has to convince readers that the proposed solution is preferable to other possible solutions. To do so, the writer examines the other possibilities and demonstrates what is wrong with them. Weisman considers the proposal that teenagers be encouraged to abstain from sexual activity. O'Malley considers study skills training, study questions, and sample exam questions as alternatives to frequent exams.

The best way to reject an alternative solution is simply to demonstrate that it does not work, as Weisman tries to do. Another way is to show that the alternative solves only part of the problem. O'Malley uses this strategy in rejecting the idea of sample exam questions.

A Reasonable Tone

Regardless of the proposal or the argument made on its behalf, proposal writers must adopt a reasonable tone. Their objective is to *advance* an argument without *having* an argument. That is, writers should avoid taking an adversarial or quarrelsome stance with their readers. The aim is to bridge any gap that may exist between writer and readers, not to widen it.

Writers can build such a bridge of shared values and concerns by showing respect for their readers and treating their concerns seriously. Writers discuss anticipated objections and reservations as an attempt to lay to rest any doubts readers may have. They consider alternative solutions as a way of showing that they have explored every possibility in order to find the best possible solution.

Most important, they do not attack those raising objections or offering other solutions by questioning their intelligence or goodwill. Frankel, Weisman, and O'Malley go out of their way to show respect for those who might question their proposed solutions or who advocate competing solutions. In contrast, while Kaus acknowledges that legal scholar Bowman has identified a serious problem in men's street hassling of women, he refers to her article as "annoying" and accuses her of "foolishness." Yet ultimately, his own solution incorporates elements of her proposal to make street harassment illegal rather than "protected" speech.

GUIDE TO WRITING

THE WRITING ASSIGNMENT

Write an essay proposing a solution to a problem. Choose a problem faced by a community or group to which you belong, and address your proposal to one or more members of the group or to an outsider who might help to solve the problem.

INVENTION AND RESEARCH

As you prepare to write a proposal, you will have to choose a problem you can write about, analyze and define the problem, identify your prospective readers, find a tentative solution, defend your solution, test your choice, offer reasons for adopting your proposal, and consider alternative solutions.

Choosing a Problem

You may already have thought of one possible problem you could write about. Even so, you will want to think about various problems before settling on a topic. The following exercise is a good way to get started.

Set a timer for ten minutes, and brainstorm your lists. If you can work on separate windows, head one "College," the next one "Neighborhood," and so on. Then save them as an invention file and print out a copy to make notes on.

Considering Problems in Various Communities. Divide a piece of paper into two columns. In the left-hand column, list all communities, groups, or organizations to which you belong. Include as many communities as possible: college, neighborhood, hometown, cultural or ethnic groups. Also include groups you participate in: sports, musical, work, religious, political, support, hobby, and so on. In the right-hand column, list any problems that exist within each group. Here is how such a chart might begin:

Community	*Problem*
My college	Poor advising or orientation
	Shortage of practice rooms in music building
	No financial aid for part-time students
	Lack of facilities for handicapped students
	Lack of enough sections of required courses
	Classes scheduled so that working students or students with children find it difficult to take courses
My neighborhood	Need for traffic light at dangerous intersection
	Unsupervised children getting into trouble
	"Megastores" driving away small businesses
	Lack of safe places for children to play

Listing Problems concerning Identity and Community Writing a proposal can give you special insight into the topic of "identity and community" by helping you to understand how members of a community negotiate their individual needs and concerns. You may already have made a chart of communities to which you belong and problems in those communities. The following categories may help you to think of additional problems in those or other communities that you could add to your list:

- Disagreement over conforming to community standards
- Conflicting economic, cultural, or political interests within the community
- Problems with equity or fairness between men and women, rich and poor, different ethnic groups
- Lack of respect or trust among the members of the community
- Struggles for leadership of the community

Listing Problems concerning Work and Career Proposals are frequently written on the job. Based on your work experience, make a chart listing the workplace in the left column and problems you have encountered there in the right column, like this one:

Workplace	*Problem*
Restaurant	Inadequate training
	Conflicts with supervisor
	Unfair shift assignments
Department store	Inadequate inventory
	Computer glitches
	Overcomplicated procedures
Office	Unfair workloads
	Changing requirements
	Inflexible work schedules
	Lack of information about procedures
	Difficulty in scheduling vacations
	Outdated technology

Choose one problem from your list that you consider especially important. It should be one that seems solvable (though you need not know the exact solution now) and that concerns others in the group or community. It should also be a problem that you can explore in detail and are willing to discuss in writing.

Proposing to solve a problem in a group or community to which you belong gives you an inestimably important advantage: You can write as an expert, an insider. You know about the history of the problem, have felt the urgency to solve it, and perhaps have already thought of possible solutions. Equally important, you will know precisely to whom to address the proposal, and you can interview others in the group to get their views of the problem and to understand how they might resist your solution. From such a position of knowledge and authority comes confident, convincing writing.

Should you want to propose a solution for a social problem of national scope, concentrate on one with which you have direct experience and for which you can suggest a detailed plan of action. Even better, focus on unique local aspects of the problem. For example, if you would like to propose a solution to the lack of affordable child care for children of college students or working parents, you have a great advantage if you are a parent who has experienced the frustration of finding professional, affordable child care. Moreover, it may well be that even though such a problem is national in scope, it can *only* be solved campus by campus, business by business, or neighborhood by neighborhood.

Analyzing and Defining the Problem

Before you can begin to consider solutions, you must analyze the problem carefully and then try to define it. Keep in mind that you will have to demonstrate to readers that the problem is serious and that you have a more than casual understanding of its causes and consequences. If you find that you cannot do so, you will want to select some other problem to write about.

If you can, save these responses as a computer file. Later, as you begin to draft, you can call up the file on a second window and easily transfer details you want to use in your draft.

Analyzing. *Start by writing a few sentences in response to these questions:*

- Does the problem really exist? How can I tell?
- What caused this problem? Can I identify any immediate causes? Any deeper causes? Is the problem caused by a flaw in the system, a lack of resources, individual misconduct or incompetence? How can I tell?
- What is the history of the problem?
- What are the bad effects of the problem? How is it hurting members of the community or group? What goals of the group are endangered by the existence of this problem? Does it raise any moral or ethical questions?
- Who in the community or group is affected by the problem? Be as specific as possible: Who is seriously affected? Minimally affected? Unaffected? Does anyone benefit from its existence?
- What similar problems exist in this same community or group? How can I distinguish my problem from these?

Defining. *Write a definition of the problem, being as specific as possible.* Identify who or what seems responsible for it, and give one recent example.

Identifying Your Readers

In a few sentences, describe your readers, stating your reason for directing your proposal to them. Then take ten minutes to write about these readers. Whom do you wish to address—everyone in the community or group, a committee, an individual, an outsider? You want to address the person or group who can implement the solution you propose. The following questions will help you to develop a profile of your readers.

- How informed are my readers likely to be about the problem? Have they shown any awareness of it?

- Why would this problem be important to them? Why would they care about solving it?
- Have they supported any other proposals to solve the problem? If so, what do their proposals have in common with mine?
- Do they ally themselves with any group, and would that alliance cause them to favor or reject my proposal? Do we share any values or attitudes that could bring us together to solve the problem?
- How have they responded to other problems? Do their past reactions suggest anything about how they might respond to my proposal?

Finding a Tentative Solution

Solving problems takes time. Apparent solutions often turn out to be impossible. After all, a solution has to be both workable and acceptable to the community or group involved. Consequently, you should strive to come up with several possible solutions whose advantages and disadvantages you can weigh. You may have noticed that the most imaginative solutions sometimes occur to you only after you have struggled with a number of other possibilities.

Look back at the way you defined the problem and described your readers. Then, with these factors in mind, list as many possible solutions as you can think of. For ideas, reflect on the following problem-solving questions:

Using a word processor, you might create a separate file for solutions or add them to your definition file.

- What solutions to this problem have already been tried?
- What solutions have been proposed for related problems? Might they solve this problem as well?
- Is a solution required that would disband or change the community or group in some way?
- What solution might eliminate some of the causes of the problem?
- What solution would eliminate any of the bad effects of the problem?
- Maybe the problem is too big to be solved all at once. Try dividing it into several parts. What solutions might solve these parts?
- If a series of solutions is required, which should come first? Second?
- What solution would ultimately solve the problem?
- What might be a daring solution? What would be the most conservative solution, acceptable to nearly everyone in the community or group?

Give yourself enough time to let your ideas percolate, continuing to add to your list of possible solutions and to consider the advantages and disadvantages of each one in light of your prospective readers. If possible, discuss your solutions with members of the community or group who can help you consider the advantages and disadvantages of each one.

Choosing the Most Promising Solution. *In a sentence or two, state what you would consider the best possible way of solving the problem.*

Determining Specific Steps. *Write down the steps necessary to carry out your solution.* This list will provide an early test of whether your solution can, in fact, be implemented.

Defending Your Solution

Proposals have to be feasible—that is, they must be both reasonable and practical. Imagine that one of your readers opposes your proposed solution and confronts you with the following statements. *Write several sentences refuting each one.*

- It won't really solve the problem.
- I'm comfortable with things as they are.
- We can't afford it.
- It will take too long.
- People won't do it.
- Too few people will benefit.
- I don't even see how to get started on your solution.
- It's already been tried, with unsatisfactory results.
- You're making this proposal because it will benefit you personally.

Answering these questions should help you to prepare responses to possible objections. If you feel that you need a better idea of how others are likely to feel about your proposal, talk to a few people involved with the problem. The more you know about your readers' concerns, the better you will be able to anticipate their reservations and preferred alternative solutions.

Testing Your Choice

Now examine the problem and your chosen solution to see whether they will result in a strong proposal. Start by asking the following questions:

- Is this a significant problem? Do other people in the community or group really care about it, or can they be persuaded to care?
- Will my solution really solve the problem? Can it be implemented?
- Can I answer objections from enough people in the community or group to win support for my solution?

As you plan and draft your proposal, you will probably want to consider these questions again. If at any point you decide that you cannot answer them with a confident yes, you may want to find another solution or even to write about some other problem.

Testing Your Choice: A Collaborative Activity

Get together with two or three other students and describe your chosen topics to one another. Assess their awareness of the problem, and "try out" your solution on them.

Presenters: Each of you take turns explaining your topic and readers, defining the problem briefly, and outlining your solution.

Listeners: Briefly tell the presenter whether you think the proposed solution seems appropriate and feasible. Suggest objections or reservations you believe readers may have. What alternative solutions might they prefer?

Offering Reasons for Your Proposal

To make a convincing case for your proposed solution, you must offer your readers good reasons for adopting your proposal.

You might create a separate computer file for reasons or add them to an earlier file.

Listing Reasons. *Write down every plausible reason you could give that might persuade readers to accept your proposal.* These reasons should answer your readers' key question: "Why is this the best solution?"

Choosing the Strongest Reasons. *Keeping your readers in mind, look over your list, and put an asterisk next to the strongest reasons.* If you do not consider at least two or three of your reasons strong, you will probably have difficulty developing a strong proposal and should reconsider your topic.

Developing Your Strongest Reasons. *Now look at your strongest reasons and explain briefly why you think each one will be effective with your particular readers. Then write about each reason for around five minutes, developing your argument for it.*

Considering Alternative Solutions

List alternative solutions that might be offered, and consider the advantages and disadvantages of each one relative to your solution. Even if your readers are likely to consider your proposal reasonable, they will probably want to compare your proposed solution with other possible solutions. You might find it helpful to chart the information as follows:

Using a word processor, you might call up your previous solutions file and add advantages and disadvantages for each.

Possible Solutions	*Advantages*	*Disadvantages*
My solution		
Alternative solution 1		
Alternative solution 2		

Doing Research

For guidelines on library and Internet research, see Chapter 21.

So far you have relied largely on your own knowledge and instincts for ideas about solving the problem. You may now feel that you need to do some research to learn more about the causes of the problem and to find more technical information about implementing the solution.

If you are proposing a solution to a problem about which others have written, you will want to find out how they have defined it and what solutions they have proposed. You may need to acknowledge these solutions in your essay, either accommodating or refuting them. Now is a good time—before beginning to draft—to get any additional information you need. If you are proposing a solution to a local problem, you will want to talk to some of those who may be aware of the problem. Informally interview several people. Find out whether they are aware of the problem or know anything about its history and current ill effects. Try out your solution on them. Discover whether they have other solutions in mind.

Try keeping computer files for your research notes. Keep one file of all sources that you consult. Organize your other research files in whatever way makes sense to you.

PLANNING AND DRAFTING

To help you to plan your essay and to begin drafting, review what you have done so far, set some specific goals for yourself, and prepare an outline.

Seeing What You Have

Print out a hard copy of what you have written on a word processor for easier reviewing.

Reread your invention notes, asking yourself whether you have a good topic—an interesting problem with a feasible solution. If at this point you doubt the significance of the problem or question the success of your proposed solution, you might want to look for a new topic. If you are unsure about these basic points, you cannot expect to produce a persuasive draft.

If your invention material seems thin but promising, however, you may be able to strengthen it with additional invention writing. Consider the following questions:

- Could I make a stronger case for the seriousness of the problem?
- Could I find more reasons for readers to support my solution?
- Are there any other ways of refuting attractive alternative solutions or troubling questions about my own proposed solution?

Setting Goals

Before beginning to draft, think seriously about the overall goals of your proposal. Not only will the draft be easier to write once you have clear goals, but it will almost surely be more convincing as well.

Following are some goal-setting questions to consider now. You may find it useful to return to them while drafting, for they are designed to help you to focus on exactly what you want to accomplish with this proposal.

Your Readers

- What do my readers already know about this problem?
- Are they likely to welcome my solution or resist it?
- Can I anticipate any specific reservations or objections they may have?
- How can I gain readers' enthusiastic support? How can I get them to want to implement the solution?
- What kind of tone would be most appropriate? How can I present myself so that I seem both reasonable and authoritative?

The Beginning

- How can I immediately engage my readers' interest? Should I open with a dramatic scenario, like O'Malley? With statistics that highlight the seriousness of the problem? By quoting an authority on the problem, like Kaus? With a question, like Weisman? With a historical reference, like Frankel?
- What information should I give first?

Defining the Problem

- How much do I need to say about the problem's causes or history?
- How can I show the seriousness of the problem? Should I use statistics, like Weisman? Stress negative consequences, like O'Malley?
- Is it an urgent problem? How can I emphasize this? Should I redefine the problem?
- How much space should I devote to defining the problem? Only a little space, like O'Malley, or much space, like Frankel?

Proposing a Solution

- How can I present my solution so that it looks like the best way to proceed? Should I show how to implement it in stages? Focus on reasons to support it, like O'Malley?
- How can I make the solution seem easy to implement? Or should I acknowledge that the solution may be difficult to implement and argue that it will be worth the effort?

Anticipating Objections

- Should I mention every possible objection to my proposed solution? How might I choose among these objections?
- Has anyone already raised these objections? Should I name the person?
- Should I accommodate certain objections?
- What specific reasons can I give for refuting each objection? How can I support these reasons?
- How can I refute the objections without seeming to attack anyone?

Rejecting Alternative Solutions

- How many alternative solutions do I need to mention? Which ones should I discuss?
- Should I indicate where these alternatives come from? Like Kaus, should I name the people who proposed them?
- What reasons should I give for rejecting the alternative solutions? Like O'Malley, can I offer any support for my reasons?
- How can I reject these other solutions without seeming to criticize their proponents? Both Weisman and O'Malley succeed at rejecting other solutions respectfully.

The Ending

- How should I conclude? Should I end by restating the problem and summarizing the solution? By arguing that the solution is workable and might bring about cultural change, as Kaus does? By arguing that some readers' preferred solution is sure to fail, as Weisman does? By making a historical comparison, as Frankel does? Or simply by summarizing my solution and its advantages, as O'Malley does?
- Is there something special about the problem that I should remind readers of at the end?

- Should I end with an inspiring call to action, like Frankel, or with a scenario suggesting the consequences of a failure to solve the problem?
- Would a shift to humor or satire be an effective way to end?

Outlining

After setting goals for your proposal, you will be ready to make a working outline. The basic outline for a proposal is quite simple:

Outlining on a word processor makes it particularly easy to experiment with different ways of planning your essay.

The problem
The solution
The reasons for accepting the solution

This simple plan is nearly always complicated by other factors, however. In outlining your material, you must take into consideration many other details, such as whether readers already recognize the problem, how much agreement exists on the need to solve the problem, how many alternative solutions are available, how much attention must be given to the other solutions, and how many objections should be expected.

Here is a possible outline for a proposal where readers may not understand the problem fully and other solutions have been proposed:

Presentation of the problem
  Its existence
  Its seriousness
  Its causes
Consequences of failing to solve the problem
Description of the proposed solution
List of steps for implementing the solution
Discussion of reasons to support the solution
  Acknowledgment of objections
  Accommodation or refutation of objections
Consideration of alternative solutions and their disadvantages
Restatement of the proposed solution and its advantages

See p. 266 for another sample outline.

Your outline will of course reflect your own writing situation. As you develop it, think about what your readers know and feel and about your own writing goals. Once you have a working outline, you should not hesitate to change it as necessary while writing. For instance, you might find it more effective to hold back on presenting your own solution until you have dismissed other possible solutions. Or you might find a better way to order the reasons for adopting your proposal. The purpose of an outline is to identify the basic features of your proposal and to help you to organize them effectively, not to lock you in to a particular structure.

Most of the information you will need to develop each feature can be found in your invention writing and research notes. How much space you devote to each feature is determined by the topic, not the outline. Do not assume that each entry on your outline must be given one paragraph—each of the reasons for supporting the solution may require a paragraph, but you might instead present the reasons, objections, and refutations all in one paragraph.

Drafting

Call up your invention material on an alternate window as you draft on the main window. Shift back and forth to cut and paste invention material into your draft.

After reviewing your outline, start drafting the proposal. Let the outline guide you as you write, but do not hesitate to change it if you find that drafting takes you in an unexpected direction. If you get stuck while you are drafting, return to the invention activities earlier in this chapter. As you draft, keep in mind the two main goals of proposal writing: (1) to establish that a problem exists and is serious enough to require a solution and (2) to demonstrate that your proposed solution is feasible and is the best possible alternative. You might want to review the general advice on drafting on pp. 13–14.

CRITICAL READING GUIDE

Now is the time for your draft to get a good critical reading. All writers find it helpful to have someone else read and comment on their drafts. Your instructor may schedule such a reading as part of your coursework; otherwise, you can ask a classmate, friend, or family member to read it over. If your campus has a writing center, you might ask a tutor to read and comment on your draft. In this section are guidelines designed to be used by *anyone* reviewing an essay proposing a solution to a problem. (If you are unable to get someone else to review your draft, turn to the section on Revising for guidance on reading your own draft with a critical eye.)

Swap copies of your drafts with another student, either by exchanging disks or by sending the computer files over a network. Add your comments either next to the essay, if you can divide the window, or at the end of the document.

If You Are the Writer. To provide focused, helpful comments, your critical reader must know your intended audience and purpose. At the top of your draft, write out the following information:

- *Audience.* Who are your readers? How much do they know about the problem?
- *Purpose.* What do you hope will happen as a result of your proposal?

If You Are the Reader. Use the following guidelines to help you give critical comments to others on proposals to solve problems:

See pp. 268–69 to review the basic features.

1. *Read for a First Impression.* Read first to get a basic understanding of the problem and the proposed solution to it. After reading the draft, briefly write out your impressions. How convincing do you think the essay will be for its particular readers? What do you notice about the way the problem is presented and the solution argued for?

continued

continued

2. *Evaluate How Well the Problem Is Defined.* Decide whether the problem is stated clearly. Does the writer give enough information about its causes and consequences? What more might be done to establish its seriousness? Is there more that readers might need or wish to know about it?
3. *Consider How Clearly the Solution Is Presented.* Does the presentation of the solution seem immediately clear and readable? How could the presentation be strengthened? Has the writer laid out steps for implementation? If not, might readers expect or require them? Does the solution seem practical? If not, why?
4. *Assess Whether a Convincing Argument Is Advanced for the Solution.* Look at the reasons offered for advocating this solution. Are they sufficient? Which are likely to be most and least convincing to the intended readers? What kind of support does the writer provide for each reason? How believable do you think readers will find it?

   Consider the treatment of objections to the proposed solution. Which refutations seem most convincing? Which seem least convincing? Are there other objections or reservations that the writer should acknowledge?

   Are alternative solutions discussed and either accommodated or refuted? Which are the most convincing reasons given against other solutions? Which are least convincing, and why?
5. *Evaluate the Appropriateness of the Tone.* Has the writer argued forcefully for the proposal without offending readers? Has the writer sought out common ground with readers who may advocate alternative solutions? Are such solutions accommodated or rejected without a personal attack on those who propose them? Point out places where the tone seems unnecessarily sharp.
6. *Consider the Effectiveness of the Organization.* Evaluate the *overall plan* of the proposal, perhaps by outlining it briefly. Would any parts be more effective earlier or later? Look closely at the way the writer has ordered the argument for the solution—the presentation of the reasons and the accommodation or refutation of objections and alternative solutions. How might the sequence be revised to strengthen the argument? Point out any gaps in the argument.

   Is the *beginning* engaging? If not, how might it be revised to capture readers' attention? Does it adequately forecast the main ideas and the plan of the proposal? Suggest other ways the writer might begin.

   Evaluate the *ending.* Does it frame the proposal by echoing or referring to something at the beginning? If not, how might it do so? Does the ending convey a sense of urgency? Suggest a stronger way to conclude.
7. *Give the Writer Your Final Thoughts.* What is the strongest part of this proposal? What part most needs more work?

REVISING

This section will help you to identify problems in your draft and to revise and edit to solve them.

Identifying Problems

To identify problems in your draft, you need to read it objectively, analyze its basic features, and study any comments you have received from others.

Getting an Overview. Consider the draft as a whole, trying to see it objectively. It may help to do so in two steps:

Even if your essay is saved to a computer file, reread from a hard copy. Add notes to yourself and quick revisions as you read through the draft.

1. *Reread.* If at all possible, put the draft aside for a day or two before rereading it. When you reread, start by reconsidering your audience and your purpose. Then read the draft straight through, trying to see it through the eyes of your intended readers.
2. *Outline.* Make a scratch outline to get an overview of the essay's development. This outline can be sketchy—words and phrases instead of complete sentences—but it should identify the basic features as they appear.

Charting a Plan for Revision. Use a two-column chart to keep track of any problems you need to solve. In the left-hand column, list the basic features of proposals. As you analyze your draft and study any comments from others, note in the right-hand column the problems you want to solve. Here is an example:

Basic Features	*Problems to Solve*
Definition of the problem	
Presentation of the solution	
Argument for the solution	
Acknowledgment of alternative solutions	
Tone	
Organization	

Analyzing the Basic Features of Your Draft. Turn now to the questions for analyzing a draft on pp. 279–80. Using these as guidelines, identify problems in your draft. Note anything you need to solve on your revision chart.

Studying Critical Comments. Review any comments you have received from other readers, and add to your chart any points that need attention. Try not to react defensively to these comments; by letting you see how others respond to your draft, they provide valuable information about how you might improve it.

Solving the Problems

Having identified problems in your draft, you now need to find solutions and to carry them out. You have three ways of finding solutions:

Before revising, copy your original draft to a second file. Should you change your mind about material you delete while revising, it will still be available to you.

1. Review your invention notes for additional information and ideas.
2. Do further invention to answer questions your readers raised.
3. Look back at the readings in this chapter to see how other writers have solved similar problems.

The following suggestions will get you started on solving some of the problems common to writing proposals. For now, focus on solving the problems identified on your chart. Avoid tinkering with grammar and punctuation; that will come later, when you edit.

Definition of the Problem

- **Is the definition of the problem unclear?** Consider sketching out its history, including past attempts to deal with it, discussing its causes and consequences more fully, dramatizing its seriousness more vividly, or comparing it to other problems that readers may be familiar with.

Presentation of the Solution

Use your computer to analyze problems with your essay. For example, if a reader feels that the plan for implementing your solution is not adequately described, highlight it by putting it in bold type. Then consider breaking it down into steps or adding additional ones.

- **Is the description of the solution inadequate?** Try outlining the steps or phases in its implementation. Help readers see how easy the first step will be, or acknowledge the difficulty of the first step.

Argument for the Solution

- **Does the argument seem weak?** Try to think of more reasons for readers to support your proposal.
- **Does your refutation of any objection or reservation seem unconvincing?** Consider accommodating it by modifying your proposal.
- **Have you left out any likely reader objections to the solution?** Acknowledge those objections and either accommodate or refute them.
- **Have you neglected to mention alternative solutions that some readers are likely to prefer?** Do so now. Consider whether you want to accommodate or reject these alternatives. For each one, try to acknowledge its good points but argue that it is not as effective a solution as your own. You may in fact want to strengthen your own solution by incorporating into it some of the good points from alternatives.

Use your word processor's cut-and-paste or block-and-move functions to shift material around. Make sure that you revise transitions so that material fits smoothly in its new spot.

Tone

- **Does your tone seem too adversarial?** Revise to acknowledge your readers' fears, biases, and expectations.

Organization

- **Is the argument or the essay hard to follow?** Find a better sequence for the major parts. Try to put reasons why you recommend the solution in a more convincing order—leading up to the strongest one rather than putting it first, perhaps. Shift your refutation of objections or alternative solutions so that it does not interrupt the main argument. Add explicit cues to keep the reader on track: previews of what comes next, transitional phrases and sentences, brief summaries of points just made.

For more on cues, see Chapter 13.

- **Is the beginning weak?** Look for a better place to start. Would an anecdote or an example of the problem engage readers more effectively?
- **Is the ending weak?** Consider framing your proposal by mentioning something from the beginning of your essay or ending with a call for action that expresses the urgency of implementing your solution.

EDITING AND PROOFREADING

Use your word processor's spell-check function cautiously. Keep in mind that it will not find all misspellings, particularly misused homonyms (such as *there* for *their* or *they're*), typographical errors that are themselves words (such as *fro* for *for*), and many proper nouns and specialized terms. Proofread these carefully yourself. Also proofread for words that should have been deleted when you edited a sentence.

In working on your draft so far, you may have corrected some obvious errors, but matters of grammar and style have not been a priority. Now is the time to check carefully for errors in usage, punctuation, and mechanics, as well as to consider matters of style. You may find that studying your draft in separate passes—first for paragraphs, then for sentences, and finally for words—will help you to recognize problems.

Our own research has turned up several errors that are especially common in writing that proposes solutions. Here are some guidelines that can help you as you edit your draft for these errors.

Checking for Ambiguous Use of *This* and *That*. Using *this* and *that* vaguely to refer to other words or ideas can confuse readers. Because you must frequently refer to the problem and the solution in a proposal, you will often use pronouns to avoid the monotony or wordiness of repeatedly referring to them by name. Check your draft carefully for ambiguous use of *this* or *that*. Often the easiest way to edit such usage is to add a specific noun after *this* or *that*, as Patrick O'Malley did in the following example from his essay in this chapter:

> Another possible solution would be to help students prepare for midterm and final exams by providing sets of questions from which the exam questions will be selected or announcing possible exam topics at the beginning of the course. *This solution* would have the advantage of reducing students' anxiety about learning every fact in the textbook. . . .

O'Malley avoids an ambiguous *this* in the second sentence by repeating the noun *solution*. (He might just as well have used *preparation* or *action* or *approach*.)

The following sentences from proposals have been edited to avoid ambiguity:

- **Students would not resist a reasonable fee increase of about $40 a year. This ^increase would pay for the needed dormitory remodeling.**
- **Compared to other large California cities, San Diego has the weakest programs for conserving water. This ^neglect and our decreasing access to Colorado River water give us reason to worry.**
- **Compared to other proposed solutions to this problem, that ^one is clearly the most feasible.**

Checking for Sentences That Lack an Agent. A writer proposing a solution to a problem usually needs to indicate who exactly should take action to solve it. Such actors are called "agents." An agent is a person who is in a position to take action. Look at this sentence from O'Malley:

To get students to complete the questions in a timely way, *professors* would have to collect and check the answers.

In this sentence, *professors* are the agents. They have the authority to assign and collect study questions, and they would need to take this action in order for this solution to be successfully implemented. Had O'Malley instead written "the answers would have to be collected and checked," the sentence would lack an agent. Naming an agent makes his argument convincing, demonstrating to readers that O'Malley has thought through one of the key parts of any proposal: who is going to take action.

The following sentences from student proposals illustrate how you can edit agentless sentences:

Your staff should plan a survey
◆ **~~A survey could be planned~~ to find out more about students' problems in scheduling the courses they need.**

The registrar should extend
◆ **~~Extending~~ the deadline to mid-quarter. ~~would make sense.~~**

Sometimes it is appropriate to write agentless sentences, however. Study the following examples from O'Malley's essay:

These exams should be given weekly, or at least twice monthly.

Exams could be collected and responded to only every third or fourth week.

Still another solution might be to provide frequent study questions for students to answer.

Even though these sentences do not name explicit agents, they are all fine because it is clear from the larger context who will perform the action. In each case, it is obvious that the action will be carried out by a professor.

A WRITER AT WORK

STRENGTHENING THE ARGUMENT

This section focuses on student writer Patrick O'Malley's successful efforts to strengthen the argument for the proposed solution in his essay "More Testing, More Learning." Read the following three paragraphs from his draft. Then compare these with paragraphs 4–6 in his revision on pp. 262–63. As you read, take notes on the differences you observe between his draft and the revised version.

The predominant reason students perform better with multiple exams is that they improve their study habits. Greater regularity in test taking means greater regularity in studying for tests. Students prone to cramming will be forced to open their textbooks more often, keeping them away from long, "kamikaze" nights of studying. Regularity prepares them for the "real world" where you rarely take on large tasks at long intervals. Several tests also improve study habits by reducing procrastination. An article about procrastination from the Journal of Counseling Psychology reports that "students view exams as difficult, important, and anxiety provoking." These symptoms of anxiety leading to procrastination could be solved if individual test importance was lessened, reducing the stress associated with the perceived burden.

With multiple exams, this anxiety decrease will free students to perform better. Several, less important tests may appear as less of an obstacle, allowing the students to worry less, leaving them free to concentrate on their work without any emotional hindrances. It is proven that "the performance of test-anxious subjects varies inversely with evaluation stress." It would also be to the psychological benefit of students if they were not subjected to the emotional ups and downs of large exams where they are virtually worry-free one moment and ready to check into the psychiatric ward the next.

Lastly, with multiple exams, students can learn how to perform better on future tests in the class. Regular testing allows them to "practice" the information they learned, thereby improving future test scores. In just two exams, they are not able to learn the instructor's personal examination style, and are not given the chance to adapt their study habits to it. The American Psychologist concludes: "It is possible to influence teaching and learning by changing the type of tests."

One difference you may have noted between O'Malley's draft and revision paragraphs is the sequencing of specific reasons readers should accept the solution and take action on it. Whereas the draft moves in three paragraphs from improving study habits to decreasing anxiety to performing better on future tests, the revision moves from learning more and performing better on major exams to improving study habits to decreasing anxiety. O'Malley made the change after a response from a classmate and a conference with his instructor helped him to see that his particular readers (professors) would probably be most convinced by the improved quality of students' learning, not improvements in their study habits and feelings. As he continued thinking about his argument and discovering further relevant research, he shifted his emphasis from the psychological to the intellectual benefits of frequent exams.

You may also have noticed that the paragraphs of the revision are better focused than in the draft. The psychological benefits (reduced anxiety as a result of less procrastination) are now discussed mainly in a single paragraph (the third), whereas in the draft they are mixed in with the intellectual benefits in the first two paragraphs. O'Malley also uses more precise language in his revision; for example, changing "future tests" to "major exams, projects, and papers."

Another change you may have noticed is that all of the quoted research material in the draft has been replaced in the revision. Extending his library research to support his argument, O'Malley discovered the very useful Harvard report. As he found a more logical sequence, more precise terms, and fuller elaboration for his argument, he saw different ways to use the research studies he had turned up initially and quoted in the draft.

A final difference is that in the revision, O'Malley argues his reasons more effectively. Consider the draft and revised paragraphs on improved study habits. In the draft paragraph, O'Malley shifts abruptly from study habits to procrastination to anxiety. Except for study habits, none of these topics is developed, and the quotation adds nothing to what he has already said. By contrast, the revised paragraph focuses strictly on study habits. O'Malley keeps the best sentences from the draft for the beginning of the revised paragraph, but he adds several new sentences to help to convince readers of the soundness of his argument that frequent exams improve students' study habits. These new sentences serve several functions: They anticipate a possible objection ("It might be argued . . ."), note a contrast between complex academic learning and familiar survival skills, and assert claims about the special requirements of regular academic study. The quotation from the Harvard report supports, rather than merely repeats, O'Malley's claims, and it effectively concludes the paragraph.

THINKING CRITICALLY ABOUT WHAT YOU HAVE LEARNED

By this point, you have had considerable experience with proposals—reading them, talking about them, and writing one of your own. So now is a good time to think critically about what you have learned about this genre. What did you learn about solving problems you encountered when writing a proposal? How did reading other proposals influence your own? What role do proposals play in shaping our society and our lives?

Reflecting on Your Writing

Write a page or two telling your instructor about a problem you encountered in writing an essay that proposes a solution and how you solved it. Before you begin, gather all of your writing—invention and planning notes, drafts, any critical comments from classmates and your instructor, revising notes and plans, and final revision. Review these materials, and refer to them as you complete this writing task.

1. Identify *one* writing problem you had to solve as you worked on your proposal essay. Do not be concerned with grammar and punctuation; concentrate, instead, on problems unique to developing a proposal essay. For example, did you puzzle over how to convince readers that your proposed solution would actually solve the problem you identified? Did you find it difficult to outline the steps required to implement the solution? Did you have trouble coming up with alternative solutions that your readers might favor?
2. How did you recognize the writing problem? When did you first discover it? What called it to your attention? If you did not become aware of the problem until someone else pointed it out to you, can you now see hints of it in your invention writings? If so, where specifically? When you first recognized the problem, how did you respond?

3. Reflect on how you went about trying to solve the problem. Did you reword a passage, cut or add details about the problem or solution, or move paragraphs or sentences around? Did you reread one of the essays in this chapter to see how another writer handled the problem, or did you look back at the invention suggestions? If you discussed the writing problem with another student, a tutor, or your instructor, did talking about it help? How useful was the advice you got?
4. Finally, write your explanation of the problem and how you tried to solve it. Be as specific as possible in reconstructing your efforts. Quote from your invention notes, your draft, others' critical comments, your revision plan, and your revised essay to show the various changes your writing underwent as you tried to solve the problem. If you are still uncertain about your solution, say so. The point is not to prove that you have solved the problem perfectly but rather to show what you have learned about problem solving in the process of writing a proposal.

Reviewing What You Learned from Reading

Your own essay has doubtless been influenced to some extent by one or more of the proposals you have read in this chapter, as well as by classmates' essays you may have read. For example, these other proposals may have helped you to decide how to show your readers the seriousness of the problem you focused on, or they may have suggested how you could convince readers that they should support your proposed solution and ignore alternative solutions. Write a page or so explaining to your instructor how the readings in this chapter influenced your revised essay. Before you begin, take time to reflect on what you have learned from the readings in this chapter, and consider some ways in which your reading has influenced your writing.

1. Reread the final revision of your essay; then look back at the selections you read before completing it. Do you see any specific influences? For example, if you were impressed with the way one of the readings defined the problem, built a bridge of shared concerns with readers, detailed the steps in implementing the solution, argued against an alternative solution, or demonstrated that the solution would not cost too much, look to see where you might have been striving for similar effects in your own writing. Also look for ideas you got from your reading, writing strategies you were inspired to try, specific details you were led to include, and effects you sought to achieve.
2. Now write an explanation of these influences. Did one selection have a particularly strong influence, or were several selections influential in different ways? Quote from the selections and from your final revision to show how your proposal essay was influenced by your reading of other proposals in this chapter. Finally, point out any ways you discovered to improve your revised essay still further while reviewing the readings in this chapter.

Considering the Social Dimensions of Proposals to Solve Problems

Proposals to solve problems are essential to our society. Businesspeople, school administrators, and government officials especially depend on proposals to decide where to direct resources and energy. Proposals enable us as individuals and as a society to make things better. We probably value this kind of thinking and writing because it makes us feel effective. It convinces us that difficulties can be overcome, that we can make practical, material changes that will improve our lives and the lives of others. We tell ourselves that with a little time, hard work, and ingenuity, we *can* make a difference. And this attitude has produced many positive changes in our culture—improvements in civil rights, in gender equality, in business and applied sciences as diverse as bridge building and environmental protection. Even so, thorny problems persist in the very areas where the most gains have been accomplished.

Who Defines the Problem? First, when someone proposes a solution, that proposal shapes our thinking about some aspect of our own and others' lives by labeling it a problem. Yet the individuals most directly affected by the solution may not even accept this definition and may not want to see any change. Most men who harass women on the street, for example, do not see their behavior as a "problem," yet they would, if Kaus's proposal became reality, be subject to misdemeanor citations. Similarly, not all students regard infrequent testing as a problem, but O'Malley's proposed solution would affect them nonetheless.

This question of definition becomes particularly difficult when a relatively powerless constituency in our society—the homeless, illegal immigrants, unwed teenage mothers—is designated a "problem" by politicians and others in the mainstream. Writers (and readers) of proposals must exercise caution in such circumstances. For example, many politicians and citizens consider immigration from Mexico a problem; we hear arguments that immigrants take American jobs and sometimes require expensive social services such as schooling and medical care. In California, Arizona, and Texas, however, many farmers and business owners rely on legal and illegal immigrant workers to keep their production costs low, and studies have shown that workers pay more in taxes on their wages than they absorb in social services. Immigrants themselves view their migration not as a problem but as an opportunity, for which they may take considerable risks in getting across the border. Those who agree that there is a problem advocate solutions that range from building high fences and training more attack dogs to strengthening the Mexican economy so that jobs will be available to the Mexican people.

The Frustrations of Effecting Real Change. No matter how well researched and well argued, many proposals are simply never carried out. The head of a personnel department might spend weeks drawing up a persuasive and feasible proposal for establishing a company day care center, only to have upper management decide not to commit the necessary resources. A team of educators and social scientists might spend several years researching and writing a comprehensive, book-length proposal for dealing with the nation's drastic illiteracy rate but never see their solutions carried out because of a lack of coordination among the country's various educational institutions and governing bodies. In fact, it might be argued that the most successful proposals often operate on the smallest scale. For example, a proposal suggesting ways for a single community to increase literacy rates would probably have a better chance of implementation and ultimate success than the more far-reaching national proposal. (Yet this observation is not to rule out the value of the national proposal, on which the local proposal might, in fact, be based.)

Further, in choosing among competing alternative proposals, decision makers—who usually hold the power of the purse strings and necessarily represent a fairly conservative position—often go for the one that is cheapest, most expedient, and least disruptive. They may also choose small, incremental changes over more fundamental, radical solutions. While sometimes the most pragmatic choice, such immediately feasible solutions may also merely patch over a problem, failing to solve it structurally. They may even inadvertently maintain the status quo. Worse, they can cause people to give up all attempts to resolve a problem after superficial treatments fail.

For Discussion. Following are some questions that can help you to think critically about the role of essays proposing solutions. As you read and, perhaps, discuss these questions in class, note down your responses. Then write a page or so for your instructor, presenting your thoughts about the social dimensions of proposal writing.

1. Some people believe that Americans value solving problems because it makes them feel effective and progressive. It could be argued, however, that Americans tend to avoid problems. What do you think?

2. Consider whether the proposals you have read attempt fundamental or superficial change. For which proposals is this question easy to answer, and for which is it hard? What about your own proposal? If you find it more difficult than you thought to answer this question, or if you and your classmates disagree, how can you account for the difficulty and the disagreement?
3. How specifically would the proposals you have read and written actually make things better? Whose interests would be served by these solutions? Who would be affected without their own stated interests' being served?
4. Because proposal writing invites writers to select problems that are solvable, they might inadvertently attempt to solve a minor problem that is actually only a small part of a major problem. Do any of these proposals—including yours—reveal this misdirection? If so, which ones, and what do you think is the major problem in each case? Do you think the minor problem is worth solving as a first step toward solving the major problem, or is it perhaps an unfortunate diversion?
5. How do the proposals you have read and written challenge the status quo? If they do, what existing situation do they challenge, and just how do they challenge it? What roadblocks might deter these challenges? Might the proposals be more successfully carried out on a local scale?
6. Do any of these proposals try to improve the status of a group that is not particularly powerful? If so, what do you think is motivating the proposal writer? Is there any evidence that the writer is a member of this group or has consulted members of the group? What gives the writer authority to speak for them?
7. Many commentators argue that we should not try to solve fundamental social problems by "throwing money at them." Do you think this objection is a legitimate criticism of most proposals to solve such problems? Or is it a manipulative justification for allowing the rich and powerful to maintain the status quo? What else, besides money, is required to solve serious social problems? Where are these other resources to come from?

A college student evaluates a history course for a campus publication. She explains that the course includes three one-hour lectures per week by the professor plus a one-hour-per-week discussion led by a teaching assistant (TA). She states her judgment that although the lectures were boring, hard to follow, and seemingly unrelated to the assigned reading, the discussions were stimulating and helped students to grasp what was important about the week's lectures and readings. To support her judgment, she describes a typical lecture and contrasts it to a typical discussion. She praises the TA for his innovative "term game," in which two teams of students compete to identify important concepts brought up in the week's lectures and reading, and for reviewing drafts via E-mail. She concludes by recommending the course but wishing that the TA had been responsible for the lectures as well as the discussions.

For a conference on innovations in education, an elementary school teacher evaluates *Schoolhouse Rock,* an animated educational television series developed in the 1970s and recently reinvented in several new formats: books, CD-ROM learning games, and CDs. She praises the original series as an entertaining and inventive way of presenting information, giving two reasons the series was an effective teaching tool: Witty lyrics and catchy tunes made the information memorable, and cartoonlike visuals made the lessons painless. She supports each reason by showing and discussing videotaped examples of popular *Schoolhouse Rock* segments such as "Conjunction Junction," "We the People," and "Three Is a Magic Number." She ends by expressing her hope that teachers and developers of multimedia educational software will learn from the example of *Schoolhouse Rock.*

For the travel section of a local newspaper, a motorcycle enthusiast writes an article called "Hog Heaven" evaluating the tour at the Harley-Davidson factory and museum in York, Pennsylvania. He argues that Harley fans will enjoy the two dozen antique bikes on display and that people interested in business will be fascinated by the Harley plant because it includes both a classic assembly line (in which each worker performs an isolated operation on the motorcycles as they move along the conveyor belt) and a Japanese-inspired assembly team (in which three workers assemble an entire motorcycle from beginning to end in whatever way they think works best). He points out that, surprisingly, productivity is substantially higher for the assembly teams (forty-five minutes to finish a bike) than for the assembly-line workers (one hour and forty minutes). He concludes by reemphasizing that the tour offers something for everyone and, in addition, is free.

CHAPTER 8

Justifying an Evaluation

Evaluation involves making judgments. Many times each day, we make judgments about subjects as diverse as the weather, food, music, computer programs, sports events, politicians, and films. In everyday conversation, we often express judgments casually ("I liked it" or "I didn't like it") seldom giving our reasons (for example, "I hate cafeteria food because it is bland and overcooked") or supporting them with specific examples ("Take last night's spaghetti. That must have been a tomato sauce because it was red, but it did not have the tang of tomatoes. And the noodles were so overdone, they were mushy").

When we write an evaluation, however, we know most readers expect that instead of merely asserting a judgment, we will provide an argument to back it up. We know that unless we argue convincingly, readers who disagree will simply dismiss our judgments as personal preferences. To earn our readers' respect, we must make ourselves credible as judges.

Evaluators can establish their credibility in several ways. One way is by making the reasons for your judgment explicit and by providing specific support to illustrate and give credence to them. You can also establish credibility by demonstrating knowledge of the particular subject being evaluated as well as the general category to which the subject belongs. For example, if you were evaluating a new Arnold Schwarzenegger action film, you would want to reassure readers that you are judging the particular film against your experience of other action films by Schwarzenegger and comparable films like those by Sylvester Stallone and Jean-Claude Van Damme. Showing readers you understand how the particular subject relates to other subjects of its kind helps establish your credibility by demonstrating that your judgment is based on standards that readers recognize as appropriate for judging that kind of subject. For example, most people would agree that taste and consistency are appropriate standards for judging spaghetti served in the school cafeteria, but would reject the high noise level and the uncomfortable seating in the cafeteria as appropriate reasons for evaluating cafeteria food (although these reasons would be appropriate for judging the cafeteria itself).

As you can see, reading and writing evaluations contributes to your intellectual growth by teaching you to develop reasoned, well-supported arguments for your judgments. Evaluations also contribute by requiring you to look critically at the standards underlying your own judgments as well as those of other people. In the process, you learn to appreciate how fundamentally important values are in determining what we think and how crucial it is for us to examine with a critical eye our cherished but often unconscious values.

In college and on the job, you will have many opportunities to write evaluations. If your college has a system of course evaluations, you will regularly evaluate your classes and instructors. You may also occasionally be asked to evaluate your own efforts and accomplishments in your courses. In addition, you will have to evaluate books and journal articles for courses in which you must write research papers. You may need to judge a scientific hypothesis against the results of an experiment you have conducted or assess the value of conflicting interpretations of a historical event or a short story. On the job, you will be evaluated and may eventually evaluate others for promotions, awards, or new jobs. You may also be expected to evaluate various plans and proposals, and your success at these important writing tasks may in some measure determine whether you advance in your career.

Writing in Your Other Courses

As a college student, you may be asked to evaluate books, scholarly articles, artwork, scientific experiments, or current events, as these actual essay assignments indicate:

- *For an astronomy course:* Write an essay of no more than three double-spaced typed pages. First, explain the two theories for the origin of the universe—the big bang theory and the pulsating universe theory. Second, give your reasons for preferring one theory over the other. Support your argument with specific references to the textbook presentation of the two theories.
- *For a political science course:* Write a research paper evaluating the two major presidential candidates' performances during one of their scheduled televised debates. If possible, record the debate so that you can analyze it closely and quote the candidates directly. Make a file of newspaper and magazine clippings on the debate, along with reports of polls taken before and after it. Take notes on the postdebate television commentary. Use this material to support your judgment of who won the debate.
- *For a twentieth-century American history course:* Review one of the books on the Vietnam War that is on reserve in the library for this class. Your review should describe the approach taken in the book and evaluate both the accuracy of its facts and the quality of its interpretation.
- *For a sociolinguistic course:* Evaluate one of the languages listed below according to the standards we have studied this term: standardization, vitality, historicity, autonomy, reduction, mixture, and de facto norms.

Haitian Creole	Black English
Provençal	Cockney
Singapore English	the language of Shakespeare's plays
Old English	Tok Pisin

Practice Evaluating a Subject: A Collaborative Activity

This activity invites you to practice making an evaluation before you have to write an essay justifying your evaluation. Your purpose is simply to find a subject that everyone in your group knows well enough to evaluate and to discuss the reasons you would give when evaluating a subject of this kind. Here are some guidelines:

Part 1. Get together with two or three other students, and find a subject that you all know well enough to evaluate (such as music, action movies, computer games, football, or science fiction novels). For example, if everyone in your group likes a particular style of music (such as country, blues, heavy metal, or rap), find an artist or a recording in this genre with which you are all familiar. Note that for this purpose you do not have to agree on a judgment. Instead, your aim is to see whether you can agree on which reasons should be used for evaluating your subject.

Together, list all the reasons you can think of for either liking or disliking the performer or CD. For example, suppose your group decides to evaluate Me'Shell Ndegéocello's second CD, *Peace beyond Passion.* Among the reasons you list might be the following: the songs explore important social issues such as racism, religious intolerance, homophobia, and sexism; the bitter tone of the social commentary does not go with the slick, upbeat melodies of some of the songs; and some of the lyrics are hard to understand.

Part 2. Now take ten more minutes to discuss what you have learned about the kinds of reasons your group agrees are appropriate for evaluating this subject.

- Which reasons were easiest for your group to agree on as appropriate or inappropriate for evaluating your subject, and which were hardest to agree on? To return to our example, upon reflection, you may think it was easy for your group to agree on the value of the social commentary in a recording like *Peace beyond Passion,* but harder to agree about the importance of understanding all the lyrics. Or someone in your group may have liked the contrast between the songs' bitter lyrics and upbeat tunes while another person may have felt that the upbeat tunes undermined the seriousness of the songs.
- First focus on the reasons your group found *easiest* to agree on. Discuss how you would explain (or defend) their appropriateness or inappropriateness. For example, if you agree on the value of social commentary in a recording like Ndegéocello's, why do you think social commentary is an appropriate standard for evaluating her music?
- Then focus on the reasons your group found *hardest* to agree on. Discuss why your group found these particular reasons so hard to agree on. For example, if you disagree on the value of social commentary in a recording like Ndegéocello's, why do some group members think it is an appropriate standard while others think it is inappropriate? Where do you imagine your ideas about what is and is not an appropriate standard for evaluating a subject like yours come from? What do you think might make you change your mind, or do you feel so strongly that nothing could change your mind?

READINGS

Terrence Rafferty writes movie reviews every week for the *New Yorker* magazine. As a seasoned movie reviewer, Rafferty recognizes that most people read reviews primarily to help them decide whether or not to see a new movie. He also knows that while it is important to offer specific support so that readers can understand the reasons for his judgment, he must not give away too much, especially when he is reviewing a mystery like *Devil in a Blue Dress.*

As you read Rafferty's review, think about what he chooses to tell readers and what he withholds from them. Consider also whether his review tells enough about the movie for you to decide whether you want to see it. To understand the choices Rafferty is making, you do not have to see the film yourself; however, it is available on video should you wish to see it.

BLACK EYE

Terrence Rafferty

1 Ezekiel Rawlins, the hero of four detective novels by Walter Mosley, is one of the most reluctant private eyes in the long history of the genre. He goes by the nickname Easy, and it fits. Trouble is not his business; he's just an ordinary, hardworking black man—a veteran of the Second World War—who's trying to keep up the mortgage payments on his small Los Angeles house. In the opening scenes of Carl Franklin's *Devil in a Blue Dress,* which is based on Mosley's first book, we see Easy (Denzel Washington) sitting in a bar in the middle of the day and looking through the want ads; he has been laid off from his job at an aircraft plant and has started to worry about the possibility of losing his home. His desperate financial circumstances make him receptive to the kind of quick-money proposition that he wouldn't normally entertain: a shady-looking white man, DeWitt Albright (Tom Sizemore), offers him a hundred dollars to locate a woman named Daphne Monet, the runaway fiancée of a wealthy local politician. Albright suspects that Daphne is lying low in the black part of town; to find her there, he needs the services of someone like Easy, who knows his way around and can make inquiries discreetly, without slamming into a stone wall of racial mistrust. Fishy as all this sounds to Easy, he accepts the job. A hundred bucks is a hundred bucks, and in his position he can't afford to be too particular about how he earns it.

2 The story is set in 1948. Both the time and the place evoke the world of Raymond Chandler's famous detective, Philip Marlowe, and it's tempting to think of Mosley's hero as a black Marlowe. Mosley's work is full of homages to the master of hardboiled L.A. crime fiction: the plots of all the Rawlins adventures are dense, murky, and rather chaotic, with either a corpse or a gun-toting goon popping up out of nowhere whenever the action begins to flag or the mystery threatens to become comprehensible; and monikers like DeWitt Albright and Daphne Monet are purest Chandler. (Carl Franklin pays his respects to genre ancestors, too: the movie, especially in its night scenes, borrows some of the death-fragrant atmosphere of Howard Hawks's 1946 Marlowe movie, *The Big Sleep.*) But the character of Easy Rawlins feels like a wholly original conception, for the simple reason that he isn't a professional investigator: he has neither the special skills of a trained detective like Marlowe nor anything like Marlowe's dogged, chivalric sense of mission. The sly joke of the books, and of this movie, is that Easy's unique qualifications for the role that has been thrust upon him derive entirely from his blackness. Because he lives in a community that, in 1948, is virtually a separate

society—another country—within the United States, he possesses knowledge to which white people have no access: the secrets of what is to them a mysterious, and even impenetrable, culture. Mosley's detective stories are based on the witty perception that to be black in America is *necessarily* to be a private eye—to see what the larger society can't, or won't.

3 *Devil in a Blue Dress* doesn't make a big deal of the social vision that informs its mystery-thriller narrative. The screenplay, by Franklin, streamlines the novel's outrageously convoluted plot, and his elegant direction keeps the picture moving forward at a confident, unhurried pace, which allows the story's ironies to sneak up on us slowly, like the huge, harsh Southern California sun rising on the groggy survivors of a long, sleepless night. When the movie is over, the details of the mystery—who killed whom, and why—fade pretty quickly, but the smoky after-hours mood created by Franklin and his wonderfully subtle cinematographer, Tak Fujimoto, lingers, and so does our sense of the cleverness and the aptness of Mosley's take on the private-eye genre. Chandler, like Hammett before him and Ross Macdonald after, used his tough-guy detective as an instrument to reveal the elusive links between the highest and the lowest levels of society. (What connects them, indissolubly, is their tenacious unwillingness to reveal themselves to outsiders; the thug and the mogul recognize each other as adepts of different cults.) There's an undogmatic awareness of class built into the hardboiled formula. As the private eye shuffles between backstreet dives and mansions on hills, he often discovers that the guns of the underworld have been doing the dirty work of the wealthy and powerful, and when the case is finished he's frequently left with the dismaying realization that he, too, has been manipulated—that the function of his skilled labor is, and always was, to clean up rich folks' messes. *Devil in a Blue Dress* spikes the genre's inherent cynicism with a bitter dash of racial exploitation; in the end, it isn't lost on Easy, or on the audience, that all his perilous, unsought exertions have been in the service of resolving the problems of ambitious whites.

4 The beauty of the film is that it treats even the most savage implications of the story matter-of-factly. Franklin, who, like Mosley, is black, isn't *shocked* by racism; it's just part of the reality of the characters' lives—something that unfairly limits possibilities for security and happiness without altogether eliminating them. The violent action of *Devil in a Blue Dress* is balanced by the movie's persuasive evocation of the vigorous, lively community that Easy belongs to and (sometimes) draws strength from. A lot of friends are from his original home town, Houston, and they're a funny, varied bunch: there's respectable-looking Odell (Albert Hall), who wears wire-rimmed glasses and gray suits and drinks himself into placid, pleasant stupors; fat, sloppy, sentimental Dupree (Jernard Burks) and his randy girlfriend, Coretta (Lisa Nicole Carson); and Junior (David Wolos-Fonteno), a dim-witted hulk who works as a night-club bouncer. Easy's best, and most alarming, friend is Mouse (Don Cheadle), a dapper little man with a mouth full of gold teeth. He smiles quickly and often, and kills with comparable alacrity. Easy knows that his buddy is a stone psychopath, and he spends an awful lot of energy trying to dissuade Mouse from casual homicide, but the two of them go way back: he can count on Mouse to be on his side. And in Easy's situation there's obviously some benefit in keeping company with a fearless, conscience-less killer.

5 Cheadle makes his entrance about halfway into the picture, and hits the ground running. His grinning, chattering, twitchy performance is a virtuoso comic turn, a disturbing and hilarious portrayal of feral amorality. But, miraculously, he doesn't overpower the movie or its leading man. Franklin's control of tone is expert; even the introduction of this flamboyantly grotesque element doesn't throw the picture off its stride—

it gallops along steadily, refusing to be shaken or surprised. (This director's ability to negotiate sudden plot twists and volatile shifts of mood was part of what made his nifty 1992 suspense sleeper *One False Move* so fresh and so distinctive.) Washington's acting has a similar quality: he takes things as they come. His work in *Devil in a Blue Dress* is deeply satisfying, because he's playing a character whose world view doesn't jibe with contemporary notions of how black men should operate in white society, and he explores Easy's wary, essentially nonconfrontational personality with genuine curiosity and sympathy. He doesn't mock the character as a shuffling, foolish Uncle Tom; nor does he try to curry favor by making Easy more courageous than an amiable, sane black workingman—struggling to make ends meet and to get a little joy out of life—could plausibly have been in the late forties. Washington finds the humor and the quiet heroism in the character's adaptability, and the practical intelligence in his cautious manner. The actor's relaxed star presence works unobtrusively to dispose of any lingering impression that Easy's fear is a sign of weakness. This man looks very, very comfortable with himself, so assured that he doesn't need to swagger. When he's afraid, we feel instinctively that he has good reason to be—that he's careful because he's not stupid.

6 Fundamentally, *Devil in a Blue Dress* is a modest, skillful, unfussy genre picture that is content to tell an exciting story and to let its more serious concerns remain just below the surface, gently complicating the smooth-flowing rhythms of the narrative. The movie, like its deceptively ordinary hero, gets by on cunning, precision, and a flexible, accommodating kind of determination, and it gives those small virtues the respect that they're entitled to. It's the most enjoyable private-eye movie in a long time, because Mosley and Franklin and Washington have the sense to look for their pleasures within the genre's home ground, on its familiar but not yet exhausted turf. *Devil in a Blue Dress* is an exuberant demonstration of the value of knowing your way around.

Connecting to Culture and Experience

Rafferty observes that African Americans lived in "a community that, in 1948, [was] virtually a separate society—another country—within the United States," a "mysterious, and even impenetrable, culture" from the perspective of white people (paragraph 2). During the same period, many Americans proudly described the United States in very different terms, as the great melting pot. Today, some people reject the melting pot as an appropriate image, opting instead for the image of America as a tossed salad in which everyone's cultural identity remains distinctive.

Discuss with other students which of these images of the United States—or some other image—best fits your experience. Take turns briefly telling each other about a specific experience that represents for you the image you have of America. Or if you have more than one image of America, think of different experiences to represent these different images. Consider also how you feel about these various images of America: Do any of them make you feel proud, unhappy, confused, angry, bored?

Analyzing Writing Strategies

1. At the beginning of this chapter, we made the following generalizations about evaluative essays. Consider which of these statements is true of Rafferty's review.
   - It asserts a judgment.
   - It tries to establish credibility with readers by convincing them that the judgment is based on knowledge of the particular subject as well as the general category to which the subject belongs.

- It tries to establish credibility by making the reasons for its judgment explicit and providing support that illustrates and gives credence to them.
- It tries to establish credibility by demonstrating that the judgment is not merely the writer's personal preference but is based on standards that many people consider appropriate for judging the subject.
- It requires writers and readers to look critically at their own underlying values as well as others'.

2. Rafferty's reputation as a movie reviewer depends, in part, on his demonstrating to readers that he is knowledgeable, not only about the film he is reviewing but also about films in general and about the private-eye genre in particular. The principal way he does this is through **comparison.** Reread paragraphs 2 and 3, underlining the comparisons. What effect do you think this strategy has on readers who recognize the comparisons and readers who do not recognize them? If some people in your class recognize them and others do not, compare your responses.

   Then, consider Rafferty's observation that the comparisons are not his but Mosley's and Franklin's, as a way to pay respect or homage to earlier writers and filmmakers in the genre whom they admire. Why do you think he makes this point? How do you think it affects his effort to earn readers' respect for his expertise?

Considering Topics for Your Own Essay

List several movies that you would enjoy reviewing, and choose one from your list that you recall especially well. Of course, if you were actually to write about this movie, you would need to see it several times (preferably on video) in order to develop your reasons and find supporting examples. For this activity, however, you do not have to view your film again. Just be sure it is one about which you have a strong judgment. Then, consider how you would argue for your judgment. Specifically, what reasons do you think you would give your readers? Why do you assume that your readers would recognize the standards these reasons reflect as appropriate for evaluating this particular film?

Commentary

Like most evaluations, movie reviews answer the fundamental question: What is it worth? People read reviews primarily to learn whether a film is worth their time and money. In addition, they read reviews to learn something about the film. Not only does the information help them decide whether to see the film, but for films they decide to see, certain kinds of information can whet their appetites and enhance the viewing experience. Readers need enough information to help them decide if they would enjoy the film, but too much information would spoil the surprise.

Understanding these needs, writers try to develop an effective **argumentative strategy.** This strategy deploys three of the basic features of evaluative essays: a well-defined subject, a clear overall judgment, and a well-supported argument.

Look first at how Rafferty **presents his subject.** In the first paragraph, he gives readers essential information about the film's story and characters: naming and describing the detective, setting the scene, and identifying the mystery. In the first four sentences alone, Rafferty names the author and title of the novel, the director and title of the film, and the film star and the detective hero he plays.

All of this information is necessary to give readers a context for the judgment. But we can infer from the different kinds of information Rafferty presents that he anticipates his readers to range from those who know very little to those who know a great deal about the private-eye genre. For example, Rafferty explains the detective's nickname and notes that the film is based on the first of Mosley's Easy Rawlins novels, suggesting that he assumes that some readers have never heard of Easy Rawlins or Mosley. In contrast, his use of the phrase "Trouble is not his business" indicates that Rafferty expects other, knowledgeable readers to recognize and appreciate his wordplay on "Trouble Is My Business," the title of a famous short story by Raymond Chandler. Rafferty uses in-jokes like this to keep his more expert readers entertained while he brings his less expert readers up to speed on the information they need.

In addition to presenting information about the film, Rafferty also asserts his judgment and gives reasons to support it. Rafferty's argumentative strategy, however, leads him to put off **stating his overall judgment**—the thesis of his essay—until the end. Movie reviewers often use the **thesis statement** to summarize the argument rather than to introduce it. Like Rafferty, they assume that most readers will not be able to understand the judgment, much less determine whether or not to accept it, until they have some basic information about the film.

For more on thesis statements, see pp. 465–66.

Although Rafferty does not state his thesis until the final paragraph, he does make a series of evaluative statements throughout the essay. The first evaluative assertion appears in the middle of the second paragraph, where he praises "the character of Easy Rawlins" as "a wholly original conception." The next evaluative statement comes in the third paragraph, where he praises Franklin's screenplay and "elegant" direction, the cinematographer's subtlety, and Mosley's "take on the private-eye genre." Rafferty sprinkles evaluative statements throughout the rest of the essay. But it is not until the final paragraph that he asserts his overall judgment: "Fundamentally, *Devil in a Blue Dress* is a modest, skillful, unfussy genre picture. . . . It's the most enjoyable private-eye movie in a long time."

Rafferty **argues for his judgment** by giving several reasons that show how the film is finely balanced. For example, he argues in paragraph 2 that although the film is firmly rooted in the detective tradition, it is also original, both in its "reluctant" African-American detective and in its social vision. In paragraph 4, he asserts: "The beauty of the film is that it treats even the most savage implications of the story matter-of-factly." And in paragraph 5, he reasons that Franklin's fine direction strikes a balance between the nearly over-the-top performance of Cheadle as Mouse and the "quiet heroism," "practical intelligence," and "cautious manner" of Washington's Easy Rawlins.

The following paragraph-by-paragraph outline shows how Rafferty's argumentative strategy unfolds:

Information about the detective is presented, and the scene for the story is set. (paragraph 1)

The film is compared to major works in the private-eye tradition. (2)

The film's social vision is comparable to traditional detective fiction but is at the same time original in its African-American detective and social vision. (3)

The beauty of the film is achieved by balancing the violence against the vitality of the African-American community. (4)

Franklin's expert direction balances the performances of Cheadle and Washington. (5)

Conclusion asserts an overall judgment of the film. (6)

Because Rafferty was writing originally with his *New Yorker* readers in mind, we can infer that he bases his argumentative strategy on certain assumptions about the **standards** his primarily white, college-educated, upper-middle-class audience would think are appropriate for evaluating a film of this kind. In addition to the standards people generally apply to films—"virtuoso" acting, well-paced screenplay, "elegant" direction, and "subtle" cinematography—Rafferty expects at least some of his readers to value the fact that the film pays respect to the private-eye genre while also making an original contribution. Finally, his emphasis on balance suggests that Rafferty may also be sending a subtle message to readers that the film may make them think about race in America, but it will not challenge or upset them. In fact, his evaluation seems designed to reassure readers that the potential for anger and violence is under control—in balance. Seeing this film will simply be "enjoyable," like a good summer read.

Amitai Etzioni is a sociology professor and former White House adviser. He has written many books and articles, including *An Immodest Agenda: Rebuilding America before the Twenty-First Century* (1984), *The Moral Dimension: Toward a New Economics* (1988), and *The Spirit of Community: Rights, Responsibilities, and the Communitarian Agenda* (1993). He is also the founder of a new journal, *The Responsive Community.*

This evaluative essay was first published in the *Miami Herald.* According to the original headnote, Etzioni's teenage son Dari, one of his five children, helped him to write this evaluation—although the headnote does not say what Dari contributed. As you read the essay, you will see that Etzioni also acknowledges learning from another of his children, Oren. Given that Etzioni is a respected professor and author, how do you think his credibility in this evaluation is affected by his admission that he got help from two of his children?

WORKING AT McDONALD'S

Amitai Etzioni

McDonald's is bad for your kids. I do not mean the flat patties and the white-flour buns; I refer to the jobs teen-agers undertake, mass-producing these choice items. 1

As many as two-thirds of America's high school juniors and seniors now hold down part-time paying jobs, according to studies. Many of these are in fast-food chains, of which McDonald's is the pioneer, trend-setter and symbol. 2

At first, such jobs may seem right out of the Founding Fathers' educational manual for how to bring up self-reliant, work-ethic-driven, productive youngsters. But in fact, these jobs undermine school attendance and involvement, impart few skills that will be useful in later life, and simultaneously skew the values of teen-agers—especially their ideas about the worth of a dollar. 3

It has been a longstanding American tradition that youngsters ought to get paying jobs. In folklore, few pursuits are more deeply revered than the newspaper route and the sidewalk lemonade stand. Here the youngsters are to learn how sweet are the fruits 4 of labor and self-discipline (papers are delivered early in the morning, rain or shine), and the ways of trade (if you price your lemonade too high or too low . . .).

5 Roy Rogers, Baskin Robbins, Kentucky Fried Chicken, *et al.*, may at first seem nothing but a vast extension of the lemonade stand. They provide very large numbers of teen jobs, provide regular employment, pay quite well compared to many other teen jobs and, in the modern equivalent of toiling over a hot stove, test one's stamina.

6 Closer examination, however, finds the McDonald's kind of job highly uneducational in several ways. Far from providing opportunities for entrepreneurship (the lemonade stand) or self-discipline, self-supervision and self-scheduling (the paper route), most teen jobs these days are highly structured—what social scientists call "highly routinized."

7 True, you still have to have the gumption to get yourself over to the hamburger stand, but once you don the prescribed uniform, your task is spelled out in minute detail. The franchise prescribes the shape of the coffee cups; the weight, size, shape and color of the patties; and the texture of the napkins (if any). Fresh coffee is to be made every eight minutes. And so on. There is no room for initiative, creativity, or even elementary rearrangements. These are breeding grounds for robots working for yesterday's assembly lines, not tomorrow's high-tech posts.

8 There are very few studies of the matter. One of the few is a 1984 study by Ivan Charper and Bryan Shore Fraser. The study relies mainly on what teen-agers write in response to questionnaires rather than actual observations of fast-food jobs. The authors argue that the employees develop many skills such as how to operate a food-preparation machine and a cash register. However, little attention is paid to how long it takes to acquire such a skill, or what its significance is.

9 What does it matter if you spend 20 minutes to learn to use a cash register, and then—"operate" it? What "skill" have you acquired? It is a long way from learning to work with a lathe or carpenter tools in the olden days or to program computers in the modern age.

10 A 1980 study by A. V. Harrell and P. W. Wirtz found that, among those students who worked at least 25 hours per week while in school, their unemployment rate four years later was half of that of seniors who did not work. This is an impressive statistic. It must be seen, though, together with the finding that many who begin as part-time employees in fast-food chains drop out of high school and are gobbled up in the world of low-skill jobs.

11 Some say that while these jobs are rather unsuited for college-bound, white, middle-class youngsters, they are "ideal" for lower-class, "non-academic," minority youngsters. Indeed, minorities are "over-represented" in these jobs (21 percent of fast-food employees). While it is true that these places provide income, work and even some training to such youngsters, they also tend to perpetuate their disadvantaged status. They provide no career ladders, few marketable skills, and undermine school attendance and involvement.

12 The hours are often long. Among those 14 to 17, a third of fast-food employees (including some school dropouts) labor more than 30 hours per week, according to the Charper-Fraser study. Only 20 percent work 15 hours or less. The rest: between 15 and 30 hours.

13 Often the stores close late, and after closing one must clean up and tally up. In affluent Montgomery County, Md., where child labor would not seem to be a widespread economic necessity, 24 percent of the seniors at one high school in 1985 worked as much as five to seven days a week; 27 percent, three to five. There is just no way such amounts of work will not interfere with school work, especially homework. In an

informal survey published in the most recent yearbook of the high school, 58 percent of the seniors acknowledged that their jobs interfere with their school work.

14 The Charper-Fraser study sees merit in learning teamwork and working under supervision. The authors have a point here. However, it must be noted that such learning is not automatically educational or wholesome. For example, much of the supervision in fast-food places leans toward teaching one the wrong kinds of compliance: blind obedience, or shared alienation with the "boss."

15 Supervision is often both tight and woefully inappropriate. Today, fast-food chains and other such places of work (record shops, bowling alleys) keep costs down by having teens supervise teens with often no adult on the premises.

16 There is no father or mother figure with which to identify, to emulate, to provide a role model and guidance. The work-culture varies from one place to another: Sometimes it is a tightly run shop (must keep the cash registers ringing); sometimes a rather loose pot party interrupted by customers. However, only rarely is there a master to learn from, or much worth learning. Indeed, far from being places where solid adult work values are being transmitted, these are places where all too often delinquent teen values dominate. Typically, when my son Oren was dishing out ice cream for Baskin Robbins in upper Manhattan, his fellow teen-workers considered him a sucker for not helping himself to the till. Most youngsters felt they were entitled to $50 severance "pay" on their last day on the job.

17 The pay, oddly, is the part of the teen work-world that is most difficult to evaluate. The lemonade stand or paper route money was for your allowance. In the old days, apprentices learning a trade from a master contributed most, if not all, of their income to their parents' household. Today, the teen pay may be low by adult standards, but it is often, especially in the middle class, spent largely or wholly by the teens. That is, the youngsters live free at home ("after all, they are high school kids") and are left with very substantial sums of money.

18 Where this money goes is not quite clear. Some use it to support themselves, especially among the poor. More middle-class kids set some money aside to help pay for college, or save it for a major purchase—often a car. But large amounts seem to flow to pay for an early introduction into the most trite aspects of American consumerism: flimsy punk clothes, trinkets and whatever else is the last fast-moving teen craze.

19 One may say that this is only fair and square; they are being good American consumers and spend their money on what turns them on. At least, a cynic might add, these funds do not go into illicit drugs and booze. On the other hand, an educator might bemoan that these young, yet unformed individuals, so early in life driven to buy objects of no intrinsic educational, cultural or social merit, learn so quickly the dubious merit of keeping up with the Joneses in ever-changing fads, promoted by mass merchandising.

20 Many teens find the instant reward of money, and the youth status symbols it buys, much more alluring than credits in calculus courses, European history or foreign languages. No wonder quite a few would rather skip school—and certainly homework—and instead work longer at a Burger King. Thus, most teen work these days is not providing early lessons in the work ethic; it fosters escape from school and responsibilities, quick gratification and a short cut to the consumeristic aspects of adult life.

21 Thus, parents should look at teen employment not as automatically educational. It is an activity—like sports—that can be turned into an educational opportunity. But it can also easily be abused. Youngsters must learn to balance the quest for income with the needs to keep growing and pursue other endeavors that do not pay off instantly—above all education.

22 Go back to school.

Connecting to Culture and Experience

Etzioni argues in this essay that McDonald's-type jobs do not teach the kinds of skills young people need to learn to prepare for employment in a "high-tech" world, skills like entrepreneurship, self-discipline, and initiative (paragraphs 6 and 7).

With other students, discuss the skills you believe you need to learn for the kind of job or career you envision for yourself. Review the essay to make a complete list of the skills Etzioni mentions. Then discuss each skill to determine whether it is important to you. Add to Etzioni's list any other skills you think are important.

Analyzing Writing Strategies

1. To see how Etzioni **presents the subject,** reread the essay, underlining the factual details about who works at fast-food restaurants and what they do on the job. If you can, identify the source of Etzioni's information: his own firsthand observation, conversations with others who have worked at fast-food jobs (such as his sons), or published research.

   Then, based on your own knowledge of fast-food restaurants, consider which details you accept and which you think may be inaccurate or only partly true. Also consider what Etzioni may have left out and why—is it because he assumes that readers already know it, because it is not important, or because it would not support his judgment?
2. Notice that Etzioni refers to two different research studies, one by Ivan Charper and Bryan Shore Fraser and another by A. V. Harrell and P. W. Wirtz. Skim the essay, noting the paragraphs in which Etzioni refers to each study. Then, choose one of the studies, and describe specifically how Etzioni uses it to **support** his argument. Conclude your analysis by assessing the effectiveness of Etzioni's use of this particular study.

Considering Topics for Your Own Essay

In this essay, Etzioni is evaluating a kind of job he thinks is inappropriate for high school students. List the kinds of jobs you know enough about to evaluate. Then, choose one job from your list, and consider the standards you would use to evaluate it. If you do not have sufficient firsthand knowledge to evaluate any particular job, consider what kind of work or career you might want to know more about. Etzioni gathered information about fast-food jobs from his children and from published research. How could you learn more about the job you have chosen?

Commentary

In contrast to Rafferty, who waits until the final paragraph to assert an overall judgment, Etzioni puts his **thesis statement** up front, in the opening sentence: "McDonald's is bad for your kids." His thesis also makes very clear who he is addressing in this essay—the parents, rather than the kids themselves. Although in the last sentence of the essay, Etzioni shifts his audience to address teens directly, perhaps for dramatic effect.

Not only does Etzioni begin by making his thesis explicit and addressing his readers directly, but in paragraph 3 he also announces his **argumentative strategy** and forecasts his plan for the essay. He explains that he will counterargue by showing that contrary to what many parents assume, McDonald's-type jobs do not teach kids to become "self-reliant, work-ethic-driven, productive youngsters." Then, he will argue directly for his overall judgment by demonstrating the ways in which fast-food jobs harm teenagers. He names the three main reasons he will develop for his judgment: Fast-food jobs are bad for kids because they (1) "undermine school attendance and involvement," (2) "impart few skills that will be useful later in life," and (3) "skew the values of teenagers—especially their ideas about the worth of a dollar."

This **forecasting statement** helps readers by telling them what to expect. But curiously, the essay does not bring up the reasons in the order they are listed here. Instead of beginning by showing how fast-food jobs undermine school attendance and involvement, Etzioni begins with his second point, that fast-food jobs impart few skills. He probably begins with skills because he needs to counterargue against the assumption that McDonald's-type jobs are comparable to the traditional paper route and sidewalk lemonade stand—jobs that many parents (perhaps nostalgically) believe are good for kids.

For more on forecasting, see pp. 466–67.

He also needs to show readers that he and they share certain fundamental **standards** for judging the worth of jobs for young people. He makes clear, for example, that the qualities he values in jobs are those that teach young people to savor the "fruits of labor and self-discipline" and to learn "the ways of trade" (paragraph 4). He explains that he disapproves of McDonald's-type jobs precisely because they are not what they seem: They do not teach these old-fashioned skills. Interestingly, instead of seeing fast-food jobs as an "extension of the lemonade stand," Etzioni claims they are "the modern equivalent of toiling over a hot stove" (paragraph 4). He admits that such jobs can develop "stamina" but asserts that they teach little else. It is surprising that Etzioni uses this particular comparison because some readers may take offense at this characterization of kitchen work, especially women who have traditionally been the ones to toil over hot stoves.

By analyzing Etzioni's essay, we can also see how writers of evaluative essays argue for their judgment with **reasons and support**. As you will see when you begin writing your own evaluative essay, the guide to invention and research later in this chapter suggests that you construct a chart of reasons and support to help you develop your argument. The following chart, based on an analysis of part of Etzioni's argument, shows how he marshals support to back one of his reasons.

Reasons	*Support*
McDonald's-type jobs are bad because they "impart few skills that will be useful in later life" (paragraph 3).	• The franchise prescribes every detail • The Charper-Fraser study shows that fast-food employees develop many skills, such as operating a cash register, but the skills are quick to learn and not terribly useful for other kinds of work. • The Harrell-Wirtz study found that many teens who begin in fast-food jobs continue in "low-skill jobs."

Notice that in addition to backing reasons with support, Etzioni also explains his reasons by defining and illustrating key terms like *useful* and *skills.* He lists various skills and identifies which he considers useful. He also contrasts the "highly routinized" skills learned for fast-food jobs to the more useful skills learned in other jobs: "entrepreneurship" learned in setting up a lemonade stand; "self-discipline, self-supervision and self-scheduling" learned from having a newspaper route; and traditional crafts such as "learning to work with a lathe or carpenter tools" and the contemporary skill of programming computers. Like Etzioni, you will need to think about not only how to support your reasons but also how to explain them so that your readers can follow your argument.

James Wolcott is the cultural critic for the *New Yorker* who often evaluates television programs, as in this essay, which originally appeared in April 1996. Here Wolcott reviews a program called *Night Stand.* You may have seen it, but Wolcott must assume that because it is not on a major network and is not especially popular, many, if not most, of his readers will be unfamiliar with the show. As you read the review, consider whether Wolcott tells readers enough about the program so that they can understand his judgment of it.

Also notice as you read the essay that Wolcott refers to a debate about television talk shows. One of the articles he mentions is the one by Barbara Ehrenreich reprinted in Chapter 6.

TALKING TRASH
James Wolcott

1 At first, the furor over "trash TV" (those daytime talk shows hosted by Ricki Lake, Geraldo Rivera, Richard Bey, Jerry Springer, Jenny Jones, Sally Jessy Raphael, Maury Povich, Montel Williams, and the others vying for Oprah's throne) divided along ideological lines, like a *Crossfire* panel.[1] On the right, wearing a gray suit and a grumpy expression, was William Bennett, the former Secretary of Education and "drug czar," the author of the best-seller *The Book of Virtues,* and the co-director (with Jack Kemp) of Empower America.[2] Having weighed in against gangsta rap, Bennett called a press conference in which he condemned daytime talk shows as degrading spectacles and specimens of "cultural rot," which fostered promiscuity and other forms of bad posture. His "J'accuse" was seconded by Republicans ranging from Colin Powell to Bruce Willis, with moderate Democrats such as Senators Sam Nunn and Joseph Lieberman making worried noises as well.[3] On the left, pundits beseeched us to look beyond the tawdry theatrics (e.g., black girls calling each other ho's) and pay heed to the Underlying Social Issues. The *Times* columnist Frank Rich chastised Bennett for not being equally indignant about the tobacco giants, such as Philip Morris, that sponsor these programs (through their food divisions). In *Time,* Barbara Ehrenreich claimed that economic deprivation sometimes drove talk-show guests to shame themselves, and that the backlash against trash TV was an attempt to neuter the working class—a position also

[1] *Crossfire* is a political talk show.

[2] Jack Kemp was a vice-presidential candidate in 1996. He has served as a congressman and as secretary of housing and urban development.

[3] *J'accuse* is French for "I accuse." It was the title of a tract by Emile Zola that unmasked a conspiracy in the infamous Dreyfus case in late-nineteenth-century France. Colin Powell served as chairman of the Joint Chiefs of Staff under Presidents Bush and Clinton. Bruce Willis is an actor and supporter of Republican party causes.

adopted by Ellen Willis in *The Nation*. She wrote, "On talk shows, whatever their drawbacks, the proles get to talk."

2 Meanwhile, TV has its own methods of policing itself. It chews its excesses and spits them out like bubble gum. The sharpest, funniest, and sanest critique of trash TV is a satire called *Night Stand* (syndicated nationally, and shown locally Saturday nights on WWOR–Channel 9), an imaginary talk show hosted by Dick Dietrick, played by Timothy Stack. Unlike E!'s popular series *Talk Soup,*[4] which serves tacky clips from talk shows in bite-size McNuggets, *Night Stand,* created by Stack, Paul Abeyta, and Peter Kaikko, doesn't peer through a porthole of smug irony. It presents sleaze and corruption as viable life-style alternatives. The program is taped in Los Angeles before a studio audience, with professional actors cast as the dysfunctional guests, and has become a cult favorite among standup comics and others with keen antennae. (Bill Maher, the host of *Politically Incorrect,* has called it "the funniest show on TV.") Each hour-long show consists of two segments, featuring such burning non-issues as "So You Think You're a Lesbian?" and "Addicted to Strip Clubs"; guests are I.D.'d onscreen with punchy tags ("BETH ANN MCCLEAR—Sexually Abused Christian Author/Centerfold"). The show also employs the guerilla tactics of trash TV—the ambush interview, the hidden camera, the inciting of catfights—and it captures the kangaroo-court, revival-tent ritualism of that realm, where bad guys are booted, sinners repent, and souls are healed.

3 Yet no one would mistake *Night Stand* for a real talk show. Its healthy sparkle is pure Hollywood. Unlike the human driftwood on daytime talk shows, the men and women on *Night Stand* are tan and buff, a master race of test-tube babies that didn't turn out so smart. These lap dancers, defrocked ministers, and shopaholics all speak as if they had attended self-help seminars, showing big rows of perfect teeth as they discuss the demons that possess them. The show's put-on humor is somewhere between the old Steve Allen show and *Fernwood 2-Night,* with double-entendres that Benny Hill might have happily squirrelled away.[5]

4 What lends *Night Stand* its touch of the idiot sublime is Stack's characterization of Dick Dietrick. He has a limber quality all his own, a guarded yet elastic self-deprecation reminiscent of George Plimpton's early writing or of Dick Martin rocking back on his heels on *Laugh-In.*[6] Lanky, boneless, pseudo-debonair, Stack's Dietrick is a one-man anthology of talk-show insincerity; the studio is his used-car lot, loaded with lemons. He can switch with seamless ease from badgering his guests to offering sympathy. He opens each segment with a brief topic intro, intoned with the news-bulletin urgency of Ted Koppel. On a recent *Night Stand,* the case of a white stripper losing a job to a black stripper raised the issue of affirmative action. "For those of you not familiar with affirmative action," Dick explained, "it's a government program originally set up to give minorities jobs that white people didn't want. Well, things are different now, white people have changed their minds, and they want those jobs back." As the show

[4] E! is the Entertainment channel. *Talk Soup* is a comedy program that makes fun of daytime talk shows.

[5] Steve Allen had several comedy programs on television in the 1950s and 1960s, including the original *Tonight Show. Fernwood 2-Night* was a comedy program starring Martin Mull that pretended to be a real talk show in the 1970s. Benny Hill was a British comic who had a comedy program on U.S. television in the 1970s.

[6] George Plimpton wrote several articles and books including *Paper Lion,* which described his attempt to play football with a professional team. Dick Martin was cohost of *Laugh-In,* a popular, fast-paced comedy show of the 1960s.

proceeds, Dick uses his body English to keep the dialogue in play: he fans his hand after he releases a tricky question, like a magician casting a spell, then does a Phil Donahue slouch as he awaits the answer; he snaps his fingers over his head, Sally Jessy Raphael style, to chastise his audience for hearing a dirty message in his innocent questions. ("Oh, *no,* no, people, no!")

5 Dietrick's professional aplomb is undercut by his verbal haplessness. He is subject to malapropisms ("Let's cut to the heart of the meat of the matter") and has a spotty sense of history, referring to "the late Paul McCartney," to "the day Elvis was shot," and to events "indelibly paper-clipped" in the mind. With his female guests, he often drifts off into erotic reverie: "So anyway you're in bed, probably in pajamas or a nightgown or a peekaboo teddy that rides high over your graceful yet powerful hips. Then what happened?" Yet at the end of each segment he pulls himself together and addresses a sermonette to the camera (a takeoff on Jerry Springer): "So, what have we learned about fame? Well, we've learned that fame is usually limited to the well-known. . . . You see, people are always watching you when you're famous. And as a result things you take for granted are hardships for people like me. For example, I can't buy Preparation H without people gawking at me. I can't stiff a waiter. I can't hang around a Catholic girls' school waiting for that three-o'clock bell."

6 Snatches of autobiography sneak into each episode of *Night Stand:* Dick's busted marriage and alimony payments. His bachelor life at Casa de Tuna, where he has been accused of nude bathing on the patio. His thing for white cotton panties ("the land of cotton"). His late nights alone with his remote-control clicker. In his sports jackets and loafers, Dietrick is the Sears-catalogue model of a classic underachiever. When one of his guests accuses him of being a third-rate talk-show host, he snaps, "I'll have you know I'm a *second*-rate talk-show host!" His proud, defensive second-rateness is what makes him a symptomatic American loser. He's the quintessential white guy who can't dance but snaps his fingers extra hard, a throwback to the "What kind of man reads *Playboy?*" ad, swirling a drink in a goblet beneath a black velvet bullfight painting. It's a persona that might be too dank and pathetic to enjoy if Stack didn't invest the role with such dry geniality.

7 *Night Stand,* like such recent pieces of pop sociology as *To Die For* and *Natural Born Killers,*[7] portrays the TV audience as a nation of trained seals—fame junkies who clap on cue and crane their necks to see themselves on the studio monitors. There's no quality filter to celebrity today: serial killers and opera singers occupy the same glittery plane. On *Night Stand,* sitcom has-beens are hurrahed like Oscar winners, and even an attractive woman who appears only in the background of infomercials is treated like a star. ("Julianne, welcome to the show. I can see by the looks on the people in the audience that they almost recognize you.") In *To Die For* and *Natural Born Killers* the mass appetite for celebrity and notoriety is diagnosed as a national soul malady, but *Night Stand* doesn't trouble its empty little head over such matters. Like *Mad* magazine, it takes pop-culture garbage as a given—something beyond reform or redemption and full of absurd goodies. It assumes that all Americans crave the same thing: cheap attention. After a religious groupie recounts to Dick how she decided to cash in on her notoriety, getting herself an agent and a new body, then posing naked everywhere she could ("It did wonders for my self-esteem"), he exclaims, "What a positive person!"

[7] *To Die For* and *Natural Born Killers* are films that had been recently released at the time this essay was written.

In the world according to Dick, the only categorical imperative is to create good TV. Good TV means embarrassment ("Let's dredge up the heartache and trauma of that moment, if you don't mind") and conflict, no matter how contrived. When a gossip columnist announced that he was collaborating with a former maid to detail her exploitation at the hands of the former sitcom star Cindy Williams,[8] Dick said, "I think writing a book is good therapy, but facing your demons is good television." (Enter a scowling Cindy Williams.) And when a beauty-pageant consultant tried to play peacemaker between two beauty queens, Dick pointed a finger and issued a stern rebuke: "Don't *ever* stop a fight on my show." . . . 8

Right and left alike have exploited the trash-TV phenomenon for their own ends. The right used trash TV to occupy a moral high ground that they vacated the moment they got bored. . . . The left used trash TV to pose as the defenders of the downtrodden by arguing that the domestic squabblers on daytime talk represent the authentic voice of the working class—even though it has been documented that these shows are plagued with impostors and deadbeats hired through classified ads. (The real working class is out working.) With both sides platitudinizing, Timothy Stack's Dick Dietrick emerges as the only honest phony around. And *Night Stand* is further evidence that in the nineties comedy is the only place where anyone can be both truthful and silly about race, sex, and class. Everything else is editorial. 9

Connecting to Culture and Experience

What do you think Wolcott means when he writes: "There's no quality filter to celebrity today: serial killers and opera singers occupy the same glittery plane" (paragraph 7)? With other students, see how many recent celebrities you can name in a minute. Then look over your list to see what makes the people you named celebrities. Do any of them fit into the serial killer or opera singer category? Into what other categories would you put celebrities? What do you think makes the people in these categories worthy of the fame they now have?

Wolcott suggests that television watching is the reason we lack an adequate "quality filter to celebrity." Consider your own experience as a television viewer. How do you think television may have influenced your attitudes about fame and celebrity? What other influences can you think of?

Analyzing Writing Strategies

1. Reread paragraphs 1 and 9 to see how Wolcott uses **framing** in his evaluation of the television talk show *Night Stand*. Framing an essay simply means returning at the end to a topic that was introduced at the beginning. Framing is only one of the many ways writers begin and end evaluative essays. To see some other possibilities, turn to another essay in this chapter. How would you describe what that writer does to open and close the essay? Compare the effectiveness of these different ways of beginning and ending by considering how they serve each writer's argumentative strategy.
2. Look closely at paragraphs 4–6, where Wolcott cites specific **examples** from *Night Stand* to support his reasons for admiring Timothy Stack's characterization

[8] Cindy Williams is a comic actress who became famous as Shirley in the popular 1970s sitcom *Laverne and Shirley*.

of talk show host Dick Dietrick. To see how often Wolcott quotes from specific episodes, underline each quotation. Then, choose one quotation, and briefly explain how it supports the point Wolcott is making. Finally, reflect on the usefulness of such extensive quoting, especially for readers unfamiliar with the subject being evaluated.

Considering Topics for Your Own Essay

Wolcott reviews a television program; however, notice that he is not reviewing a single episode but the entire series. If you were asked to evaluate some type of series—such as the *Star Trek* or *Die Hard* movies, Rembrandt's or Van Gogh's self-portraits, Sherlock Holmes mysteries, or a television show—what series would you choose? What do you think your judgment would be of the series you have chosen? What standards do you think would be appropriate for evaluating a series such as the one you have chosen?

Commentary

For a discussion of comparison and contrast, see Chapter 18.

Comparison and contrast is not a required feature of evaluative writing, but it is commonly used for a variety of purposes. We have seen Rafferty use comparison and contrast to establish his credibility as a movie reviewer. He also uses it to put readers at ease by reassuring them that although *Devil in a Blue Dress* has some original elements, they will recognize it as a good private-eye story. We have also seen Etzioni use comparison and contrast to support his argument that McDonald's-type jobs are not as good as some old-fashioned jobs for young people. Etzioni, like Rafferty, uses comparison and contrast to build a bond of shared values and standards with readers.

Wolcott constructs his **argumentative strategy** around comparison and contrast. For example, he sets up a contrast between the satirical talk show *Night Stand* and position papers like Bennett's and Ehrenreich's to make the point that satire is a more effective (not to mention more entertaining) way of commenting on the value of television talk shows than explicit editorials: "The sharpest, funniest, and sanest critique of trash TV" (paragraph 2). He argues that *Night Stand* works so well as satire precisely because of its implicit use of comparison and contrast—exaggerating the features of other "real" television talk shows.

Wolcott evaluates *Night Stand* by comparing it to other examples of satire (what he calls "put-on humor") such as the old Steve Allen show and *Fernwood 2-Night* (paragraph 3). More important, he compares *Night Stand* to the television talk shows it satirizes. In paragraph 3, for example, he contrasts the typical talk show guests (whom he derogatorily calls "human driftwood") to *Night Stand*'s "master race" of Hollywood actors. And in paragraphs 4 and 5, he compares Timothy Stack's performance as the *Night Stand* host to several actual talk show hosts. Finally, he compares *Night Stand* to recent films that have attempted to satirize the "mass appetite for celebrity" (paragraph 7). He asserts that *Night Stand* is actually better than these films because it is not as serious in its criticism: "Like *Mad* magazine, it takes pop-culture garbage as a given—something beyond reform or redemption and full of absurd goodies" (paragraph 7).

When you plan your argumentative strategy, be sure to consider what you might compare or contrast with your subject. As you can see, comparison is a writing strategy that can be enormously useful in evaluative essays.

Christine Romano wrote the following evaluation of an essay taking a position when she was a first-year college student. She focuses not on the writing strategies or basic features of an essay taking a position but rather on its logic—on whether the argument is likely to convince its intended readers. She evaluated an essay by Jessica Statsky, "Children Need to Play, Not Compete," which appears on p. 218 of this book. The standards for Romano's evaluation come from Evaluating the Logic of an Argument in Chapter 12, pp. 458–61. You might want to review these guidelines before you read Romano's evaluation. If you have not read Statsky's essay, pause to do so now, thinking about what seems most and least convincing about her argument. Keep in mind that she was trying to convince parents that competitive sports are not good for their children. Statsky and her instructor agreed that she would plan her essay as an article to be published in a magazine for parents.

As you read the following essay, notice how carefully Romano applies the standards for logical arguments outlined in Chapter 12. Notice also that she evaluates Statsky's position paper in terms of whether it is likely to be considered logical and convincing by the intended readers—parents with young children.

"CHILDREN NEED TO PLAY, NOT COMPETE" BY JESSICA STATSKY: AN EVALUATION

Christine Romano

1 Parents of young children have a lot to worry about and to hope for. In "Children Need to Play, Not Compete," Jessica Statsky appeals to their worries and hopes in order to convince them that organized competitive sports may harm their children physically and psychologically. Statsky states her thesis clearly and fully forecasts the reasons she will offer to justify her position: Besides causing physical and psychological harm, competitive sports discourage young people from becoming players and fans when they are older and inevitably put parents' needs and fantasies ahead of children's welfare. Statsky also carefully defines her key terms. By *sports,* for example, she means to include both contact and noncontact sports that emphasize competition. The sports may be organized locally at schools or summer sports camps or nationally, as in the examples of Peewee Football and Little League Baseball. She is concerned only with children six to twelve years of age.

2 In this essay, I will evaluate the logic of Statsky's argument, considering whether the support for her thesis is appropriate, believable, consistent, and complete. While her logic *is* appropriate, believable, and consistent, her argument also has weaknesses. I will focus on two: Her argument seems incomplete because she neglects to anticipate parents' predictable questions and objections, and she fails to support certain parts of it fully.

3 Statsky provides appropriate support for her thesis, and this suitability is a strength of her logic. Throughout her essay, she quotes authorities eleven times and reports anecdotes or examples from them six times. These quotes and references are woven skillfully into her argument and seem relevant to the reasons she gives for her position. Even though she relies for support on large amounts of different kinds of information (she refers to seven separate sources, both books and newspapers), she seems to have chosen the quotes, examples, and statistics she uses carefully to support the reasons

why she believes competitive sports are bad for children. For example, in paragraph 3, Statsky offers the reason that "overly competitive sports" may damage children's growing bodies and that contact sports, in particular, may be especially hazardous. She supports this reason by paraphrasing Koppett that muscle strain or even lifelong injury may result when a twelve-year-old throws curve balls. She then quotes Tutko on the dangers of tackle football. The opinions of both experts are obviously appropriate. They are relevant to her reason, and we can easily imagine that they would worry many parents.

4 Not only is Statsky's support appropriate, but it is also believable. Statsky quotes authorities to support her argument in paragraphs 3–6, 8, 9, and 11. The question is whether readers would find these authorities credible. Since Statsky relies almost entirely on authorities to support her argument, readers must believe these authorities for her argument to succeed. I have not read Statsky's sources, but I think there are good reasons to consider them authoritative. First of all, the newspaper authors she quotes write for two of America's most respected newspapers, the *New York Times* and the *Los Angeles Times*. These newspapers are read across the country by political leaders and financial experts and by people interested in the arts and popular culture. Both have sports reporters who not only report on sports events but also take a critical look at sports issues. In addition, both newspapers also have reporters who specialize in children's health and education. Second, Statsky gives background information about the authorities she quotes, which is intended to increase the person's believability in the eyes of parents of young children. In paragraph 3, she tells readers that Thomas Tutko is "a psychology professor at San Jose State University and coauthor of the book *Winning Is Everything and Other American Myths*." In paragraph 5, she announces that Martin Rablovsky is "a former sports editor for the *New York Times*," and she notes that he has watched children play organized sports for many years.

5 In addition to quoting authorities, Statsky relies on examples and anecdotes to support the reasons for her position. If examples and anecdotes are to be believable, they must seem representative to readers, not bizarre or highly unusual or completely unpredictable. Readers can imagine a similar event happening elsewhere. For anecdotes to be believable, they should, in addition, be specific and true to life. All of Statsky's examples and her one anecdote fulfill these requirements, and her readers would find them believable. For example, early in her argument, in paragraph 4, Statsky reasons that fear of being hurt greatly reduces children's enjoyment of contact sports. Both the example and the anecdote to support her reasoning come from Tosches's investigative report on Peewee Football. In the example, a mother of an eight-year-old player says that the children become frightened and pretend to be injured in order to stay out of the game. In the anecdote, a seven-year-old makes himself vomit to avoid playing. Because these echo the familiar "I feel bad" or "I'm sick" excuse children give when they do not want to go somewhere (especially school) or do something, most parents would find them believable. They could easily imagine their own children pretending to be hurt or ill if they were fearful or depressed. The anecdote is also specific. Tosches reports what the boy said and did and what the coach said and did.

6 Other examples provide support for all the major reasons Statsky gives for her position:

- That competitive sports pose psychological dangers—children becoming serious and unplayful when the game starts (paragraph 5)
- That adult fantasies of winning put children at risk—parents fighting each other at a Peewee Football game and a coach setting fire to an opposing team's jersey (paragraph 8)

- That organized sports should emphasize cooperation and individual performance instead of winning—a coach banning scoring but finding that parents would not support him and a city basketball league in which all children play an equal amount of time and scoring is easier (paragraph 11)

All of these examples are appropriate to the reason they support. They are also believable. Together, they help Statsky achieve her purpose of convincing parents that organized, competitive sports may be bad for their children and that there are alternatives.

7 If readers are to find an argument logical and convincing, it must be consistent and complete. While there are no inconsistencies or contradictions in Statsky's argument, it is seriously incomplete because it neglects to support fully one of its reasons, it fails to anticipate many predictable questions parents would have, and it pays too little attention to noncontact competitive team sports. The most obvious example of thin support comes in paragraph 11, where Statsky asserts that many parents are ready for children's team sports that emphasize cooperation and individual performance. Yet the example of a Little League official who failed to win parents' approval to ban scores raises serious questions about just how many parents are ready to embrace noncompetitive sports teams. The other support, a brief description of City Sports for Kids in New York City, is very convincing but will only be logically compelling to those parents who are already inclined to agree with Statsky's position. Parents inclined to disagree with Statsky would need additional evidence. Most parents know that big cities receive special federal funding for evening, weekend, and summer recreation. Brief descriptions of six or eight noncompetitive teams in a variety of sports in cities, rural areas, suburban neighborhoods—some funded publicly, some funded privately—would be more likely to convince skeptics. Statsky is guilty here of failing to accept the burden of proof, a logical fallacy.

8 Statsky's argument is also incomplete in that it fails to anticipate certain objections and questions that some parents, especially those she most wants to convince, are almost sure to raise. In the first sentences of paragraphs 6, 9, and 10, Statsky does show that she is thinking about her readers' questions. She does not go nearly far enough, however, to have a chance of influencing two types of readers: those who themselves are or were fans of and participants in competitive sports and those who want their six-to-twelve-year-old children involved in mainstream sports programs despite the risks, especially the national programs that have a certain prestige. Such parents might feel that competitive team sports for young children create a sense of community with a shared purpose, build character through self-sacrifice and commitment to the group, teach children to face their fears early and learn how to deal with them through the support of coaches and team members, and introduce children to the principles of social cooperation and collaboration. Some parents are likely to believe and to know from personal experience that coaches who burn opposing teams' jerseys on the pitching mound before the game starts are the exception, not the rule. Some young children idolize teachers and coaches, and team practice and games are the brightest moments in their lives. Statsky seems not to have considered these reasonable possibilities, and as a result her argument lacks a compelling logic it might have had. By acknowledging that she was aware of many of these objections—and perhaps even accommodating more of them in her own argument, as she does in paragraph 10, while refuting other objections respectfully—she would have strengthened her argument.

9 Finally, Statsky's argument is incomplete because she overlooks examples of noncontact team sports. Track, swimming, and tennis are good examples that some readers

would certainly think of. Some elementary schools compete in track meets. Public and private clubs and recreational programs organize competitive swimming and tennis competitions. In these sports, individual performance is the focus. No one gets trampled. Children exert themselves only as much as they are able to. Yet individual performances are scored, and a team score is derived. Because Statsky fails to mention any of these obvious possibilities, her argument is weakened.

The logic of Statsky's argument, then, has both strengths and weaknesses. The support she offers is appropriate, believable, and consistent. The major weakness is incompleteness—she fails to anticipate more fully the likely objections of a wide range of readers. Her logic would prevent parents who enjoy and advocate competitive sports from taking her argument seriously. Such parents and their children have probably had positive experiences with team sports, and these experiences would lead them to believe that the gains are worth whatever risks may be involved. Many probably think that the risks Statsky points out can be avoided by careful monitoring. For those parents inclined to agree with her, Statsky's logic is likely to seem sound and complete. An argument that successfully confirms readers' beliefs is certainly valid, and Statsky succeeds admirably at this kind of argument. Because she does not offer compelling counterarguments to the legitimate objections of those inclined not to agree with her, however, her success is limited.

Connecting to Culture and Experience

Romano reasons in paragraph 8 that some parents "feel that competitive team sports for young children create a sense of community with a shared purpose, build character through self-sacrifice and commitment to the group, teach children to face their fears early and learn how to deal with them through the support of coaches and team members, and introduce children to the principles of social cooperation and collaboration."

With other students, discuss this view of the role of sports in developing a child's sense of community. Begin by telling one another about your own, your siblings', or your children's experiences with team sports between the ages of six and twelve. If participating in sports at this young age helped to create a sense of community, explain how sports contributed. If you think team sports failed to create community or had some other effect, explain the effect it did have. Then, discuss how each of you is defining the term *community,* and consider whether you are using it in the same way that Romano uses it in her essay.

Analyzing Writing Strategies

1. Notice that Romano gives readers two **forecasting statements** (in paragraphs 2 and 7). Underline the key terms used in the forecasting statements. To see whether Romano keeps her promises to readers, check the forecasts against the essay by underlining the key terms used to identify each of the reasons she gives for her judgment as it is taken up and developed in the body of her essay. Then, reflect on what you have learned from Romano's essay about using key terms for **cueing the reader** in the forecasting statement and in the body of the essay.
2. Evaluate Romano's argument according to the standards for judging the writer's credibility on pages 462–64 in Chapter 12. Briefly explain your judgment of how well Romano shows her knowledge of the subject, builds common ground with readers, and responds to objections and opposing arguments.

3. Turn to the Writer at Work section on pages 331–32 in this chapter to see how Romano analyzed her readers and tried to anticipate and accommodate their different standards of judgment. Note what Romano changed when she revised her draft. Finally, reflect on why it is important for writers evaluating a subject to anticipate the standards their readers are likely to apply to the subject, as Romano tries to do in this essay.

Considering Topics for Your Own Essay

List several written texts you would consider evaluating. For example, you might include in your list an essay from one of the chapters in this book. If you choose an argument from Chapters 6 through 10, you could evaluate it for either logic, emotional appeals, or credibility. Guidelines for evaluating arguments in these ways can be found in Chapter 12, pp. 458–64. You might prefer to evaluate a children's book you read when you were younger or one you now read to your own children, a magazine for people interested in a particular topic like computers or cars, a scholarly article you read for a research paper, or a short story from Chapter 10. You need not limit yourself to texts written on paper; also consider texts available online such as the Internet webzine *Slate*. Choose one possibility from your list, and consider the basis on which you would evaluate the text. What standards do you think your readers would agree are appropriate for evaluating this subject?

Commentary

Following her instructor's suggestion that students apply the critical reading strategy of Evaluating the Logic of an Argument to one of the argument essays in Chapters 6 through 10, Romano decided to write about Statsky's essay. She had been impressed by the thoroughness of Statsky's research when she first read the essay several weeks before. She also liked the idea of working with **standards** she knew her instructor would agree are appropriate for judging the subject. Applying these standards, she did not have to worry that her evaluation would be based on personal preference rather than generally accepted standards. In her essay, as you can see, she also took special care to try to evaluate Statsky's logic from the point of view of her intended readers. Furthermore, by working with the critical reading strategy in Chapter 12, Romano developed a much better understanding of logical reasoning and the standards by which logic could be evaluated.

We can also see in Romano's essay that writers evaluating a subject do not need to give their subject unqualified praise or blame, although doing so is a great temptation. After all, few arguments are all good or all bad. Critical readers are likely to see an unqualified **judgment** as either-or thinking—a logical fallacy, or error in reasoning, that weakens an argument partly by undermining the writer's credibility. Romano spends most of her essay praising "Children Need to Play, Not Compete" for the "strengths" of its logic, but she devotes the last third to discussing the argument's "weaknesses."

For more on topic sentences, see pp. 470–75.

Romano's essay also shows clearly how writers can make rather complex evaluations readable by carefully using **topic sentences** to cue readers. A topic sentence announces the topic of the paragraph it introduces. Every paragraph in Romano's essay begins with a topic sentence that lets readers know what is coming. Here are a few examples:

Statsky provides appropriate support for her thesis, and this suitability is a strength of her logic. (paragraph 3)

Other examples provide support for all the major reasons Statsky gives for her position: . . . (6)

If readers are to find an argument logical and convincing, it must be consistent and complete. (7)

Topic sentences may also refer to the topic of the previous paragraph. For example, paragraph 5 begins with a transitional phrase ("In addition to quoting authorities") that refers to the preceding paragraph and is followed immediately by a forecast ("Statsky relies on examples and anecdotes") indicating what is to come not only in paragraph 5 but continuing into paragraph 6 as well. The opening sentence of paragraph 4 is another nice example of using topic sentences both as a transition that summarizes the previous topic and as a preview of the next topic to be developed: "Not only is Statsky's support appropriate, but it is also believable."

When you draft and revise your own evaluative essay, you will want to make sure that you have used topic sentences to make it easier for your readers to follow the logic of your argument.

PURPOSE AND AUDIENCE

When you evaluate something, you seek to influence readers' judgments and possibly their actions. Your primary aim is to convince readers that your judgment is well informed and reasonable and, therefore, that they can feel confident in making decisions based on it. Good readers do not simply accept reviewers' judgments, however, especially on important subjects. More likely, they read reviews to learn more about a subject so that they can make an informed decision themselves. Consequently, most readers care less about the forcefulness with which you assert your judgment than about the reasons and support you give for it.

Effective writers develop an argumentative strategy designed for their particular readers. Your argumentative strategy determines every writing decision you make, from what you reveal about the subject to the way you construct your argument—which reasons you use, how you explain your reasoning, how much and what kind of support you give.

You may want to acknowledge directly your readers' knowledge of the subject, perhaps revealing that you understand how they might judge it differently. You might even let readers know that you have anticipated their objections to your argument. In responding to objections, reservations, or different judgments, you could agree to disagree on certain points but try to convince readers that on other points you do share the same or at least similar standards.

SUMMARY OF BASIC FEATURES

A Well-Presented Subject

The subject must be clearly identified if readers are to know what is being evaluated. Most writers name it explicitly. When the subject is a film or a book, naming is easy. When it is something more general, naming may be difficult. Etzioni, for example, uses the name McDonald's in the first sentence to indicate the kind of job he is evaluating. A little later in the essay, he lists the names of several other fast-food chains, but the McDonald's name is so well known, it easily stands for the entire class of fast-food restaurant jobs.

In general, evaluations should provide only enough information to give readers a context for the judgment. However, certain kinds of evaluations—such as movie, television, and book reviews—usually require more information than other kinds of evaluations because reviewers have to assume that readers will be unfamiliar with the subject and are reading, in part, to learn more about it. For example, readers of movie reviews usually want to know who the actors and director are, where the film takes place, and generally what happens in it. This is basically what Rafferty tells readers about *Devil in a Blue Dress.* For a recently released film (like *Devil in a Blue Dress*), the writer must decide how much of the plot to reveal—trying not to spoil the suspense while explaining how well or how poorly the suspense is managed. For a classic film or a new film everyone is talking about (such as *Independence Day*), reviewers may be released from this constraint. They can probably assume that most readers are already familiar with the general plot outline and mostly want to know the reviewer's judgment of the film.

A Clear, Authoritative Judgment

Evaluation essays are focused around a judgment—an assertion that something is good or bad or that it is better or worse than something else of the same kind. This judgment is the thesis of the essay. The thesis statement may appear at the beginning of the evaluation, as it does in the first sentence of Etzioni's essay: "McDonald's is bad for your kids." Or it may appear later in the essay, serving to summarize instead of introduce the argument, as in Rafferty's film review. Whether the thesis appears at the beginning or at the end, it must be clear and emphatic.

Although readers expect a definitive judgment, they also appreciate a balanced one that acknowledges both good and bad qualities of the subject. Romano praises the strengths and criticizes the weaknesses of Statsky's logic. Even Etzioni, who is highly critical of fast-food jobs, admits that they do "provide very large numbers of teen jobs, provide regular employment," and "pay quite well compared to many other teen jobs" (paragraph 5).

One of the ways writers establish their authority as judges is by using the writing strategy of comparison and contrast to demonstrate that they know a lot not only about the specific subject but also about the general class of subjects they are evaluating. For example, Rafferty refers to other private-eye films and stories. His references are designed to convince readers that he is an expert on the subject and that he

continued

continued

therefore knows what kinds of standards knowledgeable people normally apply when evaluating this kind of film. In fact, most of the writers in this chapter rely on comparison and contrast. Etzioni contrasts today's fast-food restaurant jobs to the kinds of jobs that used to be available for kids and that, Etzioni argues, provided a better training ground for them. Wolcott compares the satiric talk show he is reviewing both to other satires and to position papers critical of television talk shows.

A Well-Supported Argument for the Judgment

An evaluation cannot merely state its judgment; it must argue for it. To be convincing, an evaluative argument must give reasons and support based on appropriate standards.

Writers assert the reasons for their judgment and also often explain their reasons in some detail. For example, one of the reasons Etzioni gives for his judgment that McDonald's-type jobs are bad for teenagers is that they "impart few skills that will be useful in later life." He then specifies the skills fast-food jobs teach young people and explains exactly why he thinks they are not useful, contrasting them to the kinds of skills that would be useful. Etzioni's explanation hinges on the key terms "skills" and "useful," both of which he defines and illustrates for readers.

Some of the selections in this chapter rely primarily on textual support—describing, quoting, paraphrasing, and summarizing aspects of a television program (Wolcott), a film (Rafferty), or an essay (Romano). Etzioni uses other kinds of support, including facts, statistics, expert testimony, and personal anecdote.

Sometimes reviewers counterargue. They need to be aware of their readers, anticipating arguments that readers might make for their own judgments as well as objections that they might have to the writer's argument. Etzioni, for example, tries to convince readers that they cannot equate fast-food jobs with the old-fashioned lemonade stand and newspaper route but that they are correct in valuing those traditional jobs because they taught young people useful skills. Whether or not they use counterargument, reviewers need to anticipate the standards their readers would use and expect *them* to use in evaluating a subject. If writers and readers have differing viewpoints on a subject, writers should at least acknowledge their readers' point of view and explain why their own differs.

GUIDE TO WRITING

THE WRITING ASSIGNMENT

Write an essay evaluating a particular subject. State your judgment clearly, and back it up with a convincing argument based on standards of value that your readers will be likely to agree are appropriate for judging this kind of subject.

INVENTION AND RESEARCH

The following activities will help you to choose a subject, explore it, consider your judgment, analyze your readers, test your choice, reconsider your judgment, and develop your argument. These activities are easy to complete. Doing them over several days will give your ideas time to ripen and grow. Keep a written record of your invention and research to use later when you draft and revise.

Choosing a Subject

You may already have thought of a subject and decided how you would judge it. Nevertheless, it is wise to take a few minutes to consider some additional possibilities. That way you can feel sure that you have made the best possible choice and also have one or two alternatives if your first choice does not work.

Listing Possible Subjects. Make a list of the subjects you think you might be interested in evaluating. The following categories will help you to think of possibilities.

Set a timer for ten minutes, and brainstorm your list with the monitor's brightness turned down. Enter as many possibilities as you can. Then, turn the brightness up, check that the items make sense, and save them or print out a copy to make notes on.

- *Culture:* television program, magazine or newspaper, computer game, band, songwriter, film, actor, recording, performance, dance club, coffeehouse, artist, museum exhibit, individual work of art
- *Written work:* poem, short story, novel, magazine article, newspaper column, letter to the editor, textbook, autobiography, essay from this book
- *Education:* school, program, teacher, major department, library, academic or psychological counseling service, writing center, campus publication, sports team
- *Government:* government department or official, proposed or existing law, agency or program, candidate for public office
- *Leisure:* amusement park, museum, restaurant, resort, sports team, sports equipment, national or state park

Listing Subjects concerning Identity and Community The following are ideas for an evaluative essay on issues of identity and community.

- Evaluate one of the following in terms of its contribution to your sense of self-worth: your performance as a student, your athletic ability, your physical appearance, your ability to concentrate and complete tasks, your introversion (shyness) or extroversion (outgoingness), your ability to express or control your anger
- Evaluate how well one of the following contributes to your town or city: community center, public library, health clinic, college campus, athletic team, festival, neighborhood watch or block parent program, meals-on-wheels program, theater or symphony
- Evaluate how well one of the following contributes to your religious community: religious school, youth or senior group, a religious leader, a particular sermon, bingo, revival meeting, choir, building and grounds
- Evaluate how well one of the following aspects of local government serves the needs of the community: mayor, city council, police, courts, department of motor vehicles, social services, park system, zoning commission
- Evaluate how well the needs of the community are met by a particular school, teacher, principal, school board, teachers union, or school program

Listing Subjects concerning Work and Career Following are some suggestions for an evaluative essay on issues involving work and career.

- Evaluate a job you have had or currently have in terms of one or more of the following: hiring procedures, training program, possibilities for advancement, relationship between staff and management, relationships among coworkers, treatment of women and minorities, benefits package
- Evaluate either yourself as a worker or someone else you have observed closely, such as a coworker or supervisor
- Evaluate a local job training program, either one in which you have studied or one where you can observe and interview other students
- Evaluate the work done by city or campus employees about which you have first-hand knowledge—the police, trash collectors, road repair workers, emergency services, class schedulers, advisers, cafeteria workers, dorm counselors

Making a Choice. *Review your list, and choose the subject that seems most promising.* Choose a subject that you could evaluate with some authority, either one that you already know quite well or one that you could study. Although your judgment of this subject need not be fully formed at this point, you should have some sense of how you would evaluate it.

Exploring Your Subject

Write for five minutes, exploring what you know about the subject. Before considering your judgment of this subject, think about the information you currently have about it. Also consider what kinds of questions you will need answered and where you can find the answers. If you discover that you need more information but do not have time for research or think you will not be able to get access to the information, you probably should consider choosing a different subject.

Considering Your Judgment

Now that you have refreshed your memory about the subject, you need to think about your judgment and the values on which it is based.

Stating Your Present Judgment. *Write a sentence or two stating your current judgment of the subject as clearly and simply as you can.* Your judgment now may only be tentative, or you may feel quite strongly about it. However, as you learn more about the subject, think critically about the standards on which you base your evaluation, and develop a specific argument for your particular readers, you can expect your judgment to undergo some change and your confidence in it to grow.

Exploring Your Judgment. *Write for about five minutes, reflecting on your standards for judging this subject.* Consider these questions:

- What are the standards I value or the qualities—good or bad—that are important to me in evaluating this kind of subject? (For example, Rafferty is concerned about the film's social vision, acting, and direction. Etzioni cares about whether jobs teach young people skills they need and whether jobs divert them from getting a college education.)
- Why are these standards or qualities important to me? Where did I learn to value them? Are they the standards most people use when evaluating a subject like this? How do I know?
- Do I value the same qualities in all subjects of this type or only in this particular subject? (For example, Rafferty values the social vision of the private-eye genre but recognizes that Mosley's vision differs from Chandler's and Hammett's by focusing on race rather than social and economic class.)

Analyzing Your Readers

Take ten minutes to begin thinking about your prospective readers. Contemplate what they know about the subject and how they are likely to evaluate it. Anticipating what your readers already know about the subject will enable you to decide how much you need to tell them. Knowing how they would judge the subject will help you to decide whether you share any common standards or values on which to base your argument. To convince your readers to take your judgment seriously, analyze them thoughtfully and imaginatively. The following questions should help to focus your analysis:

- Who do I envision as my readers?
- If my essay were published, in what publication would my readers be likely to see my evaluation—for example, the campus newspaper, a corporate newsletter, a particular Web site, an investment advice column? What can I infer about my readers from the fact that they read this particular publication?
- What do my readers have in common with one another and with me that relates to this subject or to my evaluation of it?
- In what role do I think of my readers? For example, are they reading primarily as parents of young children, people watching their budget, environmentalists, religious fundamentalists? How does this role affect the qualities they are likely to value in my subject?

- What are my readers likely to know about my subject? Will I be introducing the subject to them (as in a film or book review), or will they already be familiar with it, and if so, how expert are they?
- With what other subjects of the same type might they be familiar? How are they likely to judge these other subjects?
- What are the qualities—good or bad—that my readers think are important for evaluating this kind of subject? (For example, Romano knows her instructor accepts the qualities for logical argument in Chapter 12.)
- If my readers and I agree that certain qualities are important for evaluating a subject of this kind, do we have the same or a different judgment of how those qualities apply to this particular subject? (For example, readers may agree with Etzioni that jobs should teach young people useful skills but disagree about which skills are useful.)

Testing Your Choice

Pause now to decide whether you have chosen a subject about which you can make a convincing evaluative argument. Reread your invention notes to see whether you know enough about your subject or can get the information you need and also whether you feel confident in your judgment and in the appropriateness of the standards on which your judgment is based.

As you develop your argument, you should become more confident. If, however, you begin to doubt your choice, consider beginning again with a different subject selected from your list of possibilities. No one enjoys starting over, but ultimately you will waste less time and energy if you do.

→ Testing Your Choice: A Collaborative Activity

The aim of this activity is twofold: to help you to understand how much information about the subject your readers will need and to suggest how you can make your argument convincing to readers by basing it on shared values and standards of judgment. Get together with two or three other students.

Evaluators: Take turns telling your group members about your subject. Tell them the kind of subject you are evaluating (film, computer program, baseball manager, college course) plus any details that would help them think about the basis on which they would evaluate a subject of the same kind. Do not discuss your judgment of the subject. Then, sit back and listen to what your group can tell you about the standards they would use, and take careful notes.

Group Members: Briefly tell the evaluator what else you would need to know about the subject in order to evaluate it. Then discuss the standards each of you would use to judge a subject of the kind the writer is evaluating. Specifically, tell the evaluator what qualities you admire in a subject of this kind and what you would consider its serious flaws or weaknesses.

Reconsidering Your Judgment

Reread the sentences you wrote under "Stating Your Present Judgment," and consider how you could clarify and perhaps qualify your judgment. Your judgment may have changed since you began working on your subject. Consider carefully whether you would even make the same judgment now that you have thought more about what you do and do not know about the subject and after you have reflected on your own standards of judgment as well as those of your intended readers.

Developing an Argumentative Strategy

To begin thinking about an argumentative strategy—how you would present the subject and support your judgment—you need to gather reasons and support, think about how you could explain your reasons to your particular readers, and consider some comparisons and contrasts that might help to make your argument clearer and more convincing to your readers.

A partially completed Reasons/Support chart is shown on p. 303.

It might help in working out your argumentative strategy to keep track of your reasons and support on a chart. Simply divide a piece of paper into two vertical columns, heading the first "Reasons" and the second "Support." Putting your notes on a chart will help you to see at a glance where your argument is strong and where you need to give it more thought or find more support.

If you can, save your reasons and evidence as a computer file. Then, as you draft, you can call up the file in a window and transfer details to your draft.

Listing the Reasons for Your Judgment. *Enter on your chart all of the reasons you could give for your judgment.* Consider how you would answer the question, why do you like or dislike the subject you are evaluating? To identify your reasons, try completing the following statement: ________ is a good (or bad) ______ because ________. Put down all the reasons you can think of for your judgment about your subject, and then look over your list to decide which ones would be the most convincing for your particular readers. Imagine you were evaluating the Walt Disney hotel designed by Michael Graves, for instance. If your readers were professional architects, you would probably look for architectural reasons—that it is the most architecturally distinctive hotel at Walt Disney World, for instance. If, however, your readers were schoolchildren, you would surely focus on some other reasons—that it is the only hotel filled with familiar Disney characters, perhaps.

Finding Support. *After you have listed as many reasons as you can, look for support for each reason.* Support comes in many forms, including facts, quotations, statistics, examples, and expert testimony. If you are evaluating a film, written text, work of art, or piece of music, you will probably get a lot of your support from analyzing the subject itself. Examine your subject closely more than once—for example, renting a video so that you can study certain scenes and enter quotations, summaries, or paraphrases next to the relevant reason in your Reasons and Support chart. You will probably find that the amount of support you can show for each reason will vary. For some reasons you will have only one piece of support, while for others you may have many.

Justifying Your Reasons. *Write about your reasons individually and as a set, explaining why each reason is appropriate for evaluating this kind of subject.* Consider how you would justify to your readers your choice of reasons, how they work together as a set, and why you have neglected certain reasons that readers might expect you to use.

Drawing Comparisons. *Write for five minutes, considering several comparisons and contrasts you could use in your argument.* Try to think of a comparison or contrast that would fit under each reason in your chart. Remember that comparisons and contrasts are often used to establish a writer's credibility by demonstrating not only that the writer is knowledgeable but also that the argument is based on standards that readers would agree are appropriate for judging that kind of subject.

PLANNING AND DRAFTING

The following guidelines will help you to review your invention writings to see what you have so far, establish goals for drafting your essay, and make a tentative outline to guide you as you draft.

Seeing What You Have

Print out a hard copy of what you have written on a word processor for easier reviewing.

By now, you have done a great deal of thinking and writing. You have explored your subject, analyzed your readers, decided on your judgment, and developed an argumentative strategy based on standards you expect your readers will recognize as appropriate for judging that particular subject. Take some time now to reread your invention notes thoughtfully, highlighting anything you think you will be able to use in your draft and noting connections between ideas. Also keep an eye out for problems you may have overlooked earlier, and consider how you might deal with them. For example, look for places where your support is thin or contradictory or where readers are likely to question the appropriateness of your reasons.

Setting Goals

Before you begin drafting, think seriously about the overall goals of your evaluation. Having clear goals will make the draft not only easier to write but more focused as well and therefore more convincing.

Here are some questions designed to help you to focus on what exactly you want to accomplish with this evaluation. You may find it useful to return to them while you are drafting.

Your Readers

- What do I want my readers to think about the subject as a result of reading my essay? Do I want to show them how the subject I am evaluating succeeds (like Rafferty) or how it fails (like Etzioni), or do I want to demonstrate its strengths and weaknesses (like Romano)?
- Should I assume that my readers are likely to have read other evaluations of the subject or to have developed their own evaluation of it, like Etzioni? Or should I assume that I am introducing readers to the subject, like Rafferty?
- How can I gain my readers' confidence in my judgment? Should I show them how familiar I am with comparable subjects, as Wolcott and Rafferty do? Should

I indicate any special knowledge I have—personal experience or a research project, perhaps?
- What tone should I take? Should I be witty, like Wolcott? Serious, like Etzioni? Enthusiastic, like Rafferty? Thorough and balanced, like Romano?

Presentation of the Subject

- What should I name the subject? Should I name it after something readers will recognize, as Etzioni does? Should I name it after a recognized genre, as Rafferty does in referring to the private-eye genre, or after a specific style, as Wolcott does in referring to satire?
- What about the subject should I describe? What do readers need to know about the subject in order to understand my argument?
- Should I place the subject historically, as Rafferty and Etzioni try to do?
- If the subject has a plot, how much of it should I tell? Can I simply set the scene and identify the characters, as Rafferty does, without ruining the mystery?

Your Evaluative Argument

- How should I state my judgment? Should I make it a comparative judgment? Should I put it up front or wait until I have provided a context?
- How can I show that my judgment is fair and well balanced? Should I try to put my personal judgment aside and evaluate the subject according to the way I think others would judge it, as Romano does when she tries to consider how Statsky's readers would regard her argument? Can I refer to specific strengths of the subject without taking away from the larger weaknesses, as Etzioni does?
- How can I support my reasons? Can I find examples from the text to quote, paraphrase, or summarize? Can I call on authorities?
- What facts, statistics, or other support could I use?

The Organization

- How can I make my essay well organized and easy to follow? Should I forecast my reasons and use topic sentences to announce each reason as it comes up, as Romano does?
- Should I open by stating my judgment, as Etzioni does? By describing the subject, as Rafferty does? By establishing the standards I will apply, as Romano does? By comparing my subject with a subject more familiar to readers, as Wolcott does?
- How should I conclude? Should I try to frame the essay, as Wolcott does, by echoing something from the opening or from another part of the essay? Should I conclude by stating my judgment, as Rafferty and Romano do?

Outlining

Evaluations may be organized in various ways. The important thing is to include all essential parts: a presentation of the subject, the judgment, and reasons and support for the judgment. In addition, you may want to arrange your reasons in some logical order: from most obvious to least obvious, most general to most technical, least convincing to most convincing, least important to most important.

Outlining on a word processor makes it particularly easy to experiment with different ways of organizing your essay.

For readers unfamiliar with the subject, your outline might look something like Rafferty's:

Presentation of the subject

Comparison to known works in the private-eye genre

Reason 1: The film is traditional as well as original

Supporting examples and comparisons

Reason 2: Violence is counterbalanced by the sense of community

Supporting examples

Reason 3: Franklin's direction balances the acting by Cheadle and Washington

Supporting examples and comparisons

Conclusion asserting an overall judgment of the film

For readers already familiar with the subject, your outline might look like Romano's:

Presentation of the subject

Forecast of reasons

- Reason 1: the standard of appropriateness support
- Reason 2: the standard of believability support
- Reason 3: the standard of consistency support
- Reason 4: the standard of completeness support

Concluding summary

Many other organizations are possible. Whichever you choose, remember that an outline should serve only as a guide. It can help you to organize your invention materials and provide a sense of direction as you draft, but feel free to depart from it if you see a better way of developing your argumentative strategy.

Drafting

Before you begin to draft your evaluation, reread all your notes and, if possible, take a last look at your subject so that it is fresh in your mind. If you are evaluating a written text (such as an essay or a story), reread it. If you are writing about a film, see it again.

Call up invention material in an alternate window as you draft on the main window, shifting back and forth to cut and paste invention material into your draft.

Start drafting, focusing on your readers and ways to convince them to share your judgment of the subject. If you run into trouble, reconsider each element in your evaluation. Perhaps you should think of better reasons or add more support for the reasons you give. You may need to take another look at your standards to assure yourself that they really are appropriate. If you get stuck, turn back to the invention activities in this chapter to see if you can fill out your material. You might also want to review the general advice about drafting on pp. 13–14.

CRITICAL READING GUIDE

Swap copies of your drafts with another student, either by exchanging disks or by sending the computer files over a network. Add your comments either next to the essay, if you can divide the screen, or at the end of the document.

Now is the time to get a good critical reading. All writers find it helpful to have someone else read their drafts and give them critical comments. Your instructor may arrange such a reading as part of your coursework; if not, you can ask a classmate, friend, or family member to read your draft. If your college has a writing center, you might ask a tutor to read and comment on your draft. The following guidelines are designed to be used by *anyone* giving advice on revising an evaluation essay. (If you cannot get someone else to read your draft, turn to Revising, which includes guidelines for reading your own draft with a critical eye.)

If You Are the Writer. To provide helpful comments, your critical reader must know your intended audience and your purpose. Briefly write this information at the top of your draft, answering the following questions:

- *Audience.* Who are your readers? What do you assume they already know about the subject? According to what standards do you expect them to judge a subject of this kind?
- *Purpose.* What do you want your readers to think about your subject from reading this essay? What do you want them to think about you?

See pp. 315–16 to review the basic features.

If You Are the Reader. Use the following guidelines to help you to give critical comments to others on evaluative essays.

1. *Read for a First Impression.* First, read the purpose and audience statement at the top of the draft, and then read the essay quickly to get a sense of the writer's judgment on the subject and an understanding of the basic argument. Your primary responsibility in giving a critical reading is to help the writer to improve the argument for the intended readers—even if you disagree with the writer's judgment. If you disagree, however, you should say so right away so that you will be able to put aside your own views as you go on to analyze and evaluate the argument. Briefly explain what you personally think is most and least convincing in the argument and also what you expect the intended readers to find most and least convincing.
2. *Analyze the Way the Subject Is Presented.* Locate where in the draft the subject is presented. It may be discussed in several places, serving both to explain the subject and to support the argument. Point to any places where you do not understand what is being said about the subject or where you need more detail or explanation. Ask questions. If you are surprised by the way the writer has presented the subject, briefly explain how you usually think of this particular subject or subjects of this kind. Also indicate if any of the information about the subject seems unnecessary. Finally, and most important, let the writer know if any of the information about the subject seems inaccurate or only partly true.

continued

continued

3. *Determine If the Judgment Is Clear and Authoritative.* Find the most explicit statement of the writer's judgment, and underline it. If you cannot find a thesis statement, let the writer know. If the thesis is restated in several places, examine each restatement closely for consistency. Look specifically at the value terms that are being used to see if they are ambiguous or waffling. (For example, while Rafferty clearly praises Franklin's direction when he calls it "elegant," the words he uses to praise the film—"modest, skillful, unfussy"—may not seem as complimentary.)

   Remember that even though many evaluative essays point out the good as well as the bad qualities of the subject, they also make an explicit overall judgment. If the writer's overall judgment seems fuzzy or inconsistent, suggest how it might be made clearer or qualified to account for the subject's strengths and weaknesses.
4. *Evaluate Whether the Argument Is Well Supported.* Highlight the reasons in the draft. Reasons in an evaluation may take the form of judgments of the subject's good and bad qualities, judgments that in turn need to be explained and supported. Look closely at the reasons that seem most problematic, and briefly explain what bothers you—for example, that the reason does not seem appropriate for judging this kind of subject, that you do not fully understand the reason or how it applies to this particular subject, that the connection between a particular reason and its support is not clear or convincing to you. Be as specific and constructive as you can, not only pointing out what does not work but also suggesting what the writer might do to solve the problem. For example, if the reason seems inappropriate, explain why you think so, and indicate what kinds of reasons you expect the intended readers to recognize as acceptable for judging this kind of subject.

   Also look for faulty logical reasoning (perhaps applying the ABC test for evaluating an argument, as Romano does). Note if the writer is basing the argument on idiosyncratic, trivial, or inaccurate standards of judgment. Indicate if the writer has failed to accept the burden of proof and simply asserts a judgment rather than giving reasons and support for them. Tell the writer if you detect either-or reasoning (seeing only the good or the bad qualities) or if comparisons seem weak or misleading. Challenge a writer you think is being unfair, perhaps criticizing something minor as though it were major or emphasizing something beyond the control of the parties involved.
5. *Assess the Effectiveness of the Organization.* Note any places where the essay seems disorganized or confusing. Suggest where adding topic sentences might help to make the essay easier to read. Consider whether any reasons ought to be reordered.

   Look at the *beginning*. Is it engaging? If not, can you see any other passages in the draft that might be more interesting? Does it provide sufficient background information?

   Look at the *ending*. Does it leave you thinking about the subject? Point to any passage elsewhere in the draft that might work as a conclusion.

REVISING

This section will help you to identify problems in your draft and revise and edit to solve them.

Identifying Problems

To identify problems in your draft, you need to read it with a critical eye, analyze its basic features, and study any comments you have received from others.

Even if your essay is saved to a computer file, reread from a hard copy. Add notes to yourself and quick revisions as you read through the draft.

Getting an Overview. Consider the draft as a whole, trying to judge it objectively. It may help to do so in two steps:

1. *Reread.* If possible, put the draft aside for a day or two. When you do reread it, start by reconsidering your audience and your purpose. Then, read the draft straight through, trying to see it as your intended readers will.
2. *Outline.* Make a scratch outline to get an overview of the essay's development. This outline can be sketchy—words and phrases instead of complete sentences—but it should identify the basic features as they appear in the essay.

Charting a Plan for Revision. You may want to use a two-column chart to keep track of the problems you need to solve. In the left-hand column, list the basic features of evaluative writing. As you analyze the draft and study any comments from others, note the problems you want to solve in the right-hand column. Here is an example.

Basic Features	*Problems to Solve*
Subject	
Judgment	
Argument	
Organization	

Analyzing the Basic Features of Your Own Draft. Turn to the Critical Reading Guide on pp. 325–26, and use it to identify problems you now see in your draft. Note the problems on your chart.

Studying Critical Comments. Review all of the comments you have received from other readers, and add to the chart any problems that need attention. Try not to react defensively to these comments; by letting you see how others respond to your draft, the comments provide valuable information about how you might improve it.

Solving the Problems

Having identified problems, you must now come up with solutions and implement them. Basically, you have three ways of finding solutions:

Before revising, copy your original draft to a second file. Then, should you change your mind about material you delete while revising, it will still be available.

1. Review your invention and planning notes for information and ideas to add to the draft.
2. Do further invention and research to answer questions your readers raised.
3. Look back at the readings in this chapter to see how other writers have solved similar problems.

The following suggestions will get you started on solving some of the problems common to evaluative writing. For now, focus on solving the problems identified on your chart. Try not to worry about grammar and punctuation at this time; that will come later when you edit.

Presentation of the Subject

- **Is the subject undefined or vague?** Be sure you have named it explicitly. Add details to clarify and limit the subject. If you need more information about the subject, review your invention writing to see if you have left out any details you could now add. You may also need to do further invention writing or research to answer questions your critical readers have raised or your intended readers might have.
- **Is the subject presented in too much detail?** Cut extraneous and repetitive details. If your subject has a plot, try to sketch it without giving away the whole story.
- **Is any of the information inaccurate or only partly true?** Reconsider the accuracy and completeness of the information you present. If any of the information will be surprising to readers, consider how you might reassure them that the information is accurate, perhaps by citing your sources.

Assertion of Your Judgment

- **Is your overall judgment vague or ambiguous?** Restate it so that there can be no confusion about your ultimate evaluation of the subject. Announce your thesis explicitly. If your judgment is mixed—pointing out good as well as bad qualities—let readers know that from the beginning.
- **Does your overall judgment seem too one-sided?** If your readers think your evaluation is too adulatory or too harsh, you may want to balance your praise or criticism by noting a strength or weakness in the subject.
- **Does your judgment seem unemphatic or waffling?** If readers think you come across as wishy-washy—perhaps because you are trying to show that you recognize the subject's good and bad qualities—be sure your overall judgment is stated clearly and consider eliminating unnecessary hedging words like *somewhat* or *usually.*

The Argument Supporting Your Judgment

- **Do any of the reasons and support seem inappropriate?** If readers question the appropriateness of any of the reasons or support, consider how you could convince them that it is based on an appropriate standard that others use when they evaluate subjects of this kind.
- **Are any of your reasons and support unclear?** To clarify them, you may need to explain your reasoning in more detail or use comparison or contrast to make your ideas understandable. Review your invention writing, looking for material you might add to your essay. Or you may need to do some additional exploratory

writing now to figure out how to explain your reasoning. Consider also whether any of the reasons should be combined or separated.

- **Is the support thin?** To find additional support, review your invention writing or reexamine the subject. You may also need to do library research to find information—facts, statistics, expert testimony—to support your argument.
- **Does your argument fail to carry the burden of proof?** If readers think you are merely asserting your judgment instead of making an argument, you may need to make your reasons and support more explicit.
- **Do the qualities you emphasize seem minor, or does your argument seem too one-sided?** Consider how you could better explain or justify the bases for your judgment. Perhaps you need to argue for your standards, demonstrating that the qualities you emphasize are indeed important.

If a reader feels you need more support, highlight the support in your paper by putting it in bold type. Then, look for places where you can add more support or elaborate on the support you already have.

Organization

- **Does the essay seem disorganized or confusing?** You may need to add a forecasting statement, transitions, summaries, or topic sentences. You may also need to do some major restructuring, such as moving your presentation of the subject or reordering your reasons.
- **Is the beginning weak?** See if there is a better place to start. Review your notes for an interesting quotation, image, or scene to open with.
- **Is the ending weak?** See if you can frame the essay by echoing a point made earlier.

Use your word processor's cut-and-paste function to shift material around. Revise transitions so that material fits smoothly in its new spot.

EDITING AND PROOFREADING

In working on your draft so far, you may have corrected some obvious errors, but grammar and style have not been a priority. Now is the time to find and correct any errors in mechanics, usage, punctuation, and spelling, as well as to consider matters of style. You may find that studying your draft in separate passes—first for paragraphs, then for sentences, and finally for words—will help you to recognize problems.

Research has identified several errors that are especially common in evaluative writing. The following guidelines will help you to check for two errors that often occur in evaluations.

Use your word processor's spell-check function cautiously. Keep in mind that it will not find all misspellings, particularly misused homonyms (such as *there* for *their* and *they're*), typographical errors that are themselves words (such as *fro* for *for*), and many proper nouns and specialized terms. Proofread these carefully yourself. Also proofread for words that should have been deleted when you edited a sentence.

Checking Comparisons. Whenever you evaluate something, you are likely to engage in comparison. You might want to show that a new recording is inferior to an earlier one, that one film is stronger than another, that this café is better than that one. Make a point of checking to see that all comparisons in your writing are complete, logical, and clear.

Editing to Make Comparisons Complete

◇ ***Jazz* is as good, [as] if not better than, Morrison's other novels.**

◇ **I liked the Lispector story because it's so different. [from anything I've ever read.]**

Editing to Make Comparisons Logical

◇ **Chris Rock's Pookie is more serious than any ^other role he's played.**

◇ **Ohio State's offense played much better than ~~Michigan.~~ ^Michigan's did.**

Check also to see that you say *different from* instead of *different than.*

◇ **Carrying herself with a confident and brisk stride, Katherine Parker seems different ~~than~~ ^from the other women in the office.**

◇ **Films like *Internal Affairs* that glorify violence for its own sake are different ~~than~~ ^from films like *New Jack City* that use violence to make a moral point.**

Combining Sentences. When you evaluate something, you generally present your subject in some detail—defining it, describing it, placing it in some context. Writers often give such details almost one by one, in separate sentences. Combining closely related sentences can make your writing more readable, helping readers to see how ideas relate.

◇ **In paragraph 5, the details provide a different impression, ~~It is~~ a comic or perhaps even pathetic impression, ~~This impression comes from~~ ^based on the boy's attempts to dress up like a real westerner.**

From three separate sentences, the writer combined details about the "different impression" into one sentence. He did so using two common strategies for sentence-combining:

- Changing a sentence into an appositive phrase (a noun phrase that renames the noun or pronoun that immediately precedes it: "a comic or perhaps even pathetic impression")
- Changing a sentence into a verbal phrase (phrases with verbals that function as adjectives, adverbs, or nouns: "based on the boy's attempts to dress up like a real westerner")

Using Appositive Phrases to Combine Sentences

◇ **"Something Pacific" was created by Nam June Paik, ~~He is~~ a Korean artist who is considered a founder of video art.**

◇ **One of Dylan's songs, ^"Talkin' John Birch Paranoid Blues," ridiculed the John Birch Society. ~~This song was called "Talkin' John Birch Paranoid Blues."~~**

Using Verbal Phrases to Combine Sentences

- Batman's lifesaving ropes sprung from his wristbands and belt buckle~~.~~, ~~They carried~~ carrying Vicki Vale and him out of peril.
- The coffee bar flanks the bookshelves~~.~~, ~~It entices~~ enticing readers to relax with a book.

A WRITER AT WORK

ANTICIPATING READERS' STANDARDS OF JUDGMENT

In this section, we look at how Christine Romano tries to anticipate the standards her readers would be likely to apply when evaluating the logic of an argument like Jessica Statsky's in "Children Need to Play, Not Compete." The final revision of Romano's essay appears in this chapter on pp. 309–12; Statsky's essay appears in Chapter 6 on pp. 218–21.

Because she was applying the standards from the critical reading chapter of her textbook, Romano said that she felt confident that the qualities important to her would also be important to her readers. Under Analyzing Your Readers, she identified two kinds of readers: her instructor, who she assumes will approve of her using the textbook standards, and parents of young children, the same audience Statsky is trying to convince. Romano acknowledged that parents would not know the textbook standards, but she speculated that, like her, they also would be impressed by the way Statsky supports her position. She noted also that she expects parents to be sympathetic to Statsky's position because they would not want their children to get hurt playing sports.

After writing a few minutes on Testing Your Choice, Romano did the Testing Your Choice collaborative activity in class with a few other students. One of her group members told her that he had been hurt playing in Little League and had wanted to quit but that his dad had made him go back. He remembered crying and trying to get out of going to the next game. But now he said he was glad his father insisted because years later, when playing on the high school football team, he realized that to become a serious athlete, you have to face up to the pain and not let the fear of injury prevent you from doing what you need to do. He said that this lesson is important for all kids to learn because it applies to everything in life, not just to playing sports. Based on this experience, the student told Romano his standard for judging competitive sports for young children would be how well the experience teaches them to stick it out, to conquer their pain and fear.

This student's choice of standards made Romano recognize that Statsky does not adequately anticipate such a reader's compelling reason for disagreeing with her position. When Romano planned and wrote her first draft, she tried to accommodate this student's point of view and others like it. In addition to praising the appropriateness, believability, and consistency of Statsky's argument, she also criticized the argument for being incomplete: "She neglects to anticipate parents' predictable questions and objections" (paragraph 2).

A few days later, Romano brought her first draft to class and received some helpful advice from another student. Writing in response to question 3 in the Critical Reading Guide, her workshop partner wrote that she was not sure what to underline as the thesis statement. She said that it was probably in the final paragraph, but she was not sure what the overall judgment would be. Here is the version of Romano's final paragraph that her classmate read and commented on:

> I have been able to point out both strengths and weaknesses in the logic of Statsky's support for her argument. The strengths are appropriateness, believability, and consistency. The major weakness is incompleteness--a failure to anticipate more fully the likely objections of a wide range of readers. I have been able to show that her logic would prevent certain kinds of parents from taking her argument seriously, parents whose experience and whose children's experience of team sports lead them to believe that the gains are worth whatever risks may be involved and who believe that many of the risks Statsky points out can be avoided by careful monitoring. For parents inclined to agree with her, however, her logic is likely to seem sound and complete. An argument that successfully confirms readers' beliefs is certainly valid, and Statsky succeeds admirably at this kind of argument.

Romano's workshop partner added in response to question 4 that she found Romano's essay very well supported. She said that she found the praise of the strengths of Statsky's argument convincing but also found the criticism of the weaknesses equally convincing. Therefore, she concluded by asking Romano to clarify her evaluation.

This request hit home because Romano had been trying to give Statsky's essay a mixed review but was not sure how well her own judgment was coming across. Romano was reassured by her workshop partner's judgment that her argument was convincing, but she saw that she needed to clarify which standards carry the most weight for her. She revised the last paragraph, adding this final sentence to make her thesis more explicit and let readers see exactly which standards were most important for her evaluation:

> Because she does not offer compelling counterarguments to the legitimate objections of those inclined not to agree with her, however, her success is limited.

THINKING CRITICALLY ABOUT WHAT YOU HAVE LEARNED

Now that you have read and discussed several evaluative essays and have written such an essay yourself, you can think critically about what you have learned. What problems did you encounter as you were writing, and how did you solve them? How did the essays you read influence your own writing? How do evaluations reflect and influence social attitudes?

Reflecting on Your Writing

Write a page or so telling your instructor about a problem you encountered in writing an evaluation, how you discovered it, and how you went about solving it. Begin by gathering your invention and planning notes, drafts and critical comments, revision plan, and final revision. Review these as you complete this writing task.

1. Identify *one* significant writing problem you encountered while writing the essay. Do not be concerned with grammar and punctuation; focus instead on a problem specific to writing an evaluation. For example, did you have trouble deciding how much information to include in presenting your subject? Did your initial judgment come across as vague or as too one-sided? Was it difficult to come up with clear reasons for your judgment or enough support for those reasons?
2. How did you first recognize this problem? Was it when you were thinking about how to state your judgment, trying to decide on your argumentative strategy, determining your organizational plan, or getting critical comments on a draft? What called the problem to your attention? Looking back, do you see signs of it in your invention work?
3. Reflect on how you attempted to solve the problem. If it arose during invention, did you go back to look at your subject again (rereading an essay, for example, or reviewing a movie)? Did you look for other related subjects with which to compare the subject of your evaluation? If it arose during drafting, did you do further invention to solve the problem—listing more reasons for your judgment, for example? Did you rethink your presentation of the subject? If you noticed the problem as you were revising, did you reword, reorganize, add new material, or simply cut the part that was problematic? Did you review your invention notes or return again to your subject for further support?
4. Finally, explain the problem and how you tried to solve it. Be specific by quoting from your invention writing and first draft, others' critical comments, your revision plan, and your final revision. Show the various changes your writing and thinking underwent. If you are still uncertain about your solution, say so. The point is not to prove that you have solved the problem perfectly but to show what you have learned about problem solving in writing an evaluation.

Reviewing What You Learned from Reading

You have read several evaluative essays in this chapter and perhaps also one or more drafts of evaluative essays written by classmates. Reading these essays probably influenced the evaluative essay you wrote. Write a page or so explaining how your writing has been influenced by others.

1. Consider whether any of the essays in the chapter or your classmates' drafts influenced your choice of subject or the way you organized your essay. Look for ideas you got from your reading or for writing strategies you were inspired to try. For example, did one of the essays suggest a way for you to open or close your evaluation, balance your judgment by qualifying it in some way, or introduce reasons or support?
2. Now write an explanation of these influences. You may focus on a single influence or discuss what you learned from parts of different essays. Give examples, showing how you have

built on what you have seen other writers do. You might also point out anything you would now change in your essay, based on this review of the other readings.

Considering the Social Dimensions of Writing Evaluations

Making evaluations is an important part of all occupations and professions. Manufacturers and assembly-line workers must continually evaluate their processes and products—asking questions about the quality of materials from outside suppliers, the efficiency of particular manufacturing methods, and the quality of the goods produced compared to the company's own standards and competitors' products. Instructors continually evaluate how well students understand readings and lectures, and ultimately they grade each student's achievement. Doctors and researchers on the staff of the federal Food and Drug Administration monitor the quality of the country's food production, evaluate the accuracy of advertising claims made by food manufacturers, and review the benefits and side effects of drugs. As consumers, many of us rely heavily on evaluations, such as those by the highly respected Consumers Union, which publishes in its monthly magazine, *Consumer Reports,* independent evaluations of a wide range of products.

The media or arts review—someone's judgment about the quality of movies, television programs, musical performances, books, and so forth—is a special kind of evaluation. We rely on such evaluations to help us decide what movies or performances to see, what books to buy, what exhibits to attend. They confirm or challenge our attraction to a particular television series or musical group. The best media reviewers develop impressive expertise. They come to be trusted by readers to set standards for movies, musical recordings, novels, or works of art. They educate readers, helping to shape their judgment and discrimination, building their confidence in recognizing a clumsy, passable, or outstanding work or performance. At their best, reviewers counterbalance advertising: Instead of enticing us to see every movie that comes to town, they help us to choose among the advertised movies. A trusted media or arts reviewer for a local newspaper can come to influence a community's values, building a local consensus, for example, about what constitutes a successful musical performance and encouraging tolerance or even appreciation for new kinds of music.

Elevating and Rejecting. As helpful as media and arts reviewers may be, however, the social influence they exert should also be viewed critically. For example, because they must be judgmental, praising some movies and damning, ignoring, or dismissing others, film reviewers inevitably foster an attitude of elevating and rejecting, conferring value on some movies, directors, or types of movies and devaluing the rest. This attitude of elevating and rejecting may be adopted by viewers as well, particularly those who are least confident of their judgments and who rely on reviewers to make judgments for them. They may judge too quickly, without trusting their own experience and without taking time to reflect on the possible value of something unexpected or offbeat.

Excluding and Silencing. By deciding what to review and what to ignore, media and arts reviewers determine what receives public attention and what remains invisible, and their decisions may often be based to a large extent on economic factors: Which review is likely to sell more newspapers or bring in more advertising? (In this sense, reviewers are part of a larger publicity apparatus; indeed, in our age of giant media conglomerates, a movie or music reviewer in a national magazine may well work for the same parent company that produced or distributed the film or the recording being reviewed—a situation that may not encourage the most objective viewpoint.) Local theater or musical groups without money to advertise their performances may only get a brief listing in the newspaper; but unless they are reviewed, they will be unlikely to attract enough ticket buyers to survive (and the less mainstream their offerings, the less likely they are to be reviewed). Similarly, a new artist is simply not likely to be reviewed as widely as a more established one.

For a long time, this sort of resistance to anything new and different kept many women and minority writers from being appreciated by reviewers—both in the universities and in the media—thus making it harder for them to earn a living by their work and effectively silencing their voices. This situation has changed in some ways—Rafferty, for example, seems to want to ensure that a film like *Devil in a Blue Dress* is seen by the readers of the *New Yorker*. Reviewers still have great power to determine what is considered a "successful" work of art and what is not.

Hidden Assumptions of Evaluators. Since successful reviewers exude confidence and expertise, it is easy to overlook the fact that media and arts reviews reflect a reviewer's personal preferences, values, and ideology. Even the most fair-minded reviewer writes from the perspective of a particular religion, gender, age, social class, and sexual orientation. Consider the possibility that Etzioni's criticism of McDonald's-type jobs for high school students may be based, at least in part, on snobbery. Consider, too, the possibility that Romano's receptiveness to Statsky's argument against competitive sports for children may be influenced by her own personal experience.

Experienced reviewers are also very likely to be aware of insider issues and conflicts on which they take a position. For example, a writer who is known by others in the publishing business to be extremely helpful in advising younger writers and generous in reviews of their work may obtain favorable reviews of his or her own work based as much on personality as on the work's quality. Similarly, a rock critic's knowledge that a group was experiencing strong internal conflict during the production of a recording might well influence his or her evaluation of that recording.

For Discussion. Here are some questions that can help as you think critically about the role of evaluative writing, particularly media and arts reviews. As you read and, perhaps, discuss these questions in class, take notes. Then, write a page or so about the social dimensions of reviews.

1. We have said that media and arts reviewers make an important social contribution—helping to set community standards, educating consumers, counterbalancing advertising. Reread Rafferty's and Wolcott's reviews, thinking about what they offer readers. Also think about what you tried to offer in your essay. In what ways, if any, do essays like yours and the others in this chapter make a social contribution?
2. To what extent do you rely on reviews in the magazines and newspapers you read (including your college newspaper) and on television news or entertainment shows that offer reviews? Do they influence what you decide to read or watch? Usually? Sometimes? Never? Do you read only reviews that evaluate something you have already seen or heard? If possible, read again or recall a review that influenced you in some way, and explain its influence. How, generally, have reviews contributed to the way you make judgments? Have they made you more confident? More tentative? Try to give a specific example.
3. How did your gender, age, social class, religion, and political perspective influence the subject you chose to evaluate and your evaluation of it? Select one other essay in the chapter, and consider how the same factors influenced the author (you will of course have to infer some influences). What can you conclude about the way reviewers' personal perspectives influence their reviewing?

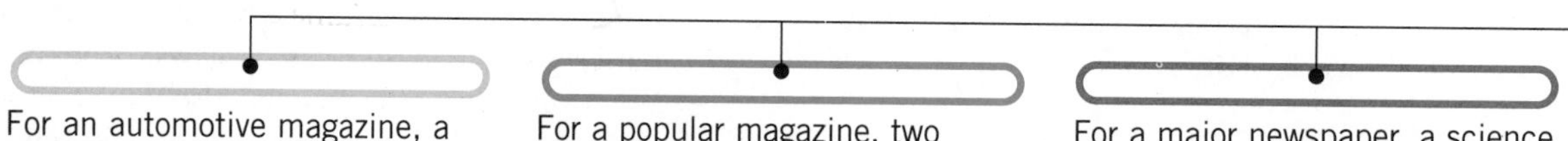

For an automotive magazine, a columnist speculates about the unexpected decline of fixed pricing at auto dealerships in the 1990s. He reports that in 1994, two thousand dealers were selling cars at fixed prices, yet by 1996, the number had dropped to around a thousand. After interviewing many dealers and recent buyers, the columnist argues that several causes might explain the decline in what was expected to be a continuing trend in automotive sales practices. Customers, it turns out, *want* to haggle over prices. They fear that they will pay too much if prices are fixed. Also, dealers learned that if they fixed selling prices on their cars, a dealer in the next town would undercut their prices. In addition to speculating about these likely causes, the columnist points out the increasing popularity of car leasing and of car-buying services. He concludes that the practice of fixed pricing will continue to decline.

For a popular magazine, two anthropologists write an article in which they speculate about the causes of the universal phenomenon known as the "afternoon lull," the period of reduced energy after the midday meal. Referring to research studies, they reject the possibility that the lull is caused either by the biochemical effects of eating or by a change in body temperature. They also reject the possibility that the lull is due to laziness or a desire for diversion. They argue instead that it is caused by a biological rhythm established during early human evolution in the tropics, where heat peaks in the early afternoon.

For a major newspaper, a science writer seeks to explain why so few women go into science. She begins by refuting the explanation that girls lack innate scientific ability. She then argues that there are at least four plausible causes for girls' disinterest in science and women's reluctance to take it up as a career. First, boys are more likely than girls to engage in physical play and active explorations of their environments, enabling them to develop an understanding of speed, motion, and mass, concepts important in physics. Second, women often feel out of place in science; classes emphasize competition; and in college, women are in the minority in science courses. Third, women in science careers do not receive fair treatment in hiring, pay, and promotions. Fourth, women learn that science careers are even more competitive now, characterized by longer hours and fewer opportunities for federal grants to support research, and so most women do not see how they can marry and have children and at the same time sustain such a career.

CHAPTER 9

Speculating about Causes

We all quite naturally try to explain causes. Because we assume that everything has a cause, we predictably ask "Why?" when we notice something new or unusual or puzzling.

Many things can be fully and satisfactorily explained. When children ask, "Why is the sky blue in the day and black at night?" parents can provide an answer. But we can answer other questions only tentatively: Why in the 1980s and 1990s has the cost of a college education increased faster than the cost of living? Why do minority groups in American society continue to suffer discrimination? Questions such as these often have only plausible, not definitive, explanations because we cannot design a scientific experiment to identify the cause conclusively. The decline in SAT scores, for example, has been attributed to the rise in television viewing among children. Although this contention is plausible, we cannot know for certain that television viewing is indeed responsible for the drop in scores.

Much of what we want to know about can never be known definitively and unarguably but can only be speculated about on the basis of the best available evidence and experience. Writing that speculates about causes plays an important role in academic and professional life, as the scenarios that open this chapter suggest. Government specialists analyze the causes of unemployment or homelessness to design policies intended to solve social problems. Business executives study the reasons for increases in sales or declines in worker productivity. Educators look at why some teaching techniques work and others do not or how family problems affect students' performance in school.

This chapter presents several essays arguing for the causes of some phenomenon or trend. A phenomenon is something notable about the human condition or social order—fear of failure, for example, or racial discrimination. A trend is a significant change occurring over some period of time, generally months or years. It can be identified by an increase or decrease—for example, a rise in the number of babies born with AIDS or a decline in the number of applicants to law school.

When you speculate about causes, you must first describe your subject and then propose some causes and argue for one (or more) as the best available explanation. You do not have to prove that your explanation is right, but you must attempt to convince readers that it is plausible by supporting your explanation with examples, facts, statistics, or anecdotes. You will probably need to anticipate readers' questions or objections to your causal argument. You may show readers that you are aware of their resistance, concede the usefulness of their questions by accommodating your own argument to them, or attempt to refute readers' objections by arguing that they are not reasonable or cannot be supported by any known evidence. When you speculate about causes, you inevitably find yourself in a situation where some of your readers believe other causes to be more plausible than the ones you are arguing for. Here, too, you must either acknowledge that you are aware of causes readers may prefer, concede the likelihood of these alternative causes, or refute them.

This chapter is designed to introduce you to one of the most common and most important writing situations you will meet in college. Speculating about why things are the way they are or why things change will help you to develop your powers of creativity as you speculate about possible causes, your powers of judgment as you weigh these possibilities and choose the most plausible ones, and your powers of reasoning as you devise an argumentative strategy to present your speculations to your readers.

Writing in Your Other Courses

As a student, you face assignments that ask you to speculate about and evaluate causes, such as the following:

- *For an American history course:* When the government forcibly moved Japanese Americans to "relocation camps" during World War II, the official reason was the danger that they would prove disloyal to the United States in its war with Japan. Some historians, however, have argued that racial prejudice and economic jealousy played a large part in the government's decision. On the basis of the assigned readings on this topic, how important do you think these unofficial reasons were?
- *For a political science course:* During 1989, Communist governments crumbled almost without resistance in the Soviet Union and much of eastern Europe, while in China the government succeeded in crushing a movement toward a more open political system. From what you have learned about the characteristics of Communist rule in the Soviet bloc and in China, why do you think the movements against the party succeeded in one case and not the other?
- *For a literature course:* Why does Huck Finn "light out for the Territory" at the novel's end? Defend your answer with evidence from the book.
- *For a biology course:* Why is AIDS concentrated among homosexuals in this country but among heterosexuals in Africa? In your answer, consider differences in such factors as sexual practices and attitudes and general standards of health and medical care.

Practice Speculating about Causes: A Collaborative Activity

To get a sense of this special kind of argument, choose a current trend, and speculate about its causes.

Part 1. Get together with two or three other students, and select one person to take notes.

1. Make a list of five or six trends—such as the decline in voter turnout in the United States, the increasing costs of a college education, or the increasing rate of smoking among young people—whose causes you are interested in speculating about. Choose one trend that interests all of you.
2. Come up with several likely causes of this trend. Just list as many as you can in different areas, including economic, cultural, or psychological causes.
3. Select three or four causes that seem most likely to provide a partial explanation for the trend. Discuss how you might support each of these causes, that is, how you would convince others that these causes are plausible or likely explanations for the trend.

Part 2. When you have finished speculating, take a few more minutes to reflect on the process you have been engaged in.

- Where did your ideas about causes come from—reading, television, your own imagination?
- How did you differentiate among the causes, rejecting some and accepting others as most likely?
- What kinds of support did you come up with? Where do you think you might find further support?

READINGS

Stephen King is America's best-known writer of horror fiction. In the following essay, excerpted from *Playboy,* King speculates about the popular appeal of horror movies. Before you begin reading, think about your own attitude toward horror films. Do you enjoy them? "Crave" them? Dislike them? Or are you indifferent?

As you read, notice how assertively King presents his assumptions about people, such as the ones in the opening sentence. How does he try to get you to accept these assumptions? Is he successful?

WHY WE CRAVE HORROR MOVIES
Stephen King

1 I think that we're all mentally ill; those of us outside the asylums only hide it a little better—and maybe not all that much better, after all. We've all known people who talk to themselves, people who sometimes squinch their faces into horrible grimaces when they believe no one is watching, people who have some hysterical fear—of snakes, the dark, the tight place, the long drop . . . and, of course, those final worms and grubs that are waiting so patiently underground.

When we pay our four or five bucks and seat ourselves at tenth-row center in a theater showing a horror movie, we are daring the nightmare. 2

Why? Some of the reasons are simple and obvious. To show that we can, that we are not afraid, that we can ride this roller coaster. Which is not to say that a really good horror movie may not surprise a scream out of us at some point, the way we may scream when the roller coaster twists through a complete 360 or plows through a lake at the bottom of the drop. And horror movies, like roller coasters, have always been the special province of the young; by the time one turns 40 or 50, one's appetite for double twists or 360-degree loops may be considerably depleted. 3

We also go to re-establish our feelings of essential normality; the horror movie is innately conservative, even reactionary. Freda Jackson as the horrible melting woman in *Die, Monster, Die!* confirms for us that no matter how far we may be removed from the beauty of a Robert Redford or a Diana Ross, we are still light-years from true ugliness. 4

And we go to have fun. 5

Ah, but this is where the ground starts to slope away, isn't it? Because this is a very peculiar sort of fun, indeed. The fun comes from seeing others menaced—sometimes killed. One critic has suggested that if pro football has become the voyeur's version of combat, then the horror film has become the modern version of the public lynching. 6

It is true that the mythic, "fairy tale" horror film intends to take away the shades of gray. . . . It urges us to put away our more civilized and adult penchant for analysis and to become children again, seeing things in pure blacks and whites. It may be that horror movies provide psychic relief on this level because this invitation to lapse into simplicity, irrationality, and even outright madness is extended so rarely. We are told we may allow our emotions a free rein . . . or no rein at all. 7

If we are all insane, then sanity becomes a matter of degree. If your insanity leads you to carve up women like Jack the Ripper or the Cleveland Torso Murderer, we clap you away in the funny farm (but neither of those two amateur-night surgeons was ever caught, heh-heh-heh); if, on the other hand, your insanity leads you only to talk to yourself when you're under stress or to pick your nose on your morning bus, then you are left alone to go about your business . . . though it is doubtful that you will ever be invited to the best parties. 8

Startling

The potential lyncher is in almost all of us (excluding saints, past and present; but then, most saints have been crazy in their own ways), and every now and then, he has to be let loose to scream and roll around in the grass. Our emotions and our fears form their own body, and we recognize that it demands its own exercise to maintain proper muscle tone. Certain of these emotional muscles are accepted—even exalted—in civilized society; they are, of course, the emotions that tend to maintain the status quo of civilization itself. Love, friendship, loyalty, kindness—these are all the emotions that we applaud, emotions that have been immortalized in the couplets of Hallmark cards and in the verses (I don't dare call it poetry) of Leonard Nimoy. 9

When we exhibit these emotions, society showers us with positive reinforcement; we learn this even before we get out of diapers. When, as children, we hug our rotten little puke of a sister and give her a kiss, all the aunts and uncles smile and twit and cry, "Isn't he the sweetest little thing?" Such coveted treats as chocolate-covered graham crackers often follow. But if we deliberately slam the rotten little puke of a sister's fingers in the door, sanctions follow—angry remonstrance from parents, aunts, and uncles; instead of a chocolate-covered graham cracker, a spanking. 10

But anticivilization emotions don't go away, and they demand periodic exercise. We have such "sick" jokes as "What's the difference between a truckload of bowling balls 11 and a truckload of dead babies?" (You can't unload a truckload of bowling balls with a pitchfork . . . a joke, by the way, that I heard originally from a ten-year-old.) Such a joke may surprise a laugh or a grin out of us even as we recoil, a possibility that confirms the thesis: If we share a brotherhood of man, then we also share an insanity of man. None of which is intended as a defense of either the sick joke or insanity but merely as an explanation of why the best horror films, like the best fairy tales, manage to be reactionary, anarchistic, and revolutionary all at the same time.

12 The mythic horror movie, like the sick joke, has a dirty job to do. It deliberately appeals to all that is worst in us. It is morbidity unchained, our most base instincts let free, our nastiest fantasies realized . . . and it all happens, fittingly enough, in the dark. For those reasons, good liberals often shy away from horror films. For myself, I like to see the most aggressive of them—*Dawn of the Dead,* for instance—as lifting a trap door in the civilized forebrain and throwing a basket of raw meat to the hungry alligators swimming around in that subterranean river beneath.

13 Why bother? Because it keeps them from getting out, man. It keeps them down there and me up here. It was Lennon and McCartney who said that all you need is love, and I would agree with that.

14 As long as you keep the gators fed.

Connecting to Culture and Experience

"The potential lyncher is in almost all of us," says Stephen King, ". . . and every now and then, he has to be let loose to scream and roll around in the grass." King seems to say that horror films perform a social function by allowing us to exercise (or possibly exorcise) our least civilized emotions.

Discuss this idea with two or three other students. Certain religious groups and politicians believe that violence like that shown in horror films inspires people, especially the impressionable young, to commit violence—a belief quite different from King's. Do you believe that media violence exorcises or inspires violence? You may find that the members of your group disagree on this issue. What reasons can you give for your positions? If you believe that media violence inspires real violence, do you support censorship of movies, television programs, books, or magazines that portray violence? For children or adults or both? If you oppose censorship, do you support movie rating systems or the television V-chip, which gives parents some control over what their children watch? Where do you stand on censoring the Internet?

These questions identify important social or civic issues: the role of the media in a democratic society, the right of free expression and access to media, and the need to control violence.

Analyzing Writing Strategies

1. At the beginning of this chapter, we discuss several attributes of arguments that speculate about causes. Consider which of these is true of King's essay.
   - It presents or defines its subject.
   - It proposes specific causes to explain the subject.
   - It argues that these causes are likely or plausible, not definitive, explanations for the subject.
   - It supports each cause with examples, facts, statistics, or anecdotes.
   - It anticipates readers' questions, objections, and alternative causes.

For more on supporting arguments, see pp. 529–37.

2. King offers several kinds of **support** for the causes he proposes. For example, in paragraph 3, in the last sentence of paragraph 12, and in paragraph 13, he provides **analogies;** in paragraph 4, an **example;** and in paragraph 6, a **comparison.** Analyze each kind of support: Notice what general statement King is trying to support in each case, and describe how the analogy, example, and comparison support the general statement. Then evaluate whether the support seems relevant to the statement for King's particular readers.

Considering Topics for Your Own Essay

Consider writing about some phenomenon of popular culture that interests you. For instance, have you ever wondered why romance novels are so popular? Police shows or soap operas or MTV? Roller blading? Singles bars? Drive-through fast-food restaurants? How might you present the phenomenon to your readers? What obvious and not-so-obvious causes might you propose to explain the popularity of the phenomenon?

Commentary

When you set goals and plan your own essay speculating about causes, two of your most basic concerns will be to come up with a tentative organization and to devise an argumentative strategy. Therefore, you can benefit from considering King's organization and argumentative strategy. A scratch outline reveals his **organization:**

We're all mentally ill, even though some of us learn how to hide it. (paragraph 1)

We go to horror movies to prove that we can face our madness. (2, 3)

We go to reassure ourselves that we are normal. (4)

We go because we enjoy seeing others in danger. (5, 6)

We go for the psychological relief that comes from giving in to our emotions. (7)

Sanity is a matter of degree. (8)

We have to give in to our emotions, and society rewards emotions that maintain the status quo. (9, 10)

But we must also give in to our antisocial emotions. (11)

Horror movies appeal to the worst in us, and they keep our worst impulses under control. (12–14)

After a brief introduction that makes provocative claims about widespread mental illness and hysterical fears, King goes immediately to his causal argument: In paragraphs 2–7, he proposes four causes of our craving for horror movies. In paragraph 8, at about the midpoint of the essay, King returns to his introductory claims, refining and qualifying them. In paragraphs 8–11, we learn much more about the illness in human nature for which horror movies provide a cure. In the final three paragraphs, King briefly restates his view of the important role horror movies play in helping us to remain sane and to maintain an orderly society. This organization seems uncomplicated and easy to follow. It allows King to present a logical, coherent argument that meets readers' expectations for a causal explanation.

This straightforward, effective organization supports a subtle **argumentative strategy.** King's purpose seems to be to convince his particular readers—*Playboy* subscribers, who are primarily men in their twenties or thirties—that horror movies have social value because they keep people's worst impulses and fears under control. Therefore, he must convince these readers that they have a dark side (which King refers to as mental illness, hysterical fear, the nightmare, irrationality, madness, fears, or anticivilization emotions) and that horror movies and presumably other portrayals of violence in the media enable them to manage or control this dark side. He begins by asserting that all people are mentally ill, and as if aware of some readers' skepticism, he returns to this part of his argument in paragraphs 8–11. Here he attempts to get readers to acknowledge that they have at least mistreated a sibling or enjoyed a sick joke. He seems to be saying, "Look, I know you may be resisting my argument, but if I acknowledge the importance of civilized emotions that hold society together, then you should be willing to acknowledge the prevalence of antisocial emotions that, uncontrolled, would lead to violence and social chaos. I'm not trying to encourage sick jokes or excuse aggression and violence, only to explain why we crave horror movies." Half of the essay is devoted to this part of King's argument.

The other half attempts to explain why we crave horror movies by offering four causes of our craving. These are to be found in paragraphs 2–7, as the scratch outline reveals. King is careful to support these causes with analogies, examples, and comparisons that he assumes will be meaningful to his readers. At the end of the essay, paragraphs 12–14 restate King's claim that we crave horror movies and that they have social value because they "keep the gators fed."

King's argumentative strategy is strengthened by his astute use of both **obvious causes** and **hidden causes.** King begins with a cause that seems obvious but is still worth mentioning: We go to horror films because we want to prove that we can sit through them, just as we ride roller coasters to show ourselves and others that we have the courage to do it (paragraph 3). This cause seems plausible, though not at all surprising. We can assume that King mentions it right away because he assumes that readers will be thinking of it. It enables him both to connect to a very common experience of his readers and to set an obvious cause aside in order to move on to the not-so-obvious causes, which are the heart of his argument.

King next entertains a very different cause: We go to horror movies "to re-establish our feelings of essential normality." This cause is much less predictable than the first. It may even be somewhat puzzling, and King might have argued it further. He asserts that horror movies are conservative and gives one example of the ugliness of their characters. Although this cause is also plausible, it moves us from obvious causes toward the one hidden (unexpected, unlikely, risky) cause that King is to argue at length—we "crave" horror movies (not just attend them casually) in order to manage our uncivilized emotions of fear, violence, and aggression.

King's readers may not accept his psychology or find his hidden cause convincingly argued, but they are almost certain to be interested in the argument itself, perhaps intrigued, maybe even shocked by either the idea or the examples. Whatever their reaction, King has not bored them with causes so obvious that they could have predicted all of them before reading the argument. In your own causal analysis essay, your first goal will be to speculate creatively about your subject so that you can come up with at least one not-so-obvious cause. Like King, you may want to place this cause last, after discussing other more obvious causes, and to argue for it at length and with ingenuity.

Joseph Berger is a *New York Times* bureau chief in White Plains, New York. His office is responsible for statewide news coverage outside the New York City and Albany areas. For twelve years a reporter on religion and education at the *Times*, he is a three-time winner of the yearly Supple Award from the Religion Newswriters Association for best reporting on religion. He has recently published a book, *The Young Scientists* (1994).

The essay reprinted here was published in 1994 in *American Enterprise*, a politically conservative journal that is read mainly by policymakers and ordinary citizens who want to understand how the conservative philosophy can shape social and economic policies. It is also read by liberals who want to find out what conservatives are thinking. As you read, consider your own views about specialized, selective high school educational programs that produce high achievement. Also notice the extended support Berger provides for the two causes he believes best explain high achievement in science.

WHAT PRODUCES OUTSTANDING SCIENCE STUDENTS

Joseph Berger

America is producing too few high-achieving high school graduates, particularly in the sciences and mathematics. This familiar lament was repeated recently in a Department of Education report, *National Excellence: A Case for Developing America's Talent,* which called for new efforts to identify talented youngsters early and provide them with more challenging curricula. But Americans have never been completely comfortable with the schools or programs that approach education this way, alternately embracing them as essential to society's progress and rejecting them as elitist. 1

A look at the record of these schools and special programs, however, should go a long way toward allaying the concerns of their detractors. They are spurring students on to extraordinary achievements and helping them learn the mental discipline that will serve them (and us) well as they undertake careers. One measure of the success of these schools and programs may be their record in producing winners of the Westinghouse Science Talent Search, the most prestigious high school science contest in the nation. Through the prism of the contest, we can take a closer look at the schools and the challenging programs they undertake. 2

The Westinghouse Search

The Westinghouse Science Talent Search was launched to identify young scientific talent, and it has been doing so with remarkable precision since 1941. Every year, approximately 1,700 students from around the country polish off projects they have been working on for as long as two years, and send in a report to the contest officials. Simply entering the contest is an impressive achievement for a high school junior. It means that the student has spent hundreds of hours probing a scientific question or testing a theory about which he has written a scientific paper of near-professional quality. The top 300 students become semifinalists, and from this group, 40 are selected to bring their projects to Washington. Ten projects are then selected as the best in the final round of judging. The 40 finalists get at least $1,000 for their efforts, and the top 3 student receives a $40,000 scholarship. Most of the winners, from semifinalists up, are guaranteed admission to the college of their choice. . . .

4 From the start, this contest was different from traditional science fairs. Its goal was not simply to choose the best project but to locate the best potential scientists. The distinction is an important one. The contest has a number of features that test the mettle of the students as well as the projects. It endeavors to explore the nimbleness and originality of the minds behind the projects, rather than just rewarding the boldness of the experiment. The contest's underlying philosophy is that students discover their scientific talents by working on science, not by listening to lectures in a classroom. . . .

5 Today there are 23 specialized science schools in the United States, and many of these are residential. This number does not include the magnet schools around the country that are placing a new emphasis on science.

6 These schools are selective and the curriculum is difficult. In special science schools and programs, students don't start with earth science as do most high school freshmen. They begin with biology or chemistry. By sophomore year, the top students are taking honors biology and chemistry. By junior year, the students are well launched on their own research at the schools or in teaching hospitals or labs in their cities. . . .

What Makes a Winner: The Method

7 "Chalk and talk is no good. Go out and do what science is," says Richard Plass, a biology teacher at Stuyvesant [High School in New York City]. Plass has never done research more sophisticated than raising guppies, but he has produced 202 Westinghouse semifinalists, nurturing more successful research projects than perhaps any other teacher in the United States. The biology teacher (not biologist) admits frankly that many of the young people he teaches are beyond him.

8 At Stuyvesant, Plass immerses his students in research at a tender age. Students in freshman biology take four periods of research lab a week in addition to the normal complement of six classes of biology. In short order, they are working on lengthy and distinctive experiments. Students start the year studying a number of common creatures. They study the organisms and their life cycles and then pick a substance or a physical or environmental phenomenon whose effects on the organism they will test. The projects are designed to nurture a love of research in the students. In addition to their work on experiments, students serve on student committees associated with their research projects in order to trade their lab experiences.

9 In their second terms, students compose a report on their experiments, complete with an abstract, a review of prior literature, a hypothesis, results, graphs, photographs, and conclusions. Students are also required to give oral presentations. Sophomore year offers a research program in chemistry. In junior year, students can choose a "Junior Research Class," sometimes called the "Westinghouse Class," which pairs them with professional scientists for more research. This class meets formally only once a week. Beyond that and the time spent on other course work, students are on their own. Students are required, as a test of their maturity, to find their own mentors in the host of hospitals and universities in New York City.

10 What comes through in examining the schools that produce the Westinghouse winners is a commitment to early training in the methods, philosophy, and ethics of research. These methods endure for a lifetime, having instilled a mental discipline that helps students tackle the world.

11 Nina Tabachnik Schor, a pediatric neurologist at Children's Hospital in Pittsburgh, exemplifies that mental discipline. She won first prize in the 1972 Westinghouse

contest and used the prize money for tuition at Yale. After graduating she enrolled in a grueling seven-year program at Cornell Medical School and Rockefeller University that led to both an M.D. and a Ph.D. in biochemistry. She credits completion of the program to the habits and persistence she developed in her youthful immersion in a Westinghouse project. "Without this background," she says, "I don't think I could have done it." Roald Hoffmann, a Nobel Prize–winning chemist at Cornell and former Westinghouse winner, credits the program for his own addiction to research.

What Makes a Winner: Students and Their Families

Schools are only part of the secret of winning the Westinghouse. The backgrounds of winning students have a number of common traits. In 1989, the year of my study, 28 percent of the winners were foreign-born immigrants and at least 2 were children of immigrants. Though precise statistics dating from the contest's inception are not available, it is clear that immigrant families have long won a disproportionate share of the prizes. In the 1940s, when the contest began, children from immigrant Jewish families captured an unexpectedly large number of prizes. During the 1980s and early 1990s, young people from Taiwan, Korea, China, Japan, and India took a disproportionate share. But since most of these students were educated almost entirely in American schools, one cannot attribute their success to a superior foreign education. 12

What differentiates these students from their peers is an immigrant grit that drives them ahead. This quality is not genetic; it is fostered by parents, and by immigrant parents more than most. A sagacious explanation for immigrant success was offered by an Israeli-born 1989 winner, Tamir Druz. "Immigrants," he said, "understand the concept of hard work. In a sense, we're more American than the Americans. We actually believe in individualism, in going out and making your own way, like the first Americans. We had a frontier too. The frontier made America what it is. Every time Americans felt tied down, they could become pioneers. Immigrants have a frontier. America is our new West." The immigrant parents I studied also appear to push their children harder than American parents. And the very experience of immigrating instills some qualities in children that lead to success. The children, accustomed to struggle, thrive on it and appear less afraid of using their initiative. 13

Many of the winners are also children of doctors or scientists; there were 18 in 1993. Actively or unwittingly such parents encourage a willingness to question, to be skeptical of authority, to have confidence in personal doubts and puzzlements. Most important, parents—scientists and nonscientists—that produce these children seem to have in common a way of child rearing that encourages children to trust their own curiosity. Children who grow up thinking that what is written on the printed page is gospel, that what a scientist or doctor says must be true, are unlikely to become scientists. In short, in cultivating young scientists, home is part of the equation. A parent who tries to coax a scientist out of a baseball player is going to fail. But the basic operating principle appears to be to let the children follow their own curiosity. 14

Conclusion

The Westinghouse has spurred improvements in science education around the country and encouraged research among the young; it has given prominence to schools such as Bronx Science and has prompted others to start research programs and research schools. The new programs and schools arose from an abundance of concerns: America's anemic performance in developing new technology, its inability to attract significant numbers of students into careers in science and math, the widespread 15 impression that American students were not up to their peers in Europe and Japan, and a general suspicion that the United States had passed its peak and was on a gentle but inexorable downward slope. . . .

Embracing whole-heartedly these schools and the methods they use to nurture talent could go a long way toward reversing the performance of America's scientific vanguard. 16

Connecting to Culture and Experience

Berger recognizes that Americans are uncomfortable with public school programs for talented youth, "alternately embracing them as essential to society's progress and rejecting them as elitist." Berger advocates such programs nevertheless and argues that because chosen students must work hard and make extraordinary achievements, the programs are justified.

Discuss with two or three other students your views on elite educational programs and the specialized schools that make them possible. Do you approve of specialized public schools with high admission standards, schools that cost more per student to operate than ordinary schools? Specifically, can you support science programs and schools of the kind Berger describes, even though they are highly selective ("elitist") and expensive? What is your reasoning? What advantages and disadvantages do you see in admittedly elitist programs? What is lost and what is gained? Even though some individuals lose out, might society as a whole benefit from programs for gifted students?

Consider that many high schools already offer a selective top academic track, where class sizes may be smaller than in regular classes. A few high schools offer the highly competitive International Baccalaureate degree program. Consider also that interscholastic sports programs and some music programs are selective and require special funding. Not just anyone can be on the football team. Coaches select students for certain characteristics and skills and demand effort and consistently high performance. If students fail to meet the coaches' expectations, they are benched or dropped from the team.

Analyzing Writing Strategies

Scratch outlines are discussed on pp. 431–32.

1. Make a scratch outline of Berger's essay. Using your outline as a guide, analyze Berger's **argumentative strategy** in convincing his particular readers—conservative and liberal policymakers—that his causal argument is plausible. (See the Commentary section following the King reading for an example of an analysis of an argumentative strategy.) What is Berger trying to accomplish in paragraphs 1–6? What, in fact, is the phenomenon he is trying to explain? How does he sequence his proposed causes in paragraphs 7–14 and go about arguing for them? How does he conclude? Given his purpose and readers, what advantages and disadvantages do you see in Berger's argumentative strategy?

For more on supporting arguments, see pp. 529–37.

2. A causal argument succeeds or fails on the strength of its **support for each cause,** the argument or reasoning that attempts to convince readers to consider the cause likely or plausible. Analyze how Berger in paragraphs 7–11 supports his first cause, certain teaching methods produce promising scientists. What approach does he take in each paragraph? How does he sequence the different kinds of support (what comes first, next, and so on)? Given his readers, how successful is he in supporting this cause?

Considering Topics for Your Own Essay

Like Berger, consider explaining the success (or failure) of some educational enterprise. Examples of educational enterprises are College Board Advanced Placement courses at your high school; home schooling; a high school or college tutoring center; health and sex education programs; school or college health clinics; the mathematics, science, history, or English curriculum at your high school; the general education requirements at your college; and college entrance or placement tests. If you were to choose one educational enterprise to speculate about, which one might it be? How might you present it to your readers? What causes might you propose to explain its success or failure?

Commentary

Whereas King can assume his readers' familiarity with his subject, horror movies, Berger must assume that his readers have little or no idea about outstanding achievement in science. Therefore, he must devote a large portion of his essay to **presenting his subject.** Fortunately, he has a lot of information about one example of exemplary science achievement—the Westinghouse Science Talent Search—and about the high school science programs that produce Westinghouse winners. He provides historical information about the Westinghouse competition and describes its procedures and goals. He cites the number of special science schools in the United States and characterizes their programs in a general way. Approximately a third of his essay (paragraphs 1–6) is devoted to presenting the subject. In planning your own essay, you will have to decide how much information your readers need about your subject in order to understand and care about your causal argument.

Berger also uses both **immediate** and **background causes** effectively. An immediate cause, in his context, is one that is close in time to students' science achievement and may be immediately responsible for it, while a background cause lies in the past, long before students became seriously interested in science. The immediate cause in Berger's argument is the special method of teaching science that he describes in paragraphs 7–11. The background cause is the set of family characteristics described in paragraphs 12–14 that seem to lead to high achievement in science—the grit and risk taking of foreign-born students and the confidence and curiosity of students with a parent who is a doctor or a scientist. (See the Commentary following the King essay for a discussion of two other types of causes, obvious and hidden.) Readers are likely to find Berger's explanation of high achievement in science more convincing because he attempts to account for both its immediate and its background causes. When you do the invention work for your own essay, you will have the opportunity to list several kinds of causes and to analyze their usefulness for explaining your subject.

Robert D. Putnam, a professor of government at Harvard University, specializes in the study of modern democracies. His most recent books are *Making Democracy Work* (1993) and *Revitalizing Trilateral Democracies* (1995). In *Making Democracy Work* he reports on a twenty-year study contrasting civic life in two Italian towns. Early in the book, he announces that his goal was to "confront basic issues about civic life and collaboration for the common good." The importance of his work has been recognized by his election as a fellow of the American Academy of Arts and Sciences.

This essay appeared in 1996 in *The American Prospect,* a politically liberal quarterly journal of politics and culture. Though its readers are primarily policymakers and ordinary citizens with liberal or progressive views, it is also read by some conservatives who are interested in getting the liberal point of view.

As you begin reading, you will notice that Putnam presents himself—in his title and through his language—as a detective seeking to explain a mystery. The mystery is his subject—the disappearance of civic America—and the explanation is his causal argument. As you read, notice that Putnam lists many possible causes and then selects only one as the most plausible. Notice also his extended, energetic attempt to make this one cause seem plausible to his readers.

THE STRANGE DISAPPEARANCE OF CIVIC AMERICA

Robert D. Putnam

1 For the last year or so, I have been wrestling with a difficult mystery. It is a classic brainteaser, with a corpus delicti, a crime scene strewn with clues, and many potential suspects. As in all good detective stories, however, some plausible miscreants turn out to have impeccable alibis, and some important clues hint at portentous developments that occurred before the curtain rose.

2 The mystery concerns the strange disappearance of social capital and civic engagement in America. By "social capital," I mean features of social life—networks, norms, and trust—that enable participants to act together more effectively to pursue shared objectives. (Whether or not their shared goals are praiseworthy is, of course, entirely another matter.) I use the term "civic engagement" to refer to people's connections with the life of their communities, not only with politics.

3 Although I am not yet sure that I have solved the mystery, I have assembled evidence that clarifies what happened. An important clue, as we shall see, involves differences among generations. Americans who came of age during the Depression and World War II have been far more deeply engaged in the life of their communities than the generations that have followed them. The passing of this "long civic generation" appears to be an important proximate cause of the decline of our civic life. This discovery does not in itself crack the case, but when combined with other data it points strongly to one suspect against whom I shall presently bring an indictment.

4 Evidence for the decline of social capital and civic engagement comes from a number of independent sources. Surveys of average Americans in 1965, 1975, and 1985, in which they recorded every single activity during a day—so-called "time-budget" studies—indicate that since 1965 time spent on informal socializing and visiting is down (perhaps by one-quarter) and time devoted to clubs and organizations is down even more sharply (by roughly half). Membership records of such diverse organizations as the PTA, the Elks club, the League of Women Voters, the Red Cross, labor unions, and even bowling leagues show that participation in many conventional voluntary associations has declined by roughly 25 percent to 50 percent over the last two to three decades. Surveys show sharp declines in many measures of collective political participation, including attending a rally or speech (off 36 percent between 1973 and 1993), attending a meeting on town or school affairs (off 39 percent), or working for a political party (off 56 percent). . . .

5 Of course, American civil society is not moribund. Many good people across the land work hard every day to keep their communities vital. Indeed, evidence suggests that America still outranks many other countries in the degree of our community

involvement and social trust. But if we examine our lives, not our aspirations, and if we compare ourselves not with other countries but with our parents, the best available evidence suggests that we are less connected with one another.

6 Reversing this trend depends, at least in part, on understanding the causes of the strange malady afflicting American civic life. This is the mystery I seek to unravel here: Why, beginning in the 1960s and accelerating in the 1970s and 1980s, did the fabric of American community life begin to fray? Why are more Americans bowling alone?

The Usual Suspects

7 Many possible answers have been suggested for this puzzle:

- Busy-ness and time pressure
- Economic hard times (or, according to alternative theories, material affluence)
- Residential mobility
- Suburbanization
- The movement of women into the paid labor force and the stresses of two-career families
- Disruption of marriage and family ties
- Changes in the structure of the American economy, such as the rise of chain stores, branch firms, and the service sector
- The sixties (most of which actually happened in the seventies), including
    - Vietnam, Watergate, and disillusion with public life
    - The cultural revolt against authority (sex, drugs, and so on)
- Growth of the welfare state
- The civil rights revolution
- Television, the electronic revolution, and other technological changes. . . .

8 I have discovered only one prominent suspect against whom circumstantial evidence can be mounted, and in this case, it turns out, some directly incriminating evidence has also turned up. This is not the occasion to lay out the full case for the prosecution, nor to review rebuttal evidence for the defense, but I want to present evidence that justifies indictment.

9 The culprit is television.

10 First, the timing fits. The long civic generation was the last cohort of Americans to grow up without television, for television flashed into American society like lightning in the 1950s. In 1950 barely 10 percent of American homes had television sets, but by 1959, 90 percent did, probably the fastest diffusion of a major technological innovation ever recorded. The reverberations from this lightning bolt continued for decades, as viewing hours grew by 17–20 percent during the 1960s and by an additional 7–8 percent during the 1970s. In the early years, TV watching was concentrated among the less educated sectors of the population, but during the 1970s the viewing time of the more educated sectors of the population began to converge upward. Television viewing increases with age, particularly upon retirement, but each generation since the introduction of television has begun its life cycle at a higher starting point. By 1995 viewing per TV household was more than 50 percent higher than it had been in the 1950s.

11 Most studies estimate that the average American now watches roughly four hours per day (excluding periods in which television is merely playing in the background). Even a more conservative estimate of three hours means that television absorbs 40 percent of the average American's free time, an increase of about one-third since 1965. Moreover, multiple sets have proliferated: By the late 1980s three-quarters of all U.S.

homes had more than one set, and these numbers too are rising steadily, allowing ever more private viewing. . . . This massive change in the way Americans spend their days and nights occurred precisely during the years of generational civic disengagement.

12 Evidence of a link between the arrival of television and the erosion of social connections is, however, not merely circumstantial. The links between civic engagement and television viewing can be instructively compared with the links between civic engagement and newspaper reading. The basic contrast is straightforward: Newspaper reading is associated with high social capital, TV viewing with low social capital.

13 Controlling for education, income, age, race, place of residence, work status, and gender, TV viewing is strongly and negatively related to social trust and group membership, whereas the same correlations with newspaper reading are positive.* Within every educational category, heavy readers are avid joiners, whereas heavy viewers are more likely to be loners. In fact, more detailed analysis suggests that heavy TV watching is one important reason *why* less educated people are less engaged in the life of their communities. Controlling for differential TV exposure significantly reduces the correlation between education and engagement.

14 Viewing and reading are themselves uncorrelated—some people do lots of both, some do little of either—but "pure readers" (that is, people who watch less TV than average and read more newspapers than average) belong to 76 percent more civic organizations than "pure viewers" (controlling for education, as always). Precisely the same pattern applies to other indicators of civic engagement, including social trust and voting turnout. "Pure readers," for example, are 55 percent more trusting than "pure viewers."

15 In other words, each hour spent viewing television is associated with less social trust and less group membership, while each hour reading a newspaper is associated with more. An increase in television viewing of the magnitude that the U.S. has experienced in the last four decades might directly account for as much as one-quarter to one-half of the total drop in social capital, even without taking into account, for example, the indirect effects of television viewing on newspaper readership or the cumulative effects of lifetime viewing hours. Newspaper circulation (per household) has dropped by more than half since its peak in 1947. To be sure, it is not clear which way the tie between newspaper reading and civic involvement works, since disengagement might itself dampen one's interest in community news. But the two trends are clearly linked.

How Might TV Destroy Social Capital?

16 **Time displacement.** Even though there are only 24 hours in everyone's day, most forms of social and media participation are positively correlated. People who listen to lots of classical music are more likely, not less likely, than others to attend Cubs games. Television is the principal exception to this generalization—the only leisure activity that seems to inhibit participation outside the home. TV watching comes at the expense of nearly every social activity outside the home, especially social gatherings and informal conversations. TV viewers are homebodies.

17 Most studies that report a negative correlation between television watching and community involvement are ambiguous with respect to causality, because they merely compare different individuals at a single time. However, one important quasi-experimental

* When social scientists "control for" education or income or other classifications in surveys or polls, they use statistical techniques to determine whether some other factor, such as education attained or level of income, contributes to the phenomenon or trend. By "controlling for" education, they have been able to show that regardless of their educational level, people who watch a lot of television are less involved in civic affairs.

study of the introduction of television in three Canadian towns found the same pattern at the aggregate level across time. A major effect of television's arrival was the reduction in participation in social, recreational, and community activities among people of all ages. In short, television privatizes our leisure time.

18 **Effects on the outlooks of viewers.** An impressive body of literature suggests that heavy watchers of TV are unusually skeptical about the benevolence of other people—overestimating crime rates, for example. This body of literature has generated much debate about the underlying causal patterns, with skeptics suggesting that misanthropy may foster couch-potato behavior rather than the reverse. While awaiting better experimental evidence, however, a reasonable interim judgment is that heavy television watching may well increase pessimism about human nature. Perhaps too, as social critics have long argued, both the medium and the message have more basic effects on our ways of interacting with the world and with one another. Television may induce passivity, as Neil Postman has claimed.

19 **Effects on children.** TV consumes an extraordinary part of children's lives, about 40 hours per week on average. Viewing is especially high among pre-adolescents, but it remains high among younger adolescents: Time-budget studies suggest that among youngsters aged 9 to 14 television consumes as much time as all other discretionary activities combined, including playing, hobbies, clubs, outdoor activities, informal visiting, and just hanging out. The effects of television on childhood socialization have, of course, been hotly debated for more than three decades. The most reasonable conclusion from a welter of sometimes conflicting results appears to be that heavy television watching probably increases aggressiveness (although perhaps not actual violence), that it probably reduces school achievement, and that it is statistically associated with "psychosocial malfunctioning," although how much of this effect is self-selection and how much causal remains much debated. The evidence is, as I have said, not yet enough to convict, but the defense has a lot of explaining to do.

20 More than two decades ago, just as the first signs of disengagement were beginning to appear in American politics, the political scientist Ithiel de Sola Pool observed that the central issue would be—it was then too soon to judge, as he rightly noted—whether the development represented a temporary change in the weather or a more enduring change in the climate. It now appears that much of the change whose initial signs he spotted did in fact reflect a climatic shift.

21 Moreover, just as the erosion of the ozone layer was detected only many years after the proliferation of the chlorofluorocarbons that caused it, so too the erosion of America's social capital became visible only several decades after the underlying process had begun. Like Minerva's owl that flies at dusk, we come to appreciate how important the long civic generation has been to American community life just as its members are retiring. Unless America experiences a dramatic upward boost in civic engagement (a favorable "period effect") in the next few years, Americans in 2010 will join, trust, and vote even less than we do today.

Connecting to Culture and Experience

Putnam is alarmed by civic disengagement and the decline of civic life in the United States since the 1960s. He defines civic engagement in paragraph 4 by category and by specific activities: The categories are informal socializing, voluntary associations, and collective political participation; the activities are visiting friends or neighbors, joining clubs or organizations (including community sports teams, like bowling leagues), attending a political rally or speech, attending a meeting concerned with town or school affairs, and working for a political party. Civic life, as Putnam defines it, seems to involve social and communal activities other than church attendance, schooling or professional training, and work. Civic activities seem to hold the promise of bringing people together across ethnic, religious, and class lines.

Discuss with two or three other students the importance of civic life in a democracy. Begin by describing the voluntary civic activities you engage in presently. (If you are going to college full time and are perhaps also working part time, the list of activities may be short.) In addition to the activities in which you currently participate, which ones seem important to you personally for sustaining civic life? That is, which ones, if any, do you hope to participate in after you finish college? To ensure that your list actually reflects your personal values about civic life, limit it to activities you can easily imagine yourself participating in, those you already know how to gain access to from observing the civic participation of your parents, relatives, neighbors, or friends.

From your lists, what can you conclude about the role and importance of civic life? (You need not reach a consensus on this question.) How might greater civic engagement improve the quality of life in the United States? How might it create what Putnam calls "social capital," the "networks, norms [standards of behavior], and trust" that enable people to cooperate in order to achieve common objectives and improve community well-being? What might be gained that is not available to us from our religious commitments, ethnic loyalties, or interactions with people at work?

Analyzing Writing Strategies

1. Putnam presents his subject, the decline of civic engagement, in paragraphs 1–6. Analyze these paragraphs to determine how he attempts to engage readers and declare the significance of his subject, define unfamiliar terms, demonstrate that the trend actually exists, and qualify his **presentation of the subject.** Given his readers, how successful is his presentation? Where does it seem most successful? Think of questions it might leave unanswered for readers.

For more on supporting arguments, see pp. 520–37.

2. To convince readers that his proposed cause is plausible, Putnam must argue for it or **support** it. He does so extensively in paragraphs 10–21. Analyze the first part of his support in paragraphs 10 and 11. What kind of support does Putnam rely on? Do you think the support will be mostly familiar or mostly new to his readers? What parts of it are likely to be new? What does Putnam do to convince readers that the support is actually relevant to the cause he wants them to consider?

Considering Topics for Your Own Essay

Like Putnam, consider writing about some trend in civic life. Possible trends might include the declining voting rate, the increase in Christian evangelicals or fundamentalists on school boards, increases in violence in some cities and decreases in others, the decline in public services like libraries, declining support for public schools, the increase in home schooling, or the increase of ethnic tensions. How might you present the trend to readers who are familiar with it but have not thought deeply about it? How might you collect evidence to demonstrate that what you are observing is indeed a trend, a sustained increase or decrease over time? What causes might you propose to explain the increase or decrease?

Commentary

Putnam takes care to **anticipate causes that readers are likely to prefer** to his own as an explanation for the decline in civic engagement. In paragraph 7, he provides a comprehensive list of alternative causes, a list that includes his own preferred cause as the last item. He neither refutes nor accommodates any of these causes; he merely announces the one he prefers and implies that though the others may exert some small influence on the trend, they are not worth serious attention. This strategy establishes Putnam's authority to write about this trend: He knows so much about it that he can anticipate nearly any cause an informed reader might think of proposing as an alternative explanation to his own.

Note that he considers alternative causes at the beginning of his argument. Writers speculating about causes may take up alternatives as they argue for their preferred causes or toward the end of their arguments. Usually writers refute two or three alternative causes, arguing as convincingly as they can that the alternatives are not likely or plausible; or they may accommodate the alternatives, acknowledging their usefulness in explaining some aspect of the trend. (Neither King nor Berger addresses alternative causes, though Kim Dartnell does in the next essay.) When you plan your own essay, you will have an opportunity to think hard about alternative causes and come up with convincing arguments to refute or accommodate them.

For more about anticipating readers' concerns, see pp. 537–42.

Putnam also **anticipates readers' likely questions or objections** to his argument that increased television viewing is the best possible explanation for the decline in civic engagement. Even in presenting his subject, Putnam anticipates an objection in paragraph 5, where he acknowledges that American civil society has some life left in it: "Many good people across the land work hard every day to keep their communities vital. Indeed, evidence suggests that America still outranks many other countries in the degree of our community involvement and trust." We can assume that Putnam anticipated that after he had made the case for a sharp decline in civic engagement in paragraph 4, some readers, especially those active in civic life, would object that he had failed to recognize the extent of civic engagement still present in America.

As Putnam's argument progresses in paragraphs 10–21, he frequently anticipates readers' questions or objections. For example, in paragraphs 14 and 15, Putnam attempts to support his argument by reporting research showing that people who read more newspapers than average and watch less television than average are much more likely to belong to civic organizations. At the end of these paragraphs, Putnam reports that fewer than half as many households receive a newspaper today as did in 1947 and then seems to anticipate an astute reader's objection that this sharp decline was the result of civic disengagement rather than the cause of it. He acknowledges, "To be sure, it is not clear which way the tie between newspaper reading and civic involvement works." Putnam then insists, however, that "the two trends are clearly linked." Putnam also anticipates readers' objections or questions in paragraphs 10, 18, and 19.

Chapter 22 provides detailed information on citing sources.

Putnam writes not solely for academics or policy professionals but for a wider audience of educated citizens interested in social and economic issues, an audience similar to the one Max Frankel writes for in his essay for the *New York Times Magazine* reprinted in Chapter 7. Consequently, Putnam follows a journalistic tradition of not citing sources within his essay or appending a list of works cited. His authority to do so rests on his having published a book on the topic of his essay. Readers who question his sources or want to learn more from them can read his book. If you research the trend you speculate about, your instructor will probably expect you to cite your sources, however. The next essay by Kim Dartnell offers an example of formal **citation of sources** and a **references** list.

Kim Dartnell looks at the plight of homeless women in the following essay, written when she was a first-year college student. Like Putnam's essay, it illustrates how a writer can use library research to present a trend, determine its causes, and support an argument for the causes.

Before reading the essay, recall what you know about the homeless in America and homeless women in particular. What reasons can you think of for Americans to be without homes?

WHERE WILL THEY SLEEP TONIGHT?

Kim Dartnell

On January 21, 1982, in New York City, Rebecca Smith froze to death, after living for five months in a cardboard box. Rebecca was one of a family of thirteen children from a rural town in Virginia. After graduating from high school as the valedictorian of her class and giving birth to a daughter, she spent ten years in mental institutions, where she underwent involuntary shock treatment for schizophrenia. It was when she was released to her sister's custody that Rebecca began wandering the streets of New York, living from day to day. Many social workers tried unsuccessfully to persuade her to go into a city shelter, and she died only a few hours before she was scheduled to be placed in protective custody (Hombs & Snyder, 1982, p. 56). 1

Rebecca Smith's story is all too typical of those of the increasing number of homeless women in America. Vagrant men have always been a noticeable problem in American cities, and their numbers have increased in the 1980s. Vagrancy among women is a relatively new problem of any size, however. In 1979, New York City had one public shelter for homeless women. By 1983, it had four. Los Angeles has recently increased the number of beds available to women in its skid-row shelters (Stoner, 1983, p. 571). Even smaller communities have noticed an increase in homeless women. It is impossible to know their number or the extent of their increase in the 1980s, but everyone who has studied the problem agrees that it is serious and that it is getting worse (Hombs & Snyder, 1982, p. 10; Stoner, 1984, p. 3). 2

Who are these women? Over half of all homeless women are under the age of forty. Forty-four percent are black, 40 percent white. The statistics for homeless men are about the same (Stoner, 1983, p. 570). These women are almost always unemployed and poorly educated, unlike Rebecca Smith, and few are homeless by choice. An expert in the field has written, "Homeless women do not choose their circumstances. They are victims of forces over which they have lost control" (pp. 568, 569). The women try in various ways to cope with their dangerous lifestyle. To avoid notice, especially by the police, some have one set of nice clothes that they wash often. They shower in shelters or YWCAs and try to keep their hairstyle close to the latest fashions. An extreme is the small number of women who actually sleep sitting up on park benches to avoid wrinkling their clothes. On the other end of the spectrum are the more noticeable "bag ladies," who purposely maintain an offensive appearance and body odor to protect themselves from rape or robbery (Stoner, 1983, pp. 568, 569). 3

Why has there been such an increase in the number of vagrant American women? There are several causes of this trend. For one thing, more and more women are leaving their families because of rape, incest, and other forms of abuse. To take one example, 4 the Christian Housing Facility, a private organization in Orange County, California, that provides food, shelter, and counseling to victims of abuse, sheltered 1,536 people in 1981, a 300 percent increase from the year before (Stoner, 1983, p. 573). It is unclear whether such increases are due to an actual increase of abuse in American families or whether they result from the fact that it is more socially acceptable for a woman to be on her own today. Another factor is that government social programs for battered women have been severely cut back, leaving victims of abuse no choice but to leave home.

Evictions and illegal lockouts force some women onto the streets. Social welfare cutbacks, unemployment, and desertion all result in a loss of income. Once a woman cannot pay her rent, she is likely to be evicted, often without notice. 5

Another problem is a lack of inexpensive housing. Of today's homeless women, over 50 percent lived in single rooms before they became vagrants. Many of the buildings containing single-room or other cheap apartments have been torn down to make way for more profitable use of the land or renovated into more expensive housing. Hotels are being offered new tax incentives that make it economically unfeasible to maintain inexpensive single rooms. This is obviously a serious problem, one that sends many women out onto the streets every year. 6

Alcoholism has been cited as a major reason for the increase in the number of homeless women. I don't feel this is a major contributing factor, however. First, there hasn't been a significant general increase in alcoholism to parallel the rise in homeless women; second, alcoholism occurs at all levels of financial status, from the executive to the homeless. Rather, I would suggest that alcoholism is usually a result of homelessness rather than the cause. 7

Probably the biggest single factor in the rising number of homeless women is the deinstitutionalization of the mentally ill. One study estimated that 90 percent of all vagrant women may be mentally ill (Stoner, 1983, p. 567), as was the case with Rebecca Smith. The last few years have seen an avalanche of mental patients released from institutions. Between 1955 and 1980, the number of patients in mental institutions dropped by 75 percent, from about 560,000 to about 140,000. There are several reasons for this decline. New psychotonic drugs can now "cure" patients with mild disturbances. Expanded legal rights for patients lead to early release from asylums. Government-funded services such as Medicare allow some patients to be released into nursing or boarding homes. The problem is that many of these women have not really known any life outside the hospital and suddenly find themselves thrust out into an unreceptive world, simply because they present no threat to society or are "unresponsive to treatment." Very few of them are ever referred to community mental health centers, as deinstitutionalization policies assumed. Instead, many go straight out onto the streets. Others may live with family or in some other inexpensive housing at first, but sooner or later they are likely to end up in the streets as well. 8

Although deinstitutionalization seems to have been the biggest factor in the increase in vagrant women, there is some evidence that the main cause is economic. Unemployment hit 10.1 percent in 1982, the highest it has been since 1940. Yet that same year saw $2.35 billion cut from food-stamp programs. Reductions in another federal welfare program, Aid to Families with Dependent Children (AFDC), hit women particularly hard because four out of five AFDC families are headed by women, two-thirds of whom have not graduated from high school (Hombs & Snyder, 1982). Together with inflation, unemployment, and loss of other welfare benefits, these cuts have effectively forced many women into homelessness and can be expected to continue to do so at a greater rate in the years to come. 9

The United States may be one of the world's most prosperous nations, but for Rebecca Smith and others like her, the American dream is far from being fulfilled. 10

References

Hombs, M. E., & Snyder, M. (1982). *Homelessness in America.* Washington, DC: Community for Creative Non-Violence.

Stoner, M. R. (1983). The plight of homeless women. *Social Service Review, 57,* 565–581.

Stoner, M. R. (1984). An analysis of public and private sector provisions for homeless people. *Urban and Social Change Review, 17,* 2–10.

Connecting to Culture and Experience

Dartnell speculates about possible causes for the increasing numbers of homeless women in the early 1980s. Homelessness continues to be a social problem in the 1990s. Questions remain about how it might be reduced and what programs are required to combat it.

Discuss with two or three other students your experience with homelessness and your ideas about what might be done to reduce it or alleviate the suffering of the homeless. Begin by reporting your observations of the homeless. Where do you see them, and what seems to be their condition? You might focus on one or two specific individuals. Mention whether you have ever talked to a homeless person or visited a homeless shelter.

Then, exchange views on what might be done to reduce homelessness or provide better care for the homeless. Should we accept the fact that in a free-market economy like ours, homelessness, like poverty, will always be with us? If not, what social and economic adjustments are needed to reduce homelessness? Should these be federal or local initiatives? Tax-supported or private programs? If you accept the inevitability of homelessness, what level of care or support do you think is appropriate? Who should provide it?

Analyzing Writing Strategies

Scratch outlines are discussed on pp. 431–32.

1. Make a scratch outline of Dartnell's essay in order to evaluate its **organization.** Notice particularly the sequence of causes in paragraphs 4–9. What is the logic behind this sequence? What are its advantages or disadvantages?
2. In **presenting the subject** of an essay speculating about the causes of a trend, the writer must always demonstrate that the trend exists and may also need to describe or **define the trend.** Notice how Dartnell defines the trend in paragraph 3. What does she assume that her readers—other students who may be aware of homelessness but have not thought deeply about it—know and do not know about homeless women? What kinds of information does she offer? How successful is she in defining women's homelessness for her readers?

Considering Topics for Your Own Essay

Think of a troubling social trend you might write about. Possibilities include the increasing inequality of wealth among Americans, increasing reliance by employers on contingent workers, increasing violence among young men, increasing suicides by young men, increasing numbers of children born to unmarried teenagers, increasing costs of a college education, increasing resentment of immigrants, increasing numbers of women with children who must work full time, increasing complexity of lifestyles, and decreasing support for the arts. What causes might you come up with to explain the trend?

Commentary

Chapter 21 provides support for library and Internet research.

Dartnell's essay illustrates how important a small amount of **research** can be for an essay explaining the causes of a social trend. She uses only three sources, all located on one visit to the library, but they provide adequate documentation for both the trend and her proposed causes. Her sources are two essays she found in social science journals and a book on the general topic of homelessness in America. Dartnell depends on these sources for her evidence—statistics and the particular case of Rebecca Smith. She also uses the authority of her sources to bolster her argument, quoting from Stoner in paragraph 3, for example, to persuade readers that they should not blame homeless women for their plight but rather see them as victims.

From her own experience and her reading, Dartnell knew that many people believe homeless women have brought their plight on themselves by becoming alcoholic. Anticipating that this will be an **alternative cause that her readers will prefer,** she attempts to refute it in paragraph 7 by arguing that "there hasn't been a significant general increase in alcoholism to parallel the rise in homeless women" and that "alcoholism occurs at all levels of financial status, from the executive to the homeless."

To open and close her essay, Dartnell relies in part on **framing**—referring in the closing to something mentioned in the opening. Dartnell's reference is to Rebecca Smith, whose case she uses effectively in her opening to dramatize the significance of her subject.

PURPOSE AND AUDIENCE

The chief purpose of an essay speculating about causes is to convince readers that the proposed causes are plausible. Therefore, you must construct a coherent, logical, authoritative argument that readers will take seriously. Sometimes, like Putnam, you may want readers to look at a phenomenon or a trend in a new way, to go beyond obvious or familiar explanations. At other times, you may, like Dartnell and Berger, hope to influence policy decisions regarding a social problem.

Your audience will also affect your purpose. If you think that your readers are only mildly curious about the subject, you might write partly to stimulate their interest. If you expect that they will be strongly opposed to your speculations or very skeptical of them, you could try to show that you understand their point of view. If you believe that the distance between you and them is unbridgeable, you could even accentuate your differences, explaining why you think their views are implausible.

SUMMARY OF BASIC FEATURES

A Presentation of the Subject

First, it is necessary to describe the subject, sometimes quite extensively, depending on what the writer thinks the readers know or need to know. Writers sometimes devote a large portion of the essay to the subject—describing it with specific details and examples and establishing that it actually exists (or existed) by citing facts, statistics, and statements by authorities.

In writing about a phenomenon he knows will be familiar to his readers, Stephen King simply asserts the popular fascination with horror movies in his title. If he had been concerned that his readers might not accept this assertion as being true, he could have cited statistics to demonstrate the popularity of horror movies. In the original essay from which this selection was excerpted, King also describes a number of particular examples of the genre in all of their gory detail. Because we all know what horror movies are—whether we have seen them or studiously avoided them—we do not need such detailed description to understand his analysis of why people, at least some of them, "crave" this type of film. But such details can still be useful for engaging readers' interest in the subject or impressing them with its importance.

Unlike King, who can assume that his readers are somewhat familiar with horror movies, Joseph Berger presents his less familiar and not so immediately engaging subject—outstanding achievement in science—in considerable detail. Taking the Westinghouse Science Talent Search as an example, he describes its history, programs, and goals.

In an essay about a trend, a writer must always demonstrate that the trend exists. Kim Dartnell uses well-documented statistics to demonstrate that the number of homeless women is increasing. Because some readers are likely to be unfamiliar with her subject, she also describes some typical homeless women and presents the case of an individual woman as an example. Robert Putnam also uses statistics to demonstrate that there has been a continuous decline in civic engagement since the 1960s.

In some cases, the writer may have to show that the subject is in fact a trend—an established, significant change—as opposed to a fad or a fluctuation, a short-term, superficial change. A new form of exercise might become a fad if many people try it out for a few months. But this brief popularity would not make it a trend. It might, however, be considered part of a trend—a general increase in health consciousness, for example.

It may also be necessary to provide other details about a trend. When did it start? Is it completed or continuing? Is it decelerating or accelerating? What is the source of these details? Is the source authoritative? A thorough presentation of the trend may have to answer all these questions.

continued

continued

A Convincing Causal Argument

At the heart of an essay that analyzes the causes of a phenomenon or a trend is the causal argument itself—presentation of the causes, presentation of evidence in support of each cause, and anticipation of objections and alternative causes. Causal arguments are tricky. Effects have a way of being mistaken for causes. A proposed cause may turn out to have originated only after a trend started. Since skeptical readers are quick to spot these errors in reasoning, writers must take care in constructing their arguments.

In proposing causes, writers need to be very sensitive to their readers. First, they must present their causes in a logical order that will be easy to follow. Dartnell, writing for nonexperts, begins with an immediate and concrete cause (abuse) and concludes with a background and perpetuating cause (economics). To hold readers' interest, writers must also avoid emphasizing causes that readers would consider obvious or predictable.

For more on supporting arguments, see pp. 529–37.

Providing Support for Proposed Causes. Writers must marshal support for each cause they propose. They may use statistics, factual cases and examples, and anecdotes. Dartnell offers statistical evidence of the economic forces behind female homelessness. She also includes a factual case: the opening narrative about a particular homeless woman. Berger details the science program at Stuyvesant High School and the success story of one scientist to support his argument that a certain kind of curriculum and teaching method produces high achievement in science.

For more on anticipating readers' concerns, see pp. 537–42.

Anticipating Readers' Objections and Preferred Causes. Most important, writers must anticipate readers' possible objections to and questions about the proposed causes and must show that they have considered (and rejected) any other possible causes. Dartnell refutes the objection that many homeless women choose their condition, and she not only presents evidence that alcoholism is not a cause of increased homelessness but also goes on to suggest that it is usually an effect instead. In addition to anticipating objections, writers may need to consider alternative causes that their readers might prefer, as Putnam does when he lists several alternative causes and implicitly rejects all of them as less important than the one he favors.

GUIDE TO WRITING

THE WRITING ASSIGNMENT

Think of some important or intriguing phenomenon or trend, and explain why it might have occurred. Describe your subject, demonstrate its existence if necessary, and propose possible causes for it. Your purpose is to convince your readers that the proposed causes are plausible.

INVENTION AND RESEARCH

The following activities will help you to find a subject, explore what you know about it, and do any necessary research.

Finding a Subject

Consider both phenomena and trends as possible subjects. A *phenomenon* is something notable about the human condition or the social order—fear of speaking to a group, for example, or opposition to gun control legislation. A *trend* is a significant change extending over many months or years. It can be identified by some sort of increase or decrease—a rise in the birthrate, a decline in test scores.

Some subjects can be approached as either phenomena or trends. For example, you could speculate about the causes of the increasing suicide rate among young people, or you could ignore the increase and simply speculate about the causes of such suicides.

Listing Phenomena. First, list any current phenomena that you might want to write about. Here are some possibilities to consider. Start with some of them, and see if they bring to mind other topics of interest to you.

Set a timer for ten minutes, and brainstorm your lists on a computer with the monitor brightness turned all the way down. Try to enter as many possibilities as you can think of. Then turn the brightness up, make sure all the items are clear to you, and save them as an invention file. If you would like, print out a copy to make notes on.

- College—a noisy library, a shortage of parking, an instructor's skill or popularity, cheating, a successful or unsuccessful class or course
- Personal life—competitiveness, idealism, creativity, popularity, jealousy, laziness, workaholics, contentiousness, rage
- Politics and government—hostility to politicians, low voter turnout, influence of political action committees (PACs), high cost of running for public office, negative campaigning
- Environment—failure to reduce pollution, the garbage crisis, difficulty of starting and maintaining recycling programs, concern about food safety
- Life stages—the "terrible twos," teenage alienation or rebellion, postponement of motherhood, midlife crisis, abrupt career changes
- The arts—popularity of rap or jazz, decline of musical theater, impulse to censor the arts
- Continuing influence or popularity of a book, movie, actor, novelist, social activist, athlete, politician, religious leader, television program

Listing Trends. List all the trends you can think of, from the past as well as the present. Consider both trends you have studied and can research and ones you know firsthand. Try to think of trends you would like to understand better, and be sure that the possibilities you list are trends, not fads or short-term fluctuations. To start, consider the following possibilities:

- Shifting patterns in education—increasing interest in computer science or in teaching as a career, increase in home schooling, increase in community college enrollments, declining numbers of math and science majors, increase in the number of African-American students attending black colleges
- Changes in patterns of leisure or entertainment—increasing consumption of fast food, declining interest in a particular style of music, increase in competitive cycling, increase or decrease in a magazine's circulation
- Shifts in religious practices—decreasing support for television evangelists, increasing incidence of women ministers or rabbis, increasing interest in Asian religions, increased membership in fundamentalist churches
- New patterns of political behavior—increase in conservatism or liberalism, a growing desire for isolation from world affairs, developing power of minorities and women
- Societal changes—increases in the number of working women with children, single-parent households, telecommunicating
- Changes in politics or world affairs—spreading influence of capitalism, increasing terrorist activity, increasing numbers of women elected to political office, growing ethnic conflicts
- Changes in economic conditions—increasing cost of medical care, decline in standard of living, increasing gap between wealthiest and poorest Americans
- Completed artistic movements or historical trends—impressionism, pop art, the struggle for female suffrage, industrialization

Listing Subjects concerning Identity and Community These suggestions may bring to mind topics related to identity and community.

Phenomena

- A particular conflict in a community to which you belong
- The popularity of athletes or other groups of students in high school
- The lack of understanding and sympathy between the young and the old
- The obsession of many young women and men with their weight and body image
- The continued high level of teenage pregnancy despite the widespread availability of birth control

Trends

- Increasing prejudice against new immigrants
- Increasing incidence of people abandoning or abusing aged relatives
- Increasing incidence of domestic violence—against spouses, children, or parents
- Increasing popularity of twelve-step, self-help programs
- Increasing popularity of sororities and fraternities on college campuses
- Increasing use of plastic surgery to enhance self-image

- Increasing numbers of young people choosing to remain virgins until they marry
- Increasing rate of smoking among young people

Listing Subjects concerning Work and Career The following suggestions will help you to think of subjects related to work and career.

Phenomena

- Students expecting to have less financial success than their parents
- People preferring to own their own business even though they must work harder for more hours each day
- Students working part time while attending college
- Students aspiring to careers in business
- The importance or difficulty of arranging working internships while in college
- Older students attending college

Trends

- Rising unemployment among youth
- Increase in full-time and part-time contingent or temporary workers
- Increase in service-related careers

Choosing a Subject. *Look over your list. Pick one subject to write about, and describe it briefly.* You may or may not already have some ideas about why this phenomenon or trend occurred. As you analyze it in detail, you will have the opportunity to consider possible causes and to decide which ones are the most important.

Of the two types of subjects, a trend may be more challenging because you must nearly always do research to demonstrate that it actually exists, that something has been increasing or decreasing over an extended period of time. (Usually one or two references will be adequate.) Since a trend begins at a specific point, you must take care that the causes you propose as the sources of the trend actually precede its onset. You may also need to differentiate between causes that launched the trend and those that perpetuate it.

Exploring What You Know about Your Subject

Write for around ten minutes about the subject you have chosen to analyze, noting everything you know about it. Figure out why you are interested in it, and decide where you might find more information about it.

Considering Causes

If you can, save your work exploring and considering causes as a computer file. Later, as you begin to draft, you can call up the file in a second window and easily transfer details you want to use in your draft.

Think now about what might have caused your selected phenomenon or trend, listing possible causes and then analyzing the most promising.

Listing Possible Causes. *Write down all the things you can think of that might have caused your subject.* Consider each of the following:

- Immediate causes (those responsible for making the phenomenon or trend begin when it did)
- Remote, background causes (those from before the phenomenon or trend began)

- Perpetuating causes (those that may have contributed to sustaining or continuing the phenomenon or trend)
- Obvious causes
- Hidden causes

Selecting the Most Promising Causes. *Review your list, and select five or six causes that seem to you to provide a plausible explanation of your subject.* Since you will next need to analyze these causes, it might be helpful to list them in table form. On a piece of paper, or using your word processor's table function, list the causes in a column at the left, leaving five or six lines below each cause.

See pp. 376–77 for an example of such a table.

Analyzing Promising Causes. *Next to each potential cause listed in your table, explain why you think it is real and important.* Consider the following questions as you analyze each cause:

- Is it a necessary cause? Without it, could the subject have occurred anyway?
- Is it a sufficient cause? Could it alone have caused this subject?
- Would this cause affect everybody the same way?
- Would this cause always lead to phenomena or trends like this one?
- Can you think of any particular anecdotes or examples that demonstrate the cause's importance?
- Have any authorities you know of suggested that it is an important cause?
- Is it actually a result of the subject rather than a cause?
- Is it a remote or background cause or an immediate cause?
- Is it a perpetuating cause, continuing to sustain the trend?
- Is it an obvious cause or a hidden cause?

Researching Your Subject

In exploring your subject, you may have found that you already know enough to describe or define it adequately for your readers. Should you need to know more, however, consult library or Internet sources or a faculty or community expert.

If you are speculating about the causes of a *trend,* you will also need to do some research to confirm that it actually is a trend and not just a fluctuation or a fad. To do so, you will need to find factual, and probably statistical, evidence of an increase or decrease over time—and also of the date when this change began. (Recall that Dartnell provides statistical evidence that the number of homeless women is increasing and that Putnam offers statistics to demonstrate that civic engagement has been falling for three decades.) If you are unable to confirm a trend, select another that you can confirm.

On pp. 573–74 is a list of sources especially useful for researching trends.

Testing Your Choice

Now that you have explored your subject, considered its possible causes, confirmed its existence, and described it in some detail, take some time to review your material and decide whether your subject is workable. Start by asking the following questions:

- Does the subject still interest you?
- Do you believe you can describe and define it in a way that will interest readers and show them that it is a phenomenon or a trend?

- Were you able to come up with several causes that together provide a plausible explanation for the trend?
- Are the causes you have come up with not simply obvious ones?
- Would you like to research the subject further?

If your subject does not seem promising, return to your list of possible subjects to select another.

Testing Your Choice: A Collaborative Activity

One good way of testing your subject and beginning to develop your causal argument is to try out your subject and causes on a group of two or three other students.

Presenters: Briefly identify your subject, and ask the listeners what causes immediately come to their minds to explain your subject. Make a list of these as the listeners talk. Finally, tell the listeners the causes you propose to argue for, and ask them whether they accept these as likely or plausible. Take notes about their objections and questions. (When you plan and draft your essay, these lists and notes may suggest further causes you want to argue for, and they will help you to anticipate your readers' likely questions and objections to your proposed causes.)

Listeners: Respond imaginatively to the request for causes that you initially think explain the presenter's subject. When the presenter tells you the causes he or she proposes to argue for, praise those that seem plausible, but also ask all the questions and raise all the objections you can think of. In this way, you will help the presenter to anticipate readers' likely questions and objections.

Researching Causes

Keep one file as a bibliography, listing all sources you consult. Organize other research files, by subtopic or as quote, summary, and paraphrase files. Copy quotations exactly and indicate the source for each.

Some causal arguments can be made fully and convincingly on the basis of your own knowledge and intuition. In fact, you may have to rely on your own ideas to explain very recent phenomena or emerging trends. Most subjects, however, will have already been noticed by others, and you will want to learn what they have said about the causes. Doing research can be helpful in several ways:

- To confirm or challenge your own ideas
- To identify further causes to add to your own explanation
- To provide support for causes you want to argue for
- To identify causes your readers may prefer to the ones you find plausible
- To reveal some of the reservations readers may have about the causes you suggest

As you discover causes others have proposed, add the most interesting or most plausible ones to your table. Analyze these as you did your own proposed causes. In your essay, you may want to accommodate them—integrate them in full or in part into your own argument.

As you gather evidence about causes, remember to record the information you will need to acknowledge your sources.

For guidelines on acknowledging sources, see pp. 603–620.

Considering Your Readers

Write a careful analysis of your readers. Because you will be trying to make a convincing case for some particular readers, you should know as much as possible about them. Only after you have analyzed your readers can you confidently decide how to present these causes in your essay—which you will emphasize, which will require the most convincing evidence, which will be obvious. Take a few minutes to answer the following questions:

- Who are my readers? (Describe them briefly.)
- What do they know about my subject? Will I have to prove its existence to them? How extensively will I have to define or describe it for them?
- What attitudes might they have about my subject? Do they care about it? Are they indifferent to it? Might they understand it differently from the way I understand it?
- Will they be in agreement with my argument already? Skeptical but convinceable? Resistant and perhaps even antagonistic?
- What causes would they be most likely to think of?
- Which of my possible causes might they be skeptical of, and why?
- What else do I know about my readers?

Developing Your Argument

Again, saving your preliminary arguments as a computer file may help you to draft your essay more efficiently.

Try to argue in writing for your most plausible causes. Once you have figured out what to expect of your readers, review your table of causes and analyses, and make a list of all the causes that you believe provide a plausible explanation of your subject. To try out your arguments for these causes, write about each one for around five minutes, summing up all the support you have found. Develop your argument with your readers in mind; remember that you must convince them that your causes are plausible or likely.

Anticipating and Refuting Objections

Try refuting the most likely objections to your causes. You should expect readers to evaluate your essay critically, considering your reasons and evidence carefully before accepting your explanation. It would be wise, therefore, to account for any possible objections they could raise. Consider the two most likely objections, and figure out ways to refute them. Write out a few sentences to prepare your refutation.

Refuting Alternative Causes

Try refuting alternative causes your readers may prefer to your own proposed causes. As they read your essay, your readers may think of other causes that seem more plausible to them than your causes. Try to think of two or three such causes now, and write a few sentences about each one, explaining why you did not consider it or why you specifically reject it. Why are these causes less plausible than your own?

PLANNING AND DRAFTING

You should now review what you have learned about your topic and start to plan your first draft by setting goals and making an outline.

Seeing What You Have

Pause now to reflect on your notes. Reread everything carefully in order to decide whether you can really prove that your subject exists (or existed) and can offer a convincing explanation of its causes.

Setting Goals

It is a good idea at this point to print out a hard copy of what you have written on a word processor for easier reviewing.

Before you begin your draft, consider some specific goals for your essay. Not only will the draft be easier to write once you have established goals, but it is also likely to be more convincing.

The following questions will help you to set goals. You may find it useful to return to them while you are drafting, for they are designed to help you to focus on specific elements of an essay speculating about causes.

Your Readers

- What are my readers likely to know about the subject?
- How can I interest them in understanding its causes?
- How can I present myself so that my readers will consider me informed and authoritative?

The Beginning

- What opening would make readers take this subject seriously and really want to think about its causes?
- Should I personalize it? Should I begin with a case, as Dartnell does, or by citing statistics?

Presentation of the Subject

- Do I need to demonstrate that my subject really exists?
- If I am analyzing a trend, do I need to demonstrate that it is not just a fluctuation or a fad?
- How much and what kind of evidence do I need for these points?

The Causal Argument

- How many causes should I propose? Should I mention or give evidence for minor causes?
- How can I present my proposed causes in the most effective order? Should I arrange them from most important to least important or vice versa? From most obvious to least obvious or vice versa? From immediate to remote or vice versa?

- Do I need to make other distinctions among causes, such as between a cause that starts a trend and one that keeps it going?
- How much and what kind of support do I need to offer to make each cause plausible to readers? Are any causes so obvious that support is unnecessary? Do I need to demonstrate to readers that all of my causes existed before the phenomenon or trend began?
- How can I refute readers' objections to my proposed causes?
- How can I refute alternative causes readers might propose?

The Ending

- How should I end my essay? Should I frame it by referring to the beginning? Do I need to summarize my causes? Should I conclude with a conjecture about larger implications?

Outlining

A causal analysis may contain as many as four basic parts:

1. A presentation of the subject
2. A presentation of proposed causes and support for them
3. A consideration of readers' objections, questions, or reservations
4. A consideration and refutation of alternative causes

Outlining on a word processor makes it particularly easy to experiment with different ways of ordering the four parts of a causal analysis.

These parts can be organized in various ways. If your readers are not likely to think of any causes other than the ones you are proposing, you could begin by describing the subject and indicating its importance or interest. Then, state your first proposed cause, supporting it convincingly and accommodating or refuting readers' likely questions and objections. Follow the same pattern for any other causes you propose. Your conclusion could then mention—and elucidate—the lack of other explanations for your subject.

Presentation of the subject

First proposed cause with support and refutation of objections, if any

Second proposed cause with support and refutation of objections, if any (etc.)

Conclusion

If you need to account for alternative causes that are likely to occur to readers, you could discuss them first and give your reasons for rejecting them before offering your own proposed causes. Many writers save their own causes for last, hoping that readers will remember them best.

Presentation of the subject

Alternative causes and reasons for rejecting them

Proposed causes with support and refutation of objections, if any

Conclusion

Another option is to put your own causes first, followed by alternatives. This pattern helps you to show the relative likelihood of your causes over the others. You might then end with a restatement of your causes.

Presentation of the subject

Proposed causes with support and refutation of objections, if any

Alternative causes compared with your causes

Concluding restatement of your proposed causes

There are, of course, many other possible ways to organize a causal analysis, but these outlines should help you to start planning your own essay.

Drafting

As you begin drafting your essay, keep in mind the following tips on writing an essay of causal analysis.

Call up invention material in an alternate window as you draft, shifting back and forth to cut and paste invention material into your draft.

- Remember that in writing about causes, you are dealing with probabilities rather than certainties; therefore, you must resist the urge to claim that you have the final, conclusive answer and instead simply assert that your explanation is plausible. Qualify your statements, and acknowledge opposing views.
- Try to enliven your writing and to appeal to your readers' interests and concerns. Causal analysis is potentially rather dry.
- Remember that your outline is just a plan. Writers often make major discoveries and reorganize as they draft. Be flexible. If you find your writing taking an interesting, unexpected turn, follow it to see where it leads. You will have an opportunity to look at it critically later.
- If you run into a problem as you draft, see whether any of the invention activities earlier in this chapter will help. If, for instance, you are having difficulty making the subject seem important or interesting, analyze your readers further, find a way to personalize the subject with a quotation or an anecdote, or look for some attention-getting statistical evidence.
- If you are finding it difficult to refute objections or alternative causes, try composing a dialogue between yourself and an imaginary reader who does not agree with you.
- If you find that you need more information, you might want to interview an expert, survey a group, or do further research in the library or on the Internet.

You might want to review the general advice on drafting on pp. 13–14.

CRITICAL READING GUIDE

At this point, your draft should get a good critical reading. All writers find it helpful to have someone else read their drafts and give them critical comments. Your instructor may arrange such a reading as part of your coursework; otherwise, you can ask a classmate, friend, or family member to read it over. If your campus has a writing center, you might ask a tutor there to read and comment on your draft. (If you are unable to have someone else read over your draft, turn ahead to the Revising section, which gives guidelines for reading your own draft with a critical eye.)

Swap copies of your drafts with another student, either by exchanging disks or sending the computer files over a network. Add your comments either next to the essay, if you can divide the window, or at the end of the document.

If You Are the Writer. To provide focused, helpful comments, your reader must know your intended audience and purpose. Briefly write out this information at the top of your draft.

- *Audience.* Who are your readers? What do you assume they already know and think about your subject and its causes? Do you expect them to be receptive, skeptical, resistant, antagonistic?
- *Purpose.* What do you hope to accomplish with your readers?

If You Are the Reader. Reading a draft critically means reading it more than once, first to get a general impression and then to analyze its basic features. Here are some guidelines to assist you in preparing critical comments on essays that speculate about the causes of phenomena or trends.

1. *Read for a First Impression.* Read the essay straight through. As you read, try to notice any words or passages that contribute to your first impression, weak ones as well as strong ones.

   After you have finished reading the draft, write a few sentences giving your impressions. Did the essay hold your interest? What most surprised you? What did you like best? Did you find the causal argument convincing?

See pp. 359–60 to review the basic features.

2. *Evaluate How Well the Subject Is Presented.* How well does the draft present the phenomenon or trend? Does it give enough information to make readers understand and care about the subject? Does it establish that the subject actually exists? If the subject is a trend, does it demonstrate a significant increase or decrease over time? Where might additional details, examples, facts, or statistics help?
3. *Consider Whether the Causes and Support Are Convincing.* Look first at the proposed causes, and list them. Do there seem to be too many? Too few? Do any seem either too obvious (not worth mentioning) or too obscure (remote in time or overly complicated)?

   Next, examine the support for each cause—anecdotes, facts, statistics, reference to authorities, and so on. Which evidence is most convincing? Which seems unconvincing? Where would more evidence or a different kind strengthen the argument? Might readers expect additional evidence that a cause existed before the phenomenon or trend began?

Check for errors in reasoning. Does the argument mistakenly take something for a cause just because it occurred before or at the start of the phenomenon or trend? Are any of the proposed causes of the subject actually effects of it instead?

4. *Assess Whether Readers' Likely Objections and Questions Are Anticipated Adequately.* Look for places where the writer has acknowledged readers' possible objections to or questions about the proposed causes. How well are objections handled? Should any of them be taken more seriously? Can you see other ways of either accommodating or refuting objections? Do any of the refutations attack or ridicule the persons raising the objections? What other questions or objections might readers raise?
5. *Assess Whether Alternative Causes Are Adequately Acknowledged.* If causes likely to be preferred by readers are acknowledged, are they presented fairly? Is it clear why they have been rejected? Do the refutations seem convincing? Do any of the refutations attack or ridicule the persons proposing the causes? Can you think of other plausible causes?
6. *Consider Whether the Organization Is Effective.* Given the expected readers, are the causes presented in an effective order? Raise specific questions about the order. Suggest a different order.

   Reread the *beginning*. Will it engage the readers? Imagine at least one other way to open. Look for sections of the essay that could be moved to the beginning—an intriguing anecdote, for instance, or a surprising statistic.

   Study the *ending*. Does the essay conclude decisively and memorably? Think of an alternative ending. Could something be moved to the end?
7. *Give the Writer Your Final Thoughts.* What is this draft's strongest part? What about it is most memorable? What is weak, most in need of further work?

REVISING

This section will help you to identify problems in your draft and to revise and edit to solve them.

Identifying Problems

To identify problems in your draft, you need to get an objective overview of it, analyze its basic features in detail, and assess any critical comments on it made by other readers.

Even if your essay is saved as a computer file, reread from a hard copy. Add notes to yourself and quick revisions as you read through the draft.

Getting an Overview. Begin by considering your draft as a whole, trying to see it as objectively as you can. The following steps make this overview possible.

1. *Reread.* If at all possible, put the draft aside for a day or two before rereading it. When you go back to it, start by reconsidering your audience and your purpose. Then, read the draft straight through, trying to see it as your intended readers will.

2. *Outline.* Make a scratch outline of the draft to chart its development. Words and phrases will do as long as they identify the subject and any important details, the proposed causes, and any objections you hope to respond to and alternative causes you intend to refute.

Charting a Plan for Revision. Once you have an overview of your draft, use a double-column chart to keep track of specific problems you need to solve. In the left-hand column, list the basic features of essays speculating about causes. As you analyze your draft and study any comments you have received from others, use the right-hand column to note any problems with each feature. Here is an example:

Basic Features	*Problems to Solve*
Presentation of the subject	
Presentation of causes and support	
Response to possible objections and questions	
Response to alternative causes	
Organization	

Analyzing the Basic Features of Your Draft. Turn now to the Critical Reading Guide, and use it to identify problems in your draft. Note specific points on your chart.

Studying Critical Comments. Review any comments you have received from other readers. Try not to react defensively to these comments. Rather, look at them as information that can help you to improve your draft. Add to the chart any problems readers have identified.

Solving the Problems

Before revising, copy your original draft to a second file. Then, should you change your mind about material you delete while revising, it will still be available.

You now need to come up with solutions to the problems in your draft and to implement them. Basically, you have three ways of finding solutions:

1. Review your invention and planning notes for other information and ideas.
2. Do additional invention or research.
3. Look back at the readings in this chapter to see how other writers have solved similar problems.

The following suggestions will help to get you started on addressing some of the problems common to writing that speculates about causes.

Presentation of the Subject

- **Is your subject unclear, or is its existence not clearly established?** Discuss it in greater detail. Consider adding anecdotes, statistics, citations from authorities, or other details. If your subject is a trend, be sure you show evidence of a significant increase or decrease over an extended period.

Presentation of Causes and Evidence

- **Have you proposed what seem like too many causes?** Clarify the role each one plays: Is it obvious? Hidden? Immediate, remote, or perpetuating? (You need not use these labels.) In addition, you may need to emphasize one or two causes or delete some that seem too obvious, too obscure, or relatively minor.
- **Have you proposed what seem like too few causes for a complex subject?** Try to think of other possible causes, especially hidden or remote ones. Do further research if necessary.
- **Is your support skimpy or weak?** Look for more or stronger support.
- **Have you made errors in reasoning?** Correct them. For example, if you cannot argue convincingly that a proposed cause not only occurred before the phenomenon or trend began but also contributed to it, you will have to delete that cause or at least present it more tentatively. If you have confused a cause with an effect, clarify their relationship.

Response to Possible Objections and Questions

- **Are any refutations of objections to your proposed causes unconvincing?** Try to provide stronger evidence. If you cannot do so, you may want to accommodate the objections.
- **Do any refutations attack or ridicule people?** Revise to focus on the objections, not the people making them.
- **Have readers raised questions about your argument?** You may need to provide more information about your subject or more evidence for proposed causes.
- **Have readers made any additional objections to your argument?** Consider whether you need to accommodate or refute them. That is, can you acknowledge their validity and incorporate them into your own argument, or can you give reasons why they are wrong?

Use your computer to help you to analyze problems with your essay. For example, if a reader feels that you need to revise the order in which you present your causes, highlight each cause in your paper by putting it in bold type. Then try arranging the causes in a different order.

Response to Alternative Causes

- **Do any refutations of alternative causes seem unconvincing?** Try to provide stronger evidence, or consider accommodating the alternative causes.
- **Do any refutations attack or ridicule people?** Revise to focus on specific alternative causes that you believe to be implausible rather than the people who are proposing these causes.
- **Have readers suggested any causes you had not considered?** Decide whether they are plausible and should be integrated into your argument. If they seem implausible, decide whether to mention and refute them.

Use your word processor's cut-and-paste or block-and-move function to shift material around. Make sure that you revise transitions so that material fits smoothly in its new spot.

Organization

- **Did your readers find the argument disorganized or hard to follow?** Consider reordering it by arranging the causes in order of increasing rather than decreasing importance, grouping related causes together, or moving the refutations of alternative causes to precede your own causes. Your plan may be more understandable if you forecast it at the beginning. Provide summaries, transitions, and other cues for readers.

- **Is the beginning dull?** Try opening with a surprising fact or an engaging anecdote or by emphasizing your subject's puzzling nature.
- **Is the ending weak?** Try to make it more emphatic or more interesting, perhaps by restating your main cause or causes, framing (referring to something mentioned at the beginning), or inviting readers to speculate further.

EDITING AND PROOFREADING

Use your word processor's spell-check function cautiously. Keep in mind that it will not find all misspellings, particularly misused homonyms (such as *there* for *their* and *they're*), typographical errors that are themselves words (such as *fro* for *for*), and many proper nouns and specialized terms. Proofread these carefully yourself. Also proofread for words that should have been deleted when you edited a sentence.

In working on your draft so far, you may have corrected some obvious errors, but grammar and style have not been a priority. Now is the time to check carefully for errors in usage, punctuation, and mechanics and to consider any ways you might adjust your writing style to suit your purpose and your audience. You may find that studying your draft in separate passes—first for paragraphs, then for sentences, and finally for words—will help you to recognize problems.

Our research on student writing that speculates about causes has revealed several errors in mechanics and usage that are especially likely to occur. The following guidelines are designed to help you to check and edit your draft for these errors.

Checking Your Use of Numbers. Whether to indicate the scope of a phenomenon or to cite the increase or decrease of a trend, writers who are speculating about causes often cite dates, percentages, fractions, and other numbers. Look, for example, at these excerpts from Kim Dartnell's essay:

> In 1979, New York City had one public shelter for homeless women. In 1983, it had four.

> Between 1955 and 1980, the number of patients in mental institutions dropped by 75 percent, from about 560,000 to 140,000.

Dartnell spells out numbers that can be written as one or two words but uses figures for numbers that require more than two words. She uses figures for dates and percentages.

Conventions for presenting numbers in writing are easy to follow. The following sentences, taken from student papers that speculate about causes, have each been edited to demonstrate conventional ways of using numbers in academic writing.

Spelling Out Numbers and Fractions of One or Two Words

- **According to the World Health Organization, as many as ~~1~~ ^one person in every ~~50~~ ^fifty may be infected with HIV.**
- **Maybe ~~2/3~~ ^two-thirds of the smoke from a cigarette is released into the air.**

Using Figures for Numbers and Fractions of More than Two Words

- **That year the Japanese automobile industry produced only** 4,837 **~~four thousand eight hundred thirty-seven~~ vehicles, mostly trucks and motorbikes.**

- **This study shows that Americans spend an average of** 5⅓ **~~five and one-third~~ hours a day watching television.**

Writing Percentages and Dates with Figures

- **Comparing 1980 to 1960, we can see that time spent viewing television increased** 28 **~~twenty-eight~~ percent.**

Spelling Out Numbers That Begin a Sentence

- Thirty **~~30~~ percent of commercial real estate in Washington, D.C., is owned by foreigners.**

Checking for "Reason Is Because" Constructions. When you speculate about causes, you need to offer reasons and support for your speculations. Consequently, papers that speculate about causes often contain sentences constructed around a "reason is because" pattern.

Redundant The *reason* we lost the war *is because* troop morale was down.

Since *because* means "for the reason that," the sentence says essentially that "the reason is the reason." If you find this pattern in your writing, there are two easy ways to edit out the redundancy:

Clear The reason we lost the war is that troop morale was down.

Clear We lost the war because troop morale was down.

- **Her research suggests that one reason women attend women's colleges is** that **~~because~~ they want to avoid certain social pressures.**

- Older **~~A reason older~~ Americans watch so much television ~~is~~ because they tend to be sedentary.**

A WRITER AT WORK

ANALYZING CAUSES

When a writer is planning an essay explaining causes, analyzing the causes is the most important part of invention and research. Because the causes are the heart of the argument, each one must be rigorously analyzed during the invention stage to compose a convincing argument.

Here we will look at the table of causes and analyses that Kim Dartnell developed for her essay on homeless women.

When Dartnell began this invention activity, she intended to write about the trend of homelessness in general, without considering men and women separately. After she had started to do some research, however, she realized not only that the number of homeless women was increasing but also that there had been several recent reports on the subject.

Before going to the library, she entered the first four causes on her table and completed a partial analysis. After she decided to focus on women, she added the other causes and completed the analysis.

TABLE OF CAUSES AND ANALYSES

Causes	Analyses
1. Unemployment	Necessary cause for this trend. Could be sufficient, would affect everybody the same way, causes loss of income. Immediate cause that has grown in importance recently.
2. Inflation	Relates to unemployment--as such, may be necessary but not sufficient by itself, especially affects unemployed and poor. Perpetuating, immediate, hidden cause.
3. Alcoholism	Not necessary, not sufficient. Common conception is all homeless are drunks. Refute this cause since alcohol use hasn't risen in proportion to homelessness. Alcoholism is found at all levels of society, and so can't say that it causes homelessness. May be a result of unemployment or homelessness. No one really knows what causes alcoholism--or what it causes.
4. Cutbacks in welfare	Necessary cause, could be sufficient. Affects women especially, causes loss of income, homelessness. Immediate cause--with no money, people forced to beg or move in with others.

Causes	Analyses
5. Abuse	There's always been abuse. Neither necessary nor sufficient. Affects women and children more. Research shows it's risen in proportion to homelessness (Stoner).
6. Release from institutions	Many women being released from mental institutions. Necessary, may be sufficient. Immediate cause for the mentally ill. May be coupled with economic problems. Rebecca Smith is a good example. Evidence shows this is increasing as homelessness increases. Couldn't be a result. Perpetuates the trend. (Use Stoner, Hombs & Snyder data.)
7. Evictions	Necessary and sufficient cause, due to economic reasons. Immediate cause. Affects females more, but also affects men. As evictions increase, more homeless. Perpetuating cause.
8. Lack of housing	Necessary and sufficient, but related to economic reasons. Cheap housing is harder to find due to redevelopment and gentrification. Renovation affects those already without housing more. Could mention Rebecca Smith. Perpetuating cause.

Once she had analyzed all these possible causes, Dartnell could decide how to use them to make the most convincing explanation. She had to decide which causes to emphasize, which ones to combine, which ones to omit, and how to order the causes to produce the most effective argument. Last, she had to try to find any potential objections to her arguments, which she would then have to answer. As it happened, she decided to use all of these causes except for alcoholism, which she would mention and refute.

She begins her essay with a discussion of abuse because she considers it the one cause of homelessness that most affects women. She then discusses evictions and housing, treating each of these causes in a separate paragraph. Next she mentions—and refutes—alcoholism as a cause. Only then does she develop the cause for which she had the most evidence, deinstitutionalization. Finally, she combines several causes—unemployment, inflation, welfare cutbacks—into one paragraph on economic causes.

These causes could be presented in a different order—deinstitutionalization might be effectively placed either first or last, for example—but Dartnell's plan serves her topic well. By covering her topic so comprehensively and discussing it in a clear, logically organized manner, she presents a convincing argument.

THINKING CRITICALLY ABOUT WHAT YOU HAVE LEARNED

By now you have worked extensively with causal speculation about phenomena and trends—reading about it, talking about it, writing about it. You can continue to learn about causal speculation by taking time to reflect on your experiences and attitudes. What problems did you encounter? How did the essays in this chapter influence your work? What effect does causal speculation have on the way we think about ourselves and the world around us?

Reflecting on Your Writing

Write a page or so telling your instructor about a problem you had in writing an essay speculating about causes and how you solved that problem. Before you begin, gather all of your writing—invention, planning notes, drafts, any critical comments from classmates and your instructor, revising notes and plans, and final revision. Review these, and refer to them as you complete this writing task.

1. Identify *one* problem you needed to solve as you worked on your essay. Do not be concerned with grammar and punctuation; concentrate instead on problems unique to developing an essay speculating about causes. For example, did you puzzle over how to present your subject in a way that would interest your readers? Did you have trouble demonstrating that a trend exists? Was it difficult to decide on a logical sequence for presenting causes? Did you worry about the need to evaluate alternative causes?
2. How did you recognize the problem? When did you first discover it? What called it to your attention? If you did not become aware of the problem until someone else pointed it out to you, can you now see hints of it in your invention writings? If so, where specifically? When you first recognized the problem, how did you respond?
3. Reflect also on how you went about solving the problem. Did you work on the wording of a passage, cut or add causes or refutations, conduct further research, move paragraphs or sentences around? Did you reread one of the essays in this chapter to see how another writer handled the problem, or did you look back at the invention suggestions? If you talked about the problem with another student, a tutor, or your instructor, did talking about it help? How useful was the advice you got?
4. Finally, write your explanation of the problem and how you tried to solve it. Be as specific as possible in reconstructing your efforts. Quote from your invention, your draft, others' critical comments, your revision plan, or your revised essay to show the various changes your writing underwent as you tried to solve the problem. Taking time to explain how you identified a particular problem, how you went about solving it, and what you learned from this experience can help you in solving future writing problems.

Reviewing What You Learned from Reading

Your own essay has undoubtedly been influenced to some extent by one or more of the essays in this chapter and by essays written by classmates that you may have read. These other essays may have helped you to decide on an appropriate subject or to recognize the importance of discovering both immediate and background causes of your trend or phenomenon. They may have suggested ways to bring up alternative causes in relation to the ones you prefer or demonstrated how to argue against a prominent alternative cause likely to be favored by your readers. Write a page or so explaining to your instructor how the readings in this chapter influenced your revised essay. Before you do, take time to reflect on what you have learned about causal speculation from the readings and consider how they may have influenced your own writing.

1. Reread the final revision of your essay; then look back at the selections you read before completing your essay. Do you see any specific influences? For example, if you were impressed with the way one of the readings established its trend, presented causes in a logical order, used personal experience and observation to support a cause, argued convincingly against an alternative cause, or addressed readers in a considerate tone, look to see where you may have been striving for similar effects in your own writing. Also, look for ideas you got from your reading, writing strategies you were inspired to try, specific details you were led to include, effects you sought to achieve.
2. Now write an explanation of these influences. Did one selection have a particularly strong influence, or were several selections influential in different ways? Quote from the readings and from your final revision to show how your causal explanation was influenced by the other causal essays you read. Finally, point out anything you would now improve in your essay based on your review of this chapter's selections.

Considering the Social Dimensions of Causal Speculation

Persuasive writing, as we have defined it in this text, deals with probabilities and possibilities, not with certainties. Causal speculation is persuasive writing par excellence because it confronts aspects of social life that we do not yet understand and may never fully understand. Without this great social resource, we would feel helpless in the face of threatening social problems. They would seem like random acts of a chaotic universe. Instead, when confronted with the alarming evidence that the teenage suicide rate is high and even increasing, we can start speculating about why so many teenagers are ending their own lives. We can evaluate competing causes and decide which are the most plausible. Finally, we can take action, feeling reassured that our knowledge is sound, even though it is speculative and likely to change over time. Nevertheless, cautious readers and writers need to be aware of several problems posed by causal speculation.

The Power of Authority. First, we need to keep in mind that what seems to be the best current explanation for the causes of a trend or a phenomenon is not necessarily the only explanation. Speculating about causes tends to give greater voice to certain interests and to minimize or silence others. Some analyses, particularly those of "experts" such as economists and demographers, are often granted more authority than analyses favored by parents, teachers, community and religious leaders, or the persons most directly affected. For example, Dartnell apparently did not talk to homeless women directly.

In addition, we need to remember that causal reasoning is always shaped by the analyst's ideology—the set of beliefs, values, and attitudes that determines a person's worldview. For example, Stephen King—a horror writer himself—has a real interest in establishing the horror genre as a legitimate literary and cinematic form; it is not surprising, then, that he would emphasize psychological benefits as a basis for the popularity of horror movies rather than a more negative factor. Kim Dartnell is clearly sympathetic to the plight of homeless women; a less sympathetic analyst might come up with a completely different explanation for the causes of their homelessness.

Even the way we define a phenomenon or a trend can color our explanation of its causes. For example, following the original acquittal of the police officers accused of beating motorist Rodney King in Los Angeles during the spring of 1992, many people took to the streets, starting fires and looting. While some observers called the disturbance a "riot," others more sympathetically called it an "uprising." These two terms reflect opposite ways of understanding what happened, pointing to entirely different sets of possible causes. A great deal is at stake when society must decide whether the causes were linked to frustration with racism and unequal justice, on the one hand, or to lack of an adequate police "presence" and respect for the law, on the other hand.

Causes and Blame. An even tougher problem is that causal explanations sometimes become exercises in assigning blame. Worse, causal explanation may even be used to blame parties who are adversely affected by the conditions they supposedly have caused. For example, not long ago, a woman's "provocative" attire could be cited in court as a cause (and possible justification) for her being raped. Similarly, the homeless are sometimes blamed for causing their own plight. In cases like these, causal explanation often becomes a way to avoid confronting our social responsibility and allows us to put off working toward solving serious social problems.

For Discussion. The following questions can help you to think critically about the role of causal speculation in our society, focusing on the reading by Putnam or Dartnell. Review these two readings. Then, as you read through and, perhaps, discuss these questions in class, note down your thoughts and reactions. Finally, write a page or so for your instructor presenting your own thoughts about how causal speculation affects our lives.

1. We have said that because causal explanation deals with possibilities instead of certainties, writers must be somewhat tentative about their speculations. However, if causal argument is to be convincing, it cannot be too timid. Compare the Putnam and Dartnell essays. Which seems more assertive? What accounts for your response?
2. We have also said that if readers are not alert, they may begin to think that the explanation offered is the only possible one. Is either Putnam's or Dartnell's argument so seductive that you find yourself accepting it without question? Explain briefly.
3. Americans are often divided about whether individuals are primarily responsible for their circumstances or whether social, economic, and political conditions best explain people's difficulties and suffering. Where does Dartnell position herself on this issue? Explore your own position as well, focusing on the particular cases Dartnell writes about. If you were to write about the causes of homelessness, which kinds of causes—individual or social—would you emphasize? Why?
4. Dartnell writes a causal argument about a social issue in which she is not personally involved and relies totally on sources, rather than on her own personal experience. She is white, middle-class, and well educated. How might her causal analysis reflect her own social position? The people directly affected by social problems seldom get to write causal analyses about their own plight; in our society, analysis is typically left to the experts. Imagine how extended interviews with homeless people might have changed the causal arguments in Dartnell's essay. What is there about causal analysis as practiced in our society that invites experts to speculate about the lives of people who are very distant from them in terms of experience, income, education, and ethnicity?

A student writes an essay agreeing that Ernest Hemingway's "Big Two-Hearted River" is about healing but arguing that instead of relying on the healing power of nature or Christianity the story's hero, Nick, tries to heal himself by practicing the four qualities of Stoicism: virtue, endurance, self-sufficiency, and self-discipline. He defines virtue as being in harmony with nature and shows several ways in which Nick acts virtuously. He also gives examples that show Nick practicing endurance and exercising self-sufficiency. He concludes by referring to two passages that illustrate Nick's efforts to control himself physically, mentally, spiritually, and emotionally. He shows that every action Nick takes is deliberate and orderly and that Hemingway's spare language and sentence structure mirror Nick's efforts at self-discipline.

Writing about Charles Dickens's classic story *A Christmas Carol* for the Sunday magazine section of a local newspaper, an essayist argues that although the story seems to criticize capitalism for neglecting the needy, it actually justifies business as usual when accompanied by individual acts of charity. She further argues that Scrooge's great flaw is not the fact that he possesses more wealth than most people but that he does not spend his money. She shows that as a miser, Scrooge must be reeducated to do what we all must do at Christmastime—be good consumers and buy lots of gifts. To support this idea, she draws readers' attention to all the bright and shiny objects Scrooge sees as he views the scenes of Christmases Past as well as the lavish gifts he purchases for the Cratchit family. She concludes by noting the irony that Scrooge's generosity at the end of the story—usually seen as embodying the true spirit of Christmas—really endorses the spirit of commercialism because, ultimately, money *does* buy him love.

For a conference on the history of psychotherapy, a therapist presents a paper on Charlotte Perkins Gilman's story "The Yellow Wallpaper" as an indictment of Dr. S. Weir Mitchell's popular therapy for women that Gilman herself underwent. She supports her argument with quotes from Gilman's story and autobiography, as well as from Mitchell's 1881 *Lectures on the Diseases of the Nervous System, Especially in Women*. She explains the three major elements of Mitchell's therapy and shows how they are represented in Gilman's story: (1) absolute isolation from family and friends; (2) bed rest—including severe restrictions on reading, writing, and painting—designed to make the patient eager "to do the things she once felt she could not do"; and (3) a strong dose of moralizing by the physician. She ends by pointing out the story's irony—that the main character becomes psychotic to escape from the therapy itself.

CHAPTER 10

Interpreting Stories

Stories have a special place in most cultures. Elders relate family and cultural history through stories; lessons are taught through moral fables and parables. The bonds of family and community are often strengthened by sharing stories.

Stories have the power to stimulate feeling and imagination, allowing us to escape our everyday routine and become aware of the wider world around us. They can lead us to look at others with sensitivity and, for a brief time, to see the world through another person's eyes. They can also lead us to see ourselves differently, to gain insight into our innermost feelings and thoughts.

The stories you will read in this chapter may remind you of the stories about remembered events you read and wrote in Chapter 2. Like those autobiographical stories, these stories all happen to be narrated in the first person ("I"), although fictional stories may use third-person narrators as well. The major difference is that in autobiography, "I" is the author speaking, whereas in fiction "I" is imaginary, simply a character in the story. Whether a story is true or imagined, its success depends largely on how well it conveys the significance of the event to readers. As you may remember, autobiographical stories convey significance primarily through vivid descriptive detail showing people in particular places engaged in some kind of dramatic action. Fictional stories work the same way, only the people are called the *characters,* places are called the *setting,* the dramatic action is called the *plot,* and the significance is called the *theme* or *meaning.*

In this chapter, we do not ask you to write a fictional story (although your instructor may give you that opportunity). Instead, you will be writing about the meaning you find in a story you have read. Learning to write about stories may help you to write other kinds of college or professional essays based on close reading. But the essay interpreting a story—like the lab report in biology, the ethnography in anthropology, and the law brief—is a special kind of writing, designed for studying literature. Like these other academic and professional genres, literary interpretation has its own specialized language, with words such as *plot, theme, metaphor,* and *simile.* But the specialized language is continually evolving as people who write and read literary interpretations try to find new ways to extend and deepen their understanding of the literature.

You can expect your readers to appreciate any insight into the story you can give them. They will be interested not only in your overall interpretation but also in what you have to say about particular scenes, characters, even bits of dialogue. They will expect you to quote from the story and also to explain how you understand the words you quoted. Although readers may not agree with your interpretation, your ideas will stimulate their thinking and enhance their enjoyment of the story.

Writing in Your Other Courses

Many colleges require students to read and write about literature as part of their general education. In addition, some of your other courses may include assignments asking you to use the course material to analyze and interpret a novel, short story, film, or other cultural text, as the following assignments suggest.

- *For a health services course:* For a change from the technical reading you have done this term, you may choose to do your final project on a movie or television series that portrays illness and disability. The media play an important role in educating the public and may also have an effect on people's views of health care providers. Your analysis should focus on how the movie represents the illness, the patient's experience, and possibly also the relationship between the patient and caregivers—family and friends as well as professionals. For example, consider whether the portrayal of the patient (or the health care provider) is idealized. Look at the ways in which the illness affects the patient's self-concept or how other people relate to the patient.

  Excellent movies available on video include *Rainman* (which deals with autism), *Coming Home* (paraplegia), *Steel Magnolias* (diabetes), *Terms of Endearment* (terminal cancer), *The Three Faces of Eve* (multiple personality disorder), *Philadelphia* (AIDS), as well as *Lost Weekend* and *Leaving Las Vegas* (alcoholism).
- *For an ethnic studies course:* You have studied the facts about the immigrant experience—when the great waves of immigration occurred, how many people came to America, where they came from, and where they settled. To understand the experience fully, however, you need the immigrant's perspective. Read one of the books on the reserve list in the library, and write an essay interpreting the meaning of the experience for that particular author.
- *For an American history course:* Write an essay analyzing Nathaniel Hawthorne's short story "My Kinsman, Major Molineux" in light of Mason Locke Weems's book *The Life of Washington.* Although Hawthorne wrote his story in 1832, it is set in the mid-1700s, *before* the American Revolution, and we know that he read Weems's best-selling biography, which was published in 1809.

  In your essay, explain what you think Hawthorne is saying about the idea of the public hero in the new national mythology of the early republic. To support your interpretation, refer to Hawthorne's story and to Weems's mythic biography. To begin thinking about this topic, you might compare Robin's heroic image of his important kinsman with the exemplary characteristics of George Washington, as depicted by Weems. Consider also what a "shrewd youth" like Robin could expect to gain from his hero and what the two stories tell us about the routes to success in the early years of the republic.

Practice Interpreting a Story: A Collaborative Activity

This activity invites you to practice interpreting a story before you have to write an essay arguing for your interpretation. As you read and discuss a story with two or three other students, you will see that there are various ways of interpreting it. Your purpose is to try to assert what you think is significant or interesting about the story and also to help your readers to see what you now see in the story.

Part 1. Choose a story that interests everyone in the group. Your instructor may assign a story or may invite you to choose one from the anthology that follows. If there is time, you may enjoy having someone in the group read the story aloud.

After reading the story, write for two or three minutes to get some ideas about it. You need not try to find an interpretation of its overall meaning. Instead, look for more specific interpretations—for example, why a character does or says something at a certain point in the story, why a scene is described in particular words, or why the story ends as it does.

Then choose one idea and take three or four minutes to present it to the others in your group, briefly explaining how it helps you to understand some aspect of the story. Give an example from the story to illustrate your idea—for instance, you could quote an especially significant passage or summarize what happens in an important scene.

After all group members have explained and illustrated their assertions, discuss the various interpretations for about five minutes. You could try to extend or develop one of the ideas, connect or contrast several ideas, or find additional support for an idea in the story or find a passage that seems to contradict it.

Part 2. After discussing your interpretations, take another five minutes to talk about what you did to develop ideas about the story by considering the following questions:

- Was it hard to think of an idea you could use to interpret the story, or did several ideas come to mind right away? If you had to choose from among several ideas, how did you make the choice?
- How well do you think you explained your interpretation? Were your partners able to see how you got this interpretation from a particular passage in the story?
- Did the discussion help you to see how you could extend your idea, connect it to or contrast it with other ideas, find further support in the story for it or find a passage that seems to contradict it?
- How did you like discussing your own and other people's interpretations about the story? Did discussing interpretations of the story help to make it more or less interesting for you? Why?

AN ANTHOLOGY OF SHORT STORIES

Following are four well-known short stories: "The Monkey Garden" by Sandra Cisneros, "The Use of Force" by William Carlos Williams, "The Hammer Man" by Toni Cade Bambara, and "Araby" by James Joyce. Your instructor may invite the whole class or small groups to discuss one or more of these stories. You may also be asked to choose one of these stories for your interpretive essay.

Sandra Cisneros (b. 1954) has published the poetry collection *My Wicked Wicked Ways* and two short-story collections, *Woman Hollering Creek* and *The House on Mango Street.* As you read "The Monkey Garden," notice its fantastic setting—a child's imaginary garden based on the Chicago neighborhood in which Cisneros grew up.

THE MONKEY GARDEN
Sandra Cisneros

1 The monkey doesn't live there anymore. The monkey moved—to Kentucky—and took his people with him. And I was glad because I couldn't listen anymore to his wild screaming at night, the twangy yakkety-yak of the people who owned him. The green metal cage, the porcelain table top, the family that spoke like guitars. Monkey, family, table. All gone.

2 And it was then we took over the garden we had been afraid to go into when the monkey screamed and showed its yellow teeth.

3 There were sunflowers big as flowers on Mars and thick cockscombs bleeding the deep red fringe of theater curtains. There were dizzy bees and bow-tied fruit flies turning somersaults and humming in the air. Sweet sweet peach trees. Thorn roses and thistle and pears. Weeds like so many squinty-eyed stars and brush that made your ankles itch and itch until you washed with soap and water. There were big green apples hard as knees. And everywhere the sleepy smell of rotting wood, damp earth and dusty hollyhocks thick and perfumy like the blue-blond hair of the dead.

4 Yellow spiders ran when we turned rocks over and pale worms blind and afraid of light rolled over in their sleep. Poke a stick in the sandy soil and a few blue-skinned beetles would appear, an avenue of ants, so many crusty lady bugs. This was a garden, a wonderful thing to look at in the spring. But bit by bit, after the monkey left, the garden began to take over itself. Flowers stopped obeying the little bricks that kept them from growing beyond their paths. Weeds mixed in. Dead cars appeared overnight like mushrooms. First one and then another and then a pale blue pickup with the front windshield missing. Before you knew it, the monkey garden became filled with sleepy cars.

5 Things had a way of disappearing in the garden, as if the garden itself ate them, or, as if with its old-man memory, it put them away and forgot them. Nenny found a dollar and a dead mouse between two rocks in the stone wall where the morning glories climbed, and once when we were playing hide and seek, Eddie Vargas laid his head beneath a hibiscus tree and fell asleep there like a Rip Van Winkle until somebody remembered he was in the game and went back to look for him.

6 This, I suppose, was the reason why we went there. Far away from where our mothers could find us. We and a few old dogs who lived inside the empty cars. We made a club-house once on the back of that old blue pickup. And besides, we liked to jump from the roof of one car to another and pretend they were giant mushrooms.

Somebody started the lie that the monkey garden had been there before anything. We liked to think the garden could hide things for a thousand years. There beneath the roots of soggy flowers were the bones of murdered pirates and dinosaurs, the eye of a unicorn turned to coal. 7

This is where I wanted to die and where I tried one day but not even the monkey garden would have me. It was the last day I would go there. 8

Who was it that said I was getting too old to play the games? Who was it I didn't listen to? I only remember that when the others ran, I wanted to run too, up and down and through the monkey garden, fast as the boys, not like Sally who screamed if she got her stockings muddy. 9

I said, Sally, come on, but she wouldn't. She stayed by the curb talking to Tito and his friends. Play with the kids if you want, she said, I'm staying here. She could be stuck-up like that if she wanted to, so I just left. 10

It was her own fault too. When I got back Sally was pretending to be mad . . . something about the boys having stolen her keys. Please give them back to me, she said, punching the nearest one with a soft fist. They were laughing. She was too. It was a joke I didn't get. 11

I wanted to go back with the other kids who were still jumping on cars, still chasing each other through the garden, but Sally had her own game. 12

One of the boys invented the rules. One of Tito's friends said you can't get the keys back unless you kiss us and Sally pretended to be mad at first but she said yes. It was that simple. 13

I don't know why, but something inside me wanted to throw a stick. Something wanted to say no when I watched Sally going into the garden with Tito's buddies all grinning. It was just a kiss, that's all. A kiss for each one. So what, she said. 14

Only how come I felt angry inside. Like something wasn't right. Sally went behind that old blue pickup to kiss the boys and get her keys back, and I ran up three flights of stairs to where Tito lived. His mother was ironing shirts. She was sprinkling water on them from an empty pop bottle and smoking a cigarette. 15

Your son and his friends stole Sally's keys and now they won't give them back unless she kisses them and right now they're making her kiss them, I said all out of breath from the three flights of stairs. 16

Those kids, she said, not looking up from her ironing. 17

That's all? 18

What do you want me to do, she said, call the cops? And kept on ironing. 19

I looked at her a long time, but couldn't think of anything to say, and ran back down the three flights to the garden where Sally needed to be saved. I took three big sticks and a brick and figured this was enough. 20

But when I got there Sally said go home. Those boys said, leave us alone. I felt stupid with my brick. They all looked at me as if *I* was the one that was crazy and made me feel ashamed. 21

And then I don't know why but I had to run away. I had to hide myself at the other end of the garden, in the jungle part, under a tree that wouldn't mind if I lay down and cried a long time. I closed my eyes like tight stars so that I wouldn't, but I did. My face felt hot. Everything inside hiccupped. 22

I read somewhere in India there are priests who can will their heart to stop beating. I wanted to will my blood to stop, my heart to quit its pumping. I wanted to be dead, to turn into the rain, my eyes melt into the ground like two black snails. I wished and wished. I closed my eyes and willed it, but when I got up my dress was green and I had a headache. 23

I looked at my feet in their white socks and ugly round shoes. They seemed far away. They didn't seem to be my feet anymore. And the garden that had been such a good place to play didn't seem mine either. 24

William Carlos Williams (1883–1963) is one of the most important poets of this century, best known for his long poem *Paterson* (1946–1958). He also wrote essays, plays, novels, and short stories. "The Use of Force" was published initially in *The Doctor Stories* (1933), a collection loosely based on Williams's experiences as a pediatrician.

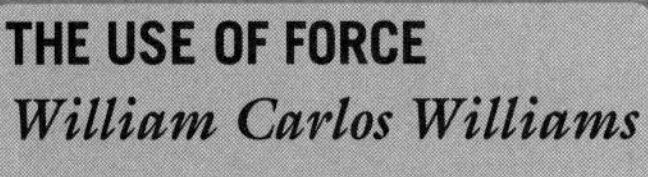

THE USE OF FORCE

William Carlos Williams

They were new patients to me, all I had was the name, Olson. Please come down as soon as you can, my daughter is very sick. 1

When I arrived I was met by the mother, a big startled-looking woman, very clean and apologetic, who merely said, Is this the doctor? and let me in. In the back, she added. You must excuse us, doctor, we have her in the kitchen where it is warm. It is very damp here sometimes. 2

The child was fully dressed and sitting on her father's lap near the kitchen table. He tried to get up, but I motioned for him not to bother, took off my overcoat and started to look things over. I could see that they were all very nervous, eyeing me up and down distrustfully. As often, in such cases, they weren't telling me more than they had to, it was up to me to tell them; that's why they were spending three dollars on me. 3

The child was fairly eating me up with her cold, steady eyes, and no expression to her face whatever. She did not move and seemed, inwardly, quiet; an unusually attractive little thing, and as strong as a heifer in appearance. But her face was flushed, she was breathing rapidly, and I realized that she had a high fever. She had magnificent blonde hair, in profusion. One of those picture children often reproduced in advertising leaflets and the photogravure sections of the Sunday papers. 4

She's had a fever for three days, began the father, and we don't know what it comes from. My wife has given her things, you know, like people do, but it don't do no good. And there's been a lot of sickness around. So we tho't you better look her over and tell us what is the matter. 5

As doctors often do I took a trial shot at it as a point of departure. Has she had a sore throat? 6

Both parents answered me together, No . . . No, she says her throat don't hurt her. 7

Does your throat hurt you? added the mother to the child. But the little girl's expression didn't change nor did she move her eyes from my face. 8

Have you looked? 9

I tried, said the mother, but I couldn't see. 10

As it happens we had been having a number of cases of diphtheria in the school to which this child went during that month and we were all, quite apparently, thinking of that, though no one had as yet spoken of the thing. 11

Well, I said, suppose we take a look at the throat first. I smiled in my best professional manner and asking for the child's first name I said, come on, Mathilda, open your mouth and let's take a look at your throat. 12

Nothing doing. 13

Aw, come on, I coaxed, just open your mouth wide and let me take a look. Look, I said opening both hands wide, I haven't anything in my hands. Just open up and let me see. 14

Such a nice man, put in the mother. Look how kind he is to you. Come on, do what he tells you to. He won't hurt you. 15

At that I ground my teeth in disgust. If only they wouldn't use the word "hurt" I might be able to get somewhere. But I did not allow myself to be hurried or disturbed but speaking quietly and slowly I approached the child again. 16

As I moved my chair a little nearer suddenly with one catlike movement both her hands clawed instinctively for my eyes and she almost reached them too. In fact she knocked my glasses flying and they fell, though unbroken, several feet away from me on the kitchen floor. 17

Both the mother and father almost turned themselves inside out in embarrassment and apology. You bad girl, said the mother, taking her and shaking her by one arm. Look what you've done. The nice man . . . 18

For heaven's sake, I broke in. Don't call me a nice man to her. I'm here to look at her throat on the chance that she might have diphtheria and possibly die of it. But that's nothing to her. Look here, I said to the child, we're going to look at your throat. You're old enough to understand what I'm saying. Will you open it now by yourself or shall we have to open it for you? 19

Not a move. Even her expression hadn't changed. Her breaths however were coming faster and faster. Then the battle began. I had to do it. I had to have a throat culture for her own protection. But first I told the parents that it was entirely up to them. I explained the danger but said that I would not insist on a throat examination so long as they would take the responsibility. 20

If you don't do what the doctor says you'll have to go to the hospital, the mother admonished her severely. 21

Oh yeah? I had to smile to myself. After all, I had already fallen in love with the savage brat, the parents were contemptible to me. In the ensuing struggle they grew more and more abject, crushed, exhausted while she surely rose to magnificent heights of insane fury of effort bred of her terror of me. 22

The father tried his best, and he was a big man, but the fact that she was his daughter, his shame at her behavior and his dread of hurting her made him release her just at the critical times when I had almost achieved success, till I wanted to kill him. But his dread also that she might have diphtheria made him tell me to go on, go on though he himself was almost fainting, while the mother moved back and forth behind us raising and lowering her hands in an agony of apprehension. 23

Put her in front of you on your lap, I ordered, and hold both her wrists. 24

But as soon as he did the child let out a scream. Don't, you're hurting me. Let go of my hands. Let them go I tell you. Then she shrieked terrifyingly, hysterically. Stop it! Stop it! You're killing me! 25

Do you think she can stand it, doctor! said the mother. 26

You get out, said the husband to his wife. Do you want her to die of diphtheria? 27

Come on now, hold her, I said. 28

Then I grasped the child's head with my left hand and tried to get the wooden tongue depressor between her teeth. She fought, with clenched teeth, desperately! But now I also had grown furious—at a child. I tried to hold myself down but I couldn't. I know how to expose a throat for inspection. And I did my best. When finally I got the wooden spatula behind the last teeth and just the point of it into the mouth cavity, she opened up for an instant but before I could see anything she came down again and gripping the wooden blade between her molars she reduced it to splinters before I could get it out again. 29

Aren't you ashamed, the mother yelled at her. Aren't you ashamed to act like that in front of the doctor?

Get me a smooth-handled spoon of some sort, I told the mother. We're going through with this. The child's mouth was already bleeding. Her tongue was cut and she was screaming in wild hysterical shrieks. Perhaps I should have desisted and come back in an hour or more. No doubt it would have been better. But I have seen at least two children lying dead in bed of neglect in such cases, and feeling that I must get a diagnosis now or never I went at it again. But the worst of it was that I too had got beyond reason. I could have torn the child apart in my own fury and enjoyed it. It was a pleasure to attack her. My face was burning with it.

The damned little brat must be protected against her own idiocy, one says to oneself at such times. Others must be protected against her. It is a social necessity. And all these things are true. But a blind fury, a feeling of adult shame, bred of a longing for muscular release are the operatives. One goes on to the end.

In a final unreasoning assault I overpowered the child's neck and jaws. I forced the heavy silver spoon back of her teeth and down her throat till she gagged. And there it was—both tonsils covered with membrane. She had fought valiantly to keep me from knowing her secret. She had been hiding that sore throat for three days at least and lying to her parents in order to escape just such an outcome as this.

Now truly she was furious. She had been on the defensive before but now she attacked. Tried to get off her father's lap and fly at me while tears of defeat blinded her eyes.

Toni Cade Bambara (1939–1995) was born in New York City. In addition to writing several collections of short stories (including *Gorilla, My Love* and *The Sea Birds Are Still Alive*) and the novel *The Salt Eaters,* she was deeply involved in improving life in urban communities and recording African-American culture. The following story was originally published in 1966.

THE HAMMER MAN
Toni Cade Bambara

I was glad to hear that Manny had fallen off the roof. I had put out the tale that I was down with yellow fever, but nobody paid me no mind, least of all Dirty Red who stomped right in to announce that Manny had fallen off the roof and that I could come out of hiding now. My mother dropped what she was doing, which was the laundry, and got the whole story out of Red. "Bad enough you gots to hang around with boys," she said. "But fight with them too. And you would pick the craziest one at that."

Manny was supposed to be crazy. That was his story. To say you were bad put some people off. But to say you were crazy, well, you were officially not to be messed with. So that was his story. On the other hand, after I called him what I called him and said a few choice things about his mother, his face did go through some piercing changes. And I did kind of wonder if maybe he sure was nuts. I didn't wait to find out. I got in the wind. And then he waited for me on my stoop all day and all night, not hardly speaking to the people going in and out. And he was there all day Saturday, with his sister bringing him peanut-butter sandwiches and cream sodas. He must've gone to the bathroom right there cause every time I looked out the kitchen window, there he was. And Sunday, too. I got to thinking the boy was mad.

"You got no sense of humor, that's your trouble," I told him. He looked up, but he didn't say nothing. All at once I was real sorry about the whole thing. I should've settled for hitting off the little girls in the school yard or waiting for Frankie to come in so we could raise some kind of hell. This way I had to play sick when my mother was around cause my father had already taken away my BB gun and hid it.

4 I don't know how they got Manny on the roof finally. Maybe the Wakefield kids, the ones who keep the pigeons, called him up. Manny was a sucker for sick animals and things like that. Or maybe Frankie got some nasty girls to go up on the roof with him and got Manny to join him. I don't know. Anyway, the catwalk had lost all its cement and the roof always did kind of slant downward. So Manny fell off the roof. I got over my yellow fever right quick, needless to say, and ventured outside. But by this time I had already told Miss Rose that Crazy Manny was after me. And Miss Rose, being who she was, quite naturally went over to Manny's house and said a few harsh words to his mother, who, being who she was, chased Miss Rose out into the street and they commenced to get with it, snatching bottles out of the garbage cans and breaking them on the johnny pumps and stuff like that.

5 Dirty Red didn't have to tell us about this. Everybody could see and hear all. I never figured the garbage cans for an arsenal, but Miss Rose came up with sticks and table legs and things, and Manny's mother had her share of scissor blades and bicycle chains. They got to rolling in the streets and all you could see was pink drawers and fat legs. It was something else. Miss Rose is nutty but Manny's mother's crazier than Manny. They were at it a couple of times during my sick spell. Everyone would congregate on the window sills or the fire escape, commenting that it was still much too cold for this kind of nonsense. But they watched anyway. And then Manny fell off the roof. And that was that. Miss Rose went back to her dream books and Manny's mother went back to her tumbled-down kitchen of dirty clothes and bundles and bundles of rags and children.

6 My father got in on it too, cause he happened to ask Manny one night why he was sitting on the stoop like that every night. Manny told him right off that he was going to kill me first chance he got. Quite naturally this made my father a little warm, me being his only daughter and planning to become a doctor and take care of him in his old age. So he had a few words with Manny first, and then he got hold of the older brother, Bernard, who was more his size. Bernard didn't see how any of it was his business or my father's business, so my father got mad and jammed Bernard's head into the mailbox. Then my father started getting messages from Bernard's uncle about where to meet him for a showdown and all. My father didn't say a word to my mother all this time; just sat around mumbling and picking up the phone and putting it down, or grabbing my stickball bat and putting it back. He carried on like this for days till I thought I would scream if the yellow fever didn't have me so weak. And then Manny fell off the roof, and my father went back to his beer-drinking buddies.

7 I was in the school yard, pitching pennies with the little boys from the elementary school, when my friend Violet hits my brand-new Spaudeen over the wall. She came running back to tell me that Manny was coming down the block. I peeked beyond the fence and there he was all right. He had his head all wound up like a mummy and his arm in a sling and his leg in a cast. It looked phony to me, especially that walking cane. I figured Dirty Red had told me a tale just to get me out there so Manny could stomp me, and Manny was playing it up with costume and all till he could get me.

8 "What happened to him?" Violet's sisters whispered. But I was too busy trying to figure out how this act was supposed to work. Then Manny passed real close to the fence and gave me a look.

9 "You had enough, Hammer Head," I yelled. "Just bring your crummy self in this yard and I'll pick up where I left off." Violet was knocked out and the other kids went

into a huddle. I didn't have to say anything else. And when they all pressed me later, I just said, "You know that hammer he always carries in his fatigues?" And they'd all nod waiting for the rest of a long story. "Well, I took it away from him." And I walked off nonchalantly.

Manny stayed indoors for a long time. I almost forgot about him. New kids moved into the block and I got all caught up with that. And then Miss Rose finally hit the numbers and started ordering a whole lot of stuff through the mail and we would sit on the curb and watch these weird-looking packages being carried in, trying to figure out what simpleminded thing she had thrown her money away on when she might just as well wait for the warm weather and throw a block party for all her godchildren.

After a while a center opened up and my mother said she'd increase my allowance if I went and joined because I'd have to get out of my pants and stay in skirts, on account of that's the way things were at the center. So I joined and got to thinking about everything else but old Hammer Head. It was a rough place to get along in, the center, but my mother said that I needed to be be'd with and she needed to not be with me, so I went. And that time I sneaked into the office, that's when I really got turned on. I looked into one of those not-quite-white folders and saw that I was from a deviant family in a deviant neighborhood. I showed my mother the word in the dictionary, but she didn't pay me no mind. It was my favorite word after that. I ran it in the ground till one day my father got the strap just to show how deviant he could get. So I gave up trying to improve my vocabulary. And I almost gave up my dungarees.

Then one night I'm walking past the Douglas Street park cause I got thrown out of the center for playing pool when I should've been sewing, even though I had already decided that this was going to be my last fling with boy things, and starting tomorrow I was going to fix my hair right and wear skirts all the time just so my mother would stop talking about her gray hairs, and Miss Rose would stop calling me by my brother's name by mistake. So I'm walking past the park and there's ole Manny on the basketball court, perfecting his lay-ups and talking with himself. Being me, I quite naturally walk right up and ask what the hell he's doing playing in the dark, and he looks up and all around like the dark had crept up on him when he wasn't looking. So I knew right away that he'd been out there for a long time with his eyes just going along with the program.

"There was two seconds to go and we were one point behind," he said, shaking his head and staring at his sneakers like they was somebody. "And I was in the clear. I'd left the man in the backcourt and there I was, smiling, you dig, cause it was in the bag. They passed the ball and I slid the ball up nice and easy cause there was nothing to worry about. And . . ." He shook his head. "I muffed the goddamn shot. Ball bounced off the rim. . . ." He stared at his hands. "The game of the season. Last game." And then he ignored me altogether, though he wasn't talking to me in the first place. He went back to the lay-ups, always from the same spot with his arms crooked in the same way, over and over. I must've gotten hypnotized cause I probably stood there for at least an hour watching like a fool till I couldn't even see the damn ball, much less the basket. But I stood there anyway for no reason I know of. He never missed. But he cursed himself away. It was torture. And then a squad car pulled up and a short cop with hair like one of the Marx Brothers came out hitching up his pants. He looked real hard at me and then at Manny.

"What are you two doing?"

"He's doing a lay-up. I'm watching," I said with my smart self.

Then the cop just stood there and finally turned to the other one who was just getting out of the car.

"Who unlocked the gate?" the big one said.

"It's always unlocked," I said. Then we three just stood there like a bunch of penguins watching Manny go at it. 18

"This on the level?" the big guy asked, tilting his hat back with the thumb the way big guys do in hot weather. "Hey you," he said, walking over to Manny. "I'm talking to you." He finally grabbed the ball to get Manny's attention. But that didn't work. Manny just stood there with his arms out waiting for the pass so he could save the game. He wasn't paying no mind to the cop. So, quite naturally, when the cop slapped him upside his head it was a surprise. And when the cop started counting three to go, Manny had already recovered from the slap and was just ticking off the seconds before the buzzer sounded and all was lost. 19

"Gimme the ball, man." Manny's face was all tightened up and ready to pop. 20

"Did you hear what I said, black boy?" 21

Now, when somebody says that word like that, I gets warm. And crazy or no crazy, Manny was my brother at that moment and the cop was the enemy. 22

"You better give him back his ball," I said. "Manny don't take no mess from no cops. He ain't bothering nobody. He's gonna be Mister Basketball when he grows up. Just trying to get a little practice in before the softball season starts." 23

"Look here, sister, we'll run you in too," Harpo said. 24

"I damn sure can't be your sister seeing how I'm a black girl. Boy, I sure will be glad when you run me in so I can tell everybody about that. You must think you're in the South, mister." 25

The big guy screwed his mouth up and let one of them hard-day sighs. "The park's closed, little girl, so why don't you and your boyfriend go on home." 26

That really got me. The "little girl" was bad enough, but that "boyfriend" was too much. But I kept cool, mostly because Manny looked so pitiful waiting there with his hands in a time-out and there being no one to stop the clock. But I kept my cool mostly cause of that hammer in Manny's pocket and no telling how frantic things can get what with a bigmouth like me, a couple of wise cops, and a crazy boy too. 27

"The gates are open," I said real quiet-like, "and this here's a free country. So why don't you give him back his ball?" 28

The big cop did another one of those sighs, his specialty I guess, and then he bounced the ball to Manny who went right into his gliding thing clear up to the backboard, damn near like he was some kind of very beautiful bird. And then he swooshed that ball in, even if there was no net, and you couldn't really hear the swoosh. Something happened to the bones in my chest. It was something. 29

"Crazy kids anyhow," the one with the wig said and turned to go. But the big guy watched Manny for a while and I guess something must've snapped in his head, cause all of a sudden he was hot for taking Manny to jail or court or somewhere and started yelling at him and everything, which is a bad thing to do to Manny, I can tell you. And I'm standing there thinking that none of my teachers, from kindergarten right on up, none of them knew what they were talking about. I'll be damned if I ever knew one of them rosy-cheeked cops that smiled and helped you get to school without neither you or your little raggedy dog getting hit by a truck that had a smile on its face, too. Not that I ever believed it. I knew Dick and Jane was full of crap from the get-go, especially them cops. Like this dude, for example, pulling on Manny's clothes like that when obviously he had just done about the most beautiful thing a man can do and not be a fag. No cop could swoosh without a net. 30

"Look out, man," was all Manny said, but it was the way he pushed the cop that started the real yelling and threats. And I thought to myself, Oh God here I am trying to 31 change my ways, and not talk back in school, and do like my mother wants, but just have this last fling, and now this—getting shot in the stomach and bleeding to death in Douglas Street park and poor Manny getting pistol-whipped by those bastards and whatnot. I could see it all, practically crying too. And it just wasn't no kind of thing to happen to a small child like me with my confirmation picture in the paper next to my weeping parents and schoolmates. I could feel the blood sticking to my shirt and my eyeballs slipping away, and then that confirmation picture again; and my mother and her gray hair; and Miss Rose heading for the precinct with a shotgun; and my father getting old and feeble with no one to doctor him up and all.

And I wished Manny had fallen off the damn roof and died right then and there and saved me all this aggravation of being killed with him by these cops who surely didn't come out of no fifth-grade reader. But it didn't happen. They just took the ball and Manny followed them real quiet-like right out of the park into the dark, then into the squad car with his head drooping and his arms in a crook. And I went on home cause what the hell am I going to do on a basketball court, and it getting to be nearly midnight?

I didn't see Manny no more after he got into that squad car. But they didn't kill him after all cause Miss Rose heard he was in some kind of big house for people who lose their marbles. And then it was spring finally, and me and Violet was in this very boss fashion show at the center. And Miss Rose bought me my first corsage—yellow roses to match my shoes.

James Joyce (1882–1941), a native of Dublin, Ireland, is considered one of the most influential writers of the early twentieth century. The following story, one of his most often anthologized, first appeared in the collection *Dubliners* in 1914. Like his novel *Portrait of the Artist as a Young Man*, published two years later, it relies for much of its detail on scenes from Joyce's own boyhood.

ARABY
James Joyce

North Richmond Street, being blind,[1] was a quiet street except at the hour when the Christian Brothers' School set the boys free. An uninhabited house of two storeys stood at the blind end, detached from its neighbours in a square ground. The other houses of the street, conscious of decent lives within them, gazed at one another with brown imperturbable faces.

The former tenant of our house, a priest, had died in the back drawing-room. Air, musty from having been long enclosed, hung in all the rooms, and the waste room behind the kitchen was littered with old useless papers. Among these I found a few paper-covered books, the pages of which were curled and damp: *The Abbot,* by Walter Scott, *The Devout Communicant* and *The Memoirs of Vidocq.*[2] I liked the last best because its leaves were yellow. The wild garden behind the house contained a central apple-tree and a few straggling bushes under one of which I found the late tenant's rusty bicycle-pump. He had been a very charitable priest; in his will he had left all his money to institutions and the furniture of his house to his sister.

[1] A dead end. The young Joyce in fact lived for a time on North Richmond Street in Dublin.

[2] *The Devout Communicant* is a collection of religious meditations. *The Abbot* is a historical romance set in the court of Mary, Queen of Scots, a Catholic, who was beheaded for plotting to assassinate her Protestant cousin, Queen Elizabeth I. *The Memoirs of Vidocq* is a collection of sexually suggestive stories about a French criminal turned detective.

When the short days of winter came dusk fell before we had well eaten our dinners. When we met in the street the houses had grown sombre. The space of sky above us was the colour of ever-changing violet and towards it the lamps of the street lifted their feeble lanterns. The cold air stung us and we played till our bodies glowed. Our shouts echoed in the silent street. The career of our play brought us through the dark muddy lanes behind the houses where we ran the gauntlet of the rough tribes from the cottages, to the back doors of the dark dripping gardens where odours arose from the ashpits, to the dark odorous stables where a coachman smoothed and combed the horse or shook music from the buckled harness. When we returned to the street light from the kitchen windows had filled the areas. If my uncle was seen turning the corner we hid in the shadow until we had seen him safely housed. Or if Mangan's sister came out on the doorstep to call her brother in to his tea we watched her from our shadow peer up and down the street. We waited to see whether she would remain or go in and, if she remained, we left our shadow and walked up to Mangan's steps resignedly. She was waiting for us, her figure defined by the light from the half-opened door. Her brother always teased her before he obeyed and I stood by the railings looking at her. Her dress swung as she moved her body and the soft rope of her hair tossed from side to side. 3

Every morning I lay on the floor in the front parlour watching her door. The blind was pulled down to within an inch of the sash so that I could not be seen. When she came out on the doorstep my heart leaped. I ran to the hall, seized my books and followed her. I kept her brown figure always in my eye and, when we came near the point at which our ways diverged, I quickened my pace and passed her. This happened morning after morning. I had never spoken to her, except for a few casual words, and yet her name was like a summons to all my foolish blood. 4

Her image accompanied me even in places the most hostile to romance. On Saturday evenings when my aunt went marketing I had to go to carry some of the parcels. We walked through the flaring streets, jostled by drunken men and bargaining women, amid the curses of labourers, the shrill litanies of shop-boys who stood on guard by the barrels of pigs' cheeks, the nasal chanting of street-singers, who sang a *come-all-you* about O'Donovan Rossa,[3] or a ballad about the troubles in our native land. These noises converged in a single sensation of life for me: I imagined that I bore my chalice safely through a throng of foes. Her name sprang to my lips at moments in strange prayers and praises which I myself did not understand. My eyes were often full of tears (I could not tell why) and at times a flood from my heart seemed to pour itself out into my bosom. I thought little of the future. I did not know whether I would ever speak to her or not or, if I spoke to her, how I could tell her of my confused adoration. But my body was like a harp and her words and gestures were like fingers running upon the wires. 5

One evening I went into the back drawing-room in which the priest had died. It was a dark rainy evening and there was no sound in the house. Through one of the broken panes I heard the rain impinge upon the earth, the fine incessant needles of water playing in the sodden beds. Some distant lamp or lighted window gleamed below me. I was thankful that I could see so little. All my senses seemed to desire to veil themselves and, feeling that I was about to slip from them, I pressed the palms of my hands together until they trembled, murmuring: *"O love! O love!"* many times. 6

At last she spoke to me. When she addressed the first words to me I was so confused that I did not know what to answer. She asked me was I going to *Araby*. 7

[3] A contemporary leader of an underground organization opposed to British rule of Ireland.

I forgot whether I answered yes or no. It would be a splendid bazaar, she said she would love to go.[4]

"And why can't you?" I asked.

While she spoke she turned a silver bracelet round and round her wrist. She could not go, she said, because there would be a retreat that week in her convent. Her brother and two other boys were fighting for their caps and I was alone at the railings. She held one of the spikes, bowing her head towards me. The light from the lamp opposite our door caught the white curve of her neck, lit up her hair that rested there and, falling, lit up the hand upon the railing. It fell over one side of her dress and caught the white border of a petticoat, just visible as she stood at ease.

"It's well for you," she said.

"If I go," I said, "I will bring you something."

What innumerable follies laid waste my waking and sleeping thoughts after that evening! I wished to annihilate the tedious intervening days. I chafed against the work of school. At night in my bedroom and by day in the classroom her image came between me and the page I strove to read. The syllables of the word *Araby* were called to me through the silence in which my soul luxuriated and cast an Eastern enchantment over me. I asked for leave to go to the bazaar on Saturday night. My aunt was surprised and hoped it was not some Freemason affair.[5] I answered few questions in class. I watched my master's face pass from amiability to sternness; he hoped I was not beginning to idle. I could not call my wandering thoughts together. I had hardly any patience with the serious work of life which, now that it stood between me and my desire, seemed to me child's play, ugly monotonous child's play.

On Saturday morning I reminded my uncle that I wished to go to the bazaar in the evening. He was fussing at the hallstand, looking for the hatbrush, and answered me curtly:

"Yes, boy, I know."

As he was in the hall I could not go into the front parlour and lie at the window. I left the house in bad humour and walked slowly towards the school. The air was pitilessly raw and already my heart misgave me.

When I came home to dinner my uncle had not yet been home. Still it was early. I sat staring at the clock for some time and, when its ticking began to irritate me, I left the room. I mounted the staircase and gained the upper part of the house. The high cold empty gloomy rooms liberated me and I went from room to room singing. From the front window I saw my companions playing below in the street. Their cries reached me weakened and indistinct and, leaning my forehead against the cool glass, I looked over at the dark house where she lived. I may have stood there for an hour, seeing nothing but the brown-clad figure cast by my imagination, touched discreetly by the lamplight at the curved neck, at the hand upon the railings and at the border below the dress.

When I came downstairs again I found Mrs. Mercer sitting at the fire. She was an old garrulous woman, a pawnbroker's widow, who collected used stamps for some pious purpose. I had to endure the gossip of the tea-table. The meal was prolonged beyond an hour and still my uncle did not come. Mrs. Mercer stood up to go: she was sorry she

[4] Such traveling bazaars—featuring cafés, shopping stalls, and entertainment—were common at the time. Araby was the name of an English bazaar that visited Dublin when Joyce was a boy.

[5] The Freemasons is a secretive fraternal order with a long history, whose members have included many artists, philosophers, and politicians, and to which the Catholic church has traditionally been opposed.

couldn't wait any longer, but it was after eight o'clock and she did not like to be out late, as the night air was bad for her. When she had gone I began to walk up and down the room, clenching my fists. My aunt said:

"I'm afraid you may put off your bazaar for this night of Our Lord." 18

At nine o'clock I heard my uncle's latchkey in the halldoor. I heard him talking to himself and heard the hallstand rocking when it had received the weight of his overcoat. I could interpret these signs. When he was midway through his dinner I asked him to give me the money to go to the bazaar. He had forgotten. 19

"The people are in bed and after their first sleep now," he said. 20

I did not smile. My aunt said to him energetically: 21

"Can't you give him the money and let him go? You've kept him late enough as it is." 22

My uncle said he was very sorry he had forgotten. He said he believed in the old saying: "All work and no play makes Jack a dull boy." He asked me where I was going and, when I had told him a second time he asked me did I know *The Arab's Farewell to his Steed*. When I left the kitchen he was about to recite the opening lines of the piece to my aunt. 23

I held a florin tightly in my hand as I strode down Buckingham Street towards the station. The sight of the streets thronged with buyers and glaring with gas recalled to me the purpose of my journey. I took my seat in a third-class carriage of a deserted train. After an intolerable delay the train moved out of the station slowly. It crept onward among ruinous houses and over the twinkling river. At Westland Row Station a crowd of people pressed to the carriage doors; but the porters moved them back, saying that it was a special train for the bazaar. I remained alone in the bare carriage. In a few minutes the train drew up beside an improvised wooden platform. I passed out on to the road and saw by the lighted dial of a clock that it was ten minutes to ten. In front of me was a large building which displayed the magical name. 24

I could not find any sixpenny entrance and, fearing that the bazaar would be closed, I passed in quickly through a turnstile, handing a shilling to a weary-looking man. I found myself in a big hall girdled at half its height by a gallery. Nearly all the stalls were closed and the greater part of the hall was in darkness. I recognised a silence like that which pervades a church after a service. I walked into the centre of the bazaar timidly. A few people were gathered about the stalls which were still open. Before a curtain, over which the words *Café Chantant*[6] were written in coloured lamps, two men were counting money on a salver. I listened to the fall of the coins. 25

Remembering with difficulty why I had come I went over to one of the stalls and examined porcelain vases and flowered tea-sets. At the door of the stall a young lady was talking and laughing with two young gentlemen. I remarked their English accents and listened vaguely to their conversation. 26

"O, I never said such a thing!" 27

"O, but you did!" 28

"O, but I didn't!" 29

"Didn't she say that?" 30

"Yes. I heard her." 31

"O, there's a . . . fib!" 32

Observing me the young lady came over and asked me did I wish to buy anything. The tone of her voice was not encouraging; she seemed to have spoken to me out of a 33

[6] A music hall.

sense of duty. I looked humbly at the great jars that stood like eastern guards at either side of the dark entrance to the stall and murmured:

"No, thank you."

The young lady changed the position of one of the vases and went back to the two young men. They began to talk of the same subject. Once or twice the young lady glanced at me over her shoulder.

I lingered before her stall, though I knew my stay was useless, to make my interest in her wares seem the more real. Then I turned away slowly and walked down the middle of the bazaar. I allowed the two pennies to fall against the sixpence in my pocket. I heard a voice call from one end of the gallery that the light was out. The upper part of the hall was now completely dark.

Gazing up into the darkness I saw myself as a creature driven and derided by vanity; and my eyes burned with anguish and anger.

READINGS

The following two essays were written by students in a composition course like yours. Studying their essays may help you to see possibilities for your own essay and will familiarize you with the basic features of essays that interpret stories. The students wrote their essays on "Araby," the preceding short story by James Joyce. Although it may help to read "Araby" before reading the student essays, you do not need to read the story to see how the essays work. The Commentary that follows the first student essay and the questions in Analyzing Writing Strategies that follow the second essay will help you to learn how writers construct and support arguments for their interpretations.

Sally Crane composed the following essay after a class discussion of "Araby." As her title suggests, Crane focuses on what the final scene tells about the boy's character. Other students in the class believe the boy changes at the end of the story, but Crane argues that he is just as much in the dark at the end of the story as he was at the beginning. Interpretations often come out of discussion or reading other people's essays. When you are trying to get ideas for your own essay, talk to others who have read the story. Listening to their ideas may help you to come up with ideas of your own.

GAZING INTO THE DARKNESS
Sally Crane

1 Readers of "Araby" often focus on the final scene as the key to the story. They assume the boy experiences some profound insight about himself when he gazes "up into the darkness." I believe, however, that the boy sees nothing and learns nothing—either about himself or others. He's not self-reflective; he's merely self-absorbed.

2 The evidence supporting this interpretation is the imagery of blindness and the ironic point of view of the narrator. There can seem to be a profound insight at the end of the story only if we empathize with the boy and adopt his point of view. In other words, we must assume that the young boy is narrating his own story. But if the real narrator is the grown man looking back at his early adolescence, then it becomes possible to read the narrative as ironic and to see the boy as confused and blind.

The story opens and closes with images of blindness. The street is "blind" with an "uninhabited house . . . at the blind end." As he spies on Mangan's sister, from his own house, the boy intentionally limits what he is able to see by lowering the "blind" until it is only an inch from the window sash. At the bazaar in the closing scene, the "light was out," and the upper part of the hall was "completely dark." The boy is left "gazing up into the darkness," seeing nothing but an inner torment that burns his eyes. 3

This pattern of imagery includes images of reading, and reading stands for the boy's inability to understand what is before his eyes. When he tries to read at night, for example, the girl's "image [comes] between him and the page," in effect blinding him. In fact, he seems blind to everything except this "image" of the "brown-clad figure cast by [his] imagination." The girl's "brown-clad figure" is also associated with the houses on "blind" North Richmond Street, with their "brown imperturbable faces." The houses stare back at the boy, unaffected by his presence and gaze. 4

The most important face he tries and fails to read belongs to Mangan's sister. His description of her and interpretation of the few words she says to him can be seen as further evidence of his blindness. He sees only what he wants to see, the "image" he has in his mind's eye. This image comes more from what he's read than from anything he's observed. He casts her simultaneously in the traditional female roles of angel and whore: 5

> While she spoke she turned a silver bracelet round and round her wrist. She could not go, she said, because there would be a retreat that week in her convent. . . . She held one of the spikes, bowing her head towards me. The light from the lamp opposite our door caught the white curve of her neck, lit up her hair that rested there and, falling, lit up the hand upon the railing. It fell over one side of her dress and caught the white border of a petticoat, just visible as she stood at ease.

Her angelic qualities are shown in her plans to attend a convent retreat and in her bowed head. Her whorish qualities come through in the way she flirtatiously plays with the bracelet, as if she were inviting him to buy her an expensive piece of jewelry at the bazaar. The "white curve of her neck" and the "white border of a petticoat" combine the symbolic color of purity, associated with the Madonna, with sexual suggestiveness. The point is that there is no suggestion here or anywhere else in the story that the boy is capable of seeing Mangan's sister as a real person. She only exists as the object of his adoring gaze. In fact, no one seems to have any reality for him other than himself.

He is totally self-absorbed. But at the same time, he is also blind to himself. He says repeatedly that he doesn't understand his feelings: "Her name sprang to my lips at moments in strange prayers and praises which I myself did not understand. My eyes were often full of tears (I could not tell why)." His adoration of her is both "confused" and confusing to him. He has no self-understanding. 6

The best insight we have into the boy comes from the language he uses. Much of his language seems to mimic the old priest's romantic books: "Her name sprang like a summons to all my foolish blood"; "I imagined that I bore my chalice safely through a throng of foes"; "my body was like a harp and her words and gestures were like fingers running upon the wires." Language like this sounds as though it comes out of a popular romance novel, something written by Danielle Steele perhaps. The mixing of romance with soft porn is unmistakable. Perhaps the boy has spent too much time reading the priest's "sexually seductive stories" from *The Memoirs of Vidocq.* 7

I think this language is meant to be ironic, to point to the fact that the narrator is not the young boy himself but the young boy now grown and looking back at how "foolish" he was. This interpretation becomes likely when you think of "Araby" as a fiction- 8 alized autobiography. In autobiographical stories, remembered feelings and thoughts are combined with the autobiographer's present perspective. The remembered feelings and thoughts in this story could be seen as expressing the boy's point of view, but we read them ironically through the adult narrator's present perspective. The romantic, gushy language the boy uses is laughable. It reveals the boy's blindness toward everyone, including himself. He sees himself as Sir Galahad, the chivalric hero on his own grail quest to Araby. The greatest irony comes at the end when his quest is shown to be merely a shopping trip; and Araby, merely a suburban mall.

9 Most people interpret the ending as a moment of profound insight, and the language certainly seems to support this interpretation: "Gazing up into the darkness I saw myself as a creature driven and derided by vanity; and my eyes burned with anguish and anger." But here again we see the narrator using inflated language that suggests an ironic stance. So even in the moment of apparent insight, the boy is still playing a heroic role. He hasn't discovered his true self. He's just as self-absorbed and blind in the end as he was at the beginning.

Commentary

This commentary offers a comprehensive overview of the main features and strategies of Sally Crane's essay interpreting "Araby." After reading it, you should be able to carry out your own analysis of the next essay by David Ratinov, an essay that offers a different interpretation of "Araby."

Like position papers, evaluations, proposals, and causal speculations, essays interpreting stories make arguments. They state a thesis—an assertion about the meaning or significance of the story—and give reasons and support to convince readers that the interpretation is plausible.

Readers can interpret a story like "Araby" in many different ways. For example, some readers might argue that the story shows the power of the artistic imagination because the main character uses his imagination to escape his stultifying environment. Other readers might disagree, arguing instead that he is not confined by his environment but by an imagination influenced too much by unrealistic stories of knights in shining armor. Readers might also focus their interpretation on the way women are represented in the story—perhaps arguing that Mangan's sister is idealized, or that she is blamed for seducing the innocent boy, or that the story's confusion about her reflects society's conflicting attitudes toward women.

For more on thesis statements, see pp. 465–66, and for more on evaluating a thesis statement, see pp. 526–29.

The thesis statement, as these examples illustrate, must be **arguable,** neither a statement of fact nor an obvious assertion with which most everyone would agree. Being arguable is one of three standards used to evaluate a thesis. The other two standards are that it be clear and appropriately qualified. In the thesis statement at the beginning of her essay, Sally Crane assures readers that her thesis meets the first standard of arguability by indicating that she disagrees with other readers (like David Ratinov) who think the main character learns something important at the end of the story:

> Readers of "Araby" often . . . assume the boy experiences some profound insight about himself when he gazes "up into the darkness." I believe, however, that the boy sees nothing and learns nothing—either about himself or others. He's not self-reflective; he's merely self-absorbed.
>
> The evidence supporting this interpretation is the imagery of blindness and the ironic point of view of the narrator. (paragraphs 1–2)

Crane asserts her belief that the boy is unchanged at the end, no more self-aware or insightful than he was at the beginning.

In addition to being arguable, Crane's thesis also meets the second standard of a good thesis: It is **clear** and **unambiguous.** Readers may not accept her interpretation, but her language is not likely to confuse them. Some readers, however, will probably think her thesis does not satisfy the third standard, that the thesis be **appropriately qualified,** because she makes the broad generalization: "the boy sees *nothing* and learns *nothing.*" To qualify a thesis, writers typically add hedging words like "usually" and "most" in place of absolutes like "nothing" and "all." However, writers who can offer readers convincing support for their generalization do not hedge. They generalize confidently, letting readers decide for themselves whether the thesis is appropriate or needs to be qualified.

For more on forecasting, see pp. 466–67.

Not only does a good thesis statement assert the interpretation, but it also uses **key terms** to **forecast** the reasons and support that will be offered and to indicate the order in which they will come up in the essay. The first term, *sees nothing,* introduces the first reason Crane thinks that the boy ultimately "learns nothing," because throughout the story he cannot understand his own feelings and motivations or anyone else's with any accuracy. In the first sentence of the second paragraph, Crane announces that she will support this reason by showing how the story uses "imagery of blindness." The second key term, *self-absorbed,* announces the second reason Crane thinks the boy lacks insight, because of his excessive egotism or vanity. Crane promises to support this reason by showing that "the ironic point of view of the narrator" casts doubt on everything the boy says about himself, including his final words. Crane's point is that the supposed revelation at the end is simply another example of the boy's supreme egotism, not an escape from it.

We can easily see how this **argumentative strategy** unfolds by making a scratch outline of the argument:

Paragraph 1 presents the thesis statement asserting that the boy learns nothing at the end because he sees nothing and is too self-absorbed.

Paragraph 2 forecasts the support that will be offered for each reason.

Paragraph 3 argues for reason 1—that the boy "sees nothing"—by showing images of blindness and darkness throughout the story.

Paragraph 4 argues for reason 1 by showing images of "reading" that demonstrate how the boy misreads everything.

Paragraph 5 argues for reason 1 by showing that the boy misreads Mangan's sister.

Paragraph 6 makes a transition from reason 1 to reason 2—that the boy is "self-absorbed"—by showing that the boy is blind even to his own feelings.

Paragraph 7 argues for reason 2 by showing that the boy's language mimics romantic fiction.

Paragraph 8 argues for reason 2 by demonstrating that the narrator's point of view is ironic toward the boy, representing him as a clueless romantic.

Crane's plan seems logical because each part follows smoothly without gaps or surprises. Though readers may have reservations about accepting every part of the argument, they have no trouble following along from one step to the next. Within a paragraph, readers hope to find, sentence by sentence, the same logical progression. We sometimes refer to this progression as *coherence*. Readers appreciate an argument that is **logical** and **coherent** as well as inventive and well supported. Consider paragraph 3 sentence by sentence. The first sentence announces the topic—that the story has "images of blindness"—and forecasts that these images appear principally in the story's opening and closing. The second sentence presents imagery from the opening, the third from somewhere near the middle, and the fourth and fifth from the closing. Each sentence presents one or more images of blindness. Readers have no trouble following along; at no sentence do they pause and ask, "Now, why is the writer telling me this?"

For more on textual evidence, see pp. 536–37, and for more on paraphrasing and summarizing, see pp. 452–55.

The most common kinds of **support** in essays arguing for an interpretation come from the story itself through quotations, summaries, and paraphrases of important passages. This support, sometimes called textual evidence, must relate clearly to the reason it illustrates, and it must be integrated smoothly into the writing. Looking again at paragraph 3, you can see that Crane achieves both these goals. Notice how she integrates quoted words and phrases into her sentences. She uses ellipsis marks (. . .) to indicate that she has left some words out of her quotation either because they are not relevant to the point she is making or they do not fit grammatically into her sentence. In paragraph 4, you can also see how she uses brackets to change the form of quoted words to make them fit grammatically into her sentence: "the girl's image [comes] between him and the page." In the original, the verb is not *comes* but the past-tense form *came*. Since Crane is writing in the present tense, the conventional tense for writing about stories, she changes the tense of the word she is quoting and puts brackets around it to indicate that there has been a change. By carefully integrating quotes into her sentences, Crane supplies support and makes her writing flow smoothly.

For more on quoting and the use of ellipsis marks, see pp. 596–603.

Notice, however, that Crane generally does not let the quoted words speak for themselves. She follows the quote with one or more sentences explaining precisely what the quoted words mean and how they support her point. You can see this strategy most clearly in paragraph 5 after the long, indented quotation. (Following the style of the Modern Language Association, quotations of more than four lines are presented this way.) Crane uses paraphrase and quotation to point to specific language in the indented passage, and explains what she thinks this language means and how it relates to her thesis. Such explanation is essential because readers often interpret particular words and phrases differently. In writing an interpretive essay, you should assume that readers have read the story, but you cannot expect them to understand it exactly as you do or know what you are trying to prove by a particular reference to the text.

For more on cueing, see pp. 465–75.

Contributing to the coherence of an argument are the **cues** writers provide for readers. One important kind of cue is the topic sentence, often the first sentence in the paragraph. The **topic sentence** announces the topic of the paragraph (or group of paragraphs). For example, paragraph 3 begins "The story opens and closes with images of blindness." Another important cue is the **transition** connecting the topic of one paragraph with the topic of the next. A good example appears at the beginning of paragraph 6: "He is totally self-absorbed. But at the same time, he is also blind to himself." The first sentence reiterates the point of the preceding paragraph, and the second announces what the point of this new paragraph will be. Transitions may also appear within paragraphs, connecting ideas or examples. Notice, for instance, near the end of paragraph 4: "In fact, he seems blind to everything except this 'image' of the 'brown-clad figure cast by [his] imagination.' The girl's 'brown-clad figure' is also associated with . . ." Here, the word *also* cues the reader that the writer is making an additional point about the phrase "brown-clad figure."

One final word about the conclusion. Crane **frames** the essay by coming back at the end to the point she made at the beginning: that readers who see the ending as a moment of insight are wrong. Her concluding paragraph repeats the essay's basic argument so that there can be no confusion about her interpretation. Essays interpreting stories may also conclude on a more general note, for example, by suggesting possible implications of the interpretation.

David Ratinov wrote the following **essay** for his first-year composition class. Like Sally Crane, Ratinov is curious about what the boy's final statement might mean. But unlike Crane, Ratinov has come to the conclusion that the boy does gain insight, as the final statement seems to indicate, from seeing the hypocrisy of other characters in the story. Notice how his interpretation differs from Crane's.

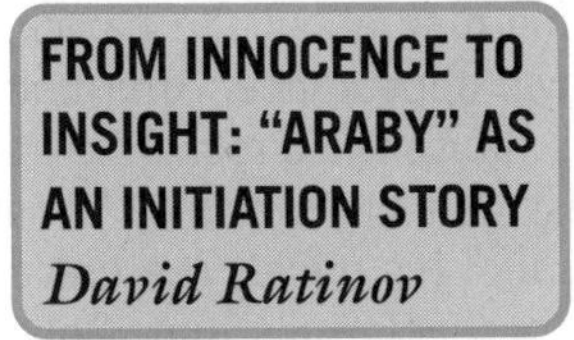

1 "Araby" tells the story of an adolescent boy's initiation into adulthood. The story is narrated by a mature man reflecting upon his adolescence and the events that forced him to face the disillusioning realities of adulthood. The minor characters play a pivotal role in this initiation process. The boy observes the hypocrisy of adults in the priest and Mrs. Mercer; and his vain, self-centered uncle introduces him to another disillusioning aspect of adulthood. The boy's infatuation with the girl ultimately ends in disillusionment, and Joyce uses the specific example of the boy's disillusionment with love as a metaphor for disillusionment with life itself. From the beginning, the boy deludes himself about his relationship with Mangan's sister. At Araby, he realizes the parallel between his own self-delusion and the hypocrisy and vanity of the adult world.

2 From the beginning, the boy's infatuation with Mangan's sister draws him away from childhood toward adulthood. He breaks his ties with his childhood friends and luxuriates in his isolation. He can think of nothing but his love for her: "From the front window I saw my companions playing below in the street. Their cries reached me weakened and indistinct and, leaning my forehead against the cool glass, I looked over at the dark house where she lived." The friends' cries are weak and indistinct because they are distant emotionally as well as spatially. Like an adult on a quest, he imagines he carries his love as if it were a sacred object, a chalice: "Her image accompanied me even in places the most hostile to romance. . . . I imagined that I bore my chalice safely through a throng of foes." Even in the active, distracting marketplace, he is able to retain this image of his pure love. But his love is not pure.

3 Although he worships Mangan's sister as a religious object, his lust for her is undeniable. He idolizes her as if she were the Virgin Mary: "her figure defined by the half-opened door . . . The light from the lamp opposite our door caught the white curve of her neck, lit up her hair that rested there, and falling, lit up the hand upon the railing." Yet even this image is sensual with the halo of light accentuating "the white curve of her neck." The language makes obvious that his attraction is physical rather than

spiritual: "Her dress swung as she moved her body and the soft rope of her hair tossed from side to side." His desire for her is strong and undeniable: "her name was like a summons to all my foolish blood"; "my body was like a harp and her words and gestures were like fingers running upon the wires." But in order to justify his love, to make it socially acceptable, he deludes himself into thinking that his love *is* pure. He is being hypocritical, although at this point he does not know it.

4 Hypocrisy is characteristic of the adults in this story. The priest is by far the most obvious offender. What is a man of the cloth doing with books like *The Abbott* (a romantic novel) and *The Memoirs of Vidocq* (a collection of sexually suggestive tales)? These books imply that he led a double life. Moreover, the fact that he had money to give away when he died suggests that he was far from saintly. Similarly, at first glance Mrs. Mercer appears to be religious, but a closer look reveals that she too is materialistic. Her church work—collecting used stamps for some "pious purpose" (presumably to sell for the church)—associates her with money and profit. Even her name, Mercer, identifies her as a dealer in merchandise. In addition, her husband is a pawnbroker, a profession that the church frowns upon. Despite being linked to money, she pretends to be pious and respectable. Therefore, like the priest, Mrs. Mercer is hypocritical.

5 The uncle, as the boy's only living male relative, is a failure as a role model and the epitome of vanity. He is a self-centered old man who cannot handle responsibility: When the boy reminds him on Saturday morning about the bazaar, the uncle brushes him off, devoting all his attention to his own appearance. After being out all afternoon the uncle returns home at 9:00, talking to himself. He rocks the hallstand when hanging up his overcoat. These details suggest that he is drunk. "I could interpret these signs" indicates that this behavior is typical of his uncle. The uncle is the only character in the story the boy relies upon, but the uncle fails him. Only after the aunt persuades him does the uncle give the boy the money he promised. From the priest, Mrs. Mercer, and his uncle, the boy learns some fundamental truths about adulthood, but it is only after his visit to Araby that he is able to recognize what he has learned.

6 Araby to the adolescent represents excitement, a chance to prove the purity of his love and, more abstractly, his hope; however, Araby fulfills none of these expectations. Instead, the boy finds himself in utter disillusionment and despair. Araby is anything but exciting. The trip there is dreary and uneventful, lonely and intolerably slow—not the magical journey he had expected. When he arrives, Araby itself is nearly completely dark and in the process of closing. With his excitement stunted, he can barely remember why he came (to prove the purity of his love by buying a gift for Mangan's sister).

7 The young lady selling porcelain and her gentleman friends act as catalysts, causing the boy to recognize the truth of his love for Mangan's sister. Their conversation is flirtatious—a silly lovers' game that the boy recognizes as resembling his own conversation with Mangan's sister. He concludes that his love for her is no different than the two gentlemen's "love" for this "lady." Neither love is pure. He too had only been playing a game, flirting with a girl and pretending that it was something else and that he was someone else.

8 His disillusionment with love is then extended to life in general. Seeing the last rays of hope fading from the top floors of Araby, the boy cries: "I saw myself as a creature driven and derided by vanity; and my eyes burned with anguish and anger." At last he makes the connection—by deluding himself, he has been hypocritical and vain like the adults in his life. Before these realizations he believed that he was driven by some-

thing of value (such as purity of love), but now he realizes that his quest has been in vain because honesty, truth, and purity are only childish illusions and he can never return to the innocence of childhood.

Analyzing Writing Strategies

1. Find the **thesis statement** in Ratinov's essay, and underline its key terms. Next, find and circle each use of these key terms in the essay. Can you find all of the key terms in the essay, or do any drop out of sight? Finally, decide whether Ratinov's key terms enable him to satisfy the three standards of a well-written thesis statement: that the thesis be arguable rather than factual or obvious, clear rather than vague or ambiguous, and appropriately qualified rather than exaggerated.
2. Look at paragraph 4. What part of the argument that Ratinov **forecasts** in the first paragraph does this paragraph attempt to develop? Explain briefly how this part of the argument is developed.
3. Underline the first sentence in each paragraph, beginning with paragraph 2. Look closely at these sentences to discover how they connect the preceding paragraph to the one they introduce. Bracket the words or phrases in the sentence that actually create this connection. Besides creating a connection, what other function do these opening sentences have?
4. To be **logical** and **coherent,** not only should every paragraph lead to the next, but within a paragraph each sentence should lead to the next. Underline the topic sentence of paragraph 2 and then examine each sentence in the paragraph to discover whether it is related to that topic and whether each sentence leads logically to the next one. How can you tell whether the writing in this paragraph is logical and coherent?
5. Underline the quoted material in paragraph 3 to see the proportion of the paragraph in which Ratinov uses **quotations** as support. Quotes cannot just be dropped into an argument. The writer must indicate what the quotation means and how it relates to the reason it illustrates and develops. In Evaluating the Logic of an Argument on pp. 458–59, we call this the test of appropriateness. Quotations used as support must pass this test. How does Ratinov indicate that the quotations in this paragraph are appropriate and clearly related to his point?
6. Look at the concluding paragraph. Compare it sentence by sentence to the opening paragraph to discover how it frames the essay. In particular, are the key terms repeated in the last paragraph? If so, how does this repetition and other aspects of the **framing** assist the reader? Does the concluding paragraph repeat the reasons introduced in the opening paragraph, or does it also add something new to the argument? If so, what?

PURPOSE AND AUDIENCE

When you write an essay interpreting a story, you make an assertion about the meaning or significance of the story. Since your readers may have other very different interpretations, you cannot simply tell them what you think and expect them to accept your interpretation or even to understand it fully. You need to give readers reasons for your interpretation and support your reasons with examples from the story that will make your interpretation clear and convincing. Ideally, your readers will see something new in the story after reading your essay. But even if they continue to read the story differently from the way you read it, you may still be able to get them to acknowledge that your interpretation reflects an imaginative, thoughtful reading of the story.

Interpreting a story, then, is not a competition for the "correct" interpretation. Your aim is to develop an interpretation that is insightful, a way of reading the story that seems plausible and enriches readers' understanding and appreciation of the

SUMMARY OF BASIC FEATURES

An Insightful Interpretation

An interpretation is an assertion about the meaning or significance of the story. A good interpretation illuminates the story for readers. This assertion is usually presented explicitly in a thesis statement near the beginning of the essay and may be summarized again at the conclusion. The thesis statement must be arguable, not a simple statement of fact that anyone who reads the story will know (such as stating that the boy in "Araby" lives in Dublin with his aunt and uncle). Nor should the thesis be obvious, a conclusion that most readers would draw from reading the story (the boy has a crush on Mangan's sister). A good thesis statement also meets two additional criteria: that it be clear, not vague or ambiguous, and that it be appropriately qualified, not overgeneralized or exaggerated.

In addition to announcing the interpretation, a good thesis statement also forecasts the reasons and support the writer will use in the essay to develop and illustrate the thesis. Inexperienced writers sometimes are afraid they are ruining the surprise by announcing their thesis and forecasting their argument at the beginning. But readers familiar with this kind of writing have come to expect writers to preview the argument in the opening paragraphs. Explicit forecasting is a convention of literary interpretation similar in purpose to the abstract that precedes many articles in scientific journals. Explicitness does not mean that you have to sacrifice subtlety or complexity in your interpretation. All it means is that you are striving to make your ideas as comprehensible as possible to readers.

Ratinov's opening paragraph provides a good example of explicit forecasting. He explains his interpretation, beginning with his thesis in the opening sentence: "'Araby' tells the story of an adolescent boy's initiation into adulthood." In the sentences that follow, Ratinov previews his argument. The last sentence in the paragraph provides a succinct summary of his reasoning: "At Araby, he realizes the parallel between his own self-delusion and the hypocrisy and vanity of the adult world." Together with *initiation,* the key term in the opening sentence, the last sentence sets out three additional key terms: *self-delusion, hypocrisy,* and *vanity.* These additional key terms signal for readers the steps in Ratinov's argument, specifying what he means when he asserts that the boy's experience can be understood as an initiation or coming-of-age story. We can briefly summarize Ratinov's reasoning as follows: (1) The boy story. Readers do not require you to come up with a startling new reading, though they would be pleased if you did. Your readers will be disappointed, however, if your essay is unfocused, if the key terms in your thesis statement are unclear, if you do not give readers reasons for your interpretation or you do not support them with examples and quotations from the story, or if your essay fails to provide the necessary cues to keep readers on track. Readers will be especially disappointed if they think you are retelling the plot rather than developing your own interpretation of the story.

realizes he has *deluded* himself, (2) he has this realization when he sees his own *hypocrisy* mirrored in the hypocritical behavior of other characters in the story, and (3) he blames his self-delusion and hypocrisy on his own *vanity* or egotism. For key terms to be useful to readers, they must be clear and consistent. Moreover, the ideas that the key terms signal should be explicitly connected to the thesis and be well supported.

A Well-Supported Argument

In addition to asserting the interpretation, writers must present an argument for it. They can usually assume their readers will be familiar with the story, but they can never assume readers will understand their interpretation, let alone accept it.

Writers argue for their interpretation not so much to convince readers to adopt it but rather to convince them that it is a plausible interpretation. An essential strategy writers typically follow is to show readers how they read the story, referring to specific details and explaining what they think these details mean in light of the thesis.

The primary source of support for your argument, then, is the story itself. Writers quote, summarize, and paraphrase passages from the story. They do more than just refer readers to a specific passage, however: They explain the meaning of the passage and its relevance to their thesis. We can see an example of the way writers explain their textual support in the following passage from Ratinov's essay where he describes what happens when the boy's uncle finally comes home from work, having forgotten that the boy was waiting for him:

> When the boy reminds him on Saturday morning about the bazaar, the uncle brushes him off, devoting all his attention to his own appearance. After being out all afternoon the uncle returns home at 9:00, talking to himself. He rocks the hallstand when hanging up his overcoat. These details suggest that he is drunk. "I could interpret these signs" indicates that this behavior is typical of his uncle. The uncle is the only character in the story the boy relies upon, but the uncle fails him. (paragraph 5)

Notice that Ratinov summarizes the most important details, paraphrasing some of the language, and that he quotes sparingly—only one especially telling phrase. Everything else in this paragraph is Ratinov's commentary. Like Ratinov and Crane, you will want to combine explanatory commentary with quotation, summary, and paraphrase to support and elaborate your argument.

GUIDE TO WRITING

THE WRITING ASSIGNMENT

Write an essay interpreting some aspect of a short story. Aim to convince readers that your view of the story is insightful and can be supported by an imaginative reading of specific passages from the story.

INVENTION

Choose a short story, analyze it, write to explore your annotations, formulate a tentative thesis statement, test your choice, revise your thesis statement, and find additional support for your thesis in the story. To make these activities as useful as possible, spread them out over several days and keep a written record of your work.

Choosing a Story

Choose a story that fascinates, surprises, or puzzles you, one that will be worth spending time on because it excites your imagination. You may have chosen a story already, or your instructor may have assigned you one. If so, go on to the next section, Analyzing the Story.

If you need to choose a story on your own, read several stories before deciding on one to write about. Do not choose a story that seems obvious to you. Your instructor can help you to decide if you have made a good choice.

Considering Stories concerning Identity and Community If you are studying the topic of identity and community, you will see immediately how the stories in this chapter relate to these concerns. Almost any story you choose to write about would allow you to think more about how people develop their individuality and their connections to others. Here are a few widely anthologized stories you might consider writing about:

"The Open Boat" by Stephen Crane
"A Rose for Emily" by William Faulkner
"My Kinsman, Major Molineux" by Nathaniel Hawthorne
"A Clean, Well-Lighted Place" by Ernest Hemingway
"The Lottery" by Shirley Jackson
"The Ones Who Walk Away from Omelas" by Ursula Le Guin
"The Metamorphosis" by Franz Kafka
"A Pair of Tickets" by Amy Tan
"Everyday Use" by Alice Walker

Considering Stories concerning Work and Career "The Use of Force" (in this chapter) would be useful in writing about the topic of work and career. Here are some additional stories you might consider for exploring this topic:

"Sonny's Blues" by James Baldwin
"The Yellow Wallpaper" by Charlotte Perkins Gilman
"The Birthmark" by Nathaniel Hawthorne
"Shiloh" by Bobbie Ann Mason
"Bartleby the Scrivener" by Herman Melville
"Picasso" by Gertrude Stein
"The Catbird Seat" by James Thurber
"A&P" by John Updike
"Why I Live at the P.O." by Eudora Welty

Analyzing the Story

To help you analyze the story, this section offers suggestions for interpreting to use as you annotate for potentially meaningful details. As you annotate the story, your goal will be to decide on a thesis, an assertion about the meaning or significance of the story, for which you can develop a reasoned, well-supported argument.

Choosing a Suggestion for Interpreting. *Review the list below and select a suggestion for interpreting that will help you examine closely some aspect of the story that seems significant or about which you have questions.* For example, if on first reading the story, you wondered why a character acts in a particular way, look at the suggestions for interpreting character. If you were struck by the language used to describe the scene, look at the suggestions for interpreting setting. If you noticed any kind of pattern in the events in the story, look at the suggestions under plot structure. If you had questions about the way the story is narrated, look at the suggestions for interpreting point of view. If you recognized a familiar motif (for example, that it seems to be a coming-of-age story) or theme (that it is about alienation), look at the suggestions for interpreting literary motif or theme.

You may want to read and annotate the story several times, keeping in mind the different suggestions for interpreting, before you decide on a thesis you feel confident asserting. Notice also that rereading the story with different suggestions for interpreting in mind can help you to discover how different aspects of the story work together and can lead you to construct a more fully developed thesis.

Character

To interpret the character psychologically:

- Identify the character's motivations, inner conflicts, doubts.
- Consider whether the character changes or learns anything in the course of the story.

- Focus on how the character relates to other characters, noting how the character deals with intimacy, commitment, responsibility.
- Note whether the character seems depressed, manic, abusive, fearful, egotistical, or paranoid. Look for another character who may represent the character's alter ego—the "flip side" of the character's personality.

To interpret the character ethically or morally:

- Decide what you consider to be the character's virtues or vices.
- Consider what influences your judgment of the character—something in the story (such as what the narrator or another character says), something you bring to the story (your views of right and wrong, based on your family upbringing or religious teachings), or something else.
- See whether any of the other characters have different moral values that could be compared and contrasted to the character's values.

To interpret the character from a social perspective:

- Consider how the character fits into and is defined by society—in terms of race, ethnicity, socio-economic class, sexual orientation, or gender.
- Notice who in the story exercises power over whom, what causes the difference in power, what its effects are, and whether the balance of power changes during the story.

Setting

To interpret the setting in relation to the action and to the characters:

- Consider how the setting signals what is happening and whether it comments (possibly ironically) on the action.
- Notice how the setting affects the mood—for example, how it heightens suspense or foreboding.
- Look for cause-and-effect connections between the setting and what characters are thinking, doing, or feeling.

To interpret the setting historically or culturally:

- Think of how the historical period or cultural context in which the story is set might affect what happens and does not happen and why.
- Imagine how the meaning might be different if the historical time or cultural situation were different.

To interpret the setting metaphorically or symbolically:

- Assume that the setting is a projection of the thoughts and feelings of the narrator, and consider what the setting tells you about the narrator's state of mind.
- Assume that the setting symbolizes the social relations among characters in the story, and consider what the setting tells you about these relationships.

- Assume that the setting stands for something outside the character's control (such as nature, God, or some aspect of the society), and consider what the setting tells you about the pressures and rules under which the characters function.

Plot Structure

To interpret the plot as realistic (resembling real-life experience):

- Think of the story as a sequence of stages or steps leading somewhere, mark where each new stage begins, and consider how the sequence could be understood.
- Think of the story as having a main plot as well as subplots that mirror, undercut, or comment in some way on the main plot.

To interpret the plot as surrealistic (having symbolic rather than literal meaning):

- Think of the story as a series of images, more like a collage or a dream rather than a realistic portrayal of actual events, and look for ways of understanding the arrangement of these images.

Point of View

To interpret the point of view in terms of what the narrator can see:

- Consider whether the narrator is a character in the story or a godlike, disembodied voice who knows what every character thinks, feels, and does.
- Identify any important insights or ideas the narrator has.
- Consider how factors such as the narrator's gender, age, and ethnicity may influence what he or she notices as important.
- Consider what the narrator is not able to see or distorts—for example, certain truths about himself or herself, about other characters, or about what happens in the story.

To interpret the point of view in terms of how the narrator represents what he or she sees:

- Characterize the narrator's tone at various points in the story—for example, as satirical, celebratory, angry, bitter, or optimistic.
- Infer what there is about the narrator (or about the situation) that could account for each tone you identified.
- Consider what special agenda or motive may have led the narrator to this particular way of describing characters and scenes or telling the story.
- Imagine how your interpretation might differ if the story were narrated from another character's point of view or from a godlike point of view.

Literary Motif or Theme

To interpret the story in terms of a traditional story motif (or an ironic reversal of the tradition), consider whether it could be seen as:

- A coming-of-age (rite-of-passage) story
- A heroic quest (for love, truth, fame, fortune, salvation of oneself or the community)
- A story about a character's disillusionment or fall from innocence

- A story about selling one's soul to the devil
- A story about storytelling (or some other art) or about becoming a writer or an artist

To interpret the story in terms of a common literary theme (treated seriously or playfully), consider whether the following themes are found in the story:

- The American dream
- Appearance versus reality
- Culture clash
- The horror of war
- Freedom versus fate
- Love and hate
- The retreat into or the endangerment of nature
- Alienation
- Moral disorder of the city
- The family
- The power of the imagination

Annotating with the Suggestions for Interpreting in Mind. *Annotate any details in the story that relate to the suggestions for interpreting you have chosen.* To annotate, simply underline, bracket, or highlight words and phrases that seem significant. Circle words to be defined and write their definition in the margins. Draw lines to connect related words and images. Make marginal notes indicating what you are learning about the story by annotating with the suggestions for interpreting in mind. Write down any further questions you have as you annotate.

Writing to Explore Your Annotations

Write at least a page exploring what you have discovered about the story from analyzing it with the suggestions for interpreting in mind. If you reread the story several times with different suggestions for interpreting, you may be able to write several pages.

It may help to begin by reviewing the suggestions for interpreting you used and writing your thoughts about each suggestion. For example, if you were using the suggestions to interpret character psychologically, you could begin by explaining what you now think are the character's motivations, inner conflicts, and doubts. Then you could go on to discuss how the character changes—what precipitated the change, how it proceeded, how you can tell the character has changed, and why the change is significant.

You may also find it productive to write about patterns of words, figures of speech, characters, or events you found as you were annotating. For example, David Ratinov discovered as he reflected on the annotations he had made using the suggestions for interpreting character that several minor characters, in addition to the main character, are hypocritical. You can see in the Writer at Work section on pp. 422–25 that Ratinov wrote half a page exploring the hypocrisy of just two of these characters.

Formulating a Tentative Thesis Statement

Using the suggestions for interpreting, you have annotated the story and explored your annotations. Your aim now is to list assertions you can support with details from the story, explore the connections among these assertions, and draft a thesis statement.

Listing Assertions. *Write several assertions stating what you have discovered using one or more of the suggestions for interpreting to annotate the story and to explore your annotations.* The only requirement is that you feel confident that you could find specific details and quotations in the story to support each assertion. Do not worry about how these assertions relate to one another or even about whether they are contradictory. Simply write down every assertion that you can make based on your analysis of the story.

The suggestions for interpreting you used to annotate the story and explore your annotations should lead you, as they led Ratinov, to make some assertions about the story. For example, writing about several of the characters in "Araby" convinced Ratinov that he could confidently assert that "all the adult characters are hypocrites."

Writing to Develop Connections among Your Assertions. *Write for ten minutes contemplating what the assertions you listed enable you to say about the story and how they could be related to one another.* As you write, you may decide to drop some of the assertions, reformulate others, or add new assertions. Focus your writing on these questions:

- Could any of these assertions serve as reasons for any of my other assertions or for some new, more general assertion I can make now?
- What are the key terms in these assertions and how would I explain to readers what these key terms enable me to say about the story?

Drafting a Thesis Statement. *Now that you have made some assertions, thought about what their key terms enable you to say about the story, and considered how they could work together, write a few sentences stating your thesis and the reasons you will use to argue for it.* Try completing the following sentence for each reason:

I think _______ about the story because _______.

Formulating a thesis statement (even one you know you will revise) can be a challenge. It may help to recall the thesis statements David Ratinov and Sally Crane wrote and to think about how they worded their key terms (italicized):

"Araby" tells the story of an adolescent boy's *initiation* into adulthood . . . [by which] he realizes the parallel between his own *self-delusion* and the *hypocrisy* and *vanity* of the adult world.

I believe, however, that the boy *sees nothing* and *learns nothing*—either about himself or others. He's not self-reflective; he's merely *self-absorbed*.

Testing Your Choice

Now that you have developed a tentative thesis statement, you need to be sure that it says what you want it to say and that you will be able to find support for it in the story. Reread the story with your thesis statement in mind. If your thesis still seems worth arguing, you have probably made a good choice. On the other hand, if your thesis seems obvious, not really arguable, unclear, or not appropriately qualified, you may need to return to Formulating a Tentative Thesis Statement or even to Analyzing the Story to try to enrich your analysis and invent a more promising thesis.

If you decide your thesis is too obvious and you cannot improve it, or you have lost confidence in it and fear you will not be able to find adequate support for it, you may need to find a new thesis or even choose a different story and start over. If you are thinking of starting over, discuss the possibility with your instructor before doing so.

→ Testing Your Choice: A Collaborative Activity

At this point, you may find it helpful to get together with two or three other students who have read your story to get responses to one another's thesis statements. Your partners' reactions will help you to determine whether you have a thesis for which you can construct a well-reasoned and well-supported argument.

Writers: Each of you take turns reading your tentative thesis statement aloud. Then take notes as your partners tell you what your thesis statement leads them to expect from your essay.

Listeners: Note down what you think are the key terms in the thesis statement. Begin by telling the writer if any of the key terms seem unclear (vague or ambiguous) or not appropriately qualified (overgeneralized or exaggerated).

Then briefly explain what the thesis statement leads you to expect will be argued in the essay. For example, if you were a member of David Ratinov's group, you might have said that the thesis led you to expect his essay to demonstrate three things—the boy is self-deluded, the adults are hypocritical or vain, and the boy ultimately realizes that he is like the adults—and that these three reasons argue the main point that the boy undergoes a process of initiation or a rite of passage.

Finally, tell the writer whether the thesis seems arguable or whether it states a fact or an obvious conclusion that any reader would reach after reading the story.

Try to make concrete suggestions on how the writer could improve the thesis statement.

Revising the Thesis Statement

Try to improve your thesis statement. Consider whether you want to change your argument to alter the thesis or the reasons you will offer for it. Clear up any ambiguity or vagueness in your key terms and qualify them more appropriately if necessary. Make explicit why you think your thesis is arguable by indicating how other readers disagree.

Finding Additional Support for Your Thesis

If you do not have enough support for your reasons, reread the story, making additional annotations in passages where you find details you might be able to use. With your key terms in mind, evaluate the support you already have to determine whether it is sufficient to explain and illustrate each reason. Wherever support is lacking, fill it in by doing further annotating. If you cannot find support for any of your reasons, you need to reconsider whether you should use that reason.

If you find details in the story that contradict any of your reasons, do not ignore the contradiction. Instead, analyze the details to see how you should modify your argument.

PLANNING AND DRAFTING

You now need to review your notes, set goals, and make an outline before writing a first draft.

Seeing What You Have

Print out a hard copy of what you have written on a word processor for easier reviewing.

Review your invention writing and annotated text. If some time has elapsed since you last read the story, you may want to reread it now. As you review what you have discovered about the story, consider whether your thesis is arguable and whether you have stated it clearly and directly. Also decide whether you have sufficient support and whether you have overlooked anything important that might contradict or weaken your argument.

If you cannot clearly explain your reasons, or if you do not have specific support for them, you may not be ready to write a complete draft. You may be able to begin drafting the parts involving reasons you can explain and for which you have solid support and return to annotating with other suggestions for interpreting in mind to bolster the rest of your argument. But if your thesis still seems obvious or not arguable, you may need to reconsider the direction in which you are going and possibly begin again.

Setting Goals

Before you start to draft, consider what you want to say about the story you are interpreting. The following questions will help you set goals for your essay that will enable you to get across to your readers exactly what you want to tell them about the story.

Your Readers

- Are my readers likely to know this story? If not, how much do I need to tell them about the story so that they can follow my argument? If so, how can I lead them to accept my interpretation as reasonable?
- How can I sequence my reasons and support so that my readers will find it easy to follow? What cues can I provide to help readers follow my organization?

- How can I integrate quotations smoothly into my writing?
- What questions might my readers raise about my argument? How should I answer them?
- How can I make my argument sound authoritative and thoughtful?

The Beginning

- Should I begin by describing the story or establishing a context for my interpretation of the story?
- How can I explicitly state my thesis and forecast my plan, as Crane and Ratinov do, without sounding stilted or mechanical?

The Argument

- Have I used key terms that accurately forecast the reasons for my thesis?
- How much textual support must I include for my argument to be convincing?
- Should I acknowledge readers' possible questions or differing interpretations, as Crane does? How much should I counterargue?

The Ending

- Should I repeat my key terms, as the writers in this chapter do?
- Should I restate my thesis?
- Should I end with a provocative question suggested by my interpretation of the story?

Outlining

Outlining on a word processor makes it easy to experiment with ways of ordering information.

At this point, you should try to develop a plan for your draft by composing an informal scratch outline, a simple list of your reasons and support in the order you will introduce them. Make sure that the forecast in your thesis statement accurately predicts the order in which the reasons and support will appear in the essay. Remember that an outline is meant to be a tentative plan; you may make further discoveries as you draft that will require you to change your plan.

Drafting

Call up invention material in an alternate window as you draft, shifting back and forth to cut and paste invention material into your draft.

Begin to draft, keeping in mind that you are trying to convince readers that your thesis is plausible. Explain your reasons fully and directly, making explicit the connection between each reason and your thesis and between each reason and the support you offer readers. Remember that your readers may have different ways of interpreting the passages to which you refer. Indicate exactly why you are citing specific details from the story and how you interpret the writer's choice of words. You might want to review the general advice on drafting on pp. 13–14.

CRITICAL READING GUIDE

Swap copies of your drafts with another student, either by exchanging disks or sending the computer files over a network. Add your comments either next to the draft, if you can split the window, or at the end of the document.

Now is the time to try to get a good critical reading. Most writers find it helpful to have someone else read and comment on their drafts, and your instructor may schedule such a reading as part of your coursework. Otherwise, you can ask a classmate, friend, or family member to read your essay using this guide. If your campus has a writing center, you might ask a tutor there to read and comment on your draft. The guidelines that follow are designed to be used by *anyone* reviewing an essay interpreting a story. (If you are unable to have someone else read over your draft, turn ahead to the Revising section, which gives guidelines for reading your own draft with a critical eye.)

If You Are the Writer. To provide focused, helpful comments, your reader must know your intended audience and purpose. The reader must also have read the story you were writing about. Attach a copy of the story to your draft if you think your reader may not already have one, and write out brief answers to the following questions at the top of your draft:

- *Audience.* How do you think your interpretation builds on or contradicts the interpretations your readers are likely to have of the story?
- *Purpose.* What specifically do you want your readers to learn about the story from reading your essay?

If You Are the Reader. Use the following guidelines when preparing critical comments on an essay interpreting a story.

1. *Read for a First Impression.* Read first to grasp the thesis. As you read, mark in the margin any passages that are particularly well written and convincing as well as any that seem unclear or unsupported. After you have finished this first quick reading of the draft, briefly write out your impressions. You may interpret the story quite differently, but your goal now is to help the writer present his or her interpretation of the story as effectively as possible. Without looking back at the essay, give a one-sentence summary of the essay's thesis. Also, indicate generally whether you think this interpretation makes sense.
2. *Comment on the Thesis Statement and How Well It Forecasts the Argument.* Find the thesis statement, and underline what seem to you to be its key terms. If you cannot find the thesis statement or cannot identify the key terms, let the writer know. Evaluate the thesis statement on the basis of whether it seems to make an arguable assertion (rather than a statement of fact or an obvious point), is clear (neither ambiguous nor vague), and is appropriately qualified (neither overgeneralized nor exaggerated).

   Then skim the rest of the essay, underlining each key term as it is brought up. If you cannot find a key term later in the essay but you do see where the reason it stands for is developed and supported, write the key term in the margin

continued

continued

to let the writer know that it should be added. If a reason introduced by a key term in the thesis statement is left out of the essay altogether, tell the writer. Also note any important reasons that are developed in the essay but not announced in the thesis statement.

3. *Indicate Whether the Reasons Are Clearly Explained and Well Supported.* Look closely at the section where each reason is developed. Note whether the reason is explained and connected to the essay's thesis. If you think it should be developed further, ask questions or suggest how it could be expanded. Also indicate where support from the story is lacking. Let the writer know if you do not see what a particular quotation means or how it supports his or her point.
4. *Evaluate the Essay's Logic and Coherence.* Comment on anything in the essay that contradicts the thesis or the reasons for it. Note where logical connections between reasons could be strengthened or made more explicit. Also note any gaps in the logic, places where connections have been left out.
5. *Suggest How the Organization Could Be Improved.* Consider the overall plan, perhaps by making a scratch outline. Note any places where the argument is hard to follow or where transitions are missing or do not work well. Look again at the *beginning* and note whether it adequately anticipates the rest of the essay. Look at the *ending* and note whether it is too abrupt, repetitive, or goes off in a new and surprising direction.

REVISING

This section will help you to identify problems in your draft and to revise and edit to solve them.

Identifying Problems

Even if your essay is saved to a computer file, reread from a hard copy. Add notes to yourself and quick revisions as you read through the draft.

To identify problems in your draft, you need to get an overview of it, analyze its basic features, and study any critical comments you have received from other readers.

Getting an Overview. First consider the draft as a whole, following these two steps:

1. *Reread.* If at all possible, put the draft aside for a day or two. When you do reread, start by reconsidering your purpose. Then read the draft straight through, trying to see it as your intended readers will.
2. *Outline.* Make a scratch outline to get an overview of the essay's development. This outline should identify the key terms and the ideas they stand for as well as the kinds of support you use to develop each idea. (See the example on p. 401).

Charting a Plan for Revision. You may wish to make a double-column chart to keep track of any problems you need to solve. In the left-hand column, list the basic features of essays interpreting stories. As you analyze your draft and study any comments you have received, note the problems you want to solve in the right-hand column next to the appropriate feature. Here is an example:

Basic Features	*Problems to Solve*
Thesis	
Argument	
Organization	

Analyzing the Basic Features of Your Own Draft. Turn now to the Critical Reading Guide, and use it to identify problems in your draft. Make note on your revision chart of any problems you need to solve.

Studying Critical Comments. Review all of the comments you have received from other readers, and add to your chart any problems that need attention. Try not to react too defensively to these comments; by letting you see how others respond to your draft, they provide valuable information about how you might improve it.

Solving the Problems

Having identified problems, you now need to come up with solutions and implement them. You have three ways of finding solutions:

1. Review your invention and planning notes for additional information and ideas.
2. Do further invention to answer questions your readers raised.
3. Look back at the student essays by Crane and Ratinov to see how other writers have solved similar problems.

Before revising or sharing your draft with another reader, copy your original draft to a second file. Then, should you change your mind about material you delete while revising, it will still be available to you.

The following suggestions will get you started solving some of the problems common to writing interpretations of stories. For now, focus on solving the problems identified on your chart. Avoid tinkering with grammar and punctuation; that will come later when you edit.

The Thesis

- **Is the thesis statement hard for readers to find?** State explicitly at the beginning what your essay will demonstrate, announcing your thesis and forecasting the reasons you will use to explain and argue for it.
- **Is your thesis statement perceived as unarguable?** Revise the thesis to make it clear that you are not stating a simple fact about the story or making an obvious point but rather are making an assertion with which others disagree, as Crane does.
- **Are your key terms unclear or not appropriately qualified?** Revise your key terms to avoid ambiguity and vagueness. If you need to limit or qualify your thesis or reasons, add words like *some* or *usually.*
- **Do the key terms in the thesis statement disappear later in the essay?** Delete a key term from the thesis statement if you do not discuss the reason later in the essay. If you do discuss it, find the paragraph where it comes up, and rewrite the topic sentence using the key term.

The Argument

- **Does the thesis or do any of the reasons used to argue for it seem superficial or thin?** Try developing your reasons more fully by comparing or contrasting related reasons; classifying your reasons or dividing them into their subparts; or discussing the social, political, and cultural implications of your way of interpreting the story. Consider elaborating on your reasons by rereading the story with another related suggestion for interpreting in mind.

Use your computer to help you to analyze problems with your essay. For example, if a reader feels that you need more support for your interpretation, highlight the support in your paper by putting it in bold type. Then look for places where you need to add more support.

- **Does support seem lacking?** Add detail by quoting, paraphrasing, or summarizing other passages. Focus your discussion more closely on the writer's choice of words, explaining what particular word choices mean in relation to your reasons. Consider using other kinds of support, such as information about the story's historical or cultural context.
- **Does the connection between a reason and its support seem vague?** Clarify your point by explaining why you think the support you have given illustrates it. Do not simply quote from the story. Explain how you interpret the quotation, which words seem significant, and how they demonstrate the point you are making.
- **Are there contradictions or gaps in your argument?** You may need to rewrite sections of your essay to eliminate contradictions or fill in gaps. Before cutting anything, consider whether the contradiction is real or apparent. If it is only apparent, explain more fully and more clearly how your reasons relate logically to one another and to your thesis. To fill in gaps, you may have to lay out your train of thought more explicitly so that readers can more easily follow your logic.

The Organization

Use your word processor's cut-and-paste or block-and-move function to shift material around. Revise so that material fits smoothly in its new spot.

- **Is the essay hard to follow?** You should provide more explicit cues: better forecasting, topic sentences, logical transitions, brief summaries.
- **Does the opening fail to prepare readers for your argument?** You may need to revise it to forecast your reasons more obviously or to give readers a clearer context in which they may grasp your thesis.
- **Does the ending seem abrupt?** You may need to tie all the strands of the essay together, reiterate your thesis, or discuss its implications.

EDITING AND PROOFREADING

Use your word processor's spell-check function cautiously. Keep in mind that it will not find all misspellings, particularly misused homonyms (such as *there* for *their* or *they're*), typographical errors that are themselves words (such as *fro* for *for*), and many proper nouns and specialized terms.

In working on your draft so far, you may have corrected some obvious errors, but grammar and style have not been a priority. Now is the time to check your draft for matters of usage, punctuation, mechanics, and style. It may help you to recognize problems if you study your draft in separate passes—first for paragraphs, then for sentences, and finally for words.

Research into student papers interpreting stories has revealed two common problems worth checking for: lack of parallel structure (a matter of style) and the misuse of ellipsis marks (a matter of punctuation). The following guidelines are designed to help as you check your draft for these common problems.

Checking for Parallelism in Your Writing. When you present similar items together, present them in the same grammatical form. All items in a series should be parallel in form—all nouns, all prepositional phrases, all adverb clauses, and so on. See, for example, how Sally Crane edited her first-draft sentences to introduce parallel structure.

learns nothing—either
He's not self-reflective; he's merely

- I believe, however, that the boy sees nothing and ~~is incapable of learning~~ about himself or others. ~~because he is so~~ self-absorbed.

what he's read anything he's observed.

- This image comes more from ~~his reading~~ than from ~~his actual observation.~~

- The greatest irony comes at the end when his quest is exposed as merely a shopping trip, and Araby as merely a suburban mall.

The parallelism makes Crane's sentences easier to read and helps her to emphasize some of her points. The parallelism of "sees nothing" and "learns nothing" emphasizes the relationship between these two realities in a way that the first-draft wording did not; the same is true of "what he's read" and "anything he's observed." In the final sentence, Crane adds a parallel phrase as an ironic comment. Following are several more examples, each edited to show ways of making writing parallel.

isolation,

- To Kafka, loneliness, ~~being isolated,~~ and regrets are the price of freedom.

values

- Sarah really cares about her brother and ~~to maintain~~ their relationship.

- She lets us know that she was injured by her mother's abuse but avoids saying what she felt after the incident, how others reacted to the incident, and what ~~the~~ physical pain she endured.

Checking Your Use of Ellipsis Marks. Ellipsis marks are three spaced periods. They are used to indicate that something has been omitted from quoted text. You will often quote other sources when you interpret a story, and you must be careful to use ellipsis marks to indicate places where you delete material from a quotation. Look, for example, at the way Sally Crane uses ellipsis marks in quoting from "Araby."

Original text	North Richmond Street, being blind, was a quiet street except at the hour when the Christian Brothers' School set the boys free. An uninhabited house of two storeys stood at the blind end, detached from its neighbours in a square ground.
Quoted with ellipsis marks	The street is "blind," with an "uninhabited house . . . at the blind end."

The ellipsis marks indicate an omission in the middle of the sentence.

There are just a few simple rules to remember about using ellipsis marks:

- When you delete text in the middle of a quoted passage, use a period before the ellipses, for a total of four periods, if what remains forms a complete sentence.
- Use ellipsis marks at the end of a quotation only if the last words you are quoting do not form a complete sentence.

For more on ellipsis marks, see Chapter 22.

- Insert a single space between ellipsis points.
- Single words and brief phrases can be quoted without ellipsis marks.

The following sentences by students have been edited to correct problems with the use of ellipsis marks:

We learn that a former tenant of the boy's house, "... a priest, had died in the back drawing room. . . . He had been a very charitable priest; in his will he had left all his money to institutions and the furniture of his house to his sister."

The boys lived on "a quiet street. . . ."

The light shone on "... the white border of a petticoat. . . ."

A WRITER AT WORK

USING THE SUGGESTIONS FOR INTERPRETING TO ANALYZE A STORY AND MAKE ASSERTIONS

To develop an interpretation that your instructor and classmates will find arguable as well as insightful, you need to know what to look for as you read a story. The more experience you have participating in class discussions in which arguments are examined for different interpretations, the more confidence you will have that you can read a story and develop your own interpretation. This process, of course, takes time and hard work. To jump-start the process and increase the likelihood that you will be able to write a successful interpretation now, the Guide to Writing section offers suggestions for interpreting to help you analyze a story and develop an interpretation.

This Writer at Work section shows part of David Ratinov's invention work on "Araby." It shows that Ratinov chose the suggestions for interpreting "Character" to guide his analysis of the story. We will see how he annotated a portion of the story focusing on two characters—Mrs. Mercer and the boy's uncle. Then, we will look at a page Ratinov wrote to explore his annotations on the passages presenting Mrs. Mercer. Finally, we will see the assertions he listed under Formulating a Tentative Thesis Statement. You will be able to infer how these assertions led to the thesis statement he developed for his essay.

Let us begin by examining the annotations Ratinov made on paragraphs 13–24 of "Araby" as he reread it with the suggestions for interpreting character in mind. Notice the diversity of his annotations. In the text itself, he underlines key words, circles words to be defined, and connects related words and ideas. In the margin, he defines words; makes comments; poses questions; and expresses tentative insights, personal reactions, and judgments.

2nd mention of uncle fussing— vain? irritable? rude

On Saturday morning I reminded my uncle that I wished to go to the bazaar in the evening. He was fussing at the hallstand, looking for the hatbrush, and answered me curtly:

"Yes, boy, I know."

always unkind to the boy? uncle's effect on the boy

As he was in the hall I could not go into the front parlour and lie at the window. I left the house in bad humour and walked slowly towards the school. The air was pitilessly raw and already my heart misgave me.

uncle will be late sudden change in mood: big contrast

When I came home to dinner my uncle had not yet been home. Still it was early. I sat staring at the clock for some time and, when its ticking began to irritate me, I left the room. I mounted the staircase and gained the upper part of the house. The high cold empty gloomy rooms liberated me and I went from room to room singing. From the front window I saw my companions playing below in the street. Their cries reached me weakened and indistinct and, leaning my forehead against the cool glass, I looked over at the dark house where she lived. I may have stood there for an hour, seeing nothing but the brown-clad figure cast by my imagination, touched discreetly by the lamplight at the curved neck, at the hand upon the railings and at the border below the dress.

liberated from uncle?

isolated from friends

romantic, even sensual

merchandise

talkative

hypocritically religious

When I came downstairs again I found Mrs. Mercer sitting at the fire. She was an old garrulous woman, a pawnbroker's widow, who collected used stamps for some pious purpose. I had to endure the gossip of the tea-table. The meal was prolonged beyond an hour and still my uncle did not come. Mrs. Mercer stood up to go: she was sorry she couldn't wait any longer, but it was after eight o'clock and she did not like to be out late, as the night air was bad for her. When she had gone I began to walk up and down the room, clenching my fists. My aunt said:

boy doesn't seem to like or trust the adults

"I'm afraid you may put off your bazaar for this night of Our Lord."

uncle and Mercer both try to give a false impression aunt seems pious too

At nine o'clock I heard my uncle's latchkey in the halldoor. I heard him talking to himself and heard the hallstand rocking when it had received the weight of his overcoat. I could interpret these signs. When he was midway through his dinner I asked him to give me the money to go to the bazaar. He had forgotten.

boy knows uncle is drunk

boy's fears are justified excuses

"The people are in bed and after their first sleep now," he said.

I did not smile. My aunt said to him energetically:

aunt to the rescue

"Can't you give him the money and let him go? You've kept him late enough as it is."

hypocritical what a bore!

My uncle said he was very sorry he had forgotten. He said he believed in the old saying: "All work and no play makes Jack a dull boy." He asked me where I was going and, when I had told him a second time he asked me did I know The Arab's Farewell to his Steed. When I left the kitchen he was about to recite the opening lines of the piece to my aunt.

boy determined to go to bazaar to buy girl a gift

boy focused on his task

I held a florin tightly in my hands as I strode down Buckingham Street towards the station. The sight of the streets thronged with buyers and glaring with gas recalled to me the purpose of my journey. I took my seat in a third-class carriage of a deserted train. After an intolerable delay the train moved out of the station slowly. It crept onward among ruinous houses and over the twinkling river. At Westland Row Station a crowd of people pressed to the carriage doors; but the porters moved them back, saying that it was a

language shows boy's impatience

boy still isolated

special train for the bazaar. I remained alone in the bare carriage. In a few minutes the train drew up beside an improvised wooden platform. I passed out on to the road and saw by the lighted dial of a clock that it was ten minutes to ten. In front of me was a large building which displayed the magical name.

As you can see, annotating this section of the story with the suggestions for interpreting character in mind leads Ratinov to notice how negatively Mrs. Mercer and the uncle are portrayed. Following the instructions for Writing to Explore Your Annotations, Ratinov discovers that these characters are criticized primarily because of their hypocrisy. Here is what he wrote to explore this portion of his annotations:

```
Mrs. Mercer may be a good neighbor to the boy's aunt, but
the boy dislikes her. Joyce plants many clues that she is a
hypocrite. She thinks of herself as a good religious Christian,
but she is pious (an exaggerated Christian, not a believable
one), she collects stamps to sell for charity instead of doing
good works firsthand (my guess), and she is a gossip. Her
husband got his money in an unchristian way. Does the boy
know all this or only the narrator much later?  I'm sure the
boy senses it. He says he has to endure Mrs. Mercer and her
gossip with his aunt. Now that I look over the evidence for
the uncle's hypocrisy, it seems that his unguardianlike
actions toward the boy, his irresponsibility toward him, is
just as big a flaw as his hypocrisy. He seems to be trying
to hide something by drinking and being obsessive about his
appearance--a failure to advance at work?  He tries to
impress people with a bigger house than he can afford. Says
he believes in things that don't apply to his own actions.
I think I can show that he's a hypocrite like Mrs. Mercer.
Because the boy distrusts him, he must sense this hypocrisy.
```

As he writes about the hypocrisy of Mrs. Mercer and the uncle, Ratinov becomes increasingly confident that he has an interesting point to make for which he will be able to find support in the story. Then, following Formulating a Tentative Thesis Statement in the Guide to Writing, Ratinov lists assertions he feels confident he would be able to support. In all, he makes five separate assertions, but notice that the first assertion in his list comes from the exploratory writing about Mrs. Mercer and the uncle quoted above:

```
-- All the adult characters are hypocrites.
-- If this is just a story about romance, then all the adult
   characters wouldn't have to be so weak and flawed.
-- Mangan's sister is different from the adults, but through
   her he has to face up to what the adult world is all
   about.
-- The adults are initiating the boy into adulthood, but he
   doesn't see it until the end of the story.
```

```
-- Growing up means being able to see the world for what it
   actually is, not what you want it to be.
```

From these assertions about hypocrisy, romance, the adult world, initiation, and the connection between growing up and learning to see reality, Ratinov was able to devise the thesis statement he uses in his essay.

THINKING CRITICALLY ABOUT WHAT YOU HAVE LEARNED

Now that you have read and discussed several essays interpreting a story and have written such an essay yourself, you are in a good position to think critically about what you have learned. What problems did you encounter as you were writing, and how did you solve them? How did the essays you read influence your own writing? How does the genre of literary interpretation reflect social and cultural attitudes about stories and their meanings?

Reflecting on Your Writing

Write a page or so describing for your instructor a problem you needed to solve as you wrote your interpretive essay, how you discovered it, and how you went about solving it. Before you begin, gather your invention and planning notes, drafts and critical comments, revising plan, and final revision. Review these as you complete this writing task.

1. Identify *one* significant writing problem you encountered while writing the essay. Do not be concerned with grammar and punctuation; focus on a problem specific to writing an interpretation. For example, were you uncertain about which suggestions for interpreting to use to analyze the story? Did you wonder how best to state your thesis and forecast your argument? Did you have trouble deciding which passages from the story to quote as support?
2. How did you first recognize this problem? Was it when you were trying to analyze the story, finding the support you needed in the story, thinking about how to sequence your reasons, or getting critical comments on a draft? What called the problem to your attention? Looking back, do you see signs of it in your early invention work? If so, where specifically?
3. Think about how you solved the problem. If it arose during invention, did you consider using different suggestions for interpreting? Did you discuss the suggestions for interpreting you were using with another student or your instructor? If the problem arose during drafting, did you do further invention to solve the problem—perhaps rereading the story, examining your original annotations to see what you omitted, or thinking of other ways to connect your reasons? If you noticed the problem as you were revising, did you reword, reorganize, or simply cut the part that was problematic? Did you review your invention notes or reread a part of the story to analyze it further, perhaps using other suggestions for interpreting?
4. Finally, write your explanation of the problem and how you tried to solve it. Be specific by quoting from your invention writing, drafts, others' critical comments, your own revision plan, and your final revision. Show the various changes your writing and thinking underwent. If you are still uncertain about your solution, say so. The point is not to prove that you have solved the problem but to show what you have learned about solving problems in the process of writing.

Reviewing What You Learned from Reading

You have read several essays interpreting a story—the two selections on "Araby" and possibly also one or more student drafts on another story. Your own essay has probably been influenced by these interpretive essays. Write a page or so explaining to your instructor how your writing has been influenced by others. Before you do, take time to reflect on what you have learned from the interpretive essays you have read and consider some ways your reading has influenced your writing.

1. Review the readings in this chapter as well as your own essay. Consider whether any of the essays in the chapter or by your classmates influenced your choice of which suggestions for interpreting to use or your way of organizing your essay. Look for ideas you got from your reading or writing strategies you were inspired to try. For example, did one of the essays suggest a way you could state your thesis clearly and emphatically, forecast your reasons, use quotations to support your argument, or anticipate readers' questions? Did an essay help you to decide how to introduce quotations or how to separate and develop each reason?
2. Now write your explanation of these influences. You may focus on a single influence or discuss what you learned from parts of different essays. Give examples, showing how you have built on what you have seen other writers do. This review of readings might suggest further changes you would now consider making in your essay. If so, mention them.

Considering the Social Dimensions of Essays Interpreting Stories

Apart from the pleasure of a good read, perhaps the most compelling reason for reading stories is that it brings us more in touch with ourselves and with others. Some stories reflect our own experience; such stories are especially enjoyable because we identify with the characters and situations. Most of us also enjoy stories about other people and places. We take pleasure in getting a glimpse of how other people's experiences differ from our own. Sometimes, however, stories do not simply divert us: They also challenge us, making us see how we could reinvent ourselves as well as the society in which we live.

If, like most people, you read stories primarily for pleasure, you may be wondering why you should go to all the trouble of analyzing and interpreting them. The more we read, the more we realize that we enjoy a story not only because we are moved by the event and intrigued by the characters but also because we discover meanings that lie beneath the surface. Serious literary texts are constructed with great care, with intense imagination, and with a sensitivity to nuances of language that their writers may not even consciously recognize. Thoughtful, analytical readers can tease out meanings that expand their and our appreciation of these texts. Interpreting, as we hope you have discovered, can be not only rewarding but also fun. It is a kind of intellectual play that can heighten the pleasure of reading. To see why this is so, we need to think about how language, particularly literary language, works and how we make sense of it.

Language and Meaning. Readers often think of reading as deciphering the writer's message, as if the black marks on the page were a code. Linguists have shown that this way of thinking about language is true—to some degree. Writers and readers who speak the same language and belong to the same culture do share a linguistic code, but that code is complex. There is no simple, one-to-one correspondence between a word and its meaning. Words are by nature ambiguous; they can have multiple meanings and numerous connotations. No single meaning can be said to be exactly the *right* one, although some meanings are probably more plausible or more interesting to readers than other meanings.

Even if we were to ask the author what he or she meant, we would not necessarily discover what the story *really* means. As we know from our own writing experience, writers wrestle with words to figure out what they want to say, and their intended meaning may not be fully communicated to every reader or even clear to themselves. Fiction writers generally expect readers to find a profusion of possible meanings in their stories.

Readers, like writers, in effect rewrite the text as they read, constructing a mental representation of it based on their associations with particular words and images. This process is especially true for literary writing, which is typically rich in figurative language and concrete details that stimulate our imagination.

Assumptions about Stories. Interpreting stories leads us to make a number of assumptions about short fiction that should be examined with a critical eye. The most basic assumption is that stories do, in fact, convey meaning. Some artists and critics claim that a work of art does not *convey* anything; it just *is*. This idea might be easier to accept for abstract art than for stories that realistically portray life experience. When we read a story, we seem naturally to look for characters, situations, and themes we recognize and relate to. But what feels natural is really learned. From early childhood, we are taught to extract meaning from fairy tales, parables, fables, and family stories. We are taught to look for correspondences between stories and real life.

We are also taught that published writers are authoritative, that their precepts are wise and worth following. This assumption about the writer's authority encourages us to assume that if we could know what the writer intended, we would understand the meaning of the story. At the same time, it encourages readers to be passive, playing the role of the child obediently taking in the writer's wisdom. But if readers interpret stories by constructing meaning, they cannot be passive.

Interpreting, as we have suggested throughout this chapter, is anything but passive. As a reader, you may analyze the story's language for figurative as well as literal meanings. You may think critically about characters' motivations and relationships. You may question what you are told by a narrator (who seems to speak with the authority of the author). You may be suspicious of endings that seem too pat or reductive. You may think of meanings in broad social and political terms. In other words, you may discover no single, fixed meaning but rather multiple, perhaps contradictory, meanings. You may find this discovery exciting, but it may also leave you with more questions than answers.

Because readers assume that stories bear some relation to real life, they also assume that characters will behave as the people in their lives do—in a way that makes sense psychologically and is consistent with their personality or "essential" self. You may remember that in thinking critically about autobiographical writing in Chapter 2, we invited you to consider the possibility that there is no single essence that defines the self. Instead, the self might be constituted by the many different roles we play in different situations. If this way of thinking about the self is useful, we might want to think of literary characters differently too. We might be less inclined to interpret characters in static terms and be more inclined to see them in terms of the social and cultural roles they play.

For Discussion. The following questions will stimulate your thinking and discussion about analyzing and interpreting stories. Jot down your thoughts in case your instructor asks you to write a page reflecting on what you have learned.

1. In discussing the relation between language and meaning, we have suggested that the process of reading is inevitably a process of interpretation because language is essentially ambiguous. Words invite multiple meanings and associations, and this property of language is especially true of "literary" language, which is heavily nuanced and evocative. For some readers, interpreting is fun, but others find the uncertainty discomforting. They may be unhappy because they associate ambiguity with lack of clarity, having been taught to value clarity and coherence in writing. Readers may also be uncomfortable because they associate ambiguity with relativism in politics and morality.

Examine your own and your classmates' attitudes about ambiguity. Are you uncomfortable with the possibility that a story has no single "right" meaning? If so, to what degree? How do you account for your own feelings about ambiguity? How do you understand other people's feelings?

2. If there is no one indisputably "right" interpretation—not even the author's—how do we decide which interpretations have merit? Reflect on your experience interpreting stories for high school and college classes, including those you read and wrote about for this assignment. When you were planning and writing your own essay, did you consider more than one interpretation? If so, how did you decide which one to develop? How do you think your instructor evaluates—and how do you evaluate—an interpretation of a story? What basis should be used for deciding whether an interpretation is strong or weak, more or less convincing?
3. Examine critically the related assumptions that stories represent real-life experience and that reading stories can tell us something about life. Use one of the stories you read in this chapter as a test case: Ask yourself how the situation in this story differs from real life and how the characters differ from real people. What are the limitations of thinking of this story as though it were the same as an experience that actually happened? How can we talk about a story's relation to social reality if we recognize that it is really only words on a page?

CHAPTER 11

A Catalog of Invention Strategies

Writers are like scientists: They ask questions, systematically inquiring about how things work, what they are, where they occur, and how more information can be learned about them. Writers are also like artists in that they use what they know and learn to create something new and imaginative.

The invention and inquiry strategies described in this chapter are not mysterious or magical. They are tricks of the trade available to everyone, and they should appeal to your common sense and experience in solving problems. Developed by writers, psychologists, and linguists, they represent the ways writers, engineers, scientists, composers—in fact, all of us—creatively solve problems.

Once you have mastered these strategies, you can use them to tackle any writing situation you encounter in college or on the job. The best way to learn them is to use them as you write an actual essay. Chapters 2–10 show you when these strategies can be most helpful and how to make the most efficient use of them. The Guides to Writing in those chapters offer easy-to-use adaptations of these general strategies, adaptations designed to satisfy the special requirements of each kind of writing.

The strategies for invention and inquiry in this chapter are grouped into two categories:

Mapping: A brief visual representation of your thinking or planning

Writing: The composition of phrases or sentences to discover information and ideas and to make connections among them

These invention and inquiry strategies can be powerful tools as you think about your topic and plan your writing. They will help you to explore and research a topic fully before you begin drafting and then to solve problems as you are drafting and revising. In this chapter, strategies are arranged alphabetically within each of the two categories.

MAPPING

Mapping involves making a visual record of invention and inquiry. Many writers find that mapping helps them to think about a topic. In making maps, they usually use key words and phrases to record material they want to remember, questions they need to answer, and new sources of information they want to check. The maps show the ideas, details, and facts they are examining. They also show possible ways whereby materials can be connected and focused. Maps might be informal graphic displays with words and phrases circled and connected by lines to show relationships, or they might be formal sentence outlines. Mapping can be especially useful because it provides a visual representation of your thinking and planning. Mapping strategies include clustering, listing, and outlining.

Clustering

Clustering is a strategy for revealing possible relationships among facts and ideas. Unlike listing (the next mapping strategy), clustering requires a brief period of initial planning. You must first come up with a tentative division of the topic into subparts or main ideas. Clustering works as follows:

1. In a word or phrase, write your topic in the center of a piece of paper. Circle it.
2. Also in words or phrases, write down the main parts or central ideas of your topic. Circle these, and connect them to the topic in the center.
3. Next, think of facts, details, examples, or ideas related in any way to these main parts. Cluster these around the main parts.

Clustering can be useful for any kind of writing. You can use it in the early stages of planning an essay to find subtopics and to organize information. You may try out and discard several clusters before finding one that is promising. Many writers use clustering to plan brief sections of an essay as they are drafting or revising. (A model of clustering is on page 431.)

Listing

Listing is a familiar activity. We make shopping lists and lists of errands to do or people to call. Listing can also be a great help in planning an essay. It enables you to recall what you already know about a topic and suggests what else you may need to find out. It is an easy way to get started with your invention writing, instead of just worrying about what you will write. A list rides along on its own momentum, the first item leading naturally to the next.

A basic activity for all writers, listing is especially useful to those who have little time for planning—for example, reporters facing deadlines and college students taking essay exams. Listing lets you order your ideas quickly. It can also serve as a first step in discovering possible writing topics.

Listing is a solitary form of brainstorming, a popular technique of problem solving in groups. When you work with a group to generate ideas for a collaborative writing project, you are engaged in true brainstorming. Here is how listing works best for invention work:

1. Give your list a title that indicates your main idea or topic.
2. Write as fast as you can, relying on short phrases.
3. Include anything that seems *at all* useful. Do not try to be judgmental at this point.

4. After you have finished, or even as you write, reflect on the list and organize it in the following way. This step is very important, for it may lead you to further discoveries about your topic.
   Put an asterisk next to the most promising items.
   Number key items in order of importance.
   Put items in related groups.
   Cross out items that do not seem promising.
   Add new items.

Outlining

Outlining, like listing and clustering, is both a way of planning and a means of inventing. An outline may, of course, be used to organize an essay. Yet as soon as you start to make an outline, you will begin to see new possibilities in your subject, discovering new ways of dividing or grouping information and seeing where you need additional information to develop your ideas. Outlining also lets you see at a glance whether your plan is appropriate.

There are three main forms of outlining: scratch, topic, and sentence. (Keep in mind that clustering is also a type of outlining.)

A scratch outline is an informal outline, little more than a rough list of the main points (and sometimes the subpoints) of an essay. You have no doubt made scratch outlines many times—both to clarify a difficult reading passage and to plan essays or essay exams. As an example, here is a *scratch outline* for Max Frankel's essay in Chapter 7.

Universal E-Mail: Worthy of a "New Frontier" Commitment

Problem

President needs to challenge the nation to provide E-mail for all

a description of E-mail and how it works

the uses of E-mail

E-mail must become universal

Solution

government ensured that postal mail and telephones would be available to all

government incubation leads to privatization

government subsidies will be required to provide the less affluent with access to E-mail

there are no technical barriers to universal E-mail

national politicians must take the lead

E-mail for all may strengthen community and the economy

Frankel may have made such a scratch outline before he began drafting his essay. Notice that the items in a scratch outline do not necessarily coincide with paragraphs. Sometimes two or more items may be developed in the same paragraph or one item may be covered in two or more paragraphs.

Scratch outlines are especially helpful for organizing information while you are still gathering it and for deciding how to revise an essay after it has been drafted. The writing guide for each chapter in Part I reminds you when you might use scratch outlining most profitably.

Topic and sentence outlines are more formal than scratch outlines. They follow a conventional format of numbered and lettered headings and subheadings. Some instructors require such an outline with term or research papers. Here is a *topic outline* of Frankel's essay.

Universal E-Mail: Worthy of a "New Frontier" Commitment

I. Goal of universal access to E-mail

II. Description of E-mail messages

  A. Sent to one person or thousands

  B. Typed on keyboards and sent out over Internet routes

III. Economic and social potential of E-mail

  A. Needs to be universal

  B. May come to belong exclusively to the affluent

IV. Proposal for government intervention

  A. Promote compatibility of systems

  B. Subsidize availability in the home

  C. Subsidize availability in public places

V. Lack of technological barriers

VI. Vast constituency of people with little or no access to or knowledge of computers
    A. Challenge industry to provide more and cheaper terminals
    B. Subsidize public use with fees for private use

VII. Great new enterprise and means of promoting unity

Notice that the Roman numerals and capital letters are followed by periods. Topic outlines contain words or brief phrases, not sentences. Items are not followed by a period, but the first word of each item is capitalized. Items at the same level of indentation should be grammatically parallel. Under item IV, for instance, the A and B items both begin with verbs:

A. Promote compatibility of systems
B. Subsidize availability in the home

The items would not be grammatically parallel if B began with an infinitive phrase (*to* plus a verb), like this:

A. Promote compatibility of systems
B. To subsidize availability in the home

Here is a *sentence outline* of Frankel's essay. Each item is a complete sentence, the first word capitalized and the last word followed by a period.

Universal E-Mail: Worthy of a "New Frontier" Commitment

I. The president or a candidate for president should set a goal of providing E-mail to every citizen by 2010.

II. E-mail is an inexpensive form of instant communication via computers and telephone wires.
    A. E-mail messages can be sent to one person or thousands.
    B. E-mail messages are mostly typed at computer keyboards and sent over the best available Internet routes.

III. E-mail is going to be an important instrument of commerce and will create electronic communities.
    A. E-mail must be universal in order to fulfill its promise.
    B. E-mail is in danger of bypassing most of the population and becoming the exclusive realm of affluent, educated people.

IV. The government should step in and lead a drive to make E-mail available to everyone.
    A. The government should promote universal compatibility of E-mail systems.
    B. The government should provide induced subsidies to develop inexpensive E-mail technologies for the home.
    C. The government should provide interim subsidies to make E-mail available in public places.

V. There are no technical barriers to achieving universal E-mail.

VI. People without computers, or with little knowledge of computers, constitute a vast political constituency.

  A. Political leaders should challenge the computer industry to provide cheaper terminals and to invent pay terminals.

  B. Political leaders should ask industry leaders to subsidize universal access with fees for profitable private uses of the Internet.

VII. E-mail for all will provide a great new enterprise and a means of promoting national unity.

Sentence outlines can be considerably more detailed, to the point where they contain most of the information in the essay; but for an essay the length of Frankel's, they are usually about as detailed as this one. Should you want to make a more detailed outline, you would probably need to include more levels of information than the preceding two outlines contain. When you subdivide topics, keep in mind that every level must have at least two items. Follow this convention for identifying levels:

I. (Main topic)
  A. (Subtopic of I)
  B.
    1. (Subtopic of I.B)
    2.
      a. (Subtopic of I.B.2)
      b.
        (1) (Subtopic of I.B.2.b.)
        (2)
          (a) (Subtopic of I.B.2.b.(2))
          (b)
          (c)

WRITING

Writing is itself a powerful tool for thinking. As you write, you can recall details, remember facts and ideas, find connections in new information you have collected, examine assumptions, and critically question what you know.

Unlike most mapping strategies, writing strategies of invention invite you to produce complete sentences. Sentences provide considerable generative power. Because they are complete statements, they take you further than listing or clustering. They enable you to explore ideas and define relationships, to bring ideas together or show how they differ, to identify causes and effects. Sentences can follow one another naturally and develop a logical chain of thought.

This section presents several invention and inquiry strategies that invite you to formulate complete sentences and thus produce brief exploratory pieces of writing.

Some are guided, systematic strategies; others are more flexible. Even though they call for complete sentences that are related to one another, they do not require planning or polishing.

These writing strategies include cubing, dialoguing, dramatizing, journals, looping, questioning, and quick drafting.

Cubing

Cubing is useful for quickly exploring a writing topic, probing it from six different perspectives. It is known as cubing because a cube has six sides. These are the six perspectives in cubing:

Describing. What does your subject look like? What size is it? What is its color? Its shape? Its texture? Name its parts.

Comparing. What is your subject similar to? Different from?

Associating. What does your subject make you think of? What connections does it have to anything else in your experience? Be creative here—include every connection you can think of.

Analyzing. How is your subject made? Where did it come from? Where is it going? How are its parts related?

Applying. What can you do with your subject? What uses does it have?

Arguing. What arguments can you make for your subject? Against it?

Here are some guidelines to help you use cubing productively.

1. Select a topic, subject, or part of a subject. This can be a person, a scene, an event, an object, a problem, an idea, or an issue. Hold it in focus.
2. Limit your writing to three to five minutes for each perspective. The whole activity should take no more than half an hour.
3. Keep going until you have written about your subject from *all six* perspectives. Remember that cubing offers the special advantage of enabling you to generate *multiple* perspectives quickly.
4. As you write from each perspective, begin with what you know about your subject. However, do not limit yourself to your present knowledge. Indicate what else you would like to know about your subject, and suggest where you might find that information.
5. Reread what you have written. Look for bright spots, surprises. Recall the part that was easiest for you to write. Recall the part where you felt a special momentum and pleasure in the writing. Look for an angle or an unexpected insight. These special parts may suggest a focus or a topic within a larger subject, or they may provide specific details to include in a draft.

Dialoguing

A dialogue is a conversation between two or more people. You can use dialoguing to search for topics, find a focus, explore ideas, or consider opposing viewpoints. When you write a dialogue as an invention strategy, you need to make up all parts of the conversation. Imagine two particular people talking, hold a conversation yourself with some imagined person, or simply talk out loud to yourself. Follow these steps:

See pp. 55–58 for an example of dialogue used for invention.

1. Write a conversation between two speakers. Label the speakers "A" and "B," or make up names for them.
2. If you get stuck, you might have one of the speakers ask the other a question.
3. Write brief responses in order to keep the conversation moving fast. Do not spend much time planning or rehearsing responses. Write what first occurs to you, just as in a real conversation, where people take quick turns to prevent any awkward silences.

Dialogues can be especially useful with personal experience and persuasive essays because they help you to remember conversations and anticipate objections.

Dramatizing

Dramatizing is an invention activity developed by the philosopher Kenneth Burke as a way of thinking about how people interact and as a way of analyzing literature and the arts.

Thinking about human behavior in dramatic terms can be very productive for writers. Drama has action, actors, setting, motives, and methods. Since stars and acting go together, you can use a five-pointed star to remember these five points of dramatizing:

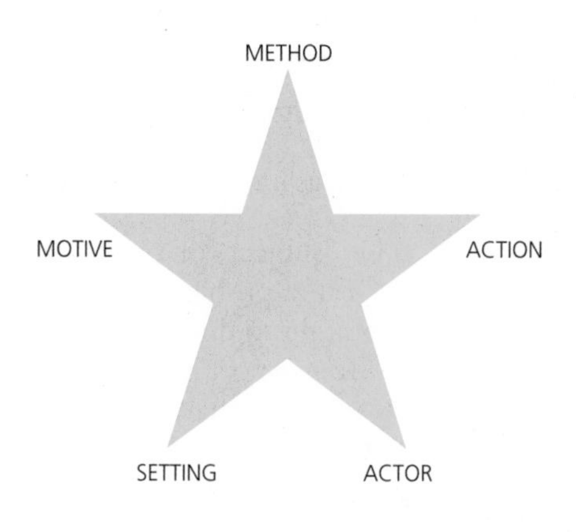

Each point on the star provides a different perspective on human behavior. We can think of each point independently and in combination. Let us begin by looking at each point to see how it helps us to analyze people and their interactions.

Action. An action is anything that happens, has happened, will happen, or could happen. Action includes events that are physical (running a marathon), mental (thinking about a book you have read), and emotional (falling in love). This category also refers to the results of activity (a term paper).

Actor. The actor is involved in the action—either responsible for it or simply affected by it. (The actor does not have to be a person. It can be a force, something that causes an action. For example, if the action is a rise in the price of gasoline, the actor could be increased demand or short supply.) Dramatizing may also include a number of coactors working together or at odds.

Setting. The setting is the situation or background of the action. We usually think of setting as the place and time of an event, but it may also be the historical background of an event or the childhood of a person.

Motive. The motive is the purpose or reason for an action—the actor's intention. Actions may have multiple, even conflicting, motives.

Method. The method explains how an action occurs, including the techniques an actor uses. It refers to whatever makes things happen.

Each of these points suggests a simple invention question:

Action: What?

Actor: Who?

Setting: When and where?

Motive: Why?

Method: How?

This list looks like the questions reporters typically ask. But dramatizing goes further: It enables us to ask a much fuller set of invention questions that we generate by considering relations between and among these five elements. We can think about actors' motives, the effect of the setting on the actors, the relations between actors, and so on.

You can use this invention strategy to learn more about yourself or about other significant people in your life. You can use it, as well, to explore, analyze, or evaluate characters in stories or movies. Moreover, dramatizing is especially useful in analyzing the readers you want to inform or convince.

To use dramatizing, imagine the person you want to understand better in a particular situation. Holding this image in mind, write answers to any questions in the following list that apply. You may draw a blank on some questions, have little to say to some, and find a lot to say to others. Be exploratory and playful with the questions. Write responses quickly, relying on words and phrases, even drawings.

- What is the actor doing?
- How did the actor come to be involved in this situation?
- Why does the actor do what he or she does?
- What else might the actor do?
- What is the actor trying to accomplish?
- How do other actors influence—help or hinder—the main actor?
- What do the actor's actions reveal about him or her?
- What does the actor's language reveal about him or her?
- How does the event's setting influence the actor's actions?
- How does the time of the event influence what the actor does?
- Where did this actor come from?
- How is this actor different from what he or she used to be?
- What might this actor become?
- How is this actor like or unlike the other actors?

Journals

Professional writers often use journals to keep notes, and so might you. Starting a writer's journal is quite easy. Buy a special notebook, or open a new file on your computer, and start writing. Here are some possibilities:

- Keep a list of new words and concepts you learn in your courses. You could also write about the progress and direction of your learning in particular courses—the experience of being in the course, your feelings about what is happening and what you are learning.
- Respond to your reading, both assigned and personal. Write about your personal associations as you read, your reflections, reactions, evaluations. Summarize important passages. Copy memorable passages and comment on them. (Copying and commenting has been practiced by students and writers for centuries in special journals called *commonplace books.*)
- Write to prepare for particular class meetings. Write about the main ideas you have learned from assigned readings and about the relationship of these new ideas to other ideas in the course. After class, write to summarize what you have learned. List questions you have about the ideas or information discussed in class. Journal writing of this kind involves reflecting, evaluating, interpreting, synthesizing, summarizing, and questioning.
- Record observations and overheard conversations.
- Write for ten or fifteen minutes every day about whatever is on your mind. Focus these meditations on your new experiences as you try to understand, interpret, and reflect on them.
- Write sketches of people who catch your attention.
- Organize your time. Write about your goals and priorities, or list specific things to accomplish and what you plan to do.
- Keep a log over several days or weeks about a particular event unfolding in the news—a sensational trial, an environmental disaster, a political campaign, a campus controversy, the fortunes of a sports team.

You can use a journal in many ways. All of the writing in your journal has value for learning, observing experience closely, and organizing your life. You may also be able to use it in other writing.

Looping

Looping—the strategy of writing quickly but returning to your topic—is especially useful for the first stages of exploring a topic. From almost any starting point, no matter how general or unfocused, looping enables you to find a center of interest and eventually a thesis. The steps are simple:

1. Write down your area of interest. You may know only that you have to write about another person or a movie or a cultural trend that has caught your attention. Or you may want to search for a topic in a broad historical period or one related to a major political event. Although you may wander from this topic as you write, you will want to keep coming back to it. Your purpose is to find a focus for writing, perhaps even a thesis.

2. Write nonstop for ten minutes. Start with the first thing that comes to mind. Write rapidly, without looking back to reread or to correct anything. *Do not stop writing. Keep your pencil moving.* Continuous writing is the key to looping. If you get stuck for a moment, rewrite the last sentence. Trust the act of writing to lead you to new insights. Follow diversions and digressions, but keep returning to your topic now and then.
3. After ten minutes, pause to reread what you have written. Decide what is most important—a single insight, a pattern of ideas, an emerging theme, a visual detail, anything at all that stands out. Some writers call this a "center of gravity" or a "hot spot." To complete the first loop, express this center in a single sentence.
4. Beginning with this sentence, write nonstop for ten minutes.
5. Summarize in one sentence again to complete the second loop.
6. Keep looping until one of your summary sentences produces a focus or thesis. You may need only two or three loops; you may need more.

Questioning

Asking questions about a subject is a way to learn about it and decide what to write. When you first encounter a subject, however, your questions may be scattered. Also, you are not likely to think right away of all the important questions you ought to ask. The advantage of having a basic list of questions for invention, like the ones for cubing and for dramatizing discussed earlier in this chapter, is that it provides a systematic approach to exploring a subject.

The questions that follow come from classical rhetoric (what the Greek philosopher Aristotle called *topics*) and a modern approach to invention called *tagmemics*. Based on the work of American linguist Kenneth Pike, tagmemics provides questions about different ways we make sense of the world, all the ways we sort and classify experience and come to understand it.

Here are the steps in using questions for invention:

1. In a sentence or two, identify your subject. A subject could be any event, person, problem, project, idea, or issue—in other words, anything you might write about.
2. Start by writing a response to the first question in the following list, and move right through the list. Try to answer each question at least briefly with a word or a phrase. Some questions may invite several sentences or even a page or more of writing. You may draw a blank on a few questions. Skip them. Later, when you have more experience with questions for invention, you can start anywhere in the list.
3. Write your responses quickly, without much planning. Follow digressions or associations. Do not screen anything out. Be playful.

What Is Your Subject?

- What is your subject's name? What other names does it have? What names did it have in the past?
- What aspects of the subject do these different names emphasize?
- Imagine a still photograph or a moving picture of your subject. What would it look like?
- What would you put into a time capsule to stand for your subject?

- What are its causes and results?
- How would it look from different vantage points or perspectives?
- What particular experiences have you had with the subject? What have you learned?

What Parts or Characteristics Does Your Subject Have and How Are They Related?

- Name the parts or characteristics of your subject.
- Describe each one, using the questions in the preceding subject list.
- How is each part or characteristic related to the others?

How Is Your Subject Similar to and Different from Other Subjects?

- What is your subject similar to? In what ways are the subjects alike?
- What is your subject different from? In what ways are the subjects different?
- Of all the things in the world, what seems to you most unlike your subject? In what ways are the two things unlike each other? Now, just for fun, note how they are alike.

How Much Can Your Subject Change and Still Remain the Same?

- How has your subject changed from what it once was?
- How is it changing now—moment to moment, day to day, year to year?
- How much can it change and still remain the same?
- What are some different forms your subject takes?
- What does it become when it is no longer itself?

Where Does Your Subject Fit in the World?

- When and where did your subject originate?
- What would happen if at some future time your subject ceased to exist?
- When and where do you usually experience the subject?
- What is this subject a part of, and what are its parts?
- What is the relationship between the subject and that of which it is a part?
- What do other people think of your subject?

Quick Drafting

Sometimes you know what you want to say or have little time for invention. In these situations, quick drafting may be a good strategy. There are no special rules for quick drafting, but you should rely on it only if you know your subject well, have had experience with the kind of writing you are doing, and will have a chance to revise your draft. Quick drafting can help you to discover what you already know about the subject and what you need to find out. It can also help you to develop and organize your thoughts.

CHAPTER 12

A Catalog of Reading Strategies

Writers need to read critically to write well. Not only must they read drafts of their own essays, but they must also often rely on information they find in books, articles, letters, computer files, and other documents. When you work with such sources, you need to read critically—gathering, analyzing, selecting, and organizing the information you find in order to integrate the information into your own text.

This chapter presents strategies to help you *read with a critical eye.* Reading critically means not just comprehending passively and remembering what you read but also scrutinizing actively and making thoughtful judgments about your reading. When you read a text critically, you need to alternate between understanding and questioning—on the one hand, striving to understand the text on its own terms; on the other hand, taking care to question its ideas and authority.

The strategies here complement and supplement reading strategies presented in Part I. Critical reading is central to your success with the writing assignments in those chapters. The Connecting to Culture and Experience activity following each reading selection helps you to think about the text you are reading in light of your own experience and awareness of important social issues. The questions for Analyzing Writing Strategies help you to understand how a text works and to evaluate how well it works to achieve its purpose with readers. The Guide to Writing in each chapter includes materials to help you to read other students' drafts and your own critically to reveal problems and possibilities.

Reading is, after all, inextricably linked to writing, and the reading strategies in this chapter can help you in your work as both reader and writer. The strategies here include the following:

- *Annotating:* Recording your reactions to, interpretations of, and questions about a text as you read it
- *Taking inventory:* Listing and grouping your annotations and other notes to find meaningful patterns
- *Outlining:* Listing the main ideas of each paragraph in your own words
- *Contextualizing:* Placing a text in its historical, biographical, and cultural contexts
- *Reflecting on challenges to your beliefs and values:* Critically examining the bases of your personal responses to a text
- *Paraphrasing:* Putting what you have read into your own words

- *Summarizing:* Distilling the main ideas or gist of a text
- *Exploring the significance of figurative language:* Examining how metaphors, similes, and symbols are used in a text to convey meaning and evoke feelings
- *Looking for patterns of opposition:* Analyzing the values and assumptions embodied in the language of a text
- *Evaluating the logic of an argument:* Determining whether a thesis is well reasoned and adequately supported
- *Recognizing emotional manipulation:* Identifying texts that unfairly and inappropriately use emotional appeals based on false or exaggerated claims
- *Judging the writer's credibility:* Considering whether writers represent different points of view fairly and know what they are writing about

These critical reading strategies can help you to connect information from different sources and relate it to what you already know; distinguish fact from opinion; uncover hidden assumptions; examine your own beliefs and values; and subject both what you read and what you know to reasoned argument. You can readily learn these strategies and apply them not only to the selections in Part I of this text but also to your other college reading. Although mastering the strategies will not make critical reading easy, it can make your reading much more satisfying and productive and thus help you to handle even difficult material with confidence.

ANNOTATING

Annotations are the marks—underlines, highlights, symbols, and comments—you make directly on the text you are reading. *Annotating* can be used to record immediate reactions and questions, outline and summarize main points, and evaluate and relate the reading to other ideas and points of view. Especially useful for studying and preparing to write, it is also an essential element of many other critical reading strategies. Your annotations can take many forms:

Writing comments, questions, or definitions in the margins

Underlining or circling words, phrases, or sentences

Connecting ideas with lines or arrows

Numbering related points in sequence

Bracketing sections of the text

Making note of anything that strikes you as interesting, important, or questionable

Most readers annotate in layers, adding further annotations on second and third readings. Annotations can be light or heavy, depending on the reader's purpose and the difficulty of the material. Your purpose for reading also determines how you use your annotations.

The following selection is excerpted from the letter and annotated to illustrate some of the ways you can annotate as you read. Since annotating is the first step for all critical reading strategies in this catalog, these annotations are referred to throughout the chapter. Add your own annotations, if you like.

Martin Luther King Jr. (1929–1968) first came to national notice in 1955, when he led a successful boycott against the policy of restricting African-American passengers to rear seats on city buses in Montgomery, Alabama, where he was minister of a Baptist church. He subsequently formed a national organization, the Southern Christian Leadership Conference, that brought people of all races from all over the country to the South to fight nonviolently for racial integration. In 1963, King led demonstrations in Birmingham that were met with violence; a bomb was detonated in a black church, killing four little girls. King was arrested for his role in organizing the protests, and while in prison, he wrote the famous "Letter from Birmingham Jail" to answer the criticism of local clergy.

King begins by discussing his disappointment with the lack of support he has received from white moderates, such as the group of clergy who published their criticism in the local newspaper. As you read the following excerpt from the letter, try to infer from King's written response what the clergy's specific criticisms might have been. Also, notice the tone King uses to answer his critics. Does the writing seem apologetic, conciliatory, accusatory? Or would you characterize it in some other way?

AN ANNOTATED SAMPLE FROM "LETTER FROM BIRMINGHAM JAIL"
Martin Luther King Jr.

¶1. White moderates block progress.

1 I must confess that over the past few years I have been gravely disappointed with the white moderate. I have almost reached the regrettable conclusion that the Negro's [great stumbling block in his stride toward freedom] is not the White Citizen's Counciler or the Ku Klux Klanner, but the white moderate, who is more devoted to "order" than to justice; who prefers a negative peace which is the absence of tension to a positive peace which is the presence of justice; who constantly says: "I agree with you in the goal you seek, but I cannot agree with your methods of direct action"; who paternalistically believes he can set the timetable for another man's freedom; who lives by a mythical concept of time and who constantly advises the Negro to wait for a "more convenient season." Shallow understanding from people of good will is more frustrating than absolute misunderstanding from people of ill will. Lukewarm acceptance is much more bewildering than outright rejection.

order vs. justice

negative vs. positive

ends vs. means

treating others like children

¶2. Tension necessary for progress.

2 I had hoped that the white moderate would understand that law and order exist for the purpose of establishing justice and that when they fail in this purpose they become the [dangerously structured dams that block the flow of social progress.] I had hoped that the white moderate would understand that the present tension in the South is a necessary phase of the transition from an

[obnoxious negative peace,] in which the Negro passively accepted his unjust plight, to a [substantive and positive peace,] in which all men will respect the dignity and worth of human personality. Actually, we who engage in nonviolent direct action are not the creators of tension. We merely bring to the surface the hidden tension that is already alive. We bring it out in the open, where it can be seen and dealt with. [Like a boil that can never be cured so long as it is covered up but must be opened with all its ugliness to the natural medicines of air and light, injustice must be exposed, with all the tension its exposure creates, to the light of human conscience and the air of national opinion before it can be cured.]

Tension already exists anyway.

True?

Simile: hidden tension is like a boil

3 In your statement you assert that our actions, even though peaceful, must be condemned because they precipitate violence. But is this a logical assertion? Isn't this like condemning a robbed man because his possession of money precipitated the evil act of robbery? Isn't this like condemning Socrates because his unswerving commitment to truth and his philosophical inquiries precipitated the act by the misguided populace in which they made him drink hemlock? Isn't this like condemning Jesus because his unique God-consciousness and never-ceasing devotion to God's will precipitated the evil act of crucifixion? We must come to see that, as the federal courts have consistently affirmed, it is wrong to urge an individual to cease his efforts to gain his basic constitutional rights because the question may precipitate violence. [Society must protect the robbed and punish the robber.]

¶13. Questions clergymen's logic: condemning his actions = condemning victims, Socrates, Jesus.

Yes!

4 I had also hoped that the white moderate would reject the myth concerning time in relation to the struggle for freedom. I have just received a letter from a white brother in Texas. He writes: "All Christians know that the colored people will receive equal rights eventually, but it is possible that you are in too great a religious hurry. It has taken Christianity almost two thousand years to accomplish what it has. The teachings of Christ take time to come to earth." Such an attitude stems from a tragic misconception of time, from the strangely irrational notion that there is something in the very flow of time that will inevitably cure all ills. Actually, time itself is neutral; it can be used either destructively or constructively. More and more I feel that the people of ill will have used time much more effectively than have the people of good will. We will have to repent in this generation not merely for the [hateful words and actions of the bad people] but for the [appalling silence of the good people.] Human progress never rolls in on [wheels of inevitability;] it comes

example of a white moderate

Silence is as bad as hateful words and actions.

metaphor

¶14. Time must be used to do right.

through the tireless efforts of men willing to be co-workers with God, and without this hard work, time itself becomes an ally of the forces of social stagnation. [We must use time creatively, in the knowledge that the time is always ripe to do right.] Now is the time to make real the promise of democracy and transform our pending [national elegy] into a creative [psalm of brotherhood.] Now is the time to lift our national policy from the [quicksand of racial injustice] to the [solid rock of human dignity.]

not moving

metaphors

You speak of our activity in Birmingham as extreme. At first I was rather disappointed that fellow clergymen would see my nonviolent efforts as those of an extremist. I began thinking about the fact that I stand in the middle of two opposing forces in the Negro community. One is a [force of complacency,] made up in part of Negroes who, as a result of long years of oppression, are so drained of self-respect and a sense of "somebodiness" that they have adjusted to segregation; and in part of a few middle-class Negroes, who because of a degree of academic and economic security and because in some ways they profit by segregation, have become insensitive to the problems of the masses. The other [force is one of bitterness and hatred,] and it comes perilously close to advocating violence. It is expressed in the various black nationalist [groups that are springing up] across the nation, the largest and best-known being Elijah Muhammad's Muslim movement. Nourished by the Negro's frustration over the continued existence of racial discrimination, this movement is made up of people who have lost faith in America, who have absolutely repudiated Christianity, and who have concluded that the white man is an incorrigible "devil."

5

King accused of being an extremist

¶15. King in middle of two extremes: complacent & angry.

Malcolm X?

I have tried to stand between these two forces, saying that we need emulate neither the "do-nothingism" of the complacent nor the hatred and despair of the black nationalist. For there is the more excellent way of love and nonviolent protest. I am grateful to God that, through the influence of the Negro church, the way of nonviolence became an integral part of our struggle.

6

¶16. King offers better choice.

How did nonviolence become part of King's movement?

If this philosophy had not emerged, by now many streets of the South would, I am convinced, be flowing with blood. And I am further convinced that if our white brothers dismiss as "rabble-rousers" and "outside agitators" those of us who employ nonviolent direct action, and if they refuse to support our nonviolent efforts, millions of Negroes will, out of frustration and despair, seek solace and security in black-nationalist ideologies—a development that would inevitably lead to a frightening racial nightmare.

7

¶17. King's movement prevented racial violence. Threat?

Gandhi? The church?

comfort

If . . . then . . .

Oppressed people cannot remain oppressed forever. The yearning for freedom eventually manifests itself, and that is what has happened to the American Negro. Something within has reminded him of his birthright of freedom, and something without has reminded him that it can be gained. Consciously or unconsciously, he has been caught up by the *Zeitgeist,* and with his black brothers of Africa and his brown and yellow brothers of Asia, South America and the Caribbean, the United States Negro is moving with a sense of great urgency toward the [promised land of racial justice.] If one recognizes this [vital urge that has engulfed the Negro community,] one should readily understand why public demonstrations are taking place. The Negro has many [pent-up resentments] and latent frustrations, and he must release them. So let him march; let him make prayer pilgrimages to the city hall; let him go on freedom rides—and try to understand why he must do so. If his repressed emotions are not released in nonviolent ways, they will seek expression through violence; this is not a threat but a fact of history. So I have not said to my people: "Get rid of your discontent." Rather, I have tried to say that this normal and healthy discontent can be [channeled into the creative outlet of nonviolent direct action.] And now this approach is being termed extremist. 8

worldwide uprising against injustice

spirit of the times

Not a threat?

¶8. Discontent is normal & healthy but must be channeled.

But though I was initially disappointed at being categorized as an extremist, as I continued to think about the matter I gradually gained a measure of satisfaction from the label. Was not Jesus an extremist for love: "Love your enemies, bless them that curse you, do good to them that hate you, and pray for them which despitefully use you, and persecute you." Was not Amos an extremist for justice: "Let justice roll down like waters and righteousness like an ever-flowing stream." Was not Paul an extremist for the Christian gospel: "I bear in my body the marks of the Lord Jesus." Was not Martin Luther an extremist: "Here I stand; I cannot do otherwise, so help me God." And John Bunyan: "I will stay in jail to the end of my days before I make a butchery of my conscience." And Abraham Lincoln: "This nation cannot survive half slave and half free." And Thomas Jefferson: "We hold these truths to be self-evident, that all men are created equal. . . ." So the question is not whether we will be extremists, but what kind of extremists we will be. Will we be extremists for hate or for love? Will we be extremists for the preservation of injustice or for the extension of justice? In 9

Hebrew prophet

Christ's disciple

Founded Protestantism

English preacher

No choice but to be extremists. But what kind?

that dramatic scene on Calvary's hill three men were crucified. We must never forget that all three were crucified for the same crime—the crime of extremism. Two were extremists for immorality, and thus fell below their environment. The other, Jesus Christ, was an extremist for love, truth and goodness, and thereby rose above his environment. Perhaps the South, the nation and the world are in dire need of creative extremists.

¶9. Creative extremists are needed.

Disappointed in the white moderate

I had hoped that the white moderate would see this need. Perhaps I was too optimistic; perhaps I expected too much. I suppose I should have realized that few members of the oppressor race can understand the deep groans and passionate yearnings of the oppressed race, and still fewer have the vision to see that [injustice must be rooted out] by strong, persistent and determined action. I am thankful, however, that some of our white brothers in the South have grasped the meaning of this social revolution and committed themselves to it. They are still all too few in quantity, but they are big in quality. Some—such as Ralph McGill, Lillian Smith, Harry Golden, James McBride Dabbs, Ann Braden and Sarah Patton Boyle—have written about our struggle in eloquent and prophetic terms. Others have marched with us down nameless streets of the South. They have languished in filthy, roach-infested jails, suffering the abuse and brutality of policemen who view them as "dirty nigger-lovers." Unlike so many of their moderate brothers and sisters, they have recognized the urgency of the moment and sensed the need for [powerful "action" antidotes] to combat the [disease of segregation.]

10

¶10. Some whites have supported King.

Who are they?

what they did

left unaided

CHECKLIST: Annotating

1. Mark the text using notations like these:
   - circle words to be defined in the margin
   - underline key words and phrases
   - bracket important sentences and passages
   - use lines or arrows to connect ideas or words
2. Write marginal comments like these:
   - number and summarize each paragraph
   - define unfamiliar words
   - note responses and questions
   - identify interesting writing strategies
   - point out patterns
3. Layer additional markings on the text and comments in the margins as you reread for different purposes.

TAKING INVENTORY

See pp. 422–25 for an example of an inventory used to analyze a story.

An inventory is simply a list or grouping of items. *Taking inventory* helps you to analyze your annotations for different purposes. When you take inventory, you make various kinds of lists to explore patterns of meaning you find in the text. For instance, in reading and annotating the passage by Martin Luther King Jr., you might have noticed that many famous people are named or that certain similes and metaphors are used. By listing the names (Socrates, Jesus, Luther, Lincoln, etc.) and then grouping them into categories (people who died for their beliefs, leaders, teachers, and religious figures) you could better understand why the writer refers to these particular people. Obviously, taking inventory of your annotations would be very helpful in writing about a text you are reading.

CHECKLIST: Taking Inventory

1. Examine your annotations for patterns or repetitions such as recurring images, stylistic features, repeated words and phrases, repeated examples or illustrations, and reliance on particular writing strategies.
2. List and group the items in the pattern.
3. Decide what the pattern indicates about the reading.

OUTLINING

Outlining is an especially helpful critical reading strategy for understanding the content and structure of a reading. *Outlining,* which identifies the text's main ideas, may be part of the annotating process, or it may be done separately. Writing an outline in the margins of the text as you read and annotate makes it easier to find information later. Writing an outline on a separate piece of paper gives you more space to work with and therefore usually includes more detail.

The key to outlining is distinguishing between the main ideas and the supporting material such as reasons, examples, factual evidence, and explanations. The main ideas form the backbone, which holds the various parts and pieces of the text together. Outlining the main ideas helps you uncover this structure.

Making an outline, however, is not simple. The reader must exercise judgment in deciding which are the most important ideas. Because importance is relative, different readers can make different—and equally reasonable—decisions based on what interests them in the reading. Outlining may be further complicated when readers use their own words rather than select words from the text. Rephrasing can create a slight or significant shift in meaning or emphasis. Reading is never a passive or neutral act; the process of outlining shows how constructive reading can be.

You may make either a formal, multileveled outline with Roman (I, II) and Arabic (1, 2) numerals together with capital and lowercase letters or an informal scratch outline that lists the main idea of each paragraph. A formal outline is harder to make and much more time consuming than a scratch outline. You might choose to make a formal outline of a reading about which you are writing an in-depth analysis or evaluation. For example, here is a formal outline a student wrote for a paper evaluating the logic of the King excerpt. Notice that the student uses Roman numerals for the main ideas or claims, capital letters for the reasons, and Arabic numerals for supporting evidence and explanation.

```
I. The Negro's great stumbling block in his stride
   toward freedom is . . . the white moderate
   A. Because the white moderate is more devoted to
      "order" than to justice (paragraph 2)
      1. Law and order should exist to establish
         justice
      2. Likens law and order to dangerously
         structured dams that block the flow of social
         progress
   B. Because the white moderate prefers a negative
      peace (absence of tension) to a positive peace
      (justice) (paragraph 2)
      1. The tension already exists
      2. It is not created by nonviolent direct action
      3. Boil simile: Compares society that does not
         eliminate injustice to a boil that hides its
         infections. Both can be cured only by
         exposure.
   C. Because even though the white moderate agrees
      with the goals, he does not support the means to
      achieve them (paragraph 3)
      1. Rebuts the argument that the means--
         nonviolent direct action--are wrong because
         they precipitate violence
      2. Analogy of the robbed man condemned because
         he had money
      3. Comparison with Socrates and Jesus
   D. Because the white moderate paternalistically
      believes he can set a timetable for another
      man's freedom (paragraph 4)
      1. Rebuts the white moderate's argument that
         Christianity will cure man's ills and man
         must wait patiently for that to happen
      2. Argues that time is neutral and that man
         must use time creatively for constructive
         rather than destructive ends
II. Creative extremism is preferable to moderation
   A. Classifies himself as a moderate (paragraphs 5-8)
      1. I stand between two forces: the white
         moderate's complacency and the Black Muslim's
         rage
      2. If nonviolent direct action were stopped,
         more violence, not less, would result
```

3. "Millions of Negroes will, out of frustration and despair, seek solace and security in black-nationalist ideologies" (paragraph 7)
4. Repressed emotions will be expressed--if not in nonviolent ways, then through violence (paragraph 8)

B. Redefines himself as a "creative extremist" (paragraph 9)
   1. Extremism for love, truth, and goodness is creative extremism
   2. Identifies himself with creative extremists like Jesus, Amos, Paul, Martin Luther, John Bunyan, Abraham Lincoln, and Thomas Jefferson

C. Not all white people are moderates, many are creative extremists (paragraph 10)
   1. Lists names of white writers
   2. Refers to white activists

Making a scratch outline, in contrast to a formal outline, takes less time but still requires careful reading. A scratch outline will not record as much information as a formal outline, but it is sufficient for most critical reading purposes. To make a scratch outline, you need to locate the topic of each paragraph. The topic is usually stated in a word or phrase, and it may be repeated or referred to throughout the paragraph. For example, the opening paragraph of the King excerpt (p. 443) makes clear that its topic is the white moderate.

After you have found the topic of the paragraph, figure out what is being said about it. To return to our example: If the white moderate is the topic of the opening paragraph, then what King says about the topic can be found in the second sentence, where he announces the conclusion he has come to—namely, that the white moderate is "the Negro's great stumbling block in his stride toward freedom." The rest of the paragraph specifies the ways the white moderate blocks progress.

When you make an outline, you can use the writer's words, your own words, or a combination of the two. An outline appears in the margins of the selection, with numbers for each paragraph (see pp. 443–47). Here is the same outline on a separate piece of paper, slightly expanded and reworded:

¶1 White moderates block progress in the struggle for racial justice
¶2 Tension is necessary for progress
¶3 The clergymen's criticism is not logical
¶4 King justifies urgent use of time
¶5 Clergymen accuse King of being extreme, but he claims to stand between two extreme forces in the black community
¶6 King offers a better choice

```
¶7 King's movement has prevented racial violence
   by blacks
¶8 Discontent is normal and healthy but must be
   channeled creatively rather than destructively
¶9 Creative extremists are needed
¶10 Some whites have supported King
```

CHECKLIST: Outlining

1. Reread each paragraph systematically, identifying the topic and what is being said about it. Do not include examples, specific details, quotations, or other explanatory and supporting material.
2. List the main ideas in the margin of the text or on a separate piece of paper.

CONTEXTUALIZING

All texts were written sometime in the past and therefore may embody historical and cultural assumptions, values, and attitudes different from your own. To read critically, you need to become aware of these differences. *Contextualizing* is a critical reading strategy that enables you to make inferences about a reading's historical and cultural context and to examine the differences between its context and your own. Contextualizing is best done in three steps:

1. Annotate any language or ideas in the text that seem to express attitudes, assumptions, or values that strike you as different from your own.
2. Reflect on what you know about the time and place in which the selection was written. Your knowledge may come from other reading, television or film, school, or elsewhere. (If you know nothing about the historical and cultural context, you could do some library research.)
3. In a paragraph or two, explore the differences you see between the writer's assumptions, values, and attitudes and those current in your culture today. Consider how these differences affect your understanding and judgment of the reading.

The excerpt from "Letter from Birmingham Jail" is a good example of a text that benefits from being read contextually. If you knew little about the history of slavery and segregation in the United States, Martin Luther King Jr., or the civil rights movement, it would be very difficult to understand the passion for justice and impatience with delay expressed in this essay. Most Americans have read histories about slavery and its aftermath and may also have seen television documentaries showing King and his followers being attacked by dogs, doused by fire hoses, and beaten by helmeted police. Such images provide a sense of the violence, fear, and hatred to which King is responding in this essay. Comparing the context of King's letter, written in 1963, to the present reveals that conditions have improved, though much remains to be done. As in King's time, many African Americans today are still pressing for fair treatment and equal opportunity.

CHECKLIST: Contextualizing

1. Annotate the text for attitudes, assumptions, or values that are different from your own.
2. Reflect on the historical and cultural situation represented in the reading selection and in other sources.
3. Write about differences between the writer's attitudes, assumptions, and values and those in your culture today.

REFLECTING ON CHALLENGES TO YOUR BELIEFS AND VALUES

To read critically, you need to scrutinize your own assumptions and attitudes as well as those expressed in the text you are reading. Our assumptions and attitudes are so ingrained, however, that we are usually not aware of them. A good strategy for getting at these underlying beliefs and values is to identify and reflect on the ways the text challenges you and how it makes you feel—disturbed, threatened, ashamed, combative, or some other way.

1. Identify challenges by annotating the text, marking each point where you feel that your own beliefs and values are being opposed, criticized, or unfairly characterized.
2. Select one or two of the most troubling challenges you have identified, and write a few paragraphs trying to understand why you feel as you do. Do not defend your feelings; instead, analyze them to see where they come from.

For example, here is what one student wrote about the King passage:

In paragraph 1, Dr. King criticizes readers who are "more devoted to 'order' than to justice." This criticism upsets me because today I think I would choose order over justice. When I analyze my feelings and try to figure out where they come from, I realize that what I feel most is fear. I am terrified by the violence in society today. I'm afraid of sociopaths who don't respect the rule of law, much less the value of human life.

I know Dr. King was writing about a time when the law itself was unjust. Then, order was apparently used to keep people from protesting and changing the law. But things are different now. Today, justice seems to serve criminals more than law-abiding citizens. That's why I'm for order over justice.

CHECKLIST: Reflecting on Challenges to Your Beliefs and Values

1. Identify challenges by marking the text where you feel your beliefs and values are being opposed, criticized, or unfairly characterized.
2. Try to understand why you feel challenged. Don't defend your feelings; but instead analyze them to see where they come from.

PARAPHRASING

Paraphrasing is restating something you have read using your own words. As a critical reading strategy, paraphrasing can help to clarify the meaning of an obscure or ambiguous passage. It is one of the three ways of integrating other people's ideas and information into your own writing, along with *quoting* (reproducing exactly the language of the source text) and *summarizing* (distilling the main ideas or gist of the source text). You might choose to paraphrase rather than quote when the source's language is not especially arresting or memorable. You might paraphrase short passages but summarize longer ones.

Here is how one student paraphrased the first five sentences of a paragraph from an article on Native American writing systems.

Original

> The Native American groups that, despite all obstacles, have developed traditions of literacy in their own languages seem to share certain characteristics. All of them, of course, have preserved some sort of social organization, at least at the local community level. It would seem that such groups have also found one or more functions for their own literacy. Thus the spread of Fox, Winnebago, Cherokee, and Mahican literacy occurred at the same time that these several tribes were divided by migrations. In all four cases it seems reasonable to suppose that the first individuals to become literate were motivated by a desire to communicate with relatives who had departed for the west or, as the case may be, had lingered behind in the east.

Paraphrase

Native American groups had to overcome many obstacles in order to develop writing systems in their own languages. The groups that did develop writing are alike in several ways: They maintained their social structure, and they were able to put writing to good use. For example, writing became more common in the Fox, Winnebago, Cherokee, and Mahican tribes after they were separated through migration. Tribal members probably wanted to write to relatives they could no longer see regularly.

The first thing to note about the paraphrase is that it contains *all* the information in the original. It is not just a summary. It is a complete reproduction in the student's own words. Although it has the same number of sentences as the original, the information is grouped in somewhat different ways. Without changing the information significantly, paraphrase aims to clarify and simplify the original.

CHECKLIST: Paraphrasing

1. Reread the passage to be paraphrased, looking up unknown words in a college dictionary.
2. Translate the passage into your own words, putting quotation marks around any words or phrases quoted from the original.
3. Revise to ensure coherence.

SUMMARIZING

Summarizing is one of the most widely used strategies for critical reading because it helps the reader understand and remember what is most important in the reading. Another advantage of summarizing is that it creates a condensed version of the reading's ideas and information, which can be referred to later or inserted into the reader's own written text. Along with quoting and paraphrasing, summarizing enables us to refer to and integrate other writers' ideas into our own writing.

A summary is a relatively brief restatement, in the reader's own words, of the reading's main ideas. Summaries vary in length, depending on the reader's purpose. Some summaries are very brief—a sentence or even a subordinate clause. For example, if you were referring to the excerpt from "Letter from Birmingham Jail" and simply needed to indicate how it relates to your other sources, your summary might focus on only one aspect of the reading. It might look something like this: "There have always been advocates of extremism in politics. Martin Luther King Jr., in 'Letter from Birmingham Jail,' for instance, defends nonviolent civil disobedience as an extreme but necessary means of bringing about racial justice." If, on the other hand, you were surveying the important texts of the civil rights movement, you might write a longer, more detailed summary that not only identifies the reading's main ideas but also shows how the ideas relate to one another.

Many writers find it useful to outline the reading as a preliminary to writing a summary. A paragraph-by-paragraph scratch outline (like that illustrated on pp. 450–51) lists the reading's main ideas following the sequence in which they appear in the original. But writing a summary requires more than merely stringing together the entries in an outline. A summary has to make explicit the logical connections between the ideas. To write a summary, you do more than translate the author's meaning into your own words, as you would when writing a paraphrase. Writing a summary shows how reading critically is a truly constructive process of interpretation involving both close analysis and creative synthesis.

To summarize, you need to separate the main ideas from the supporting material, usually by making an outline of the reading. You should use mostly your own words, but you may quote selected words and phrases. You may also want to cite the title and refer to the author by name, indicating with verbs like *expresses, acknowledges,* and *explains* the writer's purpose and strategy at each point in the argument.

Following is a sample summary of the King excerpt. It is based on the outline on pp. 449–50 but is much more detailed. Most important, it fills in connections between the ideas that King left for readers to make.

King expresses his disappointment with white moderates who, by opposing his program of nonviolent direct action, have become a barrier to progress toward racial justice. He acknowledges that his program has raised tension in the South, but he explains that tension is necessary to bring about change. Furthermore, he argues that tension already exists. But because it has been unexpressed, it is unhealthy and potentially dangerous.

He defends his actions against the clergy's criticisms, particularly their argument that he is in too much of a hurry. Responding to charges of extremism, King claims that he has

```
actually prevented racial violence by channeling the natural
frustrations of oppressed blacks into nonviolent protest. He
asserts that extremism is precisely what is needed now--but
it must be creative, rather than destructive, extremism. He
concludes by again expressing disappointment with white moder-
ates for not joining his effort as some other whites have.
```

CHECKLIST: Summarizing

1. Make an outline.
2. Write a paragraph or more that presents the main ideas largely in your own words. Use the outline as a guide, but reread parts of the original text as necessary.
3. To make the summary coherent, fill in connections between ideas.

EXPLORING THE SIGNIFICANCE OF FIGURATIVE LANGUAGE

Figurative language—metaphor, simile, and symbolism—enhances literal meaning by embodying abstract ideas in vivid images and by evoking feelings and associations.

Metaphor implicitly compares two different things by identifying them with each other. For instance, when King calls the white moderate "the Negro's great stumbling block in his stride toward freedom" (paragraph 1), he does not mean that the white moderate literally trips the Negro who is attempting to walk toward freedom. The sentence makes sense only if understood figuratively: The white moderate trips up the Negro by frustrating every effort to achieve justice. Similarly, in paragraph 2, King uses the image of a dam to express the abstract idea of the blockage of justice.

Simile, a more explicit form of comparison, uses *like* or *as* to signal the relationship of two seemingly unrelated things. King uses simile when he says that injustice is "like a boil that can never be cured so long as it is covered up" (paragraph 2). This simile makes several points of comparison between injustice and a boil. It suggests that injustice is a disease of society as a boil is a disease of the body and that injustice, like a boil, must be exposed or it will fester and infect the entire body.

Symbolism compares two things by making one stand for the other. King uses the white moderate as a symbol for supposed liberals and would-be supporters of civil rights who are actually frustrating the cause.

How these figures of speech are used in a text reveals something of the writer's feelings about the subject. Noting figures of speech as you annotate and taking inventory of any patterns they reveal can help you to read between the lines of a text, to recognize meanings that may not be stated directly.

The following list provides one systematic way to explore the patterns of figurative language.

1. Annotate and then list all the figures of speech you find in the reading—metaphor, simile, and symbolism.
2. Group the figures of speech that appear to express similar feelings and attitudes, and label each group.
3. Write one or two paragraphs exploring the meaning of these patterns. What do they tell you about the text?

Listing figures of speech in the King excerpt yields many examples, among them the following:

```
order is a dangerously structured dam that blocks
     the flow
social progress should flow
stumbling block in the stride toward freedom
injustice is like a boil that can never be cured
the light of human conscience and air of national opinion
time is something to be used, neutral, an ally, ripe
quicksand of racial injustice
the solid rock of human dignity
human progress never rolls in on wheels of inevitability
men are co-workers with God
groups springing up
promised land of racial justice
vital urge engulfed
pent-up resentments
normal and healthy discontent can be channeled into the
     creative outlet of nonviolent direct action
root out injustice
powerful action is an antidote
disease of segregation
```

Here is one way these figures can be grouped:

```
Sickness: segregation is a disease; action is healthy,
     the only antidote; injustice is like a boil
Underground: tension is hidden; resentments are pent up,
     repressed; injustice must be rooted out; extremist
     groups are springing up; discontent can be
     channeled into a creative outlet
Blockage: forward movement is impeded by obstacles--
     the dam, stumbling block; human progress never
     rolls in on wheels of inevitability; social
     progress should flow
```

In writing about these patterns and thinking about what they mean, you might recognize patterns of blockage and underground as suggesting frustration and inertia. The simile of injustice being like a boil suggests that there is something bad, a disease, inside society. The cure is to expose, to root out, the blocked hatred and injustice and release the tension or emotion that has long been repressed. This implies that repression itself is the evil, not simply what is repressed.

CHECKLIST: Exploring the Significance of Figurative Language

1. Annotate and then list all the figures of speech you find.
2. Group them and label each group.
3. Explore the meaning of the patterns you have found.

LOOKING FOR PATTERNS OF OPPOSITION

All texts carry within themselves voices of opposition. These voices may echo the views and values of critical readers the writer anticipates or predecessors to which the writer is responding in some way; they may even reflect the writer's own conflicting values. Careful readers look closely for such a dialogue of opposing voices within the text.

When we think of oppositions, we ordinarily think of polarities: *yes* and *no, up* and *down, black* and *white, new* and *old*. Some oppositions, however, may be more subtle. The excerpt from "Letter from Birmingham Jail" is rich in such oppositions: *moderate* versus *extremist, order* versus *justice, direct action* versus *passive acceptance, expression* versus *repression*. These oppositions are not accidental; they form a significant pattern that gives a critical reader important information about the essay.

A careful reading will show that King always values one of the two terms in an opposition over the other. In the passage, for example, *extremist* is valued over *moderate* (paragraph 9). This preference for extremism is surprising. The critical reader should ask why, when white extremists like the Ku Klux Klan have committed so many outrages against African Americans, King would prefer extremism. If King is trying to convince his readers to accept his point of view, why would he represent himself as an extremist? Moreover, why would a clergyman advocate extremism instead of moderation?

Studying the pattern of oppositions enables you to answer these questions. You will see that King sets up this opposition to force his readers to examine their own values and realize that they are in fact misplaced. Instead of working toward justice, he says, those who support law and order maintain the unjust status quo. By getting his readers to think of white moderates as blocking rather than facilitating peaceful change, King brings them to align themselves with him and perhaps even embrace his strategy of nonviolent resistance.

Here is a useful way to look for patterns of oppositions:

1. Annotate words and phrases that indicate oppositions or polarities.
2. Divide a piece of paper in half lengthwise by drawing a line down the middle, or set up a two-column table on your computer. In the left-hand column, list words and phrases you marked in the text. Enter in the right-hand column the word or phrase that is the opposite of each word or phrase in the left-hand column. You may have to paraphrase or even supply this opposite word or phrase if it is not stated directly in the text.
3. For each pair of words or phrases, note with an asterisk which one the writer seems to prefer.
4. Study the words or phrases that seem to be valued. Do the same for the other list. How do they contribute to your understanding—and acceptance—of the argument? What do they tell you about what the writer *wants* you to believe?

A list of oppositions in the King text might yield the following examples. The ones King seems to value are marked with asterisks.

```
 white moderate              *extremist
 order                       *justice
 negative peace              *positive peace
 absence of justice          *presence of justice
 goals                       *methods
*direct action                passive acceptance
*exposed tension              hidden tension
*robbed                       robber
*individual                   society
*words                        silence
*expression                   repression
*extension of justice         preservation of injustice
*extremist for love,          extremist for immorality
     truth, and justice
```

CHECKLIST: Looking for Patterns of Opposition

1. Annotate the selection for oppositions.
2. List the pairs on a separate page.
3. For each pair of words, put an asterisk next to the word that is preferred in the selection.
4. Examine the pattern of preferred terms to discover the system of values the pattern implies, and do the same for the unpreferred terms.

EVALUATING THE LOGIC OF AN ARGUMENT

An argument includes a thesis backed by reasons and support. The *thesis* asserts an idea the writer wants readers to accept, a position on a controversial issue, or a solution to a problem. The *reasons* tell readers why they should accept the thesis, and the *support* (such as facts, examples, and quotations) gives readers grounds for accepting it. For an argument to be considered logically acceptable, it must meet three conditions in what we call the ABC test:

For more on argument, see Chapter 19. For an example of the ABC test, see pp. 309–312.

A. The reasons and support must be *appropriate* to the thesis.
B. All of the reasons and support must be *believable*.
C. The reasons and support must be *consistent* with one another as well as *complete*.

Testing for Appropriateness

As a critical reader, you must decide whether the argument's reasons and support are actually appropriate and clearly related to the thesis. To test for appropriateness, ask, how does each reason or piece of support relate to the thesis? Is the connection between reasons and support and the thesis clear and compelling? Or is the argument irrelevant or only vaguely related to the thesis?

Readers question the appropriateness of reasons and support most often when the writer argues by analogy or by invoking authority. For example, in paragraph 2, King argues that if law and order fail to establish justice, "they become the dangerously structured dams that block the flow of social progress." The analogy asserts the following logical relationship: Law and order are to progress toward justice what a dam is to water. If you do not accept this analogy, the argument fails the test of appropriateness. King uses both analogy and authority in the following passage: "Isn't this like condemning Socrates because his unswerving commitment to truth and his philosophical inquiries precipitated the act by the misguided populace in which they made him drink hemlock?" (paragraph 3). Not only must you judge the appropriateness of comparing the Greek populace's condemnation of Socrates to the white moderates' condemnation of King's actions, but you must also judge whether it is appropriate to accept Socrates as an authority on this subject. Since Socrates is generally respected for his teaching on justice, his words and actions are likely to be considered appropriate to King's situation in Birmingham.

Several common flaws or logical fallacies, including the following, can cause an argument to fail the test of appropriateness:

- *False analogy,* when two cases are not sufficiently parallel to lead readers to accept the thesis.
- *False use of authority,* when writers invoke as expert in the field being discussed a person or people whose expertise or authority lies not in the given field but in another.
- *Non sequitur* (Latin for "it does not follow"), when one statement is not logically connected to another.
- *Red herring,* when a writer raises an irrelevant issue to draw attention away from the central issue.
- *Post hoc, ergo propter hoc* (Latin for "after this, therefore because of this"), when the writer implies that because one event follows another, the first caused the second. Chronology is not the same as causality.

Testing for Believability

You must also look critically at each statement giving reasons or support for the thesis to see whether it is believable. You may find some reasons or support self-evidently true and the truth of others less certain. To test for believability, ask, on what basis am I being asked to accept this reason or support as true? If it cannot be proved true or false, how much weight does it carry?

In judging facts, statistics, examples, and authorities, consider the following points.

Facts are statements that can be proved objectively to be true. The believability of facts depends on their *accuracy* (they should not distort or misrepresent reality), their *completeness* (they should not omit important details), and the *trustworthiness* of their sources (sources should be qualified and unbiased). King, for instance, asserts as fact that the African American will not wait much longer for racial justice (paragraph 8). His critics might question the factuality of this assertion by asking, is it true of all African Americans? How much longer will they wait? How does King know what African Americans will and will not do?

Statistics, often mistaken as facts, are actually only interpretations of numerical data. The believability of statistics depends on the *comparability* of the data (apples cannot be compared to oranges), the *precision* of the methods employed to gather and analyze data (representative samples should be used and variables accounted for), and the *trustworthiness* of the sources (sources should be qualified and unbiased).

Examples and *anecdotes* are particular instances that if accepted as believable lead readers to accept the general reason or thesis. The believability of examples depends on their *representativeness* (whether they are truly typical and thus generalizable) and their *specificity* (whether particular details make them seem true to life). Even if a vivid example or gripping anecdote does not convince readers, it strengthens argumentative writing by clarifying the meaning and dramatizing the point. In paragraph 5 of the King excerpt, for example, King supports his generalization that some African-American nationalist extremists are motivated by bitterness and hatred by citing the specific example of Elijah Muhammad's Muslim movement. Conversely, in paragraph 9, he refers to Jesus, Paul, Luther, and others as examples of extremists motivated by love and Christianity. These examples support his assertion that extremism is not in itself wrong and that any judgment of extremism must be based on its motivation and cause.

Authorities are people to whom the writer attributes expertise on a given subject. Not only must such authorities be appropriate, as mentioned earlier, but they must be believable as well. The believability of authorities depends on their *credibility,* on whether the reader accepts them as experts on the topic at hand. King cites authorities repeatedly throughout his essay. He refers to religious leaders (Jesus and Luther) as well as to American political leaders (Lincoln and Jefferson). These figures are certain to have a high degree of credibility among King's readers.

In addition, you should be aware of the following fallacies in reasoning that undermine the believability of an argument:

- *Begging the question,* when the believability of the reasons and support depends on the believability of the thesis. Another name for this kind of fallacy is *circular reasoning.*
- *Failing to accept the burden of proof,* when the writer asserts a thesis but provides no reasons or support for it.
- *Hasty generalization,* when the writer asserts a thesis on the basis of a single reason or an isolated example.
- *Sweeping generalization,* when the writer fails to qualify the applicability of the thesis and asserts that it applies to all instances instead of to some instances.
- *Overgeneralization,* when the writer fails to qualify the thesis and asserts that it is certainly true rather than that it may be true.

Testing for Consistency and Completeness

In looking for consistency, you should be concerned that all the parts of the argument work together and that none of the reasons or support contradict any of the other reasons or support. In addition, the reasons and support, taken together, should be sufficient to convince readers to accept the thesis or at least take it seriously.

To test for consistency and completeness, ask, are any of the reasons and support contradictory? Do they provide sufficient grounds for accepting the thesis? Has the writer failed to counterargue by acknowledging or refuting any opposing arguments or important objections?

A critical reader might regard as contradictory King's characterizing himself first as a moderate between the forces of complacency and violence and later as an extremist opposed to the forces of violence. King attempts to reconcile this apparent contradiction by explicitly redefining extremism in paragraph 9. Similarly, the fact that King fails to examine and refute every legal recourse available to his cause might allow a critical reader to question the sufficiency of his argument.

In evaluating the consistency and completeness of an argument, you should also be aware of the following fallacies:

- *Slippery slope,* when the writer argues that taking one step will lead inevitably to a next step, one that is undesirable.
- *Equivocation,* when a writer uses the same term in two different senses in an argument.
- *Oversimplification,* when an argument obscures or denies the complexity of the issue.
- *Either-or reasoning,* when the writer reduces the issue to only two alternatives that are polar opposites.
- *Double standard,* when two or more comparable things are judged according to different standards. This often involves holding the opposing argument to a higher standard than the one to which the writer holds his or her own argument.

CHECKLIST: Evaluating the Logic of an Argument: The ABC test

1. *Test for Appropriateness* by checking to be sure that each reason and support is clearly and directly related to the thesis.
2. *Test for Believability* by deciding whether you can accept the reasons and support as true.
3. *Test for Consistency and Completeness* by ascertaining whether there are any contradictions in the argument and also whether any important objections or opposing arguments have been ignored.

RECOGNIZING EMOTIONAL MANIPULATION

Many different kinds of essays appeal to readers' emotions. Tobias Wolff's remembered event essay (in Chapter 2) may be terrifying to some readers, David Noonan's profile of brain surgery (in Chapter 4) may be shocking, and Richard Estrada's position paper (in Chapter 6) may be annoying to some readers because of his accommodating tone.

Writers often try to arouse emotions in readers to excite their interest, make them care, or move them to take action. There is nothing wrong with appealing to readers' emotions. What is wrong is manipulating readers with false or exaggerated appeals. As a critical reader, you should be suspicious of writing that is overly or falsely sentimental, that cites alarming statistics and frightening anecdotes, that demonizes others and identifies itself with revered authorities, or that uses symbols (flag-waving) or emotionally loaded words (such as *racist*).

King, for example, uses the emotionally loaded word *paternalistically* to refer to the white moderate's belief that "he can set the timetable for another man's freedom" (paragraph 1). In the same paragraph, King uses symbolism to get an emotional reaction from readers when he compares the white moderate to the "Ku Klux Klanner." To get readers to accept his ideas, he also relies on authorities whose names evoke the greatest respect, such as Jesus and Lincoln. Some readers might consider the discussion of African-American extremists in paragraph 7 of the King excerpt to be a veiled threat designed to frighten readers into agreement. Or some readers might object that comparing King's crusade to that of Jesus and other leaders of religious and political groups is pretentious and manipulative.

Following are some fallacies that may occur when the emotional appeal is misused:

- *Loaded or slanted language,* when the writer uses language that is calculated to get a particular reaction from readers.
- *Bandwagon effect,* when it is suggested that great numbers of people agree with the writer and you would be alone if you continued to disagree.
- *False flattery,* when readers are praised in order to get them to accept the writer's point of view.
- *Veiled threat,* when the writer tries to alarm or frighten readers into accepting the thesis.

CHECKLIST: Recognizing Emotional Manipulation

1. Annotate any places in the text where you sense emotional appeals are being used.
2. Identify the kinds of emotional appeals you found, and assess whether they are unfairly manipulative.

JUDGING THE WRITER'S CREDIBILITY

Writers often try to persuade readers to respect and believe them. Because readers may not know them personally or even by reputation, writers must present an image of themselves in their writing that will gain their readers' confidence. This image cannot be made directly but must be made indirectly, through the arguments, language, and system of values and beliefs expressed or implied in the writing. Writers establish credibility in their writing in three ways:

By showing their knowledge of the subject

By building common ground with readers

By responding fairly to objections and opposing arguments

Testing for Knowledge

Writers demonstrate their knowledge through the facts and statistics they marshal, the sources they rely on for information, and the scope and depth of their understanding. As a critical reader, you may not be sufficiently expert on the subject yourself to know whether the facts are accurate, the sources are reliable, and the understanding is sufficient. You may need to do some research to see what others say about the subject. You can also check credentials—the writer's educational and professional qualifications, the respectability of the publication in which the selection first appeared, any reviews of the writer's work—to determine whether the writer is a respected authority in the field. For example, King brings with him the authority that comes from being a member of the clergy and a respected leader of the Southern Christian Leadership Conference.

Testing for Common Ground

One way writers can establish common ground with their readers is by basing their reasoning on shared values, beliefs, and attitudes. They use language that includes their readers *(we)* rather than excludes them *(they)*. They qualify their assertions to keep them from being too extreme. Above all, they acknowledge differences of opinion and try to make room in their argument to accommodate reasonable differences. As a critical reader, you will want to notice such appeals.

King creates common ground with readers by using the inclusive pronoun *we*, suggesting shared concerns between himself and his audience. Notice, however, his use of masculine pronouns and other references ("the Negro . . . he," "our brothers"). Although King addressed his letter to male clergy, he intended it to be published in the local newspaper, where it would be read by an audience of both men and women. By using language that excludes women, a common practice at the time the selection was written, King misses the opportunity to build common ground with half his readers.

Testing for Fairness

Writers display their character by how they handle opposing arguments and objections to their argument. As a critical reader, you want to pay particular attention to how writers treat possible differences of opinion. Be suspicious of those who ignore differences and pretend that everyone agrees with their viewpoint. When objections or opposing views are represented, consider whether they have been distorted in any way; if they are refuted, be sure they are challenged fairly—with sound reasoning and solid support.

One way to gauge the author's credibility is to identify the tone of the argument, for it conveys the writer's attitude toward the subject and toward the reader. Examine the text carefully for indications of tone: Is the text angry? Sarcastic? Evenhanded? Shrill? Condescending? Bullying? Do you feel as if the writer is treating the subject—and you, as a reader—with fairness? King's tone might be characterized in different passages as patient (he doesn't lose his temper), respectful (he refers to white moderates as "people of good will"), or pompous (comparing himself to Jesus and Socrates).

The following fallacies can undermine the ethical appeal:

- *Guilt by association,* when someone's credibility is attacked by associating that person with another person whom readers consider untrustworthy.
- *Ad hominem attack,* when the writer attacks opponents personally instead of finding fault with their argument. (*Ad hominem* is Latin for argument "against the man.")
- *Straw man,* when the writer directs the argument against a thesis that nobody actually asserts or that everyone agrees is weak. This often involves misrepresentation or distortion of the opposing argument.

CHECKLIST: Judging the Writer's Credibility

1. Annotate for the writer's knowledge of the subject, how well common ground is established, and whether the writer deals fairly with objections and opposing arguments.
2. Decide what in the essay you find credible and what you question.

Cueing the Reader

Readers need guidance. To guide readers through a piece of writing, a writer can provide four basic kinds of cues or signals:

1. Thesis and forecasting statements, to orient readers to ideas and organization
2. Paragraphing, to group related ideas and details
3. Cohesive devices, to connect ideas to one another and bring about coherence and clarity
4. Transitions, to signal relationships or shifts in meaning

This chapter examines how each of these cueing strategies works.

ORIENTING STATEMENTS

To help readers to find their way, especially in difficult and lengthy texts, you can provide two kinds of orienting information: a thesis statement, which declares the main point, and a forecasting statement, which both states the thesis and previews subordinate points, showing the order in which they will be discussed in the essay.

Thesis Statements

Although they may have a variety of forms and purposes, all essays are essentially assertive. That is, they assert or put forward the writer's point of view on a subject. We call this point of view the essay's *thesis,* or main idea.

To help readers understand what is being said about a subject, writers often provide a thesis statement early in the essay. The *thesis statement* operates as a cue by letting readers know which is the most important general idea among the writer's many ideas and observations. Like the focal point of a picture, the thesis statement directs the reader's attention to the one idea that brings all the other ideas and details into perspective. Here are two thesis statements from essays in Part I:

> What seems on the surface to be irrational, intoxicated behavior is in fact part of nature's master strategy—a vital force that has helped humans survive, thrive, and multiply through thousands of years.
>
> —Anastasia Toufexis, Chapter 5

> It seems to me that what Native Americans are saying is that what would be intolerable for Jews, blacks, Latinos and others is no less offensive to them. Theirs is a request not only for dignified treatment, but for fair treatment as well. For America to ignore the complaints of a numerically small segment of the population because it is small is neither dignified nor fair.
>
> —Richard Estrada, Chapter 6

Explicit arguments are those in the kinds of writing in Chapters 6–10; implicit arguments are those in Chapters 2–5.

Most thesis statements, like Toufexis's, can be expressed in a single sentence; others may require two or more sentences, like Estrada's. In some kinds of writing, such as stories about remembered events, writers imply the thesis rather than state it directly. For example, Paul Auster (Chapter 2) conveys the significance of Ralph's death through description that turns the literal storm into a symbolic one.

Readers naturally look for something that will tell them the point of an essay, a focus for the many diverse details and ideas they encounter as they read. The lack of an explicit thesis statement can make this task more difficult. Therefore, careful writers keep readers' needs and expectations in mind when deciding how to state the thesis as clearly and directly as possible.

Another important decision is where to place the thesis statement. Most readers expect to find some information early on that will give them a context for the essay. They expect the essay to open with a thesis statement, and they need that statement to orient them, particularly if they are reading about a new and difficult subject. A thesis statement placed at the beginning of an essay helps to give readers a sense of control over the subject, enabling them to anticipate the content of the essay and more easily understand the relationships among its various ideas and details.

Occasionally, however, particularly in fairly short, informal essays and in some argumentative essays, a writer may save a direct statement of the thesis until the conclusion, as Estrada does. Ending with the thesis has the effect of bringing together the various strands of information or supporting details introduced over the course of the essay and making clear the essay's main idea. In many such cases, a concluding thesis is also used to suggest future developments or possibilities.

Exercise 13.1

Read the essay by Anastasia Toufexis (Chapter 5), Richard Estrada (Chapter 6), or Stephen King (Chapter 9); then briefly explain how its thesis statement brings the ideas and details of the essay into perspective.

Forecasting Statements

A special kind of thesis statement, a *forecasting statement,* not only identifies the thesis but also gives an overview of the way that thesis will be developed. For example, note the role of the forecasting statement in this opening paragraph from an essay by William Langer on the bubonic plague:

> In the three years from 1348 through 1350 the pandemic of plague known as the Black Death, or, as the Germans called it, the Great Dying, killed at least a fourth of the population of Europe. It was undoubtedly the worst disaster that has ever befallen mankind. Today we can have no real conception of the terror under which

> people lived in the shadow of the plague. For more than two centuries plague has not been a serious threat to mankind in the large, although it is still a grisly presence in parts of the Far East and Africa. Scholars continue to study the Great Dying, however, as a historical example of human behavior under the stress of universal catastrophe. In these days when the threat of plague has been replaced by the threat of mass human extermination by even more rapid means, there has been a sharp renewal of interest in the history of the 14th-century calamity. With new perspective, students are investigating its manifold effects: demographic, economic, psychological, moral and religious.
>
> —William Langer, "The Black Death"

This paragraph informs us that Langer's article is about the effects of the Black Death. His thesis, however, is not stated explicitly. It is implied by the forecasting statement that concludes the paragraph. With this sentence, Langer states that the study of the plague is currently focused on five particular categories. As a reader would expect, Langer then goes on to divide his essay into analyses of these five effects, taking them up in the order in which they appear in the forecasting statement.

Exercise 13.2

Read an essay in Chapter 5, underlining the forecasting statement. If you do not find any sentences that perform this function, try drafting one yourself. Reflect on the usefulness of this cueing device.

PARAGRAPHING

Paragraph Cues

The indentation that signals the beginning of a new paragraph is a relatively modern printing convention. Old manuscripts show that paragraph divisions were not always marked. To make reading easier, scribes and printers began to use the symbol ¶ to mark paragraph breaks. Later, indenting became common practice, but even that relatively modern custom has changed in some forms of writing today. Instead of indenting, most business writers now distinguish one paragraph from another by leaving a line of space above and below each paragraph.

The lack of paragraph cues makes reading extremely difficult. To illustrate this fact, the paragraph indentations have been removed from the following introductory section of a chapter in Stephen Jay Gould's book *Ever Since Darwin*. Even with proper paragraphing, this passage might be difficult for some readers because it contains unfamiliar information and technical language. Without paragraphing, however, Gould's logic is hard to follow, and the reader's mind and eye long for a momentary rest. (Each of the thirty sentences in the passage is numbered at the beginning.)

> (1) Since man created God in his own image, the doctrine of special creation has never failed to explain those adaptations that we understand intuitively. (2) How can we doubt that animals are exquisitely designed for their appointed roles when we watch a lioness hunt, a horse run, or a hippo wallow? (3) The theory of natural selection would never have replaced the doctrine of divine creation if evident,

admirable design pervaded all organisms. (4) Charles Darwin understood this, and he focused on features that would be out of place in a world constructed by perfect wisdom. (5) Why, for example, should a sensible designer create only on Australia a suite of marsupials to fill the same roles that placental mammals occupy on all other continents? (6) Darwin even wrote an entire book on orchids to argue that the structures evolved to ensure fertilization by insects are jerry-built of available parts used by ancestors for other purposes. (7) Orchids are Rube Goldberg machines; a perfect engineer would certainly have come up with something better. (8) This principle remains true today. (9) The best illustrations of adaptation by evolution are the ones that strike our intuition as peculiar or bizarre. (10) Science is not "organized common sense"; at its most exciting, it reformulates our view of the world by imposing powerful theories against the ancient, anthropocentric prejudices that we call intuition. (11) Consider, for example, the cecidomyian gall midges. (12) These tiny flies conduct their lives in a way that tends to evoke feelings of pain or disgust when we empathize with them by applying the inappropriate standards of our own social codes. (13) Cecidomyian gall midges can grow and develop along one of two pathways. (14) In some situations, they hatch from eggs, go through a normal sequence of larval and pupal molts, and emerge as ordinary, sexually reproducing flies. (15) But in other circumstances, females reproduce by parthenogenesis, bringing forth their young without any fertilization by males. (16) Parthenogenesis is common enough among animals, but the cecidomyians give it an interesting twist. (17) First of all, the parthenogenetic females stop at an early age of development. (18) They never become normal, adult flies, but reproduce while they are still larvae or pupae. (19) Secondly, these females do not lay eggs. (20) The offspring develop live within their mother's body—not supplied with nutrients and packaged away in a protected uterus but right inside the mother's tissues, eventually filling her entire body. (21) In order to grow, the offspring devour the mother from the inside. (22) A few days later, they emerge, leaving a chitinous shell as the only remains of their only parent. (23) And within two days, their own developing children are beginning, literally, to eat them up. (24) *Micromalthus debilis,* an unrelated beetle, has evolved an almost identical system with a macabre variation. (25) Some parthenogenetic females give birth to a single male offspring. (26) This larva attaches itself to his mother's cuticle for about four or five days, then inserts his head into her genital aperture and devours her. (27) Greater love hath no woman. (28) Why has such a peculiar mode of reproduction evolved? (29) For it is unusual even among insects, and not only by the irrelevant standards of our own perceptions. (30) What is the adaptive significance of a mode of life that so strongly violates our intuitions about good design?

—Stephen Jay Gould, *Ever Since Darwin*

A major difficulty in reading this passage without paragraph breaks is the need to hold the meaning of each sentence "in suspension" as you read ahead, because the meaning of a succeeding sentence may affect the meaning of an earlier sentence. For instance, sentence 2 clarifies the meaning of the first sentence by giving specific examples; sentence 3 restates the idea, and sentences 4–7 clarify and illustrate it. Without paragraphing, you are forced to remember each sentence separately and even to anticipate such close connections among sentences in order to make sense of the text.

Paragraphing helps readers by signaling when a sequence of related sentences begins and ends. Such paragraph signals tell you when you can stop holding meaning in suspension. Writers must constantly consider their readers' need for this kind of closure. Gould, for example, begins a new paragraph with sentence 8 to draw a sharp distinction between the examples and the general principle. Similarly, he begins a new paragraph with sentence 24 to signal a shift from a description of the reproductive mode of the cecidomyian gall midge to that of *Micromalthus debilis.* In this way, paragraphing keeps readers from being overloaded with information and at the same time helps them to follow the development of ideas.

Paragraphing also helps readers to judge what is most important in what they are reading. Writers typically emphasize important information by placing it at the two points where readers are most attentive—the beginning and the end of a paragraph. Many writers put information to orient readers at the beginning of a paragraph and save the most important information for last, as Gould does when he ends a paragraph with sentence 27.

See pp. 470–75 for a discussion of topic sentences.

You can give special emphasis to information by placing it in a paragraph of its own. Gould puts sentences 11 and 12 together in a separate paragraph. These two sentences could have been attached to either the preceding or following paragraph. But Gould gives them a separate paragraph to emphasize the general point he wants to make. In addition, this paragraph serves as an important transition between the general discussion of how science explains things that go against intuition and the specific example of the bizarre adaptation of the cecidomyian gall midge.

Exercise 13.3

The original Gould passage is divided into six paragraphs as follows: sentences 1–7, 8–10, 11–12, 13–23, 24–27, 28–30. Put a paragraph symbol ¶ in your book before the opening sentence of each paragraph. Later exercises will ask you to analyze aspects of Gould's paragraphing.

Paragraph Conventions

Some writing situations call for fairly strict paragraphing conventions. Readers may not be conscious of these conventions, but they would certainly notice if the custom were not observed. For example, readers would be surprised if a newspaper did not have narrow columns and short paragraphs. This paragraphing convention is not accidental; it is designed to make newspaper reading easy and fast and to allow the reader to take in an entire paragraph at a glance. Short paragraphs predominate in business writing. Most memo readers do not want an excess of details or qualifications. Instead, they prefer a concise overview.

College instructors, in contrast, expect students to qualify their ideas and support them with specifics. They care not so much about how long it takes to read a paragraph as about how well developed the writing is. Therefore, paragraphs in college essays usually have several sentences. In fact, it is not unusual to find paragraphs that are quite long, as this example from an undergraduate history essay on the status of women in Victorian England illustrates:

> A genteel woman was absolutely dependent upon the two men in her life: first her father, and then her husband. From them came her economic and social status; they were the center of her thoughts and the objects of any ambitions she might have. The ideal woman did not live for herself; she barely had a self, because her entire existence was vicarious. Legally, a woman had almost no existence at all. Until her marriage, a daughter was completely in the power of her father; upon her marriage, she was legally absorbed by her husband. Any money she had became his, as did all of her property, including her clothes and even those things that had been given her as personal gifts before her marriage. Any earnings she might make by working belonged to her husband. A woman could not be sued for debt separately from her husband because legally they were the same person. She could not sign a lease or sue someone in court without having her husband be the complainant, even in cases of long separation. In cases of a husband's enmity, she had almost no legal protection from him. Under English law, divorces could be obtained, in practice, only by men. A man could divorce his wife on the grounds of adultery, but the reverse was not the case.

If any rule for paragraphing is truly universal, it is this: Paragraphs should be focused, unified, and coherent. That is, the sentences in a paragraph should be meaningfully related to one another, and the relationships among the sentences should be clear. The following sentences, though they may look like a paragraph, do not constitute a meaningful paragraph because they lack focus, unity, and coherence.

> Maturity and attitude go together because both determine why you want to become a model. I went to the university for two years, not because I wanted to but because I was pushed into it. I used to think models were thought of as dumb blondes, but after being here at the university I realized that people still have respect for modeling and know all the hard work put in it.

Even though each of these sentences mentions modeling or the university or both, the two topics are not connected. With each sentence, the focus shifts—from the general desire to become a model to the writer's attending university to the stereotypical attitude of people toward models. There is no paragraph unity because no single idea links the sentences. The various elements of the writing do not "stick together" to form a coherent meaning, and the reader may well become disoriented. The topic sentence strategies discussed in the next section are useful for ensuring paragraph coherence.

Exercise 13.4

Look again at the Gould passage earlier in this chapter. Analyze how Gould's paragraphing helps you to follow his meaning. Is each paragraph focused, unified, and coherent? How could you have paragraphed this passage differently?

Topic Sentence Strategies

A *topic sentence* lets readers know the focus of a paragraph in simple and direct terms. It is a cueing strategy for the paragraph, much as a thesis or forecasting statement is for the whole essay. Because paragraphing usually signals a shift in focus, readers expect some kind of reorientation in the opening sentence. They need to know whether the new paragraph will introduce another aspect of the topic or develop one already introduced.

Announcing the Topic. Some topic sentences simply announce the topic. Here are a few examples taken from Barry Lopez's book *Arctic Dreams:*

> A polar bear walks in a way all its own.

> What is so consistently striking about the way Eskimos used parts of an animal is the breadth of their understanding about what would work.

> Distinctive landmarks that aid the traveler and control the vastness, as well as prominent marks on the land made inadvertently in the process of completing other tasks, are very much apparent in the Arctic.

> The Mediterranean view of the Arctic, down to the time of the Elizabethan mariners, was shaped by two somewhat contradictory thoughts.

These topic sentences do more than merely identify the topic; they also indicate how the topic will be developed in subsequent sentences—by citing examples, describing physical features, presenting reasons and evidence, relating anecdotes, classifying, defining, comparing, or contrasting.

The following paragraph shows how one of Lopez's topic sentences (underlined) is developed:

> <u>What is so consistently striking about the way Eskimos used parts of an animal is the breadth of their understanding about what would work.</u> Knowing that muskox horn is more flexible than caribou antler, they preferred it for making the side prongs of a fish spear. For a waterproof bag in which to carry sinews for clothing repair, they chose salmon skin. They selected the strong, translucent intestine of a bearded seal to make a window for a snowhouse—it would fold up for easy traveling and it would not frost over in cold weather. To make small snares for sea ducks, they needed a springy material that would not rot in salt water—baleen fibers. The down feather of a common eider, tethered at the end of a stick in the snow at an aglu, would reveal the exhalation of a quietly surfacing seal. Polar bear bone was used anywhere a stout, sharp point was required, because it is the hardest bone.
>
> —Barry Lopez, *Arctic Dreams*

Exercise 13.5

Read Adam Paul Weisman's essay in Chapter 7. Mark the paragraphs that begin with topic sentences. Then explain how these sentences help you to anticipate the paragraph's topic and method of development.

Forecasting Subtopics. Other topic sentences actually give readers a detailed overview of subtopics that follow. The paragraph featured here, though a bit dated, provides a nice example. The forecasting statement announces the subtopics in the opening sentence that appear later in the paragraph. To show this, we have underscored the subtopics in the first sentence and connected them by dotted lines to the point in the paragraph where they subsequently appear.

Notice that the subtopics are taken up in the same order as in the opening sentence: education first, followed by economic independence, power of office, and so on. This correlation makes the paragraph easy to follow. Even so, one subtopic may be developed in a single sentence while another requires two or more sentences. Notice also that the last two subtopics—equality of status and recognition as human beings—are not directly brought up but are implied in the final sentence.

> Oppressed groups are denied education, economic independence, the power of office, representation, an image of dignity and self-respect, equality of status, and recognition as human beings. Throughout history women have been consistently denied all of these, and their denial today, while attenuated and partial, is nevertheless consistent. The education allowed them is deliberately designed to be inferior, and they are systematically programmed out of and excluded from the knowledge where power lies today—e.g., in science and technology. They are confined to conditions of economic dependence based on the sale of their sexuality in marriage, or a variety of prostitutions. Work on a basis of economic independence allows them only a subsistence level of life—often not even that. They do not hold office, [they] are represented in no positions of power, and authority is forbidden them. The image of woman fostered by cultural media, high and low, then and now, is a marginal and demeaning existence, and one outside the human condition—which is defined as the prerogative of man, the male.
>
> —Kate Millett, *Sexual Politics*

Asking a Rhetorical Question. Occasionally, writers put topic sentences in a question-and-answer format, posing a rhetorical question in one sentence that is then answered in the next sentence. Question-and-answer topic sentences do not always appear at the beginning of a paragraph. A question at the end of one paragraph may combine with the answer in the first sentence of the following paragraph. Here is a paragraph illustrating the rhetorical question strategy:

> Why, then, do so many people believe in astrology? One obvious reason is that people read into the generally vague astrological pronouncements almost anything they want to, and thus invest them with a truth which is not inherent in the pronouncements themselves. They're also more likely to remember true "predictions," overvalue coincidences, and ignore everything else. Other reasons are its age (of course, ritual murder and sacrifice are as old), its simplicity in principle and comforting complexity in practice, and its flattering insistence on the connection between the starry vastness of the heavens and whether or not we'll fall in love this month.
>
> —John Allen Paulos, *Innumeracy: Mathematical Illiteracy and Its Consequences*

Exercise 13.6

Look at the selection by Anastasia Toufexis in Chapter 5 or the one by Mickey Kaus in Chapter 7. Where does the writer use the rhetorical question as a topic sentence strategy? How well does it work? Explain briefly.

Making a Transition. Not all topic sentences simply point forward to what will follow. Some also refer to earlier sentences. Such sentences work both as topic sentences, stating the main point of the paragraph, and as transitions, linking that paragraph to the previous one. Here are a few topic sentences from "Quilts and Women's Culture" by Elaine Hedges that use specific transitions (underscored) to tie the sentence to a previous statement:

> Within its broad traditionalism and anonymity, however, variations and distinctions developed.

> Regionally, too, distinctions were introduced into quilt making through the interesting process of renaming.

> With equal inventiveness women renamed traditional patterns to accommodate to the local landscape.

> Finally, out of such regional and other variations come individual, signed achievements.

> Quilts, then, were an outlet for creative energy, a source and emblem of sisterhood and solidarity, and a graphic response to historical and political change.

Sometimes the first sentence of a paragraph serves as a transition, and a subsequent sentence states the topic. The underscored sentences in the following example illustrate this strategy:

> . . . What a convenience, what a relief it will be, they say, never to worry about how to dress for a job interview, a romantic tryst, or a funeral!
>
> Convenient, perhaps, but not exactly a relief. Such a utopia would give most of us the same kind of chill we feel when a stadium full of Communist-bloc athletes in identical sports outfits, shouting slogans in unison, appears on TV. Most people do not want to be told what to wear any more than they want to be told what to say. In Belfast recently four hundred Irish Republican prisoners "refused to wear any clothes at all, draping themselves day and night in blankets," rather than put on prison uniforms. Even the offer of civilian-style dress did not satisfy them; they insisted on wearing their own clothes brought from home, or nothing. Fashion is free speech, and one of the privileges, if not always one of the pleasures, of a free world.
>
> —Alison Lurie, *The Language of Clothes*

Occasionally, whole paragraphs serve as transitions, linking one sequence of paragraphs with those that follow. This transition paragraph summarizes what went before (evidence of contrast) and sets up what will follow (evidence of similarity):

> Yet it was not all contrast, after all. Different as they were—in background, in personality, in underlying aspiration—these two great soldiers had much in common. Under everything else, they were marvelous fighters. Furthermore, their fighting qualities were really very much alike.
>
> —Bruce Catton, "Grant and Lee: A Study in Contrasts"

Positioning the Topic Sentence. Although topic sentences may occur anywhere in a paragraph, stating the topic in the first sentence has the advantage of giving readers a sense of how the paragraph is likely to be developed. The beginning of the paragraph is therefore the most common position for a topic sentence.

A topic sentence that does not open a paragraph is most likely to appear at the end. When a topic sentence concludes a paragraph, it usually summarizes or generalizes preceding information. In the following example, the topic is not stated explicitly until the last sentence.

> Even black Americans sometimes need to be reminded about the deceptiveness of television. Blacks retain their fascination with black characters on TV: Many of us buy *Jet* magazine primarily to read its weekly television feature, which lists *every* black character (major or minor) to be seen on the screen that week. Yet our fixation with the presence of black characters on TV has blinded us to an important fact that *Cosby,* which began in 1984, and its offshoots over the years demonstrate convincingly: There is very little connection between the social status of black Americans and the fabricated images of black people that Americans consume each day. The representation of blacks on TV is a very poor index to our social advancement or political progress.
>
> —Henry Louis Gates Jr., "TV's Black World Turns—but Stays Unreal"

When a topic sentence is used in a narrative, it often appears as the last sentence as a way to evaluate or reflect on events:

> I hadn't known she could play the piano. She wasn't playing very well, I guess, because she stopped occasionally and had to start over again. She concentrated intensely on the music, and the others in the room sat absolutely silently. My mother was facing me but didn't seem to see me. She seemed to be staring beyond me toward something that wasn't there. All the happy excitement died in me at that moment. Looking at my mother, so isolated from us all, I saw her for the first time as a person utterly alone.
>
> —Russell Baker, *Growing Up*

In rare cases, the topic sentence for one paragraph may appear at the end of the preceding paragraph, as in this example:

> . . . And apart from being new, psychoanalysis was particularly threatening.
>
> French psychiatrists tended to look at the sufferings of their patients either as the result of organic lesions or moral degeneration. In either case, the boundary between the "healthy" doctor and the "sick" patient was clear. Freud's theory makes it hard to draw such lines by insisting that if the psychiatrist knew himself better, he would find more points in common with the patient than he might have thought.
>
> —Sherry Turkle, *Psychoanalytic Politics*

In addition, it is possible for a single topic sentence to introduce two or more paragraphs. Subsequent paragraphs in such a series have no separate topic sentences of their own. Here is a two-paragraph sequence in which the topic sentence opens the first paragraph:

> Anthropologists Daniel Maltz and Ruth Borker point out that boys and girls socialize differently. Little girls tend to play in small groups or, even more common, in pairs. Their social life usually centers around a best friend, and friendships are made, maintained, and broken by talk—especially "secrets." If a little girl tells her friend's secret to another little girl, she may find herself with a new best friend. The secrets themselves may or may not be important, but the fact of telling them is all-important. It's hard for newcomers to get into these tight groups, but anyone who is admitted is treated as an equal. Girls like to play cooperatively; if they can't cooperate, the group breaks up.
>
> Little boys tend to play in larger groups, often outdoors, and they spend more time doing things than talking. It's easy for boys to get into the group, but not everyone is accepted as an equal. Once in the group, boys must jockey for their status in it. One of the most important ways they do this is through talk: verbal display such as telling stories and jokes, challenging and sidetracking the verbal displays of other boys, and withstanding other boys' challenges in order to maintain their own story—and status. Their talk is often competitive talk about who is best at what.
>
> —Deborah Tannen, *That's Not What I Meant!*

Exercise 13.7

Now that you have seen several topic sentence strategies, look again at the Gould passage earlier in this chapter and identify the strategies he uses. Then evaluate how well his topic sentences work to orient you as a reader.

COHESIVE DEVICES

Cohesive devices guide readers, helping them to follow your train of thought by connecting key words and phrases throughout a passage. Among such devices are pronoun reference, word repetition, synonyms, repetition of sentence structure, and collocation.

Pronoun Reference

One common cohesive device is pronoun reference. As noun substitutes, pronouns refer to nouns that either precede or follow them and thus serve to connect phrases or sentences. The nouns that come before the pronouns are called *antecedents.* In the following paragraph, the pronouns (*it* or *its*) form a chain of connection with their antecedent, *George Washington Bridge.*

> In New York from dawn to dusk to dawn, day after day, you can hear the steady rumble of tires against the concrete span of the George Washington Bridge. The bridge is never completely still. It trembles with traffic. It moves in the wind. Its great veins of steel swell when hot and contract when cold; its span often is ten feet closer to the Hudson River in summer than in winter.
>
> —Gay Talese, "New York"

This example has only one pronoun-antecedent chain, and the antecedent comes first, so all the pronouns refer back to it. When there are multiple pronoun-antecedent chains with references forward as well as back, writers have to make sure that readers will not mistake one pronoun's antecedent for another's.

Word Repetition

To avoid confusion, writers often repeat words and phrases. This device is used especially if a pronoun might confuse readers:

> The first step is to realize that in our society we have permitted the kinds of vulnerability that characterize the victims of violent crime and have ignored, where we could, the hostility and alienation that enter into the making of violent criminals. No rational person condones violent crime, and I have no patience with sentimental attitudes toward violent criminals. But it is time that we open our eyes to the conditions that foster violence and that ensure the existence of easily recognizable victims.
>
> —Margaret Mead, "A Life for a Life: What That Means Today"

In the next example, several overlapping chains of word repetition prevent confusion and help the reader to follow the ideas:

> Natural selection is the central concept of Darwinian theory—the fittest survive and spread their favored traits through populations. Natural selection is defined by Spencer's phrase "survival of the fittest," but what does this famous bit of jargon really mean? Who are the fittest? And how is "fitness" defined? We often read that fitness involves no more than "differential reproductive success"—the production of more surviving offspring than other competing members of the population. Whoa! cries Bethell, as many others have before him. This formulation defines fitness in terms of survival only. The crucial phrase of natural selection means no more than "the survival of those who survive"—a vacuous tautology. (A tautology is a phrase—like "my father is a man"—containing no information in the predicate ["a man"] not inherent in the subject ["my father"]. Tautologies are fine as definitions, but not as testable scientific statements—there can be nothing to test in a statement true by definition.)
>
> —Stephen Jay Gould, *Ever Since Darwin*

Notice that Gould uses repetition to keep readers focused on the key concepts of "natural selection," "survival of the fittest," and "tautology." These key terms may vary in form—*fittest* becomes *fitness,* and *survival* changes to *surviving* and *survive*—but they serve as links in the chain of meaning.

Synonyms

In addition to word repetition, you can use *synonyms,* words with identical or very similar meanings, to connect important ideas. In the following example, the author develops a careful chain of synonyms and word repetitions:

> Over time, small bits of knowledge about a region accumulate among local residents in the form of stories. These are remembered in the community; even what is unusual does not become lost and therefore irrelevant. These narratives comprise for a native an intricate, long-term view of a particular landscape. . . . Outside the

> region this complex but easily shared "reality" is hard to get across without reducing it to generalities, to misleading or imprecise abstraction.
>
> —Barry Lopez, *Arctic Dreams*

Note the variety of synonym sequences: "region," "particular landscape"; "local residents," "community," "native"; "stories," "narratives"; "accumulate," "remembered," "does not become lost," "comprise"; "intricate, long-term view," "complex . . . reality," "without reducing it to generalities." The result is a coherent paragraph that constantly reinforces the author's point.

Sentence Structure Repetition

Writers occasionally repeat the same sentence structure to emphasize the connections among their ideas, as in this example:

> But the life forms are as much part of the structure of the Earth as any inanimate portion is. It is all an inseparable part of a whole. If any animal is isolated totally from other forms of life, then death by starvation will surely follow. If isolated from water, death by dehydration will follow even faster. If isolated from air, whether free or dissolved in water, death by asphyxiation will follow still faster. If isolated from the Sun, animals will survive for a time, but plants would die, and if all plants died, all animals would starve.
>
> —Isaac Asimov, "The Case against Man"

From the third sentence to the last, Asimov repeats the "If this . . . then that" sentence structure to emphasize his various points.

Collocation

Words collocate when they occur together in expected ways around a particular topic. For example, in a paragraph on a high school graduation, a reader might expect to encounter such words as *valedictorian, diploma, commencement, honors, cap and gown,* and *senior class.* Collocations occur quite naturally to a writer, and they usually form a recognizable network of meaning for readers. The paragraph that follows uses five collocation chains:

1. housewife, cooking, neighbor, home
2. clocks, calculated cooking times, progression, precise
3. obstinacy, vagaries, problem
4. sun, clear days, cloudy ones, sundial, cast its light, angle, seasons, sun, weather
5. cooking, fire, matches, hot coals, smoldering, ashes, go out, bed-warming pan

> The seventeenth-century housewife not only had to make do without thermometers, she also had to make do without clocks, which were scarce and dear throughout the sixteen hundreds. She calculated cooking times by the progression of the sun; her cooking must have been more precise on clear days than on cloudy ones. Marks were sometimes painted on the floor, providing her with a rough sundial, but she still had to make allowance for the obstinacy of the sun in refusing to cast its light

at the same angle as the seasons changed; but she was used to allowing for the vagaries of sun and weather. She also had a problem starting her fire in the morning; there were no matches. If she had allowed the hot coals smoldering under the ashes to go out, she had to borrow some from a neighbor, carrying them home with care, perhaps in a bed-warming pan.

—Waverly Root and Richard de Rouchement, *Eating in America*

Exercise 13.8

Now that you know more about pronoun reference, word repetition, synonyms, sentence structure repetition, and collocation, look again at the Gould passage on pp. 467–68, and identify the cohesive devices you find in it. How do these cohesive devices help you to read and make sense of the passage?

TRANSITIONS

A *transition*, sometimes called a *connective*, serves as a bridge, connecting one paragraph, sentence, clause, or word with another. Not only does a transition signal a connection, but it also identifies the kind of connection by indicating to readers how the item preceding the transition relates to the one that follows it. Transitions help readers to anticipate how the next paragraph or sentence will affect the meaning of what they have just read. There are three basic groups of transitions, based on the relationships they indicate: logical, temporal, and spatial.

Logical Relationships

Transitions help readers to follow the logic of an argument. How such transitions work is illustrated in this tightly and passionately reasoned paragraph by James Baldwin:

> The black man insists, by whatever means he finds at his disposal, that the white man cease to regard him as an exotic rarity <u>and</u> recognize him as a human being. This is a very charged and difficult moment, <u>for</u> there is a great deal of will power involved in the white man's naivete. Most people are not naturally malicious, <u>and</u> the white man prefers to keep the black man at a certain human remove <u>because</u> it is easier for him <u>thus</u> to preserve his simplicity <u>and</u> to avoid being called to account for crimes committed by his forefathers, <u>or</u> his neighbors. He is inescapably aware, <u>nevertheless</u>, that he is in a better position in the world than black men are, <u>nor</u> can he quite put to death the suspicion that he is hated by black men <u>therefore</u>. He does not wish to be hated, <u>neither</u> does he wish to change places, <u>and</u> at this point in his uneasiness he can scarcely avoid having recourse to those legends which white men have created about black men, the most unusual effect of which is that the white man finds himself enmeshed, so to speak, in his own language which describes hell, <u>as well as</u> the attributes which lead one to hell, <u>as being</u> black as night.
>
> —James Baldwin, "Stranger in the Village"

Transitions Showing Logical Relationships

- *To introduce another item in a series:* first, second; in the second place; for one thing . . . , for another; next; then; furthermore; moreover; in addition; finally; last; also; similarly; besides; and; as well as
- *To introduce an illustration or other specification:* in particular; specifically; for instance; for example; that is; namely
- *To introduce a result or a cause:* consequently; as a result, hence; accordingly; thus; so; therefore; then; because; since; for
- *To introduce a restatement:* that is; in other words; in simpler terms; to put it differently
- *To introduce a conclusion or summary:* in conclusion; finally; all in all; evidently; clearly; actually; to sum up; altogether; of course
- *To introduce an opposing point:* but; however; yet; nevertheless; on the contrary; on the other hand; in contrast; still; neither; nor
- *To introduce a concession to an opposing view:* certainly; naturally; of course; it is true; to be sure; granted
- *To resume the original line of reasoning after a concession:* nonetheless; all the same; even though; still; nevertheless

Temporal Relationships

In addition to showing logical connections, transitions may indicate temporal relationships—a sequence or progression in time—as this example illustrates:

> That night, we drank tea and then vodka with lemon peel steeped in it. The four of us talked in Russian and English about mutual friends and American railroads and the Rolling Stones. Seryozha loves the Stones, and his face grew wistful as we spoke about their recent album, "Some Girls." He played a tape of "Let It Bleed" over and over, until we could translate some difficult phrases for him; after that, he came out with the phrases at intervals during the evening, in a pretty decent imitation of Jagger's Cockney snarl. He was an adroit and oddly formal host, inconspicuously filling our teacups and politely urging us to eat bread and cheese and chocolate. While he talked to us, he teased Anya, calling her "Piglet," and she shook back her bangs and glowered at him. It was clear that theirs was a fiery relationship. After a while, we talked about ourselves. Anya told us about painting and printmaking and about how hard it was to buy supplies in Moscow. There had been something angry in her dark face since the beginning of the evening; I thought at first that it meant she didn't like Americans; but now I realized that it was a constant, barely suppressed rage at her own situation.
>
> —Andrea Lee, *Russian Journal*

Transitions Showing Temporal Relationships

- *To indicate frequency:* frequently; hourly; often; occasionally; now and then; day after day; again and again
- *To indicate duration:* during; briefly; for a long time; minute by minute

- *To indicate a particular time:* now; then; at that time; in those days; last Sunday; next Christmas; in 1997; at the beginning of August; at six o'clock; first thing in the morning; two months ago
- *To indicate the beginning:* at first; in the beginning; since; before then
- *To indicate the middle:* in the meantime; meanwhile; as it was happening; at that moment; at the same time; simultaneously; next; then
- *To indicate the end and beyond:* eventually; finally; at last; in the end; subsequently; later; afterward

Spatial Relationships

Spatial transitions orient readers to the objects in a scene, as illustrated in this paragraph:

> On Georgia 155, I crossed Troublesome Creek, then went through groves of pecan trees aligned one with the next like fenceposts. The pastures grew a green almost blue, and syrupy water the color of a dusty sunset filled the ponds. Around the farmhouses, from wires strung high above the ground, swayed gourds hollowed out for purple martins.
>
> The land rose again on the other side of the Chattahoochee River, and Highway 34 went to the ridgetops where long views over the hills opened in all directions. Here was the tail of the Appalachian backbone, its gradual descent to the Gulf. Near the Alabama stateline stood a couple of LAST CHANCE! bars. . . .
>
> —William Least Heat Moon, *Blue Highways*

Transitions Showing Spatial Relationships

- *To indicate closeness:* close to; near; next to; alongside; adjacent to; facing
- *To indicate distance:* in the distance; far; beyond; away; there
- *To indicate direction:* up/down; sideways; along; across; to the right/left; in front of/behind; above/below; inside/outside; toward/away from

Exercise 13.9

Return to the Gould passage on p. 467–68, and underline the logical, temporal, and spatial transitions. How do they help to relate the many details and ideas?

Narrating

Narration is a basic writing strategy for presenting action. You can use narration for a variety of purposes: to illustrate and support ideas with anecdotes, to entertain readers with suspenseful or revealing stories, to analyze causes and possible effects with scenarios, and to explain procedures with process narrative. This chapter focuses on narrative techniques—how to sequence narrative action, shape narrative structure, and present the narrative from various points of view. Finally, it looks at one special narrative form, how to present a process.

SEQUENCING NARRATIVE ACTION

Narration presents a sequence of actions taking place over a period of time. The most common way of ordering a narrative is to present the actions chronologically, beginning with the first action and going straight through to the last.

On occasion, however, writers complicate the narrative sequence by referring to an event that occurred earlier, in a *flashback*, or to one that will occur later, in a *flashforward*.

The following excerpt from "Death of a Pig," an essay by E. B. White, shows how writers typically organize narratives chronologically. The essay from which the passage is taken tells us what happened when the pig White was raising became ill and died. In the pages that follow, this passage is referred to often to illustrate the ways in which writers control readers' sense of passing time in a narrative and shape actions into meaningful stories.

> It was about four o'clock in the afternoon when I first noticed that there was something wrong with the pig. He failed to appear at the trough for his supper, and when a pig (or a child) refuses supper a chill wave of fear runs through any household, or ice-household. After examining my pig, who was stretched out in the sawdust inside the building, I went to the phone and cranked it four times. Mr. Dameron answered. "What's good for a sick pig?" I asked. (There is never any identification needed on a country phone; the person on the other end knows who is talking by the sound of the voice and by the character of the question.)
>
> "I don't know, I never had a sick pig," said Mr. Dameron, "but I can find out quick enough. You hang up and I'll call Henry."

Mr. Dameron was back on the line again in five minutes. "Henry says roll him over on his back and give him two ounces of castor oil or sweet oil, and if that doesn't do the trick give him an injection of soapy water. He says he's almost sure the pig's plugged up, and even if he's wrong, it can't do any harm."

I thanked Mr. Dameron. I didn't go right down to the pig, though. I sank into a chair and sat still for a few minutes to think about my troubles, and then I got up and went to the barn, catching up on some odds and ends that needed tending to. Unconsciously I held off, for an hour, the deed by which I would officially recognize the collapse of the performance of raising a pig; I wanted no interruption in the regularity of feeding, the steadiness of growth, the even succession of days. I wanted no interruption, wanted no oil, no deviation. I just wanted to keep on raising a pig, full meal after full meal, spring into summer into fall. I didn't even know whether there were two ounces of castor oil on the place.

Shortly after five o'clock I remembered that we had been invited out to dinner that night and realized that if I were to dose a pig there was no time to lose. The dinner date seemed a familiar conflict: I move in a desultory society and often a week or two will roll by without my going to anybody's house to dinner or anyone's coming to mine, but when an occasion does arise, and I am summoned, something usually turns up (an hour or two in advance) to make all human intercourse seem vastly inappropriate. I have come to believe that there is in hostesses a special power of divination, and that they deliberately arrange dinners to coincide with pig failure or some other sort of failure. At any rate, it was after five o'clock and I knew I could put off no longer the evil hour.

When my son and I arrived at the pigyard, armed with a small bottle of castor oil and a length of clothesline, the pig had emerged from his house and was standing in the middle of his yard, listlessly. He gave us a slim greeting. I could see that he felt uncomfortable and uncertain. I had brought the clothesline thinking I'd have to tie him (the pig weighed more than a hundred pounds) but we never used it. My son reached down, grabbed both front legs, upset him quickly, and when he opened his mouth to scream I turned the oil into his throat—a pink, corrugated area I had never seen before. I had just time to read the label while the neck of the bottle was in his mouth. It said Puretest. The screams, slightly muffled by oil, were pitched in the hysterically high range of pig-sound, as though torture were being carried out, but they didn't last long; it was all over rather suddenly, and, his legs released, the pig righted himself.

—E. B. White, "Death of a Pig"

Exercise 14.1

Write a one-page narrative about something memorable you did that lasted a few hours. You might recall a race you ran in, an unusual activity you participated in, or an adventure in a strange place. Reflect on what you did, listing the events in the order in which they occurred. In your narrative, follow the chronological sequence set out in your list.

Narrative Time Signals

To sequence actions for their readers, writers rely on three methods: time markers, verb tense markers, and references to calendar or clock time.

Time Markers. A common way of showing the passage of time is with temporal transitions, words and phrases that locate an action at a particular point in time or that relate one point to another. Some familiar time markers are *then, when, at that time, before, after, while, next, later, first,* and *second.* Look back at the passage from "Death of a Pig" to see how White uses time markers. Notice, for example, that he uses *when* in the first sentence to indicate the initial point at which he recognized something was seriously wrong. *After* in the third sentence signals the relationship between two actions, examining the pig and calling for advice.

Time markers are particularly crucial when a writer is explaining procedures to be followed or analyzing the steps in a complicated process, as you can see in this passage from an explanatory essay about the predatory relationship between wasps and tarantulas.

> When the grave is finished, the wasp returns to the tarantula to complete her ghastly enterprise. First, she feels it all over once more with her antennae. Then her behavior becomes more aggressive. She bends her abdomen, protruding her sting, and searches for the soft membrane at the point where the spider's legs join its body—the only spot where she can penetrate the horny skeleton. From time to time, as the exasperated spider slowly shifts ground, the wasp turns on her back and slides with the aid of her wings, trying to get under the tarantula for a shot at the vital spot. During all this maneuvering, which can last for several minutes, the tarantula makes no move to save itself. Finally the wasp corners it against some obstruction and grasps one of its legs in her powerful jaws. Now at last the harassed spider tries a desperate but vain defense. The two contestants roll over and over on the ground. It is a terrifying sight and the outcome is always the same.
>
> —Alexander Petrunkevitch, "The Spider and the Wasp"

Exercise 14.2

Skim the White passage on pp. 481–82, underlining all the time markers. In each case, consider whether you would find the narrative harder to understand if the time marker had been left out.

Verb Tense Markers. Writers also rely on verb tense when they are presenting time in narrative. Tense indicates when the actions occur and whether they are complete or in progress. White, for example, sets most of his narrative in the simple past tense, deviating only when he reports actions occurring simultaneously: "When my son and I arrived at the pigyard, . . . the pig had emerged from his house and was standing in the middle of his yard" (p. 482). To convey the time relations among these actions, he uses three forms of the past tense in one sentence: *simple past,* to indicate a completed action: "my son and I arrived"; *past perfect,* to indicate that the action occurred before another action: "the pig had emerged"; *past progressive,* to indicate an ongoing action that had been in progress for some time: the pig "was standing."

Note that in addition to these past-tense forms, White also uses the present tense to distinguish habitual, continually occurring, actions: "When a pig (or a child) refuses supper a chill wave of fear runs through any household" (p. 481). In fact, whole narratives may be written primarily in the present tense. Process narratives, for example, are generally written in the present, as illustrated by the excerpt from

The pieces by Catherine Manegold and David Noonan in Chapter 4 are good examples of this use of the present tense.

"The Spider and the Wasp." In addition, contemporary writers of profiles often use the present tense to give their writing a sense of "you are there" immediacy.

Writers can use verb tense and temporal transitions in various ways to distinguish actions that occurred repeatedly from those that occurred only once. In the following passage, for example, Willie Morris uses the tense marker *would* along with the time markers *many times* and *often* to indicate recurring actions. When he moves from action that occurred repeatedly to action that occurred only once, he shifts to the simple past tense, signaling this shift with the phrase *on one occasion*.

> Many times, walking home from work, I would see some unknowing soul venture across that intersection against the light and then freeze in horror when he saw the cars ripping out of the tunnel toward him. . . . Suddenly, the human reflex would take over, and the pedestrian would jackknife first one way, then another, arms flaying the empty air, and often the car would literally skim the man, brushing by him so close it would touch his coat or his tie. . . . On one occasion, feeling sorry for the person who had brushed against the speeding car, I hurried across the intersection after him to cheer him up a little. Catching up with him down by 32nd I said, "That was good legwork, sir. Excellent moves for a big man!" but the man looked at me with an empty expression in his eyes, and then moved away mechanically and trancelike, heading for the nearest bar.
>
> —Willie Morris, *North toward Home*

Calendar and Clock Time. Most writers use calendar and clock time sparingly to signal the passage of time in a narrative, but it is a valuable device. White uses clock time to orient readers and to give a sense of duration. He tells us that the action lasted a little over an hour, beginning at about four o'clock and ending a little after five. He indicates that he called Mr. Dameron as soon as he had assessed the situation and then had to wait five minutes for him to call back. More important, he makes it clear that once he learned what to do, he spent most of the hour avoiding the task.

In the following brief example, clock time serves the writer's purpose by making readers aware of the speed with which actions were taken.

> 9:05 P.M. An ambulance backs into the receiving bay, its red and yellow lights flashing in and out of the lobby. A split second later, the glass doors burst open as a nurse and an attendant roll a mobile stretcher into the lobby. When the nurse screams, "Emergent!" the lobby explodes with activity as the way is cleared to the trauma room. Doctors appear from nowhere and transfer the bloodied body of a black man to the treatment table. Within seconds his clothes are stripped away.
>
> —George Simpson, "The War Room at Bellevue"

Exercise 14.3

Read any of the essays in Chapter 2 to see how the writer signals the passage of time in the narration. How many time markers, verb tense markers, and references to calendar and clock time do you find? Identify any places where a signal should be added and any places where it seems unnecessary. What can you conclude from analyzing this particular essay about the importance of signaling in narrative?

Exercise 14.4

Look back at the narrative you wrote for Exercise 14.1. Did you use time markers, verb tense markers, or clock time? If you did, explain what they added. If you did not, how would your writing be improved if you added some? Which ones would you add, and where? Explain why you would add these particular transitions at these places.

SHAPING NARRATIVE STRUCTURE

In addition to clearly sequencing the action, writers of effective narrative create a structure to give their stories interest and focus. They shape the narrative around a central conflict, building suspense by manipulating the narrative pace.

Conflict and Suspense

The basic device writers use to turn a sequence of actions into a story is *conflict.* Conflict adds the question "So what?" to "What happened next?" It provides motivation and purpose for the characters' actions. In this way, conflict gives narrative its dramatic structure.

The conflict in most narrative takes the form of a struggle between the main character and an opposing force. This force may take many forms—another person or creature, nature, society's rules and values, or internal characteristics such as conflicting values or desires.

Conflict focuses the action. Instead of the simple "and then . . . and then . . . and then" structure of a timeline, conflict provides a "one thing leads to another" structure. Narratives with conflict also have suspense. Suspense seduces readers by heightening their desire to find out what will happen, how the conflict will be resolved. Readers look forward with anticipation or trepidation to the climax, the highest point of tension where the conflict is most focused and explicit.

We can see these concepts illustrated in the excerpt from "Death of a Pig." The opposing forces seem to be the man and the pig, but the conflict is really more elemental—between health and illness or life and death. We see the conflict as an internal drama within the narrator himself, who initially resists acknowledging that the routine of his life—not to mention the pig's—has been disrupted. Suspense grows as he begins to face reality and consider what he can do to save the pig. The climax of the story occurs when the narrator finally takes action, but his efforts to forestall the inevitable are hopeless and the pig dies, resolving the conflict.

Exercise 14.5

Look back at the essay you read for Exercise 14.3, and try to identify its conflict and its climax. At what points do you feel the tension grow? When do you have a sense of anticipation or suspense? How do these feelings affect your enjoyment of the story?

Narrative Pace

Although you may place actions in the context of clock time, few writers really try to reproduce time as it is measured by clocks. Clock time moves at a uniform rate. If every action were emphasized equally, readers would be unable to distinguish the importance of particular actions. Such a narrative would be monotonous and unnatural.

Pacing techniques allow writers to represent the passage of narrative time. You can pace narratives by emphasizing more important actions and deemphasizing less important ones. To emphasize a sequence of action, you can heighten tension, thus making the action last longer or seem more intense. Common techniques for increasing suspense are to concentrate on specific narrative action and to present action through dialogue.

Specific Narrative Action. The writer George Plimpton participated in the Detroit Lions football training camp in order to write a book about professional football. In this passage from his book, Plimpton tells what happened when he had his big chance in a practice scrimmage.

> Since in the two preceding plays the concentration of the play had been elsewhere, I had felt alone with the flanker. Now, the whole heave of the play was toward me, flooding the zone not only with confused motion but noise—the quick stomp of feet, the creak of football gear, the strained grunts of effort, the faint *ah-ah-ah,* of piston-stroke regularity, and the stiff calls of instruction, like exhalations. "Inside, inside! Take him inside!" someone shouted, tearing by me, his cleats thumping in the grass. A call—a parrot squawk—may have erupted from me. My feet splayed in hopeless confusion as Barr came directly toward me, feinting in one direction, and then stopping suddenly, drawing me toward him for the possibility of a buttonhook pass, and as I leaned almost off balance toward him, he turned and came on again, downfield, moving past me at high speed, leaving me poised on one leg, reaching for him, trying to grab at him despite the illegality, anything to keep him from getting by. But he was gone, and by the time I had turned to set out after him, he had ten yards on me, drawing away fast with his sprinter's run, his legs pinwheeling, the row of cleats flicking up a faint wake of dust behind.
>
> —George Plimpton, *Paper Lion*

Although the action lasted only a few moments, Plimpton gives a close-up of it. He focuses on what we are calling *specific narrative action*—specific and concrete movements, gestures, and activities. Instead of writing "Someone ran by me shouting," he writes:

> "Inside, inside! Take him inside!" someone shouted, tearing by me, his cleats thumping in the grass.

The underlined verbs and verb phrases identify a player's specific actions: shouting, tearing by, thumping his cleats. In the long fifth sentence Plimpton gives us another series of specific narrative actions: "feet splayed," "came directly toward me," "feinting in one direction," "stopping suddenly," "drawing me toward him," "leaned almost off balance," "turned and came on again," and then "moving," "leaving," "reaching," and "trying" in quick succession. The specific actions slow the narrative pace and heighten the tension. In addition, because they are concrete, they enable us to visualize what is happening.

Exercise 14.6

Look at the selection by Maya Angelou in Chapter 3. Note particularly what happens in paragraph 18. How does Angelou's use of specific narrative action here contribute to the overall effectiveness of the selection?

Exercise 14.7

Look back at the narrative you wrote for Exercise 14.1. How effectively have you used specific narrative action to pace your narrative and make it concrete? Revise a sentence or a series of sentences, emphasizing a particular part of your narrative by adding specific narrative action. Then, compare the two versions, analyzing the different effects of pacing.

Dialogue. Writers use dialogue to reveal conflict directly, without the narrator's intruding commentary. Dialogue is not a mere record of conversation; it is a carefully crafted representation of conversation. Dialogue gives readers insight into the personality and motives of the characters.

Richard Wright uses dialogue to show what happens when a white man confronts a black delivery boy. Notice that the dialogue does not have the free give-and-take of conversation. Instead, it is a series of questions that get evasive answers: "he said," "I lied," "he asked me," "I lied." The dialogue is tense, revealing the extent of the boy's fear and defensiveness.

> I was hungry and he knew it; but he was a white man and I felt that if I told him I was hungry I would have been revealing something shameful.
>
> "Boy, I can see hunger in your face and eyes," he said.
>
> "I get enough to eat," I lied.
>
> "Then why do you keep so thin?" he asked me.
>
> "Well, I suppose I'm just that way, naturally," I lied.
>
> "You're just scared, boy," he said.
>
> "Oh, no, sir," I lied again.
>
> I could not look at him. I wanted to leave the counter, yet he was a white man and I had learned not to walk abruptly away from a white man when he was talking to me. I stood, my eyes looking away. He ran his hand into his pocket and pulled out a dollar bill.
>
> "Here, take this dollar and buy yourself some food," he said.
>
> "No, sir," I said.
>
> "Don't be a fool," he said. "You're ashamed to take it. God, boy, don't let a thing like that stop you from taking a dollar and eating."
>
> The more he talked the more it became impossible for me to take the dollar. I wanted it, but I could not look at it. I wanted to speak, but I could not move my tongue. I wanted him to leave me alone. He frightened me.
>
> "Say something," he said.
>
> —Richard Wright, *Black Boy*

Wright does not try to communicate everything through dialogue. He intersperses information that supports the dialogue—description, reports of the boy's thoughts and feelings, some movement—to help readers understand the unfolding drama.

You can also use dialogue to reveal a person's character and show the dynamics of interpersonal relationships. Notice the way Lillian Hellman uses dialogue to write about a longtime friend, Arthur Cowan:

> Cowan said, "What's the matter with you? You haven't said a word for an hour." I said nothing was the matter, not wishing to hear his lecture about what was. After an hour of nagging, by the repetition of "Spit it out," "Spit it out," I told him about a German who had fought in the International Brigade in the Spanish Civil War, been badly wounded, and was now very ill in Paris without any money and that I had sent some, but not enough.
>
> Arthur screamed, "Since when do you have enough money to send anybody a can to piss in? Hereafter, I handle all your money and you send nobody anything. And a man who fought in Spain has to be an ass Commie and should take his punishment."
>
> I said, "Oh shut up, Arthur."
>
> And he did, but that night as he paid the dinner check, he wrote out another check and handed it to me. It was for a thousand dollars.
>
> I said, "What's this for?"
>
> "Anybody you want."
>
> I handed it back.
>
> He said, "Oh, for Christ sake take it and tell yourself it's for putting up with me."
>
> "Then it's not enough money."
>
> He laughed. "I like you sometimes. Give it to the stinking German and don't say where it comes from because no man wants money from a stranger."
>
> —Lillian Hellman, *Pentimento*

Hellman's dialogue is realistic, showing the way people talk to one another, the rhythms of interactive speech and its silences. But the dialogue does something more: It gives readers real insight into the way Hellman and Cowan were with each other, their conflicts and their shared understanding. Such dialogue allows readers to listen in on private conversations.

In the passage, Hellman not only uses quotes but also an alternative method of presenting dialogue, summarizing. In summarizing, writers choose their own words instead of quoting actual words used; this method allows them to condense dialogue as well as to emphasize what they wish. When Hellman writes, "I told him about a German . . . ," she is summarizing her actual spoken words.

Exercise 14.8

Read Gerald Haslam's essay about his great-grandmother in Chapter 3, paying attention to his use of dialogue. What does the dialogue reveal about the great-grandmother's character and about the boy's relationship with her?

Exercise 14.9

Write several paragraphs of narrative, including some dialogue, about an incident that occurred between you and someone you feel close to or know well—a friend, a relative, an enemy, a boss. Try to compose a dialogue that conveys the quality of your relationship.

Read over your dialogue, and reflect on the impression it gives. In a sentence or two, state what you think the dialogue reveals about your relationship with this person.

TAKING A POINT OF VIEW

In narrative writing, point of view refers to the narrator's relationship to the action as a participant (first-person point of view) or as an observer (third-person).

First person is used to narrate action in which the writer participated. For instance, when Piri Thomas writes, "Big-mouth came at me and we grabbed each other and pushed and pulled and shoved," he is using the first-person point of view. Third person is used to narrate action performed by people other than the narrator. When Paul Theroux writes, "The Suns fought for it. One man gained possession, but he was pounced upon and the ball shot up and ten Suns went tumbling after it," he is using the third-person point of view. Because they are telling about their own experiences, autobiographers typically write first-person narrative, using the first-person pronouns *I* and *we*, as Piri Thomas does. When writers tell another person's story, as in biography, they use the third-person pronouns *he*, *she*, and *they* instead of the first-person *I* or *we*.

Of course, first-person narrators may observe and report on the actions of others, using a third-person point of view, when the writer is neither participating in the action nor introducing personal thoughts or feelings. Similarly, a third-person narrative may occasionally interject personal thoughts or feelings. For example, rather than saying, "Many people think San Francisco is a great city" or simply asserting, "San Francisco is a great city," the writer might make explicit his or her point of view by saying, "I think San Francisco is a great city."

Exercise 14.10

Compare the profiles in Chapter 4 written by David Noonan and Brian Cable, noting particularly each writer's point of view, first-person or third-person. Take a paragraph from each profile and rewrite it, using the other point of view. In each case, what is the effect of the change of point of view?

Exercise 14.11

Write about a brief incident involving you and one other person from your own (first-person) point of view. Then, write about the incident from the third-person point of view, as though another person is telling it. What impact does a change in point of view have on your story?

PRESENTING A PROCESS

Process narrative typically explains how something is done or how to do it. For example, in *Oranges,* a book about the Florida citrus industry, John McPhee tells how the technical operation of bud grafting is done. He is not writing directions for readers to follow. If he were, his narrative would be much more detailed and precise. Instead, he tells us as much as he thinks nonspecialists need or want to know.

> One of Adams' men was putting Hamlin buds on Rough Lemon stock the day I was there. He began by slicing a bud from a twig that had come from a registered budwood tree—of which there are forty-five thousand in groves around Florida, each

> certified under a state program to be free from serious virus disease and to be a true strain of whatever type of orange, grapefruit, or tangerine it happens to be. Each bud he removed was about an inch long and looked like a little submarine, the conning tower being the eye of the bud, out of which would come the shoot that would develop into the upper trunk and branches of the ultimate tree. A few inches above the ground, he cut a short vertical slit in the bark of a Rough Lemon liner; then he cut a transverse slit at the base of the vertical one, and, lifting the flaps of the wound, set the bud inside. The area was bandaged with plastic tape. In a couple of weeks, Adams said, the new shoot would be starting out of the bud and the tape would be taken off. To force the growth of the new shoot, a large area of the bark of the Rough Lemon would be shaved off above the bud union. Two months after that, the upper trunk, branches, and leaves of the young Rough Lemon tree would be cut off altogether, leaving only a three-inch stub coming out of the earth, thick as a cigar, with a small shoot and a leaf or two of the Hamlin flippantly protruding near the top.
>
> —John McPhee, *Oranges*

In contrast to the McPhee example, the following process narrative provides both information and directions. This selection comes from an article written for the *American Journal of Physiology.* Notice all the precise detail, technical terminology, and careful, step-by-step narrating. Because objectivity is important to such writing, the writers use the passive voice.

> Ten 20- to 25-kg male baboons *(Papio anubis)* were tranquilized with ketamine, 10 mg/kg, intubated, mechanically ventilated, and anesthetized with halothane, 1.5 vol%. Instrumentation was implanted through a thoracotomy in the fifth left intercostal space. A miniature pressure transducer (Konigsberg P22, Konigsberg Instruments, Pasadena, CA) was implanted in the left ventricle through a stab wound in the apex, and a pair of ultrasonic transducers was implanted on opposing endocardial surfaces of the left ventricle. Tygon catheters were implanted in the left atrium and aorta. The transducer wires and catheters were run subcutaneously and buried in the interscapular area.
>
> —Steven F. Vatner and Michael Zimpfer, "Brainbridge Reflex in Conscious, Unrestrained, and Tranquilized Baboons"

Exercise 14.12

Read the selection by Brian Cable in Chapter 4 carefully, noting the way the author tells about the funeral home's process of dealing with a "client." Why do you think Cable includes this process narrative in his essay? Write a few sentences explaining Cable's purpose.

Exercise 14.13

Write a simple process narrative, explaining how to do something—make a sandwich, build a doghouse, write a poem, perform a scientific experiment, perform a simple procedure on your job, fly a kite. Address your narrative to someone who knows nothing about performing the task you are telling about.

Describing

The most effective description creates some dominant impression, a mood or an atmosphere that reinforces the writer's purpose. Writers often attempt to create a dominant impression—for example, when they describe a place in order to set a scene and make readers aware of its atmosphere. Naming, detailing, and comparing—all the choices about what to include and what to call things—come together to create this effect, as the following passage by Mary McCarthy illustrates. Notice that McCarthy directly states the idea she is trying to convey in the last sentence of the paragraph.

> Whenever we children came to stay at my grandmother's house, we were put to sleep in the sewing room, a bleak, shabby, utilitarian rectangle, more office than bedroom, more attic than office, that played to the hierarchy of chambers the role of a poor relation. It was a room seldom entered by the other members of the family, seldom swept by the maid, a room without pride; the old sewing machine, some cast-off chairs, a shadeless lamp, rolls of wrapping paper, piles of pins, and remnants of material united with the iron folding cots put out for our use and the bare floor boards to give an impression of intense and ruthless temporality. Thin, white spreads, of the kind used in hospitals and charity institutions, and naked blinds at the windows reminded us of our orphaned condition and of the ephemeral character of our visit; there was nothing here to encourage us to consider this our home.
>
> —Mary McCarthy, *Memories of a Catholic Girlhood*

Everything in the room made McCarthy and her brothers feel unwanted, discarded, orphaned. The room itself is described in terms applicable to the children. (Like them, it "played to the hierarchy of chambers the role of a poor relation.") The objects she names, together with their distinguishing details—"cast-off chairs," "shadeless lamp," "iron folding cots," "bare floor boards," "naked blinds"—contribute to this overall impression, thus enabling McCarthy to convey her purpose to her readers.

Sometimes writers comment directly in a description. McCarthy, for instance, states that the sewing room gave "an impression of intense and ruthless temporality," everything serving to remind the children that they were orphans and did not live there. Often, however, writers want description to speak for itself. They *show* rather than tell, letting the descriptive language evoke the impression by itself. Such is the case in the following description by George Orwell of a room for hire:

> Hanging from the ceiling there was a heavy glass chandelier on which the dust was so thick that it was like fur. And covering most of one wall there was a huge hideous piece of junk, something between a sideboard and a hall-stand, with lots of carving and little drawers and strips of looking-glass, and there was a once-gaudy carpet ringed by the slop-pails of years, and two gilt chairs with burst seats, and one of those old-fashioned armchairs which you slide off when you try to sit on them. The room had been turned into a bedroom by thrusting four squalid beds in among the wreckage.
>
> —George Orwell, *The Road to Wigan Pier*

Exercise 15.1

In a paragraph or two, describe a room where you have spent a lot of time in a way that conveys its atmosphere. Then write a few sentences describing the dominant impression you want your description to make, explaining your purpose in describing the room this way.

NAMING

All writers name things they wish to describe. In the following passage, for example, Annie Dillard identifies the face, chin, fur, underside, and eyes of a weasel she once encountered in the woods:

> He was ten inches long, thin as a curve, a muscled ribbon, brown as fruitwood, soft-furred, alert. His face was fierce, small and pointed as a lizard's; he would have made a good arrowhead. There was just a dot of chin, maybe two brown hairs' worth, and then the pure white fur began that spread down his underside. He had two black eyes I didn't see, any more than you see a window.
>
> —Annie Dillard, *Teaching a Stone to Talk*

The underscored nouns name the parts of the weasel on which Dillard focuses attention. The nouns she uses are concrete: They refer to actual, tangible parts of the animal. The nouns are also fairly specific: They identify parts of one particular animal, the weasel she saw.

In looking for the right word to name something, you can usually choose from a variety of words. Some may be concrete (referring to tangible objects or actual instances), while others are abstract (referring to ideas or qualities). *Nose, tooth,* and *foot* are concrete words, whereas *love, faith,* and *justice* are abstract.

Some words may be specific (referring to a particular instance or individual), while others are general (referring to a class that includes many particular instances). *Specific* and *general* are relative terms. That is, the specificity of a word cannot be measured absolutely but only by contrasting it with other words that could be substituted for it. For example, *vegetable* is more specific than *food* but more general than *carrot.*

Compare the following description to Dillard's, noting how each writer has made particular word choices:

> The expression of this snake's face was hideous and fierce; the pupils consisted of a vertical slit in a mottled and coppery iris; the jaws were broad at the base, and the nose terminated in a triangular projection.
>
> —Charles Darwin, *The Voyage of the* Beagle

Like Dillard, Darwin uses the word *face,* though he specifies the *expression* on the snake's face. He could have used *eyes,* as Dillard does, but he uses the more specific *pupils* and *iris* instead. *Chin,* however, would not substitute for *jaws* because *jaws* refers to the bone structure of the lower face, while *chin* refers to something different—the prominence of the lower jaw. Darwin could have used the technical terms *maxilla* and *mandible,* the names of the upper and lower jawbones. He chose not to, even though they are more specific than *jaws,* possibly because they might be unfamiliar to readers or more specific than necessary. As a rule of thumb, most writers prefer more specific nouns for naming, but they adjust the degree of specificity to the particular needs of their readers.

In addition to naming perceivable objects and features, writers name sensations (*stink* and *plunk*) and qualities (the *sweetness* of the lumber):

> When the sun fell across the great white pile of the new Telephone Company building, you could smell the stucco burning as you passed; then some liquid sweetness that came to me from deep in the rings of the freshly cut lumber stacked in the yards, and the fresh plaster and paint on the brand-new storefronts. Rawness, sunshiny rawness down the end streets of the city, as I thought of them then—the hot ash-laden stink of the refuse dumps in my nostrils and the only sound at noon the resonant metal plunk of a tin can I kicked ahead of me as I went my way.
>
> —Alfred Kazin, *A Walker in the City*

Exercise 15.2

Go to a place where you can sit for a while and observe the scene. It might be a landscape or a cityscape, indoors or outdoors, crowded or solitary. Write for five minutes, listing everything in the scene that you can name.

Then, for each noun in your list, try to think of two or three other nouns you could use in its place. Write these other names down.

Finally, write a paragraph describing the scene. Use the nouns you think go together best, assuming that your readers are unfamiliar with the scene.

Exercise 15.3

Read "Father," the essay by Jan Gray in Chapter 3, and notice how much naming she does in her description. In a few sentences, explain why you think Gray uses so much naming in this passage. What impression does it make on you? How specific is her naming? How subjective or objective is it?

DETAILING

Although nouns can be quite specific, adding details is a way of making them more specific and thus describing something more precisely. Naming answers the questions "What is it?" and "What are its parts or features?" Detailing answers questions like these:

- What size is it?
- How many are there?
- What is it made of?
- Where is it located?
- What is its condition?
- How is it used?
- Where does it come from?
- What is its effect?
- What is its value?

To add details to names, add modifiers—adjectives and adverbs, phrases and clauses. Modifiers make nouns more specific by supplying additional information. Notice how many modifying details about size, shape, color, texture, value, and number Annie Dillard provides in her description of the weasel.

> He was ten inches long, thin as a curve, a muscled ribbon, brown as fruitwood, soft-furred, alert. His face was fierce, small and pointed as a lizard's; he would have made a good arrowhead. There was just a dot of chin, maybe two brown hairs' worth, and then the pure white fur began that spread down his underside. He had two black eyes I didn't see, any more than you see a window.
>
> —Annie Dillard, *Teaching a Stone to Talk*

Like names, details can be more or less specific. For example, because "ten inches long" is a measurable quantity, it is more precise than the relative term *small*. Other detailing words like *good* and *pure* are also relative. Even *brown,* although it is more precise than the general word *color,* could be specified further, as Dillard does, by comparing it to the color of fruitwood.

Modifiers are also used to identify a person's character traits, as the following passage illustrates:

> By no amount of agile exercising of a wishful imagination could my mother have been called lenient. Generous she was; indulgent, never. Kind, yes; permissive, never.
>
> —Maya Angelou, *Gather Together in My Name*

Exercise 15.4

Choose something that you can examine closely, such as a car, an animal, or a desk. Study this object for at least five minutes. Then describe it for someone who has never seen it, using as many specific naming and detailing words as you can.

Exercise 15.5

Look at Gerald Haslam's description of his great-grandmother in Chapter 3. What modifiers does he use? How does this detailing contribute to the overall impression of her that the selection gives you?

COMPARING

Whereas naming and detailing call on your powers of observation, comparing brings your imagination into play. Comparison makes language even more precise, description even more evocative. Look again at Annie Dillard's description of a weasel to see how she uses comparison:

> He was ten inches long, thin as a curve, a muscled ribbon, brown as fruitwood, soft-furred, alert. His face was fierce, small and pointed as a lizard's; he would have made a good arrowhead. There was just a dot of chin, maybe two brown hairs' worth, and then the pure white fur began that spread down his underside. He had two black eyes I didn't see, any more than you see a window.
>
> —Annie Dillard, *Teaching a Stone to Talk*

In this passage, Dillard uses two kinds of comparison: simile and metaphor. Both figures of speech compare things that are essentially dissimilar. A *simile* expresses the similarity directly by using the words *like* or *as* to announce the comparison. Dillard uses a simile when she writes that the weasel was "thin as a curve." A *metaphor*, by contrast, is an implicit comparison by which one thing is described as though it were the other. Dillard uses a metaphor when she describes the weasel as "a muscled ribbon."

Here are more examples of comparison used descriptively:

> Sometimes I rambled to pine groves, standing like temples, or like fleets at sea, full-rigged, with wavy boughs, and rippling with light.
>
> —Henry David Thoreau, *Walden*

> On the walls are white spiders like tight buttons of surgical cotton suspended on long hairy legs.
>
> —Barry Lopez, "Perimeter"

By comparing, a writer enhances a description by showing readers the subject in a surprising new way that can be suggestive and revealing. Although we call this strategy comparing, it includes both comparing and contrasting because differences can be as illuminating as likenesses. When two things are compared, they are put into a context that causes them to play off each other in unexpected ways.

As useful as comparison is, there are a few pitfalls to avoid with this strategy. Be sure that the connection between the two things you are comparing is clear and appropriate to your description. Avoid using clichéd expressions, comparisons that are so overused that they have become predictable and consequently do not reveal anything new. For example, the following comparisons have been worn out and thus do not enrich a description:

The kiss was as sweet as honey.

I am as busy as a bee.

That picture stands out like a sore thumb.

Exercise 15.6

Look at David Noonan's "Inside the Brain" in Chapter 4. Mark each metaphor and each simile. Then reflect on how these comparisons contribute to your understanding of the human brain and the procedure being performed.

Exercise 15.7

Reread Jan Gray's essay about her father in Chapter 3, noting the use of naming, describing, and comparing. What impression do you get of Gray's father from this description? How do these three strategies contribute to this impression?

USING SENSORY DESCRIPTION

If there are three basic descriptive strategies—naming, detailing, and comparing—there are many language resources, and some limitations, for reporting sensory impressions. These resources help to convey sight, sound, smell, touch, and taste.

When writers describe scenes and people, they seem to rely on the sense of sight more than the other senses. *Describere,* the Latin root for *describe,* even means "to sketch or copy." Certainly our vocabulary for reporting what we see is larger and more varied than our vocabulary for reporting any other sensory impression.

As for the other senses, quite a few nouns and verbs designate sounds; a smaller number of nouns, but few verbs, describe smells; and very few nouns or verbs convey touch and taste. Furthermore, writers do not find it as easy to name these nonvisual sensations because, unlike sights, they are not readily divided into constituent features. For example, we have many names to describe the visible features of a car but few to describe the sounds a car makes. Nevertheless, writers detail the qualities and attributes of nonvisual sensations—the loudness or tinniness or rumble of an engine, for instance.

The Sense of Sight

When people describe what they see, they identify the objects in their field of vision. As the following passages illustrate, these objects may include animate beings as well as inanimate objects. Details may range from words delineating appearance to those evaluating it.

The first selection, by Henry David Thoreau, depicts a nature scene with a lot of activity; the second passage, by Tracy Kidder, describes Mrs. Zajac, a grade school teacher.

As I sit at my window this summer afternoon, hawks are circling about my clearing; the tantivy of wild pigeons, flying by twos and threes athwart my view, or perching restless on the white pine boughs behind my house, gives a voice to the air; a fish hawk dimples the glassy surface of the pond and brings up a fish; a mink steals out of the marsh before my door and seizes a frog by the shore; the sedge is bending under the weight of the reed-birds flitting hither and thither. . . .

—Henry David Thoreau, *Walden*

She was thirty-four. She wore a white skirt and yellow sweater and a thin gold necklace, which she held in her fingers, as if holding her own reins, while waiting for children to answer. Her hair was black with a hint of Irish red. It was cut short to the tops of her ears, and swept back like a pair of folded wings. She had a delicate cleft chin, and she was short—the children's chairs would have fit her. . . . Her hands kept very busy. They sliced the air and made karate chops to mark off boundaries. They extended straight out like a traffic cop's, halting illegal maneuvers yet to be perpetrated. When they rested momentarily on her hips, her hands looked as if they were in holsters.

—Tracy Kidder, *Among Schoolchildren*

Exercise 15.8

Write a few sentences describing one of your teachers or friends, using Kidder's description of Mrs. Zajac as a model. Do not rely on memory for this exercise: Describe someone who is before you as you write. You can even look in the mirror and describe yourself. Then read what you have written and identify the dominant impression of this description. Which words contribute most to creating the impression? Which words, if any, seem to contradict or weaken it?

The Sense of Hearing

In reporting auditory impressions, writers seldom name the objects from which the sounds come without also naming the sounds themselves: the murmur of a voice, the rustle of the wind, the squeak of a hinge, the sputter of an engine. *Onomatopoeia* is the term for names of sounds that echo the sounds themselves: *squeak, murmur, hiss, boom, plink, tinkle, twang, jangle, rasp, chirr.* Sometimes writers make up words like *sweesh* and *cara-wong* to imitate sounds they wish to describe. Qualitative words like *powerful* and *rich* as well as relative terms like *loud* and *low* often specify sounds further. For detailing sounds, writers sometimes use the technique called *synesthesia,* applying words commonly used to describe one sense to another, such as describing sounds as *sharp* and *soft.*

To write about the sounds along Manhattan's Canal Street, Ian Frazier uses many of these describing and naming techniques. He also uses comparison when he refers metaphorically to the horns getting "tired and out of breath."

The traffic on Canal Street never stops. It is a high-energy current jumping constantly between the poles of Brooklyn and New Jersey. It hates to have its flow pinched in the density of Manhattan, hates to stop at intersections. Along Canal Street, it moans and screams. Worn break shoes of semitrucks go "Ooohhhh nooohhhh" at stoplights, and the sound echoes in the canyons of warehouses and

Chinatown tenements. People lean on their horns from one end of Canal Street to the other. They'll honk nonstop for ten minutes at a time, until the horns get tired and out of breath. They'll try different combinations: shave-and-a-hair-cut, long-long-long, short-short-short-long. Some people have musical car horns; a person purchasing a musical car horn seems to be limited to a choice of four tunes—"La Cucaracha," "Theme from *The Godfather,*" "Dixie," and "Hava Nagila."

—Ian Frazier, "Canal Street"

Exercise 15.9

Find a noisy spot—a restaurant, a football game, a nursery school, a laundry room—where you can perch for half an hour or so. Listen attentively to the sounds of the place, and make notes about what you hear. Then, write a paragraph describing the place through its sounds. When you are done, read your description and identify the dominant impression. Which words contribute most to creating this impression, and which detract from it?

The Sense of Smell

The English language has a meager stock of words to express the sense of smell. In addition to the word *smell,* fewer than a dozen commonly used nouns name this sensation: *odor, scent, vapor, aroma, fragrance, perfume, bouquet, stench, stink.* Although there are other, rarer words like *fetor* and *effluvium,* few writers use them, probably for fear that their readers will not know them. Few verbs describe receiving or sending odors—*smell, sniff, waft*—but a fair number of detailing adjectives are available: *redolent, pungent, aromatic, perfumed, stinking, musty, rancid, putrid, rank, foul, acrid, sweet,* and *cloying.*

In the next passage, Frank Conroy uses comparing in addition to naming and detailing. Notice how he describes the effect the odor has on him.

The perfume of the flowers rushed into my brain. A lush aroma, thick with sweetness, thick as blood, and spiced with the clear acid of tropical greenery. My heart pounded like a drowning swimmer's as the perfume took me over, pouring into my lungs like ambrosial soup.

—Frank Conroy, *Stop-Time*

Naming the objects from which smells come can also be very suggestive.

My mother worked on and off, primarily as a *costurera* [seamstress] or cleaning homes or taking care of other people's children. We sometimes went with her to the houses she cleaned. They were nice, American, white-people homes. . . . The odor of these houses was different, full of fragrances, sweet and nauseating. On 105th Street the smells were of fried lard, of beans and car fumes, of factory smoke and home-made brew out of backyard stills. There were chicken smells and goat smells in grassless yards filled with engine parts and wire and wood planks, cracked and sprinkled with rusty nails. These were the familiar aromas: the funky earth, animal and mechanical smells which were absent from the homes my mother cleaned.

—Luis J. Rodriguez, *Always Running: Gang Days in L.A.*

Exercise 15.10

Choose a place with noticeable, distinctive smells where you can stay for ten or fifteen minutes. You may choose an eating place (a cafeteria, a doughnut shop), a place where something is being manufactured (a sawmill, a bakery), or some other place that has distinctive odors (a fishing dock, a garden, a locker room). Take notes while you are there on what you smell, and then write a paragraph describing the place through its smells. What dominant impression were you trying to create in your description?

The Sense of Touch

Few nouns and verbs name tactile sensations besides words like *touch, feel, tickle, brush, scratch, sting, itch,* and *tingle.* Probably as a consequence, writers describing the sense of touch tend not to name the sensation directly or even to report the act of feeling. Nevertheless, a large stock of words describe temperature *(hot, warm, mild, tepid, cold, arctic),* moisture content *(wet, dry, sticky, oily, greasy, moist, crisp),* texture *(gritty, silky, smooth, crinkled, coarse, soft, leathery),* and weight *(heavy, light, ponderous, buoyant, feathery).* Read the following passages with an eye for descriptions of touch.

> The midmorning sun was deceitfully mild and the wind had no weight on my skin. Arkansas summer mornings have a feathering effect on stone reality.
>
> —Maya Angelou, *Gather Together in My Name*

> It was an ordeal for me to walk the hills in the dead of summer for then they were parched and dry and offered no shade from the hot sun and no springs or creeks where thirst could be quenched.
>
> —William O. Douglas, *Go East, Young Man*

Exercise 15.11

Briefly describe the feel of a cold shower, a wool sweater, an autumn breeze, bare feet on hot sand, or some other tactile sensation. What dominant impression were you trying to create with this description?

The Sense of Taste

Other than *taste, savor,* and *flavor,* few words name the gustatory sensations directly. Certain words do distinguish among types of tastes—*sweet (saccharine, sugary, cloying); sour (acidic, tart); bitter (acrid, biting); salty (briny, brackish)*—and several other words describe specific tastes *(piquant, spicy, pungent, peppery, savory, toothsome).*

In addition to these words, the names of objects tasted and other details may indicate the intensity and quality of a taste. Notice Ernest Hemingway's descriptive technique in the following selection:

> As I ate the oysters with their strong taste of the sea and their faint metallic taste that the cold wine washed away, leaving only the sea taste and the succulent texture, and as I drank their cold liquid from each shell and washed it down with the crispy taste of the wine, I lost the empty feeling and began to be happy and to make plans.
>
> —Ernest Hemingway, *A Moveable Feast*

Exercise 15.12

Describe the taste of a particular food or meal as Hemingway does. What dominant impression were you trying to create?

Exercise 15.13

Read "Uncle Willie" in Chapter 3, and bracket any instances where Angelou uses sensory language—sight, hearing, smell, touch, taste—to describe the scene and the people. What dominant impression do you get from this description? How do you think sensory description helps to create this impression?

ASSUMING A VANTAGE POINT

To write effectively about a scene, you need to take a vantage point—that is, select the point or position from which to describe the scene. By presenting objects and features from a particular vantage point, you create a perspective that enables readers to enter the scene.

A Stationary Vantage Point

A writer who describes a scene entirely from one spot is said to assume a fixed or stationary vantage point. In the following passage, the author takes a position in a subway station and describes what he sees without moving from that spot.

> Standing in a subway station, I began to appreciate the place—almost to enjoy it. First of all, I looked at the lighting: a row of meager electric bulbs, unscreened, yellow, and coated with filth, stretched toward the black mouth of the tunnel, as though it were a bolt hole in an abandoned coal mine. Then I lingered, with zest, on the walls and ceiling: lavatory tiles which had been white about fifty years ago, and were now encrusted with soot, coated with the remains of a dirty liquid which might be either atmospheric humidity mingled with smog or the result of a perfunctory attempt to clean them with cold water; and, above them, gloomy vaulting from which dingy paint was peeling off like scabs from an old wound, sick black paint leaving a leprous white subsurface. Beneath my feet, the floor was a nauseating dark brown with black stains upon it which might be stale oil or dry chewing gum or some worse defilement; it looked like the hallway of a condemned slum building. Then my eye traveled to the tracks, where two lines of glittering steel—the only positively clean objects in the whole place—ran out of darkness into darkness above an unspeakable mass of congealed oil, puddles of dubious liquid, and a mishmash of old cigarette packets, mutilated and filthy newspapers, and the debris that filtered down from the street above through a barred grating in the roof. As I looked up toward the sunlight, I could see more debris sifting slowly downward, and making an abominable pattern in the slanting beam of dirt-laden sunlight. I was going on to relish more features of this unique scene: such as the advertisement posters on the walls—here a text from the Bible, there a half-naked girl, here a woman wearing a hat consisting of a hen sitting on a nest full of eggs, and there a pair of girl's legs walking up the keys of a cash register—all scribbled

> over with unknown names and well-known obscenities in black crayon and red lipstick; but then my train came in at last.
>
> —Gilbert Highet, "The Subway Station"

Although Highet stays in one spot, he shifts his field of vision. Using these shifts to order the description of what he sees, he looks first at the lights, then at the walls and ceilings, at the floor, at the tracks, toward the sunlight, and finally at the posters on the wall. He seems to describe things as they catch his attention. Sometimes writers give details in a more orderly pattern—for example, from left to right, from top to bottom, or from big to small.

A Moving Point of View

Instead of remaining fixed in one spot, a writer may move through a scene. In the following description, the writer tells what he sees as he drives along a highway:

> The highway, without warning, rolled off the plateau of green pastures and entered a wooded and rocky gorge; down, down, precipitously down to the Kentucky River. Along the north slope, man-high columns of ice clung to the limestone. The road dropped deeper until it crossed the river at Brooklyn Bridge. The gorge, hidden in the table and wholly unexpected, was the Palisades. At the bottom lay only enough ground for the river and a narrow strip of willow-rimmed houses on stilts and a few doublewides rose from the damp flats like toadstools. Next to one mobile home was a partly built steel boat longer than the trailer.
>
> —William Least Heat Moon, *Blue Highways*

See pp. 478–80 for a discussion of transitions and a list of those commonly used to indicate spatial relationships.

Notice how the writer uses spatial transitions like *down, along, from,* and *next* to orient readers to his movements.

Combined Vantage Points

Sometimes writers use more than one stationary vantage point or combine stationary and moving vantage points. In these cases, the writer needs to orient the readers to any change in position. Willie Morris begins with a moving vantage point and then uses several stationary points:

> One walked up the three flights through several padlocked doors, often past the garbage which the landlords had neglected to remove for two or three days. Once inside our place, things were not bad at all. There was a big front room with an old floor, a little alcove for a study, and to the back a short corridor opening up into a tiny bedroom for my son and a larger bedroom in the back. The kitchen was in the back bedroom. I had not been able to find a view of an extensive body of water at popular prices, but from the back window, about forty yards out, there *was* a vista of a big tank, part of some manufacturing installation in the building under it, and the tank constantly bubbled with some unidentified greenish substance. From this window one could see the tarred rooftops of the surrounding buildings, and off to the right a quiet stretch of God's earth, this being the parking lot next door.
>
> —Willie Morris, *North toward Home*

Exercise 15.14

Look back at the paragraph you wrote for Exercise 15.1. What vantage point did you take in that description? How do you think the vantage point you chose contributes to the dominant impression the description creates? Try rewriting a few sentences taking another vantage point. How does this vantage point change the dominant impression?

Exercise 15.15

Look at Brian Cable's profile, "The Last Stop," in Chapter 4. Mark places in the text where you notice that a particular vantage point is used or that a vantage point shifts. What effect does the use of a vantage point have on Cable's descriptions of the mortuary?

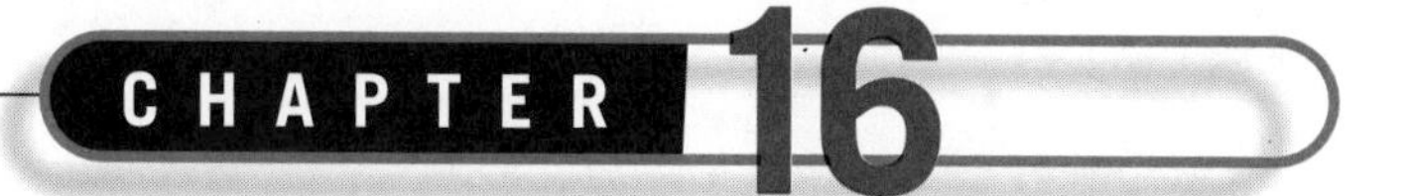

CHAPTER 16

Defining

Defining is an essential strategy for all writing. Autobiographers, for example, must occasionally define objects, conditions, events, and activities for readers likely to be unfamiliar with particular terms. In the following example from Chapter 3, the definition is underlined.

> My father's hands are grotesque. He suffers from psoriasis, a chronic skin disease that covers his massive, thick hands with scaly, reddish patches that periodically flake off, sending tiny pieces of dead skin sailing to the ground.
>
> —Jan Gray, "Father"

When writers share information or explain how to do something, they must often define important terms for readers who are unfamiliar with the subject. This example comes from Chapter 4.

> After the scalp and the skull, the next layer protecting the brain is the dura. A thin, tough, leathery membrane that encases the brain, the dura (derived from the Latin for *hard*), is dark pink, almost red.
>
> —David Noonan, "Inside the Brain"

To convince readers of a position or an evaluation or to move them to act on a proposal, a writer must often define concepts important to an argument. This example comes from Chapter 6.

> There is nothing wrong, or new, in believing one's own position is fairer, more realistic or just smarter than the opposition's. But "getting it" suggests something more, possession of a special wisdom denied to others.
>
> —Guy Molyneux, "The Declining Art of Political Debate"

As these examples illustrate, there are many kinds of definitions and many forms that they can take. This chapter illustrates the major kinds and forms of definitions, from dictionary definitions to various types of sentence definitions, the most common in writing. When writers use sentence definitions, they rely on various sentence patterns to provide concise definitions. Finally, the chapter provides illustrations of multisentence extended definitions, including definition by etymology, or word history, and by stipulation.

DICTIONARY DEFINITIONS

The most familiar source of definitions is the dictionary, where words are defined concisely using other words. In a short space, dictionaries tell us a lot about words, including what they mean, how they are pronounced, how they look in context in a sample phrase or clause, where they originated, and what forms they take as they function differently in sentences. Here is an example from *The American Heritage Dictionary:*

definition
part of speech
syllabication
pronunciation
illustrative use
etymology
other forms

in-trep-id (ĭn-trĕp′ĭd) *adj.* Marked by resolute courage; fearless and bold: *an intrepid mountaineer.* [Fr. *intrépide* < Lat. *intrepidus: in-*, not + *trepidus*, alarmed.]—**in′tre-pid′i-ty** (-trə-pĭd′ĭ-tē), **in-trep′id-ness** *n.* —**in-trep′id-ly** *adv.*

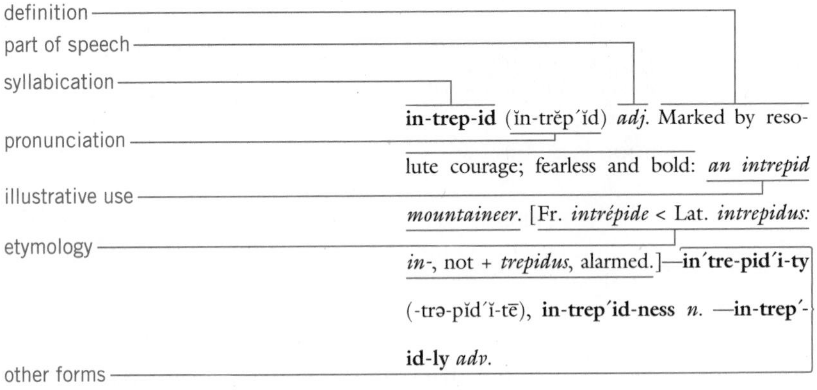

Other dictionary entries may include still more information. For example, if a word has more than one meaning, all of its meanings will be presented. From the context in which you read or hear the word, you can nearly always tell which meaning applies.

A good dictionary is an essential part of your equipment as a college student. It should always be within reach when you are reading so that you can look up unfamiliar words in order to understand what you read and to expand your vocabulary. When you are writing, you can use a dictionary to check spellings and the correct forms of words as well as to make sure of the meanings of words you may not have used before.

You may want to ask your instructor for advice about which dictionary to buy in your college bookstore. A good current dictionary like *The American Heritage Dictionary* or *Merriam-Webster's Collegiate Dictionary* is most useful. Although a hardcover dictionary will cost quite a bit more than a paperback, it will be a sound and relatively inexpensive investment (about $20). Hardcover dictionaries have several advantages, including more entries, fuller entries, larger type, and a thumb index.

To present a great deal of information in a small space, dictionaries have to rely on many abbreviations, codes, and symbols. These differ somewhat from one dictionary to the next, but most dictionaries provide a key to their system of abbreviations. You will also find a range of interesting topics and lists at the beginning and end of some dictionaries: articles on usage and language history, reviews of punctuation rules, biographical entries, and geographic entries.

For desk use, you are most likely to buy an *abridged* dictionary, which does not include many technical or obsolete words. Much larger *unabridged* dictionaries contain every known current and obsolete word in the language. Two unabridged dictionaries are preeminent: the *Oxford English Dictionary* and *Webster's Third New*

International Dictionary. The latter is the standard reference for American English. Libraries have these impressive dictionaries available for specialized use.

A special dictionary called a *thesaurus* can be useful for a writer, but only if it is used judiciously. A thesaurus is a dictionary of synonyms, words with identical or very similar meanings. Your motive for searching out synonyms should be to use just the right word, not to impress readers. Writers who strain to impress readers with unusual words risk embarrassing themselves by using a word in the wrong context.

Here is an example from *Roget's II: The New Thesaurus.* It offers alternatives to *brave,* used as an adjective. Among the synonyms for *brave* is *intrepid,* noted in the dictionary definition on the preceding page.

> **brave** *adjective*
> Having or showing courage: *a brave effort to rescue the drowning child.* **Syns:** audacious, bold, courageous, dauntless, doughty, fearless, fortitudinous, gallant, game, gutsy *(Informal)*, gutty, heroic, intrepid, mettlesome, plucky, stout, stouthearted, unafraid, undaunted, valiant, valorous.

Some thesauruses also offer antonyms, words opposite in meaning to the word of interest. (An antonym of *brave,* for example, would be *cowardly.*)

The great limitation of a thesaurus is that it does not tell you which synonym is most appropriate for a particular situation. *Brave* and *intrepid* are not simply interchangeable. Which word you might use would depend on your readers, your purpose, your subject, and the exact meaning you hoped to convey in the sentence in which the word appears. In the list from *Roget's II,* the only clue to appropriateness is the information that *gutsy* is informal. You would need to check each word in the list in a good dictionary to select the most appropriate one. A thesaurus is most useful, therefore, when it reminds you of a familiar synonym, one whose shades of meaning you already know.

To overcome the limitations of a thesaurus, writers can turn to a dictionary of synonyms, which provides words in a set as the thesaurus does but defines and contrasts each synonym and illustrates it with a quotation. An excellent source is *Webster's New Dictionary of Synonyms,* which provides enough information to let you make an appropriate choice among words with similar meanings. Your college bookstore will have this book for about the cost of a hardcover dictionary. The entry for *brave,* for example, notes eleven common synonyms for *brave* as an adjective, ranging from *courageous* to *audacious.* Each synonym is defined and then quoted in context from a respected source, as this portion of the entry shows:

> **brave** *adj* **Brave, courageous, unafraid, fearless, intrepid, valiant, valorous, dauntless, undaunted, doughty, bold, audacious** are comparable when they mean having or showing no fear when faced with something dangerous, difficult, or unknown. **Brave** usually indicates lack of fear in alarming or difficult circumstances rather than a temperamental liking for danger <the *brave* soldier goes to meet Death, and meets him without a shudder—*Trollope*> <he would send an explosion ship into the harbor . . . a *brave* crew would take her in at night, right up against the city, would light the fuses, and try to escape—*Forster*> **Courageous** implies stouthearted resolution in contemplating or facing danger and may suggest a temperamental readiness to meet dangers or difficulties <I am afraid . . . because I do not wish to die. But my spirit masters the trembling flesh and the qualms of the mind. I am more than brave, I am *courageous*—*London*> <a man is *courageous* when he does things which others might fail to do owing to fear—*Russell*> **Unafraid**

simply indicates lack of fright or fear whether because of a courageous nature or because no cause for fear is present <enjoy their homes *unafraid* of violent intrusion—*MacArthur*> <a young, daring, and creative people—a people *unafraid* of change—*MacLeish*> **Fearless** may indicate lack of fear, or it may be more positive and suggest undismayed resolution <joyous we too launch out on trackless seas, *fearless* for unknown shores—*Whitman*> <he gives always the impression of *fearless* sincerity . . . one always feels that he is ready to say bluntly what every one else is afraid to say—*T. S. Eliot*> **Intrepid** suggests either daring in meeting danger or fortitude in enduring it <with the *intrepid* woman who was his wife, and a few natives, he landed there, and set about building a house and clearing the scrub—*Maugham*> <the *intrepid* guardians of the place, hourly exposed to death, with famine worn, and suffering under many a perilous wound—*Wordsworth*>

This entry shows that *brave* and *intrepid* are very close in meaning but that *intrepid* would be the better choice if you wanted to suggest "daring in meeting danger" rather than "lack of fear" in facing danger when it comes. You might call a person setting off on a solo sea voyage in a small craft an *intrepid* sailor, but a flight attendant who faced down a potential hijacker is better described as *brave.*

To summarize our advice about dictionaries: Use a respected hardcover dictionary to look up the meanings of new words you encounter and to check spellings and usage. Consult an inexpensive paperback thesaurus for a quick look at sets of synonyms. Consult a respected hardcover dictionary of synonyms to discriminate among synonyms and pick the most appropriate word. These resources will enable you to choose just the right words for your essays and to use correct spellings and word forms.

SENTENCE DEFINITIONS

Every field of study and every institution and activity has its own unique concepts and terms. Coming to a new area for the first time, a participant or a reader is often baffled by the many unfamiliar names for objects and activities. In college, a basic course in a field often seems like an entire course in definitions of new terms. In the same way, newcomers to a sport like sailing or rock climbing often need to learn much specialized terminology. In such cases, writers of textbooks and sailing or rock-climbing manuals rely on brief sentence definitions, involving a variety of sentence strategies.

Here are some sentence strategies from one widely used introductory college biology text, Sylvia Mader's *Inquiry into Life.* These examples illustrate some of the sentence strategies an author may use to name and define terms for readers.

The most obvious sentence strategies simply announce a definition. (In each of the following examples, the word being defined is in italics, and the definition is underlined.)

Homo habilis means handyman.

Somatic mutations are mutations that affect the individual's body cells.

At the time of ejaculation, sperm leaves the penis in a fluid called *seminal fluid.*

Thus an ecosystem contains both a *biotic* (living) and an *abiotic* (nonliving) environment.

> The human blastula, termed the *blastocyst,* consists of a hollow ball with a mass of cells—the inner cell mass—at one end.

All of these sentence strategies declare in a straightforward way that the writer is defining a term. Other strategies, signaled by certain sentence relationships, are less direct but still quite apparent.

> *Fraternal twins,* which originate when two different eggs are fertilized by two different sperm, do not have identical chromosomes.

> *Hemophilia* is called the bleeder's disease because the afflicted person's blood is unable to clot.

> When a mutagen leads to an increase in the incidence of cancer, it is called a *carcinogen.*

> If the thyroid fails to develop properly, a condition called *cretinism* results.

These sentence definitions—all of which appear in subordinate clauses—add details, express time and cause, or indicate conditions or tentativeness. In all these examples from *Inquiry into Life,* however, the clauses play a specific defining role in the sections of the text where they appear. In this specialized way, they are part of a writer's repertoire for sentence definitions.

Another common defining strategy is the appositive phrase. Here one word or expression defines another word or expression in a brief inserted phrase called an *appositive.* Sometimes the appositive contains the definition; other times it contains the word to be defined.

> Sperm are produced in the testes, but they mature in the *epididymus,* a tightly coiled tubule about twenty feet in length that lies just outside each testis.

> Breathing consists of taking air in, *inspiration,* and forcing air out, *expiration.*

Finally, in a comparative definition, two or more terms are defined in part by comparing or contrasting them with each other. For these multiple definitions, writers rely on a great variety of syntactic and stylistic strategies, including the two illustrated here: (1) a series of phrases following either the main verb or a colon and (2) contrasting clauses beginning with words or phrases like *even though, in spite of,* or *whereas.* The various parts of the comparison are always grammatically parallel, that is, similar in form.

> The special senses include the *chemoreceptors* for taste and smell, the *light receptors* for sight, and the *mechanoreceptors* for hearing and balance.

> Whereas *miscarriage* is the unexpected loss of an embryo or fetus, *abortion* is the purposeful removal of an embryo or fetus from the womb.

Exercise 16.1

Look up any three of the following words in a dictionary. Define each one in a sentence. Try to use a different sentence pattern, like the ones just illustrated in the text, for each of your definitions.

clinometer	senile dementia	buyer's market
ecumenism	caricature	Shakespearean sonnet
harangue	mnemonic	edema
ectomorph	testosterone	samba

Exercise 16.2

Turn to the essay by David Noonan in Chapter 4, and analyze the sentence definitions in paragraphs 2, 6, 9, 13, and 18. (Some of these paragraphs contain more than one sentence definition.) Classify each definition as one of the sentence types identified in the text. What purpose do all these definitions serve in the selection as a whole?

EXTENDED DEFINITIONS

At times, a writer may need to go further than a brief sentence definition and provide readers with a fuller definition extending over several sentences. Here, for example, is how Earl Shorris defines a common Spanish term:

> Fulano is a very old Spanish word for someone of uncertain identity, a so-and-so, that less than memorable person the English call a bloke or a chap, the one known in American English as a guy or you-know (as in whatsisname). Fulano, zutano, and mangano play the role of Tom, Dick, and Harry or the butcher, the baker, the candlestick maker. Fulano isn't real, no one bears that name; Fulano doesn't play first base or marry your niece; he pays no taxes, eats no food, and leaves no mess behind; he's nobody. If by some error of madness, alcohol, or utter failure of the imagination, a child were named Fulano, his life would be a trial, for he would be no one and everyman, rich and poor, short and tall, Colombian, Cuban, Dominican, Mexican, Puerto Rican, Spanish, and so on.
>
> —Earl Shorris, *Latinos: A Biography of the People*

This extended definition relies on a variety of strategies—word history, comparisons, examples, even a hypothetical "incorrect" usage of the word.

A linguistics text provides another example of the way an important concept may require extended definition:

> **Prosodic meaning.** The way a sentence is said, using the prosody of the language, can radically alter the meaning. Any marked change in emphasis, for example, can lead to a sentence being interpreted in a fresh light. Each of the following sentences carries a different implication, as the stress (indicated by capitals) moves:

> John's bought a red CAR (not a red bicycle).
> John's bought a RED car (not a green one).
> JOHN'S bought a red car (not Michael).
>
> The prosody informs us of what information in the sentence can be taken for granted (is "given") and what is of special significance (is "new").
>
> —David Crystal, *The Cambridge Encyclopedia of Language*

Extended definitions may also include *negative definitions*—explanations of what the thing being defined is *not:*

> It's important to be clear about the reverse definition, as well: what dinosaurs are not. Dinosaurs are not lizards, and vice versa. Lizards are scaly reptiles of an ancient bloodline. The oldest lizards antedate the earliest dinosaurs by a full thirty million years. A few large lizards, such as the man-eating Komodo dragon, have been called "relics of the dinosaur age," but this phrase is historically incorrect. No lizard ever evolved the birdlike characteristics peculiar to each and every dinosaur. A big lizard never resembled a small dinosaur except for a few inconsequential details of the teeth. Lizards never walked with the erect, long-striding gait that distinguishes the dinosaurlike ground birds today or the birdlike dinosaurs of the Mesozoic.
>
> —Robert T. Bakker, *The Dinosaur Heresies*

When drafting an essay, you will need to choose a definition strategy that will help you to accomplish your goals and will also be appropriate for your readers. You need not even be consciously aware that you are making particular choices while you are writing a first draft. Later, though, when you are revising the draft, you will have a special advantage if you can look critically at the way you have defined key terms. If your repertoire of defining strategies includes all the variations illustrated in this chapter, you will be able to revise with confidence and power.

Though it happens fairly rarely, some published essays and reports are concerned primarily with the definition of a little-understood or problematic concept or thing. Usually, however, definition is only a part of an essay. A long piece of writing, like a term paper, a textbook, or a research report, may include many kinds of brief and extended definitions, all of them integrated with other writing strategies.

Exercise 16.3

Choose one term that names some concept or feature of central importance in an activity or a subject you know well. Choose a word with a well-established definition. Write an extended definition of several sentences for this important term. Write for readers your own age who will be encountering the term for the first time when they read your definition.

Exercise 16.4

Return to "Inside the Brain," David Noonan's essay in Chapter 4, and analyze the extended definition of *sterile field* in paragraph 6. How does he define this term? What purpose does the definition have within the whole selection?

HISTORICAL DEFINITIONS

Occasionally, a writer will trace the history of a word, from its first use to its adoption into other languages to its shifting meanings over the centuries. Such a strategy can be a rich addition to an essay, bringing surprising depth and resonance to the definition of a concept. A historical definition usually begins with the roots of a word but extends well beyond the word's origins to trace its history over a long period of time. Such a history should always serve a writer's larger purpose, as the example here shows.

In this example, from a book discussing the recent rise of witchcraft and paganism in America, the writer uses a historical definition of the word *pagan* as a background for her own definition and also as a way of instructing us in how we should feel about the new pagans.

> *Pagan* comes from the Latin *paganus,* which means a country dweller and is itself derived from *pagus,* the Latin word for village or rural district. Similarly, *heathen* originally meant a person who lived on the heaths. Negative associations with these words are the end result of centuries of political struggles during which the major prophetic religions, notably Christianity, won a victory over the older polytheistic religions. In the West, often the last people to be converted to Christianity lived on the outskirts of populated areas and kept to the old ways. These were the Pagans and heathens—the word *Pagan* was a term of insult, meaning "hick."
>
> *Pagan* had become a derogatory term in Rome by the third century. Later, after the death of Julian, the last Pagan emperor, in A.D. 362, the word *Pagan* came to refer to intellectual Pagans like Julian. Gore Vidal, in his extraordinary novel *Julian,* wrote a fictional description of this event in which the Pagan orator Libanius, after attending the funeral of a Christian notable, writes in his journal: "There was a certain amount of good-humored comment about 'pagans' (a new word of contempt for us Hellenists) attending Christian services. . . ." Julian, by the way, has long been one of Neo-Paganism's heroes, and an early Neo-Pagan journal was called *The Julian Review.* Centuries later the word *Pagan* still suffers the consequences of political and religious struggles, and dictionaries still define it to mean a godless person or an unbeliever, instead of, simply, a member of a different kind of religion.
>
> *Pagan* is also often associated with hedonism. This makes some sense, since many ancient Pagan religions incorporated sexuality into ecstatic religious practice. One scholar, writing on the use of mystical experience by young people in the 1960s, observed that a characteristic of many groups was "the idea of paganism—the body is a temple in which there is nothing unclean, a shrine to be adorned for the ritual of love." New attitudes toward sexuality play a part in some, but not all, Neo-Pagan groups, and the old Pagan religions had their share of ascetics, but generally, Neo-Pagans seem to have healthy attitudes toward sex.
>
> I use *Pagan* to mean a member of a polytheistic nature religion, such as the ancient Greek, Roman, or Egyptian religions, or, in anthropological terms, a member of one of the indigenous folk and tribal religions all over the world. People who have studied the classics or have been deeply involved with natural or aboriginal peoples are comparatively free of the negative and generally racist attitudes that surround the word *Pagan.*
>
> —Margot Adler, *Drawing Down the Moon*

Exercise 16.5

Any good dictionary tells the origins of words. Historical, or etymological, dictionaries, however, give much more information, enough to trace changes in use of a word over long periods of time. The preeminent historical dictionary of our language is the *Oxford English Dictionary.* Less imposing is *A Dictionary of American English,* and more accessible still is *A Dictionary of Americanisms.* Look up the historical definition of any one of the following words in *A Dictionary of Americanisms,* and write several sentences on its roots and development.

basketball	bonanza	eye-opener	picayune
bazooka	bushwhack	filibuster	podunk
bedrock	canyon	gerrymander	rubberneck
blizzard	carpetbag	jazz	sashay
bogus	dugout	pep	two-bits

STIPULATIVE DEFINITIONS

The historical definition of *pagan* in the preceding section concludes with a stipulative definition: "I use *Pagan* to mean a member of a polytheistic nature religion. . . ." *To stipulate* means to seek or assert agreement on something. In a stipulative definition, the writer declares a certain meaning, generally not one found in the dictionary.

Stipulative definitions have a variety of important functions, several of which are illustrated here. In the next example, a prominent historian of science proposes a stipulative definition of the word *ecology.*

> Ernst Haeckel, the great popularizer of evolutionary theory in Germany, loved to coin words. The vast majority of his creations died with him a half-century ago, but among the survivors are "ontogeny," "phylogeny," and "ecology." The last is now facing an opposite fate—loss of meaning by extension and vastly inflated currency. Common usage now threatens to make "ecology" a label for anything good that happens far from cities or anything that does not have synthetic chemicals in it. In its more restricted and technical sense, ecology is the study of organic diversity. It focuses on the interactions of organisms and their environments in order to address what may be the most fundamental question in evolutionary biology: "Why are there so many kinds of living things?"
>
> —Stephen Jay Gould, *Ever Since Darwin*

Important concepts in technical fields like biology may gradually take on fuzzy or overly broad popular definitions. The specialists may then have to rescue a concept by redefining it, as Gould does here. He is asking his readers to agree with him that *ecology* means "the study of organic diversity." He stipulates a redefinition and asks us to use the word only as he defines it, at least for the duration of his book.

Another use of stipulative definition is to sort through alternative definitions of a problematic concept—"pure breed of cats" in the next example—in order to reject these definitions and argue for another.

> What is a pure breed of cats, and what constitutes a pure-bred animal? These terms can have a number of meanings. One of the simplest is merely to regard as pure-bred a cat that has been properly registered with a responsible body (such as the Governing Council of the Cat Fancy [GCCF] in Britain, or the Cat Fanciers' Association [CFA] or one of the other similar associations in the United States). Such a cat will have a pedigree of similarly registered parents, grandparents and so on for a given number of generations—normally at least four. This ensures that the cat has "respectable" parentage and is likely to be a representative specimen of the breed—though it says nothing about its quality.
>
> However, the process of registration and the writing of pedigrees is, in a sense (and without meaning to be derogatory), merely window dressing. They simply set a seal upon a more fundamental definition of pure breeds of cats. This relates to the characteristics of the individuals constituting a recognized breed and how these may differ from those of other cats: from alley cats and from other recognized breeds. In one sense, a breed is a group of animals that sufficient people are mutually agreed to recognize as such. This is not enough in itself, however; the group must have coherent distinguishing features that set them apart from all other cats, and hence distinctive underlying genetic characteristics.
>
> —Michael Wright and Sally Walters, *The Book of the Cat*

Exercise 16.6

In his Chapter 7 proposal about birth control in the schools, Adam Paul Weisman offers a stipulative definition of the role schools play in students' lives (paragraph 11). Read the essay, paying particular attention to this definition. What function does it serve in the essay as a whole?

Exercise 16.7

Write several sentences of a stipulative definition for one of the following.

1. Define in your own way game shows, soap operas, police dramas, horror movies, or some other form of entertainment. Try for a stipulative definition of what your subject is generally like. In effect, you will be saying to your readers—other students in your class who are familiar with these entertainments—"Let's for now define it this way."
2. Do the same for some hard-to-define concept—such as "loyalty," "love," "bravery," "shyness," "male chauvinism," or "worthwhile college courses."
3. Think of a new development or phenomenon in contemporary romance, music, television, leisure, fashion, or eating habits, or in your line of work. Invent a name for it, and write a stipulative definition for it.

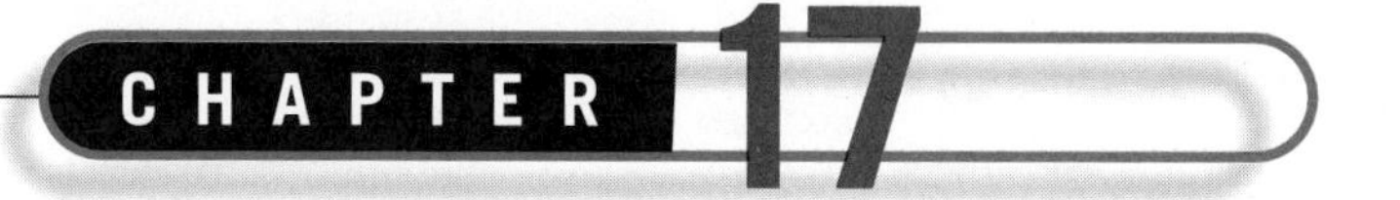

CHAPTER 17

Classifying

Classifying is an indispensable skill. In a variety of writing situations, you will face the task of sorting various snippets of material into an orderly presentation. The most common strategy for doing so is *classifying*—combining items into a number of discrete groups and then labeling each group. In many instances, classifying is a matter of *dividing* something into its constituent parts in order to consider the elements of each part separately.

In using classification and division, you will be particularly concerned with organization, principles of division, and coherence.

ORGANIZATION

As strategies, classification and division serve primarily as means of organization, of creating a framework for the presentation of information, whether in a few paragraphs of an essay or an entire book. Other strategies—definition, illustration, contrast—are often used to develop a topic in detail.

In the following passage, for example, Thomas Sowell uses classification as an organizing strategy in his discussion of immigrants in the United States. He classifies American immigrant groups into four discrete categories—refugees, sojourners, settlers, and captives:

> It has often been said that we are a nation of immigrants. In a sense that is true; but the blanket term "immigrants" covers over many important distinctions among the various peoples who came to America. The famine Irish and the east European Jewish victims of pogroms were essentially refugees who fled in whole family units, burning their bridges behind them, and arrived in the United States committed to becoming Americans. Others have come as sojourners, mostly men, and with the intention of returning to their native lands, so that Americanization in language, culture, or citizenship had a low priority for them. The earliest emigrations from Italy, China, Japan, and Mexico were largely of this character, as is much of today's migration back and forth between Puerto Rico and the mainland of the United States. There were also immigrants who were neither refugees nor sojourners, but simply people who chose to come to the United States to settle at a place and time of their choice. Such immigrants—the Germans or Scandinavians, for example—were far less likely to concentrate in the port cities where they landed and more likely to choose a long-run

settlement site suited to their conditions. Finally, there were those who did not choose to come at all but who were brought as captives—African slaves—and whose geographic distribution and occupational roles were suited to the convenience of others.

—Thomas Sowell, *Ethnic America: A History*

A writer can divide a topic into parts for a variety of purposes. See how Ernest Hemingway uses the strategy to open a chapter in *Death in the Afternoon,* his classic book on bullfighting in Spain. To help us to understand how a bullfight develops, Hemingway describes it as divided into three acts, each of which is named for the major action (the trial of the lances, the banderillas, and the death). Hemingway subdivides the third act further, into three parts (or scenes, to continue his analogy between a bullfight and a play). Finally, he summarizes his discussion in terms of a three-act "tragedy."

There are three acts to the fighting of each bull and they are called in Spanish los tres tercios de la lidia, or the three thirds of the combat. The first act, where the bull charges the picadors, is the suerte de varas, or the trial of the lances. Suerte is an important word in Spanish. It means, according to the dictionary: Suerte, f., chance, hazard, lots, fortune, luck, good luck, haphazard; state, condition, fate, doom, destiny, kind, sort; species, manner, mode, way, skillful manœuvre; trick, feat, juggle, and piece of ground separated by landmark. So the translation of trial or manœuvre is quite arbitrary, as any translation must be from the Spanish.

The action of the picadors in the ring and the work of the matadors who are charged with protecting them with their capes when they are dismounted make up the first act of the bullfight. When the president signals for the end of this act and the bugle blows the picadors leave the ring and the second act begins. There are no horses in the ring after the first act except the dead horses which are covered with canvas. Act one is the act of the capes, the pics and the horses. In it the bull has the greatest opportunity to display his bravery or cowardice.

Act two is that of the banderillas. These are pairs of sticks about a yard long, seventy centimetres to be exact, with a harpoon-shaped steel point four centimetres long at one end. They are supposed to be placed, two at a time, in the humped muscle at the top of the bull's neck as he charges the man who holds them. They are designed to complete the work of slowing up the bull and regulating the carriage of his head which has been begun by the picadors: so that his attack will be slower, but surer and better directed. Four pair of banderillas are usually put in. If they are placed by the banderilleros or peones they must be placed, above all other considerations, quickly and in the proper position. If the matador himself places them he may indulge in a preparation which is usually accompanied by music. This is the most picturesque part of the bullfight and the part most spectators care for the most when first seeing fights. The mission of the banderilleros is not only to force the bull by hooking to tire his neck muscles and carry his head lower but also, by placing them at one side or another, to correct a tendency to hook to that side. The entire act of the banderillas should not take more than five minutes. If it is prolonged the bull becomes discomposed and the fight loses the tempo it must keep, and if the bull is an uncertain and dangerous one he has too many opportunities to see and charge men unarmed with any lure, and so develops a tendency to search for the man, the bundle, as the Spanish call him, behind the cloth when the matador comes out for the last act with the sword and muleta.

The president changes the act after three or at most four pairs of banderillas have been placed and the third and final division is the death. It is made up of three parts. First the brindis or salutation of the president and dedication or toasting of the death of the bull, either to him or to some other person by the matador, followed by the work of the matador with the muleta. This is a scarlet serge cloth which is folded over a stick which has a sharp spike at one end and a handle at the other. The spike goes through the cloth which is fastened to the other end of the handle with a thumb screw so that it hangs in folds along the length of the stick. Muleta means literally crutch, but in bullfighting it refers to the scarlet-serge-draped stick with which the matador is supposed to master the bull, prepare him for killing and finally hold in his left hand to lower the bull's head and keep it lowered while he kills the animal by a sword thrust high up between his shoulder blades.

These are the three acts in the tragedy of the bullfight, and it is the first one, the horse part, which indicates what the others will be and, in fact, makes the rest possible. It is in the first act that the bull comes out in full possession of all of his faculties, confident, fast, vicious and conquering. All his victories are in the first act. At the end of the first act he has apparently won. He has cleared the ring of mounted men and is alone. In the second act he is baffled completely by an unarmed man and very cruelly punished by the banderillas so that his confidence and his blind general rage goes and he concentrates his hatred on an individual object. In the third act he is faced by only one man who must, alone, dominate him by a piece of cloth placed over a stick, and kill him from in front, going in over the bull's right horn to kill him with a sword thrust between the arch of his shoulder blades.

—Ernest Hemingway, *Death in the Afternoon*

The way a topic is divided can be illustrated with a diagram showing its parts and subparts. Here is such a diagram of Hemingway's organization:

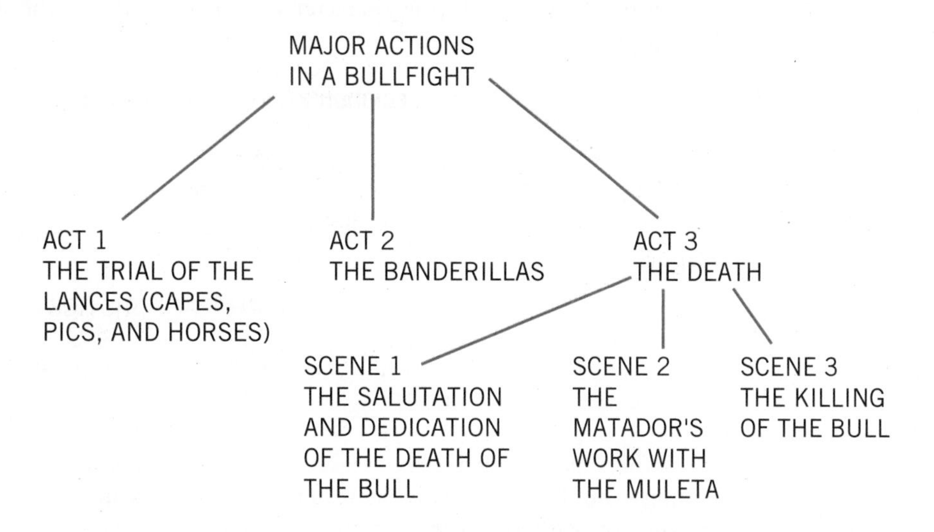

Using this division, the various actions of the bullfight can be classified according to the "act" in which they occur.

PRINCIPLES OF DIVISION

When you divide materials, be sure the division meets several basic requirements. First, it must be appropriate to your writing purpose. Do not divide material simply to have smaller bits of information; rather, use division to help you make a point about your topic. In addition, your divisions should be consistent, exclusive, and complete. These qualities may be defined as follows:

Consistency: Resulting parts must be based on the same principle of division.

Exclusiveness: Parts resulting from the division should not overlap.

Completeness: No important parts should be omitted in the division.

The Hemingway excerpt illustrates each of these requirements. The *point* of Hemingway's division is to suggest the formalized, tragic drama of a bullfight and to highlight the contribution of the key action in each act to the noble defeat of the bull. This division is *consistent* in that the parts, or acts—the trial of the lances, the banderillas, and the death—are all formed on the same principle. Each one is a primary segment of the drama and revolves around a particular major action. The division is *exclusive* because there is no overlap: Actions in one act do not usually occur again in other acts. It is *complete* because Hemingway's acts include all the actions responsible for the defeat of the bull. (Note that the subdivision of the third act into the major activities of the matador fulfills these same requirements.)

The principle of division you use depends on your purpose. Most topics can be divided in a number of ways. For example, based on the purpose of the study, sociologists might divide the respondents to a survey according to age, education, income, or geographic location. Similarly, a gardener choosing deciduous trees for a midwestern park might be concerned with, among other matters, variations in leaf coloration or in shade-giving characteristics and thus divide the subject into the following groupings:

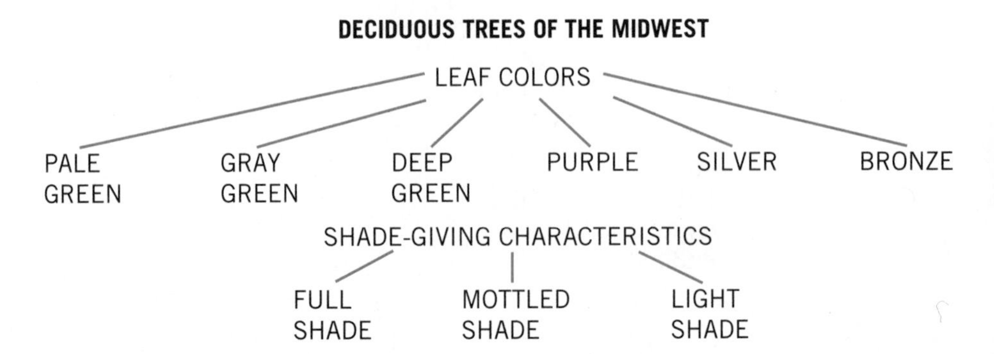

Writers likewise divide topics according to principles based on their purposes for writing. The division itself is the result of the writer's analysis of the topic and of all information gathered regarding the topic plus any ideas or insights the writer may have. Only after fully and thoughtfully analyzing the topic and carefully defining a principle of division can the writer be sure that the division or system of classification will be consistent, exclusive, and complete.

Exercise 17.1

Diagram the division in the first example in this chapter, the selection by Thomas Sowell. Then decide whether the division is consistent, exclusive, and complete. What would you say is the point of the division?

Exercise 17.2

Pick at least two of the following topics, and divide each one according to two or three different principles of division: teachers, dreams, crimes, poets, lies, restaurants, movies, popular music groups, ways of avoiding writing, football offenses, field hockey defenses. Diagram each division, and then state its point. Be sure that each division is consistent, exclusive, and complete.

MAINTAINING COHERENCE

Whenever you divide information into parts, you have to take care to present the material in a way that readers can follow easily. Biologist Sylvia Mader's *Inquiry into Life* includes many good examples of cues a writer can provide to bring coherence to a discussion and to guide readers sufficiently. In the following example, Mader offers a straightforward three-part division to identify the parts of the human ear. In the larger context of the chapter in which it appears, the purpose of this division is to name and classify the parts so that readers will be able to follow a discussion of how the ear functions.

> The ear has three divisions: outer, middle, and inner. The **outer ear** consists of the **pinna** (external flap) and **auditory canal.** The opening of the auditory canal is lined with fine hairs and sweat glands. In the upper wall are modified sweat glands that secrete earwax to help guard the ear against the entrance of foreign materials such as air pollutants.
>
> The **middle ear** begins at the **tympanic membrane** (eardrum) and ends at a bony wall in which are found two small openings covered by membranes. These openings are called the **oval** and **round windows.** The posterior wall of the middle ear leads to many air spaces within the **mastoid process.**
>
> Three small bones are found between the tympanic membrane and the oval window. Collectively called the **ossicles,** individually they are the **hammer** (malleus), **anvil** (incus), and **stirrup** (stapes) because their shapes resemble these objects. The hammer adheres to the tympanic membrane, while the stirrup touches the oval window. . . .
>
> Whereas the outer ear and middle ear contain air, the inner ear is filled with fluid. The **inner ear,** anatomically speaking, has three areas: the first two, called the vestibule and semicircular canals, are concerned with balance; and the third, the cochlea, is concerned with hearing.
>
> The **semicircular canals** are arranged so that there is one in each dimension of space. The base of each canal, called the **ampulla,** is slightly enlarged. Within the ampullae are little hair cells.
>
> The **vestibule** is a chamber that lies between the semicircular canals and the cochlea. It contains two small sacs called the **utricle** and **saccule.** Within both of these

are little hair cells surrounded by a gelatinous material containing calcium carbonate granules, or **otoliths.**

—Sylvia Mader, *Inquiry into Life*

Mader's plan for her division is *spatial,* moving from outside to inside. (Note, in contrast, that Hemingway's division of the bullfight into three acts follows a *temporal* plan, moving through time.) In the initial statement of the division, Mader forecasts the plan of the presentation and names the three divisions in the order in which she will take them up: outer, middle, and inner ear. She then introduces each division in a new paragraph and always with the same syntax at the beginning of a sentence: "The outer ear . . . ," "The middle ear . . . ," "The inner ear . . ." Such strategies help readers to understand and to follow an explanation easily and without confusion.

Exercise 17.3

General strategies for coherence are discussed in Chapter 13.

Look again at the example by Ernest Hemingway to examine the strategies he uses to present a coherent division of information. Does the initial statement of the division name all the groups and forecast the order in which they will be discussed? What other writing strategies does Hemingway use to steer the reader through the presentation?

USING CLASSIFICATION WITH OTHER WRITING STRATEGIES

The following example, which illustrates the relationship of classification and division to other essential writing strategies, is from a book explaining the new physics to nonphysicists.

There are two kinds of mass, which means that there are two ways of talking about it. The first is gravitational mass. The gravitational mass of an object, roughly speaking, is the weight of the object as measured on a balance scale. Something that weighs three times more than another object has three times more mass. Gravitational mass is the measure of how much force the gravity of the earth exerts on an object. Newton's laws describe the effects of this force, which vary with the distance of the mass from the earth. Although Newton's laws describe the effects of this force, they do not define it. This is the mystery of action-at-a-distance. . . .

The second type of mass is inertial mass. Inertial mass is the measure of the resistance of an object to acceleration (or deceleration, which is negative acceleration). For example, it takes three times more force to move three railroad cars from a standstill to twenty miles per hour (positive acceleration) than it takes to move one railroad car from a standstill to twenty miles per hour. . . . Similarly, once they are moving, it takes three times more force to stop three cars than it takes to stop the single car. This is because the inertial mass of the three railroad cars is three times more than the inertial mass of the single railroad car.

Inertial mass and gravitational mass are equal. This explains why a feather and a cannonball fall with equal velocity in a vacuum. The cannonball has hundreds of times more gravitational mass than the feather (it weighs more) but it also has hundreds of times more resistance to motion than the feather (its inertial mass). Its attraction to the earth is hundreds of times stronger than that of the feather, but then so is its inclination not to move. The result is that it accelerates downward at the same rate as the feather, although it seems that it should fall much faster.

The fact that inertial mass and gravitational mass are equal was known three hundred years ago, but physicists considered it a coincidence. No significance was attached to it until Einstein published his general theory of relativity.

—Gary Zukav, *The Dancing Wu Li Masters: An Overview of the New Physics*

Zukav divides his topic into two kinds of mass: gravitational and inertial. Then he defines each one. In the first paragraph, to define gravitational mass, he relies in part on the illustration of an ordinary balance scale. In the second paragraph, to define inertial mass, he contrasts the action of three railroad cars with that of one railroad car. These two paragraphs show how naturally dividing and classifying work together with definition, illustration, and contrast.

Dividing his material into two parts serves to emphasize his point: that inertial mass and gravitational mass (the two parts) are equal. He then illustrates this point by contrasting a feather with a cannonball.

As this example and the others in this chapter indicate, classification and division are basically a strategy for organizing rather than developing an essay. Writers need to use it with other writing strategies in order to *explain* a topic.

Exercise 17.4

Analyze the following classifications, each from a selection in Part I of this book. First, within the context of the whole selection, decide the point of the division and the principle used. Then, decide whether the division is consistent, exclusive, and complete. To focus your analysis, try diagramming the division.

"Birth Control in the Schools," paragraphs 2–5 (Chapter 7)

"Sticks and Stones and Sports Team Names," paragraphs 2–4, 11–13 (Chapter 6)

"Universal E-Mail: Worthy of a 'New Frontier' Commitment," paragraphs 2, 5 (Chapter 7)

Exercise 17.5

Choose one of the following writing activities. Each one asks for some division; state briefly what point your division might make. In addition, be sure that your groupings are consistent, exclusive, and complete. Include in your writing appropriate strategies of coherence: forecasting, paragraphing (optional in a brief piece), repeated sentence patterns, and so on.

1. Write several sentences in which you identify the major periods in your life. Label and briefly define each period.
2. Describe a familiar activity (running, sleeping, eating Chinese food, a task at work) in a new way by dividing it into stages. Label and define each stage.
3. Develop in writing one of the classification systems you created in Exercise 17.2.

CHAPTER 18

Comparing and Contrasting

Comparison and contrast make writing more memorable. Consequently, whenever you analyze and evaluate two or more things, it is useful to compare them. You might compare two people you know well, three motorcycles you are considering buying for a cross-country tour, four Stephen King novels, three tomato plants being grown under different laboratory conditions, or two theories about the causes of inflation and unemployment. But as soon as you begin to compare two things, you usually begin to contrast them as well, for rarely are two things alike in all respects. The contrasts, or differences, among the three motorcycles are likely to be more enlightening than the similarities, many of which may be so obvious as to need no analysis. *Comparison,* then, brings similar things together for examination, to see how they are alike. *Contrast* is a form of comparison that emphasizes their differences.

The use of comparison and contrast is more than a writing strategy, of course. It is a way of thinking and learning. According to a basic principle of learning theory, we acquire new concepts most readily if we can see how they are similar to or different from concepts we already know.

Professional writers say that comparison and contrast is a basic strategy they would not want to be without. In some writing situations (like the ones we mentioned), it has no substitute. Indeed, some writing is essentially extended comparison. But for all kinds of writing situations, writers regularly alternate comparison and contrast with other writing strategies when they present information.

Chances are that you will confront many test questions and essay assignments asking you to compare and contrast—two poems, three presidents, four procedures. This strategy is popular in all academic disciplines, for it is one of the best ways to challenge students intellectually.

TWO WAYS OF COMPARING AND CONTRASTING

There are two ways to organize comparison and contrast in writing: in chunks and in sequence. In *chunking,* each object of the comparison is presented separately; in *sequencing,* the items are compared point by point. For example, a chunked comparison of two motorcycles would first detail all pertinent features of the Pirsig 241X and then consider all features of the Kawazuki 500S, whereas a sequenced comparison would analyze the Pirsig and the Kawazuki feature by feature. In a chunked comparison, the discussion is organized around each separate item being compared. In a sequenced comparison, it is organized around characteristics of the items being compared.

In the following example of chunked comparison, Jane Tompkins contrasts popular nineteenth-century "sentimental" novels with the "Western" novels that provided a reaction against them:

> The female, domestic, "sentimental" religion of the best-selling women writers—Harriet Beecher Stowe, Susan Warner, Maria Cummins, and dozens of others—whose novels spoke to the deepest beliefs and highest ideals of middle-class America, is the real antagonist of the Western.
>
> You can see this simply by comparing the main features of the Western with the sentimental novel. In these books . . . a woman is always the main character, usually a young orphan girl, with several other main characters being women too. Most of the action takes place in private spaces, at home, indoors, in kitchens, parlors, and upstairs chambers. And most of it concerns the interior struggles of the heroine to live up to an ideal of Christian virtue—usually involving uncomplaining submission to difficult and painful circumstances, learning to quell rebellious instincts, and dedicating her life to the service of God through serving others. In these struggles, women give one another a great deal of emotional and material support, and they have close relationships verging on what today we would identify as homosocial and homoerotic. There's a great deal of Bible reading, praying, hymn singing, and drinking of tea. Emotions other than anger are expressed very freely and openly. Often there are long, drawn-out death scenes in which a saintly woman dies a natural death at home. . . .
>
> The elements of the typical Western plot arrange themselves in stark opposition to this pattern, not just vaguely and generally but point for point. First of all, in Westerns (which are generally written by men), the main character is always a full-grown adult male, and almost all of the other characters are men. The action takes place either outdoors—on the prairie, on the main street—or in public places—the saloon, the sheriff's office, the barber shop, the livery stable. The action concerns physical struggles between the hero and a rival or rivals, and culminates in a fight to the death with guns. In the course of these struggles the hero frequently forms a bond with another man—sometimes his rival, more often a comrade—a bond that is more important than any relation he has with a woman and is frequently tinged with homoeroticism. There is very little free expression of the emotions. The hero is a man of few words who expresses himself through physical action—usually fighting. And when death occurs it is never at home in bed but always sudden death, usually murder.
>
> —Jane Tompkins, *West of Everything: The Inner Life of Westerns*

The two items being compared—sentimental novels and Westerns—are discussed separately, first one and then the other. Tompkins signals the shift from the first discussion to the contrasting one by a transitional sentence that begins a new paragraph. Each point of contrast is presented in the same order.

Schematically, a chunked comparison looks simple enough. As the preceding example shows, it is easy to block off such a discussion in a text and then provide a clean transition between the various parts. And yet it can in fact be more complicated for a writer to plan than a sequenced comparison. Sequenced comparison may be closer to the way people perceive and think about similarities or differences in things. For example, you may have realized all at once that two navy blazers are different, but you would identify the specific differences—buttons, tailoring, fabric—one at a time. A sequenced comparison would point to the differences in just this way—one at a time—whereas a chunked comparison would present all the features of one blazer and then do the same for the second. A writer using the chunked strategy, then, must organize all the points of comparison before starting to write. With sequencing, however, the writer can take up each point of comparison as it comes to mind.

In the next example, from a natural history of the earth, David Attenborough uses sequencing to contrast bird wings and airplane wings:

> Bird wings have a much more complex job to do than the wings of an aeroplane, for in addition to supporting the bird they must act as its engine, rowing it through the air. Even so the wing outline of a bird conforms to the same aerodynamic principles as those eventually discovered by man when designing his aeroplanes, and if you know how different kinds of aircraft perform, you can predict the flight capabilities of similarly shaped birds.
>
> Short stubby wings enable a tanager and other forest-living birds to swerve and dodge at speed through the undergrowth just as they helped the fighter planes of the Second World War to make tight turns and aerobatic manoeuvres in a dogfight. More modern fighters achieve greater speeds by sweeping back their wings while in flight, just as peregrines do when they go into a 130 kph dive, stooping to a kill. Championship gliders have long thin wings so that, having gained height in a thermal up-current, they can soar gently down for hours and an albatross, the largest of flying birds, with a similar wing shape and a span of 3 metres, can patrol the ocean for hours in the same way without a single wing beat. Vultures and hawks circle at very slow speeds supported by a thermal and they have the broad rectangular wings that very slow flying aircraft have. Man has not been able to adapt wings to provide hovering flight. He has only achieved that with the whirling horizontal blades of a helicopter or the downward-pointing engines of a vertical landing jet. Hummingbirds have paralleled even this. They tilt their bodies so that they are almost upright and then beat their wings as fast as 80 times a second producing a similar down-draught of air. So the hummingbird can hover and even fly backwards.
>
> —David Attenborough, *Life on Earth*

In this example, note the limited, focused basis for the comparison: the shape of wings. Attenborough specifies this basis in the second sentence of the passage (underscored here). Though birds and planes both fly, they have almost nothing else in common. They are so obviously different that it would even seem silly to compare them in writing. But Attenborough finds a valid—and fascinating—basis for comparison and develops it in a way that both informs and entertains his readers. A successful comparison always has these qualities: a valid basis for comparison, a limited focus, and information that will catch a reader's attention.

Exercise 18.1

Write several sentences comparing and contrasting any one of the following subjects. Be careful to limit the basis for your comparison, and underline the sentence that states that basis.

Two ways of achieving the same goal (for example, travel by bus or subway, or using flattery or persuasion to get what you want)

Two seemingly unlikely subjects for comparison (for example, a child and an old man, or soccer and ballet)

Two sports or theories

Two methods of doing some task at home or on the job

Exercise 18.2

Analyze the specified comparisons in the following selections from Part I. How is each comparison organized? (It may or may not be neatly chunked or sequenced.) Why do you think the writer organizes the comparison in that way? What is the role of the comparison in the whole piece? How effective is it?

"On Being a Real Westerner," paragraphs 3, 4 (Chapter 2)

"Inside the Brain," paragraphs 21–23 (Chapter 4)

"Love," paragraph 14 (Chapter 5)

"In Defense of Talk Shows," paragraphs 7–9 (Chapter 6)

Exercise 18.3

Some of the selections in Part I are organized around comparisons. Identify and evaluate the comparisons in "Path Dependence" in Chapter 5 and "Talking Trash" in Chapter 8. (Remember that the comparison may be stated or implied.)

ANALOGY

An *analogy* is a special form of comparison in which one part of the comparison is used simply to explain the other. See how John McPhee uses two different analogies—the twelve-month calendar and the distance along two widespread arms—to explain the duration of geologic time.

> In like manner, geologists will sometimes use the calendar year as a unit to represent the time scale, and in such terms the Precambrian runs from New Year's Day until well after Halloween. Dinosaurs appear in the middle of December and are gone the day after Christmas. The last ice sheet melts on December 31st at one minute before midnight, and the Roman Empire lasts five seconds. With your arms spread wide again to represent all time on earth, look at one hand with its line of life.

> The Cambrian begins in the wrist, and the Permian Extinction is at the outer end of the palm. All of the Cenozoic is in a fingerprint, and in a single stroke with a medium-grained nail file you could eradicate human history. Geologists live with the geologic scale. Individually, they may or may not be alarmed by the rate of exploitation of the things they discover, but, like the environmentalists, they use these repetitive analogies to place the human record in perspective—to see the Age of Reflection, the last few thousand years, as a small bright sparkle at the end of time.
>
> —John McPhee, *Basin and Range*

Scientists have always made good use of analogy—in both their thinking and their writing. Physics, in particular, is full of concepts that strain the comprehension of the nonscientist. The uncertainty principle, for example, is very difficult for anybody but a physicist to define. See how Gary Zukav does so with an analogy, likening the uncertainty principle to a movie projector that is always slightly out of focus.

> The uncertainty principle reveals that as we penetrate deeper and deeper into the subatomic realm, we reach a certain point at which one part or another of our picture of nature becomes blurred, and there is no way to reclarify that part without blurring another part of the picture! It is as though we are adjusting a moving picture that is slightly out of focus. As we make the final adjustments, we are astonished to discover that when the right side of the picture clears, the left side of the picture becomes completely unfocused and nothing in it is recognizable. When we try to focus the left side of the picture, the right side starts to blur and soon the situation is reversed. If we try to strike a balance between these two extremes, both sides of the picture return to a recognizable condition, but in no way can we remove the original fuzziness from them.
>
> The right side of the picture, in the original formulation of the uncertainty principle, corresponds to the position in space of a moving particle. The left side of the picture corresponds to its momentum. According to the uncertainty principle, we cannot measure accurately, at the same time, both the position *and* the momentum of a moving particle. The more precisely we determine one of these properties, the less we know about the other. If we precisely determine the position of the particle, then, strange as it sounds, there is *nothing* that we can know about its momentum. If we precisely determine the momentum of the particle, there is no way to determine its position.
>
> —Gary Zukav, *The Dancing Wu Li Masters: An Overview of the New Physics*

Notice the strong visual image that Zukav's analogy produces: It is very easy to imagine alternating sides of the movie screen going in and out of focus. Explanatory analogies almost always use very familiar objects for comparison, ordinarily because the writer is trying to explain something very unfamiliar.

Analogies are not limited to abstract, scientific concepts, however. Writers often offer analogies to make nontechnical descriptions or explanations more vivid and entertaining. The following sports analogy from a sociological study of Hamilton, Ohio, comes from a chapter describing a hearing held to examine a school board's decision to fire one teacher, Sam Shie. In it, the writer uses analogy to describe Shie's three lawyers, comparing them to an aggressive basketball team.

> The cross-examination of Dr. Helms was conducted by Randy Rogers, the young associate of Holbrock's. Rogers was tall and strongly built, lacking by only a couple of inches the height of a professional basketball player who weakens the opposition by fouling often and drawing fouls in return. This was close to the function Rogers performed for the defense. With Hugh Holbrock, Robert Dunlevey, and Randy Rogers all ranged against Carl Morgenstern, it was sometimes hard to tell just who the underdog was at the hearings. Sam Shie, to be sure, was a lone teacher up against a community's educational establishment which was trying to purge him. But at the hearings themselves, almost all the spectators were on Shie's side; he was being supported by the Ohio Education Association, and he had three articulate, variously styled lawyers who disputed virtually everything Carl Morgenstern or one of his witnesses said. Each came at Morgenstern from a different angle with a new tactic, trying to wear him down the way a basketball team will use a full-court press, a fast break, the setting of a pick or screen, the switching of defensive assignments to bewilder an opponent. Hugh Holbrock made long, arcing, oratorical shots from outside the key, Robert Dunlevey dribbled spectacularly around any position Morgenstern took, and Randy Rogers would try to provoke Morgenstern into exchanges of anger and procedural wrangles. Rogers was surly to Morgenstern, who would respond by being loftily sardonic. A few times Morgenstern slipped and got mad at Rogers, who was polite to witnesses but steeled himself to a single pitch of fury when he was addressing Morgenstern. The rest of the time Rogers sat moodily at the defense table—in effect on the bench—while Holbrock and Dunlevey performed their own specialties.
>
> —Peter Davis, *Hometown*

Analogies are tricky. They may at first seem useful, but actually it is a rare analogy that is consistently useful at all the major points of comparison. Some are downright misleading.

Thus, most writers exercise caution with analogy. Nevertheless, you will run across analogies regularly; indeed, it would be hard to find a book without one. For certain very abstract information as well as for some writing situations, analogy is the writing strategy of choice.

Exercise 18.4

Write a one-paragraph analogy that explains a principle or process to a reader who is unfamiliar with it. Choose a principle or process that you know well. You might select a basic principle from the natural or social sciences; or you could consider a bodily movement, a physiological process, a process of social change, or a process from your job. Look for something very familiar to compare it with that will help the reader understand the principle or process without a technical explanation.

CHAPTER 19

Arguing

Arguing involves inquiry as well as advocacy. When you write an essay arguing for your point of view, you must think through your own reasons and also try to understand your readers' reasoning. If you ignore what others think, you will be unlikely to convince them to take your argument seriously, let alone to adopt your point of view.

Sometimes, reasoned argument may seem futile. The chances of convincing readers to change their views may be highly unlikely. You may even feel that many of your readers are inflexible or dogmatic, resistant to your best arguments, even impervious to facts that you believe clearly support your point of view. In such cases, you may be tempted to confront readers rather than reason with them. But whether you adopt a contentious tone or an accommodating one, you need to do more than simply assert your point of view. You must argue for your point of view and argue against—what we call counterarguing—opposing points of view.

This chapter presents the basic argumentative strategies for arguing and counterarguing. We focus first on the structure of argument—asserting a thesis, backing it up with reasons and support, and anticipating readers' concerns and objections. Then, we survey some common abuses or errors in argumentation you will want to avoid in your own writing and to be alert to as you read other people's writing.

ASSERTING A THESIS

Central to any argument is the thesis—the point of view the writer wants readers to adopt. Essays that explicitly argue for a point of view present the thesis in a thesis statement. The thesis statement may appear at the beginning of the essay or at the end, but wherever it is placed, its job is simple: to announce as clearly and straightforwardly as possible the main point the writer is trying to make in the essay.

There are five different kinds of argumentative essays in Part I of this book. Each essay asserts a different kind of thesis because each answers a different question:

Assertion of opinion: What is your position on the controversial issue? (Chapter 6: Arguing a Position)

Assertion of policy: What is your understanding of the problem and what do you think should be done to solve it? (Chapter 7: Proposing a Solution)

Chapters 6–10 contain essays that argue for each of these kinds of claims, along with guidelines for constructing an argument to support such a claim.

Assertion of evaluation: What is your judgment of the subject? (Chapter 8: Justifying an Evaluation)

Assertion of cause: What do you think made the subject the way it is? (Chapter 9: Speculating about Causes)

Assertion of interpretation: What does the story mean or what is significant about it? (Chapter 10: Interpreting Stories)

The following sample thesis statements from Chapters 6–10 illustrate the very different kinds of assertions for which you can write an argument:

> When overzealous parents and coaches impose adult standards on children's sports, the result can be activities that are neither satisfying nor beneficial to children.
> —Jessica Statsky, "Children Need to Play, Not Compete" (Chapter 6: Arguing a Position)

> Although this last-minute anxiety about midterm and final exams is only too familiar to most college students, many professors may not realize how such major, infrequent, high-stakes exams work against the best interests of students both psychologically and intellectually. . . . If professors gave additional brief exams at frequent intervals, students would be spurred to study more regularly, learn more, worry less, and perform better.
> —Patrick O'Malley, "More Testing, More Learning" (Chapter 7: Proposing a Solution)

> Fundamentally, *Devil in a Blue Dress* is a modest, skillful, unfussy genre picture. . . . It's the most enjoyable private-eye movie in a long time.
> —Terrence Rafferty, "Black Eye" (Chapter 8: Justifying an Evaluation)

> The mythic horror movie, like the sick joke, has a dirty job to do. It deliberately appeals to all that is worst in us. It is morbidity unchained, our most base instincts let free, our nastiest fantasies realized . . . and it all happens, fittingly enough, in the dark.
> —Stephen King, "Why We Crave Horror Movies" (Chapter 9: Speculating about Causes)

> "Araby" tells the story of an adolescent boy's initiation into adulthood. . . . From the beginning, the boy deludes himself about his relationship with Mangan's sister. At Araby, he realizes the parallel between his own self-delusion and the hypocrisy and vanity of the adult world.
> —David Ratinov, "From Innocence to Insight: 'Araby' as an Initiation Story" (Chapter 10: Interpreting Stories)

As these different thesis statements indicate, the kind of thesis you assert depends on the occasion in which you are writing and the question you are trying to answer for your readers. Nevertheless, to be effective, every thesis must satisfy the same three standards: it must be *arguable, clear,* and *appropriately qualified.*

Arguable Assertions

To be arguable, a thesis must have some probability of being true. It should not, however, be generally accepted as true. In addition, a thesis must be arguable on grounds shared by writer and readers.

Facts are unarguable because they are objectively verifiable. Facts are easy to verify—whether by checking an authoritative reference book, asking an authority, or observing the fact with your own eyes. For example, these statements assert facts:

Jem will be thirty years old on May 6, 2000.

I am less than five feet tall.

Eucalyptus trees were originally imported into California from Australia.

Each of these assertions can be easily verified. To find out Jem's age, you can ask him or look up his school records, among other things. To determine a person's height, you can use a tape measure. To discover where California got its eucalyptus trees, you can refer to a source in the library. There is no point in arguing over such statements (though you might question the authority of a particular source or the accuracy of someone's measurement). If a writer were to assert something as fact and attempt to support the assertion with authorities or statistics, the essay would be considered not an argument but a report of information. Facts, as you will see in the next section, are used in arguments as support for a thesis and not as the thesis itself.

Like facts, expressions of personal feelings are not arguable assertions. Whereas facts are unarguable because they can be definitively proved true or false, feelings are unarguable because they are purely subjective. Personal feelings can be explained, but it would be unreasonable to attempt to convince others to change their views or take action solely on the basis of your personal feelings.

You can declare, for example, that you love rocky road ice cream or that you detest eight o'clock classes, but you cannot offer an argument to support such assertions. All you can do is explain why you feel as you do. Even though many people agree with you about eight o'clock classes, it would be pointless to try to convince others to share your feelings. If, however, you were to restate the assertion as "Eight o'clock classes are counterproductive," you could then construct an argument that does not depend solely on your subjective feelings, memories, or preferences. Your argument could be based on reasons and support that apply to others as well as to yourself. For example, you might argue that students' ability to learn is at an especially low ebb after breakfast and provide scientific and statistical support, in addition, perhaps, to personal experience and interviews with your friends.

Clear and Exact Wording

The way a thesis is worded is as important as its arguability. The wording of a thesis, especially its key terms, must be clear and exact. Two common kinds of imprecision are vagueness and ambiguity.

Consider the following assertion: "Democracy is a way of life." The meaning of this claim is vague and uncertain, partly because the word *democracy* is abstract and partly because the phrase *way of life* is inexact. Abstract ideas like democracy, freedom, and patriotism are by their very nature hard to grasp, and they become even less clear with overuse. Too often, such words take on connotations that may obscure the meaning you want to emphasize. *Way of life* is fuzzy: What does it mean? Moreover, can a form of government be a way of life? It depends on what is meant by *way of life*. Does it refer to daily life, to a general philosophy or attitude toward life, or to something else?

Thus, a thesis is vague if its meaning is unclear; it is ambiguous if it has more than one possible meaning. For example, the statement "My English instructor is mad" can be understood in two ways: The teacher is either angry or insane. Obviously, these are two very different assertions. You would not want readers to think you mean one when you actually mean the other.

In any argumentative writing, you should pay special attention to the way you phrase your thesis and take care to avoid vague and ambiguous language.

Appropriate Qualification

In addition to being arguable and clear, the forcefulness with which a writer asserts a thesis should be appropriate to the writing situation. If you are confident that your case is so strong that readers will accept your argument without question, state your thesis emphatically and unconditionally. If, however, you expect readers to challenge your assumptions or conclusions, you must qualify your statement. Qualifying the extremity or forcefulness of a thesis makes it more likely that readers will take it seriously. Expressions like *probably, very likely, apparently,* and *it seems* all serve to qualify a thesis.

Exercise 19.1

Write an assertion of opinion that states your position on one of the following controversial issues: Should English be the "official" language of the United States? Should college athletes be paid? Should workers have the right to strike for better wages and working conditions? These issues are complicated and have been debated for a long time. Constructing a persuasive argument would obviously require careful deliberation and research. For this exercise, however, all you need to do is construct a thesis on the issue you have chosen that is arguable, clear, and appropriately qualified.

Exercise 19.2

Find the thesis in one of the argumentative essays in Chapters 6–10. Then decide whether the thesis meets the three requirements: that it be arguable, clear, and appropriately qualified.

GIVING REASONS AND SUPPORT

Whether you are arguing a position, proposing a solution, justifying an evaluation, speculating about causes, or interpreting a story, you need to give reasons and support for your thesis.

Reasons can be thought of as the main points arguing for a thesis. Often they answer the question "Why do you think so?" For example, you might value a movie highly *because* it has challenging ideas, unusual camera work, and memorable acting. You might oppose restrictions on students' speech at your college *because* they would make students reluctant to enter into frank debates on important issues, offensive speech is hard to define, and restrictions violate the free-speech clause of the First Amendment. These *because* phrases are your reasons. You may have one or many reasons, depending on your subject and your writing situation.

For your argument to succeed with your readers, you need not only to give reasons but also to provide support. The main kinds of support writers use are facts, statistics, authorities, anecdotes, scenarios, cases, and textual evidence. Following is a discussion of each kind, along with standards for judging the reliability of that particular type of support and examples from published works.

Facts

Facts may be used as support in all types of arguments. A fact is generally defined as a statement accepted as true. Facts refer to a reality that can be measured or verified by objective means. Facts are considered reliable when they meet three requirements: (1) accuracy (they should not distort or misrepresent reality), (2) completeness (they should not omit important details), and (3) trustworthiness (sources should be qualified and unbiased). Some common sources of facts are almanacs, encyclopedias, and research studies as well as direct observations and personal experience.

In this example, a scholar who studies Mexican migration to the United States counterargues the position that our immigration policy should be more restrictive. His argumentative strategy is to convince readers that what they assume to be true about illegal immigrants from Mexico is not true. In other words, their assumptions have no basis in fact.

> The case for a more restrictive immigration policy is based on three principal assumptions: that illegal aliens compete effectively with, and replace, large numbers of American workers; that the benefits to American society resulting from the aliens' contribution of low-cost labor are exceeded by the "social costs" resulting from their presence here; and that most illegal aliens entering the United States eventually settle here permanently, thus imposing an increasingly heavy, long-term burden upon the society.
>
> There is as yet no direct evidence to support any of these assumptions, at least with respect to illegal aliens from Mexico, who still constitute at least 60 to 65 percent of the total flow and more than 90 percent of the illegal aliens apprehended each year.
>
> Where careful independent studies of the impact of illegal immigration on local labor markets have been made, they have found no evidence of large-scale displacement of legal resident workers by illegal aliens. Studies have also shown that Mexican illegals make amazingly little use of tax-supported social services while they are in the United States, and that the cost of the services they do use is far outweighed by their contributions to Social Security and income tax revenues.
>
> There is also abundant evidence indicating that the vast majority of illegal aliens from Mexico continue to maintain a pattern of "shuttle" migration, most of them returning to Mexico after six months or less of employment in the United States. In fact, studies have shown that only a small minority of Mexican illegals even aspire to settle permanently in the United States.
>
> While illegal aliens from countries other than Mexico do seem to stay longer and make more use of social services, there is still no reliable evidence that they compete effectively with American workers for desirable jobs. The typical job held by the illegal alien, regardless of nationality, would not provide the average American family with more than a subsistence standard of living. In most states, it would provide less income than welfare payments.

> Certainly in some geographic areas, types of enterprises, and job categories, illegal aliens may depress wage levels or "take jobs away" from American workers. But there is simply no hard evidence that these effects are as widespread or as serious as most policy-makers and the general public seem to believe.
>
> —Wayne A. Cornelius, "When the Door Is Closed on Illegal Aliens, Who Pays?"

Notice that Cornelius refers to facts as "hard evidence." They are considered hard or solid because once accepted, a fact carries a great deal of weight in an argument. To encourage readers to accept his statements as fact, Cornelius says they come from "careful independent studies." Although he does not cite the sources of these studies here, they are included in the list of references at the end of the book in which this selection appears. Citing sources is especially important when your facts are not commonly accepted. Skeptical readers can review the research cited, as well as other relevant research, and draw their own conclusions.

Make sure that any facts you include in an argument are current, because what is accepted as factual may change as new observations and studies are completed. In addition, you should use only facts relevant to your argument, even if it means leaving out interesting peripheral information. Cornelius, for example, does not include facts about the kind of transportation Mexican illegals rely on because he wants to keep the focus on their brief periods of employment in the United States.

Exercise 19.3

Evaluate the use of fact in one essay from Chapters 6–9. Identify two or three statements presented as fact, and comment on how well they meet the three standards of accuracy, completeness, and trustworthiness.

Statistics

In many kinds of arguments about economic, educational, or social issues, statistics may be essential. When you use statistics in your own arguments, you will want to ensure that they come from reliable sources. Your readers will expect you to explain the statistics clearly and present them fairly and accurately.

The following selection comes from an argument urging that fathers take on a larger role in raising their children. Notice how the writer of this proposal uses statistics from several different studies to prove that there really is a problem.

> In terms of *time* alone, the typical American father has a long way to go to achieve parity parenthood. One famous study found that the average father interacts with his baby for less than 38 seconds a day. In 38 seconds, you cannot even change a crib sheet or sing three verses of "The Farmer in the Dell." The *most* that any father in this sample devoted to his infant in one day was 10 minutes, 26 seconds—barely time enough for a bottle and a burp.
>
> Other fathers studied have logged up to 15 minutes daily feeding their babies, compared to one and a half hours daily for mothers; almost half these fathers said that they had *never* changed the baby's diapers, and three out of four had no regular care-giving responsibilities whatsoever. With one-year-olds, fathers spend between 15 and 20 minutes per day, and although no one is quite sure how to

measure father involvement with older children, we have only to look at children's survey responses to learn that it is not enough. In one study:

- half the preschool children questioned preferred the TV to their fathers;
- one child in 10 (age 7 to 11) said that the person they fear most is their father;
- half the children wished their fathers would spend more time with them;
- among children of divorce, only one third said that they see their fathers regularly.

—Lettie Cottin Pogrebin, "Are Men Discovering the Joys of Fatherhood?"

Whenever possible, use the sources in which statistics first appeared rather than summaries or digests of others' statistics. For example, you would want to get medical statistics from a reputable and authoritative professional periodical like the *New England Journal of Medicine* rather than from a popular newsweekly. If you are uncertain about the most authoritative sources, ask a reference librarian or a professor who is knowledgeable on your topic.

Exercise 19.4

Chapter 21 provides help finding statistical data at the library.

Analyze the use of statistics in one of the following selections from Part I of this book. Identify the sources of the statistics, and consider how you would find out whether the sources are authoritative and reputable. Also look at how the writer integrates the statistics into the text: By direct quotation from the source? By paraphrase or summary? In tables or figures? Finally, decide what the statistics contribute to the argument.

"Children Need to Play, Not Compete" (Chapter 6)

"Birth Control in the Schools" (Chapter 7)

"Where Will They Sleep Tonight?" (Chapter 9)

"The Strange Disappearance of Civic America" (Chapter 9)

Authorities

To support an argument, writers often cite experts on the subject who agree with their point of view. Quoting, paraphrasing, or even just referring to a respected authority can add to a writer's credibility.

The following example comes from Loretta Schwartz-Nobel's book on starvation in America. Schwartz-Nobel cites an authority, a researcher at a well-known oceanographic institute, to support her argument that we now have the technical resources to eliminate hunger in America.

> Dr. John Ryther, a highly respected and well-known marine biologist at the Woods Hole (Massachusetts) Oceanographic Institution, points out that there are about one billion acres of coastal wetlands in the world. If only one-tenth of these wetlands were used to raise fish, the potential yield of fish using improved methods of production would be one hundred million tons a year. This is the equivalent of the yield from the entire world's commercial fisheries.
>
> Dr. Ryther has also devised a complex continuous culture system which produces oysters, seaweed, worms, flounder, and abalone. It ultimately becomes a biological sewage treatment plant returning clean water to the sea.

> If this kind of system were implemented on a large scale it could produce a million pounds of shellfish a year from each one-acre production facility. By using advanced culture techniques like those developed at Woods Hole, Dr. Ryther estimates that the yield could well be multiplied tenfold within the next three decades.
>
> —Loretta Schwartz-Nobel, *Starving in the Shadow of Plenty*

Schwartz-Nobel could simply have mentioned that a system to raise fish in coastal wetlands had been developed, without identifying who developed it or where it was developed. But because she wants readers to believe that implementing the system could help to eradicate hunger, she needs to establish the credibility of the scheme by establishing the credibility of its developer. Her method of establishing Ryther's credibility is typical: She calls him Dr. Ryther to indicate that he has a Ph.D., the highest academic qualification possible; identifies him as a specialist in marine biology; explains that he works at Woods Hole Oceanographic Institution, a place most people knowledgeable about science will recognize immediately as a very prestigious research laboratory; and lets readers know that he is a "highly respected and well-known" scientist.

You might think that citing an authority would weaken Schwartz-Nobel's own credibility with readers because it shows that she did not originate the idea. But citing authorities has the opposite effect. It strengthens her credibility because she herself is not an expert on the technical aspects of her subject. Moreover, when she acknowledges Dr. Ryther's research, Schwartz-Nobel shows that she is following the scientific tradition of using the contributions of others as the foundation for her ideas. The fact that others have been working in the same area makes her plan seem less outlandish and more legitimate.

Exercise 19.5

Analyze the way authorities are used in one of the following selections from Part I of this book. Decide whether you find the use of authorities convincing. How could you find out whether the authorities are respected? How does the writer establish each authority's credentials?

How does the writer integrate the authority's words or opinions into the text of the selection? By direct quotation? By paraphrase or summary? What role does the authority have in the piece as a whole?

"Children Need to Play, Not Compete" (Chapter 6)

"The Declining Art of Political Debate" (Chapter 6)

"Birth Control in the Schools" (Chapter 7)

Anecdotes

Anecdotes are brief stories that can effectively provide evidence in an argument. If they strike readers as true to life, their specificity may be quite convincing.

> While attending a medical meeting about a year ago, I ran into a fellow I'd known in residency. "What are you doing here, Bill?" he asked. "Giving a talk on the responses to death," I replied. "It will cover the psychological value of funerals as well as—"

"Funerals!" he exclaimed. "What a waste *they* are! I've made it plain to my wife that *I* don't want a funeral. Why spend all that money on such a macabre ordeal? And why have the kids standing around wondering what it's all about?"

"Look, Jim," I said patiently, "I've seen case after case of depression caused by the inability of patients—young and old—to work through their feelings after a death. I've found that people are often better off if they have a funeral to focus their feelings on. That lets them do the emotional work necessary in response to the loss." My friend still looked doubtful. And, as we parted company, I wondered how many other physicians are also overlooking the psychological value of funerals.

—William A. Lamers Jr., "Funerals Are Good for People"

See Chapters 2 and 14 for more on writing anecdotes.

Notice that the anecdote happened one particular time. Anecdotes are different from recurring or typical events. They are also different from scenarios, which tell about something that might happen, and cases, which summarize observations made over a period of time. Anecdotes make a special contribution to argument through their concreteness.

In the next example, a historian repeats a secondhand anecdote about the scientist Emanuel Swedenborg to argue that we should take extrasensory perception more seriously than we do.

At six o'clock one evening Swedenborg, while dining with friends in the town of Gothenburg, suddenly became excited and declared that a dangerous fire had broken out in his native city of Stockholm, some three hundred miles away. He asserted a little later that the fire had already burned the home of one of his neighbors and was threatening to consume his own. At eight o'clock of that same evening, he exclaimed with some relief that the fire had been checked three doors from his home. Two days later, Swedenborg's every statement was confirmed by actual reports of the fire, which had begun to blaze at the precise hour that he first received the impression.

Swedenborg's case is only one among hundreds of similar instances recorded in history and biography of the great, the near-great, and the obscure. At some time in their lives Mark Twain, Abraham Lincoln, Saint-Saëns, to name but a few, had, according to their biographers and in some cases their own accounts, strange sudden visions of events taking place at a distance, or events that took place, down to the last minute detail, months or years later in their own lives. In the case of Swedenborg the ability to see at a distance developed later into a powerful and sustained faculty; in most other cases, the heightened perceptivity seemed to arise only in a moment of crisis.

—Gina Cerminora, *Many Mansions*

Exercise 19.6

Analyze the use of anecdote in one of the following selections from Part I of this book. How long is the anecdote in relation to the length of the whole essay? Does the writer comment on the significance of the anecdote or leave it to the reader to infer its importance? How does the writer use the anecdote in his or her argument? Do you find the anecdote convincing?

"Children Need to Play, Not Compete," paragraphs 6, 8 (Chapter 6)

"Sticks and Stones and Sports Team Names," paragraphs 8–9 (Chapter 6)

Scenarios

Whereas an anecdote tells about something that actually happened, a scenario is a narrative that describes something that *might* happen. Writers create scenarios to make their arguments more vivid and convincing. Scenarios raise and answer the question "What if?"

The following example comes from a book on illiteracy in America. To help readers understand the plight of an illiterate person, the author creates a scenario from a dream.

> Since I first immersed myself within this work I have often had the following dream: I find that I am in a railroad station or a large department store within a city that is utterly unknown to me and where I cannot understand the printed words. None of the signs or symbols is familiar. Everything looks strange: like mirror writing of some kind. Gradually I understand that I am in the Soviet Union. All the letters on the walls around me are Cyrillic. I look for my pocket dictionary but I find that it has been mislaid. Where have I left it? Then I recall that I forgot to bring it with me when I packed my bags in Boston. I struggle to remember the name of my hotel. I try to ask somebody for directions. One person stops and looks at me in a peculiar way. I lose the nerve to ask. At last I reach into my wallet for an ID card. The card is missing. Have I lost it? Then I remember that my card was confiscated for some reason, many years before. Around this point, I wake up in a panic.
>
> This panic is not so different from the misery that millions of adult illiterates experience each day within the course of their routine existence in the U.S.A.
>
> —Jonathan Kozol, *Illiteracy in America*

Exercise 19.7

Analyze the use of scenario in Patrick O'Malley's proposal for more frequent testing, "More Testing, More Learning," reprinted in Chapter 7. How does O'Malley use the scenario? Do you find the scenario convincing?

Exercise 19.8

Writers often use scenarios to discuss the possible effects of trends or phenomena. Choose one of the following subjects, and write a scenario illustrating the possible effects.

1. The effects of cable television's popularity on commercial and public television
2. The effects of aerobic dancing and exercise on Americans
3. The effects of increasing tuition costs on college students
4. The effects on U.S. society if colleges were available only to the wealthy
5. The effects on U.S. culture if we actually ran out of gasoline

Cases

Like an anecdote, a case is an example that comes from a writer's firsthand knowledge. Cases summarize observations of people. They are meant to be typical or generalized. Case histories are an important part of the work of psychologists, doctors, and social workers. These cases may be quite lengthy, sometimes following the life of one individual over many months or years. In persuasive writing, however, cases are presented briefly as evidence for a claim or reason.

The following example, from a publication for school administrators, was written by two sociologists studying the psychological problems of adolescents, particularly alienation. Notice how they use the John Kelly case both to define alienation and to argue that it is a serious problem.

> Since the beginning of man's awareness of "self" and "other," alienation has frayed the fabric of social institutions. In recent decades the term has become a euphemism for every kind of aberrant behavior from drug use to rejection of the political system. Adolescents are especially affected by this malaise. Let us consider the case of John Kelly, for example.
>
> > When John Kelly was 10, he was curious and energetic, the mascot of his family. His inquisitiveness led him to railroad yards, museums, and bus adventures downtown alone. In school, he was charming, cooperative, and interested. At 13, John suddenly changed. His agreeable nature vanished as he quarreled endlessly with his older brothers. He became moody and sullen, constantly snapping at his parents. He began to skip school and disrupt class when he did attend. When he was finally expelled, his parents enrolled him in another junior high school, hoping the change would solve some of John's problems. Instead, his difficulties intensified as he dropped his boyhood friends, stopped communicating with his parents, and withdrew into himself. Now, 16-year-old John bears little resemblance to the loving, active child his family once knew. He has been suspended from yet another school, hangs out with an older crowd, and comes home only to sleep. His parents feel hurt, bewildered, frustrated, and frightened.
>
> As John Kelly's case makes clear, adolescent alienation is a teenager's inability to connect meaningfully with other people. At its root is aloneness, a feeling that no one else is quite like you, that you are not what other people want you to be.
>
> —James Mackey and Deborah Appleman, "Broken Connections: The Alienated Adolescent in the '80s"

When they are presented as examples and evidence in persuasive writing, cases are usually brief, rarely longer than this one. Writers nearly always know much more about their cases than they tell us. They select just the details from the case that will support the claim they are making.

To be effective, a case must ring true. Readers need specific details: dress, manner, personal history. Though the person in this case is an abstraction, meant to represent many people like him, we still recognize a real person.

Exercise 19.9

Evaluate the use of a case in either "In Defense of Talk Shows" by Barbara Ehrenreich (Chapter 6) or "Where Will They Sleep Tonight?" by Kim Dartnell (Chapter 9). Decide whether the case is relevant to the argument and whether it rings true. What does the case contribute to the essay?

Textual Evidence

When you argue claims of value (Chapter 8) and interpretation (Chapter 10), textual evidence will be very important. If you are critiquing a controversial book that your readers have not yet read, you may want to quote, paraphrase, or summarize passages so that readers can understand why you think the author's argument is not credible. If you are interpreting a novel for one of your classes, you may need to include numerous excerpts to show just how you arrived at your conclusion. In both situations, you are integrating bits of the text you are evaluating or interpreting into your own text and building your argument on these bits.

You can read "Araby" on pp. 394–98.

In the following example, a literary critic uses textual evidence to support the claim that the main character in James Joyce's story "Araby" is involved in a "vivid waiting." As you read, notice how the writer continually refers to events in the story and also regularly quotes phrases from the story.

> "'Araby,'" wrote Ezra Pound, "is much better than a 'story,' it is a vivid waiting." It is true; the boy, suspended in his first dream of love, is also held up by circumstance, and the subjective rendering of this total experience is indeed vivid. . . .
>
> Every morning the boy kept watch from his window until Mangan's sister appeared, and then with a leaping heart he ran to follow her in the street until their ways diverged, hers toward her convent school. Of an evening, when she came out on the doorstep to call her brother to tea, the boys at play would linger in the shadows to see whether she "would remain or go in"; then while she waited they would approach "resignedly," but while Mangan still teased his sister before obeying, the boy of this story "stood by the railings looking at her," seeing "her figure defined by the light from the half-opened door" and waiting upon a summons of another kind. He must wait too for his uncle's late return and for the money to fetch the girl a present from the bazaar Araby; then the special train, almost empty, waited intolerably and he arrived late. Still he drove toward his goal, paying a shilling to avoid further delay in looking for a sixpenny entrance. Once inside, he found the place half-darkened and the stalls mostly closed. Though there was nothing for him to buy, he lingered still, baffled, stultified, prolonging only pretense of interest. What awaits him as the lights are being put out is a facing "with anguish and anger" of his obsessive mood and its frustration, of himself as "a creature driven and derided by vanity"—like Stephen in *A Portrait,* "angry with himself for being young and the prey of restless foolish impulses."
>
> —Warren Beck, *Joyce's Dubliners*

Exercise 19.10

Analyze the use of evidence in one of the essays on "Araby" in Chapter 10. Identify where "Araby" is quoted, paraphrased, summarized, or merely referred to. Indicate whether the evidence is simply cited or is explained in some way.

COUNTERARGUING

Asserting a thesis and backing it with reasons and support are essential to a successful argument. Thoughtful writers go further, however, by counterarguing—anticipating and responding to their readers' objections, challenges, and questions. To anticipate readers' concerns, try to imagine other people's points of view, what they might know about the subject, and how they might feel about it. Try also to imagine how readers would respond to your argument as it unfolds step by step. What will they be thinking and feeling? What objections would they raise? What questions would they ask?

To counterargue, writers rely on three basic strategies: acknowledging, accommodating, and refuting. Writers show they are aware of readers' objections and questions (acknowledge), modify their position to accept readers' concerns they think are legitimate (accommodate), or explicitly show why readers' objections are invalid or why their concerns are irrelevant (refute). Writers may use one or more of these three strategies in the same essay. According to research by rhetoricians and communications specialists, readers find arguments more convincing when writers have anticipated their concerns in these ways. Acknowledging readers' concerns—and either accommodating or refuting them—wins readers' respect, attention, and sometimes even agreement.

Acknowledging Readers' Concerns

When you acknowledge readers' questions or objections, you show that you take their point of view seriously even if you do not agree with it. In the following example, from her book on hunger in America, Loretta Schwartz-Nobel addresses her readers directly to enlist their sympathy for neglected elderly people.

> This is South Philadelphia—a microcosm of America, a place where people have gone to work, raised children, and then retired. Their daughters are our secretaries, clerks, and teachers. Their sons are our policemen, longshoremen, bankers, doctors, and lawyers. Economically these retired people once represented America's middle class. Yet in this typical urban neighborhood with its tap dance school, businessmen's association, American Cancer Society chapter, and local fire station, a two-year survey conducted by the Albert Einstein Medical Center's Social Service Division concluded that "very few if any of the elderly were without need."
>
> These are men and women who have worked all their lives. These are our uncles, our aunts, our grandparents, our mothers, and our fathers. They live in a world of old newspaper clippings, pictures, and photographs of relatives who never visit.
>
> —Loretta Schwartz-Nobel, *Starving in the Shadow of Plenty*

Here the writer anticipates that readers—as citizens, voters, and taxpayers in any part of the country—might question whether they have any personal responsibility for elderly people in South Philadelphia. Her strategy is to counterargue that South Philadelphia is a representative American community, not a peculiar place with unique problems. She implies that we are one big American family, with familial responsibilities for aging relatives. Since she eventually argues for a national solution to what she believes is a widespread problem, her success depends on her ability to convince readers of their personal responsibility for needy elderly people anywhere in America.

In the next example, Peter Marin acknowledges his readers' possible concerns even more directly. These are the opening paragraphs in an article arguing that some of America's homeless have chosen that way of life. Marin knows that readers may immediately doubt this surprising assertion. It seems inconceivable that people would choose to sleep on sidewalks and eat out of garbage cans. He acknowledges three different doubts.

> The homeless, it seems, can be roughly divided into two groups: those who have had marginality and homelessness forced upon them and want nothing more than

> to escape them, and a smaller number who have at least in part chosen marginality, and now accept, or, in a few cases, embrace it.
>
> I understand how dangerous it can be to introduce the idea of choice into a discussion of homelessness. It can all too easily be used for all the wrong reasons by all the wrong people to justify indifference or brutality toward the homeless, or to argue that they are getting only what they deserve.
>
> And I understand, too, how complicated the notion can become: Many of the veterans on the street, or battered women, or abused and runaway children, have chosen this life only as the lesser of evils, and because, in this society, there is often no place else to go.
>
> And finally, I understand how much that happens on the street can combine to create an apparent acceptance of homelessness that is nothing more than the absolute absence of hope.
>
> Nonetheless we must learn to accept that there may indeed be people on the street who have seen so much of our world, or have seen it so clearly, that to live in it becomes impossible.
>
> —Peter Marin, "Go Ask Alice"

You might think that acknowledging readers' objections in this way—addressing readers directly, listing their possible objections, and discussing each one—would weaken an argument. It might even seem reckless to suggest objections that not all readers would think of. On the contrary, however, readers respond positively to this strategy. The writer appears to have explored the issue thoroughly. He seems thoughtful and reasonable, more interested in inquiry than advocacy, more concerned with seeking the truth about the homeless than in ignoring or overriding readers' objections in order to win their adherence to a self-serving point of view. By researching your subject and analyzing your readers, you will be able to use this strategy confidently in your own argumentative essays.

Exercise 19.11

Choose an essay in Chapter 6 or Chapter 7 that acknowledges readers, and briefly explain how it does so.

Accommodating Readers' Concerns

To argue effectively, you must often take special care to acknowledge your readers' objections, questions, and alternative positions, causes, or solutions. Occasionally, however, you may have to go even further. Instead of merely acknowledging your readers' concerns, you may decide to accept some of them and incorporate them into your own argument. This strategy can be very disarming to readers.

The following example comes from an essay speculating about the causes of people's interest in jogging. Before proposing his own cause (later in the essay), Carll Tucker acknowledges and then accommodates causes proposed by philosophers and theologists.

> Some scout-masterish philosophers argue that the appeal of jogging and other body-maintenance programs is the discipline they afford. We live in a world in which individuals have fewer and fewer obligations. The work week has shrunk.

> Weekend worship is less compulsory. Technology gives us more free time. Satisfactorily filling free time requires imagination and effort. Freedom is a wide and risky river; it can drown the person who does not know how to swim across it. The more obligations one takes on [and] the more time one occupies, the less threat freedom poses. Jogging can become an instant obligation. For a portion of his day, the jogger is not his own man; he is obedient to a regimen he has accepted.
>
> Theologists may take the argument one step further. It is our modern irreligion, our lack of confidence in any hereafter, that makes us anxious to stretch our mortal stay as long as possible. We run, as the saying goes, for our lives, hounded by the suspicion that these are the only lives we are likely to enjoy.
>
> All of these theorists seem to me more or less right. As the growth of cults and charismatic religions and the resurgence of enthusiasm for the military draft suggest, we do crave commitment. And who can doubt, watching so many middle-aged and older persons torturing themselves in the name of fitness, that we are unreconciled to death, more so perhaps than any generation in modern memory?
>
> —Carll Tucker, "Fear of Death"

Notice that Tucker's accommodation is not grudging. He admits that the theorists (and any readers who agree with them) are "more or less right," and he suggests reasons why they must be right. Considering alternative causes is very common in essays speculating about causes (Chapter 9). Writers must acknowledge alternative causes their readers may be aware of and then either accommodate or refute these alternatives. To do anything less makes writers seem uninformed and weakens their credibility.

Exercise 19.12

Exactly how does Patrick O'Malley attempt to accommodate readers in his Chapter 7 essay on more frequent exams? What seems successful or unsuccessful in his argument? What do his efforts at accommodation contribute to the essay?

Refuting Readers' Objections

Your readers' objections and views cannot always be accommodated. Sometimes they must be refuted. When you refute likely objections, you assert that they are wrong and argue against them. Refutation does not have to be delivered arrogantly or dismissively, however. Writers can refute their readers' objections in a spirit of shared inquiry in solving problems, establishing probable causes, deciding the value of something, or understanding different points of view in a controversy. Differences are inevitable. Reasoned argument provides a peaceful and constructive way for informed, well-intentioned people who disagree to work through their differences.

In the following example, an economist refutes one explanation for the increasing numbers of women in the workforce. First he describes a "frequently mentioned" explanation. Then he concedes a point ("there is little doubt") before beginning his refutation.

> One frequently mentioned but inadequately evaluated explanation for the surge of women into paid employment is the spread of time-saving household innovations such as clothes washers and dryers, frozen foods, and dishwashers. There is little doubt that it is easier to combine paid employment with home responsibilities now

> than it was fifty years ago, but it is not clear whether these time-saving innovations were the *cause* of the rise in female labor force participation or whether they were largely a *response* to meet a demand created by working women. Confusion about this point is most evident in comments that suggest that the rapid growth of supermarkets and fast-food outlets is a cause of women going to work. Similar time-saving organizations were tried at least sixty years ago, but with less success because the value of time was much lower then. The absence of supermarkets and fast-food eating places in low-income countries today also shows that their rapid growth in the United States is primarily a *result* of the rising value of time and the growth of women in the work force, not the reverse.
>
> —Victor Fuchs, "Why Married Mothers Work"

As this selection illustrates, writers cannot simply dismiss readers' concerns with a wave of the hand. Fuchs refutes one proposed cause by arguing that it is actually an effect or result of the trend. The last two sentences support his refutation.

The second example comes from a publication arguing for a revised English curriculum in the schools. In this section, the writers attempt to refute a predictable objection. Notice how they describe the objection and then assert their refutation.

> [One] argument against the teaching of literature, which enjoyed greater currency in the late 1960s and 1970s than it does now, goes something like this: Literature is an "elitist" discipline, a subterfuge for imposing ruling-class values on oppressed groups so that they will cooperate in their own exploitation. According to this argument, minority students will encounter a world view in literature classes that is either irrelevant to their own heritage or downright destructive of it. The rebuttal to this argument is straightforward: It is wrong. The treasurehouse of literature is not oppressive; it is liberating—of the constraints of time, place, and personal experience into which each of us as an individual is born. The real injustice would be to deny any child access to the wealth of insights that our best literature has to offer. To deny students the wisdom of our literary heritage may restrict their social mobility and limit the potential that schools have to create opportunities for students to develop their individual talents and to prepare for participation in our society.
>
> Of course, in literature and the arts, local districts should adopt reading lists that recognize the natural desire of communities to maintain an ethnic identity. Quite rightly, black students are inspired by Alex Haley's *Roots* and Richard Wright's *Black Boy;* Hispanic students, by Rudolfo A. Anaya's *Bless Me, Ultima* and Peter Matthiessen's *Sal Si Puedes: Cesar Chavez and the New American Revolution;* Japanese-Americans, by Yoshiko Uchida's *Samurai of Gold Hill* and Monica Sone's *Nisei Daughter;* and so on. Like all great literature, these stories confer lasting benefits—intellectual, social, and spiritual—on those who read them. Furthermore, all students will profit from such literature to understand those whose experiences of America differ from theirs. The point is, far from being "elitist," the common culture belongs to all of us. And every child in the United States—rich or poor, male or female, black, Hispanic, Asian, or white—is entitled to experience it fully.
>
> Our country was founded on the expectation that out of many traditions one nation could evolve that would be stronger and more durable than any single tradition. To argue that teaching a common core of literature in our pluralistic society is not

> feasible because there is no basis for consensus is to beg the question. It is, and always has been, precisely the task of the public schools to help form that consensus.
>
> In a society that celebrates the prerogatives of the individual, the public schools are potentially one of the most meaningful forces for social cohesion. They are the modern equivalent of the village square—a forum for identifying the shared ethos of our diverse and cosmopolitan society; a place where all our children can come together and discover what it is that unites us as a people. Well-taught literature is an essential part of that consensus building.
>
> —California State Education Department, *Handbook for Planning an Effective Literature Program*

As both of these examples illustrate, effective refutation requires a restrained tone and careful argument. Although you may not accept the refutation, you can agree that it is thoughtfully argued. You do not feel attacked personally because the writers disagree with you.

The writers of the second article make an important concession in the second paragraph. They acknowledge the value of minority literature while still arguing for a common literature in school English programs. Here, accommodation blends with refutation.

Exercise 19.13

Analyze and evaluate the use of refutation in any of the essays in Chapters 6–10. How does the writer manage the refutation? Does the objection seem to be clearly and accurately described? How does the writer assert and argue for the refutation? What seems most convincing and least convincing in the argument? What is the tone of the refutation?

Exercise 19.14

Briefly refute any of the refutations you analyzed in Exercise 19.13. State the writers' refutation accurately, and argue your refutation of it convincingly.

Exercise 19.15

Return to the thesis you wrote in Exercise 19.1. Imagine how you might develop an essay arguing for this claim with reasons and support. Then identify one objection or question you could expect readers to raise and write a few sentences refuting it.

LOGICAL FALLACIES

Fallacies are errors or flaws in reasoning. Although essentially unsound, fallacious arguments seem superficially plausible and often have great persuasive power. Fallacies are not necessarily deliberate efforts to deceive readers. A writer may introduce a fallacy accidentally by not examining their own reasons or underlying assumptions critically, by failing to establish solid support, or by using unclear or ambiguous words. Here is a summary of the most common logical fallacies (listed alphabetically):

- *Begging the question.* Arguing that a claim is true by repeating the claim in different words. Sometimes called *circular reasoning.*
- *Confusing chronology with causality.* Assuming that because one thing preceded another, the former caused the latter. Also called *post hoc, ergo propter hoc* (Latin for "after this, therefore because of this").
- *Either-or reasoning.* Assuming that there are only two sides to a question and representing yours as the only correct one.
- *Equivocating.* Misleading or hedging with ambiguous word choices.
- *Failing to accept the burden of proof.* Asserting a claim without presenting a reasoned argument to support it.
- *False analogy.* Assuming that because one thing resembles another, conclusions drawn from one also apply to the other.
- *Hasty generalization.* Offering only weak or limited evidence to support a conclusion.
- *Overreliance on authority.* Assuming that something is true simply because an expert says so and ignoring evidence to the contrary.
- *Oversimplifying.* Giving easy answers to complicated questions, often by appealing to emotions rather than logic.
- *Personal attack.* Demeaning the proponents of a claim instead of refuting their argument. Also called *ad hominen* (Latin for "against the man") *attack.*
- *Red herring.* Attempting to misdirect the discussion by raising an essentially unrelated point.
- *Slanting.* Selecting or emphasizing the evidence that supports your claim and suppressing or playing down other evidence.
- *Slippery slope.* Pretending that one thing inevitably leads to another.
- *Sob story.* Manipulating readers' emotions in order to lead them to draw unjustified conclusions.
- *Straw man.* Directing the argument against a claim that nobody actually holds or that everyone agrees is very weak.

CHAPTER 20

Field Research

Field research includes observations, interviews, and questionnaires. In universities, government agencies, and the business world, field research can be as important as library research or experimental research. If you major in education, communication, or one of the social sciences, you will probably be asked to do writing based on observations, interviews, and questionnaire results. You will also read large amounts of information based on these methods of learning about individuals, groups, and institutions.

Observations and interviews are essential for writing profiles (Chapter 4). Interviewing could be helpful, as well, in documenting a trend or phenomenon and exploring its causes (Chapter 9)—for example, you might consult an expert or conduct a survey to establish the presence of a trend. In proposing a solution to a problem (Chapter 7), you might want to interview people involved; or, if many people are affected, you might find it useful to do a questionnaire. In writing to explain an academic concept (Chapter 5), you might want to interview a faculty member who is a specialist on the subject.

OBSERVATIONS

This section offers guidelines for planning an observational visit, taking notes on your observations, writing them up, and preparing for follow-up visits. Some kinds of writing are based on observations from single visits—travel writing, social workers' case reports, insurance investigators' accident reports—but most observational writing is based on several visits. An anthropologist or a sociologist studying an unfamiliar group or activity might observe it for months, filling several notebooks with notes. If you are profiling a place (Chapter 4), you almost certainly will want to make two or more observational visits, some of them perhaps combined with interviews.

Second and third visits to observe further are important because as you learn more about a place from initial observations, interviews, or reading, you will discover new ways to look at it. Gradually, you will have more and more questions that can only be answered by follow-up visits.

Planning the Visit

To ensure that your observational visits are worthwhile, you must plan them carefully.

Getting Access. If the place you propose to visit is public, you will probably have easy access to it. If everything you need to see is within view of anyone passing by or using the place, you can make your observations without any special arrangements. Indeed, you may not even be noticed.

However, most observational visits require special access. Hence, you will need to arrange your visit, calling ahead or stopping by to get acquainted, in order to introduce yourself and state your purpose. Find out the times you may visit, and be certain you can gain access easily.

Announcing Your Intentions. State your intentions directly and fully. Say who you are, where you are from, and what you hope to do. You may be surprised at how receptive people can be to a college student on assignment. Not every place you wish to visit will welcome you, however. In addition, private businesses as well as public institutions place a variety of constraints on outside visitors. But generally, if people know your intentions, they may be able to tell you about aspects of a place or an activity you would not have thought to observe.

Taking Your Tools. Take a notebook with a firm back so that you will have a steady writing surface. Remember also to take a writing instrument. Some observers dictate their observations into a tape recorder and transcribe their notes later. You might want to experiment with this method. We recommend, though, that for your first observations you record in writing. Your instructor or other students in your class may want to see your notes, and transcribing can take a lot of time.

Observing and Taking Notes

Here are some brief guidelines for observing and taking notes.

Observing. Some activities invite multiple vantage points, whereas others seem to limit the observer to a single perspective. Take advantage of every perspective available to you. Come in close, take a middle position, and stand back. Study the scene from a stationary position and also try to move around it. The more varied your perspectives, the more you are likely to observe.

Your purpose in observing is both to describe the activity or place and to analyze it. You will want to look closely at the activity or place itself, but you will also want to think about what makes it special, what seems to be the point or purpose of it.

Try to be an innocent observer: Pretend that you have never seen anything like this activity or place before. Look at it from the perspective of your readers. Ask yourself what details would surprise, inform, and interest them.

Taking Notes. You will undoubtedly find your own style of notetaking, but here are a few pointers.

- Write on only one side of the page. Later, when you organize your notes, you may want to cut up the pages and file notes under different headings.
- Take notes in words, phrases, or sentences. Draw diagrams or sketches, if they help you to see and understand the place or activity.
- Note any ideas or questions that occur to you.
- Use quotation marks around any overheard remarks or conversations you write down.

Because you can later reorganize your notes in any way you wish, you do not need to take notes in any planned or systematic way. You might, however, want to cover the following aspects of a place:

The Setting. The easiest way to begin is to name objects you see. Just start by listing objects. Then record details of some of them—color, shape, size, texture, function, relation to similar or dissimilar objects. Although your notes will probably contain mainly visual details, you might also want to record sounds and smells. Be sure to include some notes about the shape, dimensions, and layout of the place as a whole. How big is it? How is it organized?

The People. Record the number of people, their activities, their movements and behavior. Describe their appearance or dress. Record parts of overheard conversations. Note whether you see more men than women, more members of one nationality or ethnic group than of another, more older than younger people. Most important, note anything surprising or unusual about people in the scene.

Your Personal Reactions. Include in your notes any feelings you have about what you observe. Also record, as they occur to you, any ideas or insights you have.

Reflecting on Your Observation

Immediately after your observational visit (within just a few minutes, if possible), find a quiet place to reflect on what you saw, review your notes, and add to your notes. Give yourself at least a half-hour for quiet thought.

Your notes and your recollections will suggest many more images and details from your observation. Add these to your notes.

Finally, review all your notes, and write a few sentences about your main impressions of the place. What did you learn? How did this visit change your preconceptions? What surprised you most? What is the dominant impression you get from your notes?

Writing Up Your Notes

Clustering is described in Chapter 11; inventorying is described in Chapter 12.

See Chapter 15 for a full discussion of describing strategies.

Your instructor may ask you to write up your notes as a report on the observational visit. If so, review your notes, looking for a meaningful pattern in the details you have noted down. You might find clustering or inventorying useful for discovering patterns in your notes.

Assume that your readers have never been to the place, and decide on the dominant impression you want readers to have. Use this impression to choose details for your report.

Then draft a brief description of the place. Your purpose is to select details from your notes that will convey to readers a vivid impression of the place.

Preparing for Follow-Up Visits

Rather than repeat yourself in follow-up visits, try to build on what you have already discovered. You should probably do some interviewing and reading before another observational visit so that you will have a greater understanding of the subject when you observe it again. It is also important to develop a plan for your follow-up: questions to be answered, hypotheses to be tested, types of information you would like to discover.

INTERVIEWS

Like making observations, interviewing tends to involve four basic steps: (1) planning and setting up the interview, (2) taking notes, (3) reflecting on the interview, and (4) writing up your notes.

Planning and Setting Up the Interview

The initial step in interviewing involves choosing an interview subject and then arranging and planning the interview.

Choosing an Interview Subject. First, decide whom to interview. If you are writing about some activity or enterprise in which several people are involved, choose subjects representing a variety of perspectives—a range of roles, for example. If you are profiling a single person, most, if not all, of your interviews will be with that person.

You should be flexible because you may be unable to speak to the person you initially targeted and may wind up with someone else—the person's assistant, perhaps. Do not assume that this interview subject will be of little use to you. With the right questions, you might even learn more from the assistant than you would from the person you had originally expected to see.

Arranging an Interview. You may be nervous about calling up a busy person and asking for some of his or her time. Indeed, you may get turned down. But if so, it is possible that you will be referred to someone who will see you, someone whose job it is to talk to the public.

Do not feel that just because you are a student, you do not have the right to ask for people's time. You will be surprised at how delighted people are to be asked about themselves, particularly if you reach them when they are not feeling harried. Most people love to talk—about anything! And since you are a student on assignment, some people may feel that they are performing a public service by talking with you.

When introducing yourself to arrange the interview, give a short and simple description of your project. If you talk too much, you could prejudice or limit the interviewee's response. At the same time, it is a good idea to exhibit some enthusiasm for your project. If you lack enthusiasm, the person may see little reason to talk to you.

Keep in mind that the person you are interviewing is donating time to you. Be certain that you call ahead to arrange a specific time for the interview. Be on time. Bring all the materials you need, and express your thanks when the interview is over.

Planning for the Interview. The best interview is generally the planned interview. It will help if you have made an observational visit and done some background reading beforehand. In preparation for the interview, you should do two things in particular: consider your objectives and prepare some questions.

Think about your main objectives. Do you want an orientation to the place or your topic (the "big picture") from this interview? Do you want this interview to lead you to interviews with other key people? Do you want mainly facts or information? Do you need to clarify something you have heard in another interview, observed, or read? Do you want to learn more about the person, or about the place or your topic through the person—or both? Should you trust or distrust what this person tells you?

The key to good interviewing is flexibility. You may be looking for facts, but your interview subject may not have any to offer. In that case, you should be able to shift gears and go after whatever your subject is in a position to discuss.

Composing Questions. Take care in composing the questions you prepare in advance; they can be the key to a successful interview. Any question that places unfair limits on respondents is a bad question. Two specific types to avoid are forced-choice questions and leading questions.

Forced-choice questions impose your terms on your respondents. Let us assume you are interviewing a counselor at a campus rape crisis center and want to know what he or she thinks is the motivation for rape. You could ask: "Do you think rape is an expression of sexual passion or of aggression?" But the counselor might think that neither sexual passion nor aggression satisfactorily explains rape. A better way to phrase the question would be to say, "People often fall into two camps on the issue of rape. Some think it is an expression of sexual passion, while others argue it is really not sexual but aggressive. Do you think it is either of these? If not, what is your opinion?" Phrasing the question in this way allows you to get a reaction to what others have said at the same time that it gives the interviewee freedom to set the terms for his or her response.

Leading questions assume too much. An example of this kind of question is this: "Do you think the number of rapes has increased because women are perceived as competitors in a highly competitive economy?" This question assumes that there is an increase in the occurrence of rape, that women are perceived (apparently by rapists) as economic competitors, and that the state of the economy is somehow related to acts of rape. A better way of asking the question might be to make the assumptions more explicit by dividing the question into its parts: "Do you think the number of rapes has increased? What could have caused this increase? I've heard some people argue that the economy has something to do with it. Do you think so? Do you think rapists perceive women as competitors for jobs? Could the current economic situation have made this competition more severe?"

Good questions come in many different forms. One way of considering them is to divide them into two types: open and closed. *Open questions* give the respondent range and flexibility. They also generate anecdotes, personal revelations, and expressions of attitudes. For example:

- I wonder if you would take a few minutes to tell me something about your early days in the business. I'd be interested to hear about how it got started, what your hopes and aspirations were, what problems you faced, and how you dealt with them.

- Tell me about a time you were *(name an emotion)*.
- What did you think of *(name a person or event)*?
- What did you do when *(name an event)* happened?

The best questions are those that allow the subject to talk freely but to the point. If the answer strays too far from the point, you may need to ask a follow-up question to refocus the talk. Another tack you might want to try is to rephrase the subject's answer, to say something like "Let me see if I have this right" or "Am I correct in saying that you feel . . . ?" Often, a person will take the opportunity to amplify the original response by adding just the anecdote or quotable comment you've been looking for.

Closed questions usually request specific information; for example:

- How do you *(name a process)*?
- What does *(name a word)* mean?
- What does *(a person, an object, or a place)* look like?
- How was it made?

Taking Your Tools. As for an observational visit, when you interview someone, you will need a notebook with a firm back so that you can write on it easily without the benefit of a table or desk. You might find it useful to divide several pages into two columns by drawing a line about one-third of the width of the page from the left margin. Use the left-hand column to note details about the scene, the person, the mood of the interview, and other impressions. Head this column "Details and Impressions." At the top of the right-hand column, write several questions. You may not use them, but they will jog your memory. This column should be titled "Information." In it, you will record what you learn from answers to your questions.

See pp. 148–49 for an example of notes of this sort.

Taking Notes during the Interview

Because you are not taking a verbatim transcript of the interview (if you want a literal account, use a tape recorder or shorthand), your goals are to gather information and to record a few quotable bits of information, comments, and anecdotes. In addition, because the people you interview may be unused to giving interviews and so will need to know you are paying attention, it is probably a good idea to do more listening than notetaking. You may not have much confidence in your memory, but if you pay close attention, you are likely to recall a good deal of the conversation afterward. Take some notes during the interview: a few quotations; key words and phrases; details of the scene, the person, and the mood of the interview. Remember that *how* something is said is as important as *what* is said. Look for material that will give texture to your writing—gesture, verbal inflection, facial expression, body language, physical appearance, dress, hair, anything that makes the person an individual.

Reflecting on the Interview

As soon as you finish the interview, find a quiet place to reflect on it and review your notes. This reflection is essential because so much happens in an interview that you cannot record at the time. Spend at least a half-hour adding to your notes and thinking about what you learned.

At the end of this time, write a few sentences about your main impressions from the interview. What did you learn? What surprised you most? How did the interview change your attitude or understanding about the person or place? How would you summarize your impressions of the person?

Writing Up Your Notes

Your instructor may ask you to write up your notes. If so, review them for useful details and information. Decide what main impression you want to give of this person. Choose details that will contribute to this impression. Select quotations and paraphrases of information you learned from the person.

These strategies are discussed in Chapter 11.

To find a focus for your write-up, you might try looping or clustering. Invention questions can also help you to consider the interview subject from different perspectives.

QUESTIONNAIRES

Questionnaires let you survey the attitudes or knowledge of large numbers of people. You could carry out many face-to-face or phone interviews to get the same information, but questionnaires have the advantages of economy, efficiency, and anonymity. Some questionnaires, such as ones you filled out when applying to college, just collect demographic information: your name, age, sex, hometown, religious preference, intended major. Others, such as the Gallup and Harris polls, collect opinions on a wide range of issues. Before elections, we are bombarded with the results of these kinds of polls. Still other kinds of questionnaires, ones used in academic research, are designed to help to answer important questions about personal and societal problems.

This section briefly outlines procedures you can follow to carry out an informal questionnaire survey of people's opinions or knowledge and then to write up the results.

Focusing Your Study

A questionnaire study usually has a limited focus. You might need to interview a few people in order to find this focus.

Let us assume that you went to your campus student health clinic (SHC) and had to wait over an hour to see a nurse. Sitting there with many other students, you decide that this long wait is a problem that needs to be studied. Furthermore, it seems an ideal topic for a proposal essay (Chapter 7) you have been assigned in your writing class.

You do not have to explore the entire operation of the SHC to study this problem. You are not interested in how nurses and doctors are hired or how efficient their system of ordering supplies is. You have a particular concern: how successful the SHC is in scheduling appointments and organizing its resources to meet student needs. More specifically, do students often have to wait too long to see a nurse or doctor? You might also want to know *why* this is the case, if it is; but you can seek an answer to that question only by interviewing the SHC staff. Your primary interest is in how long students usually wait for appointments, what times are most convenient for students to schedule appointments, whether SHC resources are concentrated at those times, and similar matters. With this limited focus, you can collect valuable information using a fairly brief questionnaire.

To be certain about your focus, however, you should talk informally to several students to find out whether they think there is a problem. You might also want to talk to people at the SHC, explaining your plans and asking for their views on the problem.

Whatever your interest, be sure to limit the scope of your study. Try to focus on one or two important questions. With a limited focus, your questionnaire can be brief, and people will be more willing to fill it out. In addition, a study based on a limited amount of information will be easier to organize and report.

Writing Questions

Two basic forms of questions, closed and open, were introduced earlier in this chapter. The following section contains additional illustrations of how these types of questions may be used in the context of a questionnaire.

Closed Questions. Following are examples of some forms of closed questions for a possible student questionnaire. You will probably use more than one form in a questionnaire because you will have several kinds of information to collect.

Checklists

With your present work and class schedule, when are you able to visit the SHC? (Check as many boxes as necessary.)

☐ 8–10 A.M.

☐ 10–12 A.M.

☐ noon hour

☐ 1–3 P.M.

☐ 3–5 P.M.

Which services do you expect to use at the SHC this year?

☐ allergy desensitization

☐ immunization

☐ optometry

☐ dental care

☐ birth control

☐ illness or infection

☐ counseling

☐ health education

Two-Way Questions

Have you made an appointment this year at the SHC?

______ yes

______ no

Have you ever had to wait more than thirty minutes at the SHC for a scheduled appointment?

______ yes

______ no

If you could, would you schedule appointments at the SHC after 7 P.M.?

______ yes

______ no

______ uncertain

Multiple-Choice Questions

How frequently have you had to wait more than ten minutes at the SHC for a scheduled appointment?

______ always

______ usually

______ occasionally

______ never

From your experience so far with the SHC, how would you rate its services?

______ inadequate

______ barely adequate

______ adequate

______ better than adequate

______ outstanding

Ranking Scales

With your present work and class schedule, which times during the day (Monday through Friday) would be most convenient for you to schedule appointments at the SHC? Put 1 by the most convenient time, 2 by the next most convenient time, and so on until you have ranked all four choices.

______ mornings

______ afternoons before 5 P.M.

______ 5–7 P.M.

______ 7–10 P.M.

Open Questions. Open questions ask for a brief answer.

What services do you expect to need at the SHC this year?

____

____

____

From your experiences with appointments at the SHC, what advice would you give students about making appointments?

____

____

____

What do you believe would most improve services at the SHC?

____

____

____

You may want to use a combination of closed and open questions for your questionnaire. Both offer advantages: Closed questions will give you definite answers, but open questions can elicit information you may not have anticipated and provide lively quotations for your report.

Trying Out the Questions. As soon as you have a collection of possible questions, try them out on a few typical readers. You need to know which questions are unclear, which seem to duplicate others, and which provide the most interesting responses. These tryouts will enable you to assess which questions will give you the information you need. Readers can also help you to come up with additional questions.

Designing the Questionnaire

Write a brief, clear introduction stating the purpose of the questionnaire and explaining how you intend to use the results. Give advice on answering the questions, and estimate the amount of time needed to complete the questionnaire. If you are going to give the questionnaire to groups of people in person, you can give this information orally.

Select your most promising questions, and decide on an order. Any logical order is appropriate. You might want to begin with the least complicated questions or the most general ones. You may find it necessary or helpful to group the questions by subject matter or form. Certain questions may lead to others. You might want to place open questions at the end.

Design the questionnaire so that it looks attractive and readable. Make it look easy to complete. Do not crowd questions together to save paper. Provide plenty of space for readers to answer open questions, and remind them to use the back of the page if they need more space.

Testing the Questionnaire

Make a few copies of your first design, and ask at least three readers to complete the questionnaire. Find out how much time they needed to complete it. Talk to them about any confusion or problems they experienced. Review their responses with them to be certain that each question is eliciting the information you want it to elicit. From what you learn, reconsider your design, and revise particular questions.

Administering the Questionnaire

Decide who will fill out your questionnaire and how you can arrange for them to do so. The more readers you have, the better; but constraints of time and expense will almost certainly limit the number. You can mail questionnaires or distribute them to dormitories or workplace mailboxes, but the return will be low. It is unusual for even half the people receiving mail questionnaires to return them. If you do mail the questionnaire, be sure to mention the deadline for returning it. Give directions for returning the questionnaire, and include a stamped, self-addressed envelope, if necessary.

You might want to arrange to distribute the questionnaire yourself to some groups in class, at dormitory meetings, or at work.

Note that if you want to do a formal questionnaire study, you will need a scientifically representative group of readers (a random or stratified random sample). Even for an informal study, you should try to get a reasonably representative group. For example, to study satisfaction with the appointment schedule at the SHC, you would want to have students who had been to the clinic fairly often. You might even want to include a concentration of seniors rather than first-year students because after four years, seniors would have made more visits to the SHC. If many students commute, you would want to be sure to have commuters among your respondents.

Your report will be more convincing if you demonstrate that your respondents represent the group whose opinions or knowledge you claim to be studying. As few as twenty-five respondents could be adequate for an informal study.

Writing Up the Results

Now that you have the completed questionnaires, what do you do with them?

Summarizing the Results. Begin by tallying the results from the closed questions. Take an unused questionnaire, and tally the responses next to each choice. Suppose that you had twenty-five readers. Here is how the tally might look for the first checklist question.

> With your present work and class schedule, when are you able to visit the SHC? (Check as many boxes as necessary.)
>
> M 8–10 A.M. 卌卌卌 ||| (18)
>
> M 10–12 A.M. 卌 || (7)
>
> M noon hour 卌卌 ||| (13)
>
> M 1–3 P.M. ||| (3)
>
> M 3–5 P.M. 卌 |||| (9)

Each tally mark represents one response to that item. The totals add up to more than twenty-five because readers were asked to check *all* the times when they could make appointments.

Next, consider the open questions. Read all twenty-five answers to each question separately to see the kinds and variety of responses to each. Then decide whether you want to code any of the open questions so that you can summarize results from them quantitatively, as you would with closed questions. For example, you might want to classify the types of advice given as responses to an open question proposed earlier: "From your experiences with appointments at the SHC, what advice would you give students about making appointments?" You could then report the numbers of readers (of your twenty-five) who gave each type of advice. For an opinion question ("How would you evaluate the most recent appointment you had at the SHC?"), you might simply code the answers as positive, neutral, and negative and then tally the results accordingly for each kind of response. However, responses to open questions are perhaps most often used as a source of quotations for your report.

You can report results from the closed questions as percentages, either within the text of your report or in tables. You can find table formats in texts you may be using or even in magazines or newspapers. Conventional formats for tables in social science reports are illustrated in the *Publication Manual of the American Psychological Association*, 4th ed. (Washington, DC: American Psychological Association, 1994).

See pp. 595–603 for strategies for integrating quoted material.

You can quote responses to the open questions within your text, perhaps weaving them into your discussion like quoted material from published sources. Or you can organize several responses into lists and then comment on them. Since readers' interests can be engaged more easily with quotations than with percentages, plan to use many open responses in your report.

You can use computer spreadsheet programs to tabulate the results from closed questions and even print out tables or graphs that you can insert into your report. For a small informal study, however, such programs would probably not save you much time.

Organizing and Writing the Report. In organizing the report of your results, you might want to consider a plan that is commonly followed in the social sciences:

Statement of the problem
- Context for your study
- Your question
- Need for your study
- Brief preview of your study and plan for your report

Review of other related studies (if you know of any)

Procedures
- Designing the questionnaire
- Selecting the readers
- Administering the questionnaire
- Summarizing the results

Results: presentation of what you learned, with little commentary or interpretation

Summary and discussion: brief summary of your results and discussion of their significance (commenting, interpreting, exploring implications, and comparing to other related studies)

CHAPTER 21

Library and Internet Research

Doing research is a voyage of discovery. Research requires patience, careful planning, good advice, and even luck. The rewards are great, however. One of life's greatest intellectual pleasures is to learn about a subject and then be able to put diverse information together in a new way—for yourself and others. Each new research project leads you to unexplored regions of the library or of cyberspace. You may find yourself in a rare book room reading a manuscript written hundreds of years ago or involved in a lively discussion on the Internet with people hundreds of miles away. One moment you may be keyboarding commands, and the next, you may be threading a microfilm reader, viewing a videodisk, or squinting at the fine print in an index. You may breeze through an encyclopedia entry introducing you to a new subject or struggle with a just-published report of a highly technical research study on the same subject.

Until recently, students had to rely almost exclusively on the resources available at their college and local municipal libraries. With increased access to the Internet, however, students now have more sources of information than ever before.

This chapter is designed to help you to learn how to use the resources available in your college library and on the Internet. It gives advice on how to learn about the library and the Internet, develop efficient search strategies, keep track of your research, locate sources, and read them with a critical eye. Chapter 22 provides guidelines for using and acknowledging these sources in an essay. It also presents a sample research paper, on home schooling, written in response to an assignment to write an essay speculating about the causes of a trend.

With the help of your librarian and the guidelines in this chapter and in Chapter 22, you will be able to manage all the research assignments in this text and in your other college courses as well.

ORIENTING YOURSELF TO THE LIBRARY

Make a point of taking a tour of the library. Then, when you first research a subject, be sure you understand your research task well. Consult a reference librarian if you need help.

Taking a Tour

Your instructor may arrange a library orientation tour for your composition class. If not, you can join one of the regular orientation tours scheduled by the librarians. Even if you are already a frequent user of the library, a tour is essential because nearly all college libraries are more complex and offer more services than typical school or public libraries. On a library tour, you will learn how the library catalog and reference room are organized, how to access computer catalogs and databases, whom to ask for help if you are confused, and how to get your hands on books, periodicals, and other materials.

Pick up copies of any available pamphlets and guidelines. Nearly every library offers handouts describing the resources and services it provides. Also look for a floor map of materials and facilities. See whether your library offers any research guidelines, special workshops, or presentations on strategies for locating resources.

Consulting a Librarian

Professional librarians are master navigators of a contemporary library, which often includes the diverse resources of the Internet. Think of college librarians as advisers whose job is to help you understand the library and get your hands on sources you need to complete your research projects. Think of them also as instructors who can help you with the business of learning. Librarians at the information or reference desk are there to provide reference services, and most have years of experience answering the very questions you are likely to ask. You should not hesitate to approach them with any questions you have about locating sources. Remember, however, that they can be most helpful when you can explain your research assignment clearly.

Knowing Your Research Task

Before you go to the library to start an assigned research project, learn as much as you can about the assignment. Should you need to ask a librarian for advice, it is best to have the assignment in writing. Ask your instructor to clarify any confusing terms and to define the purpose and scope of the project. Find out how you can narrow or focus the project once you begin the research. Asking a question or two in advance can prevent hours—or even days—of misdirected work. You should try to get to the library as soon as you understand the assignment. If many of your classmates will be working on similar projects, there may be competition for a limited number of books and other resources.

A LIBRARY SEARCH STRATEGY

For your library research to be manageable and productive, you will want to work carefully and systematically. The search strategy presented in this chapter was developed by college librarians with undergraduate needs firmly in mind. Although specific search strategies may vary to fit the needs of individual research tasks, the general process presented here should help you to get started, keep track of all your research,

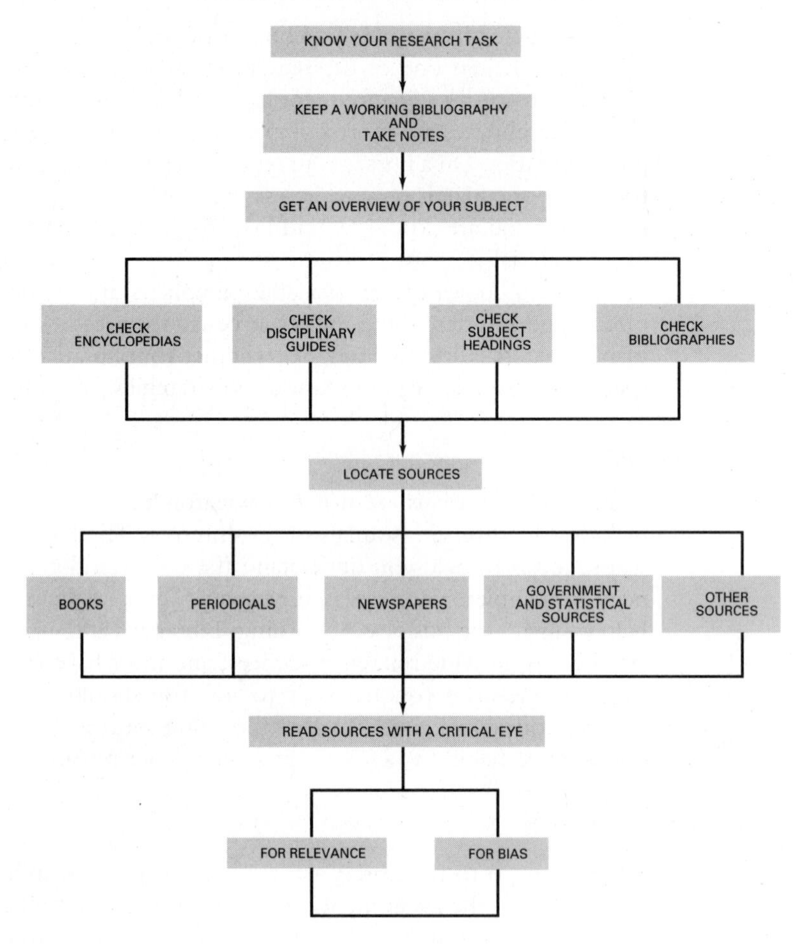

use library materials to get an overview of your subject, locate the sources you need, and read those sources with a critical eye.

KEEPING TRACK OF YOUR RESEARCH

As you research your topic, you will want to keep careful records of all your sources by setting up a working bibliography.

Keeping a Working Bibliography

A working bibliography is a preliminary, ongoing record of books, articles, pamphlets—all the sources of information you discover as you research your subject. In addition, you can use your working bibliography as a means of keeping track of any encyclopedias, bibliographies, and indexes you consult, even though you do not use these resources in an essay or a research review.

Practiced researchers keep their working bibliography on index cards, in a notebook, or in a computer file. They may keep bibliographical information separate from notes they take on the sources. Many researchers find index cards most convenient because they are so easy to alphabetize. Others find them too easy to lose and prefer instead to keep everything—working bibliography, notes, and drafts—in one notebook. Researchers who use computers set up working bibliographies in word processing programs or bibliographic management programs, such as Endnote Plus, that work in conjunction with word processing programs. With these bibliographic programs, you enter a source's publication information, and the program then formats the information according to one of the preset documentation styles (MLA, APA, etc.) or a style you create. From the formatted listings, the program can create in-text citations and insert them into your essay, as well as format your final list of works cited. Some of these programs can interact with computer indexes and other databases so that you can download source information from the database right into your bibliographic file, which then correctly formats the information.

Whether you use cards, a notebook, or a computer, the important thing is to make your entries accurate and complete. If the call number for a book is incomplete or inaccurate, for example, you will not be able to find the book in the stacks. If the volume number for a periodical is incorrect, you may not be able to locate the article. If the author's name is misspelled, you may have trouble finding the book in the library catalog.

Confirm with your instructor which documentation style is required for your assignment so that all sources listed in your working bibliography will conform to the documentation style of your essay. Chapter 22 presents two common documentation styles, one adopted by the Modern Language Association (MLA) and widely used in the humanities, and the other advocated by the American Psychological Association (APA) and used in the social sciences. Individual disciplines often have their own preferred styles of documentation.

Taking Notes

Outlining, paraphrasing, and summarizing are discussed in Chapter 12, and quoting is discussed in Chapter 22.

After you are oriented to your research topic and have found a way to focus it, you will want to begin taking notes from relevant sources. If you own the work or can obtain a copy of the relevant parts, you may want to annotate right on the page. Otherwise, you should paraphrase, summarize, and outline useful information as separate notes. In addition, you will want to write down quotations you might use in your essay.

You may already have a method of notetaking you prefer. Some researchers like to use index cards for notes as well as for their working bibliography. They use 3- by 5-inch cards for their bibliography and larger ones (4- by 6-inch or 5- by 7-inch) for notes. Some use cards of different colors to organize their notes, other people prefer to keep their notes in a notebook, and still others enter their notes into a computer. Whatever method you use, be sure to keep accurate notes.

See p. 602 for tips on avoiding plagiarism.

Care in notetaking is of paramount importance to minimize the risks of copying facts incorrectly and of misquoting. Another common error in notetaking is copying the author's words without enclosing them in quotation marks. This error could lead easily to plagiarism, the unacknowledged use of another's words or ideas. Double-check all your notes, and be as accurate as you can.

You might consider photocopying materials from sources that look especially promising. All libraries house a photocopy machine or offer a copying service. Photocopying can be costly, of course, so you'll want to be selective. It will facilitate your work, however, allowing you to reread and analyze important sources as well as to highlight material you may wish to quote, summarize, or paraphrase. Be sure to photocopy title pages or other publication information for each source you copy, or write this information on the photocopied text, especially if you are copying several excerpts. Bring paper clips or a stapler with you to the library to help to keep your photocopies organized.

GETTING STARTED

"But where do I start?" That common question is easily answered. You first need an overview of your topic. If you are researching a concept or an issue in a course you are taking, a bibliography in your textbook or other course materials provides the obvious starting point. Your instructor can advise you about other sources that provide overviews of your topic. If your topic is just breaking in the news, you will want to consult current newspapers and magazines. For all other topics—and for background information—encyclopedias and disciplinary guides are often the place to start. They let you test your interest in a topic before you start gathering sources on it, and they introduce you to diverse aspects of a subject, from which you might find a focus for your research. In a typical college essay or research project, you do not have the time or space to summarize everything that is known on a subject, but you can inquire productively into some unusual or controversial aspect of it. Keep in mind that the key to a good research paper is to choose a topic you're interested in exploring.

Consulting Encyclopedias

General encyclopedias, such as the *Encyclopaedia Britannica* and the *Encyclopedia Americana,* give basic information about many topics. The authors of articles in these encyclopedias are often prominent in their respective fields, and you might follow up on other articles or book-length works they have written. However, general encyclopedias alone are not adequate resources for college research.

Specialized encyclopedias cover topics in the depth appropriate for college writing. In addition to providing an overview of a topic, a specialized encyclopedia often includes an explanation of issues related to the topic, definitions of specialized terminology, and selective bibliographies of additional sources.

As starting points, specialized encyclopedias have two distinct advantages: (1) They provide a comprehensive introduction to key terms related to your topic, terms that are especially useful in identifying the subject headings used to locate material in catalogs and indexes, and (2) they provide a comprehensive presentation of a subject, enabling you to see many possibilities for focusing your research on one aspect of it.

The following are some specialized encyclopedias in the major academic disciplines:

ART *Encyclopedia of World Art.* 17 vols. 1959–1987.

BIOLOGY *Encyclopedia of Biological Sciences.* 1981.

CHEMISTRY	*Van Nostrand Reinhold Encyclopedia of Chemistry.* 1984.
COMPUTERS	*Encyclopedia of Computer Science and Technology.* 15 vols. 1975–.
ECONOMICS	*Encyclopedia of Economics.* 1982.
EDUCATION	*Encyclopedia of Education.* 10 vols. 1971.
ENVIRONMENT	*McGraw-Hill Dictionary of Earth Sciences.* 1984.
FOREIGN RELATIONS	*Encyclopedia of American Foreign Policy.* 1978. *Encyclopedia of the Third World.* 1992.
HISTORY	*Harvard Guide to American History.* 2 vols. 1974. *New Cambridge Modern History.* 14 vols. 1957–1980.
LAW	*Encyclopedia of Crime and Justice.* 4 vols. 1983.
LITERATURE	*Encyclopedia of World Literature in the 20th Century.* 5 vols. 1981–1993.
MUSIC	*New Grove Dictionary of Music and Musicians.* 20 vols. 1980.
PHILOSOPHY	*Encyclopedia of Philosophy.* 4 vols. 1973.
PSYCHOLOGY	*Encyclopedia of Psychology.* 1979.
RELIGION	*Encyclopedia of Religion.* 16 vols. 1987.
SCIENCE	*McGraw-Hill Encyclopedia of Science and Technology.* 20 vols. 1992.
SOCIAL SCIENCES	*International Encyclopedia of the Social Sciences.* 8 vols. 1977.
WOMEN'S STUDIES	*Women's Studies Encyclopedia.* 3 vols. 1989–1991.

You can locate any of these encyclopedias in the library by doing a title search in the online catalog for its call number. Other specialized encyclopedias can be found by looking in the catalog under the subject heading for the discipline, such as "psychology," and the subheading "dictionaries and encyclopedias."

Two particular reference sources can help you to identify other specialized encyclopedias covering your topic:

ARBA Guide to Subject Encyclopedias and Dictionaries (1986). Lists specialized encyclopedias by broad subject category, with descriptions of coverage, focus, and any special features.

First Stop: The Master Index to Subject Encyclopedias (1989). Lists specialized encyclopedias by broad subject category and provides access to individual articles within them. By looking under the key terms that describe a topic, you will find references to specific articles in any of over four hundred specialized encyclopedias.

Consulting Disciplinary Guides

Once you have a general overview of your topic, you will want to consult one of the research guides in that discipline. The following guides can help you to identify the major handbooks, encyclopedias, bibliographies, journals, periodical indexes, and computer databases in the various disciplines. You need not read any of these extensive works straight through, but you will find them to be valuable references.

ANTHROPOLOGY	*Introduction to Library Research in Anthropology.* 1991. By John M. Weeks.
ART	*Visual Arts Research: A Handbook.* 1986. By Elizabeth B. Pollard.
EDUCATION	*Education: A Guide to Reference and Information Sources.* 1989. By Lois Buttlar.
FILM	*On the Screen: A Film, Television, and Video Research Guide.* 1986. By Kim N. Fisher.
GENERAL	*Guide to Reference Books,* 11th ed. 1996. Edited by Robert Balay.
HISTORY	*A Student's Guide to History,* 6th ed. 1994. By Jules R. Benjamin.
HUMANITIES	*The Humanities: A Selective Guide to Information Sources,* 4th ed. 1994. By Ron Blazek and Elizabeth S. Aversa.
LITERATURE	*Reference Works in British and American Literature.* 2 vols. 1990. By James K. Bracken. *Literary Research Guide: A Guide to Reference Sources for the Study of Literatures in English and Related Topics,* 3rd ed. 1993. By James L. Harner.
MUSIC	*Music: A Guide to the Reference Literature.* 1987. By William S. Brockman.
PHILOSOPHY	*Philosophy: A Guide to the Reference Literature.* 1986. By Hans E. Bynagle.
POLITICAL SCIENCE	*Information Sources of Political Science,* 4th ed. 1986. By Frederick L. Holler.
PSYCHOLOGY	*Library Research Guide to Psychology: Illustrated Search Strategy and Sources.* 1984. By Nancy E. Douglas.
SCIENCE AND TECHNOLOGY	*Scientific and Technical Information Sources,* 2nd ed. 1987. By Ching-chih Chen.
SOCIAL SCIENCES	*Sources of Information in the Social Sciences: A Guide to the Literature,* 3rd ed. 1986. Edited by William H. Webb.
SOCIOLOGY	*Sociology: A Guide to Reference and Information Sources.* 1987. By Stephen H. Aby.
WOMEN'S STUDIES	*Introduction to Library Research in Women's Studies.* 1985. By Susan E. Searing.

Checking Subject Headings

To extend your research beyond encyclopedias, you need to find appropriate subject headings. Subject headings are specific words and phrases used in libraries to categorize the contents of books and periodicals. As you read about your subject in an encyclopedia or other reference book, you should keep a list of possible subject headings.

To begin your search for subject headings, consult the *Library of Congress Subject Headings* (LCSH), which can usually be found near the library catalog. This reference book lists the standard subject headings used in catalogs and indexes and in many encyclopedias and bibliographies. Here is an example from the LCSH:

Home schooling *(May Subd Geog)* ← Place names may follow heading
Here are entered works on the provision of compulsory education in the home by parents as an alternative to traditional public or private schooling. General works on the provision of education in the home by educational personnel are entered under Domestic Education.

Used for → UF Education, Home
Home-based education
Home education
Home instruction
Home teaching by parents
Homeschooling
Instruction, Home
Schooling, Home
Broader Term → BT Education
Related Term → RT Education—United States
Education—Parent participation

NT = Narrower term
SA = See also

Subject headings provide you with various key words and phrases to use as you look through catalogs and indexes. For example, our sample entry proved particularly useful because when the student found nothing listed in the library catalog under "Home schooling," she tried the other headings until "Education—Parent participation" and "Education—United States" yielded information on three books. Note, too, that this entry explains the *types* of articles that would be found under these headings and those that would be found elsewhere. Keep in mind that the terms listed in the LCSH might not be the only ones used for your subject; don't be reluctant to try other terms that you think might be relevant.

Consulting Bibliographies

A bibliography is simply a list of publications on a given subject. Just as an encyclopedia can give you background information on your subject, a bibliography gives you an overview of what has been published on the subject. Its scope may be broad or narrow. Some bibliographers try to be exhaustive, including every title they can find, but most are selective. To discover how selections were made, check the bibliography's preface or introduction. Occasionally, bibliographies are annotated, that is, they provide brief summaries of the entries and, sometimes, also evaluate them. Bibliographies may be found in a variety of places: in encyclopedias, in the library catalog, and in research guides. All specialized encyclopedias and disciplinary research guides have bibliographies.

The best way to locate a comprehensive, up-to-date bibliography on your subject is to look in the *Bibliographic Index.* A master list of bibliographies that contain fifty or more entries, the *Bibliographic Index* includes bibliographies from articles, books, and government publications. A new volume is published every year. (Because this index is not cumulative, you should check back over several years, beginning with the most current volume.)

Even if you attend a large research university, your library is unlikely to hold every book or journal article a bibliography might direct you to. The library catalog and serial record (a list of the periodicals the library holds) will tell you whether the book or journal is available.

Determining the Most Promising Sources

As you follow a subject heading into the library catalog and bibliographic and periodical indexes and discover many seemingly relevant books and articles, how do you decide which ones to track down and examine? With little to go on but author, title, date, and publisher or periodical name, you may feel at a loss; but these actually provide useful clues. Look, for example, at the entry from a card catalog on page 567. The entry shows the author, title, and subject cards for a book on home schooling. Note that from the author's birthdate and the publication date of the book, you can tell that he wrote the book late in his career. He might, therefore, offer a historical perspective. From the physical description, you can see that the book includes a bibliography, which could lead you to other sources. Finally, from the subject headings, you can see that this book focuses on learning; you can also use "Learning" to search for related books.

Now look at the following entry from *Education Index*, a periodical index:

Home schooling
Do children have to go to school? [Great Britain] C. Henson. *Child Educ (Engl)* v73 p68 Mr '96
Homegrown learning [Twin Ridges Elementary School District combines homeschooling with regular classroom instruction] D. Hill. il *Teach Mag* v7 p40-5 Ap '96
Should we open extracurriculars to home-schoolers? J. Watford; B. Dickinson. il *Am Teach* v80 p4 Mr '96

This entry lists articles that address different aspects of home schooling, briefly describing some of the articles. You can see that the first article deals with the issue from a British point of view, which might provide an interesting cross-cultural perspective for your paper. The title of the third article seems to indicate an argument or debate on the issue; that it appears in a magazine for teachers might give you a sense of that profession's attitudes toward home schooling.

When you look in catalogs and indexes, consider the following points to help you to decide whether you should track down a particular source:

- **Relevance to your topic.** Do the title, subtitle, description, subject headings, abstract, or periodical title help you to determine just how directly a particular source addresses your topic?
- **Publication date.** How recent is the source? For current controversies, emerging trends, and continuing technical or medical developments, you must see the most recent material. For historical or biographical topics, you will want to start with present-day perspectives but keep in mind that older sources also offer authoritative perspectives.

- **Description.** Does the length indicate a brief or an extended treatment of the topic? Does the work include illustrations that may elaborate on concepts discussed in the text? Does the work include a bibliography that could lead you to other works or an index that could give you an overview of what is discussed in the text? Does the abstract tell you the focus of the work?

From among the sources that look promising, select at least one book, one research report in an academic journal, and one article in a popular magazine. Or select three or four publications that seem by their titles to address different aspects of your topic or to approach it from different perspectives. Try to avoid selecting sources by the same author, from the same publisher, or in the same journal. Common sense will lead you to an appropriate decision about diversity in source materials.

LOCATING SOURCES

When you tour your college library, or else when you begin your research project, find out how best to gain access to the various resources you will need. Many libraries now offer access to their online catalog, periodical holdings, periodical and newspaper indexes, government documents, some specialized CD-ROM products, and even the holdings of other libraries through public access terminals. Check the menu screen of one of the terminals; it usually indicates the resources that are available through the system.

The following are guidelines for finding books, periodical articles, newspaper articles, government documents and statistical information, and other types of sources.

Finding Books

The primary source for books is the library catalog. Nearly every college library offers a computerized catalog, sometimes called an online catalog. The library may also maintain a card catalog consisting of cards filed in drawers. The online catalog provides more flexibility in searching subject headings and may even tell you whether the book is checked out. Another distinct advantage is its ability to print out source information, making it unnecessary for you to copy it by hand. A card catalog, however, is valuable for its accumulation of librarians' comments and notes pertaining to books and holdings unique to the library. Card catalogs might also be useful if you are uncertain of the spelling of an author name or other reference keyword (as with a dictionary, an approximate spelling will get you in the neighborhood of the source you need, whereas most online directories do not accept variant or incorrect spellings). Also, an online catalog often contains material received and cataloged only after a certain date.

Library catalogs organize sources by author, subject, and title. Each book has a computer entry or card filed under the name of each author, under the title, and under each subject heading to which the book is related. Author, title, and subject entries or cards all give the same basic information.

1. *Call number*—usually appears on a separate line in an online catalog and in the upper left-hand corner of cards in a card catalog. The call number is the numerical

code under which the book is filed in the library. Call numbers are assigned according to subject. Most college libraries use the Library of Congress subject headings and numbering system. Call numbers have at least two rows of numbers. The top row indicates the general subject classification, and the second row places the book within this classification. Subsequent rows identify the copyright and publication date for multiple editions.

2. *Author*—appears last name first, followed by birth and death dates. If there are multiple authors, there is an author entry or card under each author's name.
3. *Title*—appears exactly as it is printed on the title page of the book, except that only the first word and proper nouns and adjectives are capitalized.
4. *Publication information*—includes the place of publication (usually just the city), publisher, and year of publication. If the book was published simultaneously in the United States and abroad, both places of publication and both publishers are indicated.
5. *Physical description*—provides information about the book's length and size. A roman numeral indicates the number of pages devoted to front matter (such as a preface, table of contents, and acknowledgments).
6. *Notes*—point out any special features (for example, a bibliography or an index).
7. *Subject headings*—indicate how the book is listed in the subject catalog. These headings may be useful in finding other books related to your subject.

Here is one college library's online catalog display of the author entry for a recent book on home schooling in its collection. Notice the call number along the bottom line.

```
AUTHOR:          Guterson, David, 1951–
TITLE:           Family matters: Why home schooling makes sense/
                 David Guterson
EDITION:         1st Harvest ed.
PUBLISHER:       San Diego: Harcourt Brace & Co., c1992
PHYSICAL DESC:   x, 254 p.; 18 cm.

NOTES:           Includes bibliographical references and index.
SUBJECTS:        Education—United States
                 Education—parent participation
                 Teaching methods

LOCATION / CALL NUMBER                    STATUS

UCSD Undergrad/649.68 g 1993              Available
```

On p. 567 are the author, title, and subject cards for a book on home schooling. The title and subject cards for a book are just like the author card except that they have headings printed at the top, above the author's name. On the title card, the heading is the title (which appears again below the author's name). On the subject card, the heading is one of the subject headings from the bottom of the card.

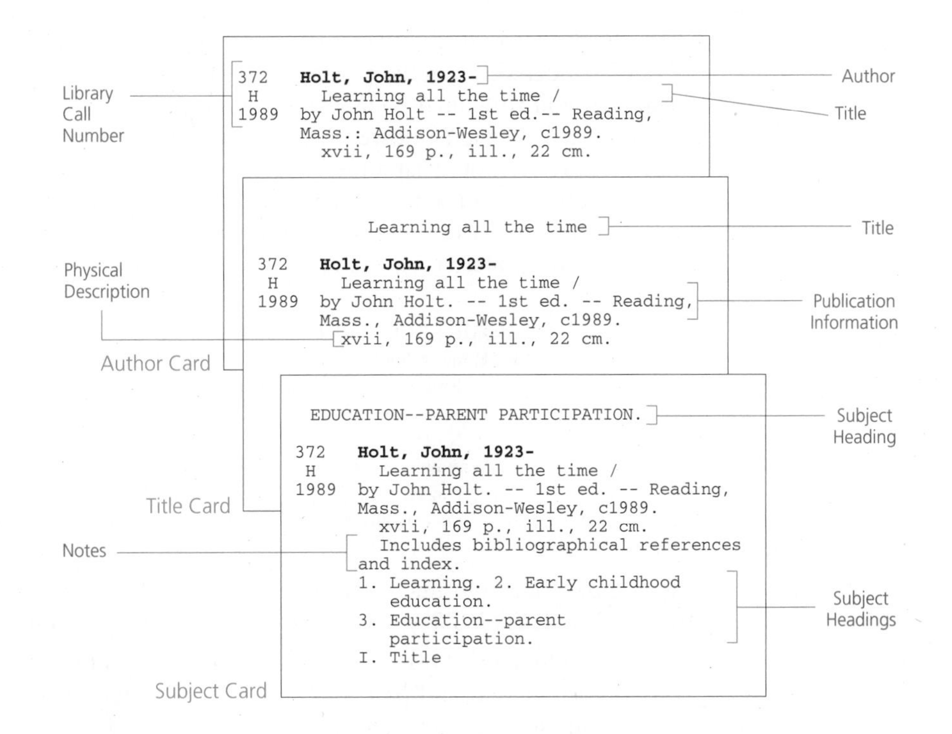

Note that for a book, a separate online entry or catalog card exists for each subject heading listed. When you search for books on a particular subject, rather than by author or title, it's a good idea to check the *Library of Congress Subject Headings* (see p. 563) for key words related to your subject, before searching the catalog for a subject heading you have formulated on your own. This extra step will often save you time later on.

Finding Periodical Articles

The most up-to-date information on a subject is usually found not in books but in articles in magazines and journals, known as periodicals because they are issued periodically on a regular basis. Articles in periodicals are usually not listed in the library catalog; to find them, you must use periodical indexes and abstracts. Indexes list articles; abstracts summarize them as well. Library catalogs list the indexes and abstracts held at the library and note whether they are available in printed form or in microform. Many indexes and abstracts, including those listed in this section, are also available as computer databases.

Computer databases are discussed on pp. 570–71.

In the lists that follow, names for computer databases are given if they differ from those of the print indexes. Because these databases are not always listed in the library catalog, check with a librarian to see what databases are available at your library.

Periodical indexes and abstracts are of two types: general and specialized.

General Indexes. These indexes list articles in nontechnical, general-interest publications and cover a broad range of subjects. Most have separate author and subject listings as well as a list of book reviews. Following are some general indexes, beginning with one you may already be familiar with:

The Readers' Guide to Periodical Literature (1900–; online and CD-ROM, 1983–); updated quarterly. Covers about two hundred popular periodicals and may help you to launch your search for sources on general and current topics. Even for general topics, however, you should not rely on it exclusively. Nearly all college libraries house far more than two hundred periodicals, and university research libraries house twenty thousand or more. The *Readers' Guide* does not even attempt to cover the research journals that play such an important role in college writing. Here is an example of an entry for "home education":

HOME EDUCATION

Home-school kids in public-school activities. D. Brockett. *The Education Digest* v61 p67–9 N '95

Pros and cons of home schooling. il *Parents* v70 p18 N '95

Why homeschooling is important for America [address, August 11, 1995] S. L. Blumenfeld. *Vital Speeches of the Day* v61 p763-6 O 1 '95

Magazine Index. On microfilm (1988–), online (1973–), and on CD-ROM as part of InfoTrac (1973–); see below. Indexes over four hundred magazines.

InfoTrac. On CD-ROM. Includes three indexes: (1) the *General Periodicals Index* (current year and past four), which covers over twelve hundred general-interest publications, incorporating the *Magazine Index* and including the *New York Times* and the *Wall Street Journal*; (2) the *Academic Index* (current year and past four), which covers four hundred scholarly and general-interest publications, including the *New York Times*; and (3) the *National Newspaper Index* (current year and past three), which covers the *Christian Science Monitor, Los Angeles Times, New York Times, Wall Street Journal,* and *Washington Post.* Some entries also include abstracts of articles. The example below is from the *General Periodicals Index.*

```
AUTHOR(s):        Hawkins, Dana
TITLE(s):         Homeschool battles: clashes grow as some in
                    the movement seek access to public
                    schools.
                   illustration photograph

Summary:          An estimated 500,000 students in the US
                    study at home, and there is an increasing
                    tension in some communities as some of the
                    'homeschoolers' attempt to use the public
                    schools on a limited basis. The parents
                    of one homeschooler in Oklahoma have sued
                    the school district to gain access.

                  U.S. News & World Report
                  p57(2)
                  Feb 12   1996   v120   n6

DESCRIPTORS:      Home schooling_Cases
                  Public schools_Cases
                  Education_Parent participation
more follows -- press <RETURN>   (Q to quit)
```

Access: The Supplementary Index to Periodicals (1979–). Indexes magazines not covered by the *Readers' Guide*, such as regional and particular-interest magazines (the environment, women's issues, etc.).

Alternative Press Index (1970–). Indexes alternative and radical publications.

Humanities Index (1974–; online and CD-ROM, 1984–). Covers 330 titles in archaeology, history, classics, literature, performing arts, philosophy, and religion.

Social Sciences Index (1974–; online and CD-ROM, 1983–). Covers four hundred titles in economics, geography, law, political science, psychology, public administration, and sociology. The complete text of certain articles is available on the CD-ROM.

Public Affairs Information Service Bulletin (PAIS) (1915–; online and CD-ROM, 1972–). Covers articles and other publications by public and private agencies on economic and social conditions, international relations, and public administration. Subject listing only.

Specialized Indexes and Abstracts. These indexes list or summarize articles devoted to technical or scholarly research. The following example from *Sociological Abstracts*, which indexes and summarizes articles from a wide range of periodicals that publish sociological research, is typical of entries found in specialized indexes:

> **91X2727**
> **Mayberry, Maralee & Knowles, J. Gary** (Dept Sociology U Nevada, Las Vegas 89154), **Family Unity Objectives of Parents Who Teach Their Children: Ideological and Pedagogical Orientations to Home Schooling,** UM *The Urban Review*, 1989, 21, 4, Dec, 209-225.
>
> ¶ The objectives of parents who teach their children at home are examined, using results from 2 qualitative studies: (1) a study conducted in Ore in 1987/88, consisting of interview & questionnaire data (N = 15 & 800 families, respectively); & (2) an ongoing ethnographic study being conducted in Utah (N = 8 families). Analysis suggests that while families have complex motives for teaching their children at home, most respondents felt that establishing a home school would allow them to maintain or further develop unity within the family. It is concluded that a family's decision to home school is often made in an attempt to resist the effects on the family unit of urbanization & modernization. Policy implications are discussed. 36 References. Adapted from the source document. (Copyright 1991, Sociological Abstracts, Inc., all rights reserved.)

Here is a list of specialized periodical indexes that cover various disciplines:

Accountant's Index (1944–).

American Statistics Index (1973–).

Applied Science and Technology Index (1958–). Online, CD-ROM.

Art Index (1929–; CD-ROM, 1984–).

Biological and Agricultural Index (1964–). CD-ROM.

Education Index (1929–). Online, CD-ROM.

Engineering Index (1920–).

Historical Abstracts (1955–; CD-ROM, 1982–).

Index Medicus (1961–). Online, CD-ROM (called MEDLINE).

MLA International Bibliography of Books and Articles in the Modern Languages and Literature (1921–). Online, CD-ROM.

Music Index. (1949–; CD-ROM, 1981–1989).

Philosopher's Index (1957–). Online.

Psychological Abstracts (1927–). Online (called PsycINFO), CD-ROM (PsycLIT).

Physics Abstracts (1898–). Online (called INSPEC).

Science Abstracts (1898–).

Sociological Abstracts (1952–). Online, CD-ROM (called Sociofile).

Many periodical indexes and abstracts use the Library of Congress subject headings, but some have their own systems. *Sociological Abstracts,* for example, has a separate volume for subject headings. Check the opening pages of the index or abstract you are using, or refer to the system documentation, to see how it classifies its subjects. Then look for periodicals under your chosen Library of Congress subject heading or the heading that seems most similar to it.

Computer Databases. Your library may subscribe to *online* database networks and may own *CD-ROM* machines that are accessed through the library's computer terminals. Most research databases—like those noted in the preceding lists—are electronic indexes listing thousands of books and articles.

You may be able to use a CD-ROM database yourself, but you will probably need a librarian to conduct an online search. When you use a CD-ROM database, check the first screen, which should let you know what information you are accessing. Some large databases may require more than one disk, usually separated by date. In such cases, the reference librarian can help you to obtain the disk you need. Although you can search a database by author or title, most likely you will use *descriptors,* or keywords describing subjects. Make your descriptors as precise as possible so that your database search results in a manageable list of sources relevant to your topic. Most databases include a thesaurus of descriptors and a set of guidelines for combining terms to narrow your search. In addition, most CD-ROMs include a browse function. When you enter a descriptor, the system automatically lists the terms that are close to it alphabetically. If you enter a very general descriptor, the system provides that general term along with subtopics. Use these subtopics to narrow your search further before you ask the system to retrieve records.

Once you have typed in your descriptors, the computer searches the database and lists every reference to them it finds. If your search is extensive, you can usually download the records to your own disk. Because you may be charged for access time and printing for an online search or be given a limit on time at the terminal and on the number of entries you can print from a CD-ROM database, you may want to talk with a librarian before consulting a database. Also keep in mind that because most electronic indexes cover only the most recent years, you may need to consult older printed versions as well.

In addition to the database versions of the indexes listed earlier, many libraries subscribe to computer services that provide abstracts or the full text of articles, either in the database (so you can see them on-screen) or by mail or fax for a fee, and that list books in particular subject areas. The use of computers for scholarly research is becoming more widespread, with new technology being developed all the time, so be sure to check with a librarian about what is available at your library. Some common computer services include the following:

ERIC (Educational Resources Information Center) (CD-ROM, 1969–). Indexes, abstracts, and provides some full texts of articles from 750 education journals. Here is an example of a work on home schooling listed in ERIC:

```
    6 of 215   Complete Record
  EJ509882   EA530056
  Why Parents Choose Home Schooling.
  Jeub, Chris
  Educational Leadership, v52 n1 p50-52 Sep  1995
  ISSN: 0013-1784
  Available from: UMI
  Language: English
  Document Type: POSITION PAPER (120);  JOURNAL ARTICLE
(080)
  Journal Announcement: CIJJAN96
  Home schooling neither isolates children nor harms their
academic growth, but approaches the true definition of
education: the passing down of culture. Public schools
have redefined family values and often fail to take reli-
gion seriously. Home-school parents see the family as a
superior social institution; many value religion's cul-
tural contribution.  (MLH)
  Descriptors: *Educational Benefits; Elementary Secondary
Education; *Family Characteristics; *Home Schooling;
*Parent Child Relationship; *Religious Factors;
*Socialization
```

Business Periodicals Ondisc (1988–) and *ABI/INFORM* (1988–). Full text of articles from business periodicals. If your library has a laser printer attached to a terminal, you can print out articles, including illustrations.

PsycBooks (1987–). A CD-ROM database that indexes books and book chapters in psychology.

Carl/Uncover (1988–). An online document delivery service that lists over three million articles from twelve thousand journals. For a fee, you can receive the full text of the article by fax, usually within a few hours.

Interlibrary networks. Known by different names in different regions, these networks allow you to search in the catalogs of colleges and universities in your area and across the country. In many cases, you can request a book by interlibrary loan. It may take several weeks for you to receive your material. You can also request a copy of an article from a journal to which your own library does not subscribe. Most libraries do not loan their journals but will copy and forward articles for a fee.

Periodicals Representing Particular Viewpoints. Some specialized periodical indexes tend to represent particular viewpoints and may help you to identify different positions on an issue.

Index to Black Periodicals (1984–). An author and subject index to articles of both a general and a scholarly nature about African Americans.

Left Index (1982–). An author and subject index to over eighty periodicals with a Marxist, radical, or left perspective. Listings cover primarily topics in the social sciences and humanities.

Chicano Index (1967–). An index to general and scholarly articles about Mexican Americans. Articles are arranged by subject with author and title indexes. (Before 1989, the title was *Chicano Periodical Index.*)

Another useful source for identifying positions is *Editorials on File,* described on p. 573.

Locating Periodicals in the Library. When you identify a promising magazine or journal article in a periodical index, you must go to the library serial record or online catalog to learn whether the library subscribes to the periodical and, if so, where you can find it. Recent issues of periodicals are usually arranged alphabetically by title on open shelves. Older issues may be bound like books and shelved by call numbers or alphabetically by title or else filmed and available in microform.

Finding Newspaper Articles

Newspapers provide useful information for many research topics in such areas as foreign affairs, economic issues, public opinion, and social trends. Libraries usually miniaturize newspapers and store them on microfilm (reels) or microfiche (cards) that must be placed in viewing machines to be read.

Newspaper indexes, such as the *Los Angeles Times Index,* the *New York Times Index,* and the *London Times Index,* help you to locate specific articles on your topic. College libraries usually have indexes to local newspapers as well.

Your library may also subscribe to newspaper article and digest services, such as the following:

National Newspaper Index. On microfilm (1989–), online (1979–), and on CD-ROM, as part of InfoTrac (see p. 568). Indexes *Christian Science Monitor, Los Angeles Times, New York Times, Wall Street Journal,* and *Washington Post.*

NewsBank (1970–). On microfiche and CD-ROM. Full-text articles from five hundred U.S. newspapers. A good source of information on local and regional issues and trends.

Newspaper Abstracts (1988–; CD-ROM, 1991–). An index and brief abstracts of articles from nineteen major regional, national, and international newspapers.

Facts on File (weekly; CD-ROM, 1980–). A digest of U.S. and international news events arranged by subject, such as foreign affairs, arts, education, religion, and sports.

Editorials on File (twice monthly). Editorials from 150 U.S. and Canadian newspapers. Each entry includes a brief description of an editorial subject followed by fifteen to twenty editorials on the subject, reprinted from different newspapers.

Editorial Research Reports (1924–). Reports on current and controversial topics, including brief histories, statistics, editorials, journal articles, endnotes, and supplementary reading lists.

African Recorder (1970–). Articles on African issues from African newspapers.

Asian Recorder (1971–). Articles on Asian issues from Asian newspapers.

Canadian News Facts (1972–). On CD-ROM. A digest of current articles from Canadian newspapers such as the *Montreal Star,* the *Toronto Star,* and the *Vancouver Sun*. Some articles are available as full text on the CD-ROM.

Foreign Broadcast Information Service (FBIS) (1980–). Foreign broadcast scripts, newspaper articles, and government statements from Asia, Europe, Latin America, Africa, Russia, and the Middle East.

Keesing's Contemporary Archives (weekly). A digest of events in all countries, compiled from British reporting services. Includes speeches and statistics. Index includes chronological, geographic, and topical sections.

Finding Government and Statistical Information

Following is a description of some government publications and sources of statistical information that may help you to find sources for a particular purpose or a particular kind of subject.

Sources for Political Subjects. Two publications that report developments in the federal government can be rich sources of information on political issues. Types of material they cover include congressional hearings and debates, presidential proclamations and speeches, Supreme Court decisions and dissenting opinions, and compilations of statistics. These publications are not always included in catalogs but are shelved in the reference area or in a government documents department in some college libraries. If these works are not listed in the library catalog, ask a reference librarian for assistance.

Congressional Quarterly Almanac (annual). A summary of legislation. Provides an overview of governmental policies and trends, including analysis as well as election results, records of roll-call votes, and the text of significant speeches and debates.

Congressional Quarterly Weekly Report. A news service that includes up-to-date summaries of committee actions, votes, and executive branch activities, as well as overviews of current policy discussions and activities within the federal government.

Sources for Researching Trends. Research can help you to identify trends to write about and, most important, provide the evidence you need to demonstrate the existence of a trend. The following resources can be especially helpful:

Statistical Abstract of the United States (annual). Issued by the Bureau of the Census. Provides a variety of social, economic, and political statistics, often

Chapter 9 provides guidance developing an argument speculating about the causes of a trend.

covering several years. Includes tables, graphs, and charts and gives references to additional sources of information.

American Statistics Index (1974–; annual with monthly supplements). Attempts to cover all federal government publications containing statistical information of research significance. Includes brief descriptions of references.

Statistical Reference Index (1980–). Claims to be "a selective guide to American statistical publications from sources other than the U.S. government." Includes economic, social, and political statistical sources.

World Almanac and Book of Facts (annual). Presents information on a variety of subjects drawn from many sources. Includes such things as a chronology of the year, climatological data, and lists of inventions and awards.

The Gallup Poll: Public Opinion (1935–). A chronological listing of the results of public opinion polls. Includes information on social, economic, and political trends.

In addition to researching the trend itself, you may want to research others' speculations about its causes. If so, the reports of federal government activities described in the preceding section may be helpful.

Finding Other Sources

Libraries hold a vast amount of useful materials other than books and periodicals. Some of the following sources and services may be appropriate for your research.

Vertical file. Pamphlets and brochures from government and private agencies.

Special collections. Manuscripts, rare books, materials of local interest.

Audio collections. Records, audiocassettes, and CDs of all kinds of music, readings, and speeches.

Video collections. Slides, filmstrips, and videocassettes.

Art collections. Drawings, paintings, and engravings.

Interlibrary loans. Many libraries will borrow books from another library and make copies of journal articles; be aware that interlibrary loans often take some time. Ask your librarian if there is a public access terminal from which you can send an electronic request for such a loan to your local interlibrary loan office.

Computer resources. Many libraries house interactive computer programs that combine text, video, and audio resources in history, literature, business, and other disciplines.

USING THE INTERNET FOR RESEARCH

The *Internet* is a global network made up of many smaller networks that enables computer users to share information and resources quickly and easily. Using the Internet, people can send and receive electronic mail (E-mail), read documents or post them for others to read, communicate with other people who share similar interests, and store, send, and receive documents, graphic images, videos, and computer applications. With a computer and a modem or a direct network connection, students can gather information about a research subject from sources all over the world. If you are interested in ecology, for example, you can locate government reports and news articles on the environment, information from environmental action groups, forums discussing a wide range of environmental topics, and information about current research in ecology. Your school may provide its students with access to the Internet, possibly at little or no cost. To find out whether you can access the Internet on campus, check with the reference librarian or computer services office. Much of the software you need to access the network is widely available free or for a small fee through campus services, computer user groups, electronic bulletin boards, or the World Wide Web.

If you cannot gain access to the Internet through your university or college, you may use your own computer and modem to access a commercial Internet service provider. Service providers charge a fee; in return, they provide all the software you need and a dial-up phone number to connect to the Internet. Some services charge a flat monthly or annual fee; others base their charges on the amount of time you are connected. Some well-known commercial online services are CompuServe, Prodigy, and America Online; until recently, these large services provided only information storage, electronic mail, and chat forums for their members, but they now provide access to the Internet as well. Using these large services can become expensive, however. In most areas of the country, less expensive local Internet service providers now exist. Check with local computer stores or computer user groups to compare pricing among the services available in your area.

Research on the Internet is very different from library research. Information is stored on many different computers, each with its own system of organization. There is no central catalog, reference librarian, or standard classification system for the vast resources on the Internet. As a result, it can be difficult to determine the sources of information and to evaluate their reliability. Depending on your topic, purpose, and audience, the sources you find on the Internet may not be as credible or as authoritative as library sources (see pp. 591–94 for information on determining the credibility of sources). When in doubt about the reliability or acceptability of online sources for a particular assignment, be sure to check with your instructor. In most cases, you will probably have to balance or supplement online sources with library sources. As with sources you locate in the library, you need to provide proper documentation for all online sources that you cite.

Citing Internet sources using MLA style is discussed on pp. 608–611; a style based on APA is discussed on pp. 616–619.

Because the Internet is so large and relatively unorganized, you may wonder how to find information relevant to your topic. Various tools have been developed to make it easier to find information on the Internet. One popular tool is the World Wide Web; others include telnet and file transfer protocol (FTP) systems and such services as gopher, MUDs, and MOOs. The following sections provide information about these tools; in addition, the Search in Progress sections show a student using them to research a topic for a position paper on the topic of censorship.

Searching the World Wide Web

The *World Wide Web* was initially developed to allow scientists to link related information wherever that information might be located. Using the Web, for example, a physicist in California who published a paper on the Internet could create a link to a related paper by a colleague in Sweden. Anyone reading the first paper could simply click on the link for instant access to the second paper.

Since it began, the World Wide Web has grown and developed rapidly to include many other uses. People may now include not only text but also graphic images, sound, animation, and even video in documents, all of which can be shared with others. New programs make it much easier to search, view, and create Web documents. Increasingly, the Web is taking over many of the functions of older tools such as telnet.

Becoming Familiar with Web Sites. There are Web sites for people interested in finding the text of a recently passed law, looking at a college catalog, listening to a jazz performance, or viewing prehistoric cave art from France. You can find Web pages that serve as indexes to information about particular topics and Web pages that allow researchers to search the Web using keywords for topics or names. Increasingly, many Web pages are interactive, allowing users to send comments or questions to the Web page author, respond to a survey, contribute to a collaborative work of fiction, or make purchases via the network.

Web Browsers A *Web browser,* also called a *Web client program,* is software that allows you to display a Web page on your computer, including any graphic images, video, or sound that is included on that page. A Web browser also allows you to navigate among Web pages. For example, you may return to previous pages by clicking on an arrow icon (such as the Back button in the top left corner of the sample home page on p. 577) or by accessing a menu that lists recently visited pages. In addition, a browser helps you to find, read, download, and save the text of documents, graphic images, video, or sounds.

The first graphical Web browser, Mosaic, was created at the University of Illinois. Currently, the most widely used graphical browsers are Netscape and Mosaic, and other programs are under development. A plain-text browser, Lynx, does not display graphics or video and is used for computer or modem connections that lack the processing speed needed for graphical browsers such as Mosaic and Netscape. Web browsers differ slightly in their format and features, though they share similarities that make them easy to use. Web browsers exist for virtually every computer platform (such as IBM, Macintosh, and UNIX), and they are widely available at no cost to students at academic institutions.

Home Pages A particular *Web site* usually consists of a home page and the pages to which it is linked. A *home page* is the page you most often find first when you access a Web site; it typically provides a title heading, a brief introduction, and a table of contents consisting of *links* to the information available at that site. In this way, it functions like the opening pages of a book. At the bottom of the home page, you will usually find the name of the person or group responsible for the site and an E-mail address to which you can send requests for further information. The illustration on page 577 shows a home page from the Ecology Action Centre. Home pages and Web sites vary greatly in content and design.

Links On a World Wide Web home page, links to other information are often indicated by underlined text (sometimes the words may be in bold type or highlighted in another way). In the example from the Ecology Action Centre, *EAC People* is one such link. Note also that the boxes on the home page are buttons that, when clicked,

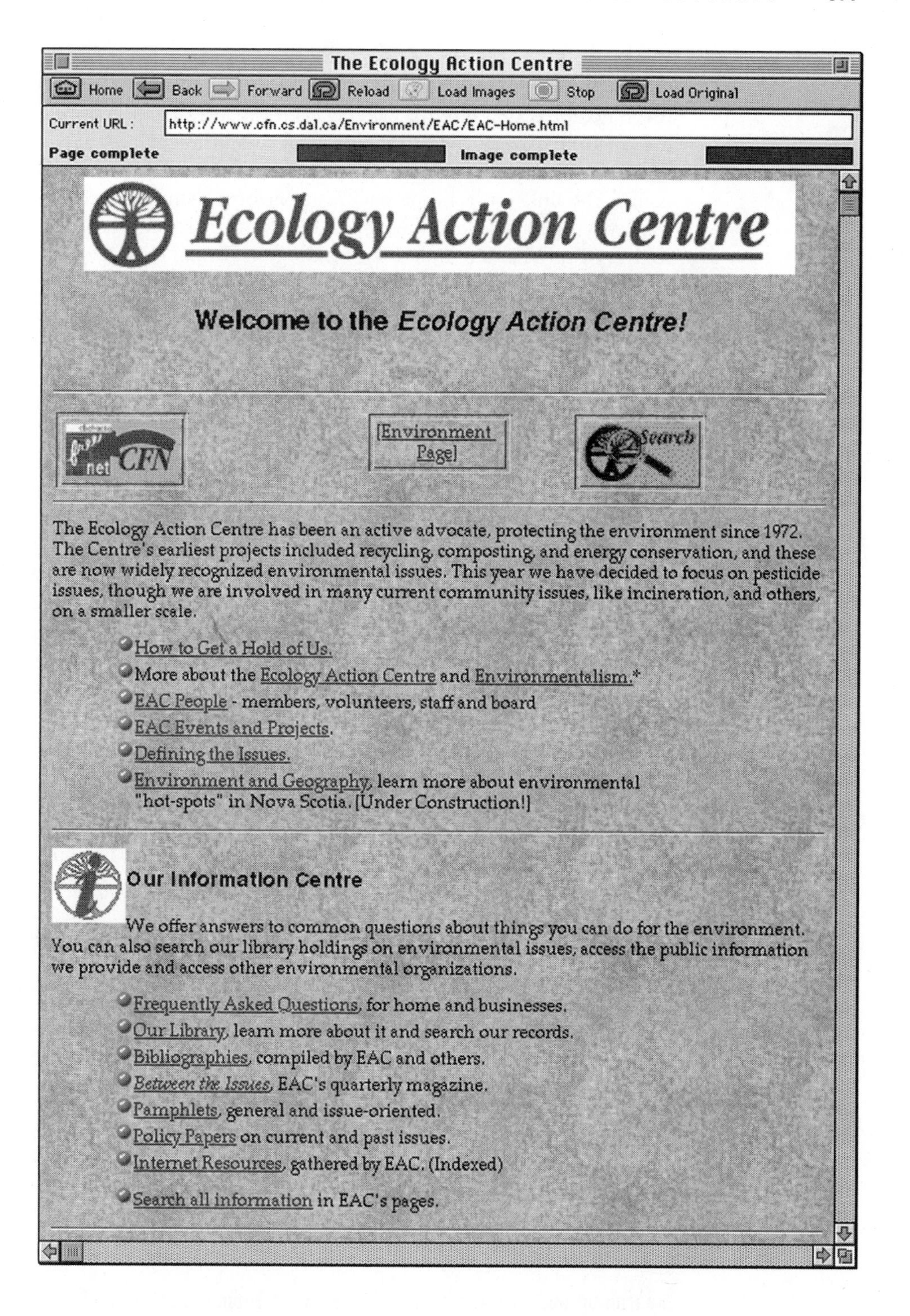

A sample home page from the Web site of the Ecology Action Centre.

link to further information. Links can also appear as icons or other graphic images. On a color monitor, links to additional information are indicated by a different color. After a color-coded link has been clicked on and the reader has looked at the linked information and returned to the original page, the link appears in a different color to show that it has been visited. In addition to providing connections to other documents, the links on a home page can perform many other functions—for example, they may open a form to be filled out by the reader, start a video, play music or sound, or provide a template for sending an E-mail message to the author.

URLs Each Web home page has its own address or *uniform resource locator (URL)*. The URL allows people anywhere in the world to locate a particular Web page. The URL for the Ecology Action Centre is typical:

http://www.cfn.cs.dal.ca /Environment/EAC/EAC-Home.html

- The first part of a URL for a Web page usually consists of the abbreviation *http://* (meaning "hypertext transfer protocol"); it tells the sending and receiving computers the type of information being sent and how to transfer it.
- The second part of the URL includes the standard *www.*, to establish that the location being accessed is on the World Wide Web, as well as the Internet address of the institution, government agency, corporation, or organization (and the country, if outside of the United States) where the document is located (*cfn.cs.dal.ca* is the address of the Ecology Action Centre).
- After a slash, the third part of the URL (which may be quite lengthy) gives the address of the directory and file where the page is found as well as the name of the specific page itself (as in *Environment/EAC/EAC-Home.html*).

Bookmarks When you find a Web page that you may want to visit again, it is a good idea to create a *bookmark* for that page. For example, in the Netscape program you create a bookmark by choosing Add Bookmark from the Bookmarks menu. The title of the Web page will be added to a list in the Bookmarks menu.

Accessing a Web Site. You may access a particular Web site in several ways:

- By typing the URL directly into the location box and then pressing Return or Enter on your keyboard
- By selecting Open Location from the file menu and typing the URL into the dialogue box
- By pasting or copying the URL into the location box from some other source, such as the computer's scrapbook or clipboard
- By selecting the URL from the bookmark menu, if you have previously saved a bookmark for that page

The method you use to access a URL may depend on your Web browser.

Searching the Web for Information on Your Topic. A Web page often provides links to additional information about a subject at other Web sites. You may also use one of the special search engines on the Web itself. *Search engines* are resources available for searching the World Wide Web. The home page of a search engine is especially set up to allow you to enter a keyword or phrase. The search engine scans the Web for your keyword and produces a list of direct links to pages containing the keyword. Usually, the list includes a brief description of each page. The program searches both the titles of Web pages and the actual text of those pages for the keyword. By clicking on one of the links on the list, you can access a specific Web page. For example, by clicking the Search button shown in the example on p. 577, you could directly access several popular search engines, such as Lycos and WebCrawler, which link to the most visited sites on the Web.

The well-known Lycos search engine offers two levels of searching: a quick search from among a relatively small selection of sites and an in-depth search of the entire collection of Web sites. A sample Lycos search form is shown on p. 580. To use Lycos, you type in one or more keywords and select the maximum number of sources, or "hits," you would like listed. Many other search engines are available in various locations, and some large Web sites with many documents in their archives provide their own search engines.

Using your Web browser, you can locate and use additional search engines for research. One of the most popular and best-maintained search engines available is Yahoo! Using Yahoo! you can easily execute a keyword search on a topic, generating a great number of returns. Yahoo! also offers eight other ways to locate information, including a What's New section that offers the latest available sites on the Web.

The following list provides information about five popular search engines.

Search Engine	*Description*	*URL**
Lycos	Offers two levels of searches	http://www.lycos.com
Infoseek Guide	Offers up-to-date news and reviews from magazines and television; allows user to post search questions	http://www2.infoseek.com
Magellan Internet Guide	Offers categories to help narrow your search and reviews and rates sites	http://www.mckinley.com
Excite	Offers weekly updates of site reviews, plus newsgroups and current news items	http://www.excite.com
Yahoo!	Offers links to categories such as Arts and Education	http://www.yahoo.com

*URLs are subject to change. All URLs in this chapter are current as of April 1998.

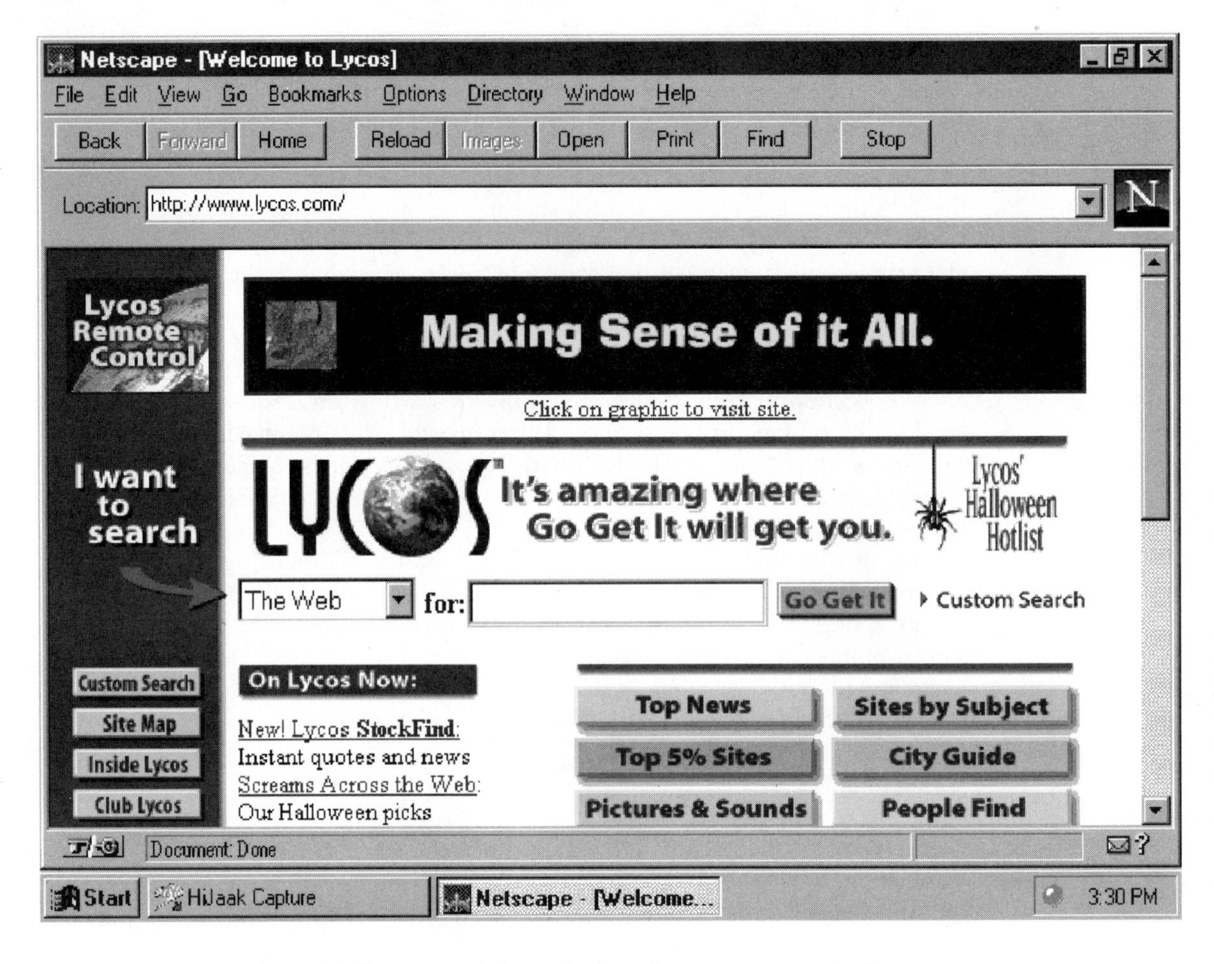

A sample Lycos search form for locating sources on a topic.

Because the World Wide Web is in demand by computer users, you might have to request access to a particular site several times before you succeed at reaching it. If you receive a message such as "Unable to locate host" or "Access denied," try again later.

In addition, the success of a Web search depends on the keywords you choose; if a search yields few sources or irrelevant ones, try rephrasing your keywords or choosing more specific ones to locate the most useful information. If your topic is ecology, for example, you may find information under the terms *ecosystem, environment, pollution,* and *endangered species,* as well as a number of other related keywords, depending on the focus of your research. As with library searches, however, you may need to narrow your topic to keep the number of sources manageable. When you find a source that seems promising, be sure to create a bookmark for the Web page so that you can return to it easily later on.

Finally, although the Web cannot provide the helpful advice and expertise of a reference librarian, you can contact authors of Web pages by E-mail to find additional resources. In addition, some search engines provide basic advice on how to conduct searches on the Internet.

Search in Progress: A Web Search

To complete the assignment in Chapter 6 in which students are asked to take a position on a controversial issue, a student writing on the topic of censorship on the Internet chooses to explore the following question: "Should state or federal governments have the power to censor activities on the Internet for purposes of eliminating criminal activity?"

Using the key term *censorship on the Internet,* or *censorship and Internet,* the student obtains the following results by using the sample search engines on our list:

1. A search of *Infoseek* yields several hundred thousand matches on the term. Because no researcher has the time to evaluate even a fraction of this number, the student reads the summaries of the top ten sources, as rated by the Web browser—in this case, Netscape. Netscape automatically provides these sources after the student presses the Enter key. When she groups these top ten sources, two categories seem to emerge:

   - Discussions of the topic in general, including descriptions of exactly what is involved in cyberspace censorship. These sites provide valuable background information concerning the development of the concept of censorship on the Internet, which the student might need, if not in her research paper, then to guide further research.
   - The legal challenges of Internet censorship and rights of its users. These sites provide discussions of what constitutes true criminal activity and what might instead be characterized as merely poor taste or a lack of judgment.

   Although some of the sources that the student locates are useful, other Web sites are out of date, particularly those that provide information about the Communications Decency Act (CDA). Passed by the U.S. Senate in June 1995 to take effect February 1, 1996, but later declared unconstitutionally vague, the CDA was concerned with removing material considered to be obscene from the Internet. Some of the Web sites the student locates have not been updated to reflect the current status of the CDA.
2. A *Magellan* search using the keywords *censorship and Internet* and the category Cyberspace Issues provides a list of thirty-one sites, ranked by relevancy. The student visits two promising sites: Sex, Censorship, and the Internet and Journoporn: Dissection of the Time Scandal.

continued

continued

3. Using *Excite,* the student comes across a review of recent school censorship cases and corresponding court rulings, which gives her access to primary legal files and various subdirectories. A related site offers her the opportunity to examine commercial software that allows parents and educators to block Internet pornography.
4. A search using the *Yahoo!* search engine is a bit more selective, yielding only nineteen topic matches. One potentially useful site provides an in-depth view of civil rights issues and the Communications Decency Act.
5. The *Lycos* search nets millions of URLs. The top ten URLs offer links to Internet monitoring tools such as Networld, which allows the student to examine some adult Internet sites firsthand. Another site invites visitors to join the Citizens' Internet Empowerment Coalition. A third site offers information on *netiquette,* Internet policies on appropriate online language, behavior, and graphics. Finally, the link to the PICS platform (Platform for Internet Content Selection) offers a rating service for parents and teachers that allows them to monitor material on the Internet themselves, without third-party censorship.

So far, the student's search has yielded a definition of cyberspace censorship, along with legal concerns regarding the protection of children versus the rights of adults to enjoy unlimited access to material available over the Internet. As a result of her search, the student decides to narrow her topic to Internet crimes, specifically, pornography available over the Internet, or *cyberporn.* Her primary source links are to legal sites and to sites that contain content considered pornographic. After reading some of the legal materials and examining examples of cyberporn, she takes the tentative position that the government should restrict Internet content in order to eliminate the danger that children might gain access to pornography on the Internet.

Using Other Tools to Access the Internet

As mentioned earlier, in addition to the World Wide Web, other tools for accessing information on the Internet include telnet and file transfer protocol (FTP) systems and such services as gopher, MUDs, and MOOs. Telnet allows you to view information on other computers, FTP enables you to download the information on your computer, and gopher allows you to do both. MUDs and MOOs provide new ways for researchers and others to interact.

Telnet. *Telnet* is a software networking tool that allows you to log on to another computer, called a *host computer,* through your modem or a direct network connection. A host computer may be in the same room or on the other side of the world. Once connected, you can access any services or information that a host computer makes available. For example, you might look through the card catalogs of various college libraries or read newspaper articles, government documents, and reports of recent scientific research. Many kinds of information can be located through telnet. Telnet makes it possible for you to use FTP and gopher to find and download information stored in thousands of host computers all over the world.

Telnet connections can be made directly to the New York Public Library and to other general libraries all over the world. You can also make telnet connections to international locations, using the World Wide Web, to obtain information on virtually any topic imaginable.

If you do not know the direct address of the telnet connection, you can use any Web browser or search engine to search for telnet sites. The following sites will help you to make telnet connections:

Title	*Summary*	*URL*
Telnet directory	Allows you to keep a telnet database of over 1,300 sites on a PC and to subscribe to a telnet mailing list via E-mail	http://www.internetdatabase.com/telnet.htm
Connecting to Internet-Accessible Online Catalogs Using Telnet	Provides tips for using telnet with both Windows and Macintosh computers and explains how to find online catalog addresses	http://www.gslis.ucla.edu/LIS/lab/unote15.html
WebTeacher Tutorials	Provides a telnet tutorial with screen shots and step-by-step instructions	http://www.webteacher.org/winnet/telnet/telnet.html
Introduction to Telnet	Functions as a user's guide to telnet resources	http://www.vonl.com/vtab24/telnet.htm

File Transfer Protocol (FTP). *File transfer protocol (FTP)* is a standard communication format that allows files to be transferred across computer networks. Although similar in function to telnet in that it allows you to log on to and read information stored in host computers, FTP can also transfer that information to your computer, provided that you are granted access. FTP also allows you to create, delete, and rename files on a remote system when you have been granted these privileges.

Generally, when people refer to FTP as a research tool, they are referring to *anonymous FTP,* a special "public space" provided by many host computers for storing documents that may be accessed freely by anyone. To retrieve a file using anonymous FTP, you log on to the host computer using the log-in name *anonymous* and any password (usually your E-mail address). You then search the directories and files of the public archives on that host computer and download the file you wish to retrieve. FTP works best when you know the location of the information you are seeking.

Because the Internet is such a large collection of networks, it can be difficult for you to find and keep track of the locations of all the information you seek. *Archie* is a system that indexes host computer files that are open to the general public and thereby provides a way of searching for specific kinds of information. Under this system, host computers register as Archie servers; once a month, each Archie server is asked to update its list of files on the system's master index.

You can conduct an online search of the Archie index by file name (or part of it) using an Archie client program, such as Anarchie, which is available online as well as from service providers and computer user groups. Following the Archie search, you would use FTP to access the host computer where the file is located.

Gopher. The *gopher* system functions like the subject cards in a library's card catalog, allowing you to browse by topic, rather than by file name or location, and to find information on the same subject grouped together. In addition, you can browse the Internet by choosing resources from menus. When you find a source that interests you, gopher can retrieve it for you to read or save without using FTP. Most gopher client programs, like World Wide Web browsers, also include the bookmark feature, which makes it easy to return to sources.

Gopher indexing services vary, particularly in the way subjects are organized and classified. Therefore, you need to be resourceful, trying out different approaches to locate information on a particular topic.

Noteworthy gopher sites that you can access using the World Wide Web include these:

Title	*Summary*	*URL*
State Departments of Education	Provides access to an alphabetical listing of state departments of education	http://ericps.ed.uiuc.edu /eece/statlink.html
FAQS	Posts frequently asked questions about gopher and answers to them	http://www.ach.uams.edu /~adh/FAQS/gopher.FAQ
Forensic and Law Enforcement Gophers	Lists law enforcement gophers available through major university networks	http://www.eskimo.com /~spban/pgopher.html

Title	*Summary*	*URL*
Publisher List	Connects to the Library of Congress, public and private universities, and private publishing houses; provides an alphabetical listing	http://eci2.ucsb.edu/infoweb/publishers.html

Originally an acronym for *Very Easy, Rodent-Oriented, Netwide Index to Computerized Archives, Veronica* is a research tool that allows you to search GopherSpace (the specific cyberspace area that can be reached by using a gopher server) by keying in a specified term. Veronica creates a temporary, easily accessed gopher menu just for your keyword, which saves you valuable time. Notable Veronica sites include these:

Title	*Summary*	*URL*
Yahoo!	Provides direct Veronica searches	http://www.yahoo.com/Computers_and_Internet/Internet/Gopher/Searching/Veronica/
VERONICA Gopher Search Sites	Helps you to create a Veronica query and allows you to search eight gopher sites, national and international	http://www.schdist81.bc.ca/veronica.html
Veronica home access page	Veronica tutorial	http://www.scs.unr.edu/veronica.html
MAP21: Veronica	Provides a detailed map of how to use Veronica and allows for practical application searches	http://www.brandonu.ca/~ennsnr/Resources/Roadmap/map21.html

Search in Progress: A Search Using Veronica

Using Veronica as a search tool, the student makes close to seventy thousand matching inquiry connections to the search term *censorship on the Internet.* Two hundred titles appear on the screen at a time.

Because the student has taken the tentative position that the government should censor the Internet, she spots a Senate contact list, giving her access to the names and numbers of senators who may be willing to give her an interview. Of course, the initial interview contact may be made through a staff assistant.

Because she does not have time to look at all of the matches to her original keyword, however, the student decides to narrow her search by choosing a more limited subject heading. She types in the term *legislation on censorship.* This time the search provides only three titles under the headings of Society and Culture, Civil Rights, and Censorship and the Net.

Thus, the Veronica search helps the student locate information concerning the details of censorship legislation, with updates, and offers her an opportunity to extend her research by contacting people who are either for or against such legislation. After reviewing the material up to this point, particularly speeches by legislators who oppose censorship legislation, the student decides to change her position and argue that the government does not have the right to censor activities on the Internet. She decides to investigate pending legislation further and make arrangements for an interview.

Searching Remote Libraries. Both gopher and the World Wide Web give researchers unprecedented access to libraries in the United States as well as in other countries. The following gopher or World Wide Web sites provide easy access to libraries around the world:

Title	*Summary*	*URL*
IPL Services For Librarians	Locates libraries and library schools on the World Wide Web and its Internet Public Library	http://www.ipl.org/svcs/
On-line Library	Provides access to the Library of Congress, World Wide Web Virtual Libraries, BRIAN on the Web (Oxford Libraries Bibliographic Resource for Accessing Networks), and Research Libraries	http://firth .natcorp.ox.ac.uk/cgi-bin /humbul/section .p1?SECTION-libraries

Title	*Summary*	*URL*
State of Wisconsin, Department of Public Instruction: Library Resource List	Provides a menu of resources	http://www.dpi.state.wi.us /dpi/dlcl/pld/lib~res.html
Database union list for Oxford academic libraries	Provides an alphabetical search tool of CD-ROMs and remote databases	http://www.rsl.ox.ac.uk /cdul/title.html
WWW Virtual Library	Provides a catalog of Internet resources	http://www.mth.uea.ac.uk /VL/Overview.html

Search in Progress: Searching Remote Libraries

Choosing the URL for On-line Library, the student begins a search of remote libraries. The student accesses the Harvard OnLine Library Information System (HOLLIS) and the New York Public Library but is unable to locate any resources by using the keywords *censorship* and *Internet.* The student has more success with the Library of Congress, however. She goes to the Library of Congress Catalogs and chooses Advanced Word Search, which gives her access to a search form. She types in *censorship* as term 1 and *Internet* as term 2. Her search yields records for two recent books on the topic of censorship on the Internet: a reference guide to media censorship and a book on Internet filters. The student prints both records so that she can search for the books in her college library.

MUDs and MOOs. *MUDs* (derived from *multi-user dungeons*) and *MOOs* (from *MUD object oriented*) began as computer games, similar to Dungeons and Dragons, in which participants could play in real time and interact with one another. These media have since become serious tools for writing and research. Students and professionals, posing as characters, can interact and become part of research projects. The following MUDs are useful resources for students.

- *The Idea Exchange,* a MUD for educational purposes, can be found at <http://www.imaginary.com/LPMud/IdeaExchange>.
- *Diversity University,* a distance learning project, is located at <http://du.org>.

Search in Progress: Posting a Query on a MUD

To find out more about objections and opposing arguments, the student connects to the mail service of the MUD Idea Exchange and addresses an E-mail message to the individual who maintains this site. The student posts a query concerning censorship on the Internet and directs it to participants who oppose her position. The student can continue the discussion by return E-mail or on the MUD itself if the topic is opened to the group.

Accessing Special-Interest Groups on the Internet

Joining Discussion Groups. To conduct research on a particular topic on the Internet, you may also find it helpful to join a *computer discussion group* on your topic. Discussion groups operate like large mailing lists. Members of a group communicate with each other through E-mail. A message sent by any group member to the list is automatically distributed to everyone who subscribes to that list.

Various discussion groups and their E-mail addresses can be found in computer publications, special-interest magazines, and print directories in the library; many are passed along by word of mouth. You may also conduct online searches to find discussion groups on particular topics. Many discussion groups are managed by special software such as a *listserv,* which automatically takes care of the details of operating the list: adding new subscribers, distributing messages, and deleting the addresses of members who leave the group (unsubscribing). You can subscribe to most discussion groups at no cost. To subscribe to a particular group, you simply send an E-mail request to the group's listserv E-mail address. Once you are a member, any messages sent to the group are automatically sent to you, and any messages you send are automatically distributed to the other members of the group.

Participating in Newsgroups. *Newsgroups* are similar to discussion groups except that membership is not required. You can read and post messages to a newsgroup even if you do not subscribe to it. Messages sent to the newsgroup are posted for anyone to read and respond to, much like a public bulletin board. Readers can browse the messages, dropping in and following a discussion that interests them and ignoring the rest.

Thousands of newsgroups currently exist on the Internet. As with discussion groups, they are organized primarily by topic. Software programs such as Nuntius and Newswatcher are widely available and make it easy to browse, read, and save newsgroup messages. Increasingly, Web browsers such as Netscape enable you to read newsgroups. You can also use search engines to search newsgroups.

Using Discussion Groups and Newsgroups. Although discussion groups and newsgroups are not authoritative sources of factual information in the same way that published library sources are, they can serve many useful functions in research and writing. A computer group can help you to conduct preliminary research on a topic or to seek general background information on a controversy—how it developed and whether it has been resolved.

- For a paper proposing changes in public schools, a group focusing on child development may alert you to some interesting new research on how play supports language development, suggesting new models for learning environments.
- For a paper explaining the concept of ecology, you may find that there are various interpretations of the concept among scholars in the field. Reading messages posted to a group on ecology can give you a good sense of the major questions, issues, and trends related to your topic.

Discussion groups and newsgroups can provide a means of conducting field research on a topic. For example, you might conduct an informal public opinion poll, sample the current thinking about a topic, or post a question you would like answered. Groups can also help you to find and evaluate useful sources on a topic.

- For a paper arguing the position that there ought to be import quotas on Japanese cars, you might send a message to a discussion group or newsgroup on trade issues, asking for recent sources of information on trade practices.
- For a paper proposing a solution to the problem of endangered species, you might post a request for help in evaluating sources: "What are the three most important books or articles to read on the preservation of critical habitats?"
- For an essay arguing the position that the government should be more flexible in seeking to preserve wetlands, you may have found two important sources that contradict each other. You might describe the contradiction and ask group members whether recent opinion has favored one point of view over the other.

Discussion groups vary from lively to nearly inactive, members may be extremely polite or openly combative, and the level of discussion may range from technical and scholarly to casual. Read enough messages from a particular group to get a sense of the tone and level of the discussion before subscribing or posting a message to the group yourself. Be polite when asking for help and gracious in thanking those who respond. Keep in mind that once your message is posted you cannot retrieve it. Because it may be read by thousands—perhaps millions—of people, compose it carefully.

→ Search in Progress: Locating Relevant Discussion Groups

The student decides to look for a discussion group on the topic of censorship. First, however, she consults her service provider's electronic mail system to see if this feature is offered. It is, and the student finds a general list of discussion groups available as well as a keyword search feature that allows her to enter the term, view the summary notes for each group, and subscribe by pressing the Enter key.

Two discussion groups that deal with the issue of censorship on the Internet seem to be currently active. Digianarch@ids.net is a group opposing censorship that the student can join temporarily. The other group, TBTF, is actually an E-mail newsletter that sends to its subscribers articles on Internet topics such as censorship.

By examining newsgroups on Usenet, under the title <alt.censorship>, the student finds an active discussion of harassing E-mail and a newly coined term, *net.cops.* If the student wants to participate in the discussion, she can respond by sending an E-mail message to the newsgroup's address.

Establishing E-Mail Contact with Experts

Another advantage of using the Internet for research is that you can contact other researchers—authors, scholars, scientists, government officials, and so on—directly by sending E-mail. Many people are willing to respond to specific requests for information. For instance, if you have additional questions after reading an article on your topic, you might send your questions to the author. To locate a person's E-mail address, try looking at published papers, books, or online documents, many of which now include the writer's E-mail address. You can also locate people by using the following directories:

- *Excite Email Lookup* at <http://www.excite.com/Reference/email.html>
- *Netfind* at <http://lut.ac.uk/dir/netfind.html>

You may also find E-mail useful for requesting an interview with an expert. In your E-mail message, introduce yourself, briefly describe the purpose and general topic of the interview, and request a time and place convenient for the person you wish to interview. You might even conduct the interview by E-mail if the interviewee cannot meet with you personally. After the interview, be sure to send a note of thanks via E-mail or regular mail.

→ Search in Progress: Locating E-Mail Addresses and Constructing an Outline

Using the URL for Excite Email Lookup, the student accesses the main screen and chooses Personal Home Pages under Related Resources. She types the keywords *Internet and Censorship* into the form and receives a list of home pages. She cannot tell from their titles whether or not they are relevant and hasn't time to look at them all, so she returns to the first screen. She chooses the Yellow Pages option and searches under the category *Computers* and the name of her city. The search yields a list of subcategories, including *Computer Consultants* and *Internet Marketing Service*. The student could contact a consultant and perhaps make arrangements for a phone interview. This search does not give direct access to experts on censorship, however, and the student is unable to locate a promising source using this method.

Consulting the sample outlines in Chapter 6 of the text, the student constructs her own preliminary outline on the topic of censorship. The following table shows the points of her outline and the Internet source that informed her thinking about or provided evidence to support each point. In addition to the sources she found on the Internet, the student also consulted library sources, using strategies discussed earlier in this chapter.

Outline	*Information*	*Source*
I. Thesis/issue	State and federal governments should not attempt to censor activities on the Internet for purposes of eliminating criminal activity.	Veronica/Infoseek
Explains/supports reason 1	Legal challenges and rights of Internet users	Infoseek

Outline	*Information*	*Source*
Explains/supports reason 2	Civil rights issues and the problems with the Communications Decency Act	Yahoo!
Refutes opposing argument	Internet crime School censorship	Magellan Excite, Lycos
Explains/supports reason 3	Adult sites/screening software/netiquette	Lycos
Explains/supports reason 4	FBI investigations	Remote libraries
Refutes opposing argument	Results of query	MUD
Concludes by reasserting position	Results of expert interview	Veronica

The following sources of information about the Internet can help you to learn more about this valuable research tool.

Kurland, Daniel. *The 'Net, the Web, and You*. Belmont: Wadsworth, 1996.

Reddick, Randy, and Elliot King. *The Online Student*. Fort Worth: Harcourt, 1996.

READING SOURCES WITH A CRITICAL EYE

From the beginning of your search, you should evaluate potential sources to determine which ones to use in your essay. Obviously, you must decide which sources provide information relevant to the topic. But you must also read sources with a critical eye to decide how credible or trustworthy they are. Just because a book or essay appears in print or online does not necessarily mean that an author's information or opinions are reliable.

Selecting Relevant Sources

Begin your evaluation of sources by narrowing your working bibliography to the most relevant works. Consider them in terms of scope, date of publication, and viewpoint.

Scope and Approach. To decide how relevant a particular source is to your topic, you need to examine the source in depth. Do not depend on title alone, for it may be misleading. If the source is a book, check its table of contents and index to see how many pages are devoted to the precise subject you are exploring. In most cases, you will want an in-depth, not a superficial, treatment of the subject. Read the preface or introduction to a book or the abstract or opening paragraphs of an article and any biographical information given about the author to determine the author's basic approach to the subject or special way of looking at it. As you attend to these elements, consider the following questions:

- Does the source provide a general or specialized view? General sources are helpful early in your research, but then you need the authority or up-to-date coverage of specialized sources. Extremely specialized works, however, may be too technical.
- Is the source long enough to provide adequate detail?
- Was the source written for general readers? Specialists? Advocates? Critics?
- Is the author an expert on the topic? Does the author's way of looking at the topic support or challenge your own views? (The fact that an author's viewpoint challenges your own does not mean that you should reject the author as a source, as you will see from our discussion of the importance of multiple viewpoints.)

Date of Publication. Although you should always consult the most up-to-date sources available on your subject, older sources often establish the principles, theories, and data on which later work is based and may provide a useful perspective for evaluating it. If older works are considered authoritative, you may want to become familiar with them. To determine which sources are authoritative, note the ones that are cited most often in encyclopedia articles, bibliographies, and recent works on the subject.

Viewpoint. Your sources should represent a variety of viewpoints on the subject. Just as you would not depend on a single author for all of your information, so you do not want to use authors who all belong to the same school of thought. For suggestions on determining authors' viewpoints, see the following section, on identifying bias.

Using sources that represent different viewpoints is especially important when developing an argument for one of the essay assignments in Chapters 6–10. During the invention work in those chapters, you may want to research what others have said about your subject to see what positions have been staked out and what arguments have been made. You will then be able to define the issue more carefully, collect arguments supporting your position, and anticipate arguments opposing it.

Identifying Bias

One of the most important aspects of evaluating a source is identifying any bias in its treatment of the subject. Although the word *bias* may sound accusatory, it simply refers to the fact that most writing is not neutral or objective and does not try or claim to be. Authors come to their subjects with particular viewpoints. In using sources, you must consider carefully how these viewpoints are reflected in the writing and how they affect the way authors present their arguments.

Although the text of the source will give you the most precise indication of the author's viewpoint, you can often get a good idea by looking at the preface or introduction or at the sources the author cites. When you examine a reference, you can often determine the general point of view it represents by considering the following elements:

Title. Does the title or subtitle indicate the text's bias? Watch for loaded words or confrontational phrasing.

Author. What is the author's professional title or affiliation? What is the author's perspective? Is the author in favor of something or at odds with it? What has persuaded the author to take this stance? How might the author's professional affiliation affect his or her perspective? What is the author's tone? Information on the author may also be available in the book or article itself or in biographical sources available in the library.

Presentation of Argument. Almost every written work asserts a point of view or makes an argument for something the author considers important. To determine this position and the reason behind it, look for the main point. What evidence does the author provide as support for this point? Is the evidence from authoritative sources? Is the evidence persuasive? Does the author accommodate or refute opposing arguments?

Publication Information. Was the book published by a commercial publisher, a corporation, a government agency, or an interest group? What is that organization's position on the topic? Is the author funded by or affiliated with the organization?

Editorial Slant. What kind of periodical or online source published the article—popular, academic, alternative? If the article is available on a Web site, is the Web page maintained by a commercial or academic organization? For periodicals, knowing some background about the publisher or periodical can help to determine bias because all periodicals have their own editorial slants. In cases where the publication title does not indicate bias, reference sources may help you to determine this information. Two of the most common are the following:

> *Gale Directory of Publications and Broadcast Media* (1990). A useful source for descriptive information on newspapers and magazines. Entries often include an indication of intended audience and political or other bias. For example, the *San Diego Union* is described as a "newspaper with a Republican orientation."
>
> *Magazines for Libraries* (1992). A listing of over 6,500 periodicals arranged by academic discipline. For each discipline, there is a list of basic indexes, abstracts, and periodicals. Each individual listing for a periodical includes its publisher, the date it was founded, the places it is indexed, its intended audience, and an evaluation of its content and editorial focus. One such listing appears on the next page.

2605. *Growing Without Schooling.* [ISSN: 0745-5305] 1977. bi-m. $25. Susannah Sheffer. Holt Assocs., 2269 Massachusetts Ave., Cambridge, MA 02140. Illus., index, adv. Sample. Circ: 5,000.

Bk. rev: 0–4, 400–600 words, signed. *Aud:* Ga, Sa.

GWS is a journal by and for home schoolers. Parents and students share their views as to why they chose home schooling and what they like about it. While lesson plans or activities are not included, home schoolers could get ideas for interesting activities from articles chronicling their experiences ("Helping Flood Victims," "Legislative Intern"). "News and Reports" offers home schoolers information on legal issues while the "Declassified Ads" suggest resources geared toward home schoolers. This is an important title for public libraries and should be available to students and faculty in teacher preparation programs.

Using and Acknowledging Sources

Information and ideas come from various sources. In addition to your own first-hand observation and analysis, your writing in college will be expected to use and acknowledge secondary sources—reading, interviews, computer bulletin boards, lectures, and other print and nonprint material. In fact, most of your college education is devoted to teaching you what Matthew Arnold called "the best that has been thought and said," along with ways of analyzing and interpreting this information so that your own understanding is informed but not limited by what others have said. Your education involves your participation in ongoing academic, cultural, and social conversations. When you bring diverse sources into your writing, your readers can see how you position yourself in these larger conversations through the ideas and information that have influenced your thinking.

When you cite material from another source, you need to acknowledge the source, usually by giving the author and page or date (depending on the documentation system) in parentheses in your text and including a list of works cited at the end of your paper. This chapter provides guidelines for using sources effectively and acknowledging them accurately. It also presents a sample research paper that follows the Modern Language Association documentation style.

USING SOURCES

Writers commonly use sources by quoting directly, by paraphrasing, and by summarizing. This section provides guidelines for deciding when to use each of these three methods and how to do so effectively.

Deciding Whether to Quote, Paraphrase, or Summarize

As a general rule, quote only in these situations: (1) when the wording of the source is particularly memorable or vivid or expresses a point so well that you cannot improve it without destroying the meaning, (2) when the words of reliable and respected authorities would lend support to your position, (3) when you wish to highlight the author's opinions, or (4) when you wish to cite an author whose opinions challenge or vary greatly from those of other experts. Paraphrase passages whose details you wish to note completely but whose language is not particularly striking.

Summarize any long passages whose main points you wish to record selectively as background or general support for a point you are making.

Quoting

Quotations should duplicate the source exactly. If the source has an error, copy it and add the notation *sic* (Latin for "thus") in brackets immediately after the error to indicate that it is not your error but your source's:

> According to a recent newspaper article, "Plagirism [*sic*] is a problem among journalists and scholars as well as students" (Berensen 62).

However, you can change quotations (1) to emphasize particular words by underlining or italicizing them, (2) to omit irrelevant information or to make the quotation conform grammatically to your sentence by using ellipsis marks, and (3) to make the quotation conform grammatically or to insert information by using brackets.

Underlining or Italicizing for Emphasis. In quotations, underline or italicize the words you want to emphasize, and add the notation *emphasis added* in parentheses at the end of the sentence.

> In a review of psychosocial literature on adolescence, Elder (1975) concludes: "Adolescents who fail to receive guidance, affection, and concern from parents—whether by parental inattention or absence—are likely to rely heavily on peers for emotional gratification, advice, and companionship, *to anticipate a relatively unrewarding future,* and to engage in antisocial activities" (emphasis added).

Using Ellipsis Marks for Omissions. Ellipsis marks—three spaced periods (. . .)—signals that something has been left out of a quotation. A writer may decide to leave certain words out of a quotation because they are not relevant to the point being made or because they add information readers will not need in the context in which the quotation is being used. When you quote only single words or phrases, you do not need to use ellipsis marks because it will be obvious that you have left out some of the original:

> More specifically, Wharton's imagery of suffusing brightness transforms Undine before her glass into "some fabled creature whose home was in a beam of light" (21).

However, when you omit words from within a quotation, you must use ellipsis marks in place of the missing words. When the omission occurs within the sentence, put a space *before* and *after* each of the three periods:

> Hermione Roddice is described in Lawrence's *Women in Love* as a "woman of the new school, full of intellectuality and . . . nerve-worn with consciousness" (17).

When the omission falls at the end of a sentence, place a sentence period *directly after* the last word, followed by three spaced periods, for a total of four periods:

> But Grimaldi's recent commentary on Aristotle contends that for Aristotle rhetoric, like dialectic, had "no limited and unique subject matter upon which it must be

> exercised. . . . Instead, rhetoric as an art transcends all specific disciplines and may be brought into play in them" (6).

A period plus ellipsis marks can indicate the omission of the rest of the sentence as well as whole sentences, paragraphs, or even pages.

When a parenthetical reference follows the ellipsis marks at the end of a sentence, place the three spaced periods after the quotation, and place the sentence period after the final parenthesis:

> But Grimaldi's recent commentary on Aristotle contends that for Aristotle rhetoric, like dialectic, had "no limited and unique subject matter upon which it must be exercised . . ." (6).

Using Brackets for Insertions or Changes. Use brackets around an insertion or a change needed to make a quotation conform grammatically to your sentence, such as a change in verb tense or a change in the capitalization of the first letter of the first word of a quotation, or to replace an unclear pronoun. In this example from an essay on James Joyce's "Araby," reprinted in Chapter 10, the writer adapts Joyce's phrases "we played till our bodies glowed" and "shook music from the buckled harness" to fit the tense of her sentences:

> In the dark, cold streets during the "short days of winter," the boys must generate their own heat by "[playing] till [their] bodies glowed." Music is "[shaken] from the buckled harness" as if it were unnatural, and the singers in the market chant nasally of "the troubles in our native land" (30).

You may also use brackets to add or substitute explanatory material in a quotation:

> Guterson notes that among Native Americans in Florida, "education was in the home; learning by doing was reinforced by the myths and legends which repeated the basic value system of their [the Seminoles'] way of life" (159).

Several kinds of changes necessary to make a quotation conform grammatically to another sentence may be made without any signal to readers: (1) A period at the end of a quotation may be changed to a comma if you are using the quotation within your own sentence, and (2) double quotation marks enclosing a quotation may be changed to single quotation marks when the quotation is enclosed within a longer quotation.

Integrating Quotations

Depending on its length, a quotation may be integrated into your text by enclosing it in quotation marks or set off from your text in a block without quotation marks.

In-Text Quotations. Incorporate brief quotations (no more than four typed lines of prose or three lines of poetry) into your text. You may place the quotation virtually anywhere in your sentence:

At the Beginning

> "To live a life is not to cross a field," Sutherland quotes Pasternak at the beginning of her narrative (11).

In the Middle

> Woolf begins and ends by speaking of the need of the woman writer to have "money and a room of her own" (4)—an idea that certainly spoke to Plath's condition, especially in her impoverished and harassed last six months.

At the End

> In *The Second Sex,* Simone de Beauvoir describes such an experience as one in which the girl "becomes as object, and she sees herself as object" (378).

Divided by Your Own Words

> "Science usually prefers the literal to the nonliteral term," Kinneavy writes, "—that is, figures of speech are often out of place in science" (177).

When you quote poetry within your text, use a slash (/) with spaces before and after to signal the end of each line of verse:

> Alluding to St. Augustine's distinction between the City of God and the Earthly City, Lowell writes that "much against my will / I left the City of God where it belongs" ("Beyond the Alps" lines 4–5).

Block Quotations. Put in block form prose quotations of five or more typed lines and poetry quotations of four or more lines. For APA style, use block form for quotations of forty words or more. If you are using MLA style, indent the quotation an inch (ten character spaces) from the left margin, as shown below. If you are using APA style, indent the block quotation five to seven spaces, keeping your indents consistent throughout your paper. Double-space between lines just as you do in your text. *Do not* enclose the passage within quotation marks. Use a colon to introduce a block quotation, unless the context calls for another punctuation mark or none at all. When quoting a single paragraph or part of one, do not indent the first line of the quotation more than the rest. In quoting two or more paragraphs, indent the first line of each paragraph an extra quarter inch (three spaces). If you are using APA style, the first line of subsequent paragraphs in the block quotation indents an additional five to seven spaces from the block quotation indent.

```
In "A Literary Legacy from Dunbar to Baraka," Margaret Walker
says of Paul Lawrence Dunbar's dialect poems:
          He realized that the white world in the United
          States tolerated his literary genius only because of
          his "jingles in a broken tongue," and they found the
```

old "darky" tales and speech amusing and within the vein of folklore into which they wished to classify all Negro life. This troubled Dunbar because he realized that white America was denigrating him as a writer and as a man. (70)

Punctuating Introductory Statements

Statements that introduce quotations take a range of punctuation marks and lead-in words. Let us look at some examples of ways writers typically introduce quotations.

Introducing a Statement with a Colon

As George Williams notes, protection of white privilege is critical to patterns of discrimination: "Whenever a number of persons within a society have enjoyed for a considerable period of time certain opportunities for getting wealth, for exercising power and authority, and for successfully claiming prestige and social deference, there is a strong tendency for these people to feel that these benefits are theirs 'by right'" (727).

Introducing a Statement with a Comma

Similarly, Duncan Turner asserts, "As matters now stand, it is unwise to talk about communication without some understanding of Burke" (259).

Introducing a Statement Using *that*

Noting this failure, Alice Miller asserts that "the reason for her despair was not her suffering but the impossibility of communicating her suffering to another person" (255).

Introducing a Statement Using *as . . . said*

The token women writers authenticated the male canon without disrupting it, for as Ruth Bleier has said, "The last thing society desires of its women has been intellectuality and independence" (73).

Punctuating within Quotations

Although punctuation within a quotation should reproduce the original, some adaptations may be necessary. Use single quotation marks for quotations within the quotation:

Original

E. D. Hirsch also recognizes the connection between family and learning, suggesting in his discussion of family background and academic achievement "that the significant part of our children's education has been going on outside rather than inside the schools" (Guterson 16–17).

Quoted Version

> Guterson claims that E. D. Hirsch "also recognizes the connection between family and learning, suggesting in his discussion of family background and academic achievement 'that the significant part of our children's education has been going on outside rather than inside the schools'" (16–17).

If the quotation ends with a question mark or an exclamation point, retain the original punctuation:

> "Did you think I loved you?" Edith later asks Dombey (566).

If a quotation ending with a question mark or an exclamation point concludes your sentence, retain the question mark or exclamation point and put the parenthetical reference and sentence period outside the quotation marks:

> Edith later asks Dombey, "Did you think I loved you?" (566).

Avoiding Grammatical Tangles

When you incorporate quotations into your writing, and especially when you omit words from quotations, you run the risk of creating ungrammatical sentences. Three common errors you should try to avoid are verb incompatibility, ungrammatical omissions, and sentence fragments.

Verb Incompatibility. When this error occurs, the verb form in the introductory statement is grammatically incompatible with the verb form in the quotation. When your quotation has a verb form that does not fit in with your text, it is usually possible to use just part of the quotation, thus avoiding verb incompatibility.

he describes seeing himself

The narrator suggests his bitter disappointment when ~~"I saw myself~~ "as a creature driven and derided by vanity" (35).

Ungrammatical Omission. Sometimes omitting text from a quotation leaves you with an ungrammatical sentence. Two ways of correcting the grammar are (1) adapting the quotation (with brackets) so that its parts fit together grammatically and (2) using only one part of the quotation.

From the moment of the boy's arrival in Araby, the bazaar is presented as a commercial enterprise: "I could not find any sixpenny entrance and . . .

hand[ed]

~~handing~~ a shilling to a weary-looking man" (34).

From the moment of the boy's arrival in Araby, the bazaar is presented as a commercial enterprise:

He

~~"I~~ "could not find any sixpenny entrance" and ~~. . .~~

so had to pay a shilling to get in (34).

~~handing a shilling to a weary-looking man" (34).~~

Sentence Fragment. Sometimes when a quotation is a complete sentence, writers neglect the introductory sentence—for example, by forgetting to include a verb. It is important to recognize that even though the quotation is a complete sentence, the statement in which it occurs may be a sentence fragment.

The girl's interest in the bazaar ~~leading~~ leads the narrator to make what amounts to a sacred oath: "If I go . . . I will bring you something" (32).

Paraphrasing and Summarizing

In addition to quoting sources, writers have the option of paraphrasing or summarizing what others have written. In a *paraphrase,* the writer accurately and thoroughly states in his or her own words all the relevant information from a passage, without any additional comments or elaborations. A paraphrase is useful for recording details of the passage when the order of the details is important but the source's wording is not. Because all the details of the passage are noted, a paraphrase is often about the same length as the original passage.

In a *summary,* the writer boils down a long passage—several pages or even a whole chapter or work—to its main ideas using his or her own words. Unlike a paraphrase, a summary conveys the gist of a source, using just enough information to record the points the summarizer chooses to emphasize. In choosing what to include in a summary, be sure not to distort the author's meaning. Whereas the length of a paraphrase depends on the length of the original and how much information you need, a summary is generally much shorter than the original passage.

To avoid plagiarizing inadvertently, you must use *your own words and sentence structures* when paraphrasing or summarizing. If you include some of the author's words, enclose them in quotation marks. Note that even though a paraphrase or a summary is restated in your own words, you still need to include a parenthetical citation that identifies the original source of the ideas. If you are uncertain about a particular paraphrase or summary, ask your instructor while you are still drafting your paper.

Here is a passage from a book on home schooling and an example of a paraphrase:

Original Passage

Bruner and the discovery theorists have also illuminated conditions that apparently pave the way for learning. It is significant that these conditions are unique to each learner, so unique, in fact, that in many cases classrooms can't provide them. Bruner also contends that the more one discovers information in a great variety of circumstances, the more likely one is to develop the inner categories required to organize that information. Yet life at school, which is for the most part generic and predictable, daily keeps many children from the great variety of circumstances they need to learn well.

—David Guterson, *Family Matters: Why Homeschooling Makes Sense,* p. 172

Paraphrase

According to Guterson (172), the discovery theorists, particularly Bruner, have identified the conditions that allow learning to take place. Because these conditions are

> specific to each individual, many children are not able to learn in the classroom. According to Bruner, when people can explore information in different situations, they learn to classify and order what they discover. The general routine of the school day, however, does not provide children with the diverse activities and situations that would allow them to learn these skills.

Here is an example of a summary of the longer section that contains the original passage:

> In looking at different theories of learning that discuss individual-based programs (such as home schooling) versus the public school system, Guterson describes the disagreements among "cognitivist" theorists. One group, the discovery theorists, believe that individual children learn by creating their own ways of sorting the information they take in from their experiences. Schools should help students develop better ways of organizing new material, not just present them with material that is already categorized, as traditional schools do. Assimilationist theorists, by contrast, believe that children learn by linking what they don't know to information they already know. These theorists claim that traditional schools help students learn when they present information in ways that allow children to fit the new material into categories they have already developed (171–75).

Introducing Cited Material

Notice in the preceding examples that the source is acknowledged by name. Even when you use your own words to present someone else's information, you must acknowledge that you borrowed the information. The only types of information that do not require acknowledgment are common knowledge (John F. Kennedy was assassinated in Dallas), familiar sayings ("Haste makes waste"), and well-known quotations ("To be or not to be. That is the question").

The documentation guidelines later in this chapter present various ways of citing the sources you quote, paraphrase, and summarize; the important thing is that your readers can tell where words or ideas that are not your own begin and end. You can accomplish this most readily by separating your words from those of the source's with signal phrases such as "According to Smith," "Peters claims," and "As Olmos asserts." When you cite a source for the first time in the actual text, use the author's full name; after that, use just the last name.

Avoiding Plagiarism

Writers—students and professionals alike—occasionally fail to acknowledge sources properly. The word *plagiarism,* which derives from the Latin word for "kidnapping," refers to the unacknowledged use of another's words, ideas, or information. Students sometimes get into trouble because they mistakenly assume that plagiarizing occurs only when another writer's exact words are used without acknowledgment. In fact, plagiarism applies to ideas and statistics as well. So keep in mind that you must indicate the source of any ideas or information you use in your research for a paper, whether you have paraphrased, summarized, or quoted directly from the source.

Some people plagiarize simply because they do not know the conventions for using and acknowledging sources. This chapter makes clear how to incorporate sources into your writing and how to acknowledge your use of those sources. Others plagiarize because they keep sloppy notes and thus fail to distinguish between their own and their sources' ideas. Either they neglect to enclose their sources' words in quotation marks, or they fail to indicate when they are paraphrasing or summarizing a source's ideas and information. If you keep a working bibliography and careful notes, you will not make this serious mistake.

Another reason some people plagiarize is that they doubt their ability to write the paper by themselves. They feel intimidated by the writing task or the deadline or their own and others' expectations. This sense of inadequacy is not experienced by students alone. In a *Los Angeles Times* article on the subject, a journalist whose plagiarizing was discovered explained why he had done it: the other writer "said what I wanted to say and he said it better." If you experience this same anxiety about your work, speak to your instructor. Do not run the risk of failing a course or being expelled because of plagiarism. Your school probably has a policy on plagiarism as part of its student conduct code; ask your instructor.

ACKNOWLEDGING SOURCES

Although there is no universally accepted system for acknowledging sources, there is agreement on both the need for documentation and the details that should be included. Writers should acknowledge sources for two reasons: to give credit to those sources and to enable readers to consult those sources for further information.

Most documentation styles combine in-text citations keyed to a separate list of works cited. The information required in the in-text citations and the order and content of the works-cited entries vary across the disciplines, but two styles predominate: the author-page system, used in the humanities and advocated by the Modern Language Association (MLA), and the author-year system, used in the natural and social sciences and advocated by the American Psychological Association (APA). Check with your instructor about which of these styles to use or whether you should use some other style.

This section presents the basic features of the MLA and APA documentation styles. In Part I of this book, you can find examples of student essays that follow MLA style (Jessica Statsky, Chapter 6; Kim Dartnell, Chapter 9) and that use the APA style (Veronica Murayama, Chapter 5; Patrick O'Malley, Chapter 7).

For more information about these documentation styles, consult the *MLA Handbook for Writers of Research Papers*, Fourth Edition (1995), or the *Publication Manual of the American Psychological Association*, Fourth Edition (1994).

The MLA System of Documentation

Parenthetical Citations in Text

The MLA author-page system requires that in-text citations include the author's last name and the page number of the passage being cited.

Dr. James is described as a "not-too-skeletal Ichabod Crane" (Simon 68).

The MLA uses no punctuation between author and page (Simon 68). Note also that the parenthetical citation comes before the final period. With block quotations, however, the citation comes after the final period, preceded by a space (see p. 598–99 for an example).

If the author's name is mentioned in your text, put the page reference in parentheses as close as possible to the quoted material without disrupting the flow of the sentence.

Simon describes Dr. James as a "not-too-skeletal Ichabod Crane" (68).

To cite a source by two or three authors, the MLA uses all the authors' last names; for works with more than three authors, it uses all the authors' names or just the first author's name followed by *et al.* in regular type (not italics or underlined).

Dyal, Corning, and Willows identify several types of students, including the "Authority-Rebel" (4).

The Authority-Rebel "tends to see himself as superior to other students in the class" (Dyal, Corning, and Willows 4).

To cite one of two or more works by the same author or authors, the MLA includes the author's last name, a shortened version of the title, and the page.

When old paint becomes transparent, it sometimes shows the artist's original plans: "a tree will show through a woman's dress" (Hellman, *Pentimento* 1).

To cite a work listed only by its title, use a shortened version of the title. Begin the shortened version with the word by which the title is alphabetized in the works-cited list.

An international pollution treaty still to be ratified would prohibit all plastic garbage from being dumped at sea ("Awash" 26).

To quote material taken not from the original source but from a secondary source that quotes the original, give the secondary source in the list of works cited, and acknowledge that the original was quoted in a secondary source in the text.

E. M. Forster says "the collapse of all civilization, so realistic for us, sounded in Matthew Arnold's ears like a distant and harmonious cataract" (qtd. in Trilling 11).

List of Works Cited

Providing full information for the parenthetical citations in the text, the list of works cited identifies all the sources the writer uses. Every source cited in the text must refer to an entry in the works-cited list. Conversely, every entry in the works-cited list must correspond to at least one parenthetical citation. Entries are alphabetized according to the first author's last name.

In the MLA style, multiple works by the same author (or same group of authors) are alphabetized by title. The author's name is given for the first entry only; in subsequent entries, three hyphens and a period are used.

Vidal, Gore. Empire. New York: Random, 1987.

---. Lincoln. New York: Random, 1984.

The information presented in a works-cited list follows this order: author, title, publication source, year, and (for an article) page range. The MLA style requires a "hanging indent," which means that the first line of a works-cited entry is not indented but subsequent lines of the entry are. The MLA specifies an indent of half an inch or five character spaces.

Books

A BOOK BY A SINGLE AUTHOR

Guterson, David. Family Matters: Why Homeschooling Makes Sense. San Diego: Harcourt, 1992.

A BOOK BY AN AGENCY OR A CORPORATION

Association for Research in Nervous and Mental Disease. The Circulation of the Brain and Spinal Cord: A Symposium on Blood Supply. New York: Hafner, 1966.

A BOOK BY MORE THAN ONE AUTHOR

Gottfredson, Stephen G., and Sean McConville. America's Correctional Crisis. Westport: Greenwood, 1987.

Dyal, James A., William C. Corning, and Dale M. Willows. Readings in Psychology: The Search for Alternatives. 3rd ed. New York: McGraw, 1975.

WORKS BY MORE THAN THREE AUTHORS

The MLA lists all the authors' names or the name of the first author followed by *et al.*

Nielsen, Niels C., Jr., et al. Religions of the World. 3rd ed. New York: St. Martin's, 1992.

A BOOK BY AN UNKNOWN AUTHOR

Use the title in place of the author.

Rand McNally Commercial Atlas. Skokie: Rand, 1993.

A BOOK WITH AN AUTHOR AND AN EDITOR

If you refer to the text itself, begin the entry with the author:

Arnold, Matthew. Culture and Anarchy. Ed. J. Dover Wilson. Cambridge: Cambridge UP, 1966.

If you cite the editor in your paper, begin the entry with the editor:

Wilson, J. Dover, ed. Culture and Anarchy. By Matthew Arnold. 1869. Cambridge: Cambridge UP, 1966.

AN EDITED COLLECTION

Carter, Kathryn, and Carole Spitzack, eds. Doing Research on Women's Communication. Norwood: Ablex, 1989.

A WORK IN AN ANTHOLOGY OR A COLLECTION

Fairbairn-Dunlop, Peggy. "Women and Agriculture in Western Samoa." Different Places, Different Voices. Ed. Janet H. Momsen and Vivian Kinnaird. London: Routledge, 1993. 211-26.

A TRANSLATION

If you refer to the work itself, begin the entry with the author:

Tolstoy, Leo. War and Peace. Trans. Constance Garnett. London: Pan, 1972.

If you cite the translator in your text, begin the entry with the translator's name:

Garnett, Constance, trans. War and Peace. By Leo Tolstoy. 1869. London: Pan, 1972.

AN ARTICLE IN A REFERENCE BOOK

Suber, Howard. "Motion Picture." Encyclopedia Americana. 1991 ed.

AN INTRODUCTION, PREFACE, FOREWORD, OR AFTERWORD

Holt, John. Introduction. Better than School. By Nancy Wallace. Burnett: Larson, 1983. 9-14.

A GOVERNMENT DOCUMENT

United States. Cong. Senate. Subcommittee on Constitutional Amendments of the Committee on the Judiciary. Hearings on the "Equal Rights" Amendment. 91st Cong., 2nd sess. S. Res. 61. Washington: GPO, 1970.

AN UNPUBLISHED DOCTORAL DISSERTATION

Bullock, Barbara. "Basic Needs Fulfillment among Less Developed Countries: Social Progress over Two Decades of Growth." Diss. Vanderbilt U, 1986.

Articles

AN ARTICLE FROM A DAILY NEWSPAPER

Wilford, John Noble. "Corn in the New World: A Relative Latecomer." New York Times 7 Mar. 1995, late ed.: C1+.

AN ARTICLE FROM A WEEKLY OR BIWEEKLY MAGAZINE

Glastris, Paul. "The New Way to Get Rich." U.S. News & World Report 7 May 1990: 26-36.

AN ARTICLE FROM A MONTHLY OR BIMONTHLY MAGAZINE

Rohn, Alfie. "Home Schooling." Atlantic Monthly Apr. 1988: 20-25.

AN ARTICLE IN A SCHOLARLY JOURNAL WITH CONTINUOUS ANNUAL PAGINATION

The volume number follows the title of the journal.

Natale, Jo Anna. "Understanding Home Schooling." Education Digest 9 (1993): 58-61.

AN ARTICLE IN A SCHOLARLY JOURNAL THAT PAGINATES EACH ISSUE SEPARATELY

The issue number appears after the volume number. A period separates the two numbers.

Epstein, Alexandra. "Teen Parents: What They Need to Know." High/Scope Resource 1.2 (1982): 6.

AN ANONYMOUS ARTICLE

"Awash in Garbage." New York Times 15 Aug. 1987, sec. 1: 26.

AN EDITORIAL

"Stepping Backward." Editorial. Los Angeles Times 4 July 1989: B6.

A LETTER TO THE EDITOR

Rissman, Edward M. Letter. Los Angeles Times 29 June 1989: B5.

A REVIEW

Anders, Jaroslaw. "Dogma and Democracy." Rev. of The Church and the Left, by Adam Minchik. New Republic 17 May 1993: 42-48.

If you don't know the author, start with the title of the review and alphabetize by that title. If the review is untitled, begin with the words *Rev. of* and alphabetize under the title of the work being reviewed.

Internet Sources

For more information on the Internet, see pp. 574–91.

The range of information available through the worldwide network of computers known as the Internet is astonishing. Setting guidelines for regulating and using this information is an ongoing process. The following models are based on the guidelines set forth in the *MLA Style Manual,* Second Edition (1998). They should help you to incorporate these new sources of information and data into your own essays.

In-text reference When citing an Internet source in the body of your text, use the author's name or the document title if the author's name is not given. Do not use the URL (Uniform Resource Locator) for your reference.

List of works cited For most sources you have accessed on the Internet, you should provide the following information:

- Name of author (if available)
- Title of document
- Name of editor, compiler, or translator (if available)
- Publication information, including date of publication; publication information for original print version (for an online book or poem, if available); sponsoring institution (for an online scholarly project or reference database); and page numbers or number of paragraphs, pages, or other numbered sections (for an online periodical, if available)
- Date of access

- URL (in angle brackets) or path followed to locate the site (slashes separate menu choices), followed by a period

If you must break a URL between lines, the break should follow the slash.

AN ARTICLE IN AN ONLINE NEWSPAPER

Fuquay, Jim. "Megabanks Fuel Concern of Consumer." Star-Telegram.com. 14 Apr. 1998. <http://www.netarrant.net/news/doc/1047/1:TOPSTORY/TOPSTORY041498.html>.

A PERSONAL WEB SITE

For a site with no title, use the title *Home page.*

Johnson, Suzanne H. Home page. 5 Oct. 1997 <http://members.aol.com/suzannehi/hello.htm>.

A BOOK OR POEM

Book:

Howells, William Dean. The Rise of Silas Lapham. 1885. 9 Apr. 1998 <http://www.tiac.net/users/eldred/wdh/rsl.html>.

Poem:

Coleridge, Samuel Taylor. "Kubla Khan." Christabel. 2nd ed. London: William Bulmer, 1816. Representative Poetry On-line. U of Toronto. 9 Apr. 1998 <http://library.utoronto.ca/www/utel/rp/poems/coleridge4.html>.

AN ARTICLE IN A REFERENCE DATABASE

Atwood, Margaret. "Memento Mori--but First, Carpe Diem." Rev. of Toward the End of Time, by John Updike. The New York Times Books on the Web. 1997. 13 Oct. 1997 <http://search.nytimes.com/books/97/10/12/reviews/971012.12atwoodt.html>.

AN ARTICLE FROM AN ONLINE JOURNAL

Killiam, Rosemary. "Cognitive Dissonance: Should Twentieth-Century Women Composers Be Grouped with Foucault's Mad Criminals?" Music Theory Online 3.2 (1997): 30 pars. 10 May 1997 <http://smt.ucsb.edu/mto/mtohome.html>.

AN ARTICLE FROM AN ONLINE MAGAZINE

Keillor, Garrison. "Why Did They Ever Ban a Book This Bad?" Salon 13 Oct. 1997. 14 Oct. 1997 <http://www.salon1999.com/feature/>.

A POSTING ON A NEWSGROUP OR ON A LISTSERV

Conrad, Ed. "Proof of Life after Death." 8 July 1996. Online posting. 9 July 1996 <sci.archeology>.

Include the name of the group, if available, after the words *Online posting*. For a posting to a Usenet newsgroup, the prefix *news* followed by a colon and the group's name should appear within the angle brackets. To make it easier for readers to locate your source, provide a citation for an archived version whenever possible.

Healy, Jack. "Intellectual Property and Fair Use." 3 July 1997. Online posting. ACW-L. 14 Oct. 1997 <http://www.ttu.edu/lists/acw-l/9707/0031.html>.

SYNCHRONOUS COMMUNICATION (MOOs, MUDs)

The author's name, if available, precedes the title.

Seminar Discussion on Netiquette. 28 May 1996. LambdaMOO. 28 May 1996 <telnet://lambda.parc.xerox.edu:8888>.

A SCHOLARLY PROJECT

The Ovid Project. Ed. Hope Greenberg. 13 Mar. 1996. U of Vermont. 13 Oct. 1997 <http://www.uvm.edu/~hag/ovid/index.html>.

AN E-MAIL MESSAGE

Somer, Tina. E-mail to the author. 9 May 1990.

Other Sources

COMPUTER SOFTWARE

SPSS/PC+ Studentware Plus. Chicago: SPSS, 1991.

NEWSBANK

Sharpe, Lora. "A Quilter's Tribute." Boston Globe 25 Mar. 1989. NewsBank: Social Relations (1989): fiche 6, grids B4-6.

MATERIAL FROM A DATABASE ON CD-ROM

If publication details are available for the work, they should be included. The electronic publication date appears at the end of the reference.

Braus, Patricia. "Sex and the Single Spender." American Demographics 15.11 (1993): 28-34. ABI/INFORM. CD-ROM. UMI-ProQuest. 1993.

PERFORMANCES

Hamlet. By William Shakespeare. Dir. Jonathan Kent. Perf. Ralph Fiennes. Belasco Theatre, New York. 20 June 1995.

A TELEVISION PROGRAM

"The Universe Within." Nova. Narr. Stacy Keach. Writ. Beth Hoppe and Bill Lattanzi. Dir. Goro Koide. PBS. WNET, New York. 7 Mar. 1995.

A FILM

Boyz N the Hood. Writ. and Dir. John Singleton. Perf. Ice Cube, Cuba Gooding Jr., and Larry Fishburne. Columbia, 1991.

A MUSIC RECORDING

Indicate the medium ahead of the name of the manufacturer for an audiocassette, audiotape, or LP; it is not necessary to indicate the medium for a compact disk.

Beethoven, Ludwig van. Violin Concerto in D Major, op. 61. U.S.S.R. State Orchestra. Cond. Alexander Gauk. David Oistrikh, violinist. Audiocassette. Allegro, 1980.

Springsteen, Bruce. "Dancing in the Dark." Born in the U.S.A. Columbia, 1984.

AN INTERVIEW

Lowell, Robert. "Robert Lowell." Interview with Frederick Seidel. Paris Review 25 (1975): 56-95.

Franklin, Ann. Personal interview. 3 Sept. 1983.

The APA System of Documentation

Parenthetical Citations in Text

The APA author-year system calls for the last name of the author and the year of publication of the original work in the citation. If the cited material is a quotation, you also need to include the page number of the original. If the cited material is not a quotation, the page number is optional. Use commas to separate author, year, and page. The page number is preceded by *p.* for a single page or *pp.* for a range.

> Dr. James is described as a "not-too-skeletal Ichabod Crane" (Simon, 1982, p. 68).

If the author's name is mentioned in your text, cite the year in parentheses directly following the author's name, and place the page reference in parentheses before the final sentence period.

> Simon (1982) describes Dr. James as a "not-too-skeletal Ichabod Crane" (p. 68).

To cite works with three to five authors, use all the authors' last names the first time the reference occurs and the last name of the first author followed by *et al.* subsequently. If a source has more than six authors, use only the last name of the first author and *et al.* at first and subsequent references.

> Dyal, Corning, and Willows (1975) identify several types of students, including the "Authority-Rebel" (p. 4).

The Authority-Rebel "tends to see himself as superior to other students in the class" (Dyal et al., 1975, p. 4).

To cite one of two or more works by the same author or authors, use the author's last name plus the year (and the page, if you are citing a quotation). When more than one work being cited was published by an author in the same year, they are alphabetized by title and then assigned lowercase letters after the date (1973a, 1973b).

When old paint becomes transparent, it sometimes shows the artist's original plans: "a tree will show through a woman's dress" (Hellman, 1973b, p. 1).

To cite a work listed only by its title, the APA uses a shortened version of the title.

An international pollution treaty still to be ratified would prohibit all plastic garbage from being dumped at sea ("Awash," 1987).

To quote material taken not from the original source but from a secondary source that quotes the original, give the secondary source in the reference list, and acknowledge that the original was quoted in a secondary source in the text.

E. M. Forster says "the collapse of all civilization, so realistic for us, sounded in Matthew Arnold's ears like a distant and harmonious cataract" (as cited in Trilling, 1955, p. 11).

List of References

The APA follows this order in the presentation of information: author; publication year; title; publication source; (for an article) page range.

When several works by the same author are listed, the APA provides the following rules for arranging the list:

- Same-name single-author entries precede multiple-author entries:
  `Aaron, P. (1990).`
  `Aaron, P., & Zorn, C. R. (1985).`
- Entries with the same first author and a different second author are alphabetized under the first author according to the second author's last name:
  `Aaron, P., & Charleston, W. (1987).`
  `Aaron, P., & Zorn, C. R. (1991).`
- Entries by the same authors are arranged by year of publication, in chronological order:
  `Aaron, P., & Charleston, W. (1987).`
  `Aaron, P., & Charleston, W. (1993).`
- Entries by the same authors with the same publication year should be arranged alphabetically by title (according to the first word after *A, An,* or *The*), and lowercase letters (*a, b, c,* and so on) are appended to the year in parentheses:
  `Aaron, P. (1990a). Basic . . .`
  `Aaron, P. (1990b). Elements . . .`

The APA recommends that only the first line of each entry be indented five to seven spaces for papers intended for publication, but student writers may choose not to indent the first line but instead use a hanging indent of five to seven spaces. Ask your instructor which format is preferred. The following examples demonstrate a hanging indent of five to seven spaces.

Books

A BOOK BY A SINGLE AUTHOR

Guterson, D. (1992). Family matters: Why homeschooling makes sense. San Diego: Harcourt Brace.

A BOOK BY AN AGENCY OR A CORPORATION

Association for Research in Nervous and Mental Disease. (1966). The circulation of the brain and spinal cord: A symposium on blood supply. New York: Hafner.

A BOOK BY MORE THAN ONE AUTHOR

The APA cites all authors' names regardless of the number.

Gottfredson, S. G., & McConville, S. (1987). *America's correctional crisis.* Westport, CT: Greenwood.

Dyal, J. A., Corning, W. C., & Willows, D. M. (1975). *Readings in psychology: The search for alternatives* (3rd ed.). New York: McGraw-Hill.

A BOOK BY AN UNKNOWN AUTHOR

Use the title in place of the author.

Rand McNally commercial atlas. (1993). Skokie, IL: Rand McNally.

When an author is designated as "Anonymous," cite as "Anonymous" in the text and alphabetize as "Anonymous" in the reference list.

A BOOK WITH AN AUTHOR AND AN EDITOR

Arnold, M. (1966). Culture and anarchy (J. Dover Wilson, Ed.). Cambridge: Cambridge University Press. (Original work published 1869)

AN EDITED COLLECTION

Carter, K., & Spitzack, C. (Eds.). (1989). Doing research on women's communication. Norwood, NJ: Ablex.

A WORK IN AN ANTHOLOGY OR A COLLECTION

Fairbairn-Dunlop, P. (1993). Women and agriculture in western Samoa. In J. H. Momsen & V. Kinnaird (Eds.), *Different places, different voices* (pp. 211-226). London: Routledge.

A TRANSLATION

Tolstoy, L. (1972). *War and peace* (C. Garnett, Trans.). London: Pan Books. (Original work published 1869)

AN ARTICLE IN A REFERENCE BOOK

Suber, H. (1991). Motion picture. In *Encyclopedia Americana* (Vol. 19, pp. 505-539). Danbury, CT: Grolier.

AN INTRODUCTION, PREFACE, FOREWORD, OR AFTERWORD

Holt, J. (1983). Introduction. In N. Wallace, *Better than school* (pp. 9-14). Burnett, NY: Larson.

A GOVERNMENT DOCUMENT

U.S. Department of Health, Education and Welfare. (1979). *Healthy people: The surgeon general's report on health promotion* (DHEW Publication No. 79-55071). Washington, DC: U.S. Government Printing Office.

AN UNPUBLISHED DOCTORAL DISSERTATION

Bullock, B. (1986). *Basic needs fulfillment among less developed countries: Social progress over two decades of growth.* Unpublished doctoral dissertation, Vanderbilt University, Nashville, TN.

Articles

AN ARTICLE FROM A DAILY NEWSPAPER

Wilford, J. N. (1995, March 7). Corn in the New World: A relative latecomer. *The New York Times,* pp. C1, C5.

AN ARTICLE FROM A WEEKLY OR BIWEEKLY MAGAZINE

Glastris, P. (1990, May 7). The new way to get rich. *U.S. News & World Report, 108,* 26-36.

AN ARTICLE FROM A MONTHLY OR BIMONTHLY MAGAZINE

Rohn, A. (1988, April). Home schooling. *Atlantic Monthly, 261,* 20-25.

AN ARTICLE IN A SCHOLARLY JOURNAL WITH CONTINUOUS ANNUAL PAGINATION

The volume number follows the title of the journal.

Natale, J. A. (1993). Understanding home schooling. Education Digest, 9, 58-61.

AN ARTICLE IN A SCHOLARLY JOURNAL THAT PAGINATES EACH ISSUE SEPARATELY

The issue number appears in parentheses after the volume number.

Epstein, A. (1982). Teen parents: What they need to know. High/Scope Resource, 1(2), 6.

AN ANONYMOUS ARTICLE

Awash in garbage. (1987, August 15). The New York Times, p. A26.

A REVIEW

Anders, J. (1993, May 17). Dogma and democracy [Review of the book The church and the left]. The New Republic, 208, 42-48.

If the review is untitled, use the bracketed information as the title, retaining the brackets.

Internet Sources

For more information on the Internet, see pp. 574–91.

APA citation guidelines for online resources are currently being discussed and evaluated. It is generally agreed that citation information must allow readers to access and retrieve the information cited. For the time being, if your source is available both in print and online, APA prefers that you cite the print version.

Except for the guidelines for citing an article from an online journal and material from an online computer service, the following models are taken from Andrew Harnack and Eugene Kleppinger, *Online! A Reference Guide for Using Internet Sources* (NY: St. Martin's Press, 1997). Harnack and Kleppinger have applied APA style guidelines from the fourth edition of the *Publication Manual of the American Psychological Association* (1993) to recent developments in online communication. Harnack and Kleppinger advise writers to consult the *Publication Manual* when citing online resources to clarify issues of content and style.

The guidelines for citing online journals and material from computer services are from the *Publication Manual.*

In-text reference When citing an Internet source in the body of your text, follow the guidelines for citing print sources (see p. 612). Instead of page numbers, however, the APA allows you to use paragraph numbers for electronic text. If paragraph numbers are not available, give a division used within the document (for example, a chapter or heading) instead.

List of references For most sources you have accessed on the Internet, you should provide the following information:

- Name of author (if available)
- Publication date (in parentheses; if unavailable, use the abbreviation *n.d.*)
- Title of document
- URL (in angle brackets) or path followed to locate the site
- Date of access (in parentheses)

A WORLD WIDE WEB SITE

Shade, L. R. (1993). Gender issues in computer networking. <http://www.mit.edu:8001/people/sorokin/women/lrs.html> (1996, May 28).

LINKAGE DATA

If you have gained access to a file through a link in another document and want to provide information about this link, you need to give the source document title, underlined for italics, after the abbreviation *Lkd.* (meaning "linked from"). Any additional linkage details, if necessary, are preceded by the word *at.*

Gwitch'in Steering Committee. (n.d.). The Arctic Wildlife Refuge: America's last great wilderness. Lkd. Alaska Web Servers at "Virtual Tourist." <http://www.tourist.com> (1996, July 11).

A TELNET SITE

The word *telnet* precedes the complete telnet address, with no closing punctuation; the access path to the telnet site follows the address.

Earthquake report for 6/27/96. (1996, July 6). Weather Underground. telnet madlab.sprl.umich.edu:3000/Latest Earthquake Reports (1996, July 11).

FTP (FILE TRANSFER PROTOCOL) SITE

The abbreviation *ftp* precedes the FTP address, with no closing punctuation. Provide the full path to follow to find the text after the address.

Altar, T. W. (1993, January 14). Vitamin B12 and vegans. ftp wiretap.spies.com Library/Article/Food/b12.txt (1996, May 28).

If you use a URL instead of command, address, and path elements, it should appear between angle brackets.

Greig, A. (1995, November 21). Home magazines and modernist dreams: Designing the 1950s house. <ftp://coombs.anu.edu.au/coombs papers/coombs archives/urban-research-program/working-papers /wp-047-1995.txt> (1996, July 11).

A GOPHER SITE

Give print publication information (if needed) with appropriate underlining for italics. Provide either a gopher command-path format, preceded by the word *gopher*, or the URL for the document.

Michaels, D. (1993, November 15). ROADMAP09: Spamming and urban legends. gopher Home Gopher Server/Connect to Gophers at other sites around the world/Use Veronica to search gopher space for documents/urban legends (1996, July 11).

Smith, C. A. (1994). National extension model of critical parenting practices. <gopher://tinman.mes.umn.edu:4242/11/Other/Other/NEM_Parent> (1996, May 28).

A POSTING ON A DISCUSSION GROUP OR NEWSGROUP (USENET)

Include the author's name (if known) and the E-mail address between angle brackets. The subject line of the posting is given as plain text after the date of publication. The newsgroup name, also enclosed in angle brackets, follows the subject line. If you do not know the author's name, begin with the author's e-mail address, in angle brackets. In your list of references, alphabetize the posting by the first letter of this E-mail address.

Conrad, E. <edconrad@prolog.net> (1996, July 8). Proof of life after death. <sci.archeology> (1996, July 9).

A LISTSERV POSTING

Provide the author's E-mail address, enclosed in angle brackets, after the author's name. Enclose the listserv address in angle brackets following the date of publication and the subject line of the posting.

Sherman, M. <mgs@vt.edu> (1995, February 15). Writing process and self-discipline. <engl3764@ebbs.english.vt.edu> (1995, February 16).

For an article or a file archived at a Web site or listserv address, provide the list address, within angle brackets, and the URL for the list's archive (indicated by *via*), also within angle brackets.

Carbone, N. <nickc@english.umass.edu> (1996, January 26). NN 960126: Follow-up to Don's comments about citing URLs. <acw-l@unicorn.acs.ttu.edu> via <http://www.ttu.edu/lists/acw-l> (1996, February 17).

E-MAIL MESSAGES

If you are using APA style, it is not necessary to list personal correspondence, including E-mail, in your reference list. Simply cite the person's name in your text, and in parentheses give the notation *personal communication* and the date.

ARTICLE FROM AN ONLINE JOURNAL

The APA requires an availability statement that includes the specific information (such as path, directory, and file name) needed to access the source. Notice that the APA uses the hyphenated spelling *on-line* and that final periods are omitted from entries that end with electronic addresses or with path, file, or item numbers.

Nielsen, R. (1995, March). Radon risks [16 paragraphs]. Carcinogens [On-line serial], 4(12). Available FTP: Hostname: princeton.edu Directory: pub/carcinogens/1995 File: radon.95.3.12.radonrisks

MATERIAL FROM AN ONLINE COMPUTER SERVICE

When citing from an online computer service using APA style, include publication information (if available), the medium, and the name of the service. So that readers can locate the article, APA provides the path number at the end of the reference.

Reece, J. S. (1978). Measuring investment center performance. Harvard Business Review [On-line], 56(3), 28-40. Available: Dialog file 107, item 673280 047658

Other sources

COMPUTER SOFTWARE

If an individual has proprietary rights to the software, cite that person's name as you would for a print text. Otherwise, cite as you would an anonymous print text.

SPSS/PC+ Studentware Plus [Computer software]. (1991). Chicago: SPSS.

MATERIAL FROM A DATABASE ON CD-ROM

For information retrieved from electronic media, follow general citation models. (For date of publication, cite the year copies of the data were first made generally available.) Insert, in brackets, the type of medium from which you are citing (CD-ROM, data file, database) after the title of the work. Give the location and name of both the producer and the distributor.

National Health Interview Survey: Current health topics, 1991--Longitudinal study of aging (Version 4) [Electronic data tape]. (1992). Hyattsville, MD: National Center for Health Statistics [Producer and Distributor].

A TELEVISION PROGRAM

Hoppe, B., & Lattanzi, B. (1995). The universe within (G. Koide, Director). In P. Apsell (Producer), Nova. Boston: WGBH.

A FILM

Singleton, J. (Writer and Director). (1991). Boyz n the hood [Film]. New York: Columbia.

A MUSIC RECORDING

Beethoven, L. van. (1806). Violin concerto in D major, op. 61 [Recorded by USSR State Orchestra]. (Cassette Recording No. ACS 8044). New York: Allegro. (1980)

Springsteen, B. (1984). Dancing in the dark. On Born in the U.S.A. [CD]. New York: Columbia.

If the recording date differs from the copyright date, APA requires that it should appear in parentheses after the name of the label. If it is necessary to include a number for the recording, use parentheses for the medium; otherwise, use brackets.

AN INTERVIEW

When using the APA style, do not list personal interviews in your references list. Simply cite the person's name (last name and initials) in your text, and in parentheses give the notation *personal communication* and the date of the interview. For published interviews, use the appropriate format for an article.

SOME SAMPLE RESEARCH PAPERS

As a writer, you will want or need to use sources on many occasions. You may be assigned to write a research paper, complete with formal documentation of outside sources. Several of the writing assignments in this book present opportunities to do library or field research—in other words, to turn to outside sources. Among the readings in Part I, the ones listed here cite and document sources. (The documentation style each follows is given in parentheses.)

"Schizophrenia: What It Looks Like, How It Feels," by Veronica Murayama, pp. 173–76 (APA)

"Children Need to Play, Not Compete," by Jessica Statsky, pp. 218–21 (MLA)

"More Testing, More Learning," by Patrick O'Malley, pp. 262–65 (APA)

"Where Will They Sleep Tonight?" by Kim Dartnell, pp. 355–57 (MLA)

AN ANNOTATED RESEARCH PAPER

Here is a student research paper speculating about the causes of a trend—the increase in home schooling. The author cites statistics, quotes authorities, and paraphrases and summarizes background information and support for her argument. She uses the MLA documentation style.

1″

½″

Dinh 1

Double-space

Cristina Dinh
Professor Cooper
English XXX
1″ 5 November 19--

Double-space

Educating Kids at Home

Title centered

Every morning, Mary Jane, who is nine, doesn't have to worry about gulping down her cereal so she can be on time for school. School for Mary Jane is literally right at her doorstep. 1″

Paragraphs indented five spaces

In this era of growing concerns about the quality of public education, increasing numbers of parents across the United States are choosing to educate their children at home. These parents believe they can do a better job teaching their children than their local schools can. _Home schooling_, as this practice is known, has become a national trend over the past twenty years. Patricia Lines, a senior research associate at the U.S. Department of Education, estimates that in 1970 the nationwide number of home-schooled children was 15,000. By the 1990-91 school year, she estimates that the number rose to between 250,000 and 350,000 (5). From 1986 to 1989, the number of home-schooled children in Oregon almost doubled, from 2,671 to 4,578 (Graves B8). Home-school advocates believe that the numbers may even be greater; many home schoolers don't give official notice of what they are doing because they are still afraid of government interference.

Author named in text; parenthetical page reference falls at end of sentence

What is home schooling, and who are the parents choosing to teach their children at home? David Guterson, a high-school teacher whose own children are home schooled, defines home schooling as "the attempt to gain an education outside of institutions" (5). Home-schooled children spend the majority of the conventional school day learning in or near

Author named and identified to introduce quotation

Dinh 2

their homes rather than in traditional schools; parents or guardians are the prime educators. Cindy Connolly notes that parents teach their children the same subjects--math, science, music, history, and language arts--that are taught in public schools but vary the way they teach these subjects. Some home-schooling parents create structured plans for their children, while others prefer looser environments (E2). While home schoolers are a diverse group--libertarians, conservatives, Christian fundamentalists--most say they home school for one of two reasons: they are concerned about the way children are taught in public schools or they are concerned about exposing their children to secular education that may contradict their religious beliefs (Guterson 5-6).

Author named in parenthetical citation; no punctuation between name and page number

The first group generally believes that children need individual attention and the opportunity to learn at their own pace in order to learn well. This group says that one teacher in a classroom of twenty to thirty children (the size of typical public-school classes) cannot give this kind of attention. These parents believe they can give their children greater enrichment and more specialized instruction than public schools can provide. At home, parents can work one-on-one with each child and be flexible about time, allowing their children to pursue their interests at earlier ages. Many of these parents, like home-schooler Peter Bergson, believe that

Quotation of more than four lines typed as a block and indented ten spaces

Brackets indicate addition to quotation

> home schooling provides more of an opportunity to continue the natural learning process that's in evidence in all children. [In school,] you change

Parenthetical citation falls after period

Double-space

Dinh 3

> the learning process from self-directed to other-directed, from the child asking questions to the teacher asking questions. You shut down areas of potential interest. (qtd. in Kohn 22)

The second, and larger, group, those who home school their children for religious reasons, accounts for about 90 percent of all home schoolers, according to the Home School Legal Defense Association and the National Association of State Boards of Education (Kohn 22). This group is made up predominantly of Christian fundamentalists but also includes Buddhists, Jews, and black Muslims.

What causes underlie the increasing number of parents in both groups choosing to home school their children? One cause for this trend can be traced back to the 1960s when many people began criticizing traditional schools. Various types of "alternative schools" were created, and some parents began teaching their children at home (Friedlander 20). As the public educational system has continued to have problems, parents have seen academic and social standards get lower. They mention several reasons for their disappointment with public schools and for their decision to home school. A lack of funding, for example, leaves children without new textbooks. One day a mother found out her sons were reading books that they read from the year before (Monday C11). Many schools also cannot afford to buy laboratory equipment and other teaching materials. At my own high school, the chemistry teacher told me that most of the lab equipment we used came from a research firm he worked for. In a 1988 Gallup poll, lack of proper financial support ranked third on the list of the problems in public schools; poor curriculum and poor standards ranked fifth on the list (Gallup and Elam 34).

Parents also cite overcrowding as a reason for taking their kids out of school. Faced with a large group of children, a teacher can't satisfy the needs of all the students. Thus, a teacher ends up gearing lessons to the students in the middle level, so children at both ends miss out. Gifted children and those with learning disabilities particularly suffer in this situation. At home, parents of these children say, they can tailor the material and the pace for each child. Studies show that home-schooling methods seem to work well in preparing children academically. For example, in 1989, 74 percent of Oregon's home-schooled kids scored above the fiftieth percentile, and 22 percent above the ninetieth percentile, on standardized tests (Graves B9).

Source of statistic cited

In addition, home-schooling parents claim that their children are more well-rounded than those in school. Because they don't have to sit in classrooms all day, home-schooled kids can pursue their own projects, often combining crafts or technical skills with academic subjects. Home schoolers participate in outside activities such as 4-H competitions, field trips with other children, parties, gym activities, Christian pageants, and Boy Scouts or Girl Scouts (Shenk D6). Some school districts even invite home-schooled children to participate in sports and to use libraries and computer facilities (Guterson 186). A school district near Seattle trains home-schooling families in computer skills, giving them access to the resources of the Internet (Hawkins 58).

Dinh 5

Many home-schooling parents believe that these activities provide the social opportunities kids need without exposing their children to the peer pressure they would have to deal with in school. Occasionally, peer values can be good; often, however, students in today's schools face many negative peer pressures. For example, many kids think that drinking and using drugs are cool. When I was in high school, my friends would tell me a few drinks wouldn't hurt and affect your driving. If I had listened to them, I wouldn't be alive today. Four of my friends were killed under the influence of alcohol. In 1975, according to the National Institute on Drug Abuse, 45 percent of high-school seniors answered "yes" when asked if they had "ever used" marijuana; in 1981, the number rose to 60 percent, a 13 percent increase over six years (Hawley K3). In 1986, 1987, and 1988 Gallup polls, use of drugs ranked first among the problems in public schools, and the number of students who use drugs was increasing (Gallup and Elam 34).

Another reason many parents decide to home school their kids is that they are concerned for their children's safety. In addition to fears that peer pressure might push their children into using drugs, many parents fear drug-related violence in and near public schools. There are stories practically every week about drug-related violence in schools--even in elementary schools. Home-schooling parents say they want to protect their children from dangerous environments. As Sam Allis notes about home-schooling parents, "There are no drugs in their bathrooms or switchblades in the hallways" (86).

Dinh 6

Paraphrase of original work cited by author in text and page number at end of sentence

Brackets used to change capitalization

Ellipsis marks used to indicate words left out of quotation

Quotation cited in another source

Single quotation marks indicate a quotation within a quotation

The major cause of the growing home-schooling trend is Christian fundamentalist dissatisfaction with "godless" public schools. Maralee Mayberry, a professor of sociology at the University of Nevada, states in a 1987 survey that 65 percent of Oregon parents who choose home schooling do so because they feel that public schools lack Christian values (Graves B9). Kohn notes that Growing without Schooling, a secular home-schooling newsletter started by education critic John Holt, has 5,000 subscribers, whereas The Parent Educator and Family Report, a newsletter put out by Raymond Moore, a Christian home-school advocate and researcher, has 300,000 subscribers (22). Luanne Shackelford and Susan White, two Christian home-schooling mothers, claim that because schools expose children to "[p]eer pressure, perverts, secular textbooks, values clarification, TV, pornography, rock music, bad movies . . . [h]ome schooling seems to be the best plan to achieve our goal [to raise good Christians]" (160). Moore claims that children in public schools are more likely to "turn away from their home values and rely on their peers for values" (qtd. in Kilgore 24). Moore believes that home-schooled kids are less vulnerable to peer pressure because they gain a positive sense of self-worth fostered by their parents.

In addition, those who cite the lack of "Christian values" are concerned about the textbooks used in public schools. For example, Kohn notes that Moore talks of parents who are "'sick and tired of the teaching of evolution in the schools as a cut-and-dried fact,' along with other evidence of so-called secular humanism"

Reference placed close to quotation, before punctuation

Dinh 7

(21), such as textbooks that contain material that contradicts Christian beliefs. Moreover, parents worry that schools decay their children's moral values. In particular, some Christian fundamentalist parents object to sex education in schools, saying that it encourages children to become sexually active early, challenging values taught at home. They see the family as the core and believe that the best place to instill family values is within the family. These Christian home-schooling parents want to provide their children not only with academic knowledge but also with a moral grounding consistent with their religious beliefs.

Other home-schooling parents object to a perceived government-mandated value system that they believe attempts to override the values, not necessarily religious in nature, of individual families. Home schooling, for these parents, is a way of resisting what John Gatto describes as unwarranted intrusion by the federal government into personal concerns.

Armed with their convictions, home-schooling parents, such as those who belong to the Christian Home School Legal Defense Association, have fought in court and lobbied for legislation that allows them the option of home schooling. In the 1970s, most states had compulsory attendance laws that made it difficult, if not illegal, to keep school-age children home from school. By 1993, thirty-two states permitted home schooling, ten allowed it with certain restrictions, and eight insisted that the home school be a legal private school (Guterson 91). Because of their efforts, Mary Jane can start her school day without leaving the house.

Title centered

Dinh 8

Double-space

Entries in alphabetical order by author

Indent five spaces

Angle brackets enclose the URL

Period after author, after title, and at end of entry

Works Cited

Allis, Sam. "Schooling Kids at Home." Time 22 Oct. 1990: 84-85.

Connolly, Cindy. "Teen-agers See Advantages to Attending School at Home." Omaha World Herald 10 Sept. 1990. NewsBank [Microform], Education, 1990, fiche 106, grids E1-E3.

Friedlander, Tom. "A Decade of Home Schooling." The Home School Reader. Ed. Mark and Helen Hegener. Tonasket: Home Education, 1988.

Gallup, Alec M., and Stanley M. Elam. "The 20th Annual Gallup Poll: Of the Public toward the Public Schools." Phi Delta Kappan Sept. 1988: 34.

Gatto, John Taylor. "The Nine Assumptions of Modern Schooling." The Education Liberator 1.3 (1995). 30 May 1996 <http://www.sepschool.org/edlib/v1n3/gatto.html>.

Graves, Bill. "Home School: Enrollment Increases in Oregon, Nation." Oregonian 4 Nov. 1990 NewsBank [Microform], Education, 1990, fiche 135, grids B8-B9.

Guterson, David. Family Matters: Why Home-schooling Makes Sense. San Diego: Harcourt, 1992.

Hawkins, Dana. "Homeschool Battles: Clashes Grow as Some in the Movement Seek Access to Public Schools." U.S. News & World Report 12 Feb. 1996: 57-58.

Hawley, Richard A. "Schoolchildren and Drugs: The Fancy That Has Not Passed." Phi Delta Kappan May 1987: K1-K3.

Kilgore, Peter. "Profile of Families Who Home School in Maine." 1987. 1-47. ERIC ED 295 280.

Kohn, Alfie. "Home schooling." Atlantic Apr. 1988: 20-25.

Lines, Patricia. Estimating the Home School Education Population. Washington: U.S. Dept. of Education, 1991.

Monday, Susan McAtee. "In-House Education." San Antonio Light 18 Mar. 1990. NewsBank [Microform], Education, 1990, fiche 27, grids C11, C13.

Dinh 9

Shackelford, Luanne, and Susan White. A Survivor's Guide to Home Schooling. Westchester: Crossway, 1988.

Shenk, Dan. "Parents Find Home-Schooling Has Special Rewards." Elkhart Truth 20 Mar. 1988. NewsBank [Microform], Education, 1988, fiche 41, grid D6.

CHAPTER 23

Essay Examinations

Essay exams are inescapable. Even though the machine-scorable multiple-choice test has sharply reduced the number of essay exams administered in schools and colleges, essay exams will continue to play a significant role in the education of liberal arts students. Many instructors—especially in the humanities and social sciences—still believe that an exam that requires you to write is the best way to find out what you have learned and, more important, how you can use what you have learned. Instructors who give essay exams want to be sure you can sort through the large body of information covered in a course, identify what is important or significant, and explain your decision. They want to see whether you understand the concepts that provide the basis for a course and whether you can use those concepts to interpret specific materials, to make connections on your own, to see relationships, to draw comparisons and find contrasts, and to synthesize diverse information in support of an original assertion. They may even be interested in your ability to justify your own evaluations based on appropriate standards of judgment and to argue your own opinions with convincing reasons and supporting evidence. Remember that your instructors want to encourage you to think more critically and analytically about a subject; they feel, therefore, that a written exam provides the best demonstration that you are doing so.

As a college student, then, you will face a variety of essay exams, from short-answer identifications that require only a few sentences to take-home exams that may involve hours of planning and writing. You will find that the writing activities and strategies discussed in Parts I and III of this book—particularly narrating, describing, defining, comparing and contrasting, and arguing—as well as the critical thinking strategies in Part II will help you to do well on these exams. This chapter provides some more specific guidelines for you to follow in preparing for and writing essay exams and analyzes a group of typical exam questions to help to determine which strategies will be most useful.

But you can also learn a great deal from your experiences with essay exams in the past, the embarrassment and frustration of doing poorly on one and the great pleasure and pride of doing well. Do you recall the best exam you ever wrote? Do you remember how you wrote it and why you were able to do so well? How can you be certain to approach such writing tasks confidently and to complete them successfully? Keep these questions in mind as you consider the following guidelines.

PREPARING FOR AN EXAM

First of all, essay exams require a comprehensive understanding of large amounts of information. Because exam questions can reach so widely into the course materials—and in such unpredictable ways—the best way to ensure that you will do well on them is to keep up with readings and assignments from the very start of the course. Do the reading, go to lectures, take careful notes, participate in discussion sections, organize small study groups with classmates to explore and review course materials throughout the semester. Trying to cram weeks of information into a single night of study will never allow you to do your best.

Then, as an exam approaches, find out what you can about the form it will take. No question is more irritating to instructors than the pestering inquiry "Do we need to know this for the exam?" but it is generally legitimate to ask whether the questions will require short or long answers, how many questions there will be, whether you may choose which questions to answer, and what kinds of thinking and writing will be required of you. Some instructors may hand out study guides for exams or even lists of potential questions. However, you will often be on your own in determining how best to go about studying.

Try to avoid simply memorizing information aimlessly. As you study, you should be clarifying the important issues of the course and using these issues to focus your understanding of specific facts and particular readings. If the course is a historical survey, distinguish the primary periods and try to see relations among the periods and the works or events that define them. If the course is thematically unified, determine how the particular materials you have been reading relate to those themes. If the course is a broad introduction to a general topic, concentrate on the central concerns of each study unit and see what connections you can discover among the various units. Try to place all you have learned into perspective, into a meaningful context. How do the pieces fit together? What fundamental ideas have the readings, the lectures, and the discussions seemed to emphasize? How can those ideas help you to digest the information the course has covered?

One good way to prepare yourself for an exam is by making up questions you think the instructor might ask and then planning answers to them with classmates. Returning to your notes and to assigned readings with specific questions in mind can help enormously in your process of understanding. The important thing to remember is that an essay exam tests more than your memory of specific information; it requires you to use specific information to demonstrate a comprehensive grasp of the topics covered in the course.

READING THE EXAM CAREFULLY

Before you answer a single question, read the entire exam so that you can apportion your time realistically. Pay particular attention to how many points you may earn in different parts of the exam; notice any directions that suggest how long an answer should be or how much space it should take up. As you are doing so, you may wish to make tentative choices of the questions you will answer and decide on the order in which you will answer them. If you have immediate ideas about how you would organize any of your answers, you might also jot down partial scratch outlines. But before you start to complete any answers, write down the actual clock time you expect to be working on each question or set of questions. Careful time management is crucial to your success on essay exams; giving some time to each question is always better than using up your time on only a few and never getting to others.

You will next need to analyze each question carefully before beginning to write your answer. Decide what you are being asked to do. If your immediate impulse is to cast about for ideas indiscriminately, it can be easy at this point to become flustered, to lose concentration, even to go blank. But if you first look closely at what the question is directing you to do and try to understand the sort of writing that will be required, you can begin to recognize the structure your answer will need to take. This tentative structure will help to focus your attention on the particular information that will be pertinent to your answer. Consider this question from a sociology final:

> Drawing from lectures on the contradictory aspects of American values, discussions of the "bureaucratic personality," and the type of behavior associated with social mobility, discuss the problems of bettering oneself in a relatively "open," complex, industrial society such as the United States.

Such a question can cause momentary panic, but you can nearly always define the writing task you face. Look first at the words that give you directions: *draw from* and *discuss.* The term *discuss* is fairly vague, of course, but here it probably invites you to list and explain the problems of bettering oneself. The categories of these problems are already identified in the opening phrases: contradictory values, bureaucratic personality, certain behavior. Therefore, you would plan to begin with an assertion (or thesis) that included the keywords in the final clause (bettering oneself in an open, complex, industrial society) and then take up each category of problem—and perhaps other problems you can think of—in separate paragraphs.

This question essentially calls for recall, organization, and clear presentation of facts from lectures and readings. Though it looks confusing at first, once you sort it out, you will find that it contains the key terms for the answer's thesis, as well as the main points of development. In the next section are some further examples of the kinds of questions often found on essay exams. Pay particular attention to how the directions and the keywords in each case can help you to define the writing task involved.

SOME TYPICAL ESSAY EXAM QUESTIONS

Following are nine categories of exam questions, divided according to the sort of writing task involved and illustrated by examples. You will notice that although the wording of the examples in a category may differ, the essential directions are very much the same.

All of the examples are unedited and were written by instructors in six different departments in the humanities and social sciences at two different universities. Drawn from short quizzes, midterms, and final exams for a variety of first- and second-year courses, these questions demonstrate the range of writing you may be expected to do on exams.

Define or Identify

Some questions require you to write a few sentences defining or identifying material from readings or lectures. Such questions almost always allow you only a few minutes to complete your answer.

You may be asked for a brief overview of a large topic, as in Question 23.1. This question, from a twenty-minute quiz in a literature course, was worth as much as 15 of the 100 points possible on the quiz.

Question 23.1

Name and describe the three stages of African literature.

Answering this question would simply involve following the specific directions. A student would probably *name* the periods in historical order and then *describe* each period in a separate sentence or two.

Other questions, like Question 23.2, supply a list of specific items to identify. This example comes from a final exam in a communication course, and the answer to each part was worth as much as 4 points on a 120-point exam.

Question 23.2

Define and state some important facts concerning each of the following:

A. demographics
B. instrumental model
C. RCA
D. telephone booth of the air
E. penny press

With no more than three or four minutes for each part, students taking this exam would offer a concise definition (probably in a sentence), then briefly expand the definition with facts relevant to the main topics in the course.

Sometimes the list of items to be identified can be quite complicated, including quotations, concepts, and specialized terms; it may also be worth a significant number of points. The next example contains the first five items in a list of fifteen that opened a literature final. Each item was worth 3 points, for a total of 45 out of a possible 130 points.

Question 23.3

Identify each of the following items:

1. projection
2. "In this vast landscape he had loved so much, he was alone."
3. Balducci

4. *pied noir*
5. the Massif Central

Although the directions do not say so specifically, it is crucial here not only to identify each item but also to explain its significance in terms of the overall subject. In composing a definition or an identification, always ask yourself a simple question: Why is this item important enough to be on the exam?

Recall Details of a Specific Source

Sometimes instructors will ask for a straightforward summary or paraphrase of a specific source—for example, a report on a book or a film. To answer such questions, the student must recount details directly from the source and is not encouraged to interpret or evaluate. In the following example from a sociology exam, students were allowed about ten minutes and required to complete the answer on one lined page provided with the exam.

Question 23.4

> In his article "Is There a Culture of Poverty?" Oscar Lewis addresses a popular question in the social sciences. What is the "culture of poverty"? How is it able to come into being, according to Lewis? That is, under what conditions does it exist? When does he say a person is no longer a part of the culture of poverty? What does Lewis say is the future of the culture of poverty?

The phrasing here invites a fairly clear-cut structure. Each of the five specific questions can be turned into an assertion and supported with illustrations from Lewis's book. For example, the first two questions could become assertions like these: "Lewis defines the culture of poverty as _______," and "According to Lewis, the culture of poverty comes into being through _______." The important thing in this case is to summarize accurately what the writer said and not waste time evaluating or criticizing his ideas.

Explain the Importance or Significance

Another kind of essay exam question asks students to explain the importance of something covered in the course. Such questions require specific examples as the basis for a more general discussion of what has been studied. This type of question often involves interpreting a literary work by concentrating on a particular aspect of it, as in Question 23.5. This question was worth 10 out of 100 points and was to be answered in seventy-five to one hundred words.

Question 23.5

> In the last scene in *The Paths of Glory,* the owner of a café brings a young German woman onto a small stage in his café to sing for the French troops, while Colonel Dax looks on from outside the café. Briefly explain the significance of this scene in relation to the movie as a whole.

In answering this question, a student's first task would be to reconsider the whole movie, looking for ways in which this one small scene illuminates or explains larger issues or themes. Then, in a paragraph or two, the student would summarize these themes and point out how each element of the specific scene fits into the overall context.

You may also be asked to interpret specific information to show that you understand the fundamental concepts of a course. The following example from a communication midterm was worth a possible 10 of 100 points and was allotted twenty minutes of exam time.

Question 23.6

> Chukovsky gives many examples of cute expressions and statements uttered by small children. Give an example or two of the kinds of statements that he finds interesting. Then state their implications for understanding the nature of language in particular and communication more generally.

Here, the student must start by choosing examples of children's utterances from Chukovsky's book. These examples would then provide the basis for demonstrating the student's grasp of the larger subject.

Questions like these are usually more challenging than definition and summary questions because you must decide for yourself the significance, importance, or implications of the information. You must also consider how best to organize your answer so that the general ideas you need to communicate are clearly developed.

Apply Concepts

Very often, courses in the humanities and the social sciences emphasize significant themes, ideologies, or concepts. A common essay exam question asks students to apply the concepts to works studied in the course. Rather than providing specific information to be interpreted more generally, such questions present you with a general idea and require you to illustrate it with specific examples from your reading.

On a literature final, an instructor posed this writing task. It was worth 50 points out of 100, and students had about an hour to complete it.

Question 23.7

> Many American writers have portrayed their characters or their poetic speaker as being engaged in a quest. The quest may be explicit or implicit, it may be external or psychological, and it may end in failure or success. Analyze the quest motif in the work of four of the following writers: Edwards, Franklin, Hawthorne, Thoreau, Douglass, Whitman, Dickinson, James, Twain.

On another literature final, the following question was worth 45 of 130 points. Students had about forty-five minutes to answer it.

Question 23.8

> Several works studied in this course depict scapegoat figures. Select two written works and two films, and discuss how their authors or directors present and analyze the social conflicts that lead to the creation of scapegoats.

Question 23.7 instructs students to *analyze*, Question 23.8 to *discuss;* yet the answers for each would be structured very similarly. An introductory paragraph would define the concept—the *quest* or a *scapegoat*—and refer to the works to be discussed. Then, a paragraph or two would be devoted to each of the works, developing specific support to illustrate the concept. A concluding paragraph would probably attempt to bring the concept into clearer focus, which is, after all, the point of answering these questions.

Comment on a Quotation

On essay exams, an instructor will often ask students to comment on quotations they are seeing for the first time. Usually, such quotations will express some surprising or controversial opinion that complements or challenges basic principles or ideas in the course. Sometimes the writer being quoted is identified, sometimes not. In fact, it is not unusual for instructors to write the quotation themselves.

A student choosing to answer the following question from a literature final would have risked half the exam—in points and time—on the outcome.

Question 23.9

> Argue for or against this thesis: "In *A Clockwork Orange,* both the heightened, poetic language and the almost academic concern with moral and political theories deprive the story of most of its relevance to real life."

The directions here clearly ask for an argument. A student would need to set up a thesis indicating that the novel either is or is not relevant to real life and then point out how its language and its theoretical concerns can be viewed in light of this thesis.

The next example comes from a midterm exam in a history course. Students had forty minutes to write their answers, which could earn as much as 70 points on a 100-point exam.

Question 23.10

> "Some historians believe that economic hardship and oppression breed social revolt; but the experience of the United States and Mexico between 1900 and 1920 suggests that people may rebel also during times of prosperity."
>
> Comment on this statement. Why did large numbers of Americans and Mexicans wish to change conditions in their countries during the years from 1900 to 1920? How successful were their efforts? Who benefited from the changes that took place?

Although here students are instructed to "comment," the three questions make clear that a successful answer will require an argument: a clear thesis stating a position on the views expressed in the quotation, specific reasons for that thesis, and support for the thesis from readings and lectures. In general, such questions do not require a "right" answer: Whether you agree or disagree with the quotation is not as important as whether you can argue your case reasonably and convincingly, demonstrating a firm grasp of the subject matter.

Compare and Contrast

Instructors are particularly fond of essay exam questions that require a comparison or contrast of two or three principles, ideas, works, activities, or phenomena. To answer this kind of question, you need to explore fully the relations between things of importance in the course, analyze each thing separately, and then search out specific points of likeness or difference. Students must thus show a thorough knowledge of the things being compared, as well as a clear understanding of the basic issues on which comparisons and contrasts can be made.

Often, as in Question 23.11, the basis of comparison will be limited to a particular focus; here, for example, students are asked to compare two works in terms of their views of colonialism.

Question 23.11

> Compare and analyze the views of colonialism presented in Memmi's *Colonizer and the Colonized* and Pontecorvo's *Battle of Algiers.* Are there significant differences between these two views?

Sometimes instructors will simply identify what is to be compared, leaving students the task of choosing the basis of the comparison, as in the next three examples from communication, history, and literature exams, respectively.

Question 23.12

> In what way is the stage of electronic media fundamentally different from all the major stages that preceded it?

Question 23.13

> What was the role of the United States in Cuban affairs from 1898 until 1959? How did its role there compare with its role in the rest of Spanish America during the same period?

Question 23.14

> Write an essay on one of the following topics:
> 1. Squire Western and Mr. Knightley
> 2. Dr. Primrose and Mr. Elton

See Chapter 18 for more on comparing and contrasting.

Whether the point of comparison is stated in the question or left for you to define for yourself, it is important to limit your answer to the aspects of similarity or difference that are most relevant to the general concepts or themes covered in the course.

Synthesize Information from Various Sources

In a course with several assigned readings, an instructor may give students an essay exam question that requires them to pull together (synthesize) information from several or even all the readings.

The following example was one of four required questions on a final exam in a course in Latin American studies. Students had about thirty minutes to complete their answer.

Question 23.15

> On the basis of the articles read on El Salvador, Nicaragua, Peru, Chile, Argentina, and Mexico, what would you say are the major problems confronting

Latin America today? Discuss the major types of problems with references to particular countries as examples.

See pp. 466–67 for information on forecasting statements.

This question asks students to do a lot in thirty minutes. They must first decide which major problems to discuss, which countries to include in each discussion, and how to use material from many readings to develop their answers. To compose a coherent essay, a student will need a carefully developed forecasting statement.

Analyze Causes

In humanities and social science courses, much of what students study concerns the causes of trends, actions, and events. Hence, it is not surprising to find questions about causes on essay exams. In such cases, the instructor expects students to analyze causes from readings and lectures. These examples come from midterm and final exams in literature, sociology, cultural studies, and communication courses, respectively.

Question 23.16

Why do Maurice and Jean not succumb to the intolerable conditions of the prison camp (the Camp of Hell) as most of the others do?

Question 23.17

Given that we occupy several positions in the course of our lives and given that each position has a specific role attached to it, what kinds of problems or dilemmas arise from those multiple roles, and how are they handled?

Question 23.18

Explain briefly the relationship between the institution of slavery and the emergence of the blues as a new African-American musical expression.

Question 23.19

Analyze the way in which an uncritical promotion of the new information technology (computers, satellites, etc.) may support, unintentionally, the maintenance of the status quo.

Chapter 9 presents strategies for analyzing causes.

These questions are presented in several ways ("what kind of problem," "explain the relationship," "analyze the way"), but they all require a list of causes in the answer. The causes would be organized under a thesis statement, and each cause would be argued and supported by referring to lectures or readings.

Criticize or Evaluate

Occasionally, instructors will invite students to evaluate a concept or a work. Nearly always, they want more than opinion: They expect a reasoned, documented judgment based on appropriate standards of judgment. Not only do such questions test students' ability to recall and synthesize pertinent information, but they also allow instructors to find out whether students understand and can apply criteria taught in the course.

On a final exam in a literature course, a student might have chosen one of the following questions about novels read in the course. Each would have been worth half the total points, with about an hour to answer it.

Question 23.20

Evaluate *A Passage to India* from a postcolonial critical standpoint.

Question 23.21

A Clockwork Orange and *The Comfort of Strangers* both attempt to examine the nature of modern decadence. Which does so more successfully?

To answer either of these questions, a student would obviously have to be very familiar with the novels under discussion and would also have to establish standards for evaluating works of literature. The student would initially have to make a judgment favoring one novel over the other (though not necessarily casting one novel as "terrible" and the other as "perfect"). The student would then give reasons for this judgment, with supporting quotations from the novels, and probably use the writing strategies of comparison and contrast to develop the argument.

This next question was worth 10 of 85 points on a communication midterm. Students were asked to answer "in two paragraphs."

Question 23.22

Eisenstein and Mukerji both argue that movable print was important to the rise of Protestantism. Cole extends this argument to say that print set off a chain of events that was important to the history of the United States. Summarize this argument, and criticize any part of it if you choose.

Evaluative questions like these involve the same sorts of writing strategies as those discussed in Chapter 8.

Here students are asked to criticize or evaluate an argument in several course readings. The instructor wants to know what students think of this argument and also, even though this is not stated, why they judge it as they do. Answering this unwritten "why" part of the question is the challenge: Students must come up with reasons and support appropriate to evaluating the arguments.

PLANNING YOUR ANSWER

The amount of planning you do for a question will depend on how much time it is allotted and how many points it is worth. For short-answer definitions and identifications, a few seconds of thought will probably be sufficient. (Be careful not to puzzle too long over individual items like these. Skip over any you cannot recognize fairly quickly; often, answering other questions will help jog your memory.) For answers that require a paragraph or two, you may want to jot down several ideas and examples to focus your thoughts and give you a basis for organizing your information.

For longer answers, though, you will need to develop a much more definite strategy of organization. You have time for only one draft, so allow a reasonable period—

See pp. 430–34 for information on clustering and outlining.

as much as a quarter of the time allotted the question—for making notes, determining a thesis, and developing an outline. Jotting down pertinent ideas is a good way to begin; then you can plan your organization with a scratch outline (just a listing of points or facts) or a cluster.

For questions with several parts (different requests or directions, a sequence of questions), make a list of the parts so that you do not miss or minimize one part. For questions presented as questions (rather than directives), you might want to rephrase each question as a writing topic. These topics will often suggest how you should outline the answer.

You may have to try two or three outlines or clusters before you hit on a workable plan. But be realistic as you outline—you want a plan you can develop within the limited time allotted for your answer. Hence, your outline will have to be selective—it will contain not everything you know on the topic but rather what you know that can be developed clearly within the time available.

WRITING YOUR ANSWER

As with planning, your strategy for writing depends on the length of your answer. For short identifications and definitions, it is usually best to start with a general identifying statement and then move on to describe specific applications or explanations. Two sentences will almost always suffice, but make sure you write complete sentences.

For longer answers, begin by stating your forecasting statement or thesis clearly and explicitly. An essay exam is not an occasion for indirectness: You want to strive for focus, simplicity, and clarity. In stating your point and developing your answer, use key terms from the question; it may look as though you are avoiding the question unless you use key terms (the same key terms) throughout your essay. If the question does not supply any key terms, you will find that you have provided your own by stating your main point. Use these key terms throughout the answer.

Strategies for cueing the reader are presented in Chapter 13.

If you have devised a promising outline for your answer, you will be able to forecast your overall plan and its subpoints in your opening sentences. Forecasting shows readers how your essay is organized and has the practical advantage of making your answer easier to read. You might also want to use briefer paragraphs than you ordinarily do and signal clear relations between paragraphs with transition phrases or sentences.

As you begin writing your answer, freely strike out words or even sentences you want to change by drawing through them neatly with a single line. Do not stop to erase, and try not to be messy. Instructors do not expect flawless writing, but they are put off by unnecessary messiness.

As you continue to write, you will certainly think of new subpoints and new ideas or facts to include later in the paper. Stop briefly to make a note of these on your original outline. If you find that you want to add a sentence or two to sections you have already completed, write them in the margin or at the top of the page, with a neat arrow pointing to where they fit in your answer.

Do not pad your answer with irrelevancies and repetitions just to fill up space. You may have had one instructor who did not seem to pay much attention to what you wrote, but most instructors read exams carefully and are not impressed by the length of an answer alone. Within the time available, write a comprehensive, specific answer without padding.

Watch the clock carefully to ensure that you do not spend too much time on one answer. You must be realistic about the time constraints of an essay exam, especially if you know the material well and are prepared to write a lot. If you write one dazzling answer on an exam with three required questions, you earn only 33 points, not enough to pass at most colleges. Being required to answer more than one question may seem unfair, but keep in mind that instructors plan exams to be reasonably comprehensive. They want you to write about the course materials in two or three or more ways, not just one way.

If you run out of time when you are writing an answer, jot down the remaining main ideas from your outline, just to show that you know the material and with more time could have continued your exposition.

Write legibly and proofread. Remember that your instructor will likely be reading a large pile of exams. Careless scrawls, misspellings, omitted words, and missing punctuation (especially missing periods needed to mark the ends of sentences) will only make that reading difficult, even exasperating. A few minutes of careful proofreading can improve your grade.

MODEL ANSWERS TO SOME TYPICAL ESSAY EXAM QUESTIONS

Here we analyze several successful answers and give you an opportunity to analyze one for yourself. These analyses, along with the information we have provided elsewhere in this chapter, should greatly improve your chances of writing successful exam answers.

Short Answers

A literature midterm opened with ten items to identify, each worth 3 points. Students had about two minutes for each item. Here are three of Brenda Gossett's answers, each one earning her the full 3 points.

Rauffenstein: He was the German general who was in charge of the castle where Boeldieu, Marical, and Rosenthal were finally sent in The Grand Illusion. He, along with Boeldieu, represented the aristocracy, which was slowly fading out at that time.

Iges Peninsula: This peninsula is created by the Meuse River in France. It is there that the Camp of Hell was created in The Debacle. The Camp of Hell is where the French army was interned after the Germans defeated them in the Franco-Prussian War.

Pache: He was the "religious peasant" in the novel The Debacle. It was he who inevitably became a scapegoat when he was murdered by Loubet, La Poulle, and Chouteau because he wouldn't share his bread with them.

The instructor said only "identify the following" but clearly wanted students both to identify the item and to indicate its significance to the work in which it appeared. Gossett does both and gets full credit. She mentions particular works, characters, and events. Although she is rushed, she answers in complete sentences. She does not misspell any words or leave out any commas or periods. Her answers are complete and correct.

Paragraph-Length Answers

One question on a weekly literature quiz was worth 20 points of the total of 100. With only a few minutes to answer the question, students were instructed to "answer in a few sentences." Here is the question and Camille Prestera's answer:

> In *Things Fall Apart,* how did Okonkwo's relationship with his father affect his attitude toward his son?

Okonkwo despised his father, who was lazy, cowardly, and in debt. Okonkwo tried to be everything his father wasn't. He was hard-working, wealthy, and a great warrior and wrestler. Okonkwo treated his son harshly because he was afraid he saw the same weakness in Nwoye that he despised in his father. The result of this harsh treatment was that Nwoye left home.

Prestera begins by describing Okonkwo and his father, contrasting the two sharply. Then she explains Okonkwo's relationship with his son Nwoye. Her answer is coherent and straightforward.

Long Answers

Many final exams include at least one question requiring an essay-length answer. John Pixley had an hour to plan and write this essay for a final exam in a literature course in response to Question 23.7.

> Many American writers have portrayed their characters or their poetic speaker as being engaged in a quest. The quest may be explicit or implicit, it may be external or psychological, and it may end in failure or success. Analyze the quest motif in the work of four of the following writers: Edwards, Franklin, Hawthorne, Thoreau, Douglass, Whitman, Dickinson, James, Twain.

John Pixley's Answer

Key term, *quest,* is mentioned in introduction and thesis.

Americans pride themselves on being ambitious and on being able to strive for goals and to tap their potential. Some say that this is what the "American Dream" is all about. It is important for one to do and be all that one is capable of. This entails a quest or search for identity, experience, and happiness. Hence, the idea of the quest is a vital one in the United States, and it can be seen as a theme throughout American literature.

First writer is identified immediately.

In eighteenth-century colonial America, Jonathan Edwards dealt with this theme in his autobiographical and personal writings. Unlike his fiery and hard-nosed sermons, these autobiographical writings present a sensitive, vulnerable man trying to find himself and his proper, satisfying place in the world. He is concerned with his spiritual growth, in being free to find and explore religious experience and happiness. For example, in Personal Narrative, he very carefully traces the stages of religious beliefs. He tells about periods of abandoned ecstasy, doubts, and rational revelations. He also notes that his best insights and growth came at times when he was alone in the wilderness, in nature. Edwards's efforts to find himself in relation to the world can also be seen in his "Observations of the Natural World," in which he relates various meticulously observed and described natural phenomena to religious precepts and occurrences. Here, he is trying to give the world and life, of which he is a part, some sense of meaning and purpose. 2

Edwards's work and the details of his quest are presented.

Transition sentence identifies second writer. Key term is repeated.

Contrast with Edwards adds coherence to essay.

Another key term from the question, *external,* is used.

Franklin's particular kind of quest is described.

Although he was a contemporary of Edwards, Benjamin Franklin, who was very involved in the founding of the United States as a nation, had a different conception of the quest. He sees the quest as being one for practical accomplishment, success, and wealth. In his Autobiography, he stresses that happiness involves working hard to accomplish things, getting along with others, and establishing a good reputation. Unlike Edwards's, his quest is external and bound up with society. He is concerned with his morals and behavior, but, as seen in Part 2 of the Autobiography, he deals with them in an objective, pragmatic, even statistical way, rather than in sensitive pondering. It is also evident in this work that Franklin, unlike Edwards, believes so much in himself and his quest that he is able to laugh at himself. His concern with society can be seen in Poor Richard's Almanac, in which he gives practical advice on how to find success and happiness in the world, how to "be healthy, wealthy, and wise." 3

Transition sentence identifies third writer. Key term is repeated.

Comparison of Whitman to Edwards and Franklin sustains coherence of essay.

Whitman's quest is defined.

Still another version of the quest can be seen in the mid-nineteenth-century poetry of Walt Whitman. The quest that he portrays blends elements of those of Edwards and Franklin. In "Song of Myself," which is clearly autobiographical, the speaker emphasizes the importance of finding, knowing, and enjoying oneself as part of nature and the human community. He says that one should come to realize that one is lovable, just as are all other people and all of nature and life. This is a quest for sensitivity and awareness, as Edwards advocates, and for great self-confidence, as Franklin advocates. Along with Edwards, Whitman sees that peaceful isolation in nature is important; but he also sees the importance of interacting with people, as Franklin does. Being optimistic and feeling good--both in the literal and figurative sense--is the object of 4 this quest. Unfortunately, personal disappointment and national crisis (i.e., the Civil War) shattered Whitman's sense of confidence, and he lost the impetus of this quest in his own life.

Transition: Key term is repeated, and fourth writer is identified.

This theme of the quest can be seen in prose fiction as well as in poetry and autobiography. One interesting example is "The Beast in the Jungle," a short story written by Henry James around 1903. It is interesting in that not only does the principal character, John Marcher, fail in his lifelong quest, but his failure comes about in a most subtle and frustrating way. Marcher believes that something momentous is going to happen in his future. He talks about his belief to only one person, a woman named May. May decides to befriend him for life and watch with him for the momentous occurrence to come about, for "the beast in the jungle" to "pounce." As time passes, May seems to know what this occurrence is and eventually even says that it has happened; but John is still in the dark. It is only long after May's death that the beast pounces on him in his recognition that the "beast" was his failure to truly love May, the one woman of his life, even though she gave him all the encouragement that she possibly, decently could. Marcher never defined the terms of his quest until it was too late. By just waiting and watching, he failed to find feeling and passion. This tragic realization, as someone like Whitman would view it, brings about John Marcher's ruin.

Quest of James character is described.

Conclusion repeats key term.

As seen in these few examples, the theme of the quest is a significant one in American literature. Also obvious is the fact that there are a variety of approaches to, methods used in, and outcomes of the quest. This is an appropriate theme for American literature seeing how much Americans cherish the right of "the pursuit of happiness."

Pixley's answer is strong for two reasons: He has the information he needs, and he has organized it carefully and presented it coherently.

Exercise 23.1

The following essay was written by Don Hepler. He is answering the same essay exam question as his classmate John Pixley. Analyze Hepler's essay to discover whether it meets the criteria of a good essay exam answer. Review the criteria mentioned earlier in this chapter under "Writing Your Answer" and in the annotated commentary of John Pixley's answer. Try to identify the features of Hepler's essay that contribute to or work against its success.

Don Hepler's Answer

The quest motif is certainly important in American literature. By considering Franklin, Thoreau, Douglass, and Twain, we can see that the quest may be explicit or implicit, external or psychological, a failure or a success. Tracing the quest motif through these four authors seems to show a developing concern in American literature with transcending materialism to address deeper issues. It also reveals a drift toward ambiguity and pessimism.

2 Benjamin Franklin's quest, as revealed by his _Autobiography_, is for material comfort and outward success. His quest may be considered an explicit one because he announces clearly what he is trying to do: perfect a systematic approach for living long and happily. The whole _Autobiography_ is a road map intended for other people to use as a guide; Franklin apparently meant rather literally for people to imitate his methods. He wrote with the assumption that his success was reproducible. He is possibly the most optimistic author in American literature because he enjoys life, knows exactly _why_ he enjoys life, and believes that anyone else willing to follow his formula may enjoy life as well.

3 By Franklin's standards, his quest is clearly a success. But his _Autobiography_ portrays only an external, not a psychological, success. This is not to suggest that Franklin was a psychological, failure. Indeed, we have every reason to believe the contrary. But the fact remains that Franklin _wrote_ only about external success; he never indicated how he really felt emotionally. Possibly it was part of Franklin's overriding optimism to assume that material comfort leads naturally to emotional fulfillment.

4 Henry David Thoreau presents a more multifaceted quest. His _Walden_ is, on the simplest level, the chronicle of Thoreau's physical journey out of town and into the woods. But the moving itself is not the focus of _Walden_. It is really more of a metaphor for some kind of spiritual quest going on within Thoreau's mind. Most of the action in _Walden_ is mental, as Thoreau contemplates and philosophizes, always using the lake, the woods, and his own daily actions as symbols of higher, more eternal truths. This spiritual quest is a success in that Thoreau is able to appreciate the beauty of nature and to see through much of the sham and false assumptions of town life and blind materialism.

5 Thoreau does not leave us with nearly as explicit a "blueprint" for success as Franklin does. Even Franklin's plan is limited to people of high intelligence, personal discipline, and sound character; Franklin sometimes seems to forget that many human beings are in fact weak and evil and so would stand little chance of success similar to his own. But at least Franklin's quest could be duplicated by another Franklin. Thoreau's quest is more problematic, for even as great a mystic and naturalist as Thoreau himself could not remain in the woods indefinitely. This points toward the idea that the real quest is all internal and psychological; Thoreau seems to have gone to the woods to develop a spiritual strength that he could keep and take elsewhere on subsequent dealings with the "real world."

The quest of Frederick Douglass was explicit in that he needed physically to get north and escape slavery, but it was also implicit because he sought to discover and redefine himself through his quest, as Thoreau did. Douglass's motives were more sharply focused than either Franklin's or Thoreau's; his very humanness was at stake, as well as his physical well-being and possibly even his life. But Douglass also makes it clear that the most horrible part of slavery was the mental anguish of having no hope of freedom. His learning to read, and his maintenance of this skill, seems to have been as important as the maintenance of his material comforts, of which he had very few. In a sense, Douglass's quest is the most psychological and abstract so far because it is for the very essence of freedom and humanity, both of which were mostly taken for granted by Franklin and Thoreau. Also, Douglass's quest is the most pessimistic of the three; Douglass concludes that physical violence is the only way out, as he finds with the Covey incident.

Finally, Mark Twain's Huckleberry Finn is an example of the full range of meaning that the quest motif may assume. Geographically, Huck's quest is very large. But again, there is a quest defined implicitly as well as one defined explicitly, as Huck (without consciously realizing it) searches for morality, truth, and freedom. Twain's use of the quest is ambiguous, even more so than the previous writers', because while he suggests success superficially (i.e., the "happily ever after" scene in the last chapter), he really hints at some sort of ultimate hopelessness inherent in society. Not even Douglass questions the good or evil of American society as deeply as Twain does; for Douglass, everything will be fine when slavery is abolished; but for Twain, the only solution is to "light out for the territories" altogether--and when Twain wrote, he knew that the territories were no more.

Twain's implicit sense of spiritual failure stands in marked contrast to Franklin's buoyant confidence in material success. The guiding image of the quest, however, is central to American values and, consequently, a theme that these writers and others have adapted to suit their own vision.

Exercise 23.2

Analyze the following essay exam questions in order to decide what kind of writing task they present. What is being asked of the student as a participant in the course and as a writer? Given the time constraints of the exam, what plan would you propose for writing the answer? Following each question is the number of points it is worth and the amount of time allotted to answer it.

1. Cortazar is a producer of fantastic literature. Discuss first what fantastic literature is. Then choose any four stories by Cortazar as examples, and discuss the fantastic elements in these stories. Refer to the structure, techniques, and narrative styles

that he uses in these four stories. If you like, you may refer to more than four, of course. (Points: 30 of 100. Time: 40 of 150 minutes.)

2. During the course of the twentieth century, the United States has experienced three significant periods of social reform—the progressive era, the age of the Great Depression, and the decade of the 1960s. What were the sources of reform in each period? What were the most significant reform achievements of each period as well as the largest failings? (Points: 35 of 100. Time: 75 of 180 minutes.)
3. Since literature is both an artistic and ideological product, writers comment on their material context through their writing.
   a. What is Rulfo's perspective of his Mexican reality, and how is it portrayed through his stories?
   b. What particular themes does he deal with, especially in these stories: "The Burning Plain," "Luvina," "They Gave Us the Land," "Paso del Norte," and "Tell Them Not to Kill Me"?
   c. What literary techniques and structures does he use to convey his perspective? Refer to a specific story as an example.

   (Points: 30 of 100. Time: 20 of 50 minutes.)
4. Why is there a special reason to be concerned about the influence of television watching on kids? In your answer, include a statement of the following:
   a. Your own understanding of the *general communication principles* involved for any television watcher.
   b. What is special about television and kids.
   c. How advertisers and producers use this information. (You should draw from the relevant readings as well as lectures.)

   (Points: 20 of 90. Time: 25 of 90 minutes.)
5. Analyze the autobiographical tradition in American literature, focusing on differences and similarities among authors and, if appropriate, changes over time. Discuss four authors in all. In addition to the conscious autobiographers—Edwards, Franklin, Thoreau, Douglass—you may choose one or two figures from among the following fictional or poetic quasi-autobiographers: Hawthorne, Whitman, Dickinson, Twain. (Points: 50 of 120. Time: 60 of 180 minutes.)
6. How does the system of (media) sponsorship work, and what, if any, ideological control do sponsors exert? Be specific and illustrative! (Points: 33 of 100. Time: 60 of 180 minutes.)
7. Several of the works studied in this course analyze the tension between myth and reality. Select two written works and two films, and analyze how their authors or directors present the conflict between myth and reality and how they resolve it, if they resolve it. (Points: 45 of 130. Time: 60 of 180 minutes.)
8. *Man's Hope* is a novel about the Spanish Civil War written while the war was still going on. *La Guerre Est Finie* is a film about Spanish revolutionaries depicting their activities nearly thirty years after the civil war. Discuss how the temporal relationship of each of these works to the civil war is reflected in the character of the works themselves and in the differences between them. (Points: 58 of 100. Time: 30 of 50 minutes.)
9. Write an essay on one of these topics: The role of the narrator in *Tom Jones* and *Pride and Prejudice* or the characters of Uncle Toby and Miss Bates. (Points: 33 of 100. Time: 60 of 180 minutes.)

CHAPTER 24

Assembling a Writing Portfolio

A writing portfolio presents your best writing. Assembling a portfolio gives you the opportunity to show your most successful work. It challenges you to evaluate and reconsider your work and to think about what you have learned. The contents of a portfolio will, of course, vary from writer to writer and may even be set by an instructor. Portfolios for college composition courses often include several pieces of work, a written statement about why they were chosen, and some reflection on what you have learned. This chapter provides guidelines for assembling a writing portfolio using the resources in *The St. Martin's Guide to Writing.*

THE PURPOSE OF A PORTFOLIO

Portfolios are widely used for many purposes, most generally to collect writing samples, art, or other documents. Artists present portfolios of their work to gallery owners and patrons. Designers and architects present portfolios of their most successful and imaginative work to show potential clients what they can do. People applying for positions that require a large amount of written communication would be expected to submit representative samples of their writing. Some colleges request applicants to submit portfolios of high school writing; outstanding portfolios sometimes qualify students for college credit or placement in advanced courses. Some college majors require graduating seniors to submit a portfolio of their best work for evaluation, sometimes leading to special recognition or rewards. No matter what the specific purpose or occasion, a portfolio can present a rich opportunity to show what you can do.

You may as a student be required to assemble a portfolio of your work, either as part of a course or as part of an application to graduate school or for a job. Whether or not you are asked to turn in a writing portfolio, you might want to consider assembling one. You could create a portfolio from all the materials of your first-year writing course, for example. You have probably produced many pages of very diverse writing, from journal entries to revised essays. Organizing it can help you to reread and think about your written work and will serve as a valuable personal record of an important year in your intellectual development. You might even wish to add to it year by year to include your best work from all your courses or perhaps from all the courses in your major. Such an effort should help you to reflect on your learning, one of the key tasks in any education.

Pausing to reflect on your learning is sometimes referred to as *metacognition,* meaning roughly "thinking about your thinking." Such reflection helps to consolidate what you have learned by reviewing the basic principles of a course. This review of your work can help you to remember it and recognize connections to other courses.

In addition, reviewing your work can develop your powers of judgment as you learn to evaluate it by the standards of judgment in various academic disciplines. This review can increase your satisfaction with your courses as you become aware of the specific ways in which your knowledge is growing. Finally, it can give you insights into your own intellectual development and help you to recognize your strengths and weaknesses and to discover your interests.

ASSEMBLING A PORTFOLIO FOR YOUR COMPOSITION COURSE

Your instructor may ask you to assemble a writing portfolio as part of your coursework. If so, the following guidelines will be helpful. They are designed to show you some resources in the *Guide* that can help you reflect on and assess the effectiveness of your writing.

Your purpose in assembling such a portfolio is to show what you have learned in the course. In a writing course using the *Guide,* that goal probably means showing various kinds of writing, including examples from all parts of the writing process. The following guidelines will help you to select work, revise one piece, consider what you have learned, and organize your portfolio.

Selecting Work

Your instructor will very likely specify a list of what to include in your portfolio. It may look something like the following list:

- A selection of your best essays, including all of your work—invention, drafts, critical responses, final revisions. Your instructor will tell you how many essays to include; some might want only one, while others may want several. To choose your best work, consider responses you have gotten from your instructor and other readers, and review carefully the Basic Features discussion in relevant chapters of the *Guide.*
- A further revision of one or more of the essays you have selected. Use the Critical Reading Guide for these assignments to get ideas and the Revising as well as the Editing and Proofreading sections to establish a plan. You might also seek advice from your campus writing center or from friends or classmates.
- Examples of your most imaginative, productive invention work completed for two or three other essays.

Reflecting on Your Work and Your Learning

Many instructors require a written statement about what you have learned about writing in the course. Some ask for this statement in the form of a letter; others may prefer an essay. Whatever form it takes, this kind of analysis is "thinking about thinking" *par excellence*. Keeping the following considerations in mind will help you to write a thoughtful statement to your instructor about what you have learned.

- *Describe the work.* Because you will need to refer to several works or parts of a work, be careful to name each one in a consistent way. In describing an essay, give its title and review briefly its purpose and topic.
- *Justify your choices.* Here begins the serious metacognitive work: When you justify what you see as your "best" work, you reveal what standards you have established for yourself about good work. These standards are fundamental to what you have learned. The *Guide* sets forth clear criteria for each kind of writing in the Basic Features sections in Chapters 2–10. Review the discussion of those features as you judge the success of your essay, and refer to them as you explain your choice.
- *Reflect on your learning.* Your instructor may ask you to consider what you learned in writing and revising a particular essay as well as what you have learned about the process of writing that essay. In either case, it will help you to anchor your reflections in the specific work you have done using the *Guide*. Consider what you have learned analyzing and discussing the readings, inventing, participating in group inquiry, planning and drafting, getting and giving critical comments, and revising. Look again at the Thinking Critically about What You Have Learned sections in Chapters 2–10. There, you will find questions that will help you to reflect on how you solved problems when revising an essay, how reading influenced your writing, and how your writing can be situated and understood in a larger social context. You may well be able to use material you have already written for these sections in the statement about your learning.

Whatever materials you include, you have some important decisions to make, and these decisions reveal a lot about you as a writer. Assembling a portfolio gives you the responsibility and the opportunity to assess your own work, a key step in taking charge of your own writing—and your own learning.

Organizing the Portfolio

Present your portfolio in an inexpensive manila folder. The contents of the folder need not be stapled; loose sheets will make it easier for your instructor to review your work. You should include a separate table of contents, however; and take care to number all pages. You should also label all of your work in the upper right corner of each page. For example, write "Draft, 1" for page 1 of a draft; "Revision 2, 1" for page 1 of a second revision; "Invention, 1" for page 1 of your best invention materials; and so on. You should also date all work. Put everything in the sequence specified by your instructor.

HOW WRITING PORTFOLIOS ARE EVALUATED

Instructors read portfolios to get an overall impression of student achievement. They look at how carefully the portfolio has been assembled: the choices made, the way the writer has justified those choices, the quality of the work, the success of revisions, and the insightfulness of reflections on the contents of the portfolio. They will probably not grade individual pieces of work, though they might comment on some of them.

Your instructor will first determine whether your portfolio is complete, looking over the table of contents and skimming the portfolio to get an impression of the care with which it was organized and presented. Labeling each piece carefully will help your instructor—or any reader—to review your work.

The essays themselves will be read with certain expectations. Essays written for the assignments in *The St. Martin's Guide to Writing* will be evaluated on how appropriately they employ the strategies of that kind of writing. In selecting work for your portfolio, therefore, and in evaluating the work yourself, you should review the Basic Features summary in the appropriate chapter. You can expect as well that your instructor will compare revisions to earlier drafts to assess how successfully you have solved problems. In selecting this work for your portfolio, you should review the Identifying Problems and Solving the Problems sections in the Revising section of the chapter. Finally, many instructors will consider how well the essay has been edited and proofread. The *Guide* includes tips for checking and editing errors that often occur in each of its writing assignments; you might want to check for these errors in particular as you do any final revision for your portfolio.

Instructors always pay special attention to the letter or essay of reflection on the portfolio contents. You can be sure that your instructor will be curious to know why you chose these particular examples of your work and eager to see the rationale you offer for your choices. A strong rationale shows that the student knows how to recognize good work and how to say precisely what makes it good. Instructors are particularly interested in students' analyses of their revisions of drafts because recognizing and solving problems in a draft is a sign of a maturing writer.

Acknowledgments

Maya Angelou. "Uncle Willie." From *I Know Why the Caged Bird Sings* by Maya Angelou. Copyright © 1969 by Maya Angelou. Reprinted by permission of Random House, Inc.

Paul Auster. "Why Write." First appeared in *The New Yorker* 12/25/95 and 1/1/96, pp. 86–89. Reprinted by permission of the author.

Toni Cade Bambara. "The Hammer Man." From *Gorilla, My Love* by Toni Cade Bambara. Copyright © 1966 by Toni Cade Bambara. Reprinted by permission of Random House, Inc.

Joseph Berger. "What Produces Outstanding Science Students." Originally titled "Science Education for the Gifted and Talented" from *The American Enterprise* (January/February 1994), pp. 16–18. Reprinted by permission of the American Enterprise Institute.

"brave." Copyright © 1989 by Houghton Mifflin Company. Reproduced by permission from *Roget's II*: The New Thesaurus, Expanded Edition.

"brave." From Webster's New Dictionary of Synonyms. Copyright © 1984 by Merriam-Webster Inc., publisher of the Merriam-Webster dictionaries. Reproduced by permission.

Janice Castro. "Contingent Workers." Originally titled "Disposable Workers." *Time* magazine, March 29, 1993. © 1993 Time Inc. Reprinted by permission.

Ward Churchill. "The Indian Chant and the Tomahawk Chop." Reprinted by permission of the author.

Sandra Cisneros. "The Monkey Garden." From *The House on Mango Street* by Sandra Cisneros. Copyright © 1984 by Sandra Cisneros. Published by Vintage Books, a division of Random House, Inc., New York, and in hardcover by Alfred A. Knopf in 1994. Reprinted by permission of Susan Bergholz Literary Services, New York. All rights reserved.

Annie Dillard. "Handled My Own Life." From *An American Childhood* by Annie Dillard. Copyright © 1987 by Annie Dillard. Reprinted by permission of HarperCollins Publishers, Inc.

Ecology Action Centre web page. Design by Ronald S. Wood; artwork by Rob Hansen. © Ecology Action Centre Halifax NS Canada. Reprinted by permission.

Barbara Ehrenreich. "In Defense of Talk Shows." *Time* (December 4, 1995). © 1995 Time Inc. Reprinted by permission.

Entry 91X2727. (Mayberry, Maralee & Knowles, J. Gary. Article from *Urban Review, Sociological Abstracts*, April 1991). Reprinted by permission.

Richard Estrada. "Sticks and Stones and Sports Team Names." From the *Los Angeles Times* (October 29, 1995). Copyright © 1995, The Washington Post Writers Group. Reprinted with permission.

Amitai Etzioni. "Working at McDonald's." Copyright © 1986 Amitai Etzioni, author of *The Spirit of Community*. Director, George Washington University Center for Communitarian Policy Studies. Reprinted by permission of the author.

Max Frankel. "Universal E-Mail: Worthy of a 'New Frontier' Commitment." *The New York Times* (May 5, 1996), pp. 40, 42. Copyright © 1996 by The New York Times Company. Reprinted by permission.

"Growing without schooling." Reprinted with permission of R.R.Bowker, a division of Cahners Publishing Company, from *Magazines for Libraries* 8th ed., by Bill Katz and Linda Sternberg Katz. Copyright © 1995 by William A. Katz.

Gerald Haslam. "Grandma." From *The Horned Toad* by Gerald Haslam. Copyright © 1983 by Gerald Haslam. Reprinted by permission of the author.

Ernest Hemingway. Excerpt from *Death in the Afternoon* by Ernest Hemingway. Copyright © 1932 Charles Scribner's Sons. Copyright renewed © 1960 by Ernest Hemingway. Reprinted with permission of Scribner, a division of Simon & Schuster.

"Home Education." From the *Reader's Guide to Periodical Literature, 1991*, page 940 (Home Education). Copyright © 1992 by The H. W. Wilson Company. Material reproduced with permission of the publisher.

"InfoTrac™." Copyright © 1996 Information Access Company. Citation reproduced by permission of Information Access Company.

"intrepid." Copyright © 1991 by Houghton Mifflin Company. Reprinted by permission from *The American Heritage Dictionary*, Second College Edition.

Chris Jeub. "Why Parents Choose Home Schooling." From *Educational Leadership*, V52, pp. 50–52 (September 1995). Copyright © 1995. All rights reserved. Reprinted by permission of the Association for Supervision and Curriculum Development.

James Joyce. "Araby." From *The Dubliners* by James Joyce. Copyright © 1916 by B. W. Heubsch. Definitive text Copyright © 1967 by the Estate of James Joyce. Used by permission of Viking Penguin, a division of Penguin Books USA Inc.

Mickey Kaus. "Street Hassle." From *The New Republic* (March 22, 1993). Copyright © 1993, The New Republic, Inc. Reprinted by permission of *The New Republic*.

Martin Luther King Jr. "Excerpt from *Letter from Birmingham Jail*." Copyright © 1963 by Martin Luther King, Jr. Copyright renewed 1991 by Coretta Scott King. Reprinted by arrangement with the heirs to the estate of Martin Luther King Jr., c/o Writers House, Inc. as agent for the proprietor.

Stephen King. "Why We Crave Horror Movies." © Stephen King. Reprinted with permission. All rights reserved.

Lycos web page. Copyright © 1996 Lycos, Inc. All rights reserved. The Lycos™ "Catalog of the Internet" copyright © 1994, 1995, 1996 Carnegie Mellon University. All rights reserved. Used by permission.

Sylvia S. Mader. Excerpt from *Inquiry into Life*, 3e by Sylvia S. Mader. Copyright © 1982 William C. Brown Communications, Inc. Dubuque, Iowa. Reprinted by permission. All rights reserved.

Catherine Manegold. "To Crystal, 12, School Serves No Purpose." *The New York Times* (April 8, 1993). Copyright © 1993 by The New Yorker Co. Reprinted by permission.

Guy Molyneux. "The Declining Art of Political Debate." From the *Los Angeles Times* (May 16, 1993). Copyright © 1993 by Guy Molyneux. Reprinted by permission of the author.

David Noonan. "Inside the Brain." Excerpt from *Neuro-Life on the Frontlines of Brain Surgery & Neurological Medicine* by David Noonan. Copyright © 1989 by David Noonan. Reprinted with the permission of Simon & Schuster.

Peter Passell. "Path Dependence." *The New York Times* (May 5, 1996). Originally titled "Why the Best Doesn't Always Win." Copyright © 1996 by The New York Times Co. Reprinted by permission.

Robert Putnam. "The Strange Disappearance of Civic America." Originally appeared in *The American Prospect* (Winter 1996): 34–48. Copyright © 1996 by Robert Putnam. Reprinted by permission of Robert D. Putnam.

Terrence Rafferty. "Black Eye." Originally in *The New Yorker* (October 2, 1995). © 1995 Terrence Rafferty. All rights reserved. Reprinted by permission.

"Soup." Originally titled "Slave" from The Talk of the Town section in *The New Yorker* magazine (January 23, 1989). © 1989 The New Yorker Magazine, Inc. Reprinted by permission.

Anastasia Toufexis. "Love: The Right Chemistry." *Time* (February 15, 1993). Originally titled "The Right Chemistry." © 1993 Time Inc. Reprinted by permission.

Adam Paul Weisman. "Birth Control in the Schools: Clinical Examination." From *The New Republic* (March 16, 1987). Copyright © 1987 by Adam Paul Weisman. Reprinted by permission of The New Republic.

William Carlos Williams. "The Use of Force." From *The Doctor Stories* by William Carlos Williams. Copyright © 1938 by William Carlos Williams. Reprinted by permission of New Directions Publishing Corp.

Tobias Wolff. "On Being a Real Westerner." From *This Boy's Life* by Tobias Wolff. Copyright © 1989 by Tobias Wolff. Used by permission of Grove/Atlantic, Inc.

James Wolcott. "Talking Trash." Originally in *The New Yorker* (April 2, 1996). © 1996 James Wolcott. Reprinted by permission.

Amy Wu. "A Different Kind of Mother." Originally published in *The Chinese American Forum* (Vol. 9, No. 1, July 1993), pp. 26–27. Copyright © 1993 by Amy Wu. Reprinted by permission of the author.

Author and Title Index

Subject Index

Submitting Papers for Publication

To Students and Instructors

We hope that we'll be able to include essays from more colleges and universities in the next edition of the *Guide* and our accompanying anthology, *Free Falling and other student essays.* Please let us see essays written using *The St. Martin's Guide* you'd like us to consider. Send them with this Paper Submission Form and the Agreement Form on the back to *The Guide,* St. Martin's Press, 345 Park Avenue South, New York, NY 10010.

PAPER SUBMISSION FORM

Instructor's name ________________________________

School ________________________________

Address ________________________________

Department ________________________________

Student's name ________________________________

Course ________________________________

Writing activity the paper represents ________________________________

This writing activity appears in chapter(s) ________________________________
of *The St. Martin's Guide to Writing*

Agreement Form

I hereby transfer to St. Martin's Press all rights to my essay,

(tentative title), subject to final editing by the publisher. These rights include copyright and all other rights of publication and reproduction. I guarantee that this essay is wholly my original work, and that I have not granted rights to it to anyone else.

Student's signature X: ______________________________

Please type

Name: ______________________________

Address: ______________________________

____

____

Phone: ______________________________

Please indicate the reader or publication source you assumed for your essay:

____

Write a few sentences about the purpose or purposes of your essay. What did you hope to achieve with your reader?

____

____

____

____

St. Martin's Press representative: ______________________________